FIFTH EDITION

MICROSOFT® VISUAL C#® 2012

AN INTRODUCTION TO OBJECT-ORIENTED PROGRAMMING

JOYCE FARRELL

COURSE TECHNOLOGY
CENGAGE Learning®

Australia • Brazil • Japan • Korea • Mexico • Singapore • Spain • United Kingdom • United States

COURSE TECHNOLOGY
CENGAGE Learning

Microsoft® Visual C#® 2012:
An Introduction to Object-Oriented
Programming, Fifth Edition
Joyce Farrell

Executive Editor: Kathleen McMahon

Senior Product Manager: Alyssa Pratt

Development Editor: Dan Seiter

Editorial Assistant: Sarah Ryan

Brand Manager: Kay Stefanski

Content Project Manager:
Jen Feltri-George

Art Director: Cheryl Pearl, GEX

Cover Designer: Lisa Kuhn/Curio Press,
LLC, www.curiopress.com

Cover Photo: ©Leigh Prather/Veer
Incorporated

Print Buyer: Julio Esperas

Copyeditor: Michael Beckett

Proofreader: Brandy Lilly

Indexer: Sharon Hilgenberg

Compositor: Integra Software
Services Pvt. Ltd.

For product information and technology assistance, contact us at
Cengage Learning Customer & Sales Support, www.cengage.com/support

For permission to use material from this text or product,
submit all requests online at **cengage.com/permissions**
Further permissions questions can be e-mailed to
permissionrequest@cengage.com

Library of Congress Control Number: 2013931000

ISBN-13: 978-1-285-09633-9

ISBN-10: 1-285-09633-9

Course Technology
20 Channel Center Street
Boston, MA 02210

Some of the product names and company names used in this book have been used for identification purposes only and may be trademarks or registered trademarks of their respective manufacturers and sellers.

Any fictional data related to people, companies, or URLs used throughout this book is intended for instructional purposes only. At the time this book was printed, any such data was fictional and not belonging to any real people or companies.

Course Technology, a part of Cengage Learning, reserves the right to revise this publication and make changes from time to time in its content without notice.

The programs in this book are for instructional purposes only. They have been tested with care, but are not guaranteed for any particular intent beyond educational purposes. The author and the publisher do not offer any warranties or representations, nor do they accept any liabilities with respect to the programs.

Cengage Learning is a leading provider of customized learning solutions with office locations around the globe, including Singapore, the United Kingdom, Australia, Mexico, Brazil, and Japan. Locate your local office at: **www.cengage.com/global**

Cengage Learning products are represented in Canada by Nelson Education, Ltd.

To learn more about Course Technology, visit
www.cengage.com/coursetechnology

Purchase any of our products at your local college store or at our preferred online store: **www.CengageBrain.com**

Printed in the United States of America
2 3 4 5 6 7 19 18 17 16 15 14

Brief Contents

Contents

Preface

Microsoft Visual C# 2012, Fifth edition provides the beginning programmer with a guide to developing programs in C#. C# is a language developed by the Microsoft Corporation as part of the .NET Framework and Visual Studio platform. The .NET Framework contains a wealth of libraries for developing applications for the Windows family of operating systems.

With C#, you can build small, reusable components that are well-suited to Web-based programming applications. Although similar to Java and C++, many features of C# make it easier to learn and ideal for the beginning programmer. You can program in C# using a simple text editor and the command prompt, or you can manipulate program components using Visual Studio's sophisticated Integrated Development Environment. This book provides you with the tools to use both techniques.

This textbook assumes that you have little or no programming experience. The writing is nontechnical and emphasizes good programming practices. The examples are business examples; they do not assume mathematical background beyond high school business math. Additionally, the examples illustrate one or two major points; they do not contain so many features that you become lost following irrelevant and extraneous details. This book provides you with a solid background in good object-oriented programming techniques and introduces you to object-oriented terminology using clear, familiar language.

Organization and Coverage

Microsoft Visual C# 2012 presents C# programming concepts, enforcing good style, logical thinking, and the object-oriented paradigm. Chapter 1 introduces you to the language by letting you create working C# programs using both the simple command line and the Visual Studio environment. In Chapter 2 you learn about data and how to input, store, and output data in C#. Chapter 3 provides a quick start to creating GUI applications. You can take two approaches:

- You can cover Chapter 3 and learn about GUI objects so that you can create more visually interesting applications in the subsequent chapters on decision making, looping, and array manipulation. These subsequent chapters confine GUI examples to the end of the chapters, so you can postpone GUI manipulation if you want.

- You can skip Chapter 3 until learning the fundamentals of decision making, looping, and array manipulation, and until studying object-oriented concepts such as classes, objects, polymorphism, inheritance, and exception handling. Then, after Chapter 11, you can return to Chapter 3 and use the built-in GUI component classes with a deeper understanding of how they work.

In Chapters 4, 5, and 6, you learn about the classic programming structures—making decisions, looping, and manipulating arrays—and how to implement them in C#. Chapters 7 and 8 provide a thorough study of methods, including passing parameters into and out of methods and overloading them.

Chapter 9 introduces the object-oriented concepts of classes, objects, data hiding, constructors, and destructors. After completing Chapters 10 and 11, you will be thoroughly grounded in the object-oriented concepts of inheritance and exception handling, and will be able to take advantage of both features in your C# programs. Chapter 12 continues the discussion of GUI objects from Chapter 3. You will learn about controls, how to set their properties, and how to make attractive, useful, graphical, and interactive programs. Chapter 13 takes you further into the intricacies of handling events in your interactive GUI programs. In Chapter 14, you learn to save data to and retrieve data from files. In Chapter 15 you learn how to interact with databases in C# programs—an increasingly valuable skill in the information-driven business world. C# supports LINQ (Language INtegrated Query) statements, which allow you to integrate SQL-like queries into C# programs.

Features

This text focuses on helping students become better programmers and understand C # program development through a variety of key features. In addition to chapter Objectives, Summaries, and Key Terms, these useful features will help students regardless of their learning styles.

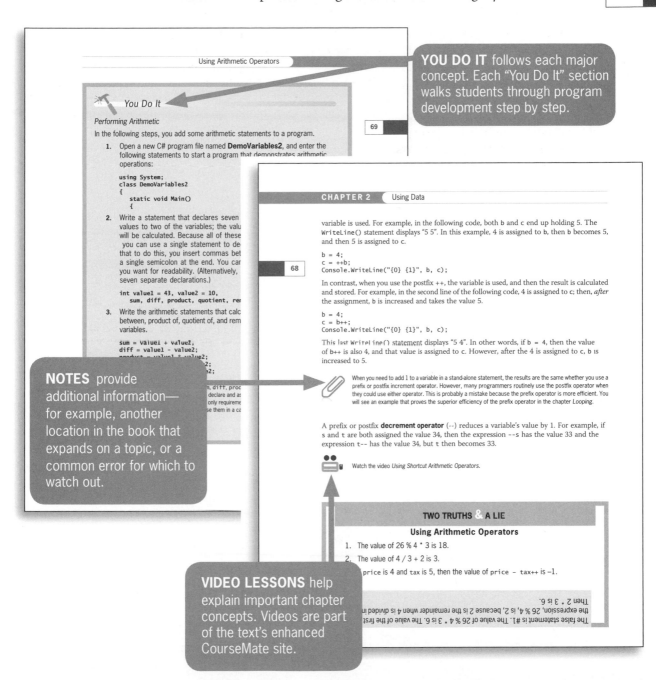

YOU DO IT follows each major concept. Each "You Do It" section walks students through program development step by step.

Using Arithmetic Operators

You Do It

Performing Arithmetic

In the following steps, you add some arithmetic statements to a program.

1. Open a new C# program file named **DemoVariables2**, and enter the following statements to start a program that demonstrates arithmetic operations:

```
using System;
class DemoVariables2
{
    static void Main()
    {
```

2. Write a statement that declares seven values to two of the variables; the value will be calculated. Because all of these you can use a single statement to de that to do this, you insert commas bet a single semicolon at the end. You can you want for readability. (Alternatively, seven separate declarations.)

```
int value1 = 43, value2 = 10,
    sum, diff, product, quotient, rem
```

3. Write the arithmetic statements that calc between, product of, quotient of, and rem variables.

```
sum = value1 + value2,
diff = value1 - value2;
product = value1 * value2;
```

NOTES provide additional information— for example, another location in the book that expands on a topic, or a common error for which to watch out.

69

68

CHAPTER 2 Using Data

variable is used. For example, in the following code, both b and c end up holding 5. The WriteLine() statement displays "5 5". In this example, 4 is assigned to b, then b becomes 5, and then 5 is assigned to c.

```
b = 4;
c = ++b;
Console.WriteLine("{0} {1}", b, c);
```

In contrast, when you use the postfix ++, the variable is used, and then the result is calculated and stored. For example, in the second line of the following code, 4 is assigned to c; then, *after* the assignment, b is increased and takes the value 5.

```
b = 4;
c = b++;
Console.WriteLine("{0} {1}", b, c);
```

This last WriteLine() statement displays "5 4". In other words, if b = 4, then the value of b++ is also 4, and that value is assigned to c. However, after the 4 is assigned to c, b is increased to 5.

> When you need to add 1 to a variable in a stand-alone statement, the results are the same whether you use a prefix or postfix increment operator. However, many programmers routinely use the postfix operator when they could use either operator. This is probably a mistake because the prefix operator is more efficient. You will see an example that proves the superior efficiency of the prefix operator in the chapter *Looping*.

A prefix or postfix **decrement operator** (--) reduces a variable's value by 1. For example, if s and t are both assigned the value 34, then the expression --s has the value 33 and the expression t-- has the value 34, but t then becomes 33.

Watch the video *Using Shortcut Arithmetic Operators.*

VIDEO LESSONS help explain important chapter concepts. Videos are part of the text's enhanced CourseMate site.

TWO TRUTHS & A LIE
Using Arithmetic Operators

1. The value of 26 % 4 * 3 is 18.

2. The value of 4 / 3 + 2 is 3.

price is 4 and tax is 5, then the value of price - tax++ is –1.

The false statement is #1. The value of 26 % 4 * 3 is 6. The value of the first the expression, 26 % 4, is 2, because 2 is the remainder when 4 is divided in Then 2 * 3 is 6.

TWO TRUTHS & A LIE quizzes appear after each chapter section, with answers provided. The quiz contains three statements based on the preceding section of text—two statements are true and one is false. Answers give immediate feedback without "giving away" answers to the multiple-choice questions and programming problems later in the chapter. Students also have the option to take these quizzes electronically through the enhanced CourseMate site.

4

TWO TRUTHS & A LIE

Programming

Two of the following statements are true, and one is false. Identify the false statement and explain why it is false.

1. A high-level programming language allows you to use a vocabulary of reasonable terms such as "read," "write," or "add" instead of the sequence of on/off switches that perform these tasks.

2. Each high-level programming language has its own syntax, or rules of the language.

3. Programmers use a computer program called code into a high-level language they can under

> The false statement is #3. Programmers use a computer program called a ... high-level language statements into machine code.

Procedural and Object-Oriented Pr

Two popular approaches to writing computer programs object-oriented programming.

When you write a **procedural program**, you use your kn to create and name computer memory locations that can steps or operations to manipulate those values. The nam called **variables** because they hold values that might var variable is referenced by using a one-word name (an **iden** example, a company's payroll program might contain a va location referenced by the name payRate might contain For instance, an organization's payroll program might u each of 100 employees. Additionally, a single employee's different values before or after a raise or before or after su During the execution of the payroll program, each value might have many operations performed on it—for exam multiplying it by another variable representing hours wo

> Examples of procedural programming languages include C a

THE DON'T DO IT ICON illustrates how NOT to do something—for example, having a dead code path in a program. This icon provides a visual jolt to the student, emphasizing that particular figures are NOT to be emulated and making students more careful to recognize problems in existing code.

Using Compound Expressions in if Statements

For example, the two code samples shown in Figure 4-14 work exactly the same way. The age variable is tested, and if it is greater than or equal to 0 and less than 120, a message is displayed to explain that the value is valid.

161

```
// using the && operator
  if(age >= 0 && age < 120)
    Console.WriteLine("Age is valid");

// using nested ifs
  if(age >= 0)
    if(age < 120)
      Console.WriteLine("Age is valid");
```

Figure 4-14 Comparison of the && operator and nested if statements

Using the && operator is never required, because nested if statements achieve the same result, but using the && operator often makes your code more concise, less error-prone, and easier to understand.

It is important to note that when you use the && operator, you must include a complete Boolean expression on each side of the operator. If you want to set a bonus to $400 when saleAmount is both over $1000 and under $5000, the correct statement is as follows:

```
if(saleAmount > 1000 && saleAmount < 5000)
    bonus = 400;
```

The following statement is incorrect and will not compile:

```
if(saleAmount > 1000 && < 5000)
    bonus = 400;
```

> **Don't Do It**
> 5000 is not a Boolean expression (it is a numeric constant), so this statement is invalid.

For clarity, many programmers prefer to surround each Boolean expression that is part of a compound Boolean expression with its own set of parentheses, For example:

```
if((saleAmount > 1000) && (saleAmount < 5000))
    bonus = 400;
```

Notice that the if clause has its own set of parentheses, and that nested within the set each Boolean expression has a set of parentheses. Use this format if it is clearer to you.

The expressions in each part of a compound, conditional Boolean expression are evaluated only as much as necessary to determine whether the entire expression is true or false. This feature is called **short-circuit evaluation**. With the && operator, both Boolean expressions must be true before the action in the statement can occur. If the first expression is false, the second expression is never evaluated, because its value does not matter. For example, if a is not greater than LIMIT in the following if statement, then the evaluation is complete because there is no need to evaluate whether b is greater than LIMIT.

```
if(a > LIMIT && b > LIMIT)
    Console.WriteLine("Both are greater than LIMIT");
```

Assessment

PROGRAMMING EXERCISES provide opportunities to practice concepts. These exercises increase in difficulty and allow students to explore each major programming concept presented in the chapter. Additional programming exercises are available in the Instructor's Resource Kit.

Review Questions

1. When you use a number such as 45 in a C# program, the number is a _____.

   a. literal constant   c. literal variable
   b. figurative constant   d. figurative variable

2. A variable declaration must contain all of the following *except* a(n) _____.

   a. data type   c. assigned value
   b. identifier   d. ending semicolon

3. Which of the following is true of variable declarations?

   a. Two variables of the same type can be de
   b. Two variables of different types can be de
   c. Two variables of the same type must be c
   d. Two variables of the same type cannot co

4. Assume that you have two variables declared a Which of the following would display *838*?

   a. `Console.WriteLine("{0}{1}{2}", var1`
   b. `Console.WriteLine("{0}{1}{0}", var1`
   c. `Console.WriteLine("{0}{1}{2}", var2`
   d. `Console.WriteLine("{0}{1}{0}", var2`

5. Assume that you have a variable declared as following would display *A 3A*?

   a. `Console.WriteLine("X{0}X", var1);`
   b. `Console.WriteLine("X{0,2}X", var1);`
   c. `Console.WriteLine("X{2,0}X", var1);`
   d. `Console.WriteLine("X{0}{2}", var1);`

6. Assume that you have a variable declared as 22 % var1?

   a. 0   c.
   b. 1   d.

7. Assume that you have a variable declared as 22 / var1?

   a. 1   c.
   b. 7   d.

Exercises

Programming Exercises

1. a. Write a console-based application named **SumFiveDoubles** that allows the user to enter five doubles and displays their sum.

   b. Write a console-based application named **SumDoubles** that allows the user to enter any number of doubles continuously until the user enters 999. Display the sum of the values entered, not including 999.

2. Write a console-based application named **EnterLowercaseLetters** that asks the user to type a lowercase letter from the keyboard. If the character entered is a lowercase letter, display "OK"; if it is not a lowercase letter, display an error message. The program continues until the user types '!'.

3. Write a console-based application named **CreditScores** that continuously prompts a user for consumer credit scores until the user enters a sentinel value. A valid credit score ranges from 300 through 850. When the user enters a valid score, add it to a total; when the user enters an invalid credit score, display an error message. Before the program ends, display the average of the credit scores entered.

4. The Anderson, Bowman, and Claxton families are running their annual garage sale. Write a console-based application named **GarageSale** that prompts the user for a family initial (*A*, *B*, or *C*). Either uppercase or lowercase initials are valid. While the user does not type *Z*, continue by prompting for the amount of a sale. Keep a running total of the amount earned by each family. After the user types *Z* or *z* for an initial, display each family's total as well as a grand total made at the garage sale.

5. a. Write a console-based application named **DisplayMultiplicationTable** that displays a table of the products of every combination of two integers from 1 through 10.

   b. Create a GUI application named **DisplayMultiplicationTableGUI** that displays the multiplication table when the user clicks a button.

6. a. Write a console-based application named **OddNums** that displays all the odd numbers from 1 through 99.

   b. Create a GUI application named **OddNumsGUI** that displays all the odd numbers from 1 through 99 when the user clicks a button.

7. a. Write a console-based application named **TableOfSquares** that displays every integer value from 1 to 20, along with its squared value.

   b. Create a GUI application named **TableOfSquaresGUI** that displays every integer from 1 to 20, along with its squared value, when the user clicks a button.

REVIEW QUESTIONS test student comprehension of the major ideas and techniques presented. Twenty questions follow each chapter.

DEBUGGING EXERCISES are included with each chapter because examining programs critically and closely is a crucial programming skill. Students can download these exercises at *www.CengageBrain.com* and through the CourseMate available for this text. These files are also available to instructors through *login.cengage.com*.

CHAPTER 2   Using Data

15. Create an enumeration named Month that holds values for the months of the year, starting with JANUARY equal to 1. Write a program named **MonthNames** that prompts the user for a month integer. Convert the user's entry to a Month value and display i

16. Create an enumeration named Planet that holds the names for the eight planets in our solar system, starting with MERCURY and ending with NEPTUNE. Write a program named **Planets** that prompts the user for a numeric position, and display the name of the planet that is in the requested position.

17. Pig Latin is a nonsense language. To create a word in pig Latin, you remove the first letter and then add the first letter and "ay" at the end of the word. For example, "dog" becomes "ogday" and "cat" becomes "atcay". Write a program named **PigLatin** that allows the user to enter a word. Output the pig Latin version.

 Debugging Exercises

CASE PROBLEMS provide opportunities to build more detailed programs that continue to incorporate increasing functionality throughout the book.

1. Each of the following files in the Chapter.02 folder of your do files has syntax and/or logical errors. In each case, determine the program. After you correct the errors, save each file using preceded with *Fixed*. For example, DebugTwo1.cs will become

    a. DebugTwo1.cs   c. DebugTwo3.cs
    b. DebugTwo2.cs   d. DebugTwo4.c

 Case Problems

1. In Chapter 1, you created two programs to display the motto for the Greenville Idol competition that is held each summer during the Greenville County Fair. Now, write a program named **GreenvilleRevenue** that prompts a user for the number of contestants entered in last year's competition and in this year's competition. Display all the input data. Compute and display the revenue expected for this year's competition if each contestant pays a $25 entrance fee. Also display a statement that indicates whether this year's competition has more contestants than last year's.

2. In Chapter 1, you created two programs to display the motto for Marshall's Murals. Now, write a program named **MarshallsRevenue** that prompts a user for the number of interior and exterior murals scheduled to be painted during the next month. Compute the expected revenue for each type of mural. Interior murals cost $500 each, and exterior murals cost $750 each. Also display the total expected revenue and a statement that indicates whether more interior murals are scheduled than exterior ones.

Features

Microsoft Visual C# 2012 is a superior textbook because it also includes the following new features:

- *C# 5.0 in Visual Studio 2012*—This edition is written and tested using the latest edition of C#.

- *You Do It*—In each chapter, step-by-step exercises help you to create multiple working programs that emphasize the logic a programmer uses in choosing statements. These sections enable students to achieve success on their own—even students in online or distance learning classes. Previous editions of the book contained a long, multipart "You Do It" section at the end of each chapter. In this edition, more and shorter sections follow important chapter topics, so the student can focus on one new concept at a time.

- *Exercises*—Each chapter concludes with meaningful programming exercises that provide additional practice of the skills and concepts you learned in the chapter. Several new exercises appear in each chapter of this edition, and all the replaced exercises and solutions are available to instructors to provide as additional student assignments or to use as the basis for lectures.

- *Cases*—Each chapter contains two running case problems. These cases represent projects that continue to grow throughout a semester using concepts learned in each new chapter. Two cases allow instructors to assign different cases in alternate semesters, or to divide students in a class into two case teams.

Microsoft Visual C# 2012 also includes the following features:

- *Early GUI applications*—Students can begin to create GUI applications in Chapter 3. The earlier introduction helps engage students who have used GUI applications their entire lives. In subsequent chapters on selections, loops, arrays, and methods, students apply concepts to applications in both console and GUI environments. This approach keeps some examples simple while increasing the understanding that input, processing, and output are programming universals, no matter what interface is used. The book is structured so that students who want to skip Chapter 3 until they understand object-oriented programming can do so with no loss of continuity.

- *Objectives*—Each chapter begins with a list of objectives so you know the topics that will be presented in the chapter.

- *Notes*—These tips provide additional information—for example, an alternative method of performing a procedure, another term for a concept, background information on a technique, or a common error to avoid.

- *Figures*—Each chapter contains many figures. Code figures are most frequently 25 lines or shorter, illustrating one concept at a time. Frequently placed screen shots show exactly how program output appears. In this edition, all C# keywords that appear in figures are bold to help them stand out from programmer-created identifiers.

- *Summaries*—Following each chapter is a summary that recaps the programming concepts and techniques covered in the chapter. This feature helps you to check your understanding of the main points in each chapter.

- *Key Terms*—Each chapter includes a list of newly introduced vocabulary, shown in the order of appearance in the text. The list of key terms provides a review of the major concepts in the chapter.

- *Two Truths and a Lie*—This short quiz appears after each main chapter section, with answers provided. This quiz contains three statements—two true and one false—and the student must identify the false one. These quizzes provide students with immediate feedback as they read, without "giving away" answers to the existing multiple-choice and programming problem questions.

- *Review Questions*—Each chapter contains 20 multiple-choice review questions that provide a review of the key concepts in the chapter.

- *Debugging Exercises*—Each chapter contains four programs that have syntax and/or logical errors for you to fix. Completing these exercises provides valuable experience in locating errors, interpreting code written by others, and observing how another programmer has approached a problem.

- *Program Code*—The downloadable student files provide code for each full program presented in the chapter figures. Providing the code allows students to run it, view the results for themselves, and experiment with multiple input values and changes to the code.

- *Glossary*—A glossary contains definitions for all key terms in the book, presented in alphabetical order.

- *Video lessons*—Each chapter includes three or more video lessons produced by the author. These short videos provide instruction, further explanation, or background about a topic covered in the corresponding chapter. These videos are especially useful for online classes, for student review before exams, and for students who are audio learners.

- *Quality*—Every program example in the book, as well as every exercise, case project, and game solution, was tested by the author and again by a Quality Assurance team using Visual Studio 2012.

Instructor Resources

The following teaching tools are available for download at our Instructor Companion Site. Simply search for this text at *login.cengage.com*. An instructor login is required.

- **Electronic Instructor's Manual:** The Instructor's Manual that accompanies this textbook includes additional instructional material to assist in class preparation, including items such as Overviews, Chapter Objectives, Teaching Tips, Quick Quizzes, Class Discussion Topics, Additional Projects, Additional Resources, and Key Terms. A sample syllabus is also available.

- **ExamView®:** This textbook is accompanied by ExamView, a powerful testing software package that allows instructors to create and administer printed, computer (LAN-based), and Internet-based exams. ExamView includes hundreds of questions that correspond to the topics covered in this text, enabling students to generate detailed study guides that include page references for further review. The computer-based and Internet testing components allow students to take exams at their computers, and they save the instructor time by grading each exam automatically. These test banks are also available in Blackboard-compatible formats.

- **PowerPoint Presentations:** This text provides PowerPoint slides to accompany each chapter. Slides may be used to guide classroom presentations, to make available to students for chapter review, or to print as classroom handouts. Files are provided for every figure in the text. Instructors may use the files to customize PowerPoint slides, illustrate quizzes, or create handouts.

- **Solutions:** Solutions to "You Do It" exercises and all end-of-chapter exercises are available.

Acknowledgments

Thank you to all of the people who make this book a success, including Dan Seiter, Development Editor; Alyssa Pratt, Senior Product Manager; and Jennifer Feltri-George, Content Project Manager. I want to acknowledge every Cengage book representative who travels the country guiding instructors in their choices of educational materials.

I am also grateful to the many reviewers who provided helpful comments and encouragement during this book's development, including Dave Curelli, Upper Cape Cod Regional Technical School; Tony Hills, Northwest State Community College; Nancy Sanchez, Baylor University; and Sylvia Unwin, Bellevue College.

Thanks, too, to my husband, Geoff, for his constant support and encouragement. Finally, this book is dedicated to the flight of angels at Rosemore Village, including (but not limited to) Amy, Becki, Carrie, Cici, Clarissa, Dawn, Emily, Jaemie, Jean, Joan, Julie, Inke, Pam, Sherri, and Tim.

Joyce Farrell

Read This Before You Begin

To the User of the Data Files

To complete the steps and projects in this book, you need data files that have been created specifically for this book. Your instructor will provide the data files to you. You also can obtain the files electronically from *www.CengageBrain.com*. Find the ISBN of your title on the back cover of your book, then enter the ISBN in the search box at the top of the Cengage Brain home page. You can find the data files on the product page that opens. Note that you can use a computer in your school lab or your own computer to complete the exercises in this book.

Using Your Own Computer

To use your own computer to complete the steps and exercises, you will need the following:

- *Software*—Microsoft Visual C# 2012, including the Microsoft .NET Framework. If your book came with a copy of the software, you may install it on your computer and use it to complete the material.

- *Hardware*—Minimum requirements identified by Microsoft are a 1.6 GHz CPU, 1 GB of RAM, 10 GB of available hard disk space, 5400 RPM hard disk drive, and DirectX 9-capable video card that runs at 1024×768 or higher display resolution.

- *Operating system*—Windows 7 or 8.

A First Program Using C#

In this chapter you will:

◎ Learn about programming

◎ Learn about procedural and object-oriented programming

◎ Learn about the features of object-oriented programming languages

◎ Learn about the C# programming language

◎ Write a C# program that produces output

◎ Learn how to select identifiers to use within your programs

◎ Improve programs by adding comments and using the `System` namespace

◎ Compile and execute a C# program using the command prompt and using Visual Studio

Programming a computer is an interesting, challenging, fun, and sometimes frustrating task. As you learn a programming language, you must be precise and careful as well as creative. Computer programmers can choose from a variety of programming languages, such as Visual Basic, Java, and C++. C# (pronounced "C Sharp") is a newer programming language that offers a wide range of options and features. As you work through this book, you will master many of them, one step at a time. If this is your first programming experience, you will learn new ways to approach and solve problems and to think logically. If you know how to program but are new to C#, you will be impressed by its capabilities.

In this chapter, you will learn about the background of programming that led to the development of C#, and you will write and execute your first C# programs.

Programming

A computer **program** is a set of instructions that tell a computer what to do. Programs are also called **software**; software comes in two broad categories:

- **System software** describes the programs that operate the computer. Examples include operating systems such as Microsoft Windows, Mac OSX, and Linux.

- **Application software** describes the programs that allow users to complete tasks such as creating documents, calculating paychecks, and playing games.

The physical devices that make up a computer system are called **hardware**. Internally, computer hardware is constructed from circuitry that consists of small on/off switches; the most basic circuitry-level language that computers use to control the operation of those switches is called **machine language**. Machine language is expressed as a series of 1s and 0s—1s represent switches that are on, and 0s represent switches that are off. If programmers had to write computer programs using machine language, they would have to keep track of the hundreds of thousands of 1s and 0s involved in programming any worthwhile task. Not only would writing a program be a time-consuming and difficult task, but modifying programs, understanding others' programs, and locating errors within programs all would be cumbersome. Additionally, the number and location of switches vary from computer to computer, which means you would need to customize a machine-language program for every type of machine on which the program had to run.

Fortunately, programming has become easier because of the development of high-level programming languages. A **high-level programming language** allows you to use a limited vocabulary of reasonable keywords. **Keywords** are predefined and reserved identifiers that have special meaning in a language. In other words, high-level language programs contain words such as "read," "write," or "add" instead of the sequence of on/off switches that perform these tasks. High-level languages also allow you to assign reasonable names to areas of computer memory; you can use names such as hoursWorked or payRate, rather than having to remember the memory locations (switch numbers) of those values.

Each high-level language has its own **syntax**, or rules of the language. For example, to produce output, you might use the verb "print" in one language and "write" in another. All languages have a specific, limited vocabulary, along with a set of rules for using that vocabulary. Programmers use a computer program called a **compiler** to translate their high-level language statements into machine code. The compiler issues an error message each time a programmer commits a **syntax error**—that is, each time the programmer uses the language incorrectly. Subsequently, the programmer can correct the error and attempt another translation by compiling the program again. The program can be completely translated to machine language only when all syntax errors have been corrected. When you learn a computer programming language such as C#, C++, Visual Basic, or Java, you really are learning the vocabulary and syntax rules for that language.

In some languages, such as BASIC, the language translator is called an interpreter. In others, such as assembly language, it is called an assembler. The various language translators operate differently, but the ultimate goal of each is to translate the higher-level language into machine language.

In addition to learning the correct syntax for a particular language, a programmer must understand computer programming logic. The **logic** behind any program involves executing the various statements and procedures in the correct order to produce the desired results. For example, you might be able to execute perfect individual notes on a musical instrument, but if you do not execute them in the proper order (or execute a B-flat when an F-sharp was expected), no one will enjoy your performance. Similarly, you might be able to use a computer language's syntax correctly, but be unable to obtain correct results because the program is not constructed logically. Examples of logical errors include multiplying two values when you should divide them, or attempting to calculate a paycheck before obtaining the appropriate payroll data.

Programmers call some logical errors **semantic errors**. For example, if you misspell a programming language word, you commit a syntax error, but if you use a correct word in the wrong context, you commit a semantic error, generating incorrect results.

To create a working program that accomplishes its intended tasks, you must remove all syntax and logical errors from the program. This process is called **debugging** the program.

Since the early days of computer programming, program errors have been called "bugs." The term is often said to have originated from an actual moth that was discovered trapped in the circuitry of a computer at Harvard University in 1945. Actually, the term "bug" was in use prior to 1945 to mean trouble with any electrical apparatus; even during Thomas Edison's life, it meant an "industrial defect." In any case, the process of finding and correcting program errors has come to be known as debugging.

TWO TRUTHS & A LIE

Programming

Two of the following statements are true, and one is false. Identify the false statement and explain why it is false.

1. A high-level programming language allows you to use a vocabulary of reasonable terms such as "read," "write," or "add" instead of the sequence of on/off switches that perform these tasks.

2. Each high-level programming language has its own syntax, or rules of the language.

3. Programmers use a computer program called a compiler to translate machine code into a high-level language they can understand.

The false statement is #3. Programmers use a computer program called a compiler to translate their high-level language statements into machine code.

Procedural and Object-Oriented Programming

Two popular approaches to writing computer programs are procedural programming and object-oriented programming.

When you write a **procedural program**, you use your knowledge of a programming language to create and name computer memory locations that can hold values, and you write a series of steps or operations to manipulate those values. The named computer memory locations are called **variables** because they hold values that might vary. In programming languages, a variable is referenced by using a one-word name (an **identifier**) with no embedded spaces. For example, a company's payroll program might contain a variable named payRate. The memory location referenced by the name payRate might contain different values at different times. For instance, an organization's payroll program might use a different value for payRate for each of 100 employees. Additionally, a single employee's payRate variable might contain different values before or after a raise or before or after surpassing 40 work hours in one week. During the execution of the payroll program, each value stored under the name payRate might have many operations performed on it—for example, reading it from an input device, multiplying it by another variable representing hours worked, and printing it on paper.

 Examples of procedural programming languages include C and Logo.

Camel casing, or **lower camel casing**, describes the style of identifiers that appear to have a hump in the middle because they start with a lowercase letter but contain uppercase letters to identify new words, as in payRate. When programmers adopt the style of capitalizing the first letter of all new words in an identifier, even the first one, as in PayRate, they call the style **Pascal casing** or **upper camel casing**. By convention, C# programmers use camel casing when creating variable names. Also, the C# programming language is case sensitive. Therefore, if you create an identifier named payRate, you cannot refer to it later using PayRate or payrate.

For convenience, the individual operations used in a computer program often are grouped into logical units called **methods**. For example, a series of four or five comparisons and calculations that together determine an employee's federal tax withholding value might be grouped as a method named CalculateFederalWithholding(). A procedural program divides a problem solution into multiple methods, each with a unique name. The program then **calls** or **invokes** the methods to input, manipulate, and output the values stored in those locations. A single procedural program often contains hundreds of variables and thousands of method calls.

Depending on the programming language, methods are sometimes called *procedures*, *subroutines*, or *functions*. In C#, the preferred term is *methods*.

In C#, methods conventionally are named using Pascal casing, and all method names are followed by a set of parentheses. When this book refers to a method, the name will be followed with parentheses. This practice helps distinguish method names from variable and class names.

Object-oriented programming (OOP) is an extension of procedural programming. OOP uses variables and methods like procedural programs do, but it focuses on objects. An **object** is a concrete entity that has attributes and behaviors. The **attributes of an object** are the features it "has"; the values of an object's attributes constitute the **state of the object**. For example, attributes of a paycheck include its payee and monetary value, and the state of those attributes might be "Alice Nelson" and $400. The **behaviors of an object** are the things it "does," or its methods; for example, a paycheck object can be written and cashed, and contains a method to calculate the check amount. Object-oriented programmers might start to design a payroll application by thinking about all the objects needed, such as employees, time cards, and paychecks, and describing their attributes and behaviors.

Programmers use the term *OO*, pronounced "oh oh," as an abbreviation for "object oriented." When discussing object-oriented programming, they use *OOP*, which rhymes with "soup."

Examples of OO languages include C#, Java, Visual Basic, and C++. You can write procedural programs in OO languages, but you cannot write OO programs in procedural languages.

With either approach, procedural or object-oriented, you can produce a correct paycheck, and both techniques employ reusable program modules. The major difference lies in the focus the programmer takes during the earliest planning stages of a project. Taking an **object-oriented approach** to a problem means defining the objects needed to accomplish a task and developing classes that describe the objects so that each object maintains its own data and carries out tasks when another object requests them. The object-oriented approach is said to be "natural"—it is more common to think of a world of objects and the ways they interact than to consider a world of systems, data items, and the logic required to manipulate them.

Object-oriented programming employs a large vocabulary; you can learn much of this terminology in the chapter called *Using Classes and Objects*.

Originally, object-oriented programming was used most frequently for two major types of applications:

- **Computer simulations**, which attempt to mimic real-world activities so that their processes can be improved or so that users can better understand how the real-world processes operate.

- **Graphical user interfaces,** or **GUIs** (pronounced "gooeys"), which allow users to interact with a program in a graphical environment.

Thinking about objects in these two types of applications makes sense. For example, a city might want to develop a program that simulates traffic patterns to better prevent congestion. By creating a model with objects such as cars and pedestrians that contain their own data and rules for behavior, the simulation can be set in motion. For example, each car object has a specific current speed and a procedure for changing that speed. By creating a model of city traffic using objects, a computer can create a simulation of a real city at rush hour.

Creating a GUI environment for users also is a natural use for object orientation. It is easy to think of the components a user manipulates on a computer screen, such as buttons and scroll bars, as similar to real-world objects. Each GUI object contains data—for example, a button on a screen has a specific size and color. Each object also contains behaviors—for example, each button can be clicked and reacts in a specific way when clicked. Some people consider the term *object-oriented programming* to be synonymous with GUI programming, but object-oriented programming means more. Although many GUI programs are object-oriented, one does not imply the other. Modern businesses use object-oriented design techniques when developing all sorts of business applications, whether they are GUI applications or not.

TWO TRUTHS & A LIE

Procedural and Object-Oriented Programming

1. Procedural programs use variables and tasks that are grouped into methods or procedures.

2. Object-oriented programming languages do not support variables or methods; instead they focus on objects.

3. Object-oriented programs were first used for simulations and GUI programs.

The false statement is #2. Object-oriented programs contain variables and methods just as procedural programs do.

Features of Object-Oriented Programming Languages

For a language to be considered object-oriented, it must support the following features:

- Classes

- Objects

- Encapsulation and interfaces

- Inheritance

- Polymorphism

A **class** describes potential objects, including their attributes and behaviors. A class is similar to a recipe or a blueprint in that it describes what features objects will have and what they will be able to do after they are created. An object is an **instance of a class**; it is one tangible example of a class.

For example, you might create a class named Automobile. Some of an Automobile's attributes are its make, model, year, and purchase price. All Automobiles possess the same attributes, but not the same values, or states, for those attributes. (Programmers also call the values of an object's attributes the **properties** of the object.) When you create specific Automobile objects, each object can hold unique values for the attributes, such as *Ford*, *Taurus*, *2013*, and *$27,000*. Similarly, a Dog has attributes that include its breed, name, age, and vaccination status; the attributes for a particular dog might be *Labrador retriever*, *Murphy*, *7*, and *current*.

When you understand that an object belongs to a specific class, you know a lot about the object. If your friend purchases an Automobile, you know it has *some* model name; if your friend gets a Dog, you know it has *some* breed. You probably don't know the current state of the Automobile's speed or of the Dog's shots, but you do know that those attributes exist for the Automobile and Dog classes. Similarly, in a GUI operating environment, you expect each window you open to have specific, consistent attributes, such as a menu bar and a title bar, because each window includes these attributes as a member of the general class of GUI windows.

 By convention, programmers using C# begin their class names with an uppercase letter and use a singular noun. Thus, the class that defines the attributes and methods of an automobile would probably be named Automobile, and the class that contains dogs would probably be named Dog. If the class requires two words, programmers conventionally use upper camel casing, as in RaceCar.

Besides attributes, objects possess methods that they use to accomplish tasks, including changing attributes and discovering the values of attributes. Automobiles, for example, have methods for moving forward and backward. They also can be filled with gasoline or be washed; both are methods that change some of an Automobile's attributes. Methods also exist for determining the status of certain attributes, such as the current speed of an Automobile and the number of gallons of gas in its tank. Similarly, a Dog can walk or run, eat, and get a bath, and there are methods for determining whether it needs a walk, food, or a bath. GUI operating system components, such as windows, can be maximized, minimized, and dragged; depending on the component, they can also have their color or font style altered.

Like procedural programs, object-oriented programs have variables (attributes) and procedures (methods), but the attributes and methods are encapsulated into objects that are then used much like real-world objects. **Encapsulation** is the technique of packaging an object's attributes and methods into a cohesive unit that can be used as an undivided entity. Programmers sometimes refer to encapsulation as using a "**black box**," a device you use without regard for the internal mechanisms. If an object's methods are well written, the user is unaware of the low-level details of how the methods are executed; in such a case, the user must understand only the **interface** or interaction between the method and object. For example, if you can fill your Automobile with gasoline, it is because you understand the interface between the gas pump nozzle and the vehicle's gas tank opening. You don't need to understand how the pump works or where the gas tank is located inside your vehicle. If you can read your speedometer, it does not matter how the display figure is calculated. In fact, if someone produces a new, more accurate speedometer and inserts it into your Automobile, you don't have to know or care how it operates, as long as the interface remains the same as the previous one. The same principles apply to well-constructed objects used in object-oriented programs.

Object-oriented programming languages support two other distinguishing features in addition to organizing objects as members of classes. One feature, **inheritance**, provides the ability to extend a class so as to create a more specific class. The more specific class contains all the attributes and methods of the more general class and usually contains new attributes or methods as well. For example, if you have created a Dog class, you might then create a more specific class named ShowDog. Each instance of the ShowDog class would contain, or inherit, all the attributes and methods of a Dog, along with additional methods or attributes. For example, a ShowDog might require an attribute to hold the number of ribbons won and a method for entering a dog show. The advantage of inheritance is that when you need a class such as ShowDog, you often can extend an existing class, thereby saving a lot of time and work.

Object-oriented languages also support **polymorphism**, which is the ability to create methods that act appropriately depending on the context. That is, programs written in object-oriented languages can distinguish between methods with the same name based on the type of object that uses them. For example, you are able to "fill" both a Dog and an Automobile, but you do so by very different means. Similarly, the procedure to "fill" a ShowDog might require different food than that for a "plain" Dog. Older, non-object-oriented languages could not make such distinctions, but object-oriented languages can.

The chapters *Using Classes and Objects* and *Introduction to Inheritance* contain much more information on the features of object-oriented programs.

Watch the video *Object-Oriented Programming*.

TWO TRUTHS & A LIE

Features of Object-Oriented Programming Languages

1. Object-oriented programs contain classes that describe the attributes and methods of objects.

2. Object-oriented programming languages support inheritance, which refers to the packaging of attributes and methods into logical units.

3. Object-oriented programming languages support polymorphism, which is the ability of a method to act appropriately based on the context.

The false statement is #2. Inheritance is the ability to extend classes to make more specific ones. Encapsulation refers to the packaging of attributes and methods.

The C# Programming Language

The **C# programming language** was developed as an object-oriented and component-oriented language. It is part of Microsoft Visual Studio, a package designed for developing applications that run on Windows computers. Unlike other programming languages, C# allows every piece of data to be treated as an object and to consistently employ the principles of object-oriented programming. C# provides constructs for creating components with properties, methods, and events, making it an ideal language for modern programming, where building small, reusable components is more important than building huge, stand-alone applications. You can find Microsoft's C# specifications at *msdn.microsoft.com*. Search for *C# specifications*.

If you have not programmed before, the differences between C# and other languages mean little to you. However, experienced programmers will appreciate the thought that was put into C# features. For example:

- C# contains a GUI interface that makes it similar to Visual Basic, but C# is considered more concise than Visual Basic.

- C# is modeled after the C++ programming language, but is considered easier to learn. Some of the most difficult features to understand in C++ have been eliminated in C#.

Some differences between C# and C++ are that pointers are not used in C# (except in a mode called unsafe, which is rarely used), object destructors and forward declarations are not needed, and using `#include` files is not necessary. Multiple inheritance, which causes many C++ programming errors, is not allowed in C#.

- C# is very similar to Java, because Java was also based on C++. However, C# is more truly object-oriented. Unlike in Java, every piece of data in C# is an object, providing all data with increased functionality.

In Java, simple data types are not objects; therefore, they do not work with built-in methods. Additionally, in Java, data can only be passed to and from methods using a copy; C# omits this limitation. You will learn more in two later chapters: *Introduction to Methods* and *Advanced Method Concepts*.

The C# programming language was standardized in 2002 by Ecma International. You can read or download this set of standards at *www.ecma-international.org/publications/standards/Ecma-334.htm*.

TWO TRUTHS & A LIE

The C# Programming Language

1. The C# programming language was developed as an object-oriented and component-oriented language.

2. C# contains several features that make it similar to other languages such as Java and Visual Basic.

3. C# contains many advanced features, so the C++ programming language was created as a simpler version of the language.

The false statement is #3. C# is modeled after the C++ programming language, but some of the most difficult features to understand in C++ have been eliminated in C#.

Writing a C# Program that Produces Output

At first glance, even the simplest C# program involves a fair amount of confusing syntax. Consider the simple program in Figure 1-1. This program is written on seven lines, and its only task is to display "This is my first C# program" on the screen.

```
class FirstClass
{
    static void Main()
    {
        System.Console.WriteLine("This is my first C# program");
    }
}
```

Figure 1-1 FirstClass console application

The statement that does the actual work in this program is in the middle of the figure:

```
System.Console.WriteLine("This is my first C# program");
```

The statement ends with a semicolon because all C# statements do.

The text "This is my first C# program" is a **literal string** of characters—that is, a series of characters that will be used exactly as entered. Any literal string in C# appears between double quotation marks.

The string "This is my first C# program" appears within parentheses because the string is an argument to a method, and arguments to methods always appear within parentheses. **Arguments** represent information that a method needs to perform its task. For example, if making an appointment with a dentist's office was a C# method, you would write the following:

```
MakeAppointment("September 10", "2 p.m.");
```

Accepting and processing a dental appointment is a method that consists of a set of standard procedures. However, each appointment requires different information—the date and time— and this information can be considered the arguments of the MakeAppointment() method. If you make an appointment for September 10 at 2 p.m., you expect different results than if you make one for September 9 at 8 a.m. or December 25 at midnight. Likewise, if you pass the argument "Happy Holidays" to a method, you will expect different results than if you pass the argument "This is my first C# program".

 Although a string can be an argument to a method, not all arguments are strings. In this book, you will see and write methods that accept many other types of data.

Within the statement System.Console.WriteLine("This is my first C# program");, the method to which you are passing the argument string "This is my first C# program" is named WriteLine(). The **WriteLine() method** displays output on the screen and positions the cursor on the next line, where additional output might be displayed subsequently. The **Write() method** is very similar to the WriteLine() method. With WriteLine(), the cursor is moved to the following line after the message is displayed. With Write(), the cursor does not advance to a new line; it remains on the same line as the output.

Within the statement System.Console.WriteLine("This is my first C# program");, Console is a class that contains the WriteLine() method. Of course, not all classes have a WriteLine() method (for instance, you can't write a line to a computer's mouse, an Automobile, or a Dog), but the creators of C# assumed that you frequently would want to display output on the screen at your terminal. For this reason, the Console class was created and endowed with the method named WriteLine(). When you use the WriteLine() method, programmers say that you *call* it or *invoke* it. Soon, you will create your own C# classes and endow them with your own callable methods.

Within the statement System.Console.WriteLine("This is my first C# program");, System is a namespace. A **namespace** is a construct that acts like a container to provide a way to group similar classes. To organize your classes, you can (and will) create your own namespaces. The **System namespace**, which is built into your C# compiler, holds commonly used classes.

 An advantage to using Visual Studio is that all of its languages use the same namespaces. In other words, everything you learn about any namespace in C# is knowledge you can transfer to Visual C++ and Visual Basic.

The dots (periods) in the statement System.Console.WriteLine("This is my first C# program"); are used to separate the names of the namespace, class, and method. You will use this same namespace-dot-class-dot-method format repeatedly in your C# programs.

In the FirstClass class in Figure 1-1, the WriteLine() statement appears within a method named Main(). Every executable C# application must contain a Main() method because that is the starting point for every program. As you continue to learn C# from this book, you will write applications that contain additional methods. You will also create classes that are not programs, and so do not need a Main() method.

Every method in C# contains a header and a body. A **method header** includes the method name and information about what will pass into and be returned from a method. A **method body** is contained within a pair of curly braces ({ }) and includes all the instructions executed by the method. The program in Figure 1-1 includes only one statement between the curly braces of the Main() method. Soon, you will write methods with many more statements. In Figure 1-1, the WriteLine() statement within the Main() method is indented within the curly braces. Although the C# compiler does not require such indentation, it is conventional and clearly shows that the WriteLine() statement lies within the Main() method.

For every opening curly brace ({) in a C# program, there must be a corresponding closing curly brace (}). The precise position of the opening and closing curly braces is not important to the compiler. In general, whitespace is optional in C#. **Whitespace** is any combination of spaces, tabs, and carriage returns (blank lines). You use whitespace to organize your program code and make it easier to read; it does not affect your program. Usually, you vertically align each pair of opening and closing curly braces and indent the contents between them, as in Figure 1-1.

The method header for the Main() method in Figure 1-1 contains three words. Two of these words are keywords. In this book, C# keywords appear in bold. A complete list of keywords appears in Table 1-1 later in this chapter. In the method header static void Main(), the keyword **static** indicates that the Main() method will be executed through a class—not by a variety of objects. It means that you do not need to create an object of type FirstClass to use the Main() method defined within FirstClass. Later in this book, you will create other methods that are nonstatic methods and that are executed by objects.

The second word in the method header in Figure 1-1 is void. In English, the word *void* means empty or having no effect. When the keyword **void** is used in the Main() method header, it does not indicate that the Main() method is empty, or that it has no effect, but rather that the method does not return any value when called. You will learn more about methods that return values (and do affect other methods) when you study methods in greater detail.

In the method header, the name of the method is Main(). Main() is not a C# keyword, but all C# applications must include a method named Main(), and most C# applications will have additional methods with other names. Recall that when you execute a C# application, the Main() method always executes first. Classes that contain a Main() method are **application classes**. Applications are executable or **runnable**. Classes that do not contain a Main() method are **non-application classes**, and are not runnable. Non-application classes provide support for other classes.

 Watch the video *The Parts of a C# Program.*

TWO TRUTHS & A LIE

Writing a C# Program that Produces Output

1. Strings are information that methods need to perform their tasks.

2. The WriteLine() method displays output on the screen and positions the cursor on the next line, where additional output might be displayed.

3. Many methods such as WriteLine() have been created for you because the creators of C# assumed you would need them frequently.

The false statement is #1. Strings are literal values represented between quotation marks. Arguments represent information that a method needs to perform its task. Although an argument might be a string, not all arguments are strings.

Selecting Identifiers

Every method that you use within a C# program must be part of a class. To create a class, you use a class header and curly braces in much the same way you use a header and braces for a method within a class. When you write `class FirstClass`, you are defining a class named `FirstClass`. A class name does not have to contain the word *Class* as `FirstClass` does; as a matter of fact, most class names you create will not contain *Class*. You can define a C# class using any identifier you need, as long as it meets the following requirements:

- An identifier must begin with an underscore, the "at" sign (@), or a letter. (Letters include foreign-alphabet letters such as Π and Ω, which are contained in the set of characters known as Unicode. You will learn more about Unicode in the next chapter.)

- An identifier can contain only letters, digits, underscores, and the "at" sign. An identifier cannot contain spaces or any other punctuation or special characters such as #, $, or &.

- An identifier cannot be a C# reserved keyword, such as `class` or `void`. Table 1-1 provides a complete list of reserved keywords. (Actually, you can use a keyword as an identifier if you precede it with an "at" sign, as in `@class`. An identifier with an @ prefix is a **verbatim identifier**. This feature allows you to use code written in other languages that do not have the same set of reserved keywords. However, when you write original C# programs, you should not use the keywords as identifiers.)

abstract	float	return
as	for	sbyte
base	foreach	sealed
bool	goto	short
break	if	sizeof
byte	implicit	stackalloc
case	in	static
catch	int	string
char	interface	struct
checked	internal	switch
class	is	this
const	lock	throw
continue	long	true
decimal	namespace	try
default	new	typeof

Table 1-1   C# reserved keywords *(continues)*

(continued)

delegate	null	uint
do	object	ulong
double	operator	unchecked
else	out	unsafe
enum	override	ushort
event	params	using
explicit	private	virtual
extern	protected	void
false	public	volatile
finally	readonly	while
fixed	ref	

Table 1-1 C# reserved keywords

The following identifiers have special meaning in C# but are not keywords: add, alias, get, global, partial, remove, set, value, where, and yield. For clarity, you should avoid using these words as your own identifiers.

Table 1-2 lists some valid and conventional class names you might use when creating classes in C#. You should follow established conventions for C# so that other programmers can interpret and follow your programs. Table 1-3 lists some class names that are valid, but unconventional; Table 1-4 lists some illegal class names.

Class Name	Description
Employee	Begins with an uppercase letter
FirstClass	Begins with an uppercase letter, contains no spaces, and has an initial uppercase letter that indicates the start of the second word
PushButtonControl	Begins with an uppercase letter, contains no spaces, and has an initial uppercase letter that indicates the start of all subsequent words
Budget2012	Begins with an uppercase letter and contains no spaces

Table 1-2 Some valid and conventional class names in C#

Class Name	Description
employee	Unconventional as a class name because it begins with a lowercase letter
First_Class	Although legal, the underscore is not commonly used to indicate new words in class names
Pushbuttoncontrol	No uppercase characters are used to indicate the start of a new word, making the name difficult to read
BUDGET2013	Unconventional as a class name because it contains all uppercase letters
Void	Although this identifier is legal because it is different from the keyword void, which begins with a lowercase v, the similarity could cause confusion

Table 1-3 Some unconventional (though legal) class names in C#

Class Name	Description
an employee	Space character is illegal
Push Button Control	Space characters are illegal
class	class is a reserved word
2011Budget	Class names cannot begin with a digit
phone#	The # symbol is not allowed; identifiers consist of letters, digits, underscores, or @

Table 1-4 Some illegal class names in C#

In Figure 1-1, the line class FirstClass contains the keyword class, which identifies FirstClass as a class.

The simple program shown in Figure 1-1 has many pieces to remember. For now, you can use the program shown in Figure 1-2 as a shell, where you replace the identifier AnyLegalClassName with any legal class name, and the line /*********/ with any statements that you want to execute.

```
class AnyLegalClassName
{
    static void Main()
    {
        /*********/;
    }
}
```

Figure 1-2 Shell program

Watch the video *C# Identifiers*.

TWO TRUTHS & A LIE

Selecting Identifiers

1. In C#, an identifier must begin with an underscore, the at sign (@), or an uppercase letter.

2. An identifier can contain only letters, digits, underscores, and the "at" sign, not special characters such as #, $, or &.

3. An identifier cannot be a C# reserved keyword.

The false statement is #1. In C#, an identifier must begin with an underscore, the at sign (@), or a letter. There is no requirement that the initial letter be capitalized, although in C#, it is a convention that the initial letter of a class name is capitalized.

Improving Programs by Adding Comments and Using the System Namespace

As you can see, even the simplest C# program takes several lines of code and contains somewhat perplexing syntax. Large programs that perform many tasks include much more code. As you work through this book, you will discover many ways to improve your ability to handle large programs. Two things you can do immediately are to add program comments and use the System namespace.

Adding Program Comments

As you write longer programs, it becomes increasingly difficult to remember why you included steps and how you intended to use particular variables. **Program comments** are nonexecuting statements that you add to document a program. Programmers use comments to leave notes for themselves and for others who might read their programs in the future.

As you work through this book, you should add comments as the first few lines of every program file. The comments should contain your name, the date, and the name of the program. Your instructor might want you to include additional comments.

Comments also can be useful when you are developing a program. If a program is not performing as expected, you can **comment out** various statements and subsequently run the program to observe the effect. When you comment out a statement, you turn it into a comment so that the compiler will ignore it. This approach helps you pinpoint the location of errant statements in malfunctioning programs.

C# offers three types of comments:

- **Line comments** start with two forward slashes (//) and continue to the end of the current line. Line comments can appear on a line by themselves, or they can occupy part of a line following executable code.

- **Block comments** start with a forward slash and an asterisk (/*) and end with an asterisk and a forward slash (*/). Block comments can appear on a line by themselves, on a line before executable code, or after executable code. When a comment is long, block comments can extend across as many lines as needed.

- C# also supports a special type of comment used to create documentation within a program. These comments, called **XML-documentation format comments**, use a special set of tags within angle brackets (< >). (XML stands for Extensible Markup Language.) You will learn more about this type of comment as you continue your study of C#.

The forward slash (/) and the backslash (\) characters often are confused, but they are distinct characters. You cannot use them interchangeably.

Figure 1-3 shows how comments can be used in code. The program covers 10 lines, yet only seven are part of the executable C# program, including the last two lines, which contain curly braces and are followed by partial-line comments. The only line that actually *does* anything visible when the program runs is the shaded one that displays "Message".

```
/* This program is written to demonstrate
   using comments */
class ClassWithOneExecutingLine
{
    static void Main()
    {
        // The next line writes the message
        System.Console.WriteLine("Message");
    }  // End of Main
} // End of ClassWithOneExecutingLine
```

Figure 1-3   Using comments within a program

Using the `System` Namespace

A program can contain as many statements as you need. For example, the program in Figure 1-4 produces the three lines of output shown in Figure 1-5. (To get the output, you have to know how to compile and execute the program, which you will learn in the next part of this chapter.) A semicolon separates each program statement.

```
class ThreeLinesOutput
{
    static void Main()
    {
        System.Console.WriteLine("Line one");
        System.Console.WriteLine("Line two");
        System.Console.WriteLine("Line three");
    }
}
```

Figure 1-4 A program that produces three lines of output

Figure 1-5 Output of `ThreeLinesOutput` program

Figure 1-5 shows the output of the `ThreeLinesOutput` program when it is run in Visual Studio. The prompt to press any key to continue is not part of the program; it is added by Visual Studio, but it does not appear if you run the program from the command prompt.

The program in Figure 1-4 shows a lot of repeated code—the phrase `System.Console.WriteLine` appears three times. When you need to repeatedly use a class from the same namespace, you can shorten the statements you type by adding a clause that indicates a namespace containing the class. You indicate a namespace with a **using clause**, or **using directive**, as shown in the shaded statement in the program in Figure 1-6. If you type `using System;` prior to the class definition, the compiler knows to use the `System` namespace when it encounters the `Console` class. The output of the program in Figure 1-6 is identical to that in Figure 1-4, in which `System` was repeated with each `WriteLine()` statement.

```
using System;
class ThreeLinesOutput
{
    static void Main()
    {
        Console.WriteLine("Line one");
        Console.WriteLine("Line two");
        Console.WriteLine("Line three");
    }
}
```

Figure 1-6   A program that produces three lines of output with a `using System` clause

At this point, a new programmer might say, "Maybe I can shorten my typing tasks even further by typing `using System.Console;` at the top of my programs, and produce output with statements like `WriteLine("Hi");`." However, `using` cannot be used with a class name like `System.Console`—only with a namespace name like `System`.

TWO TRUTHS & A LIE

Improving Programs by Adding Comments and Using the `System` Namespace

1. Line comments start with two forward slashes (//) and end with two backslashes (\\).

2. Block comments can extend across as many lines as needed.

3. You use a namespace with a `using` clause, or `using` directive, to shorten statements when you need to repeatedly use a class from the same namespace.

The false statement is #1. Line comments start with two forward slashes (//) and continue to the end of the current line.

 You Do It

Now that you understand the basic framework of a program written in C#, you are ready to enter your first C# program into a text editor so you can compile and execute it. It is a tradition among programmers that the first program you write in

(continues)

20

(continued)

any language produces "Hello, world!" as its output. To create a C# program, you can use any simple text editor, such as Notepad, or the editor that is included as part of Microsoft Visual Studio. There are advantages to using the C# editor to write your programs, but using a plain text editor is simpler when you are getting started.

Entering a Program into an Editor

1. Start any text editor, such as Notepad, and open a new document, if necessary.

2. Type the `using` statement and the header for the class:

```
using System;
class Hello
```

3. On the next two lines, type the class-opening and class-closing curly braces: {}. Many programmers type a closing brace as soon as they type the opening one to guarantee that they always type complete pairs.

4. Between the class braces, insert a new line, type three spaces to indent, and write the `Main()` method header:

```
static void Main()
```

5. On the next two lines, type the opening and closing braces for the `Main()` method, indenting them about three spaces.

6. Between the `Main()` method's braces, insert a new line and type six spaces so the next statement will be indented within the braces. Type the one executing statement in this program:

```
Console.WriteLine("Hello, world!");
```

Your code should look like Figure 1-7.

```
using System;
class Hello
{
   static void Main()
   {
      Console.WriteLine("Hello, world!");
   }
}
```

Figure 1-7 The Hello class

(continues)

(continued)

7. Choose a location that is meaningful to you to save your program. For example, you might create a folder named C# on your hard drive. Within that folder, you might create a folder named Chapter.01 in which you will store all the examples and exercises in this chapter. If you are working in a school lab, you might be assigned a storage location on your school's server, or you might prefer to store your examples on a USB drive or other portable storage media. Save the program as **Hello.cs**. It is important that the file extension be .cs, which stands for *C Sharp*. If the file has a different extension, the compiler for C# will not recognize the program as a C# program.

Many text editors attach their own filename extension (such as .txt or .doc) to a saved file. Double-check your saved file to ensure that it does not have a double extension (as in Hello.cs.txt). If the file has a double extension, rename it. If you use a word-processing program as your editor, select the option to save the file as a plain text file.

Compiling and Executing a C# Program

After you write and save a program, two more steps must be performed before you can view the program output:

1. You must compile the program you wrote (called the **source code**) into **intermediate language (IL)**.

2. The C# **just in time (JIT)** compiler must translate the intermediate code into executable code.

When you compile a C# program, your source code is translated into intermediate language. The JIT compiler converts IL instructions into native code at the last moment, and appropriately for each type of operating system on which the code might eventually be executed. In other words, the same set of IL can be JIT-compiled and executed on any supported architecture.

Some developers say that languages like C# are "semi-compiled." That is, instead of being translated immediately from source code to their final executable versions, programs are compiled into an intermediate version that is later translated into the correct executable statements for the environment in which the program is running.

You can write a program using a simple editor such as Notepad and then perform these steps from the command line in your system. You also can write a program within the Integrated Development Environment that comes with Visual Studio. Both methods can produce the same output; the one you use is a matter of preference.

- The **command line** is the line on which you type a command in a system that uses a text interface. The **command prompt** is a request for input that appears at the beginning of the command line. In DOS, the command prompt indicates the disk drive and optional path, and ends with >. You might prefer the simplicity of the command line because you do not work with multiple menus and views. Additionally, if you want to pass command-line arguments to a program, you must compile from the command line.

- The **Integrated Development Environment (IDE)** is a programming environment that allows you to issue commands by selecting choices from menus and clicking buttons. Many programmers prefer using the IDE because it provides features such as color-coded keywords and automatic statement completion.

Compiling Code from the Command Prompt

 If you will be using the IDE to write all your programs, you can read this section quickly, and then concentrate on the section titled "Compiling Code Using the Visual Studio IDE."

To compile your source code from the command line, you first locate the command prompt. There, you type csc, followed by the name of the file that contains the source code. The command csc stands for "C Sharp compiler." For example, to compile a file named ThreeLinesOutput.cs, you would type the following and then press the Enter key:

```
csc ThreeLinesOutput.cs
```

One of three outcomes will occur:

- You receive an operating system error message such as "Bad command or file name" or "csc is not recognized as an internal or external command, operable program or batch file". You can recognize operating system messages because they do not start with the name of the program you are trying to compile.

- You receive one or more program language error messages. You can recognize program language error messages because they start with the name of the program followed by a line number and the position where the error was first noticed.

- You receive no error messages (only a copyright statement from Microsoft), indicating that the program has compiled successfully.

What to Do if You Receive an Operating System Error Message at the Command Prompt

If you receive an operating system message such as "csc is not recognized…," or "Source file… could not be found," it may mean that:

- You misspelled the command csc.

- You misspelled the filename.

- You forgot to include the extension .cs with the filename.

- You are not within the correct subdirectory or folder on your command line. For example, Figure 1-8 shows the `csc` command typed in the root directory of the C drive. If the ThreeLinesOutput.cs file is stored in a folder on the C drive rather than in the root directory, then the command shown will not work because the C# file cannot be found.

Figure 1-8 Attempt to compile a program from the root directory at the command line, and error message received

- The C# compiler was not installed properly. If you are working on your own computer, you might need to reinstall C#; if you are working in a school laboratory, you need to notify the system administrator.

- You need to set a path command. To do this, you must locate the C# compiler on your hard disk. (The process for finding a file differs slightly with different systems.) If you don't find a copy of the compiler, named csc.exe, you need to obtain and install one. For more information, visit *msdn2.microsoft.com/en-us/vcsharp*.

When you find the csc.exe file, type `path` = at the command line, followed by the complete path name that describes where csc.exe is stored; then try to compile the `ThreeLinesOutput` program again. For example, if C# was stored in the default location in the folder named v4.5, you might type the following:

```
path = c:\Windows\Microsoft.NET\Framework\v4.5
```

(Your folder name might contain many more digits and additional dots.) Press Enter. Next, type `csc ThreeLinesOutput.cs` and press Enter again.

Instead of typing the `path` command, you also can change the default path if you are the system administrator on the local computer. The process varies slightly depending on your operating system.

What to Do if You Receive a Programming Language Error Message at the Command Prompt

If you receive a programming language error message, it means that the compiler was installed correctly, but that the source code contains one or more syntax errors. A syntax error occurs when you introduce typing errors into your program. Program error messages start with the program name, followed by parentheses that hold the line number and the position in the line where the compiler noticed the error. For example, in Figure 1-9, an error is found in ThreeLinesOutput.cs in line 6, position 15. In this case, the message is generated because WriteLine is typed as *writeLine* (with a lowercase *w*). The error message is "'System. Console' does not contain a definition for 'writeLine'". If a problem like this occurs, you must reopen the text file that contains the source code, make the necessary corrections, save the file, and compile it again.

```
Command Prompt

C:\C#\Chapter.01>csc ThreeLinesOutput.cs
Microsoft (R) Visual C# Compiler version 4.5
for Microsoft (R) .NET Framework 4.5
Copyright (C) Microsoft Corporation. All rights reserved.

ThreeLinesOutput.cs(6,15): error CS0117: 'System.Console' does not contain a
        definition for 'writeLine'

C:\C#\Chapter.01>_
```

Figure 1-9 Error message generated when WriteLine is mistyped in the ThreeLinesOutput program compiled from the command prompt

 The C# compiler issues warnings as well as errors. A warning is less serious than an error; it means that the compiler has determined you have done something unusual, but not illegal. If you have purposely introduced a warning situation to test a program, then you can ignore the warning. Usually, however, you should treat a warning message just as you would an error message and attempt to remedy the situation.

What to Do When the Program Compiles Successfully at the Command Prompt

If you receive no error messages after compiling the code, then the program compiled successfully, and a file with the same name as the source code—but with an .exe extension—is created and saved in the same folder as the program text file. For example, if ThreeLinesOutput.cs compiles successfully, then a file named ThreeLinesOutput.exe is created.

To run the program from the command line, you simply type the program name—for example, ThreeLinesOutput. You can also type the full filename, ThreeLinesOutput.exe, but it is not necessary to include the extension.

Compiling Code Using the Visual Studio IDE

As an alternative to using the command line, you can compile and write your program within the Visual Studio IDE. This approach has several advantages:

- Some of the code you need is already created for you.

- The code is displayed in color, so you can more easily identify parts of your program. Reserved words appear in blue, comments in green, and identifiers in black.

- If error messages appear when you compile your program, you can double-click an error message and the cursor will move to the line of code that contains the error.

- Other debugging tools are available. You will become more familiar with these tools as you develop more sophisticated programs.

If Visual Studio has been installed on your system, you can open it from the main menu, start a new project, designate it to be a *Console Project*, and give the project a name. Figure 1-10 shows a program and project named ThreeLinesOutput written in the editor of the Visual Studio IDE. Everything in the figure was generated automatically by Visual Studio except for the project name and the three lines coded in the Main() method. You can see that the environment looks like a word processor, containing menu options such as FILE, EDIT, and HELP, and buttons with icons representing options such as SAVE and UNDO. Selecting any of these menu options displays a drop-down list of additional options. Many of the options have shortcut keys that you can use instead of accessing the menus. You will learn about some of these options later in this chapter and continue to learn about more of them as you work with C# in the IDE.

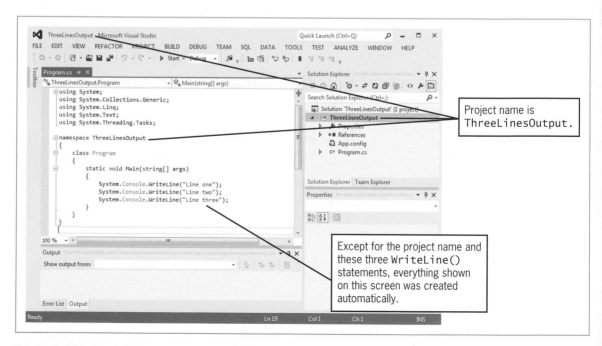

Figure 1-10 ThreeLinesOutput program as it appears in Visual Studio

One way to compile a program from Visual Studio is to select BUILD from the main menu and then select Build Solution. As an alternative, you can press the F7 key. You can also select DEBUG from the main menu, and then Start Without Debugging. The advantage of the latter option is that the program will be compiled if there are no syntax errors and then execute so that you can see the output.

What to Do if You Receive a Programming Language Error Message in the IDE

If you introduce a syntax error into a program in the IDE, you receive a programming language error message. For example, in Figure 1-11, WriteLine is spelled incorrectly because it uses a lowercase *w*. The error message displayed at the bottom of the IDE is the same one displayed for an application run at the command prompt: "'System.Console' does not contain a definition for 'writeLine'". The position is given, and as an additional visual aid, a wavy underline emphasizes the unrecognized definition. When you fix the problem and compile again, the error message is eliminated.

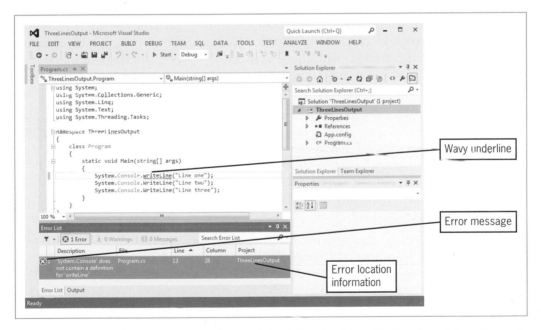

Figure 1-11 Error message generated when WriteLine is mistyped in the ThreeLinesOutput program compiled in the IDE

What to Do When the Program Compiles Successfully in the IDE

If you receive no error messages after compiling the code, then the program compiled successfully, and you can run the program. Select DEBUG from the main menu, and then select Start Without Debugging. The output appears, as you saw it in Figure 1-5 earlier in this chapter.

Noticing the Differences Between the Programs in the Text Editor and the IDE

There are a few differences between the ThreeLinesOutput programs in Figures 1-4 and 1-10. Specifically, the Visual Studio version in Figure 1-10 contains the following extra components that are highlighted in Figure 1-12:

- *Five using statements at the top of the file.* You have already learned that you can place the using System; statement in a program to eliminate naming System with every call to Console.WriteLine(). Visual Studio automatically provides you with the statement and several other commonly needed statements. In this case, you could delete all five statements from the Visual Studio version of the program, and the program would still run correctly. Conversely, you could add all five statements to the command-line version of the program, and it would also run correctly.

- *A namespace declaration and its opening and closing curly braces.* You already know that C# uses built-in namespaces like System and others that are automatically listed at the top of the Visual Studio version of programs. C# also allows you to create your own namespaces; Visual Studio assumes that you will want to create one using the name you have assigned to the project. In this case, you could remove the namespace declaration from the Visual Studio version of the program, or you could add one to the command-line version of the program. In both cases, the programs would still run correctly.

- *A class named Program.* Visual Studio assumes that you want to avoid confusion by having different names for your namespace and the class contained within it, so it assigns the generic name Program to the class that contains the Main() method. You could change this name to match the namespace identifier, or use any other legal identifier, and the program would still work correctly. In the command-line version of the program, you could change the class name to Program or any other legal identifier, and the program would also work.

- *The words string[] args between the parentheses of the Main() method header.* C# allows a program's Main() method header to be written in several ways. For example, you can include the words string[] args between the method's parentheses, or you can omit the words. The square brackets indicate an array, as you will learn when studying arrays later in this book. In this example, you could write the Main() method header with or without the extra code in either the command-line or Visual Studio version of the program, and the Main() method would still work correctly.

In summary, the Visual Studio version of the ThreeLinesOutput program provides everything you need to run the program and saves you as much typing as possible in case you want to include additional options. The command-line and Visual Studio versions of the program function identically.

ThreeLinesOutput in Notepad and executed from the command prompt:

```csharp
class ThreeLinesOutput
{
    static void Main()
    {
        System.Console.WriteLine("Line one");
        System.Console.WriteLine("Line two");
        System.Console.WriteLine("Line three");
    }
}
```

ThreeLinesOutput in and executed from the Visual Studio IDE:

```csharp
using System;
using System.Collections.Generic;
using System.Linq;
using System.Text;
using System.Threading.Tasks;

namespace ThreeLinesOutput
{
    class Program
    {
        static void Main(string[] args)
        {
            System.Console.WriteLine("Line one");
            System.Console.WriteLine("Line two");
            System.Console.WriteLine("Line three");
        }
    }
}
```

Figure 1-12 Comparing the command-line and Visual Studio versions of the ThreeLinesOutput program

Deciding Which Environment to Use

When you write, compile, and execute a C# program, you can use either a text editor and the command line or the Visual Studio IDE. You would never need to use both. You might prefer using an editor with which you are already familiar (such as Notepad) and compiling from the command line because only two files are generated, saving disk space.

On the other hand, the IDE provides many useful features, such as automatic statement completion. For example, if you type System and a dot, then a list of choices is displayed, and you can click Console instead of typing it. Similarly, after the dot that follows Console, a list of choices is displayed from which you can select WriteLine.

Additionally, in the IDE, words are displayed using different colors based on their category; for example, one color is used for C#-reserved words and a different color for literal strings. It is also easier to correct many errors using the IDE. When compiler errors or warnings are issued, you can double-click the message, and the cursor jumps to the location in the code where the error was detected. Another advantage to learning the IDE is that if you use another programming language in Visual Studio (C++ or Visual Basic), the environment will already be familiar to you.

The C# language works the same way no matter which method you use to compile your programs. Everything you learn in the next chapters about input, output, decision making, loops, and arrays will work the same way, regardless of the compilation technique you use. You can use just one technique or compile some programs in each environment as the mood strikes you. You can also mix and match techniques if you prefer. For example, you can use an editor you like to compose your programs, then paste them into the IDE to execute them. Although any program can be written using either compilation technique, when you write GUI applications that use existing objects such as buttons and labels, you will find that the extensive amount of code automatically generated by the IDE is very helpful.

 Watch the video *Writing and Compiling a Program*.

TWO TRUTHS & A LIE

Compiling and Executing a C# Program

1. After you write and save a program, you must compile it into intermediate language and then the C# just in time (JIT) compiler must translate the intermediate code into executable code.

2. You can compile and execute a C# program from the command line or within the Integrated Development Environment (IDE) that comes with Visual Studio.

3. Many programmers prefer to compile their programs from the command line because it provides features such as color-coded keywords and automatic statement completion.

The false statement is #3. Programmers who prefer the command line prefer its simplicity. Programmers who prefer the Visual Studio IDE prefer the color-coded keywords and automatic statement completion.

You Do It

Compiling and Executing a Program from the Command Line

 If you do not plan to use the command line to execute programs, you can skip to the next part of this "You Do It" section, called "Compiling and Executing a Program Using the Visual Studio IDE."

1. Go to the command prompt on your system. For example, in Windows 7, click **Start**, then click **All Programs**, click **Accessories**, and click **Command Prompt**. In Windows 8, click the **Windows Explorer** icon on the **Start** screen. In the **Libraries** window that opens, click the **File** menu, and click **Open command prompt**. In the next window, click **Open command prompt** again. Change the current directory to the name of the folder that holds your program.

    If your command prompt indicates a path other than the one you want, you can type `cd\` and then press Enter to return to the root directory. You can then type `cd` to change the path to the one where your program resides. For example, if you stored your program file in a folder named Chapter.01 within a folder named C#, then you can type the following:

    ```
    cd C#\Chapter.01
    ```

    The command `cd` is short for *change directory*.

2. Type the command that compiles your program:

    ```
    csc Hello.cs
    ```

    If you receive no error messages and the prompt returns, it means that the compile operation was successful, that a file named Hello.exe has been created, and that you can execute the program. If you do receive error messages, check every character of the program you typed to make sure it matches Figure 1-7 in the last "You Do It" section. Remember, C# is case sensitive, so all casing must match exactly. When you have corrected the errors, repeat this step to compile the program again.

3. You can verify that a file named Hello.exe was created in several ways:

    -   At the command prompt, type **dir** to view a directory of the files stored in the current folder. Both Hello.cs and Hello.exe should appear in the list.

    -   Use Windows Explorer to view the contents of the Chapter.01 folder, verifying that two Hello files are listed.

(continues)

(continued)

- Double-click the **Computer** icon, navigate to and double-click the **Chapter.01** folder, and verify that two Hello files are listed.

4. At the command prompt, type **Hello**, which is the name of the program (the name of the executable file), and then press **Enter**. Alternatively, you can type the full filename **Hello.exe**, but typing the .exe extension isn't necessary. The output should look like Figure 1-13.

Figure 1-13   Output of the Hello application

 You can use the /out compiler option between the csc command and the name of the .cs file to indicate the name of the output file. For example, if you type csc /out:Hello.exe Hello.cs, you create an output file named Hello.exe. By default, the name of the output file is the same as the name of the .cs file. Usually, this is your intention, so most often you omit the /out option.

Compiling and Executing a Program Using the Visual Studio IDE

Next, you use the C# compiler environment to compile and execute the same Hello program you ran from the command line.

1. Open Visual Studio. If there is a shortcut icon on your desktop, you can double-click it. Alternatively, in Windows 7, you can click the **Start** button, click **All Programs**, and then click **Visual Studio 2012**.

2. If this is the first time any user has opened Visual Studio, you will be asked to choose your preferred settings. Select **Visual C# Development Settings**, and click **Start Visual Studio**. The first time Visual Studio is started, it may take a few minutes to configure the environment for you. When you see the Start Page, click **New Project**.

3. In the New Project window, click **Visual C#** and then click **Console Application**. By default, the name for the project is set to ConsoleApplication1.

(continues)

(continued)

Change it to **Hello** and select the path where you want to save the project (see Figure 1-14). Click **OK**. Visual C# creates a new folder for your project named after the project title.

Many students like to walk through these "You Do It" exercises multiple times for practice. Note that Visual Studio does not allow you to create a project with the same name as one already stored in a folder. When you perform these steps additional times, either delete the first version of the project before you start the next one, store the new version in a different folder, or give the new project a different name.

This project uses Visual C#.

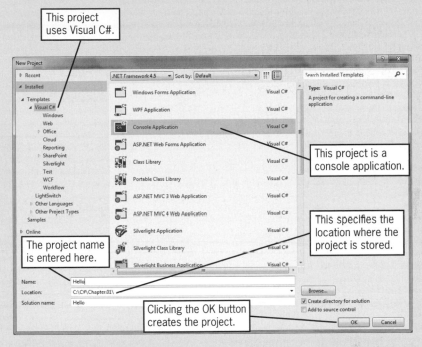

This project is a console application.

This specifies the location where the project is stored.

The project name is entered here.

Clicking the OK button creates the project.

Figure 1-14   Creating a new project

4. The Hello application editing window appears. A lot of code is already written for you in this window, including some using statements, a namespace named Hello, a class named Program, and a Main() method. To create the Hello program, you need to add only one statement to the prewritten code. Place your cursor after the opening brace of the Main() method, press **Enter** to start a new line, and add the following statement:

```
Console.WriteLine("Hello, world!");
```

(continues)

(continued)

Figure 1-15 shows the editing window after the `WriteLine()` statement has been added.

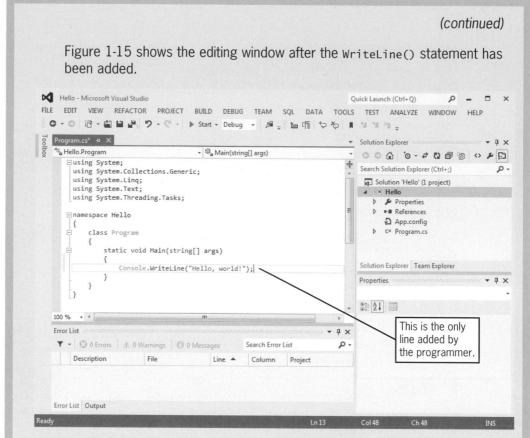

Figure 1-15   The `Hello` application editing window after the code has been added

5. Save the project by clicking **FILE** on the menu bar and then clicking **Save All**, or by clicking the **Save All** button (which shows two disks) on the toolbar.

6. To compile the program, click **BUILD** on the menu bar and then click **Build Solution**. You should receive no error messages, and the words "Build succeeded" should appear near the lower-left edge of the window.

7. Click **DEBUG** on the menu bar and then click **Start Without Debugging**. Figure 1-16 shows the output; you see "Hello, world!" followed by the message "Press any key to continue". Press any key to close the output screen.

(continues)

(continued)

Figure 1-16 Output of the `Hello` application in Visual Studio

8. Close Visual Studio by clicking **FILE** on the menu bar and then clicking **Exit**, or by clicking the **Close** box in the upper-right corner of the Visual Studio window.

9. When you create a C# program using an editor such as Notepad and compiling with the `csc` command, only two files are created—Hello.cs and Hello.exe. When you create a C# program using the Visual Studio editor, many additional files are created. You can view their filenames in several ways:

- At the command prompt, type **dir** to view a directory of the files stored in the folder where you saved the project (for example, your Chapter.01 folder). Within the folder, a new folder named Hello has been created. Type the command **cd Hello** to change the current path to include this new folder, then type **dir** again. You see another folder named Hello. Type **cd Hello** again, and **dir** again. You should see several folders and files.

- Double-click the **Computer** icon, find and double-click the correct drive, select the **C#** folder and the **Chapter.01** folder (or the path you are using), double-click the **Hello** folder, and view the contents. Double-click the second **Hello** folder and view the contents there too.

- Use Windows Explorer to view the contents of the Hello folders within the **Chapter.01** folder.

Regardless of the technique you use to examine the folders, you will find that the innermost Hello folder contains a bin folder, an obj folder, a Properties folder, and additional files. If you explore further, you will find that the bin folder contains Debug and Release folders, which include additional files. Using the Visual Studio editor to compile your programs creates a significant amount of overhead. These additional files become important as you create more sophisticated C# projects.

(continues)

(continued)

Depending on the version of Visual Studio you are using, your folder configuration might be slightly different.

If you followed the earlier instructions on compiling a program from the command line, and you used the same folder when using the IDE, you will see the additional Hello.cs and Hello.exe files in your folder. These files will have an earlier time stamp than the files you just created. If you were to execute a new program within Visual Studio without saving and executing it from the command line first, you would not see these two additional files.

Adding Comments to a Program

Comments are nonexecuting statements that help to document a program. In the following steps, you add some comments to the program you just created.

1. If you prefer compiling programs from the command line, then open the **Hello.cs** file in your text editor. If you prefer compiling programs from Visual Studio, then open Visual Studio, click **FILE**, point to **Open**, click **Project/Solution**, browse for the correct folder, double-click the **Hello** folder, and then double-click the **Hello** file.

2. Position your cursor at the top of the file, press **Enter** to insert a new line, press the **Up** arrow key to go to that line, and then type the following comments at the top of the file. Press **Enter** after typing each line. Insert your name and today's date where indicated.

    ```
    //Filename Hello.cs
    //Written by <your name>
    //Written on <today's date>
    ```

3. Scroll to the line that reads `static void Main()` and press **Enter** to start a new line. Then press the **Up** arrow; in the new blank line, aligned with the start of the `Main()` method header, type the following block comment in the program:

    ```
    /*  This program demonstrates the use of
    the WriteLine() method to display the
    message Hello, world!  */
    ```

4. Save the file, replacing the old Hello.cs file with this new, commented version.

(continues)

(continued)

5. If you prefer to compile programs from the command line, type **csc Hello.cs** at the command line. When the program compiles successfully, execute it with the command **Hello**. If you prefer compiling and executing programs from Visual Studio, click **DEBUG** and **Start Without Debugging**. Adding program comments makes no difference in the execution of the program.

6. If you are working from the command line, you can close the command-line window. If you are working from Visual Studio, you can close the output screen and then close Visual Studio.

Chapter Summary

- A computer program is a set of instructions that tell a computer what to do. Programmers write their programs, then use a compiler to translate their high-level language statements into intermediate language and machine code. A program works correctly when both its syntax and logic are correct.

- Procedural programming involves creating computer memory locations, called variables, and sets of operations, called methods. In object-oriented programming, you envision program components as objects that are similar to concrete objects in the real world; then you manipulate the objects to achieve a desired result. OOP techniques were first used for simulations and GUIs.

- Objects are instances of classes and are made up of attributes and methods. Object-oriented programming languages support encapsulation, inheritance, and polymorphism.

- The C# programming language was developed as an object-oriented and component-oriented language. It contains many features similar to those in Visual Basic, Java, and C++.

- To produce a line of console output in a C# program, you must pass a literal string as an argument to the System.Console.WriteLine() method. System is a namespace and Console is a class. Calls to the WriteLine() method can appear within the Main() method of a class you create.

- You can define a C# class or variable by using any name or identifier that begins with an underscore, a letter, or an "at" sign. These names can contain only letters, digits, underscores, and the "at" sign, and cannot be C#-reserved keywords.

- You can improve programs by adding comments, which are nonexecuting statements that you add to document a program or to disable statements when you test a program. The three types of comments in C# are line comments that start with two forward slashes (//) and continue to the end of the current line, block comments that start with a forward slash and an asterisk (/*) and end with an asterisk and a forward slash (*/), and XML-documentation comments. You can also improve programs and shorten the statements you type by using a clause that indicates a namespace where your classes can be found.

- To create a C# program, you can use the Microsoft Visual Studio environment or any text editor, such as Notepad. After you write and save a program, you must compile the source code into intermediate and machine language.

Key Terms

A computer **program** is a set of instructions that tell a computer what to do.

Software is computer programs.

System software describes the programs that operate the computer.

Application software is the programs that allow users to complete tasks.

Hardware comprises all the physical devices associated with a computer.

Machine language is the most basic circuitry-level language.

A **high-level programming language** allows you to use a vocabulary of keywords instead of the sequence of on/off switches that perform these tasks.

Keywords are predefined and reserved identifiers that have special meaning to the compiler.

A language's **syntax** is its set of rules.

A **compiler** is a computer program that translates high-level language statements into machine code.

A **syntax error** is an error that occurs when a programming language is used incorrectly.

The **logic** behind any program involves executing the various statements and methods in the correct order to produce the desired results.

Semantic errors are the type of logical errors that occur when you use a correct word in the wrong context, generating incorrect results.

Debugging a program is the process of removing all syntax and logical errors from the program.

A **procedural program** is created by writing a series of steps or operations to manipulate values.

Variables are named computer memory locations that hold values that might vary.

An **identifier** is the name of a program component such as a variable, class, or method.

Camel casing, also called **lower camel casing**, is a style of creating identifiers in which the first letter is not capitalized, but each new word is.

Pascal casing, also called **upper camel casing**, is a style of creating identifiers in which the first letter of all new words in a name, even the first one, is capitalized.

Methods are compartmentalized, named program units containing instructions that accomplish tasks.

A program **calls** or **invokes** methods.

Object-oriented programming (OOP) is a programming technique that features objects, classes, encapsulation, interfaces, polymorphism, and inheritance.

An **object** is a concrete entity that has attributes and behaviors; an object is an instance of a class.

The **attributes of an object** represent its characteristics.

The **state of an object** is the collective value of all its attributes at any point in time.

The **behaviors of an object** are its methods.

Taking an **object-oriented approach** to a problem means defining the objects needed to accomplish a task and developing classes that describe the objects so that each maintains its own data and carries out tasks when another object requests them.

Computer simulations are programs that attempt to mimic real-world activities to foster a better understanding of them.

Graphical user interfaces, or **GUIs** (pronounced "gooeys"), are program elements that allow users to interact with a program in a graphical environment.

A **class** is a category of objects or a type of object.

An **instance of a class** is an object.

The **properties** of an object are its values.

Encapsulation is the technique of packaging an object's attributes and methods into a cohesive unit that can be used as an undivided entity.

A **black box** is a device you use without regard for the internal mechanisms.

An **interface** is the interaction between a method and an object.

Inheritance is the ability to extend a class so as to create a more specific class that contains all the attributes and methods of a more general class; the extended class usually contains new attributes or methods as well.

Polymorphism is the ability to create methods that act appropriately depending on the context.

The **C# programming language** was developed as an object-oriented and component-oriented language. It exists as part of Visual Studio, a package used for developing applications for the Windows family of operating systems.

A **literal string** of characters is a series of characters enclosed in double quotes that is used exactly as entered.

An **argument** to a method represents information that a method needs to perform its task. An argument is the expression used between parentheses when you call a method.

The **WriteLine() method** displays a line of output on the screen, positions the cursor on the next line, and waits for additional output.

The **Write() method** displays a line of output on the screen, but the cursor does not advance to a new line; it remains on the same line as the output.

A **namespace** is a construct that acts like a container to provide a way to group similar classes.

The **System namespace**, which is built into your C# compiler, holds commonly used classes.

A **method header** includes the method name and information about what will pass into and be returned from a method.

The **method body** of every method is contained within a pair of curly braces ({ }) and includes all the instructions executed by the method.

Whitespace is any combination of spaces, tabs, and carriage returns (blank lines). You use whitespace to organize your program code and make it easier to read.

The keyword **static**, when used in a method header, indicates that a method will be executed through a class and not by an object.

The keyword **void**, when used in a method header, indicates that the method does not return any value.

Application classes contain a Main() method and are executable programs.

Runnable describes files that are executable.

Non-application classes do not contain a Main() method; they provide support for other classes.

A **verbatim identifier** is an identifier with an @ prefix.

Program comments are nonexecuting statements that you add to document a program.

To **comment out** a statement is to make a statement nonexecuting.

Line comments start with two forward slashes (//) and continue to the end of the current line. Line comments can appear on a line by themselves, or at the end of a line following executable code.

Block comments start with a forward slash and an asterisk (/*) and end with an asterisk and a forward slash (*/). Block comments can appear on a line by themselves, on a line before executable code, or after executable code. They can also extend across as many lines as needed.

XML-documentation format comments use a special set of tags within angle brackets to create documentation within a program.

A **using clause** or **using directive** declares a namespace.

Source code is the statements you write when you create a program.

Intermediate language (IL) is the language into which source code statements are compiled.

The C# **just in time (JIT)** compiler translates intermediate code into executable code.

The **command line** is the line on which you type a command in a system that uses a text interface.

The **command prompt** is a request for input that appears at the beginning of the command line.

An **Integrated Development Environment (IDE)** is a program development environment that allows you to select options from menus or by clicking buttons. An IDE provides such helpful features as color coding and automatic statement completion.

Review Questions

1. Programming languages such as Java and Visual Basic are _____.

    a. machine languages   c. high-level languages
    b. low-level languages   d. uninterpreted languages

2. A program that translates high-level programs into intermediate or machine code is a(n) _____.

    a. mangler   c. analyst
    b. compiler   d. logician

3. The grammar and spelling rules of a programming language constitute its _____.

    a. logic   c. syntax
    b. variables   d. class

4. Variables are _____.

    a. methods   c. grammar rules

    b. named memory locations   d. operations

5. Programs in which you create and use objects that have attributes similar to their real-world counterparts are known as _____ programs.

    a. procedural   c. authentic

    b. logical   d. object-oriented

6. Which of the following pairs is an example of a class and an object, in that order?

    a. robin and bird   c. university and Harvard

    b. chair and desk   d. oak and tree

7. The technique of packaging an object's attributes into a cohesive unit that can be used as an undivided entity is _____.

    a. inheritance   c. polymorphism

    b. encapsulation   d. interfacing

8. Of the following languages, which is least similar to C#?

    a. Java   c. C++

    b. Visual Basic   d. COBOL

9. A series of characters that appears within double quotation marks is a(n) _____.

    a. method   c. argument

    b. interface   d. literal string

10. The C# method that produces a line of output on the screen and then positions the cursor on the next line is _____.

    a. `WriteLine()`   c. `DisplayLine()`

    b. `PrintLine()`   d. `OutLine()`

11. Which of the following is a class?

    a. `System`   c. `void`

    b. `Console`   d. `WriteLine()`

12. In C#, a container that groups similar classes is a(n) _____.

    a. superclass   c. namespace

    b. method   d. identifier

13. Every method in C# contains a _____.

    a. header and a body   c. variable and a class

    b. header and a footer   d. class and an object

14. Which of the following is a method?

    a. `namespace`   c. `Main()`

    b. `class`   d. `static`

15. Which of the following statements is true?

    a. An identifier must begin with an underscore.

    b. An identifier can contain digits.

    c. An identifier must be no more than 16 characters long.

    d. An identifier can contain only lowercase letters.

16. Which of the following identifiers is not legal in C#?

    a. `per cent increase`   c. `HTML`

    b. `annualReview`   d. `alternativetaxcredit`

17. The text of a program you write is called _____.

    a. object code   c. machine language

    b. source code   d. executable documentation

18. Programming errors such as using incorrect punctuation or misspelling words are collectively known as _____ errors.

    a. syntax   c. executable

    b. logical   d. fatal

19. A comment in the form `/* this is a comment */` is a(n) _____.

    a. XML comment   c. executable comment

    b. block comment   d. line comment

20. If a programmer inserts `using System;` at the top of a C# program, which of the following can the programmer use as an alternative to `System.Console.WriteLine("Hello");`?

    a. `System("Hello");`   c. `Console.WriteLine("Hello");`

    b. `WriteLine("Hello");`   d. `Console("Hello");`

Exercises

 Programming Exercises

1. Indicate whether each of the following C# programming language identifiers is legal or illegal. If it is legal, indicate whether it is a conventional identifier for a class.

   a. quantity sold

   b. Inventory

   c. Static

   d. static

   e. void

   f. Qwjhfu

   g. #OfTimes

   h. 1492Event

   i. Blue_Shirt

   j. Condominium

   k. Base16

   l. riverDepth

2. Name at least three attributes that might be appropriate for each of the following classes:

   a. Refrigerator

   b. College

   c. AcademicRecord

3. Name a class to which each of these objects might belong:

   a. your apartment

   b. Thomas Jefferson

   c. London

4. Write, compile, and test a program named **PersonalInfo** that displays a person's name, e-mail address, and phone number.

5. Write, compile, and test a program named **Lyrics** that displays at least four lines of your favorite song.

6. Write, compile, and test a program named **Comments** that displays a statement that defines program comments. Include at least one block comment and one line comment in the program.

7. Write, compile, and test a program named **TableAndChairs** that displays a pattern similar to the following on the screen:

```
X                        X
X                        X
X          XXXXXXXXXX       X
XXXX   X            X  XXXX
X   X   X            X   X   X
X   X   X            X   X   X
```

8. Write a program named **Initials** that displays your initials in a pattern on the screen. Compose each initial with six lines of smaller initials, as in the following example:

```
     J     FFFFFF
     J     F
     J     FFF
     J     F
J    J     F
JJJJJJ     F
```

9. From 1925 through 1963, Burma Shave advertising signs appeared next to highways all across the United States. There were always four or five signs in a row containing pieces of a rhyme, followed by a final sign that read "Burma Shave." For example, one set of signs that has been preserved by the Smithsonian Institution reads as follows:

```
Shaving brushes
You'll soon see 'em
On a shelf
In some museum
Burma Shave
```

Find a classic Burma Shave rhyme on the Web and write a program named **BurmaShave** that displays the rhyme.

 Debugging Exercises

1. Each of the following files in the Chapter.01 folder of your downloadable student files has syntax and/or logical errors. In each case, determine the problem and fix the program. After you correct the errors, save each file using the same filename preceded with *Fixed*. For example, DebugOne1.cs will become FixedDebugOne1.cs.

   a. DebugOne1.cs

   b. DebugOne2.cs

   c. DebugOne3.cs

   d. DebugOne4.cs

Case Problems

The case problems in this section introduce two fictional businesses. Throughout this book, you will create increasingly complex classes for these businesses that use the newest concepts you have mastered in each chapter.

1. Greenville County hosts the Greenville Idol competition each summer during the county fair. The talent competition takes place over a three-day period during which contestants are eliminated following rounds of performances until the year's ultimate winner is chosen. Write a program named **GreenvilleMotto** that displays the competition's motto, which is "The stars shine in Greenville." Create a second program named **GreenvilleMotto2** that displays the motto surrounded by a border composed of asterisks.

2. Marshall's Murals is a company that paints interior and exterior murals for both business and residential customers. Write a program named **MarshallsMotto** that displays the company motto, which is "Make your vision your view." Create a second program named **MarshallsMotto2** that displays the motto surrounded by a border composed of repeated *M*s.

Using Data

In this chapter you will:

◎ Learn about declaring variables

◎ Display variable values

◎ Learn about the integral data types

◎ Learn about floating-point data types

◎ Use arithmetic operators

◎ Learn about the `bool` data type

◎ Learn about numeric type conversion

◎ Learn about the `char` data type

◎ Learn about the `string` data type

◎ Define named constants and enumerations

◎ Accept console input

In Chapter 1, you learned about programming in general and the C# programming language in particular. You wrote, compiled, and ran a C# program that produces output. In this chapter, you build on your basic C# programming skills by learning how to manipulate data and use data types, variables, and constants. As you will see, using variables to hold data makes computer programs flexible.

Declaring Variables

A data item is **constant** when it cannot be changed after a program is compiled—in other words, when it cannot vary. For example, if you use the number 347 within a C# program, then 347 is a constant, and every time you execute the program, the value 347 will be used. You can refer to the number 347 as a **literal constant**, because its value is taken literally at each use.

On the other hand, when you want a data item's value to be able to change, you can create a variable. A **variable** is a named location in computer memory that can hold different values at different points in time. For example, if you create a variable named heatingBill and include it in a C# program, heatingBill might contain the value 347, or it might contain 200. Different values might be used when the program is executed multiple times, or different values might be used at different times during the same execution of the program. Because you can use a variable to hold heatingBill within a program used by a utility company's automated billing system, you can write one set of instructions to compute heatingBill, yet use different heatingBill values for thousands of utility customers during one execution of the program.

Whether it is a constant or a variable, each data item you use in a C# program has a data type. A **data type** describes the format and size of (amount of memory occupied by) a data item and defines what types of operations can be performed with the item. C# provides for 15 basic or **intrinsic types** of data, as shown in Table 2-1. Of these built-in data types, the ones most commonly used are int, double, decimal, char, string, and bool. Each C# intrinsic type is an **alias**, or other name for, a class in the System namespace. (You learned about the System namespace in Chapter 1.) All of the built-in types except object and string are called **simple types**.

The meaning of the largest and smallest values for the numeric types in Table 2-1 is probably clear to you, but some of the other values require explanation. The highest char value, 0xFFFF, represents the character in which every bit is turned on. The lowest value, 0x0000, represents the character in which every bit is turned off. Any value that begins with "0x" represents a hexadecimal, or base 16, value. For any two Strings, the one with the higher Unicode character value in an earlier position is considered higher. For example, "AAB" is higher than "AAA". The String type has no true minimum.

Type	System Type	Bytes	Description	Largest Value	Smallest Value
Types that hold numbers with no decimal places					
byte	Byte	1	Unsigned byte	255	0
sbyte	Sbyte	1	Signed byte	127	−128
short	Int16	2	Signed short	32,767	−32,768
ushort	UInt16	2	Unsigned short	65,535	0
int	Int32	4	Signed integer	2,147,483,647	−2,147,483,648
uint	UInt32	4	Unsigned integer	4,294,967,295	0
long	Int64	8	Signed long integer	Approximately 9×10^{18}	Approximately -9×10^{18}
ulong	UInt64	8	Unsigned long integer	Approximately 18×10^{18}	0
Types that hold numbers with decimal places					
float	Single	4	Floating-point	Approximately 3.4×10^{38}	Approximately -3.4×10^{38}
double	Double	8	Double-precision floating-point	Approximately 1.8×10^{308}	Approximately -1.8×10^{308}
decimal	Decimal	16	Fixed-precision number	Approximately 7.9×10^{28}	Approximately -7.9×10^{28}
Types that hold other values					
char	Char	2	Unicode character	0xFFFF	0x0000
bool	Boolean	1	Boolean value (true or false)	NA	NA
string	String	NA	Unicode string	NA	NA
object	Object	NA	Any object	NA	NA

Table 2-1   C# data types

However, you can think of the empty string "" as being the lowest. Although the `Boolean` type has no true maximum or minimum, you can think of `true` as the highest and `false` as the lowest.

You name variables using the same rules for identifiers as you use for class names. Variable names must start with a letter, cannot include embedded spaces, and cannot be a reserved keyword. By convention, C# variable names start with a lowercase letter and use camel casing if they contain multiple words. As with class names, a variable name cannot be a C# keyword. Table 1-1 in Chapter 1 lists all the C# keywords.

You must declare all variables you want to use in a program. A **variable declaration** is the statement that names a variable and reserves storage for it. The declaration includes:

- The data type that the variable will store

- The variable's name (its identifier)

- An optional assignment operator and assigned value when you want a variable to contain an initial value

- An ending semicolon

For example, the following statement declares a variable of type int named myAge and assigns it an initial value of 25:

```
int myAge = 25;
```

In other words, the statement reserves four bytes of memory with the name myAge, and the value 25 is stored there. The declaration is a complete statement that ends in a semicolon.

The equal sign (=) is the **assignment operator**; any value to the right of the assignment operator is assigned to the identifier to the left. An assignment made when a variable is declared is an **initialization**; an assignment made later is simply an **assignment**. Thus, the following statement initializes myAge to 25:

```
int myAge = 25;
```

A statement such as the following assigns a new value to the variable:

```
myAge = 42;
```

Notice that the data type is not used again when an assignment is made; it is used only in a declaration.

Also note that the expression 25 = myAge; is illegal because assignment always takes place from right to left. By definition, a constant cannot be altered, so it is illegal to place one (such as 25) on the left side of an assignment operator. The assignment operator means "is assigned the value of the following expression." In other words, the statement myAge = 25 can be read as "myAge is assigned the value of the following expression: 25."

Instead of using a type name from the Type column of Table 2-1, you can use the fully qualified type name from the System namespace that is listed in the System Type column. For example, instead of using the type name int, you can use the full name System.Int32. The number 32 in the name System.Int32 represents the number of bits of storage allowed for the data type. There are 8 bits in a byte, and an int occupies 4 bytes. It's better to use the shorter alias int, however, for the following reasons:

- The shorter alias is easier to type and read.

- The shorter alias resembles type names used in other languages such as Java and C++.

- Other C# programmers expect the shorter type names.

The variable declaration `int myAge;` declares a variable of type `int` named `myAge`, but no value is assigned at the time of creation. You can make an assignment later in the program, but you cannot use the variable in a calculation or display the value of the variable until you assign a value to it.

You can declare multiple variables of the same type in separate statements. For example, the following statements declare two variables. The first variable is named `myAge` and its value is 25. The second variable is named `yourAge` and its value is 19.

```
int myAge = 25;
int yourAge = 19;
```

You also can declare multiple variables of the same type in a single statement by using the type once and separating the variable declarations with a comma, as shown in the following statement:

```
int myAge = 25, yourAge = 19;
```

Some programmers prefer to use the data type once and break the declaration across multiple lines, as in the following example:

```
int myAge = 25,
    yourAge = 19;
```

When a statement occupies more than one line, it is easier to read if lines after the first one are indented a few spaces. This book follows that convention.

When you declare multiple variables of the same type, a comma separates the variable names and a single semicolon appears at the end of the declaration statement, no matter how many lines the declaration occupies. However, when declaring variables of different types, you must use a separate statement for each type. The following statements declare two variables of type `int` (`myAge` and `yourAge`) and two variables of type `double` (`mySalary` and `yourSalary`), without assigning initial values to any of them:

```
int myAge, yourAge;
double mySalary, yourSalary;
```

Similarly, the following statements declare two `int`s and two `double`s, assigning values to two of the four named variables:

```
int    numCarsIOwn = 2,
       numCarsYouOwn;
double myCarsMpg,
       yourCarsMpg = 31.5;
```

 Watch the video *Declaring Variables.*

TWO TRUTHS & A LIE

Declaring Variables

1. A constant value cannot be changed after a program is compiled, but a variable can be changed.

2. A data type describes the format and size of a data item and the types of operations that can be performed with it.

3. A variable declaration requires a data type, name, and assigned value.

The false statement is #3. A variable declaration names a variable and reserves storage for it; it includes the data type that the variable will store, and an identifier. An assignment operator and assigned value can be included, but they are not required.

Displaying Variable Values

You can display variable values by using the variable name within a `WriteLine()` method call. For example, Figure 2-1 shows a C# program that displays the value of the variable `someMoney`. Figure 2-2 shows the output of the program when executed at the command prompt.

```csharp
using System;
class DisplaySomeMoney
{
    static void Main()
    {
        double someMoney = 39.45;
        Console.WriteLine(someMoney);
    }
}
```

Figure 2-1   Program that displays a variable value

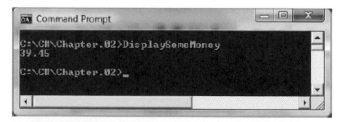

Figure 2-2   Output of `DisplaySomeMoney` program

The output shown in Figure 2-2 is rather stark—just a number with no explanation. The program in Figure 2-3 adds some explanation to the output; the result is shown in Figure 2-4. This program uses the Write() method to display the string "The money is $" before displaying the value of someMoney. Because the program uses Write() instead of WriteLine(), the second output appears on the same line as the first output.

```
using System;
class DisplaySomeMoney2
{
    static void Main()
    {
        double someMoney = 39.45;
        Console.Write("The money is $");
        Console.WriteLine(someMoney);
    }
}
```

Figure 2-3   Program that displays a string and a variable value

Figure 2-4   Output of DisplaySomeMoney2 program

If you want to display several strings and several variables, you can end up with quite a few Write() and WriteLine() statements. To make producing output easier, you can combine strings and variable values into a single Write() or WriteLine() statement in one of two ways: by concatenating them or by using a format string.

When you **concatenate** a string with another value, you join the values with a plus sign. For example, the following statement produces the same output as shown in Figure 2-4, but uses only one WriteLine() statement:

Console.WriteLine("The money is $" + someMoney);

A **format string** is a string of characters that optionally contains fixed text and contains one or more format items or placeholders for variable values. A **placeholder** consists of a pair of curly braces containing a number that indicates the desired variable's position in a list that follows the string. The first position is always position 0.

You can create a formatted string using the `String.Format()` method that is built into C#. For example, the following statements create a formatted string and then display it:

```
double someMoney = 39.45;
string mySentence = String.Format("The money is ${0} exactly", someMoney);
Console.WriteLine(mySentence);
```

The placeholder {0} holds a position into which the value of someMoney is inserted. Because someMoney is the first variable after the format string (as well as the only variable in this example), its position is 0.

C# also allows you to use a shortcut with the `Console.Write()` and `Console.WriteLine()` statements. You can format a string and output it in one step without declaring a temporary string variable and without explicitly naming the `String.Format()` method, as in the following:

```
double someMoney = 39.45;
Console.WriteLine("The money is ${0} exactly", someMoney);
```

For example, if you remove the `Write()` and `WriteLine()` statements from the program in Figure 2-3 and replace them with the shaded statement in Figure 2-5, the program produces the output shown in Figure 2-6. The placeholder {0} holds a position into which the value of someMoney is inserted. Because someMoney is the first variable after the format string (as well as the only variable in this example), its position is 0.

```
using System;
class DisplaySomeMoney3
{
    static void Main()
    {
        double someMoney = 39.45;
        Console.WriteLine("The money is ${0} exactly",
            someMoney);
    }
}
```

Figure 2-5   Using a format string

Figure 2-6   Output produced using format string

To display two variables within a single call to `Write()` or `WriteLine()`, you can use a statement like the following:

```
Console.WriteLine("The money is {0} and my age is {1}",
    someMoney, myAge);
```

The number within the curly braces in the format string must be less than the number of values you list after the format string. In other words, if you list six values to be displayed, valid format position numbers are 0 through 5. You do not have to use the positions in order. For example, you can choose to display the value in position 2, then 1, then 0. You also can display a specific value multiple times. For example, if `someMoney` has been assigned the value 439.75, the following code produces the output shown in Figure 2-7:

```
Console.WriteLine("I have ${0}. ${0}!! ${0}!!",
    someMoney);
```

Figure 2-7 Displaying the same value multiple times

The output in Figure 2-7 could be displayed without using a format string, but you would have to name the someMoney variable three separate times as follows:

```
Console.WriteLine("I have $" + someMoney + ". $" + someMoney +
    "!! $" + someMoney + "!!");
```

Besides the extra typing in this statement, you might find it harder to read than the version with the format string that includes a single set of quotation marks and a variable list at the end.

When you use a series of `WriteLine()` statements to display a list of variable values, the values are not automatically right-aligned as you normally expect numbers to be. For example, the following code produces the unaligned output shown in Figure 2-8:

```
Console.WriteLine("{0}", 4);
Console.WriteLine("{0}", 56);
Console.WriteLine("{0}", 789);
```

Figure 2-8   Displaying values with different numbers of digits without using field sizes

If you use a second number within the curly braces in a format string, you can specify alignment and field size. By default, numbers are right-aligned in their fields. If you use a negative value for the field size in a Write() or WriteLine() statement, the displayed value will be left-aligned in the field. Most often, you want numbers to be right-aligned and string values to be left-aligned. For example, the following code produces the output shown in Figure 2-9. The output created by each of the first three WriteLine() statements is a right-aligned number in a field that is five characters wide, and the output created by each of the last three statements is two left-aligned strings in a field that is eight characters wide.

```
Console.WriteLine("{0, 5}", 4);
Console.WriteLine("{0, 5}", 56);
Console.WriteLine("{0, 5}", 789);
Console.WriteLine("{0, -8}{1, -8}", "Richard", "Lee");
Console.WriteLine("{0, -8}{1, -8}", "Marcia", "Parker");
Console.WriteLine("{0, -8}{1, -8}", "Ed", "Tompkins");
```

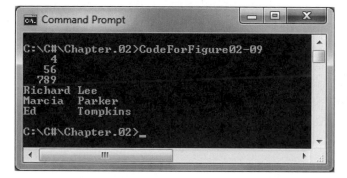

Figure 2-9   Displaying values with different numbers of digits using field sizes

Format strings can become very long. However, when you include any string in a statement in a program, you cannot extend it across multiple lines by pressing Enter. If you do, you will receive an error message: "Newline in constant". Instead, if you want to break a long string into multiple lines of code, you can concatenate multiple strings into a single entity. For example, the following two statements produce identical results. In the second, the format string is broken into two parts and concatenated using a plus sign.

```
Console.WriteLine("I have ${0}. ${0} is a lot.",
    someMoney);
Console.WriteLine("I have ${0}. " +
    "${0} is a lot. ", someMoney);
```

In the concatenated example, the + could go at the end of the first code line or the beginning of the second one. If the + is placed at the end of the first line, someone reading your code is more likely to notice that the statement is not yet complete. Because of the limitations of this book's page width, you will see examples of concatenation frequently in program code.

TWO TRUTHS & A LIE

Displaying Variable Values

1. Assuming number and answer are legally declared variables, then the following statement is valid:

   ```
   Console.WriteLine("{1}{2}", number, answer);
   ```

2. Assuming number and answer are legally declared variables, then the following statement is valid:

   ```
   Console.WriteLine("{1}{1}{0}", number, answer);
   ```

3. Assuming number and answer are legally declared variables, then the following statement is valid:

   ```
   Console.WriteLine("{0}{1}{1}{0}", number, answer);
   ```

The false statement is #1. When two values are available for display, the position number between any pair of curly braces in the format string must be 0 or 1. If three values were listed after the format string, the position numbers could be any combination of 0, 1, and 2.

Using the Integral Data Types

In C#, nine data types are considered **integral data types**—that is, types that store whole numbers. The nine types are **byte**, **sbyte**, **short**, **ushort**, **int**, **uint**, **long**, **ulong**, and **char**. The first eight always represent whole numbers, and the ninth type, char, is used for characters like 'A' or 'a'. Actually, you can think of all nine types as numbers because every Unicode character, including the letters of the alphabet and punctuation marks, can be represented as a number. For example, the character 'A' is stored within your computer as a 65. Because you more commonly think of the char type as holding alphabetic characters instead of their numeric equivalents, the char type will be discussed in its own section later in this chapter.

You will learn more about Unicode later in this chapter, and Appendix B contains further information.

The most basic of the other eight integral types is int. You use variables of type int to store (or hold) **integers**, or whole numbers. An int uses four bytes of memory and can hold any whole number value ranging from 2,147,483,647 down to -2,147,483,648. When you type a whole-number constant such as 3 or 589 into a C# program, by default it is an int.

If you want to save memory and know you need only a small value, you can use one of the shorter integer types—byte, sbyte (which stands for signed byte), short (short int), or ushort (unsigned short int). For example, a payroll program might contain a variable named numberOfDependents that is declared as type byte, because numberOfDependents will never need to hold a negative value or a value exceeding 255; for that reason, you can allocate just one byte of storage to hold the value. When you declare variables, you always make a judgment about which type to use. If you use a type that is too large, you waste storage. If you use a type that is too small, your program won't compile. Many programmers simply use int for most whole numbers.

Saving memory is seldom an issue for an application that runs on a PC. However, when you write applications for small devices with limited memory, such as smartphones, conserving memory becomes more important.

The word *integer* has only one *r*—at the end. Pronouncing it as "in-ter-ger," with an r in the middle, would mark you as unprofessional.

When you assign a value to any numeric variable, you do not use any commas or other nonnumeric characters such as dollar or percent signs; you type only digits. You can also type a plus or minus sign to indicate a positive or negative integer; a value without a sign is assumed to be positive. For example, to initialize a variable named annualSalary, you might write the following without a dollar sign or comma:

```
int annualSalary = 20000;
```

TWO TRUTHS & A LIE

Using the Integral Data Types

1. C# supports nine integral data types, including the most basic one, int.

2. Every Unicode character, including the letters of the alphabet and punctuation marks, can be represented as a number.

3. When you assign a value to any numeric variable, it is optional to use commas for values in the thousands.

The false statement is #3. When you assign a value to a numeric variable, you do not use commas, but you can type a plus or minus sign to indicate a positive or negative integer.

 You Do It

Declaring and Using Variables

In the following steps, you write a program that declares several integral variables, assigns values to them, and displays the results.

1. Open a new file. If you are using a simple text editor to write your C# programs, you will save the file as DemoVariables.cs. If you are using Visual Studio, select **Console Application**, name the project **DemoVariables**, and delete all the code in the program editing window before starting.

2. Create the beginning of a program that will demonstrate variable use. Use the System namespace, name the class **DemoVariables**, and type the class-opening curly brace.
   ```
   using System;
   class DemoVariables
   {
   ```

3. In the Main() method, declare two variables (an integer and an unsigned integer) and assign values to them.
   ```
   static void Main()
   {
       int anInt = -123;
       uint anUnsignedInt = 567;
   ```

(continues)

(continued)

4. Add a statement to display the two values.

```
Console.WriteLine("The int is {0} and the unsigned int is {1}.",
    anInt, anUnsignedInt);
```

5. Add two closing curly braces—one that closes the `Main()` method and one that closes the `DemoVariables` class. Align each closing curly brace vertically with the opening brace that is its partner. In other words, the first closing brace aligns with the brace that opens `Main()`, and the second aligns with the brace that opens `DemoVariables`.

6. Save the program and compile it. If you receive any error messages, correct the errors and compile the program again. When the file is error-free, execute the program. The output should look like Figure 2-10.

Figure 2-10 Output of `DemoVariables` program

7. Experiment with the program by introducing invalid values for the named variables. For example, change the value of `anUnsignedInt` to **–567** by typing a minus sign in front of the constant value. Compile the program. You receive the following error message:

Constant value '-567' cannot be converted to a 'uint'.

8. Correct the error either by removing the minus sign or by changing the data type of the variable to **int**, and compile the program again. You should not receive any error messages. Remember to save your program file after you make each change and before you compile.

9. Change the value of `anInt` from –123 to **–123456789000**. When you compile the program, the following error message appears:

Cannot implicitly convert type 'long' to 'int'.

The value is a `long` because it is greater than the highest allowed `int` value. Correct the error either by using a lower value or by changing the variable type to **long**, and compile the program again. You should not receive any error messages.

10. Experiment with other changes to the variables. Include some variables of type `short`, `ushort`, `byte`, and `sbyte`, and experiment with their values.

Using Floating-Point Data Types

A **floating-point** number is one that contains decimal positions. Floating-point numbers are described as having varying numbers of significant digits. A value's number of **significant digits** specifies the mathematical accuracy of the value. The concept is often used in rounding. For example, in the statement "The population of New York City is 8,000,000," there is just one significant digit—the 8. The zeros serve as placeholders and are meant to approximate the actual value.

When numbers are stored in computer memory, using a decimal point that can "float" provides a wider possible range of values. As a very simple example, suppose that the largest number you could store had only two digits with a fixed decimal point between them. Then the positive numbers that could be stored would range from 0.0 to 9.9. However, if the decimal point can float to be first, middle, or last, then the range becomes .00 through 99.

C# supports three floating-point data types: float, double, and decimal.

- A **float** data type can hold as many as seven significant digits of accuracy. For example, a float assigned the value 1234.56789 will appear as 1234.568 because it is accurate only to the seventh digit (the third digit to the right of the decimal point).

- A **double** data type can hold 15 or 16 significant digits of accuracy. For example, a double given the value 123456789.987654321 will appear as 123456789.987654 because it is accurate to only the fifteenth digit (the sixth digit to the right of the decimal point).

- Compared to floats and doubles, the **decimal** type has a greater precision and a smaller range, which makes it suitable for financial and monetary calculations. A decimal is significant to 28 or 29 digits. As Table 2-1 shows, a decimal cannot hold as large a value as a double can (the highest value is about 10^{28}; the highest value of a double is 10^{308}), but the decimal will be more accurate to more decimal places.

Just as an integer constant is an int by default, a floating-point number constant is a double by default. To explicitly store a constant as a float, you place an *F* after the number, as in the following:

```
float pocketChange = 4.87F;
```

You can use either a lowercase or uppercase *F*. You can also place a *D* (or *d*) after a floating-point value to indicate that it is a double; even without the *D*, however, it will be stored as a double by default. To explicitly store a value as a decimal, use an *M* (or *m*) after the number. (*M* stands for monetary; *D* can't be used for a decimal because it indicates double.)

Because monetary values are extremely important in business applications, many C# developers frequently use the decimal data type. This book most often uses the double type for floating-point values because floating-point numbers are double by default and do not require a modifying letter after the value. However, you should use the data type preferred by your instructor or manager, or the type that is most appropriate to your application. Some programmers prefer to use the decimal type for any measurement created by humans (for example, money or Olympic scores), and double for measurements of naturally occurring phenomena (for example, half lives of elements).

If you store a value that is too large (or too small) in a floating-point variable, you will see output expressed in **scientific notation**. Values expressed in scientific notation include an E (for exponent). For example, if you declare float f = 1234567890f;, the value is output as 1.234568E9, meaning that the numeric constant you used is approximately 1.234568 times 10 to the ninth power, or 1.234568 with the decimal point moved nine positions to the right. When the value that follows the E is negative, it means the value is very small and the decimal point should move to the left. For example, the value 1.234E-07 represents 0.0000001234.

Formatting Floating-Point Values

By default, C# always displays floating-point numbers in the most concise way possible that maintains the correct value. For example, if you declare a variable and display it as in the following statements, the output will appear as "The amount is 14".

```
double myMoney = 14.00;
Console.WriteLine("The amount is {0}", myMoney);
```

The two zeros to the right of the decimal point in the value will not appear because they add no mathematical information. To see the decimal places, you can convert the floating-point value to a string using a standard numeric format string.

Standard numeric format strings are strings of characters expressed within double quotation marks that indicate a format for output. They take the form *X0*, where *X* is the format specifier and *0* is the precision specifier. The **format specifier** can be one of nine built-in format characters that define the most commonly used numeric format types. The **precision specifier** controls the number of significant digits or zeros to the right of the decimal point. Table 2-2 lists the nine format specifiers.

Format Character	Description	Default Format (if no precision is given)
C or c	Currency	$XX,XXX.XX
		($XX,XXX.XX)
D or d	Decimal	[–]XXXXXXX
E or e	Scientific (exponential)	[–]X.XXXXXXE+xxx
		[–]X.XXXXXXe+xxx
		[–]X.XXXXXXE-xxx
		[–]X.XXXXXXe-xxx
F or f	Fixed-point	[–]XXXXXXX.XX
G or g	General	Variable; either with decimal places or scientific

Table 2-2   Format specifiers *(continues)*

(continued)

Format Character	Description	Default Format (if no precision is given)
N or n	Number	[−]XX,XXX.XX
P or p	Percent	Represents a numeric value as a percentage
R or r	Round trip	Ensures that numbers converted to strings will have the same values when they are converted back into numbers
X or x	Hexadecimal	Minimum hexadecimal (base 16) representation

Table 2-2 Format specifiers

You can use a format specifier with the ToString() method to convert a number into a string that has the desired format. For example, you can use the *F* format specifier to insert a decimal point to the right of a number that does not contain digits to the right of the decimal point, followed by the number of zeros indicated by the precision specifier. (If no precision specifier is supplied, two zeros are inserted.) For example, the first WriteLine() statement in the following code produces 123.00, and the second produces 123.000:

```
double someMoney = 123;
string moneyString;
moneyString = someMoney.ToString("F");
Console.WriteLine(moneyString);
moneyString = someMoney.ToString("F3");
Console.WriteLine(moneyString);
```

 You will learn more about creating and using methods in the chapters called *Introduction to Methods* and *Advanced Method Concepts*.

You use *C* as the format specifier when you want to represent a number as a currency value. Currency values appear with a dollar sign, appropriate commas, and the desired number of decimal places; negative values appear within parentheses. The integer you use following the *C* indicates the number of decimal places. If you do not provide a value for the number of decimal places, then two digits are shown after the decimal separator by default. For example, both of the following WriteLine() statements produce $456,789.00:

```
double moneyValue = 456789;
string conversion;
conversion = moneyValue.ToString("C");
Console.WriteLine(conversion);
conversion = moneyValue.ToString("C2");
Console.WriteLine(conversion);
```

Currency appears with a dollar sign and commas in the English culture. A **culture** is a set of rules that determines how culturally dependent values such as money and dates are formatted. You can change a program's culture by using the `CultureInfoClass`. The .NET framework supports more than 200 culture settings, such as Japanese, French, Urdu, and Sanskrit.

To display a numeric value as a formatted string, you do not have to create a separate string object. You also can make the conversion in a single statement; for example, the following code displays $12,345.00:

```
double payAmount = 12345;
Console.WriteLine(payAmount.ToString("C2"));
```

TWO TRUTHS & A LIE

Using Floating-Point Data Types

1. A floating-point number is one in which the decimal point varies each time you reference it.

2. C# supports three floating-point data types: `float`, `double`, and `decimal`.

3. To explicitly store a constant as a `float`, you may place an F after the number, but to store a constant as a `double` you need no special designation.

The false statement is #1. A floating-point number is one that contains decimal positions.

Using Arithmetic Operators

Table 2-3 describes the five most commonly used binary arithmetic operators. You use these operators to manipulate values in your programs. The operators are called **binary operators** because you use two arguments with each—one value to the left of the operator and another value to the right of it. The values that operators use in expressions are called **operands**; binary operators are surrounded by two operands.

Operator	Description	Example
+	Addition	45 + 2: the result is 47
−	Subtraction	45 − 2: the result is 43
*	Multiplication	45 * 2: the result is 90
/	Division	45 / 2: the result is 22 (not 22.5)
%	Remainder (modulus)	45 % 2: the result is 1 (that is, 45 / 2 = 22 with a remainder of 1)

Table 2-3   Binary arithmetic operators

Unlike some other programming languages, C# does not have an exponential operator. Instead, you can use the built-in method Math.Pow() that you will learn about in the chapter *Introduction to Methods*.

The operators / and % deserve special consideration. When you divide two numbers and at least one is a floating-point value, the answer is a floating-point value. For example, 45.0 / 2 is 22.5. However, when you divide integers using the / operator, whether they are integer constants or integer variables, the result is an integer; in other words, any fractional part of the result is lost. For example, the result of 45 / 2 is 22, not 22.5.

When you use the remainder (modulus) operator with two integers, the result is an integer with the value of the remainder after division takes place—so the result of 45 % 2 is 1 because 2 "goes into" 45 twenty-two times with a remainder of 1. Modulus operations should not be performed with floating-point numbers. The results are unpredictable because of the way floating-point numbers are stored in computer memory.

In older languages, such as assembler, you had to perform division before you could take a remainder. In C#, performing a division operation is not necessary before using a remainder operation. In other words, a remainder operation can stand alone.

Even though you define a result variable as a floating-point type, integer division still results in an integer. For example, the statement double d = 7 / 2; results in d holding 3, not 3.5, because the expression on the right is evaluated as integer-by-integer division before the assignment takes place. If you want the result to hold 3.5, at least one of the operands in the calculation must be a floating-point number, or else you must perform a cast. You will learn about casting later in this chapter.

When you combine mathematical operations in a single statement, you must understand **operator precedence**, or the rules that determine the order in which parts of a mathematical expression are evaluated. Multiplication, division, and remainder always take place prior to addition or subtraction in an expression. For example, the following expression results in 14:

```
int result = 2 + 3 * 4;
```

The result is 14 because the multiplication operation (3 * 4) occurs before adding 2. You can override normal operator precedence by putting the operation that should be performed first in parentheses. The following statement results in 20 because the addition within parentheses takes place first:

```
int result = (2 + 3) * 4;
```

In this statement, an intermediate result (5) is calculated before it is multiplied by 4.

Operator precedence is also called **order of operation**. A closely linked term is **associativity**, which specifies the order in which a sequence of operations with the same precedence are evaluated. Appendix A describes the precedence and associativity of every C# operator.

You can use parentheses in an arithmetic expression even if they do not alter the default order of operation. For example, even though multiplication takes place before addition without parentheses, it is perfectly acceptable to add them as follows:

```
weeklyPay = (hours * rate) + bonus;
```

You can use parentheses to make your intentions clear to other programmers who read your programs, which means they do not have to rely on their memory of operator precedence.

In summary, the order of operations for arithmetic operators is:

- *Parentheses.* Evaluate expressions within parentheses first.

- *Multiplication, division, remainder.* Evaluate these operations next from left to right.

- *Addition, subtraction.* Evaluate these operations next from left to right.

Using Shortcut Arithmetic Operators

Increasing the value held in a variable is a common programming task. Assume that you have declared a variable named `counter` that counts the number of times an event has occurred. Each time the event occurs, you want to execute a statement such as the following:

```
counter = counter + 1;
```

This type of statement looks incorrect to an algebra student, but the equal sign (=) is not used to compare values in C#; it is used to assign values. The statement `counter = counter + 1;` says "Take the value of `counter`, add 1 to it, and assign the result to `counter`."

Because increasing the value of a variable is such a common task, C# provides several shortcut ways to count and accumulate. The following two statements are identical in meaning:

```
counter += 1;
counter = counter + 1;
```

The += operator is the **add and assign operator**; it adds the operand on the right to the operand on the left and assigns the result to the operand on the left in one step. For example, if payRate is 20, then payRate += 5 results in payRate holding the value 25. Similarly, the following statements both increase bankBal by a rate stored in interestRate:

```
bankBal += bankBal * interestRate;
bankBal = bankBal + bankBal * interestRate;
```

For example, if bankBal is 100.00 and interestRate is 0.02, then both of the previous statements result in bankBal holding 102.00.

Additional shortcut operators in C# are −=, *=, and /=. Each of these operators is used to perform an operation and assign the result in one step. You cannot place spaces between the two characters that compose these operators; spaces preceding or following the operators are optional. Examples in which the shortcut operators are useful include the following:

- balanceDue −= payment subtracts a payment from balanceDue and assigns the result to balanceDue.

- rate *= 100 multiplies rate by 100 and assigns the result to rate. For example, it converts a fractional value stored in rate, such as 0.27, to a whole number, such as 27.

- payment /= 12 changes a payment value from an annual amount to a monthly amount due.

When you want to increase a variable's value by exactly 1, you can use either of two other shortcut operators—the **prefix increment operator** and the **postfix increment operator**. To use a prefix increment operator, you type two plus signs before the variable name. For example, these statements result in someValue holding 7:

```
int someValue = 6;
++someValue;
```

The variable someValue holds 1 more than it held before the ++ operator was applied. To use a postfix ++, you type two plus signs just after a variable name. Executing the following statements results in anotherValue holding 57:

```
int anotherValue = 56;
anotherValue++;
```

You can use the prefix ++ and postfix ++ with variables, but not with constants. An expression such as ++84 is illegal because 84 is constant and must always remain as 84. However, you can create a variable as in int val = 84;, and then write ++val or val++ to increase the variable's value to 85.

The prefix and postfix increment operators are **unary operators** because you use them with one operand. Most arithmetic operators, like those used for addition and multiplication, are binary operators that operate on two operands.

When you only want to increase a variable's value by 1, there is no apparent difference between using the prefix and postfix increment operators. However, these operators function differently. When you use the prefix ++, the result is calculated and stored, and then the

variable is used. For example, in the following code, both b and c end up holding 5. The
WriteLine() statement displays "5 5". In this example, 4 is assigned to b, then b becomes 5,
and then 5 is assigned to c.

```
b = 4;
c = ++b;
Console.WriteLine("{0} {1}", b, c);
```

In contrast, when you use the postfix ++, the variable is used, and then the result is calculated
and stored. For example, in the second line of the following code, 4 is assigned to c; then, *after*
the assignment, b is increased and takes the value 5.

```
b = 4;
c = b++;
Console.WriteLine("{0} {1}", b, c);
```

This last WriteLine() statement displays "5 4". In other words, if b = 4, then the value
of b++ is also 4, and that value is assigned to c. However, after the 4 is assigned to c, b is
increased to 5.

When you need to add 1 to a variable in a stand-alone statement, the results are the same whether you use a
prefix or postfix increment operator. However, many programmers routinely use the postfix operator when
they could use either operator. This is probably a mistake because the prefix operator is more efficient. You
will see an example that proves the superior efficiency of the prefix operator in the chapter *Looping*.

A prefix or postfix **decrement operator** (--) reduces a variable's value by 1. For example, if
s and t are both assigned the value 34, then the expression --s has the value 33 and the
expression t-- has the value 34, but t then becomes 33.

Watch the video *Using Shortcut Arithmetic Operators*.

TWO TRUTHS & A LIE

Using Arithmetic Operators

1. The value of 26 % 4 * 3 is 18.

2. The value of 4 / 3 + 2 is 3.

3. If price is 4 and tax is 5, then the value of price - tax++ is -1.

The false statement is #1. The value of 26 % 4 * 3 is 6. The value of the first part of
the expression, 26 % 4, is 2, because 2 is the remainder when 4 is divided into 26.
Then 2 * 3 is 6.

You Do It

Performing Arithmetic

In the following steps, you add some arithmetic statements to a program.

1. Open a new C# program file named **DemoVariables2**, and enter the following statements to start a program that demonstrates arithmetic operations:

```
using System;
class DemoVariables2
{
    static void Main()
    {
```

2. Write a statement that declares seven integer variables. Assign initial values to two of the variables; the values for the other five variables will be calculated. Because all of these variables are the same type, you can use a single statement to declare all seven integers. Recall that to do this, you insert commas between variable names and place a single semicolon at the end. You can place line breaks wherever you want for readability. (Alternatively, you could use as many as seven separate declarations.)

```
int value1 = 43, value2 = 10,
    sum, diff, product, quotient, remainder;
```

3. Write the arithmetic statements that calculate the sum of, difference between, product of, quotient of, and remainder of the two assigned variables.

```
sum = value1 + value2;
diff = value1 - value2;
product = value1 * value2;
quotient = value1 / value2;
remainder = value1 % value2;
```

Instead of declaring the variables `sum`, `diff`, `product`, `quotient`, and `remainder` and assigning values later, you could declare and assign all of them at once, as in `int sum = value1 + value2;`. The only requirement is that `value1` and `value2` must be assigned values before you can use them in a calculation.

(continues)

(continued)

4. Include five `WriteLine()` statements to display the results.

```
Console.WriteLine("The sum of {0} and {1} is {2}",
    value1, value2, sum);
Console.WriteLine("The difference between {0} and {1}" +
    " is {2}", value1, value2, diff);
Console.WriteLine("The product of {0} and {1} is {2}",
    value1, value2, product);
Console.WriteLine("{0} divided by {1} is {2}", value1,
    value2, quotient);
Console.WriteLine("and the remainder is {0}", remainder);
```

5. Add two closing curly braces—one for the `Main()` method and the other for the `DemoVariables2` class.

6. Save the file, compile the program, and execute it. The output should look like Figure 2-11.

Figure 2-11   Output of `DemoVariables2` program

7. Change the values of the `value1` and `value2` variables, save the program, and compile and run it again. Repeat this process several times. After each execution, analyze the output to make sure you understand the results of the arithmetic operations.

Using the bool Data Type

Boolean logic is based on true-or-false comparisons. An `int` variable can hold millions of different values at different times, but a **Boolean variable** can hold only one of two values—true or false. You declare a Boolean variable by using type **bool**. The following statements declare and assign appropriate values to two `bool` variables:

```
bool isItMonday = false;
bool areYouTired = true;
```

If you begin a **bool** variable name with a form of the verb "to be" or "to do," such as "is" or "are," then you can more easily recognize the identifiers as Boolean variables when you encounter them within your programs.

When you use "Boolean" as an adjective, as in "Boolean variable," you usually begin with an uppercase B because the data type is named for Sir George Boole, the founder of symbolic logic, who lived from 1815 to 1864. The C# data type **bool**, however, begins with a lowercase "b."

You also can assign values based on the result of comparisons to Boolean variables. A **comparison operator** compares two items; an expression containing a comparison operator has a Boolean value. Table 2-4 describes the six comparison operators that C# supports.

Operator	Description	true Example	false Example
<	Less than	3 < 8	8 < 3
>	Greater than	4 > 2	2 > 4
==	Equal to	7 == 7	3 == 9
<=	Less than or equal to	5 <=5	8 <= 6
>=	Greater than or equal to	7 >= 3	1 >= 2
!=	Not equal to	5 != 6	3 != 3

Table 2-4 Comparison operators

When using any of the operators that require two keystrokes (==, <=, >=, or !=), you cannot place any whitespace between the two symbols.

A frequent mistake among new programmers is attempting to create a Boolean expression for equivalency with a single equal sign. The equivalency operator uses two equal signs. For example, the following assigns either **true** or **false** to **isDiscountProvided**:

```
isDiscountProvided = custStatus == 1;
```

The second operator in the statement (==) compares **custStatus** to 1. The first operator in the statement (=) is an assignment operator that assigns the result of the comparison to the variable on the left.

Legal (but somewhat useless) declaration statements might include the following, which compare two values directly:

```
bool isSixBigger = 6 > 5;  // Value stored would be true
bool isSevenSmallerOrEqual = 7 <= 4;
   // Value stored would be false
```

72

Using Boolean values is more meaningful when you use variables (that have been assigned values) rather than constants in the comparisons, as in the following examples:

```
bool doesEmployeeReceiveOvertime = hoursWorked > 40;
bool isEmployeeInHighTaxBracket = annualIncome > 100000;
```

In the first statement, the hoursWorked variable is compared to a constant value of 40. If the hoursWorked variable holds a value less than or equal to 40, then the expression is evaluated as false. In the second statement, the annualIncome variable value must be greater than 100000 for the expression to be true.

Boolean variables become more useful after you learn to make decisions within C# programs in Chapter 4.

When you display a bool variable's value with Console.WriteLine(), the displayed value is capitalized as True or False. However, the values within your programs are true and false.

TWO TRUTHS & A LIE

Using the bool Data Type

1. If rate is 7.5 and min is 7, then the value of rate >= min is false.
2. If rate is 7.5 and min is 7, then the value of rate < min is false.
3. If rate is 7.5 and min is 7, then the value of rate == min is false.

The false statement is #1. If rate is 7.5 and min is 7, then the value of rate >= min is true.

You Do It

Working with Boolean Variables

Next, you write a program that demonstrates how Boolean variables operate.

1. Open a new file in your editor and name it **DemoVariables3**.

2. Enter the following code. In the Main() method, you declare an integer value, then assign different values to a Boolean variable. Notice that when you declare value and isSixMore, you assign types. When you reassign values to these variables later in the program, you do not redeclare them by using a type name. Instead, you simply assign new values to the already declared variables.

```
using System;
class DemoVariables3
{
   static void Main()
   {
      int value = 4;
      bool isSixMore = 6 > value;
      Console.WriteLine("When value is {0} isSixMore is {1}",
         value, isSixMore);
      value = 35;
      isSixMore = 6 > value;
      Console.WriteLine("When value is {0} isSixMore is {1}",
         value, isSixMore);
   }
}
```

3. Save, compile, and run the program. The output looks like Figure 2-12.

Figure 2-12 Output of DemoVariables3 program

4. Change the value of the variable named value and try to predict the outcome. Run the program to confirm your prediction.

Understanding Numeric Type Conversion

When you perform arithmetic with variables or constants of the same type, the result of the arithmetic retains that type. For example, when you divide two `int`s, the result is an `int`; when you subtract two `double`s, the result is a `double`. Often, however, you need to perform mathematical operations on different types. For example, in the following code, you multiply an `int` by a `double`:

```
int hoursWorked = 36;
double payRate = 12.35;
double grossPay = hoursWorked * payRate;
```

When you perform arithmetic operations with operands of dissimilar types, C# chooses a **unifying type** for the result and **implicitly** (or automatically) converts nonconforming operands to the unifying type, which is the type with the higher **type precedence**. The conversion is called an **implicit conversion** or an **implicit cast**—the automatic transformation that occurs when a value is assigned to a type with higher precedence.

For example, if you multiply an `int` and a `double`, the result is implicitly a `double`. This requirement means the result must be stored in a `double`; if you attempt to assign the result to an `int`, you will receive a compiler error message like the one shown in Figure 2-13.

Figure 2-13 Error message received when trying to compile a program that attempts to store a `double` in an `int`

The implicit numeric conversions are:

- From `sbyte` to `short`, `int`, `long`, `float`, `double`, or `decimal`
- From `byte` to `short`, `ushort`, `int`, `uint`, `long`, `ulong`, `float`, `double`, or `decimal`
- From `short` to `int`, `long`, `float`, `double`, or `decimal`
- From `ushort` to `int`, `uint`, `long`, `ulong`, `float`, `double`, or `decimal`
- From `int` to `long`, `float`, `double`, or `decimal`
- From `uint` to `long`, `ulong`, `float`, `double`, or `decimal`
- From `long` to `float`, `double`, or `decimal`
- From `ulong` to `float`, `double`, or `decimal`
- From `char` to `ushort`, `int`, `uint`, `long`, `ulong`, `float`, `double`, or `decimal`
- From `float` to `double`

Implicit conversions occur both as the result of calculations and assignments. For example, if money is declared as a double, then the following statement implicitly converts the integer 15 to a double:

```
money = 15;
```

 Conversions from int, uint, or long to float and from long to double may cause a loss of precision, but will never cause a loss of magnitude.

 A constant expression of type int, such as 25, can be converted to sbyte, byte, short, ushort, uint, or ulong. For example, sbyte age = 19; is legal. However, you must make sure that the value of the assigned constant expression is within the range of the destination type, or the program will not compile.

The error message in Figure 2-13 asks "are you missing a cast?" You may **explicitly** (or purposefully) override the unifying type imposed by C# by performing an explicit cast. An **explicit cast** involves placing the desired result type in parentheses followed by the variable or constant to be cast. For example, two explicit casts are performed in the following code:

```
double bankBalance = 191.66;
float weeklyBudget = (float) bankBalance / 4;
      // weeklyBudget is 47.915, one-fourth of bankBalance
int dollars = (int) weeklyBudget;
      // dollars is 47, the integer part of weeklyBudget
```

The value of bankBalance / 4 is implicitly a double because a double divided by an int produces a double. The double result is then converted to a float before it is stored in weeklyBudget, and the float value weeklyBudget is converted to an int before it is stored in dollars. When the float value is converted to an int, the decimal-place values are lost.

 It is easy to lose data when performing a cast. For example, the largest byte value is 255, and the largest int value is 2,147,483,647, so the following statements produce distorted results:

```
int anOkayInt = 345;
byte aBadByte = (byte)anOkayInt;
```

 If you attempt to store 256 in a byte, you will receive an error message unless you place the statement in a section of code preceded by the keyword unchecked, which tells the compiler not to check for invalid data. If you use the unchecked mode and store 256 in a byte, the results will look the same as storing 0; if you store 257, the result will appear as 1. You will see 89 when you store 345 in a byte variable and display the results, because the value 89 is exactly 256 less than 345.

 Watch the video *Numeric Type Conversion*.

TWO TRUTHS & A LIE

Understanding Numeric Type Conversion

1. If deptNum is an int with a value of 10, then double answer = deptNum is a valid statement.

2. If deptNum is an int with a value of 10, and answer is a double with a value of 4, then deptNum = answer is a valid statement.

3. If deptNum is an int with a value of 10, and answer is a double with a value of 4, then double answer = (int)value is a valid statement.

The false statement is #2. If deptNum is an int with a value of 10, and answer is a double with a value of 4, then deptNum = answer is invalid because a double cannot be implicitly converted to an int.

Using the char Data Type

You use the **char** data type to hold any single character. You place constant character values within single quotation marks because the computer stores characters and integers differently. For example, the following statements are both legal:

```
char aCharValue = '9';
int aNumValue = 9;
```

However, the following statements are both illegal:

```
char aCharValue = 9;
int aNumValue = '9';
```

A number can be a character, in which case it must be enclosed in single quotation marks and declared as a char type. A variable of type char can hold only one character, and a literal character is written using single quotation marks. To store a string of characters, such as a person's name, you must use a string; a string literal is written using double quotation marks. You will learn about strings later in this chapter.

Although a digit can be stored as a character, an alphabetic letter cannot be stored in a numeric type variable. The following code shows how you can store several characters using the char data type:

```
char myInitial = 'J';
char percentSign = '%';
char numThatIsAChar = '9';
```

When you store a digit such as '9' as a character, you cannot use it in ordinary arithmetic statements. If the value of 9 is needed for use in arithmetic, you should store it as a numeric type, such as int.

You can store any character—including nonprinting characters such as a backspace or a tab—in a char variable. To store these characters, you use two symbols in an **escape sequence**, which always begins with a backslash. The pair of symbols represents a single character. For example, the following code stores a backspace character and a tab character in the char variables aBackspaceChar and aTabChar, respectively:

```
char aBackspaceChar = '\b';
char aTabChar = '\t';
```

In the preceding code, the escape sequence indicates a unique value for each character—a backspace or tab instead of the letter *b* or *t*. Table 2-5 describes some common escape sequences that are used in C#.

Escape Sequence	Character Name
\'	Single quotation mark
\"	Double quotation mark
\\	Backslash
\0	Null
\a	Alert
\b	Backspace
\f	Form feed
\n	Newline
\r	Carriage return
\t	Horizontal tab
\v	Vertical tab

Table 2-5   Common escape sequences

The characters used in C# are represented in **Unicode**, which is a 16-bit coding scheme for characters. For example, the letter *A* actually is stored in computer memory as a set of 16 zeros and ones—namely, 0000 0000 0100 0001. (The spaces are inserted here after every set of four digits for readability.) Because 16-bit numbers are difficult to read, programmers often use a shorthand notation called **hexadecimal**, or **base 16**. In hexadecimal shorthand, 0000 becomes 0, 0100 becomes 4, and 0001 becomes 1. Thus, the letter *A* is represented in hexadecimal as 0041. You tell the compiler to treat the four-digit hexadecimal 0041 as a single character by preceding it with the \u escape sequence. Therefore, there are two ways to store the character *A*:

```
char letter = 'A';
char letter = '\u0041';
```

 For more information about Unicode, see Appendix B.

The second option, using hexadecimal, obviously is more difficult and confusing than the first option, so it is not recommended that you store letters of the alphabet using the hexadecimal method. However, you can produce some interesting values using the Unicode format. For example, letters from foreign alphabets that use characters instead of letters (Greek, Hebrew, Chinese, and so on) and other special symbols (foreign currency symbols, mathematical symbols, geometric shapes, and so on) are not available on a standard keyboard, but they are available in Unicode. You can even output the sound of a beep by displaying the hexadecimal character '\u0007'.

TWO TRUTHS & A LIE

Using the char Data Type

1. The following statement is legal in C#:

    ```
    char department = '5';
    ```

2. The following statement is legal in C#:

    ```
    char department = '\f';
    ```

3. The following statement is legal in C#:

    ```
    char department = '32';
    ```

The false statement is #3. Only a single character can appear between single quotation marks, with the exception of escape sequence characters such as '\t' and '\f'. In these cases, a single character is created using two symbols.

You Do It

Using Escape Sequences

Next, you write a short program to demonstrate the use of escape sequences.

1. Open a new file in your text editor and name it **DemoEscapeSequences**.

2. Enter the following code. The three `WriteLine()` statements demonstrate using escape sequences for tabs, a newline, and alerts.

```
using System;
class DemoEscapeSequences
{
    static void Main()
    {
        Console.WriteLine("This line\tcontains two\ttabs");
        Console.WriteLine("This statement\ncontains a new line");
        Console.WriteLine("This statement sounds three alerts\a\a\a");
    }
}
```

3. Save, compile, and execute the program. Your output should look like Figure 2-14. Additionally, if your system has speakers and they are on, you should hear three "beep" sounds caused by the three alert characters: '\a'.

Figure 2-14   Output of DemoEscapeSequences program

Using the `string` Data Type

In C#, you use the **string** data type to hold a series of characters. The value of a `string` is expressed within double quotation marks. For example, the following statement declares a `string` named `firstName` and assigns "Jane" to it:

```
string firstName = "Jane";
```

You can also initialize a string with a character array. The *Using Arrays* chapter explains more.

When you assign a literal (such as "Jane") to a `string`, you can compare the `string` to another `string` using the == and != operators in the same ways that you compare numeric or character variables. For example, the program in Figure 2-15 declares three `string` variables. Figure 2-16 shows the results: `strings` that contain "Amy" and "Amy" are considered equal, but `strings` that contain "Amy" and "Matthew" are not.

```
using System;
class CompareNames1
{
    static void Main()
    {
        string name1 = "Amy";
        string name2 = "Amy";
        string name3 = "Matthew";
        Console.WriteLine("compare {0} to {1}: {2}",
            name1, name2, name1 == name2);
        Console.WriteLine("compare {0} to {1}: {2}",
            name1, name3, name1 == name3);
    }
}
```

Figure 2-15   Program that compares two strings using == operator (not recommended)

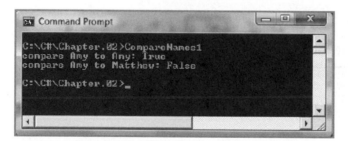

Figure 2-16   Output of CompareNames1 program

In addition to the == comparison operator, you can use several prewritten methods to compare `strings`. The advantage to using these other methods is that they have standard names; when you use most other C# classes written by others, they will use methods with the same names to compare their objects. You can compare `strings` with any of the following methods: Equals(), Compare(), and CompareTo().

The `String` class **Equals() method** requires two `string` arguments that you place within its parentheses, separated by a comma. As when you use the == operator, the Equals() method returns true or false.

The String class **Compare() method** also requires two `string` arguments, but it returns an integer. When it returns 0, the two `strings` are equivalent; when it returns a positive number, the first `string` is greater than the second; and when it returns a negative value, the first `string` is less than the second. A `string` is considered equal to, greater than, or less than another string **lexically**, which in the case of letter values means alphabetically. That is, when you compare two `strings`, you compare each character in turn from left to right. If each Unicode value is the same, then the strings are equivalent. If any corresponding character values are different, the `string` that has the greater Unicode value earlier in the string is considered greater.

The **CompareTo() method** also compares two `strings`. However, one `string` is used before the dot and method name, and the second `string` is placed within the method's parentheses as an argument. Like the Compare() method, the CompareTo() method returns a 0 when the compared `strings` are equal, a negative number if the first `string` is less, and a positive number if the second `string` (the one in parentheses) is less. Figure 2-17 shows a program that makes several comparisons using the three methods; in each case the method name is shaded. Figure 2-18 shows the program's output.

Methods like Compare() that are not preceded with an object and a dot when they are called are *static methods*. Methods like CompareTo() that are preceded with an object and a dot are *nonstatic* and are called *instance methods*. The *Advanced Method Concepts* chapter explains more.

```csharp
using System;
class CompareTwoNames
{
    static void Main()
    {
        string name1 = "Amy";
        string name2 = "Amy";
        string name3 = "Matthew";
        Console.WriteLine("Using Equals() method");
        Console.WriteLine("   compare {0} to {1}: {2}",
            name1, name2, String.Equals(name1, name2));
        Console.WriteLine("   compare {0} to {1}: {2}",
            name1, name3, String.Equals(name1, name3));
        Console.WriteLine("Using Compare() method");
        Console.WriteLine("   compare {0} to {1}: {2}",
            name1, name2, String.Compare(name1, name2));
        Console.WriteLine("   compare {0} to {1}: {2}",
            name1, name3, String.Compare(name1, name3));
        Console.WriteLine("Using CompareTo() method");
        Console.WriteLine("   compare {0} to {1}: {2}",
            name1, name2, name1.CompareTo(name2));
        Console.WriteLine("   compare {0} to {1}: {2}",
            name1, name3, name1.CompareTo(name3));
    }
}
```

Figure 2-17 Program that compares two strings using three methods

Figure 2-18   Output of CompareTwoNames program

In C#, a string is **immutable**. That is, a string's value is not actually modified when you assign a new value to it. For example, when you write `name = "Amy";` followed by `name = "Donald";`, the first literal string of characters "Amy" still exists in computer memory, but the `name` variable no longer refers to the string's memory address. The situation is different than with numbers; when you assign a new value to a numeric variable, the value at the named memory address actually changes.

The comparisons made by the `Equals()`, `Compare()`, and `CompareTo()` methods are case sensitive. In other words, "Amy" does not equal "amy". In Unicode, the decimal value of each uppercase letter is exactly 32 less than its lowercase equivalent. For example, the decimal value of a Unicode 'a' is 97 and the value of 'A' is 65.

You can use the **Length property** of a string to determine its length. For example, suppose you declare a string as follows:

```
string word = "water";
```

The value of `word.Length` is 5.

The **Substring() method** can be used to extract a portion of a string from a starting point for a specific length. For example, Figure 2-19 shows a string that contains the word *water*. The first character in a string is at position 0, and the last character is at position `Length - 1`. Therefore, after you declare `string word = "water"`, each of the statements in the figure is true. The last statement produces an error message because the combination of the starting position and length attempt to access values outside the range of the string.

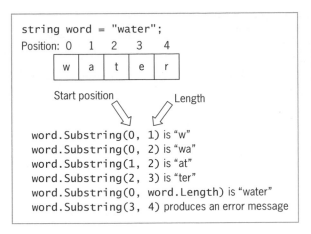

```
string word = "water";
Position: 0  1  2  3  4
         w  a  t  e  r
```

Start position   Length

word.Substring(0, 1) is "w"
word.Substring(0, 2) is "wa"
word.Substring(1, 2) is "at"
word.Substring(2, 3) is "ter"
word.Substring(0, word.Length) is "water"
word.Substring(3, 4) produces an error message

Figure 2-19 Using the Substring() method

The **StartsWith() method** is another useful string method. In the example that defines word as "water", the expression word.StartsWith("wa") is true, and the expression word.StartsWith("waet") is false.

TWO TRUTHS & A LIE

Using the string Data Type

1. If creature1 = "dog" and creature2 = "cat", then the value of String.Equals(creature1, creature2) is false.

2. If creature1 = "dog" and creature2 = "cat", then the value of String.Compare(creature1, creature2) is false.

3. If creature1 = "dog" and creature2 = "cat", then the value of creature1.CompareTo(creature2) is a positive number.

The false statement is #2. If creature1 = "dog" and creature2 = "cat", then the value of String.Compare(creature1, creature2) is a positive number.

Defining Named Constants

By definition, a variable's value can vary, or change. Sometimes you want to create a **named constant**, an identifier for a memory location whose contents cannot change. You create a named constant by adding the keyword const before the data type in a declaration. Although there is no requirement to do so, programmers usually name constants using all uppercase letters, inserting underscores for readability. This convention makes constant names stand out so that a reader is less likely to confuse them with variable names. For example, the following declares a constant named TAX_RATE that is initialized to 0.06:

```
const double TAX_RATE = 0.06;
```

You must assign a value to a constant when you create it. You can use a constant just as you would use a variable of the same type—for example, display it or use it in a mathematical equation—but you cannot assign any new value to it.

It's good programming practice to use named constants for any values that should never change; doing so makes your programs clearer. For example, when you declare a constant `const int INCHES_IN_A_FOOT = 12;` within a program, then you can use a statement such as the following:

```
lengthInInches = lengthInFeet * INCHES_IN_A_FOOT;
```

This statement is **self-documenting**; that is, even without a program comment, it is easy for someone reading your program to tell why you performed the calculation in the way you did.

Working with Enumerations

An **enumeration** is a set of constants represented by identifiers. You place an enumeration in a class outside of any methods. Very frequently, programmers place enumerations at the top of a file before any methods. You create an enumeration using the keyword `enum` and an identifier, followed by a comma-separated list of constants between curly braces. By convention, the enumerator identifier begins with an uppercase letter. For example, the following is an enumeration called DayOfWeek:

```
enum DayOfWeek
{
    SUNDAY, MONDAY, TUESDAY, WEDNESDAY,
        THURSDAY, FRIDAY, SATURDAY
}
```

By default, enumeration values are integers. You could also declare an `enum`'s type to be `byte`, `sbyte`, `short`, `ushort`, `uint`, `long`, or `ulong` by including a colon and the type after the enumeration name and before the opening curly brace of the assignment list.

Frequently, the identifiers in an enumeration are meant to hold consecutive values. When you do not supply values for the items in an `enum` list, they start with 0 and are automatically increased by 1. For example, in the DayOfWeek enumeration, SUNDAY is 0, MONDAY is 1, and so on.

 As is the convention with other constants, you might prefer to name `enum` constants using all uppercase letters and underscores for readability, as shown in the DayOfWeek enumeration here. This helps distinguish enumeration names from variables. However, the developers of C# frequently violate this convention in both their online documentation and in built-in enumerations in the language. For example, the built-in FontStyle enumeration contains constants with mixed-case names such as Bold and Italic. When you create enumerations, you should follow the convention your instructor or supervisor prefers. Another convention is to use a singular noun or noun phrase as the `enum` identifier. In other words, DayOfWeek is better than DaysOfWeek.

If you want the first **enum** constant in the list to have a value other than 0, you can assign one, as in the following:

```
enum DayOfWeek
{
    SUNDAY = 1, MONDAY, TUESDAY, WEDNESDAY,
        THURSDAY, FRIDAY, SATURDAY
}
```

In this case, SUNDAY is 1, MONDAY is 2, TUESDAY is 3, and so on.

As another option, you can assign values to each enumeration, as in the following:

```
enum SpeedLimit
{
    SCHOOL_ZONE_SPEED = 20,
    CITY_STREET_SPEED = 30,
    HIGHWAY_SPEED = 55
}
```

The names used within an **enum** must be unique, but the values assigned don't have to be.

When you create an enumeration, you clearly identify what values are valid for an item. You also make your code more self-documenting. You should consider creating an enumeration any time you have a fixed number of integral values allowed for a variable.

As a side benefit, when you use an **enum** in Visual Studio, Intellisense lists the defined values. Appendix C provides more information on Intellisense.

After you have created an enumeration, you can declare variables of the enumeration type, and you can assign enumeration values to them. For example, you can use the following statements to declare **orderDay** as data type **DayOfWeek**, and assign a value to it.

```
DayOfWeek orderDay;
orderDay = DayOfWeek.TUESDAY;
```

In the chapter called *Using Classes and Objects*, you will learn to create many additional data types that are more complex than the built-in data types.

You can convert an **enum** value to another data type or an integral type to an **enum** value by using a cast. For example, the following are valid statements:

```
int shipDay;
DayOfWeek deliverDay;
shipDay = (int)DayOfWeek.THURSDAY;
deliverDay = (DayOfWeek)shipDay;
```

Using the preceding example, you can display *THURSDAY* with the following statement:

```
Console.WriteLine(deliverDay);
```

Creating an enumeration type provides you with several advantages. For example, the DayOfWeek enumeration improves your programs in the following ways:

- If you did not create an enumerated type, you could use another type—for example, ints or Strings. The problem is that any value could be assigned to an int or String variable, but only the seven allowed values can be assigned to a DayOfWeek object.

- If you did not create an enumerated type, you could create another type to represent days, but invalid behavior could be applied to the values. For example, if you used integers to represent days, you could add, subtract, multiply, or divide two days, which is not logical. Programmers say using enums makes the values type-safe. **Type-safe** describes a data type for which only appropriate behaviors are allowed.

- The enum constants provide a form of self-documentation. Someone reading your program might misinterpret what 3 means as a day value, but there is less confusion when you use the identifier WEDNESDAY.

This discussion is meant to be a brief introduction to enumerations. At this point in your study of C#, the advantages to using enumerations are limited. Enumerations are particularly useful with switch statements, which you will learn about in the *Making Decisions* chapter.

TWO TRUTHS & A LIE

Defining Named Constants

1. The following is a valid and conventional C# constant:

    const string FIRST_HEADING = "Progress Report";

2. The following is a valid and conventional C# constant:

    const double COMMISSION_RATE;

3. By default, enumeration values are integers.

The false statement is #2. A constant must be assigned a value when it is declared.

Accepting Console Input

A program that allows user input is an **interactive program**. You can use the **Console.ReadLine() method** to create an interactive program that accepts user input from the keyboard. This method accepts all of the characters entered by a user until the user presses Enter. The characters can be assigned to a string. For example, the following statement accepts a user's input and stores it in the variable myString:

myString = Console.ReadLine();

The `Console.Read()` method is similar to the `Console.ReadLine()` method. `Console.Read()` reads just one character from the input stream, whereas `Console.ReadLine()` reads every character in the input stream until the user presses the Enter key.

If you want to use the input value as a type other than `string`, then you must use a conversion method to change the input `string` to the proper type. Two methods are available for converting strings—the `Convert` class and `Parse()` methods.

Using the Convert Class

Figure 2-20 shows an interactive program that prompts the user for a price and calculates a 6 percent sales tax. The program displays "Enter the price of an item" on the screen. Such an instruction to the user is a **prompt**. Notice that the program uses a `Write()` statement for the prompt instead of a `WriteLine()` statement so that the user's input appears on the screen on the same line as the prompt. Also notice that the prompt contains a space just before the closing quote so that the prompt does not crowd the user's input on the screen. After the prompt appears, the `Console.ReadLine()` statement accepts a string of characters and assigns them to the variable `itemPriceAsString`. Before the tax can be calculated, this value must be converted to a number. This conversion is accomplished using the `Convert` class `ToDouble()` method in the shaded statement. Figure 2-21 shows a typical execution of the program in which the user typed 28.77 as the input value.

```
using System;
class InteractiveSalesTax
{
    static void Main()
    {
        const double TAX_RATE = 0.06;
        string itemPriceAsString;
        double itemPrice;
        double total;
        Console.Write("Enter the price of an item >> ");
        itemPriceAsString = Console.ReadLine();
        itemPrice = Convert.ToDouble(itemPriceAsString);
        total = itemPrice * TAX_RATE;
        Console.WriteLine("With a tax rate of {0}, a {1} item " +
            "costs {2} more.", TAX_RATE, itemPrice.ToString("C"),
            total.ToString("C"));
    }
}
```

Figure 2-20   `InteractiveSalesTax` program

 In the program in Figure 2-20, the angle brackets at the end of the prompt are not required; they are merely cosmetic. You might prefer other punctuation such as a colon, ellipsis, or hyphen to indicate that input is required.

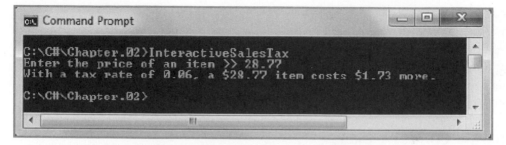

Figure 2-21   Typical execution of `InteractiveSalesTax` program

As a shortcut, you can avoid declaring and using the extra `string` variable `itemPriceAsString` in the program in Figure 2-20. Instead, you can accept and convert the input string in one step by nesting the `ReadLine()` and `ToDouble()` method calls, as in the following:

```
itemPrice = Convert.ToDouble(Console.ReadLine());
```

Table 2-6 shows `Convert` class methods you can use to change `strings` into additional useful data types. The methods use the system types (also called run-time types) in their names. For example, recall from Table 2-1 that the "formal" name for an `int` is `Int32`, so the method you use to convert a `string` to an `int` is named `Convert.ToInt32()`.

Method	Description
ToBoolean()	Converts a specified value to an equivalent Boolean value
ToByte()	Converts a specified value to an 8-bit unsigned integer
ToChar()	Converts a specified value to a Unicode character
ToDecimal()	Converts a specified value to a decimal number
ToDouble()	Converts a specified value to a double-precision floating-point number
ToInt16()	Converts a specified value to a 16-bit signed integer (a short)
ToInt32()	Converts a specified value to a 32-bit signed integer (an int)
ToInt64()	Converts a specified value to a 64-bit signed integer (a long)
ToSByte()	Converts a specified value to an 8-bit signed integer
ToSingle()	Converts a specified value to a single-precision floating-point number
ToString()	Converts the specified value to its equivalent String representation
ToUInt16()	Converts a specified value to a 16-bit unsigned integer
ToUInt32()	Converts a specified value to a 32-bit unsigned integer
ToUInt64()	Converts a specified value to a 64-bit unsigned integer

Table 2-6   Selected `Convert` class methods

Using the `Parse()` Methods

As an alternative to the `Convert` class methods, you can use a `Parse()` method to convert a string to a number. For example, to convert a `string` to a `double` in the `InteractiveSalesTax` program in Figure 2-20, you can replace the `Convert.ToDouble()` statement with either of the following `Parse()` method statements:

```
itemPrice = double.Parse(itemPriceAsString);
itemPrice = Double.Parse(itemPriceAsString);
```

Each of the previous two statements uses a `Parse()` method defined in the `Double` class. You can use the system type name `Double` or its simple type name `double`. Either version converts the `string` argument within the parentheses to the correct data type. Similar methods exist for other data types, such as `int.Parse()` and `boolean.Parse()`.

As another example, either of the following two statements reads an integer and stores it in a variable named `score` without using a temporary string to hold the input value:

```
score = int.Parse(Console.ReadLine());
score = Int32.Parse(Console.ReadLine());
```

There are some performance differences between the `Convert` and `Parse()` techniques, but they are minor and relatively technical. Until you learn more about C#, you should use the method preferred by your instructor or organization.

The term **parse** means to break into component parts. Grammarians talk about "parsing a sentence"— deconstructing it so as to describe its grammatical components. Parsing a `String` converts it to its numeric equivalent.

TWO TRUTHS & A LIE

Accepting Console Input

1. The following is valid:

   ```
   int age = Convert.ToInt(Console.ReadLine());
   ```

2. The following is valid:

   ```
   double payRate = Convert.ToDouble(Console.ReadLine());
   ```

3. The following is valid:

   ```
   int dependents = int.Parse(Console.ReadLine());
   ```

The false statement is #1. The `Convert` class method to convert a string to an integer is `ToInt32()`, not `ToInt()`.

You Do It

Writing a Program that Accepts User Input

In the next steps, you write an interactive program that allows the user to enter two integer values. The program then calculates and displays their sum.

1. Open a new file named **InteractiveAddition**, and type the first few lines needed for the Main() method:

    ```
    using System;
    class InteractiveAddition
    {
        static void Main()
        {
    ```

2. Add variable declarations for two strings that will accept the user's input values. Also, declare three integers for the numeric equivalents of the string input values and their sum.

    ```
    string name, firstString, secondString;
    int first, second, sum;
    ```

3. Prompt the user for his or her name, accept it into the name string, and then display a personalized greeting to the user, along with the prompt for the first integer value.

    ```
    Console.Write("Enter your name… ");
    name = Console.ReadLine();
    Console.Write("Hello {0}! Enter the first integer… ", name);
    ```

4. Accept the user's input as a string, and then convert the input string to an integer.

    ```
    firstString = Console.ReadLine();
    first = Convert.ToInt32(firstString);
    ```

5. Add statements that prompt for and accept the second string and convert it to an integer.

    ```
    Console.Write("Enter the second integer… ");
    secondString = Console.ReadLine();
    second = Convert.ToInt32(secondString);
    ```

6. Assign the sum of the two integers to the sum variable and display all of the values. Add the closing curly brace for the Main() method and the closing curly brace for the class.

(continues)

(continued)

```
            sum = first + second;
            Console.WriteLine("{0}, the sum of {1} and {2} is {3}",
                name, first, second, sum);
        }
    }
```

7. Save, compile, and run the program. When prompted, supply your name and any integers you want, and confirm that the result appears correctly. Figure 2-22 shows a typical run of the program.

```
Command Prompt                                    _ □ X

C:\C#\Chapter.02>InteractiveAddition
Enter your name... Emily
Hello Emily! Enter the first integer... 18
Enter the second integer... 275
Emily, the sum of 18 and 275 is 293

C:\C#\Chapter.02>
```

Figure 2-22   Typical execution of `InteractiveAddition` program

Chapter Summary

- A constant is a data value that cannot be changed after a program is compiled; a value in a variable can change. C# provides for 15 basic built-in types of data. A variable declaration includes a data type, an identifier, an optional assigned value, and a semicolon.

- You can display variable values by using the variable name within a `WriteLine()` or `Write()` method call. To make producing output easier, you can combine strings and variable values into a single `Write()` or `WriteLine()` statement by using a format string.

- C# supports nine integral data types: `byte`, `sbyte`, `short`, `ushort`, `int`, `uint`, `long`, `ulong`, and `char`.

- C# supports three floating-point data types: `float`, `double`, and `decimal`. You can use format and precision specifiers to display floating-point data to a specified number of decimal places.

- You use the binary arithmetic operators +, –, *, /, and % to manipulate values in your programs. Multiplication, division, and remainder always take place prior to addition or subtraction in an expression, unless you use parentheses to override the normal precedence. C# provides several shortcut arithmetic operators, including the binary operators +=, –=, *=, /=, and the unary prefix and postfix increment (++) and decrement (– –) operators.

- A bool variable can hold only one of two values—true or false. C# supports six comparison operators: >, <, >=, <=, ==, and !=. An expression containing a comparison operator has a Boolean value.

- When you perform arithmetic with variables or constants of the same type, the result of the arithmetic retains that type. When you perform arithmetic operations with operands of different types, C# chooses a unifying type for the result and implicitly converts nonconforming operands to the unifying type. You may explicitly override the unifying type imposed by C# by performing a cast.

- You use the char data type to hold any single character. You place constant character values within single quotation marks. You can store any character—including nonprinting characters such as a backspace or a tab—in a char variable. To store these characters, you must use an escape sequence, which always begins with a backslash.

- In C#, you use the string data type to hold a series of characters. The value of a string is expressed within double quotation marks. Although the == and != comparison operators can be used with strings that are assigned literal values, you also can use the Equals(), Compare(), CompareTo(), and Substring() methods and the Length property that belong to the String class.

- Named constants are program identifiers whose values cannot change. Conventionally, their identifiers are all uppercase, with underscores inserted for readability. Enumerations are lists of named constants. The constants are integers by default, and frequently the list holds consecutive values.

- You can use the Console.ReadLine() method to accept user input. Often you must use a Convert class method to change the input string into a usable data type.

Key Terms

Constant describes data items whose values are fixed.

A **literal constant** is a value that is taken literally at each use.

A **variable** is a named location in computer memory that can hold different values at different points in time.

A **data type** describes the format and size of a data item and defines what types of operations can be performed with the item.

Intrinsic types of data are basic types; C# provides 15 intrinsic types.

An **alias** is another name for something.

A **simple type** is one of the following in C#: byte, sbyte, short, ushort, int, uint, long, ulong, float, double, decimal, char, and bool.

A **variable declaration** is the statement that names a variable; it includes the data type that the variable will store, an identifier that is the variable's name, an optional assignment operator and assigned value when you want a variable to contain an initial value, and an ending semicolon.

The **assignment operator** is the equal sign (=); any value to the right of the assignment operator is assigned to, or taken on by, the variable to the left.

An **initialization** is an assignment made when a variable is declared.

An **assignment** is a statement that provides a variable with a value.

To **concatenate** a string with another value is to join the two values end to end using a plus sign.

A **format string** is a string of characters that contains one or more placeholders for variable values.

A **placeholder** in a format string consists of a pair of curly braces containing a number that indicates the desired variable's position in a list that follows the string.

Integral data types are those that store whole numbers.

The nine integral types are **byte**, **sbyte**, **short**, **ushort**, **int**, **uint**, **long**, **ulong**, and **char**. The first eight always represent whole numbers, and the ninth type, char, is used for characters like 'A' or 'a'.

Integers are whole numbers.

A **floating-point** number is one that contains decimal positions.

Significant digits provide a measure of the mathematical accuracy of a value.

A **float** data type can hold a floating-point number with as many as seven significant digits of accuracy.

A **double** data type can hold a floating-point number with 15 or 16 significant digits of accuracy.

The **decimal** data type is a floating-point type that has a greater precision and a smaller range than a float or double, which makes it suitable for financial and monetary calculations.

Scientific notation is a means of expressing very large and small numbers using an exponent.

Standard numeric format strings are strings of characters expressed within double quotation marks that indicate a format for output.

The **format specifier** in a format string can be one of nine built-in format characters that define the most commonly used numeric format types.

The **precision specifier** in a format string controls the number of significant digits or zeros to the right of the decimal point.

A C# **culture** is a set of rules that determines how culturally dependent values such as money and dates are formatted.

Binary operators use two arguments—one value to the left of the operator and another value to the right of it.

Operands are the values that operators use in expressions.

Operator precedence determines the order in which parts of a mathematical expression are evaluated.

Order of operation is another term for operator precedence.

Associativity specifies the order in which a sequence of operations with the same precedence are evaluated.

The **add and assign operator** (+=) adds the operand on the right to the operand on the left and assigns the result to the operand on the left in one step.

The **prefix increment operator** (++ before a variable) increases the variable's value by 1 and then evaluates it.

The **postfix increment operator** (++ after a variable) evaluates a variable and then adds 1 to it.

Unary operators are operators used with one operand.

The **decrement operator** (−−) reduces a variable's value by 1. There is a prefix and a postfix version.

A **Boolean variable** can hold only one of two values—true or false.

The **bool** data type holds a Boolean value.

A **comparison operator** compares two items; an expression containing a comparison operator has a Boolean value.

A **unifying type** is the type chosen for an arithmetic result when operands are of dissimilar types.

Implicitly means automatically.

Type precedence is a hierarchy of data types used to determine the unifying type in arithmetic expressions containing dissimilar data types.

An **implicit conversion** or **implicit cast** is the automatic transformation that occurs when a value is assigned to a type with higher precedence.

Explicitly means purposefully.

An **explicit cast** purposefully assigns a value to a different data type; it involves placing the desired result type in parentheses followed by the variable or constant to be cast.

The **char** data type can hold any single character; a literal character is contained between single quotation marks.

An **escape sequence** is two symbols beginning with a backslash that represent a nonprinting character such as a tab.

Unicode is a 16-bit coding scheme for characters.

Hexadecimal, or **base 16**, is a mathematical system that uses 16 symbols to represent numbers.

The **string** data type is used to hold a series of characters; a literal string is contained between double quotation marks.

The String class **Equals() method** determines if two strings have the same value; it requires two string arguments placed within its parentheses, separated by a comma.

The **Compare() method** requires two string arguments. When it returns 0, the two strings are equivalent; when it returns a positive number, the first string is greater than the second; and when it returns a negative value, the first string is less than the second.

Lexically means alphabetically.

The **CompareTo() method** uses a string, a dot, and the method name. When it returns 0, the two strings are equivalent; when it returns a positive number, the first string is greater than the second; and when it returns a negative value, the first string is less than the second.

Immutable describes unchangeable objects such as strings that refer to a new memory location when a new value is assigned.

The **Length property** contains a string's length.

The **Substring() method** can be used to extract a portion of a string from a starting point for a specific length.

The **StartsWith() method** is used with a string and a dot, and its parentheses contain another string. It returns true if the first string starts with the characters contained in the second string.

A **named constant** is an identifier whose value must be assigned upon declaration and whose contents cannot change.

A **self-documenting** program element is one that is self-explanatory.

An **enumeration** is a set of constants represented by identifiers.

Type-safe describes a data type for which only appropriate behaviors are allowed.

An **interactive program** is one that allows user input.

The **Console.ReadLine() method** accepts user input from the keyboard.

A **prompt** is an instruction to the user to enter data.

To **parse** an item is to break it into component parts.

Review Questions

1. When you use a number such as 45 in a C# program, the number is a _____.

   a. literal constant   c. literal variable
   b. figurative constant   d. figurative variable

2. A variable declaration must contain all of the following *except* a(n) _____.

   a. data type   c. assigned value
   b. identifier   d. ending semicolon

3. Which of the following is true of variable declarations?

   a. Two variables of the same type can be declared in the same statement.
   b. Two variables of different types can be declared in the same statement.
   c. Two variables of the same type must be declared in the same statement.
   d. Two variables of the same type cannot coexist in a program.

4. Assume that you have two variables declared as int var1 = 3; and int var2 = 8;. Which of the following would display *838*?

   a. `Console.WriteLine("{0}{1}{2}", var1, var2);`
   b. `Console.WriteLine("{0}{1}{0}", var1, var2);`
   c. `Console.WriteLine("{0}{1}{2}", var2, var1);`
   d. `Console.WriteLine("{0}{1}{0}", var2, var1);`

5. Assume that you have a variable declared as int var1 = 3;. Which of the following would display *X 3X*?

   a. `Console.WriteLine("X{0}X", var1);`
   b. `Console.WriteLine("X{0,2}X", var1);`
   c. `Console.WriteLine("X{2,0}X", var1);`
   d. `Console.WriteLine("X{0}{2}", var1);`

6. Assume that you have a variable declared as int var1 = 3;. What is the value of 22 % var1?

   a. 0   c. 7
   b. 1   d. 21

7. Assume that you have a variable declared as int var1 = 3;. What is the value of 22 / var1?

   a. 1   c. 7.333
   b. 7   d. 21

8. What is the value of the expression 4 + 2 * 3?

   a. 0   c. 18
   b. 10   d. 36

9. Assume that you have a variable declared as int var1 = 3;. If var2 = ++var1, what is the value of var2?

   a. 2   c. 4
   b. 3   d. 5

10. Assume that you have a variable declared as int var1 = 3;. If var2 = var1++, what is the value of var2?

   a. 2   c. 4
   b. 3   d. 5

11. A variable that can hold the two values true and false is of type _____.

   a. int   c. char
   b. bool   d. double

12. Which of the following is *not* a C# comparison operator?

   a. =>   c. ==
   b. !=   d. <

13. What is the value of the expression 6 >= 7?

   a. 0   c. true
   b. 1   d. false

14. Which of the following C# types *cannot* contain floating-point numbers?

   a. float   c. decimal
   b. double   d. int

15. Assume that you have declared a variable as double hourly = 13.00;. What will the statement Console.WriteLine(hourly); display?

   a. 13   c. 13.00
   b. 13.0   d. 13.000000

16. Assume that you have declared a variable as double salary = 45000.00;. Which of the following will display $45,000?

   a. Console.WriteLine(salary.ToString("c"));
   b. Console.WriteLine(salary.ToString("c0"));
   c. Console.WriteLine(salary);
   d. two of these

17. When you perform arithmetic operations with operands of different types, such as adding an int and a float, _____.

    a. C# chooses a unifying type for the result

    b. you must choose a unifying type for the result

    c. you must provide a cast

    d. you receive an error message

18. Unicode is _____.

    a. an object-oriented language   c. a 16-bit coding scheme

    b. a subset of the C# language   d. another term for hexadecimal

19. Which of the following declares a variable that can hold the word *computer*?

    a. `string device = 'computer';`

    b. `string device = "computer";`

    c. `char device = 'computer';`

    d. `char device = "computer";`

20. Which of the following compares two string variables named `string1` and `string2` to determine if their contents are equal?

    a. `string1 = string2`

    b. `string1 == string2`

    c. `Equals.String(string1,string2)`

    d. two of the above

Exercises

Programming Exercises

1. What is the numeric value of each of the following expressions, as evaluated by the C# programming language?

    a. 7 / 3 + 1   g. 81 % 9

    b. 2 + 5 * 3   h. 5 + 2 * 4 − 3 * 7

    c. 15 / 2   i. 3 * (4 + 5) / 5

    d. 15 % 2   j. 27 % 5 − 2

    e. (6 − 2) * 2   k. 15 / 2 / 2

    f. 41 / 5   l. 28 / (3 + 4)

2. What is the value of each of the following Boolean expressions?

   a. 6 < 8
   b. 7 <= 7
   c. 6 * 2 > 10
   d. 4 == 5
   e. 1 + 8 <= 9

   f. 3 + 5 == 33 / 4
   g. 7 != 6
   h. 7 != 7
   i. 3 == 4 – 1
   j. 3 * 4 / 5 == 2

3. Choose the best data type for each of the following, so that no memory storage is wasted. Give an example of a typical value that would be held by the variable and explain why you chose the type you did.

   a. the number of siblings you have
   b. your final grade in this class
   c. the population of Earth
   d. the number of passengers on a bus
   e. one player's score in a Scrabble game
   f. the year an historical event occurred
   g. the number of legs on an animal
   h. one team's score in a Major League Baseball game

4. In this chapter, you learned that although a double and a decimal both hold floating-point numbers, a double can hold a larger value. Write a C# program named **DoubleDecimalTest** that declares and displays two variables—a double and a decimal. Experiment by assigning the same constant value to each variable so that the assignment to the double is legal but the assignment to the decimal is not. In other words, when you leave the decimal assignment statement in the program, an error message should be generated that indicates the value is outside the range of the type decimal, but when you comment out the decimal assignment and its output statement, the program should compile correctly.

5. a. Write a C# program named **MilesToFeet** that declares a named constant that holds the number of feet in a mile: 5280. Also declare a variable to represent the distance in miles between your house and your uncle's house. Assign an appropriate value to the variable—for example, 8.5. Compute and display the distance to your uncle's house in both miles and feet. Display explanatory text with the values—for example, *The distance to my uncle's house is 8.5 miles or 44880 feet.*

   b. Convert the MilesToFeet class to an interactive application named **MilesToFeetInteractive**. Instead of assigning a value to the distance, accept the value from the user as input.

6. a. Write a C# program named **ProjectedSales** that includes a named constant representing next year's anticipated 10 percent increase in sales for each division of a company. (You can represent 10 percent as 0.10). Also declare

variables to represent this year's sales totals in dollars for the North and South divisions. Assign appropriate values to the variables—for example, 4000 and 5500. Compute and display, with explanatory text, next year's projected sales for each division.

b. Convert the `ProjectedSales` class to an interactive application named **ProjectedSalesInteractive**. Instead of assigning values to the North and South sales variables, accept them from the user as input.

7. The Happy Yappy Kennel boards dogs at a cost of 50 cents per pound per day. Write a program named **DogBoarding** that prompts a user for and accepts a dog's weight and number of days to be boarded. Then, display the total price for boarding.

8. Write a program named **HoursAndMinutes** that declares a `minutes` variable to represent minutes worked on a job, and assign a value to it. Display the value in hours and minutes. For example, 197 minutes becomes 3 hours and 17 minutes.

9. a. Write a program named **Eggs** that declares four variables to hold the number of eggs produced in a month by each of four chickens, and assign a value to each variable. Sum the eggs, then display the total in dozens and eggs. For example, a total of 127 eggs is 10 dozen and 7 eggs.

b. Modify the `Eggs` program to create a new one named **EggsInteractive** that prompts the user for and accepts a number of eggs for each chicken.

10. Write a program named **Dollars** that calculates and displays the conversion of an entered number of dollars into currency denominations—20s, 10s, 5s, and 1s.

11. a. Write a program named **Tests** that declares five variables to hold scores for five tests you have taken, and assign a value to each variable. Display the average of the test scores to two decimal places.

b. Modify the `Tests` program to create a new one named **TestsInteractive** that accepts five test scores from a user.

12. Write a program named **FahrenheitToCelsius** that accepts a temperature in Fahrenheit from a user and converts it to Celsius by subtracting 32 from the Fahrenheit value and multiplying the result by 5/9. Display both values.

13. Write a program named **Payroll** that prompts the user for a name, Social Security number, hourly pay rate, and number of hours worked. In an attractive format (similar to Figure 2-23), display all the input data as well as the following:

- Gross pay, defined as hourly pay rate times hours worked

- Federal withholding tax, defined as 15 percent of the gross pay

- State withholding tax, defined as 5 percent of the gross pay

- Net pay, defined as gross pay minus taxes

Figure 2-23 Typical execution of `Payroll` program

14. Write a program named **OrderReceipt** for the Magic Blender Company. The program prompts the user for a name, street address, city, state, zip code, and quantity of blenders ordered at $39.95 each. In an attractive format (similar to Figure 2-24), display all the input data as well as the following:

 • Amount due before tax, defined as number ordered times price

 • Sales tax, defined as 7 percent of the amount due

 • Net due, defined as amount due before tax, plus tax

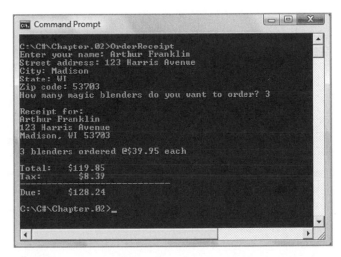

Figure 2-24 Typical execution of `OrderReceipt` program

15. Create an enumeration named Month that holds values for the months of the year, starting with JANUARY equal to 1. Write a program named **MonthNames** that prompts the user for a month integer. Convert the user's entry to a Month value and display it.

16. Create an enumeration named Planet that holds the names for the eight planets in our solar system, starting with MERCURY and ending with NEPTUNE. Write a program named **Planets** that prompts the user for a numeric position, and display the name of the planet that is in the requested position.

17. Pig Latin is a nonsense language. To create a word in pig Latin, you remove the first letter and then add the first letter and "ay" at the end of the word. For example, "dog" becomes "ogday" and "cat" becomes "atcay". Write a program named **PigLatin** that allows the user to enter a word. Output the pig Latin version.

Debugging Exercises

1. Each of the following files in the Chapter.02 folder of your downloadable student files has syntax and/or logical errors. In each case, determine the problem and fix the program. After you correct the errors, save each file using the same filename preceded with *Fixed*. For example, DebugTwo1.cs will become FixedDebugTwo1.cs.

    a. DebugTwo1.cs   c. DebugTwo3.cs

    b. DebugTwo2.cs   d. DebugTwo4.cs

Case Problems

1. In Chapter 1, you created two programs to display the motto for the Greenville Idol competition that is held each summer during the Greenville County Fair. Now, write a program named **GreenvilleRevenue** that prompts a user for the number of contestants entered in last year's competition and in this year's competition. Display all the input data. Compute and display the revenue expected for this year's competition if each contestant pays a $25 entrance fee. Also display a statement that indicates whether this year's competition has more contestants than last year's.

2. In Chapter 1, you created two programs to display the motto for Marshall's Murals. Now, write a program named **MarshallsRevenue** that prompts a user for the number of interior and exterior murals scheduled to be painted during the next month. Compute the expected revenue for each type of mural. Interior murals cost $500 each, and exterior murals cost $750 each. Also display the total expected revenue and a statement that indicates whether more interior murals are scheduled than exterior ones.

Using GUI Objects and the Visual Studio IDE

In this chapter you will:

◎ Create a Form in the Visual Studio IDE

◎ Use the Toolbox to add a Button to a Form

◎ Add Labels and TextBoxes to a Form

◎ Name Forms and controls

◎ Correct errors

◎ Decide which interface to use

You have learned to write simple C# programs that accept input from a user at the console and produce output at the command line. The environment the user sees is a program's **interface**; unfortunately, the interfaces in the applications you have written so far look dull. Most modern applications, and certainly most programs you have used on the Internet, use visually pleasing graphic objects to interact with users. These graphical user interface (GUI) objects include the labels, buttons, and text boxes you control with a mouse when interacting with Windows-type programs.

When you write a console application, you can use a simple text editor such as Notepad or you can use the Visual Studio integrated development environment (IDE). Technically, you have the same options when you write a GUI program. However, so much code is needed to create even the simplest of GUI programs that it is far more practical to develop the user interface visually in the IDE. This approach allows the IDE to automatically generate much of the code you need to develop appealing GUI programs that are easy to use.

In Visual Studio versions before .NET, each language such as C++ and Visual Basic had its own IDE, so you had to learn about a new environment with each programming language you studied. Now, you can use one IDE to create projects in all the supported languages.

Creating a Form in the IDE

Forms are GUI objects that provide an interface for collecting, displaying, and delivering information. You can use a Form to represent any window you want to display within an application. Although they are not required, Forms almost always include **controls**, which are devices such as labels, text boxes, and buttons that users can manipulate to interact with a program.

To create a Form visually using the IDE, you select New Project after starting Visual Studio and then choose Windows Forms Application, as shown in Figure 3-1. By default, Visual Studio names your first Forms application WindowsFormsApplication1. You can change the name if you want, and you can browse to choose a location to save the application. You should almost always provide a more meaningful name for applications than the default name suggested. Most of the examples in this chapter retain the default names to minimize the number of changes required if you want to replicate the steps on your computer.

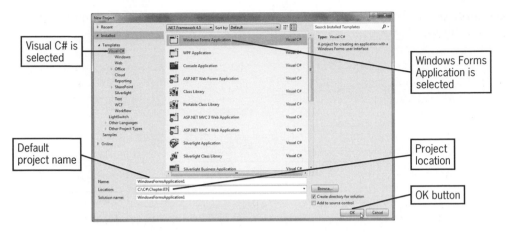

Visual C# is selected

Windows Forms Application is selected

Default project name

Project location

OK button

Figure 3-1   Choosing Windows Forms Application in the New Project window

After you click OK in the New Project window, you see the IDE main window, as shown in Figure 3-2. The main window contains several smaller windows, each of which can be resized, relocated, or closed. If a window is not currently visible, you can select it from the VIEW menu in the main menu bar. Some key features in the IDE include:

- The name of the project shown in four places: on the title bar, in two locations in the Solution Explorer, and in the Properties window. In Figure 3-2, the application has the default name `WindowsFormsApplication1`.

- The **main menu**, which lies horizontally across the top of the window, and includes a FILE menu from which you open, close, and save projects. It also contains submenus for editing, debugging, and help tasks, among others.

 As you work through any project, you should choose Save All frequently. You can select this action from the FILE menu or click the Save All button, which has an icon that looks like two overlapping disks.

- The **Toolbox tab**, which, when opened, provides lists of controls you can drag onto a Form so that you can develop programs visually, using a mouse.

- The **Form Designer**, which appears in the center of the screen. This is where you design applications visually.

- The **Solution Explorer**, for viewing and managing project files and settings.

- The **Properties window**, for configuring properties and events on controls in your user interface. For example, you can use this window to set the Size property of a Button or the Text property of a Form.

- The **Error list**, which displays any warnings and errors that occur when you build or execute a program.

If some of these features are not visible after you start a project in the IDE, you can select them from the VIEW menu.

Figure 3-2   The IDE main window

The Solution Explorer file list shows the files that are part of the current project:

- The Program.cs file contains the automatically generated `Main()` method of the application.

- The Form1.cs file contains other automatically generated code, and is where you write code describing the tasks you will assign to controls in your application.

- To the left of the Form1.cs file, you see a small triangle node. A **node** is an icon that can be used to expand or condense a list or a section of code. In Visual Studio, some nodes appear as triangles, and others appear as small plus or minus signs. When a triangle-shaped node points straight to the right, you see a condensed view. Clicking the triangle reveals hidden items or code—the triangle will point diagonally down and to the right, and you see all the items in the list (or all the hidden code). Clicking the triangle again collapses the list so you can work with a condensed view.

If you expand the Form1.cs node by clicking it, you see the following:

- A file named Form1.Designer.cs. The Windows Form Designer automatically writes code in the Designer.cs file; the code created there implements all the actions that are performed when you drag and drop controls from the Toolbox. You should avoid making manual changes to this file because you can easily corrupt a program.

- A file named Form1.resx that can hold resources such as images and audio clips; you will add such resources to your programs as you learn more about C#.

When you create a Windows Forms project, Visual C# adds a form to the project and calls it Form1. You can see Form1 in the following locations in Figure 3-3:

- On the folder tab at the top of the Form Designer area (followed by *[Design]*)
- In the title bar of the form in the Form Designer area
- In the Solution Explorer file list (with a .cs extension)

Figure 3-3 Displaying the properties of Form1

When you click the Form in the Form Designer area, you see its name in two more locations: in the Properties window in the lower-right corner, and as the Text property of the form that is in the Form Designer area. You can scroll through a list of properties in the Properties window. If you click a property, a brief description of it appears at the bottom of the Properties window. For example, Figure 3-3 displays a description of the Text property of Form1.

You can change the appearance, size, color, and window management features of a Form by setting its properties. The Form class contains approximately 100 properties; Table 3-1 lists a few of the Form features you can change. For example, setting the Text property allows you to specify the caption of the Form in the title bar, and setting the Size, BackColor, and ForeColor allow you to further customize the Form. The two left buttons at the top of the Properties list allow you to organize properties by category or alphabetically. The properties shown in Figure 3-3 are in alphabetical order. Not every property that can be used with a Form appears in the Properties window in the Visual Studio IDE—only the most frequently used properties are listed.

Property Name	Description
AcceptButton	Gets or sets the button on the form that is clicked when the user presses the Enter key
BackColor	Gets or sets the background color of the Form
CancelButton	Gets or sets the button control that is clicked when the user presses the Esc key
ForeColor	Gets or sets the foreground color of the Form
Name	Gets or sets the name of the Form
Size	Gets or sets the size of the Form
Text	Gets or sets the text associated with the control
Visible	Gets or sets a value indicating whether the control is visible

Table 3-1   Selected properties of Forms

In Figure 3-3, notice the small plus sign that appears to the left of the Size property in the Properties window. This is a node that you can click to expand or condense a property. For example, if you click the Size node, you will see an expanded list that displays the two parts of Size (Width and Height) separately. The node changes to a minus sign, which you can then click to condense the expanded list.

The property names generally appear in alphabetical order in the Properties window. A notable exception is the Name entry. Name appears in parentheses so that when the Properties list is sorted in alphabetical order, Name is near the top and easy to find. (An opening parenthesis has a lower Unicode value than any alphabetic letter; Appendix B contains information on Unicode.) For most professional applications, you will want to provide a Form with a reasonable identifier that is more descriptive than Form1.

Do not confuse a Form's Name with its Text property. If you change a Form's Name, you don't notice any difference in the visual design, but all references to the form are changed in the code. Therefore, a Form's Name property is an identifier and it must follow the rules for variable names. This means, for example, that a Form's Name cannot contain spaces and cannot start with a digit. However, a Form's Text is what appears in its title bar, and it can be any string. (In Chapter 2, you learned to enclose a string's contents in quotation marks. Although a Form's Text is a string, you do not type containing quotes when you enter a value for the Text property in the Properties list.) For example, in an accounting application, you might name a Form BudgetForm, but assign *2014 Budget Calculator* as its Text.

    Watch the video *The Visual Studio IDE*.

TWO TRUTHS & A LIE

Creating a Form in the IDE

1. The Visual Studio IDE allows you to use a visual environment for designing Forms.

2. Some key features in Visual C# include the Toolbox, Form Designer, and Solution Explorer.

3. When you create a first Windows Forms project in any folder, Visual C# names the project MyFirstForm by default.

The false statement is #3. When you create a first Windows Forms project in any folder, Visual C# names the project WindowsFormsApplication1 by default.

Using the Toolbox to Add a Button to a Form

When you open the IDE, the left border displays a Toolbox tab. (If you don't see the tab, you can select VIEW and then Toolbox from the IDE's main menu.) When you open the Toolbox, a list of tool groups is displayed. The list automatically closes when you move your mouse off the list and click elsewhere, or you can pin the Toolbox to the screen by clicking the pushpin icon at the top of the list. When you pin the Toolbox, the Form moves to the right to remain as visible as possible depending on how you have sized the windows in the IDE. Selecting All Windows Forms at the top of the Toolbox displays a complete list of available tools; selecting Common Controls displays a smaller list that is a subset of the original one. As shown in Figure 3-4, the Common Controls list contains many controls: the GUI objects a user can click or manipulate. The list includes controls you probably have seen when using Windows applications—for example, Button and CheckBox. You can drag these controls onto the Form. This chapter features only three controls from the Toolbox—Label, Button, and TextBox. You will learn about many of the other controls in the chapter called *Using Controls.*

All windows in Visual C# can be made dockable or floating, hidden or visible, or can be moved to new locations. To change the behavior of a window, click the down arrow or pushpin icon on the title bar and select from the available options. You can customize many aspects of the IDE by clicking the TOOLS menu, then clicking Options. To reset the windows to their original states, click WINDOW on the main Visual Studio menu, and then click Reset Window Layout.

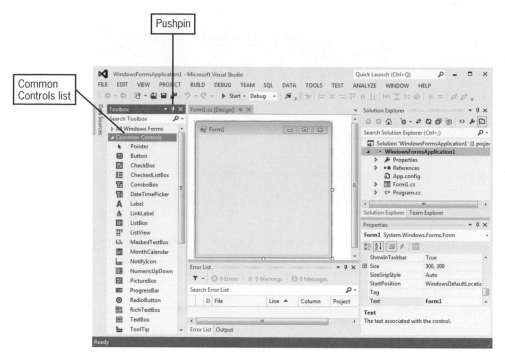

Figure 3-4   The open Toolbox in the IDE

You can drag controls onto a Form where you think they will be most useful or contribute to a pleasing design. After a control is on a Form, you can relocate it by dragging it, or delete the control by selecting it and pressing the Del key on your keyboard. You also can delete a control by right-clicking it and selecting the Delete option from the menu that appears.

In Figure 3-5, the programmer has dragged a button onto the Form. By default, its Name is button1. (You might guess that if you drag a second Button onto a Form, its Name automatically becomes button2.) In a professional application, you would probably want to change the Name property of the Button to a unique and memorable identifier.

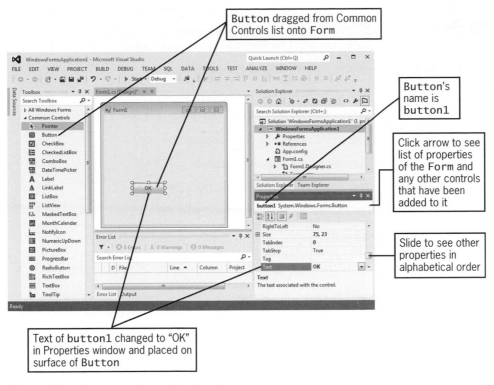

Button dragged from Common Controls list onto Form

Button's name is button1

Click arrow to see list of properties of the Form and any other controls that have been added to it

Slide to see other properties in alphabetical order

Text of button1 changed to "OK" in Properties window and placed on surface of Button

Figure 3-5 A Button dragged onto a Form

In Figure 3-5, the programmer has clicked button1, so the Properties window shows the properties for button1. (If you click the Form, the Properties window changes to show Form properties instead of Button properties.) The Text property of button1 has been changed to "OK", and the button on the Form has handles that can be used to resize it. You can scroll through the Properties list and examine other properties that can be modified for the Button. For example, you can change its BackColor, ForeColor, Font, and Size. Table 3-2 describes a few of the properties available for Button objects. This chapter discusses only a few properties of each control. You can learn about other properties in the chapter *Using Controls*.

Property Name	Description
BackColor	Gets or sets the background color for the control
Enabled	Gets or sets whether the control is enabled
Font	Gets or sets the current font for the control
ForeColor	Gets or sets the foreground color of the control
Name	Gets or sets the name of the control
Size	Gets or sets the size of the control
Text	Gets or sets the text associated with the control
Visible	Gets or sets a value indicating whether the control is visible

Table 3-2 Selected properties of Buttons

You can click a control on a Form to display its Properties list in the Properties window. Alternatively, you can click the arrow next to the current control name shown at the top of the Properties list and select the desired control to view from a drop-down list. See Figure 3-5.

Adding Functionality to a Button on a Form

Adding functionality to a Button is easy when you use the IDE. After you have dragged a Button onto a Form, you can double-click it to create a method that executes when the user clicks the Button. For example, if you have dragged a Button onto a Form and have not changed its default name from button1, code is automatically generated when you double-click the button, as shown in Figure 3-6. (The viewing windows in the figure have been resized by dragging their borders so that you can see more of the code.) You can view the Form Designer again by selecting VIEW and then Designer from the main menu. Then, you can revert to the code window by selecting VIEW and Code. As you create GUI applications, you frequently will switch back and forth between the visual environment and the code. Alternatively, you can use the tabs or press one of the shortcut keys displayed on the drop-down menu to switch the view.

Figure 3-6 The automatically generated code after clicking `button1`

 When you double-click a button to generate a click method, you generate code for the button's default event. Clicking is a button's default event because users typically expect to click a button. As you learn more about C#, you will find that you can write other events for a button. For example, perhaps you want to take a specific action if a user double-clicks or right-clicks a button.

If you scroll through the exposed code, you see many generated statements, some of which are confusing. However, to make a `Button` perform an action, you can ignore most of the statements. You only need to write code between the curly braces of the method with the following header:

```
private void button1_Click(object sender, EventArgs e)
```

Instead of automatically generating the method header that executes when a user clicks a `Button`, you could write it yourself. However, you would have to know more about both methods and event handlers because other code is also automatically written elsewhere in the project that links the `Form`'s button to the method. You will learn about these topics in later chapters.

You have seen the following two method headers used in console applications:

```
static void Main()
static void Main(string[] args)
```

The GUI application also contains a Main() method that is created automatically; you can see it by opening the Program.cs file that is part of the application.

The button1_Click() method and the two versions of the Main() method headers all use the void return type, but the methods differ in the following ways:

- The button1_Click() method has a private access specifier. An **access specifier** is a keyword that dictates which types of outside classes can use a method. By default, Visual Studio makes the button1_Click() method private, which limits the ability of other classes to use the method, but you could remove the word private and notice no difference in how the button works. You will learn more about access specifiers later in this book.

- Both versions of the Main() method are static, whereas the button1_Click() method is not. A static method executes without an object. The button1_Click() method cannot be static because it needs an object, which is the Form in which it is running. The chapter called *Using Classes and Objects* provides more detail about the keyword static.

- One version of the Main() method header contains nothing between its parentheses, and the other one contains a parameter named string[] args. The button1_Click() method contains two parameters between its parentheses, separated with a comma. These represent values about the event (the user clicking the button) that causes execution of the method. When a user interacts with a GUI object, an **event** is generated that causes the program to perform a task. When a user clicks a Button, the action fires a **click event**, which causes the Button's Click() method to execute. This chapter discusses only click events. You can learn about other events in the *Event Handling* chapter.

If you change the Name property of the button1 object in the IDE, the name of its subsequently created Click() method will also change automatically. For example, if you rename button1 to okButton, then double-click it, the name of the generated method is:

okButton_Click()

If you change a Button's Name from button1 and then place a second button on the Form, the new Button is named button1. If you leave the first Button's default name as button1, then the second Button you place on the Form is named button2, and its default Click() method is named button2_Click(). C# automatically creates a method name for each Button based on its associated object's name. Later in this chapter you will learn what to do if you create the event method first and change the control's name later.

You are not required to create a Click() method for a Button. If, for some reason, you did not want to take any action when a user clicked a Button, you simply would not include the method in your program. Alternatively, you could create an empty method that contains no statements between its curly braces and thus does nothing. However, these choices would be unusual and a poor programming practice—you usually place a Button on a Form because you expect it to be clicked at some point. You will frustrate users if you do not allow your controls to act in expected ways.

You can write any statements you want between the curly braces of the button1_Click() method. For example, you can declare variables, perform arithmetic statements, and produce output. You also can include block or line comments. The next sections of this chapter include several statements added to a Click() method.

 Watch the video *Creating a Functional Button*.

TWO TRUTHS & A LIE

Using the Toolbox to Add a Button to a Form

1. When a user clicks a Button, the action fires a click event that causes the Button's Click() method to execute.

2. If a Button's identifier is reportButton, then the name of its Click() method is reportButton.Click().

3. You can write any statements you want between the curly braces of a Button's Click() method.

The false statement is #2. If a Button's identifier is reportButton, then the name of its Click() method is reportButton_Click().

Adding Labels and TextBoxes to a Form

Suppose that you want to create an interactive GUI program that accepts two numbers from a user and outputs their sum when the user clicks a Button. To provide prompts for the user and to display output, you can add Labels to a Form, and to get input from a user, you can provide TextBoxes.

Labels are controls that you use to display text to communicate with an application's user. Just like a Button, you can drag a Label onto a Form, as shown in Figure 3-7. By default, the first Label you drag onto a Form is named label1, and the text that appears on the Label also is label1. You can change its Text property to display any string of text; depending on the amount of text you enter, you might need to change the size of the Label by dragging its resizing handles or altering its Size property. In Figure 3-7, "Enter a number" has been assigned to label1's Text property. If you want to create multiple lines of text on a Label, click the small, downward-pointing arrow to the right of the Text property value to open an editor and type the needed text in separate lines. You might want a program to start with no text appearing on a label. If so, just delete the entry from the Text property in the Properties list. If you execute a program that starts with a blank label, it will be invisible on the Form. Note that a label's Text property can be blank, but a Label's Name property cannot.

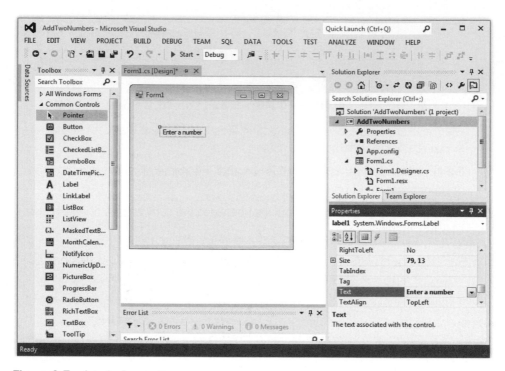

Figure 3-7   A Label on a Form

TextBoxes are controls through which a user can enter input data in a GUI application. Figure 3-8 shows a TextBox on a Form. If a user will enter data in a TextBox, you frequently want to start with its Text property empty, but you are allowed to add text to its Text property if desired.

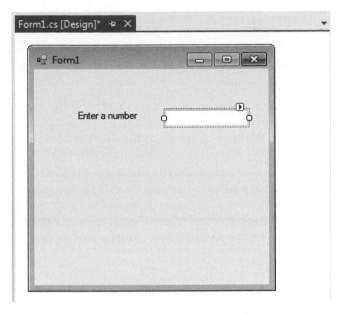

Figure 3-8   A Label and TextBox on a form

Figure 3-9 shows a Form with three Labels, two TextBoxes, and a Button. The third Label has not yet been provided with text, so it still contains "label3". You can delete the Text value in the Properties window if you want the Label to be empty at first.

Figure 3-9   A Form with several controls

When a user runs the program that displays the Form in Figure 3-9, the intention is for the user to enter two numbers in the TextBoxes. When the user clicks the Button, the sum of the two numbers will be displayed in label3. To create the code that does this, you must write code for the Button. In the Form Designer, you can double-click the Button to expose the prewritten shell of the button1_Click() method.

Figure 3-10 shows the code you can write within the button1_Click() method. The method contains declarations for three integers. When a user types a value into a TextBox in an executing program, it becomes the value for the Text property of the TextBox. Because a user might type any value, the value in a TextBox is a string by default. When you write an application in which the user is supposed to enter a number, you must convert the entered string into a number. You are familiar with this process because it's exactly the same action required when a user enters data in response to a Console.ReadLine() statement in a console application. So, for example, to convert a user's entry in a TextBox named textBox1 to an int and a user's entry in a TextBox named moneyTextBox to a double, you can make statements similar to the following:

```
int num1 = Convert.ToInt32(textBox1.Text);
double money = Convert.ToDouble(moneyTextBox.Text);
```

The last two statements in the method perform the necessary addition operation and assign a string and the concatenated sum to the Text property of the Label that displays the output.

```
private void button1_Click(object sender, EventArgs e)
{
    int num1;
    int num2;
    int sum;
    num1 = Convert.ToInt32(textBox1.Text);
    num2 = Convert.ToInt32(textBox2.Text);
    sum = num1 + num2;
    label3.Text = "Sum is " + sum;
}
```

Figure 3-10   The button1_Click() method that calculates the sum of the entries in two TextBoxes

You can execute a program from the IDE by selecting DEBUG from the main menu and then Start Without Debugging. (As an alternative, you can hold down the Ctrl key and press F5.) Figure 3-11 shows how the Form appears when the program executes and the result after the user has entered numbers and clicked the Button. The period during which you design a program is called **design time**. When you execute a program, the stage is called **run time**.

Figure 3-11   The Form when it first appears and after a user has entered two integers and clicked the Button

You can change the values in either or both of the TextBoxes in the Form and click the Button to see a new result. When you finish using the application, you can close it by clicking the Close button in the upper-right corner of the Form.

Understanding Focus and Tab Control

When a GUI program displays a Form, one of the components on the Form has focus. The control with **focus** is the one that can receive keyboard input. When a Button has focus, a thin, bright line appears around it to draw your attention, and the Button's associated event executes when you click the button or press the Enter key on the keyboard. When a TextBox has focus, a blinking cursor appears inside it.

When an application is running, the user can give focus to a component by clicking it, or can switch focus from one component to another using the Tab key. The order in which controls receive focus from successive Tab key presses is their **tab order**. By default, controls are assigned tab order based on the order in which you place them on a Form when designing a program. The first control you place on a Form has TabIndex 0, the next control has TabIndex 1, and so on. When you start a program, the control with TabIndex 0 automatically has focus. You can check a control's tab order by viewing its TabIndex property in the Properties list of the IDE. If you do not want a control to be part of the tabbing sequence for a Form, you can change its TabStop property from true to false in the Properties list.

You can change a control's TabIndex value by changing the entry next to TabIndex in the Properties list of the IDE. Alternatively, you can select VIEW from the main menu, and then select Tab Order. You see a representation of the Form with a small blue number next to each control to represent the tab values. To change the focus order for the controls, simply click each control in the desired order. Select VIEW and then Tab Order again to remove the blue numbers.

 Watch the video *Visual Studio's Automatically Generated Code.*

Formatting Data in GUI Applications

In Chapter 2, you learned about format strings that can be used to make numeric data align appropriately, display the desired number of decimal places, and display dollar signs. For example, the following displays *Total is $4.55* because the double variable myMoney is converted to currency format and placed in position 0 in a string:

```
double myMoney = 4.558;
string mySentence = String.Format("Total is {0}", myMoney.ToString("C"));
Console.WriteLine(mySentence);
```

You can use the same String.Format() method to create formatted strings in your GUI applications. For example, suppose you have retrieved a double from a TextBox with a statement similar to the following:

```
double money = Convert.ToDouble(textBox1.Text);
```

You can display the value on a label with explanatory text and as currency with two decimal places with a statement similar to the following:

```
label1.Text = String.Format("The money value is {0}",
    money.ToString("C2"));
```

If necessary, you also can use escape characters in strings that are assigned to controls such as labels. For example, a two-line label might be created using the following code:

```
label1.Text = "Hello\nthere";
```

Changing a Label's Font

The Font property for controls was described briefly in Table 3-2 earlier in this chapter. You will learn more about this property in Chapter 12, but you might want to experiment with it now to align numbers.

When you click any control on a Form and examine its Properties list, you discover that the default font for controls is Microsoft Sans Serif. This font is a **proportional font**, which means that different characters have different pitches or widths. For example, a *w* is wider than an *i*. The opposite of a proportional font is a **fixed-pitch font**, or a **monospaced font**, in which each character has the same width. You might want to use a fixed-pitch font to help align text values on controls. For example, when you stack $11.11 and $88.88 on a Label, you typically want the characters to be an equal width so that the values align.

To change the font for a Label, select the small box with an ellipsis (three dots) to the right of the existing Font name in the Properties list, and select a new Font from the dialog box that opens. For example, Courier New and Consolas are popular fixed-pitch fonts. (You can also change the font style and size if desired.)

TWO TRUTHS & A LIE

Adding Labels and TextBoxes to a Form

1. A Label and a TextBox both have a Text property.

2. When a user types a value on a Label in an executing program, it becomes the value for the Text property of the Label.

3. You can display the value on a Label using a format string.

The false statement is #2. A user does not type on a Label. When a user types a value into a TextBox in an executing program, it becomes the value for the Text property of the TextBox.

Naming Forms and Controls

Usually, you want to provide reasonable Name property values for all the controls you place on a Form. Although any identifier that starts with a letter is legal, note the following conventions:

- Start control names with a lowercase letter and use camel casing as appropriate.

- Start Form names with an uppercase letter and use camel casing as appropriate. A Form is a class and, by convention, C# class names start with an uppercase letter.

- Use the type of object in the name. For example, use names such as okButton, firstValueTextBox, or ArithmeticForm.

 Professional programmers usually do not retain the default names for Forms and controls. An exception is sometimes made for Labels that never change. For example, if three labels provide directions or explanations to the user and are never altered during a program's execution, many programmers would approve of retaining their names as label1, label2, and label3.

Most often, you will want to name controls as soon as you add them to a Form. If you rename a control after you have created an event for it, the program still works, but the name of the control no longer corresponds to its associated method, making the code harder to understand. If you simply change the method name to match the control name, the event code will generate errors. For example, assume that you have created a button named button1 and that you have double-clicked it, creating a method named button1_Click().

Then suppose that you decide to change the Name property of the Button to sumButton. Afterward, when you look at the program code, the Click() method is still named button1_Click(). To fix this, you must refactor the code. **Code refactoring** is the process of changing a program's internal structure without changing the way the program works. To refactor the code after changing the button's name, do the following:

- After you change the name of the control using the Designer, switch to view the code.

- Right-click the name of the method button1_Click().

- From the menu that appears, point to Refactor and then click Rename, as shown in Figure 3-12.

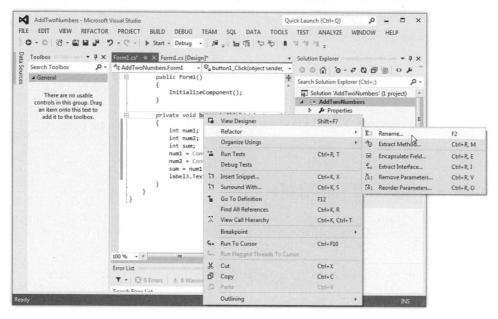

Figure 3-12   Choosing the Rename option from the Refactor menu

- When you click Rename, a dialog box opens, as shown in Figure 3-13.

- Type the new method name; for example, you can enter sumButton_Click using the button's Name, an underscore, and Click, but not adding the parentheses that appear in the method header.

- When you finish, click OK. A Preview Changes dialog box will highlight the change. You can confirm the change by clicking Apply.

Figure 3-13 The Rename dialog box

TWO TRUTHS & A LIE

Naming Forms and Controls

1. Label and TextBox names usually start with an uppercase letter, but Form names usually start with a lowercase letter.

2. Professional programmers usually do not retain the default names for Forms and controls.

3. If you rename a control after you have created an event for it, you must refactor the code.

The false statement is #1. Label and TextBox names usually start with a lowercase letter, but Form names usually start with an uppercase letter.

Correcting Errors

Just like in console-based programs, you will often generate syntax errors when you use the visual developer to create GUI applications. If you build or run a program that contains a syntax error, you see *Build failed* in the lower-left corner of the IDE. You also see an error dialog box like the one shown in Figure 3-14. When you are developing a program, you should always click No in response to "Would you like to continue and run the last successful build?" Clicking Yes will run the previous version of the program you created before inserting the mistake that caused the dialog box to appear. Instead, click No, examine the error messages and code, and correct the mistake.

Figure 3-14   Dialog box that appears when an error occurs during compilation

 When you select BUILD from the main menu, two options are Build Solution and Rebuild Solution. The Build Solution option uses only files that have changed since the most recent build, whereas Rebuild Solution works with all the files in a project, regardless of whether they have changed. The Build Solution option is usually sufficient and faster, but if you have made many changes to several parts of a project, you might choose Rebuild Solution to make sure that all files are currently coordinated.

When errors occur, they are shown in the error list at the bottom of the screen. If you do not see error messages, you can click VIEW from the IDE's main menu and then click Error List. If the list is hidden, you can drag up on the divider between the development window and the error list, and then click the Error List tab. Figure 3-15 shows a single error message, *; expected*, which means *semicolon expected*. The error list also shows the file, line, position in the line, and project in which the error occurred. If you double-click the error message, the cursor is placed at the location in the code where the error was found. A wiggly red underline will help you locate the error in the code window. In this case, a semicolon is missing at the end of a statement. You can fix the error and attempt another compilation.

Figure 3-15   The error list

You can add line numbers to your code for reference by selecting TOOLS from Visual Studio's main menu, then selecting Options. Use the triangle-shaped node to expand Text Editor, and then click the node next to C# from the list that appears. Click General, select the Line numbers check box, and then click OK.

As with console-based programs, GUI applications might compile successfully but contain logical errors. For example, you might type a minus sign instead of a plus sign in the statement that is intended to calculate the sum of two input numbers. You should be prepared to execute a program multiple times and carefully examine the output to discover any logical errors.

Deleting an Unwanted Event-Handling Method

When you are working in the Form Designer in the IDE, it is easy to inadvertently double-click a control and automatically create an event-handling method that you do not want. For example, you might double-click a Label named label1 by mistake and generate a method named label1_Click(). You can leave the automatically created method empty so that no actions result, but in a professional program you typically would not include empty methods. Such empty methods that never execute are known as **orphaned methods**. You should not just delete an orphaned method because, behind the scenes, other code might have been created that refers to the method; if so, the program will not compile. Instead of deleting the method code, you should click the control with the unwanted method so it appears in the Properties window, then click the Events button, which looks like a lightning bolt. Select the event you want to eliminate, and delete the name of the method (see Figure 3-16). This eliminates all the references to the method, and your program can again run successfully.

Figure 3-16 Deleting an event from the Properties window

Failing to Close a Form Before Attempting to Reexecute a Program

Often you will execute a GUI application and notice something you want to correct in the program. For example, you might want to reword the Text on a Label, or reposition a Button on the Form. In your haste to make the improvement, you might forget to close the application that is still running. If you make a change to the program and then try to rerun it, you get an error message that starts with the words "Could not copy...". The solution is simply to close the previous execution of the application and then try again.

Using Visual Studio Help

When working with a class that is new to you, such as Button or Form, no book can answer all of your questions. The ultimate authority on C# classes is the Visual Studio Help documentation. You should use this tool often as you continue to learn about C# in particular and the Visual Studio products in general. The Help documentation for Visual Studio is in the MSDN Library, which you can install locally on your own computer. It is also available at *http://msdn.microsoft.com*.

Two other good ways to find help while working in Visual Studio include the following:

- *F1 Search.* In the Code Editor, you can position the cursor on or just after a keyword or class member and press F1. The Help provided is context-sensitive, which means the screen you see depends on where your cursor is located.

- *Search.* On the main menu, you can click HELP and then click View Help. You will be taken to the Visual Studio Web site where you can type a topic in the Search box.

TWO TRUTHS & A LIE

Correcting Errors

1. When a program in Visual Studio has a syntax error, you see an error dialog box that asks if you want to continue with the last successful build. You should always respond No.

2. Program errors are harder to locate in the Visual Studio IDE than they are in applications written using a plain text editor.

3. If you inadvertently create a Click() method in Visual Studio, you should not delete its code. You should select the event in the Properties window and delete it there.

The false statement is #2. In the Visual Studio IDE, any displayed syntax errors include the file name, line, position in the line, and project in which the error occurred.

Deciding Which Interface to Use

You have learned to create console applications in which most of the action occurs in a
Main() method and the WriteLine() and ReadLine() methods are used for input and
output. You also have learned to create GUI applications in which most of the action occurs
within an event-handling method such as a Click() method, and Labels and TextBoxes

are used for input and output. Both types of applications can use declared variables and
constants, and, as you will learn in the next few chapters, both types of programs can
contain the basic building blocks of applications—decisions, loops, arrays, and calls to
other methods. When you want to write a program that displays a greeting or sums
some integers, you can do so using either type of interface and employing the same logic
to get the same results. So, should you develop programs using a GUI interface or a
console interface?

- GUI applications look "snazzier." It is easy to add colors and fonts to them, and they
  contain controls that a user can manipulate with a mouse. Also, users are accustomed
  to GUI applications from their experiences on the Web. However, GUI programs
  usually take longer to develop than their console counterparts because you can spend
  a lot of time setting up the controls, placing them on a Form, and adjusting their
  sizes and relative positions before you write the code that does the actual work of
  the program. GUI applications created in the IDE also require much more disk space
  to store.

Designing aesthetically pleasing, functional, and user-friendly Forms is an art; entire books are devoted
to the topic.

- Console applications look dull in comparison to GUIs, but they can often be developed
  more quickly because you do not spend much time setting up objects for a user to
  manipulate. When you are learning programming concepts like decision-making and
  looping, you might prefer to keep the interface simple so that you can better concentrate
  on the new logical constructs being presented.

In short, it doesn't matter which interface you use to develop programs while learning the
intricacies of the C# programming language. In the following "You Do It" section, you
develop an application that is similar to the one you developed at the console in Chapter 1.
In the programming exercises at the end of this chapter, you will develop programs that are
identical in purpose to programs written using the console in the chapter called *Using Data*.
Throughout the next several chapters on decisions, looping, and arrays, many concepts
will be illustrated in console applications, because the programs are shorter and the
development is simpler. However, you also will occasionally see the same concept
illustrated in a program that uses a GUI interface, to remind you that the program logic
is the same no matter which interface is used. After you complete the chapters *Using
Classes and Objects*, *Using Controls*, and *Handling Events*, you will be able to write even
more sophisticated GUI applications.

When writing your own programs, you will use the interface you prefer or one that your instructor or boss requires. If time permits, you might even want to develop programs both ways in future chapter exercises.

TWO TRUTHS & A LIE

Deciding Which Interface to Use

1. Console applications are used for declaring variables and constants and performing arithmetic, but GUI applications are not.

2. GUI programs usually take longer to develop than their console counterparts because you can spend a lot of time setting up and arranging the controls.

3. Console applications look dull compared to GUI applications, but they can often be developed more quickly because you do not spend much time setting up objects for a user to manipulate.

The false statement is #1. Both console and GUI applications can use declared variables and constants, and perform arithmetic.

 You Do It

Working With the Visual Studio IDE

In the next steps, you use the IDE to create a Form with a Button and a Label. Your first console application in Chapter 1's "You Do It" section displayed "Hello, world!" at the command prompt. This application displays "Hello, Visual World!" on a Form.

1. Open Microsoft Visual C#. You might have a desktop shortcut you can double-click, or you might click **Start** on the taskbar, point to **All Programs**, and then click **Visual Studio 2012**. Your steps might differ slightly from the ones listed here if you are using a different version of C#. If you are using a school network, you might be able to select Visual Studio from the school's computing menu.

(continues)

(continued)

2. Select **New Project**. Then, in the New Project window, select **Visual C#** and **Windows Forms Application**. Make the name of the project **HelloVisualWorld**, as shown in Figure 3-17, and select a location to store the project. Then click **OK**.

Figure 3-17 Opening a new project

3. The HelloVisualWorld development environment opens, as shown in Figure 3-18. The text in the title bar of the blank Form contains the default name Form1. If you click the Form, its Properties window appears in the lower-right portion of the screen, and you can see that the Text property for the Form is set to Form1. Take a moment to scroll through the list in the Properties window, examining the values of other properties of the Form. For example, the value of the Size property is 300, 300 by default.

(continues)

(continued)

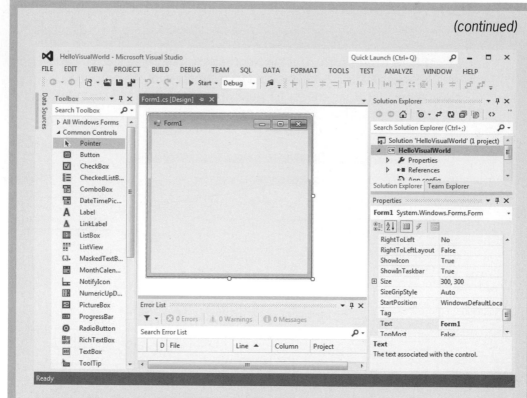

Figure 3-18   The HelloVisualWorld project development environment

 If you do not see the Properties window in the lower-right corner of your screen, click the title bar on the Form. Alternatively, click VIEW in the main menu and click Properties Window.

 If you do not see the Toolbox shown in Figure 3-18, click the Toolbox tab at the left side of the screen, and then click the pushpin near the top to pin the Toolbox to the screen. Alternatively, click VIEW from the main menu and then click Toolbox.

 If you do not see the error list at the bottom of the screen, as in Figure 3-18, you can select VIEW from the main menu and then select Error List. You might have to drag up on the divider that separates the error list from the window above it.

4. In the Properties window, change the Name of the Form to **HelloForm**. Then change the Text of the Form to **Hello Visual World**. Press **Enter**; the title of the Form in the center of the screen changes to *Hello Visual World*, as shown in Figure 3-19.

(continues)

5. Examine the Toolbox on the left side of the screen. Select
    Common Controls if it is not already selected. In the Toolbox,
    click **Button**. As you move your mouse off the Toolbox and onto the
    form, the mouse pointer changes so that it appears to carry a Button.
    Position your mouse anywhere on the form, then release the mouse
    button. The Button appears on the Form and contains the text "button1".
    When you click the Button, handles appear that you can drag to
    resize it. When you click off the Button on the Form, the handles
    disappear. Click the Button to display the properties for button1.
    Change its Name to **displayOutputButton**, and change its Text
    property to **Click here**. When you press Enter on the keyboard or
    click anywhere on the Form, the text of the Button on the Form
    changes to "Click here". See Figure 3-19.

Figure 3-19 A Form with changed Text and a Button

6. Scroll through the other displayOutputButton properties. For example,
    examine the Location property. The first value listed for Location
    indicates horizontal position, and the second value indicates vertical
    position. Drag the Button across the Form to a new position. Each time

(continued)

you release your mouse button, the value of the Form Button's Location property is updated to reflect the new location. Try to drag the Button to Location 100, 150. Alternatively, delete the contents of the Location property field and type **100, 150**. The Button moves to the requested location on the Form.

7. Save your form by clicking **FILE** on the menu bar, then clicking **Save All**. Alternatively, you can click the **Save All** button on the toolbar; its icon is two overlapping disks.

8. Although your Form doesn't do much yet, you can execute the program anyway. Click **DEBUG** on the menu bar and then click **Start Without Debugging**. The Form appears. You can drag, minimize, and restore it, and you can click its Button. The Button has not yet been programmed to do anything, but it appears to be pressed when you click it. Click the Form's **Close** button to dismiss the Form.

9. You can close a project at any time and come back to it later. Exit Visual Studio now by clicking the **Close** button in the upper-right corner of the screen, or by clicking **FILE** on the menu bar and then clicking **Exit**. If you have made more changes since the last time you saved, you will be prompted to save again. When you choose **Yes**, the program closes.

Providing Functionality for a Button

In the next steps, you make the Button on the HelloVisualWorld Form functional; it will display a message when the user clicks it.

1. Start Visual Studio. Select **FILE** from the menu, click **Open**, and browse for the **HelloVisualWorld** project. Alternatively, select **FILE** from the menu, click **Recent Files and Projects**, and select the project from the pop-up list.

2. When the Form appears, drag a Label from the Toolbox to the Form. Change its Name to **helloLabel** and its Text property to **Hello, Visual World!**. If you want your Form to match Figure 3-20 exactly, change the Label's Location property to **90, 75**.

(continues)

(continued)

Figure 3-20   The helloLabel on the Form

3.   Scroll through the Properties list for the Label and change its Visible property from True to **False**. You can still see the Label in the Designer, but the Label will be invisible when you execute the program.

4.   Double-click the Button on the Form. A new window that contains program code is displayed, revealing a newly created displayOutputButton Click() method with no statements. Between the curly braces, type the following statement that causes the Label to appear when the user clicks the Button on the Form:

```
helloLabel.Visible = true;
```

5.   Save the file, then run the program by clicking **DEBUG** on the menu bar and clicking **Start Without Debugging**, or by pressing **Ctrl+F5**. When the Form appears, click the **Click here** button to reveal the greeting.

6.   If you want, experiment with values for some of the Label properties, such as Font, BackColor, and ForeColor.

(continues)

(continued)

Adding a Second Button *to a* Form

In the next steps, you add a second Button to the Form in the HelloVisualWorld project.

1. In the IDE, switch to Design View. Drag a second button onto the Form below the first Button. Change the new Button's Name property to changeOutputButton and change its Text to **Click me last**.

2. Double-click the changeOutputButton to expose the changeOutputButton_Click() method.

3. Between the curly braces of the method, add the following code:

   helloLabel.Text = "Goodbye";

4. Save the project, then execute the program. Click the displayOutputButton to reveal "Hello, Visual World!". Then click the changeOutputButton to reveal "Goodbye".

5. Execute the program again. This time, click the second Button first. No message appears because the Label with the message has not been made visible. When you click the displayOutputButton, the Label becomes visible, but it displays "Goodbye" because the changeOutputButton's Click() method has already changed the Label's Text.

6. Return to the Form1.cs [Design] tab. Click the changeOutputButton and change its Enabled property to **False**. Now, when the program executes, the user will not be immediately able to click the second Button.

7. Double-click the displayOutputButton. Add the following statement to the method so that the changeOutputButton becomes enabled when the displayOutputButton is clicked:

   changeOutputButton.Enabled = true;

8. Save the project, then execute the program. When the Form appears, the changeOutputButton is dimmed and not clickable because it is not enabled. Click the enabled displayOutputButton to reveal the "Hello, Visual World!" message and to enable the second Button. Then click the changeOutputButton to expose the "Goodbye" message.

9. Dismiss the Form and close Visual Studio.

Chapter Summary

- Forms are GUI objects that provide an interface for collecting, displaying, and delivering information. Forms almost always include controls such as labels, text boxes, and buttons that users can manipulate to interact with a program. Every Form and control on a Form has multiple properties you can set using the IDE.

- The Toolbox displays a list of available controls you can add to a Form. The list includes Button, CheckBox, and Label. From the Toolbox, you can drag controls onto a Form where they will be most useful. After you have dragged a Button onto a Form, you can double-click it to create the method that executes when a user clicks the Button, and you can write any statements you want between the curly braces of the Click() method.

- Labels are controls that you use to display text to communicate with an application's user. TextBoxes are controls through which a user can enter input data in a GUI application. Both have a Text property; frequently an application starts with the Text empty for TextBoxes. Because a user might type any value, the value in a TextBox is a string by default.

- Usually, you want to provide reasonable Name property values for all the controls you place on a Form. Although any identifier that starts with a letter is legal, by convention you should start control names with a lowercase letter and use camel casing as appropriate, start Form names with an uppercase letter and use camel casing as appropriate, and use the type of object in the name.

- If you build or run a program that contains a syntax error, you see *Build failed* in the lower-left corner of the IDE and an error dialog box. Errors are shown in the error list at the bottom of the screen. The error list also shows the file, line, position in the line, and project in which the error occurred. If you double-click the error message, the cursor is placed at the location in the code where the error was found. If you inadvertently create an event-handling method that you do not want, you should eliminate the event using the Properties window in the IDE. The ultimate authority on C# classes is the Visual Studio Help documentation.

- Both console and GUI applications can contain variables and constants, decisions, loops, arrays, and calls to other methods. GUI applications look "snazzier," and they contain controls that a user can manipulate with a mouse. However, GUI programs usually take longer to develop than their console counterparts. When writing your own programs, you will use the interface you prefer or one that your instructor or boss requires.

Key Terms

The **interface** is the environment a user sees when a program executes.

Forms are GUI objects that provide an interface for collecting, displaying, and delivering information.

Controls are devices such as labels, text boxes, and buttons that users can manipulate to communicate with a GUI program.

The **main menu** in the IDE lies horizontally across the top of the window, and includes submenus that list additional options.

The **Toolbox tab** in the IDE provides lists of controls that can be dragged onto a Form so that you can develop programs visually, using a mouse.

The **Form Designer** in the IDE is the area where you design applications visually.

The **Solution Explorer** in the IDE provides the means to view and manage project files and settings.

The **Properties window** in the IDE provides the means to configure properties and events on controls in your user interface.

The **Error list** in the IDE displays messages about compiler errors in your code.

A **node** is an icon that appears beside a list or a section of code and that can be expanded or condensed.

An **access specifier** is a keyword that dictates what outside classes can use a method.

An **event** causes a program to perform a task.

A **click event** is the event generated when a user clicks a control in a GUI program.

Labels are controls that you use to display text to communicate with an application's user.

TextBoxes are controls through which a user can enter input data in a GUI application.

Design time is the period of time during which a programmer designs the interface and writes the code.

Run time is the period of time during which a program executes.

Focus describes the attribute of a Form control that stands out visually from the others and that reacts to keyboard input.

Tab order describes the sequence of controls selected when the user presses the Tab key.

A **proportional font** is one in which different characters have different pitches or widths.

A **fixed-pitch font** is one in which each character occupies the same width.

A **monospaced font** is one in which each character occupies the same width.

Code refactoring is the process of changing a program's internal structure without changing the way the program works.

An **orphaned method** is one that never executes in an application, and thus serves no purpose.

Review Questions

1. Which of the following is a GUI object that provides an interface for collecting, displaying, and delivering information, and that contains other controls?

   a. Form

   b. Button

   c. TextBox

   d. Label

2. In the Visual Studio IDE main window, where does the main menu lie?

   a. vertically along the left border

   b. vertically along the right border

   c. horizontally across the top of the window

   d. horizontally across the bottom of the window

3. In the IDE, the area where you visually construct a Form is the _____.

   a. Toolbox

   b. Palette

   c. Easel

   d. Form Designer

4. When you create a new Windows Forms project, by default the first Form you see is named _____.

   a. Form

   b. Form1

   c. FormA

   d. FormAlpha

5. The Form class has _____ properties.

   a. three

   b. ten

   c. about 100

   d. about 1000

6. Which of the following is not a Form property?

   a. BackColor

   b. ProjectName

   c. Size

   d. Text

7. Which of the following is a legal Form Name property?

   a. Payroll Form

   b. PayrollForm

   c. either of the above

   d. none of the above

8. Which of the following is a legal Form Text property?

   a. Payroll Form

   b. PayrollForm

   c. either of the above

   d. none of the above

9. Which of the following does not appear in the IDE's Toolbox list?

   a. Text

   b. Button

   c. Label

   d. TextBox

10. After you have dragged a `Button` onto a `Form` in the IDE, you can double-click it to _____.

a. delete it

b. view its properties

c. create a method that executes when a user clicks the `Button`

d. execute a method when a user clicks the `Button`

11. The `button1_Click()` method that is generated by the IDE _____.

a. has a `private` access specifier

b. is nonstatic

c. contains parameters between its parentheses

d. all of the above

12. A(n) _____ is generated when a user interacts with a GUI object.

a. event   c. method

b. occasion   d. error

13. If you create a `Button` named `yesButton`, the name of the method that responds to clicks on it is _____.

a. `button1_Click()`   c. `click_YesButton()`

b. `yesButton_Method()`   d. `yesButton_Click()`

14. Statements allowed in a `Click()` method include _____.

a. variable declarations   c. both of the above

b. arithmetic statements   d. none of the above

15. _____ are controls through which a user can enter input data in a GUI application.

a. `Labels`   c. `Tickets`

b. `Tags`   d. `TextBoxes`

16. The value in a `TextBox` is _____.

a. an `int`   c. a `string`

b. a `double`   d. It might be any of the above.

17. Which of the following is a legal and conventional name for a `TextBox`?

a. `Salary TextBox`   c. both of the above

b. `salaryTextBox`   d. none of the above

18. The process of changing a program's internal structure without changing the way the program works is _____.

    a. compiling   c. code refactoring

    b. debugging   d. systems analysis

19. If you inadvertently create a `Click()` method for a control that should not generate a click event, you can successfully eliminate the method by _____.

    a. deleting the method code from the Form1.cs file

    b. eliminating the method from the Events list in the Properties window

    c. adding the method to the Discard window

    d. making the method a comment by placing two forward slashes at the start of each line

20. Of the following, the most significant difference between many console applications and GUI applications is _____.

    a. their appearance   c. their ability to perform calculations

    b. their ability to accept input   d. their ability to be created using C#

Exercises

Programming Exercises

1. Write a GUI program named **DistanceGUI** that allows the user to input a distance in miles and output the value in feet. There are 5280 feet in a mile.

The exercises in this section should look familiar to you. Each is similar to an exercise in Chapter 2, where you created solutions using console input and output.

2. Write a GUI program named **ProjectedSalesGUI** that allows a user to enter the current year's sales figures for the North and South divisions of a company. Compute and display, with explanatory text, next year's projected sales for each division, which reflect 10 percent increases.

3. Write a GUI program named **EggsInteractiveGUI** that allows a user to input the number of eggs produced in a month by each of five chickens. Sum the eggs, then display the total in dozens and eggs. For example, a total of 127 eggs is 10 dozen and 7 eggs. Figure 3-21 shows a typical execution.

Figure 3-21   An EggsInteractiveGUI application

4. Write a GUI program named **TestsInteractiveGUI** that allows a user to enter scores for five tests he has taken. Display the average of the test scores to two decimal places.

5. Write a GUI program named **PayrollGUI** that prompts the user for a name, Social Security number, hourly pay rate, and number of hours worked. In an attractive format, display all the input data as well as the following:

    ● Gross pay, defined as hourly pay rate times hours worked

    ● Federal withholding tax, defined as 15 percent of the gross pay

    ● State withholding tax, defined as 5 percent of the gross pay

    ● Net pay, defined as gross pay minus taxes

6. Write a GUI program named **OrderReceiptGUI** for the Magic Blender Company. The program prompts the user for a name, street address, city, state, zip code, and quantity of blenders ordered at $39.95 each. Display all the input data as well as the following:

    ● Amount due before tax, defined as number ordered times price each

    ● Sales tax, defined as 7 percent of the amount due

    ● Net due, defined as amount due before tax, plus tax

7. Create an enumeration named Month that holds values for the months of the year, starting with JANUARY equal to 1. (Recall that an enumeration must be placed within a class but outside of any method.) Write a GUI program named **MonthNamesGUI** that prompts the user for a month integer. Convert the user's entry to a Month value and display it.

8. Pig Latin is a nonsense language. To create a word in pig Latin, you remove the first letter and then add the first letter and "ay" at the end of the word. For example, "dog" becomes "ogday" and "cat" becomes "atcay". Write a GUI program named **PigLatinGUI** that allows the user to enter a word and displays the pig Latin version.

Debugging Exercises

1. Each of the following projects in the Chapter.03 folder of your downloadable student files has syntax and/or logical errors. In each case, immediately save a copy of the project folder with a new name that begins with *Fixed* before you open the project in Visual Studio. For example, the project folder for DebugThree1 will become FixedDebugThree1. All the files within the folders have already been named with the *Fixed* prefix, so you do not need to provide new filenames for any of the files in the top-level folder. After naming the new folder, open the project, determine the problems, and fix them.

   a. DebugThree1   c. DebugThree3
   b. DebugThree2   d. DebugThree4

Case Problems

1. In Chapter 2, you created a program for the Greenville Idol competition that prompts a user for the number of contestants entered in last year's competition and in this year's competition. The program displays the revenue expected for this year's competition if each contestant pays a $25 entrance fee. The application also displays a statement that indicates whether this year's competition has more contestants than last year's. Now, create an interactive GUI program named **GreenvilleRevenueGUI** that performs all the same tasks.

2. In Chapter 2, you created a program for Marshall's Murals that prompts a user for the number of interior and exterior murals scheduled to be painted during the next month. The program computes the expected revenue for each type of mural when interior murals cost $500 each and exterior murals cost $750 each. The application also displays the total expected revenue and a statement that indicates whether more interior murals are scheduled than exterior ones. Now, create an interactive GUI program named **MarshallsRevenueGUI** that performs all the same tasks.

Making Decisions

In this chapter you will:

- ◎ Understand logic-planning tools and decision making
- ◎ Learn how to make decisions using the `if` statement
- ◎ Learn how to make decisions using the `if-else` statement
- ◎ Use compound expressions in `if` statements
- ◎ Make decisions using the `switch` statement
- ◎ Use the conditional operator
- ◎ Use the NOT operator
- ◎ Learn to avoid common errors when making decisions
- ◎ Learn about decision-making issues in GUI programs

Computer programs are powerful because of their ability to make decisions. Programs that decide which travel route will offer the best weather conditions, which Web site will provide the closest match to search criteria, or which recommended medical treatment has the highest probability of success all rely on a program's decision making. In this chapter you will learn to make decisions in C# programs.

Understanding Logic-Planning Tools and Decision Making

When computer programmers write programs, they rarely just sit down at a keyboard and begin typing. Programmers must plan the complex portions of programs using paper and pencil. Programmers often use **pseudocode**, a tool that helps them plan a program's logic by writing plain English statements. Using pseudocode requires that you write down the steps needed to accomplish a given task. You write pseudocode in everyday language, not the syntax used in a programming language. In fact, a task you write in pseudocode does not have to be computer-related. If you have ever written a list of directions to your house—for example, (1) go west on Algonquin Road, (2) turn left on Roselle Road, (3) enter expressway heading east, and so on—you have written pseudocode. A **flowchart** is similar to pseudocode, but you write the steps in diagram form, as a series of shapes connected by arrows.

 You learned the difference between a program's logic and its syntax in Chapter 1.

Some programmers use a variety of shapes to represent different tasks in their flowcharts, but you can draw simple flowcharts that express very complex situations using just rectangles and diamonds. You use a rectangle to represent any processing step and a diamond to represent any decision. For example, Figure 4-1 shows a flowchart and pseudocode describing driving directions to a friend's house. Notice how the actions illustrated in the flowchart and the pseudocode statements correspond. Figure 4-1 illustrates a logical structure called a **sequence structure**—one step follows another unconditionally. A sequence structure might contain any number of steps, but one task follows another with no chance to branch away or skip a step.

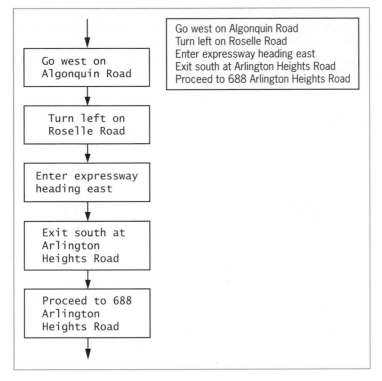

Go west on Algonquin Road
Turn left on Roselle Road
Enter expressway heading east
Exit south at Arlington Heights Road
Proceed to 688 Arlington Heights Road

Figure 4-1 Flowchart and pseudocode of a sequence structure

Sometimes, logical steps do not follow in an unconditional sequence—some tasks might or might not occur based on decisions you make. To represent a decision, flowchart creators use a diamond shape to hold a question, and they draw paths to alternative courses of action emerging from the sides of the diamonds. Figure 4-2 shows a flowchart describing directions in which the execution of some steps depends on decisions.

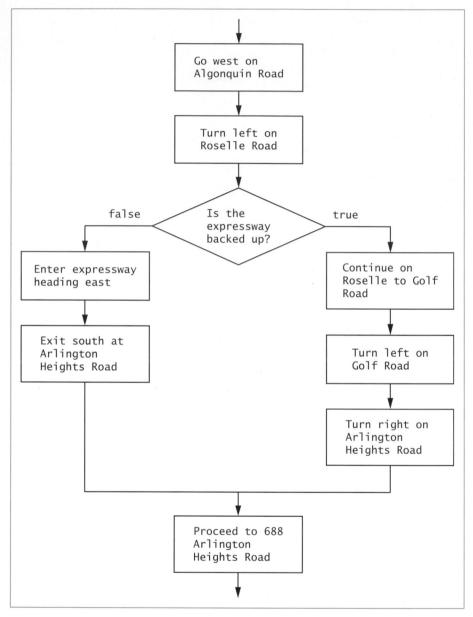

Figure 4-2   Flowchart including a decision structure

Figure 4-2 shows a **decision structure**—one that involves choosing between alternative courses of action based on some value within a program. When reduced to their most basic form, all computer decisions are true-or-false decisions. This is because computer circuitry consists of millions of tiny switches that are either "on" or "off," and the result of every decision sets one of these switches in memory. The values true and false are

Boolean values; every computer decision results in a Boolean value. For example, program code that you write never includes a question like "What number did the user enter?" Instead, the decisions might be: "Did the user enter a 1?" "If not, did the user enter a 2?" "If not, did the user enter a 3?"

TWO TRUTHS & A LIE

Understanding Logic-Planning Tools and Decision Making

1. A sequence structure has three or more alternative logical paths.

2. A decision structure involves choosing between alternative courses of action based on some value within a program.

3. When reduced to their most basic form, all computer decisions are yes-or-no decisions.

The false statement is #1. In a sequence structure, one step follows another unconditionally.

Making Decisions Using the `if` Statement

The `if` and `if-else` statements are the two most commonly used decision-making statements in C#. You use an **if statement** to make a single-alternative decision. In other words, you use an `if` statement to determine whether an action will occur. The `if` statement takes the following form:

```
if(testedExpression)
   statement;
```

where *testedExpression* represents any C# expression that can be evaluated as `true` or `false` and *statement* represents the action that will take place if the expression evaluates as `true`. You must place the `if` statement's evaluated expression between parentheses. You can leave a space between the keyword `if` and the opening parenthesis if you think that format is easier to read.

Usable expressions in an `if` statement include Boolean expressions such as `amount > 5` and `month == "May"` as well as the value of `bool` variables such as `isValidIDNumber`. If the expression evaluates as `true`, then the statement executes. Whether the expression evaluates as `true` or `false`, the program continues with the next statement following the complete `if` statement.

You learned about Boolean expressions and the **bool** data type in Chapter 2. Table 2-4 summarizes how comparison operators are used.

 In the chapter *Introduction to Methods*, you will learn to write methods that return values. A method call that returns a Boolean value also can be used as the tested expression in an **if** statement.

 In some programming languages, such as C++, nonzero numbers evaluate as **true** and 0 evaluates as **false**. However, in C#, only Boolean expressions evaluate as **true** and **false**.

For example, the code segment written and diagrammed in Figure 4-3 displays "A" and "B" when **number** holds a value less than 5. The expression **number < 5** evaluates as **true**, so the statement that displays "A" executes. Then the independent statement that displays "B" executes.

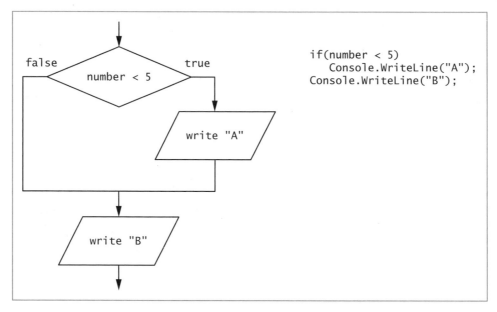

Figure 4-3   Flowchart and code including a typical **if** statement followed by a separate statement

When an evaluated expression is false, the rest of the statement does not execute. For example, when number is 5 or greater in Figure 4-3, only "B" is displayed. Because the expression number < 5 is false, the statement that displays "A" never executes.

In Figure 4-3, notice there is no semicolon at the end of the line that contains if(number < 5). The statement does not end at that point; it ends after Console.WriteLine("A");. If you incorrectly insert a semicolon at the end of if(number < 5), then the statement says, "If number is less than 5, do nothing; then, no matter what the value of number is, the next independent statement displays 'A'." Figure 4-4 shows the flowchart logic that matches the code when a semicolon is placed at the end of the if expression.

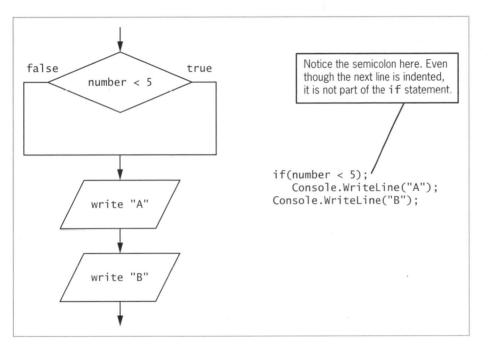

Figure 4-4   Flowchart and code including an if statement with a semicolon following the if expression

Although it is customary, and good style, to indent any statement that executes when an if Boolean expression evaluates as true, the C# compiler does not pay any attention to the indentation. Each of the following if statements displays "A" when number is less than 5. The first shows an if written on a single line; the second shows an if on two lines but with no indentation. The third uses conventional indentation.

```
if(number < 5) Console.WriteLine("A");
if(number < 5)
Console.WriteLine("A");
if(number < 5)
   Console.WriteLine("A");
```

Don't Do It
Although these first two formats work for if statements, they are not conventional and using them makes a program harder to understand.

When you want to execute two or more statements conditionally, you must place the statements within a block. A **block** is a collection of one or more statements contained within a pair of curly braces. For example, the code segment written and diagrammed in Figure 4-5 displays both "C" and "D" when number is less than 5, and it displays neither when number is not less than 5. The if expression that precedes the block is the **control statement** for the decision structure.

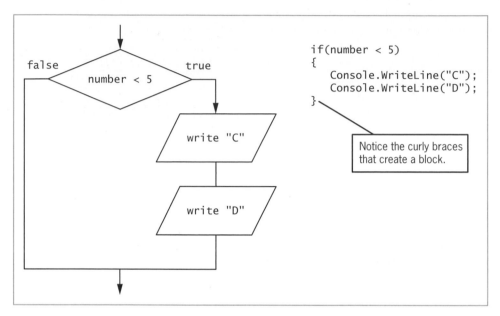

Figure 4-5   Flowchart and code including a typical if statement containing a block

Indenting alone does not cause multiple statements to depend on the evaluation of a Boolean expression in an if. For multiple statements to depend on an if, they must be blocked with braces. For example, Figure 4-6 shows two statements that are indented below an if expression. When you glance at the code, it might first appear that both statements depend on the if; however, only the first one does, as shown in the flowchart, because the statements are not blocked.

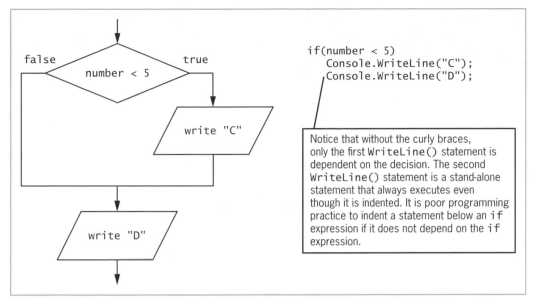

```
if(number < 5)
    Console.WriteLine("C");
    Console.WriteLine("D");
```

Notice that without the curly braces, only the first WriteLine() statement is dependent on the decision. The second WriteLine() statement is a stand-alone statement that always executes even though it is indented. It is poor programming practice to indent a statement below an if expression if it does not depend on the if expression.

Figure 4-6 Flowchart and code including an if statement that is missing curly braces or that has inappropriate indenting

When you create a block using curly braces, you do not have to place multiple statements within it. It is perfectly legal to block a single statement. Blocking a single statement can be a useful technique to help prevent future errors. When you write if statements that use curly braces even when they aren't required—and then a program later is modified to include multiple statements that depend on the if—you will naturally place the additional statements within the block that is already in place. Creating a block with braces that contain no statements also is legal in C#. You usually do so only when starting to write a program, as a reminder to yourself to add statements later.

 In C#, it is customary to align a block's opening and closing braces. Some programmers prefer to place the opening brace on the same line as the if expression instead of giving the brace its own line. This style is called the **K & R style**, named for Brian Kernighan and Dennis Ritchie, who wrote the first book on the C programming language.

You can place any number of statements within a block contained by curly braces, including other if statements. Of course, if a second if statement is the only statement that depends on the first if, then no braces are required. Figure 4-7 shows the logic for a **nested if** statement in which one decision structure is contained within another. With a nested if statement, a second if's Boolean expression is tested only when the first if's Boolean expression evaluates as true.

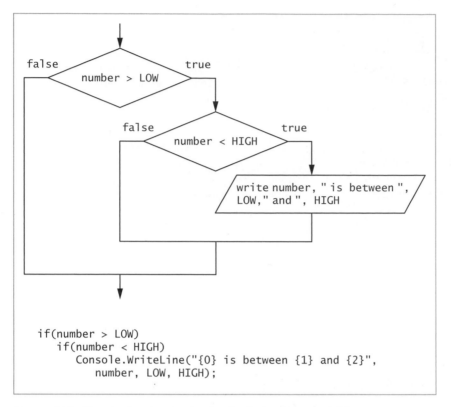

```
if(number > LOW)
   if(number < HIGH)
      Console.WriteLine("{0} is between {1} and {2}",
         number, LOW, HIGH);
```

Figure 4-7 Flowchart and code showing the logic of a nested `if`

Figure 4-8 shows a program that contains the logic in Figure 4-7. When a user enters a number greater than 5, the first tested expression is `true` and the `if` statement that tests whether the number is less than 10 executes. When the second tested expression also is `true`, the `Console.WriteLine()` statement executes. However, if the second tested expression is `false`, no output occurs. When the user enters a number less than or equal to 5, the first tested expression is `false` and the second Boolean expression is never tested, and again no output occurs. Figure 4-9 shows the output after the program is executed three times using three different input values. Notice that when the value input by the user is not between 5 and 10, no output message appears; the message is displayed only when both tested expressions are `true`.

```
using System;
class NestedDecision
{
   static void Main()
   {
      const int HIGH = 10, LOW = 5;
      string numberString;
      int number;
      Console.Write("Enter an integer ");
      numberString = Console.ReadLine();
      number = Convert.ToInt32(numberString);
       if(number > LOW)
          if(number < HIGH)
            Console.WriteLine("{0} is between {1} and {2}",
               number, LOW, HIGH);
   }
}
```

Figure 4-8   Program using nested if

Figure 4-9   Output of three executions of the NestedDecision program

A Note on Equivalency Comparisons

Often, programmers mistakenly use a single equal sign rather than the double equal sign when attempting to determine equivalency. For example, the following expression does not compare number to HIGH:

number = HIGH

Instead, it attempts to assign the value HIGH to the variable number. When it is used between the parentheses in an if statement, as in if(number = HIGH), this assignment is illegal, and the program will not compile.

The only condition under which the assignment operator would work as part of the tested expression in an `if` statement is when the assignment is made to a `bool` variable. For example, suppose that a payroll program contains a `bool` variable named doesEmployeeHaveDependents, and then uses the following statement:

```
if(doesEmployeeHaveDependents = numDependents > 0)…
```

In this case, numDependents would be compared to 0, and the result, `true` or `false`, would be assigned to doesEmployeeHaveDependents. Then the decision would be made based on the assigned value. This is not a recommended way to make a comparison because it looks confusing. If your intention was to assign a value to doesEmployeeHaveDependents and to make a decision based on the value, then your intentions would be clearer with the following code:

```
doesEmployeeHaveDependents = numDependents > 0;
if(doesEmployeeHaveDependents)…
```

Notice the difference in the following statement that uses two equal signs within the parentheses in the `if` statement:

```
if(doesEmployeeHaveDependents == numDependents > 0)…
```

This statement compares doesEmployeeHaveDependents to the result of comparing numDependents to 0, but does not change the value of doesEmployeeHaveDependents.

One of the many advantages of using the Visual Studio IDE to write programs is that if you use an assignment operator in place of an equivalency operator in a Boolean expression, your mistake will be flagged as an error immediately.

TWO TRUTHS & A LIE

Making Decisions Using the `if` Statement

1. In C#, you must place an `if` statement's evaluated expression between parentheses.

2. In C#, for multiple statements to depend on an `if`, they must be indented.

3. In C#, you can place one `if` statement within a block that depends on another `if` statement.

The false statement is #2. Indenting alone does not cause multiple statements to depend on the evaluation of a Boolean expression in an `if`. For multiple statements to depend on an `if`, they must be blocked with braces.

Making Decisions Using the `if-else` Statement

Some decisions you make are **dual-alternative decisions**; they have two possible resulting actions. If you want to perform one action when a Boolean expression evaluates as `true` and an alternate action when it evaluates as `false`, you can use an **if-else statement**. The `if-else` statement takes the following form:

```
if(expression)
    statement1;
else
    statement2;
```

You can code an `if` without an `else`, but it is illegal to code an `else` without an `if`.

Just as you can block several statements so they all execute when an expression within an `if` is `true`, you can block multiple statements after an `else` so that they will all execute when the evaluated expression is `false`.

For example, Figure 4-10 shows the logic for an `if-else` statement, and Figure 4-11 shows a program that contains the statement. With every execution of the program, one or the other of the two `WriteLine()` statements executes. The indentation shown in the `if-else` example in Figure 4-11 is not required, but it is standard. You vertically align the keyword `if` with the keyword `else`, and then indent the action statements that depend on the evaluation. Figure 4-12 shows two executions of the program.

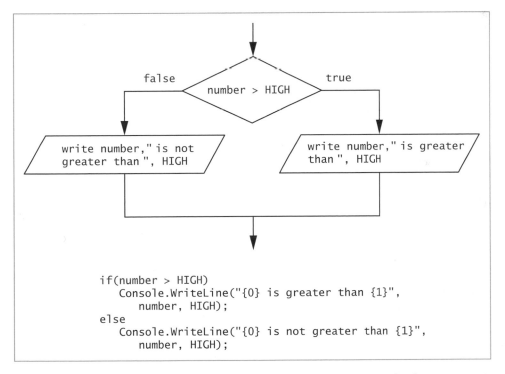

```
if(number > HIGH)
    Console.WriteLine("{0} is greater than {1}",
        number, HIGH);
else
    Console.WriteLine("{0} is not greater than {1}",
        number, HIGH);
```

Figure 4-10   Flowchart and code showing the logic of a dual-alternative `if-else` statement

156

```
using System;
class IfElseDecision
{
    static void Main()
    {
        const int HIGH = 10;
        string numberString;
        int number;
        Console.Write("Enter an integer ");
        numberString = Console.ReadLine();
        number = Convert.ToInt32(numberString);
        if(number > HIGH)
            Console.WriteLine("{0} is greater than {1}",
                number, HIGH);
        else
            Console.WriteLine("{0} is not greater than {1}",
                number, HIGH);
    }
}
```

Figure 4-11　Program with a dual-alternative if-else statement

Figure 4-12　Output of two executions of the IfElseDecision program

When if-else statements are nested, each else always is paired with the most recent unpaired if. For example, in the following code, the else is paired with the second if.

```
if(saleAmount > 1000)
    if(saleAmount < 2000)
        bonus = 100;
    else
        bonus = 500;
```

In this example, the following bonuses are assigned:

- If `saleAmount` is between $1000 and $2000, `bonus` is $100 because both evaluated expressions are `true`.

- If `saleAmount` is $2000 or more, `bonus` is $500 because the first evaluated expression is `true` and the second one is `false`.

157

- If `saleAmount` is $1000 or less, `bonus` is unassigned because the first evaluated expression is `false` and there is no corresponding `else`.

TWO TRUTHS & A LIE

Making Decisions Using the `if-else` Statement

1. Dual-alternative decisions have two possible outcomes.

2. In an `if-else` statement, a semicolon is always the last character typed before the `else`.

3. When `if-else` statements are nested, the first `if` always is paired with the first `else`.

The false statement is #3. When `if-else` statements are nested, each `else` always is paired with the most recent unpaired `if`.

 You Do It

Using `if-else` Statements

In the next steps, you write a program that requires using multiple, nested `if-else` statements to accomplish its goal—determining whether any of the three integers entered by a user are equal.

1. Open a new file or project named **CompareThreeNumbers**, and write the first lines necessary for the class:

```
using System;
class CompareThreeNumbers
{
```

(continues)

(continued)

2. Begin a `Main()` method by declaring a string for input and three integers that will hold the input values.

```
static void Main()
{
    string numberString;
    int num1, num2, num3;
```

3. Add the statements that retrieve the three integers from the user and assign them to the appropriate variables.

```
Console.Write("Enter an integer ");
numberString = Console.ReadLine();
num1 = Convert.ToInt32(numberString);
Console.Write("Enter an integer ");
numberString = Console.ReadLine();
num2 = Convert.ToInt32(numberString);
Console.Write("Enter an integer ");
numberString = Console.ReadLine();
num3 = Convert.ToInt32(numberString);
```

In the chapter *Introduction to Methods*, you will learn to write methods, avoiding repetitive code like that shown here.

4. If the first number and the second number are equal, there are two possibilities: either the first is also equal to the third, in which case all three numbers are equal, or the first is not equal to the third, in which case only the first two numbers are equal. Insert the following code:

```
if(num1 == num2)
    if(num1 == num3)
        Console.WriteLine("All three numbers are equal");
    else
        Console.WriteLine("First two are equal");
```

5. If the first two numbers are not equal, but the first and third are equal, display an appropriate message. For clarity, the `else` should vertically align under `if(num1 == num2)`.

```
else
    if(num1 == num3)
        Console.WriteLine("First and last are equal");
```

6. When `num1` and `num2` are not equal, and `num1` and `num3` are not equal, but `num2` and `num3` are equal, display an appropriate message. For clarity, the `else` should vertically align under `if(num1 == num3)`.

(continues)

(continued)

```
else
   if(num2 == num3)
      Console.WriteLine("Last two are equal");
```

7. Finally, if none of the pairs (num1 and num2, num1 and num3, or num2 and num3) is equal, display an appropriate message. For clarity, the `else` should vertically align under `if(num2 == num3)`.

```
else
   Console.WriteLine
      ("No two numbers are equal");
```

8. Add a closing curly brace for the `Main()` method and a closing curly brace for the class.

9. Save and compile the program, and then execute it several times, providing different combinations of equal and nonequal integers when prompted. Figure 4-13 shows several executions of the program.

Figure 4-13 Several executions of the `CompareThreeNumbers` program

Using Compound Expressions in if Statements

In many programming situations, you need to make multiple decisions before taking action. For example, suppose that a specific college scholarship is available under the following conditions:

- If your high school class rank is higher than 75 percent

- And if your grade-point average is higher than 3.0

- And if you are an in-state resident

- Or if you are a resident of a cooperating state

- Or if you have participated in at least five extracurricular activities and held a part-time job

No matter how many decisions must be made, you can decide on the scholarship eligibility for any student by using a series of if statements to test the appropriate variables. For convenience and clarity, however, you can combine multiple decisions into a single if statement using a combination of conditional AND and OR operators to create compound Boolean expressions.

Using the Conditional AND Operator

As an alternative to nested if statements, you can use the **conditional AND operator** (or simply the **AND operator**) to create a compound Boolean expression. The conditional AND operator is written as two ampersands (&&).

A tool that can help you understand the && operator is a truth table. **Truth tables** are diagrams used in mathematics and logic to help describe the truth of an entire expression based on the truth of its parts. Table 4-1 shows a truth table that lists all the possibilities with compound Boolean expressions. For any two expressions x and y, the expression x && y is true only if both x and y are individually true. If either x or y alone is false, or if both are false, then the expression x && y is false.

x	y	x && y
True	True	True
True	False	False
False	True	False
False	False	False

Table 4-1   Truth table for the conditional && operator

For example, the two code samples shown in Figure 4-14 work exactly the same way. The age variable is tested, and if it is greater than or equal to 0 and less than 120, a message is displayed to explain that the value is valid.

```
// using the && operator
  if(age >= 0 && age < 120)
    Console.WriteLine("Age is valid");

// using nested ifs
  if(age >= 0)
     if(age < 120)
       Console.WriteLine("Age is valid");
```

Figure 4-14 Comparison of the && operator and nested if statements

Using the && operator is never required, because nested if statements achieve the same result, but using the && operator often makes your code more concise, less error-prone, and easier to understand.

It is important to note that when you use the && operator, you must include a complete Boolean expression on each side of the operator. If you want to set a bonus to $400 when saleAmount is both over $1000 and under $5000, the correct statement is as follows:

```
if(saleAmount > 1000 && saleAmount < 5000)
   bonus = 400;
```

The following statement is incorrect and will not compile:

```
if(saleAmount > 1000 && < 5000)
   bonus = 400;
```

Don't Do It
5000 is not a Boolean expression (it is a numeric constant), so this statement is invalid.

For clarity, many programmers prefer to surround each Boolean expression that is part of a compound Boolean expression with its own set of parentheses. For example:

```
if((saleAmount > 1000) && (saleAmount < 5000))
   bonus = 400;
```

Notice that the if clause has its own set of parentheses, and that nested within the set each Boolean expression has a set of parentheses. Use this format if it is clearer to you.

The expressions in each part of a compound, conditional Boolean expression are evaluated only as much as necessary to determine whether the entire expression is true or false. This feature is called **short-circuit evaluation**. With the && operator, both Boolean expressions must be true before the action in the statement can occur. If the first expression is false, the second expression is never evaluated, because its value does not matter. For example, if a is not greater than LIMIT in the following if statement, then the evaluation is complete because there is no need to evaluate whether b is greater than LIMIT.

```
if(a > LIMIT && b > LIMIT)
   Console.WriteLine("Both are greater than LIMIT");
```

Using the Conditional OR Operator

You can use the **conditional OR operator** (or simply the **OR operator**) when you want some action to occur even if only one of two conditions is true. The OR operator is written as ||. When you use the || operator, only one of the listed conditions must be met for the resulting action to take place. Table 4-2 shows the truth table for the || operator. As you can see, the entire expression x || y is false *only* when x and y each are false individually.

x	y	x || y
True	True	True
True	False	True
False	True	True
False	False	False

Table 4-2 Truth table for the || operator

For example, if you want to display a message indicating an invalid age when the variable is less than 0 or is 120 or greater, you can use either code sample in Figure 4-15.

 You create the conditional OR operator by using two vertical pipes. On most keyboards, the pipe is found above the backslash key; typing it requires that you also hold down the Shift key.

```
// using the || operator
  if(age < 0 || age >= 120)
     Console.WriteLine("Age is not valid");

// using nested ifs
  if(age < 0)
     Console.WriteLine("Age is not valid");
  else
     if(age >= 120)
        Console.WriteLine("Age is not valid");
```

Figure 4-15 Comparison of the || operator and nested if statements

When the || operator is used in an if statement, only one of the two Boolean expressions in the tested expression needs to be true for the resulting action to occur. As with the && operator, this feature is called short-circuit evaluation. When you use the || operator and the first Boolean expression is true, the second expression is never evaluated because it doesn't matter whether the second expression is true or false.

Watch the video *Using the AND and OR Operators*.

Using the Logical AND and OR Operators

C# provides two logical operators that you generally do *not* want to use when making comparisons. However, you should learn about them because they might be used in programs written by others, and because you might use one by mistake when you intend to use a conditional operator.

The **Boolean logical AND operator** (&) and **Boolean logical inclusive OR operator** (|) work just like their && and || (*conditional* AND and OR) counterparts, except they do not support short-circuit evaluation. That is, they always evaluate both sides of the expression, no matter what the first evaluation is. This can lead to a **side effect**, or unintended consequence. For example, in the following statement that uses &&, if salesAmountForYear is not at least 10,000, the first half of the expression is false, so the second half of the Boolean expression is never evaluated and yearsOfService is not increased.

```
if(salesAmountForYear >= 10000 && ++yearsOfService > 10)
   bonus = 200;
```

On the other hand, when a single & is used and salesAmountForYear is not at least 10,000, then even though the first half of the expression is false, the second half is still evaluated, and yearsOfService is increased:

```
if(salesAmountForYear >= 10000 & ++yearsOfService > 10)
   bonus = 200;
```

Because the first half of the expression is false, the entire evaluation is false, and bonus is not set to 200. However, a side effect occurs with the & operator that does not occur when the && operator is used: yearsOfService is incremented.

In general, you should avoid writing expressions that contain side effects. If you want yearsOfService to increase no matter what the value of salesAmountForYear is, then you should increase it in a stand-alone statement before the decision is made. If you want it increased only when the sales amount exceeds 10,000, then you should increase it in a statement that depends on that decision.

The & and | operators are Boolean logical operators when they are placed between Boolean expressions. When the same operators are used between integer expressions, they are **bitwise operators** that are used to manipulate the individual bits of values.

Combining AND and OR Operators

You can combine as many AND and OR operators in an expression as you need. For example, when three conditions must be true before performing an action, you can use an expression such as if(a && b && c). When you combine && and || operators within the same Boolean expression, the && operators take precedence, meaning their Boolean values are evaluated first.

For example, consider a program that determines whether a movie theater patron can purchase a discounted ticket. Assume that discounts are allowed for children (age 12 and younger) and for senior citizens (age 65 and older) who attend G-rated movies. (To keep the comparisons simple, this example assumes that movie ratings are always a single character.) The following code looks reasonable, but it produces incorrect results because the && evaluates before the ||.

```
if(age <= 12 || age >= 65 && rating == 'G')
  Console.WriteLine("Discount applies");
```

For example, suppose that a movie patron is 10 years old and the movie rating is 'R'. The patron should not receive a discount (or be allowed to see the movie!). However, within the if statement above, the compound expression age >= 65 && rating == 'G' evaluates first. It is false, so the if becomes the equivalent of if(age <= 12 || false). Because age <= 12 is true, the if becomes the equivalent of if(true || false), which evaluates as true, and the statement "Discount applies" is displayed, which is not accurate.

You can use parentheses to correct the logic and force the expression age <= 12 || age >= 65 to evaluate first, as shown in the following code.

```
if((age <= 12 || age >= 65) && rating == 'G')
  Console.WriteLine("Discount applies");
```

With the added parentheses, the age comparisons are made first and the expression is evaluated as if(true && rating == 'G'). When the age value qualifies a patron for a discount, then the rating value must also be acceptable. Figure 4-16 shows the if statement within a complete program; note that the discount age limits now are represented as named constants. Figure 4-17 shows the execution before the parentheses were added to the if statement, and Figure 4-18 shows the output after the inclusion of the parentheses.

```
using System;
class MovieDiscount
{
    static void Main()
    {
        int age = 10;
        char rating = 'R';
        const int CHILD_AGE = 12;
        const int SENIOR_AGE = 65;
        Console.WriteLine("When age is {0} and rating is {1}",
            age, rating);
        if((age <= CHILD_AGE || age >= SENIOR_AGE) && rating == 'G')
            Console.WriteLine("Discount applies");
        else
            Console.WriteLine("Full price");
    }
}
```

Figure 4-16   Movie ticket discount program using parentheses to alter precedence of Boolean evaluations

Figure 4-17 Incorrect results when `MovieDiscount` program is executed without added parentheses

Figure 4-18 Correct results when parentheses are added to `MovieDiscount` program

You can use parentheses for clarity in a Boolean expression even when they are not required. For example, the following expressions both evaluate `a && b` first:

```
a && b || c
(a && b) || c
```

If the version with parentheses makes your intentions clearer, you should use it.

In Chapter 2, you controlled arithmetic operator precedence by using parentheses. Appendix A describes the precedence of every C# operator. For example, in Appendix A you can see that the arithmetic and relational operators have higher precedence than `&&` and `||`.

 Watch the video *Combining AND and OR Operations.*

166

TWO TRUTHS & A LIE

Using Compound Expressions in if Statements

1. If a is true and b and c are false, then the value of b && c || a is true.

2. If d is true and e and f are false, then the value of e || d && f is true.

3. If g is true and h and i are false, then the value of g || h && i is true.

The false statement is #2. If d is true and e and f are false, then the value of e || d && f is false. Because you evaluate && before ||, first d && f is evaluated and found to be false, then e || false is evaluated and found to be false.

 You Do It

Using AND and OR Logic

In the next steps, you create an interactive program that allows you to test AND and OR logic for yourself. The program decides whether a delivery charge applies to a shipment. If the customer lives in Zone 1 or Zone 2, then shipping is free, as long as the order contains fewer than 10 boxes. If the customer lives in another zone or if the order is too large, then a delivery charge applies.

1. Open a new file in your text editor or start a new project in the Visual Studio IDE. Name the file or project **DemoORAndAND**, and then enter the first few lines of the program. Define constants for ZONE1, ZONE2, and the LOWQUANTITY limit as well as variables to hold the customer's input string, which will be converted to the zone and number of boxes in the shipment.

```
using System;
class DemoORAndAND
{
    static void Main()
    {
        const int ZONE1 = 1, ZONE2 = 2;
        const int LOWQUANTITY = 10;
        string inputString;
        int quantity;
        int deliveryZone;
```

(continues)

(continued)

2. Enter statements that describe the delivery charge criteria to the user and accept keyboard values for the customer's delivery zone and shipment size.

```
Console.WriteLine("Delivery is free for zone {0} or {1}",
   ZONE1, ZONE2);
Console.WriteLine("when the number of boxes is less than {0}",
   LOWQUANTITY);
Console.WriteLine("Enter delivery zone ");
inputString = Console.ReadLine();
deliveryZone = Convert.ToInt32(inputString);
Console.WriteLine
   ("Enter the number of boxes in the shipment");
inputString = Console.ReadLine();
quantity = Convert.ToInt32(inputString);
```

3. Write a compound if statement that tests whether the customer lives in Zone 1 or 2 and has a shipment consisting of fewer than 10 boxes. Notice that the first two comparisons joined with the || operator are contained in their own set of nested parentheses.

```
if((deliveryZone == ZONE1 || deliveryZone == ZONE2) &&
   quantity < LOWQUANTITY)
      Console.WriteLine("Delivery is free");
else
   Console.WriteLine("A delivery charge applies");
```

4. Add closing curly braces for the Main() method and for the class, and save the program. Compile and execute the program. Enter values for the zone and shipment size. Figure 4-19 shows the output.

Figure 4-19 Sample execution of DemoORAndAND program

(continues)

(continued)

5. To demonstrate the importance of the nested parentheses in the `if` statement, remove the inner set of parentheses that surround the expression `deliveryZone == ZONE1 || deliveryZone == ZONE2` in the `Main()` method. Save the new version of the program, and compile it. When you execute this version of the program, the output indicates that any delivery to ZONE1 is free, but it should not be. The way the `if` statement is currently constructed, as soon as `deliveryZone == ZONE1` is `true`, the rest of the Boolean expression is not even evaluated. Reinstate the parentheses, and then save and compile the program. Execute it, and confirm that the output is again correct.

Making Decisions Using the `switch` Statement

By nesting a series of `if` and `else` statements, you can choose from any number of alternatives. For example, suppose that you want to display different strings based on a student's class year. Figure 4-20 shows the logic using nested `if` statements. The program segment tests the `year` variable four times and executes one of four statements, or displays an error message.

```
if(year == 1)
   Console.WriteLine("Freshman");
else
   if(year == 2)
      Console.WriteLine("Sophomore");
   else
      if(year == 3)
         Console.WriteLine("Junior");
      else
         if(year == 4)
            Console.WriteLine("Senior");
         else
            Console.WriteLine("Invalid year");
```

Figure 4-20   Executing multiple alternatives using a series of `if` statements

An alternative to the series of nested `if` statements in Figure 4-20 is to use the `switch` structure (see Figure 4-21). The **switch structure** tests a single variable against a series of exact matches. The `switch` structure in Figure 4-21 is easier to read and interpret than the series of nested `if` statements in Figure 4-20. The `if` statements would become harder to read if additional choices were required and if multiple statements had to execute in each case. These additional choices and statements might also increase the potential to make mistakes.

```
switch(year)
{
   case 1:
       Console.WriteLine("Freshman");
       break;
   case 2:
       Console.WriteLine("Sophomore");
       break;
   case 3:
       Console.WriteLine("Junior");
       break;
   case 4:
       Console.WriteLine("Senior");
       break;
   default:
       Console.WriteLine("Invalid year");
       break;
}
```

Figure 4-21   Executing multiple alternatives using a `switch` statement

The `switch` structure uses four new keywords:

- The keyword **switch** starts the structure and is followed immediately by a test expression (called the **switch expression**) enclosed in parentheses.

- The keyword **case** is followed by one of the possible values that might equal the `switch` expression. A colon follows the value. The entire expression—for example, `case 1:`—is a case label. A **case label** identifies a course of action in a `switch` structure. Most `switch` structures contain several `case` labels. The value that follows `case` is the **governing type** of the `switch` statement; this value can be `sbyte`, `byte`, `short`, `ushort`, `int`, `uint`, `long`, `ulong`, `char`, `string`, or an `enum` type. You learned about `enum` types in Chapter 2.

- The keyword **break** usually terminates a `switch` structure at the end of each `case`. Although other statements can end a `case`, `break` is the most commonly used.

- The keyword **default** optionally is used prior to any action that should occur if the test expression does not match any `case`.

Instead of `break`, you can use a `return` statement or a `throw` statement to end a `case`. You learn about `return` statements in the chapter *Introduction to Methods* and `throw` statements in the chapter *Exception Handling*.

The switch structure shown in Figure 4-21 begins by evaluating the year variable. If year is equal to the first case label value, which is 1, then the statement that displays "Freshman" executes. The break statement causes a bypass of the rest of the switch structure, and execution continues with any statement after the closing curly brace of the switch structure.

If the year variable is not equivalent to the first case label value of 1, then the next case label value is compared, and so on. If year does not contain the same value as any of the case label expressions, then the default statement or statements execute.

You are not required to list the case label values in ascending order, as shown in Figure 4-21, but doing so can make the statement easier for a reader to follow. However, it is more efficient to list the most common case first, reducing the number of decisions that must be made. You can even list the default case first, especially if it is the most common case, although usually it is listed last. You receive a compiler error if two or more case label values are the same in a switch statement.

In C#, an error occurs if you reach the end point of the statement list of a case section. For example, the following code is not allowed because when the year value is 1, "Freshman" is displayed, and the code reaches the end of the case.

```
switch(year)
{
    case 1:
        Console.WriteLine("Freshman");
    case 2:
        Console.WriteLine("Sophomore");
        break;
}
```

Don't Do It
This code is invalid because the end of the case is reached after "Freshman" is displayed.

Not allowing code to reach the end of a case is known as the "no fall through rule." In several other programming languages, such as Java and C++, if you write the corresponding case statement, both "Freshman" and "Sophomore" are displayed when year equals 1. In those languages, the logic falls through until the break statement. However, falling through to the next case is not allowed in C#.

A switch structure does not need to contain a default case. If the test expression in a switch does not match any of the case label values, and there is no default value, then the program simply continues with the next executable statement. However, it is good programming practice to include a default label in a switch structure; that way, you provide for actions when your data does not match any case. The default label does not have to appear last, although often it does.

You can use multiple labels to govern a list of statements. For example, in the code in Figure 4-22, "Upperclass" is displayed whether the year value is 3 or 4.

```
switch(year)
{
    case 1:
        Console.WriteLine("Freshman");
        break;
    case 2:
        Console.WriteLine("Sophomore");
        break;
    case 3:
    case 4:
        Console.WriteLine("Upperclass");
        break;
    default:
        Console.WriteLine("Invalid year");
        break;
}
```

Cases 3 and 4 are both "Upperclass".

Figure 4-22 Example `switch` structure using multiple labels to execute a single statement block

Using a `switch` structure is never required; you can always achieve the same results with nested `if` statements. The `switch` statement is not as flexible as the `if` statement because you can test only one variable, and it must be tested for equality. The `switch` structure is simply a convenience you can use when there are several alternative courses of action depending on a match with a variable. Additionally, it makes sense to use a `switch` only when there are a reasonable number of specific matching values to be tested. For example, if every sale amount from $1 to $500 requires a 5 percent commission, it is not reasonable to test every possible dollar amount using the following code:

```
switch(saleAmount)
{
    case 1:
    case 2:
    case 3:
    // ...and so on for several hundred more cases
        commRate = .05;
        break;
```

With 500 different dollar values resulting in the same commission, one test— `if(saleAmount <= 500)`—is far more reasonable than listing 500 separate cases.

Using an Enumeration with a `switch` Statement

Using an enumeration with a `switch` structure can often be convenient. Recall from Chapter 2 that an enumeration allows you to apply values to a list of constants. For example, Figure 4-23 shows a program that uses an enumeration to represent major courses of study at a college. In the enumeration list in Figure 4-23, `ACCOUNTING` is assigned 1, so the other values in the list are 2, 3, 4, and 5 in order. Suppose that students who are Accounting, CIS, or

Marketing majors are in the Business Division of the college, and English or Math majors are in the Humanities Division. The program shows how the enumeration values can be used in a `switch` structure. In the program, the user enters an integer. Next, in the shaded `switch` control statement, the input integer is cast to an enumeration value. Then, enumeration values become the governing types for each case. For someone reading the code, the purposes of `enum` values such as `ACCOUNTING` and `CIS` are clearer than their integer equivalents would be. Figure 4-24 shows a typical execution of the program.

```csharp
using System;
class DivisionBasedOnMajor
{
    enum Major
    {
        ACCOUNTING = 1, CIS, ENGLISH, MATH, MARKETING
    }
    static void Main()
    {
        int major;
        String message;
        Console.Write("Enter major code >> ");
        major = Convert.ToInt32(Console.ReadLine());
        switch((Major) major)
        {
            case Major.ACCOUNTING:
            case Major.CIS:
            case Major.MARKETING:
                message = "Major is in the Business Division";
                break;
            case Major.ENGLISH:
            case Major.MATH:
                message = "Major is in the Humanities Division";
                break;
            default:
                message = "Department number is invalid";
                break;
        }
        Console.WriteLine(message);
    }
}
```

Figure 4-23 The `DivisionBasedOnMajor` class

Figure 4-24 Typical execution of the `DivisionBasedOnMajor` program

TWO TRUTHS & A LIE

Making Decisions Using the `switch` Statement

1. In a `switch` statement, the keyword `case` is followed by one of the possible values that might equal the `switch` expression, and a colon follows the value.

2. The keyword `break` always terminates a `switch` structure at the end of each `case`.

3. A `switch` statement does not need to contain a `default` case.

The false statement is #2. The keyword `break` typically is used to terminate a `switch` structure at the end of each case, but other statements can end a case.

Using the Conditional Operator

The **conditional operator** is used as an abbreviated version of the `if-else` statement; it requires three expressions separated with a question mark and a colon. Like the `switch` structure, using the conditional operator is never required. Rather, it is simply a convenient shortcut, especially when you want to use the result immediately as an expression. The syntax of the conditional operator is:

```
testExpression ? trueResult : falseResult;
```

Unary operators use one operand; binary operators use two. The conditional operator `?:` is **ternary** because it requires three arguments: a test expression and `true` and `false` result expressions. The conditional operator is the only ternary operator in C#.

The first expression, testExpression, is evaluated as true or false. If it is true, then the entire conditional expression takes on the value of the expression following the question mark (trueResult). If the value of the testExpression is false, then the entire expression takes on the value of falseResult. For example, consider the following statement:

```
biggerNum = (a > b) ? a : b;
```

This statement evaluates a > b. If a is greater than b, then the entire conditional expression takes the value of a, which then is assigned to biggerNum. If a is not greater than b, then the expression assumes the value of b, and b is assigned to biggerNum.

The conditional operator is most often applied when you want to use the result as an expression without creating an intermediate variable. For example, a conditional operator can be used directly in an output statement such as the following:

```
Console.WriteLine((testScore >= 60) ? "Pass" : "Fail");
```

In this example, the value of the expression within the WriteLine() method parentheses is a string ("Pass" or "Fail"), which is then output.

Conditional expressions are frequently more difficult to read than if-else statements, but they can be used in places where if-else statements cannot, such as in method calls.

TWO TRUTHS & A LIE

Using the Conditional Operator

1. If j = 2 and k = 3, then the value of the following expression is 2:

   ```
   int m = j < k ? j : k;
   ```

2. If j = 2 and k = 3, then the value of the following expression is "yes":

   ```
   string ans = j < k ? "yes" : "no";
   ```

3. If j = 2 and k = 3, then the value of the following expression is 5:

   ```
   int n = j > k ? j + k : j * k;
   ```

The false statement is #3. If j = 2 and k = 3, then the value of the expression int n = j > k ? j + k : j * k; is 6 because j is not greater than k and the false result is j * k, which is 2 * 3.

Using the NOT Operator

You use the **NOT operator**, which is written as an exclamation point (!), to negate the result of any Boolean expression. Any expression that evaluates as `true` becomes `false` when preceded by the ! operator, and any `false` expression preceded by the ! operator becomes `true`.

In Chapter 2 you learned that an exclamation point and equal sign together form the "not equal to" operator.

For example, suppose that a monthly car insurance premium is $200 if the driver is younger than age 26 and $125 if the driver is age 26 or older. Each of the following `if` statements (which have been placed on single lines for convenience) correctly assigns the premium values.

```
if(age < 26) premium = 200;   else premium = 125;
if(!(age < 26)) premium = 125;   else premium = 200;
if(age >= 26) premium = 125;   else premium = 200;
if(!(age>= 26)) premium = 200;   else premium = 125;
```

The statements with the ! operator are somewhat more difficult to read, particularly because they require the double set of parentheses, but the result is the same in each case. Using the ! operator is clearer when the value of a Boolean variable is tested. For example, a variable initialized as `bool oldEnough = (age >= 25);` can become part of the relatively easy-to-read expression `if(!oldEnough)...` .

The ! operator has higher precedence than the && and || operators. For example, suppose that you have declared two Boolean variables named `ageOverMinimum` and `ticketsUnderMinimum`. The following expressions are evaluated in the same way:

```
ageOverMinimum && !ticketsUnderMinimum
ageOverMinimum && (!ticketsUnderMinimum)
```

Augustus de Morgan was a 19th-century mathematician who originally observed the following:

```
!(a && b) is equivalent to !a || !b
!(a || b) is equivalent to !(a && b)
```

TWO TRUTHS & A LIE

Using the NOT Operator

1. Assume that p, q, and r are all Boolean variables that have been assigned the value true. After the following statement executes, the value of p is still true.

   ```
   p = !q || r;
   ```

2. Assume that p, q, and r are all Boolean variables that have been assigned the value true. After the following statement executes, the value of p is still true.

   ```
   p = !(!q && !r);
   ```

3. Assume that p, q, and r are all Boolean variables that have been assigned the value true. After the following statement executes, the value of p is still true.

   ```
   p = !(q || !r);
   ```

The false statement is #3. If p, q, and r are all Boolean variables that have been assigned the value true, then after p = !(q || !r); executes, the value of p is false. First q is evaluated as true, so the entire expression within the parentheses is true. The leading NOT operator reverses that result to false and assigns it to p.

Avoiding Common Errors When Making Decisions

New programmers frequently make errors when they first learn to make decisions. As you have seen, the most frequent errors include the following:

- Using the assignment operator (=) instead of the comparison operator (==) when testing for equality

- Inserting a semicolon after the Boolean expression in an if statement instead of using it after the entire statement is completed

- Failing to block a set of statements with curly braces when several statements depend on the if or the else statement

- Failing to include a complete Boolean expression on each side of an && or || operator in an if statement

In this section, you will learn to avoid other types of errors with if statements. Programmers often make errors at the following times:

- When performing a range check incorrectly or inefficiently

- When using the wrong operator

- Using ! incorrectly

Performing Accurate and Efficient Range Checks

When new programmers must make a range check, they often introduce incorrect or inefficient code into their programs. A **range check** is a series of if statements that determine whether a value falls within a specified range. Consider a situation in which salespeople can receive one of three possible commission rates based on an integer named saleAmount. For example, a sale totaling $1000 or more earns the salesperson an 8 percent commission, a sale totaling $500 through $999 earns 6 percent of the sale amount, and any sale totaling $499 or less earns 5 percent. Using three separate if statements to test single Boolean expressions might result in some incorrect commission assignments. For example, examine the following code:

```
if(saleAmount >= 1000)
   commissionRate = 0.08;
if(saleAmount >= 500)
   commissionRate = 0.06;
if(saleAmount <= 499)
   commissionRate = 0.05;
```

Don't Do It
Although it was not the programmer's intention, both of the first two if statements are true for any saleAmount greater than or equal to 1000.

Using this code, if saleAmount is $5000, the first if statement executes. The Boolean expression (saleAmount >= 1000) evaluates as true, and 0.08 is correctly assigned to commissionRate. However, the next if expression, (saleAmount >= 500), also evaluates as true, so the commissionRate, which was 0.08, is incorrectly reset to 0.06.

A partial solution to this problem is to add an else clause to the statement:

```
if(saleAmount >= 1000)
   commissionRate = 0.08;
else if(saleAmount >= 500)
   commissionRate - 0.06;
else if(saleAmount <= 499)
   commissionRate = 0.05;
```

Don't Do It
If the logic reaches this point, the expression is always true, so it is a waste of time to make this decision.

 The last two logical tests in this code are sometimes called else-if statements because each else and its subsequent if are placed on the same line. When the else-if format is used to test multiple cases, programmers frequently forego the traditional indentation and align each else-if with the others.

With this code, when saleAmount is $5000, the expression (saleAmount >= 1000) is true and commissionRate becomes 0.08; then the entire if structure ends. When saleAmount is not greater than or equal to $1000 (for example, $800), the first if expression is false and the else statement executes and correctly sets commissionRate to 0.06.

This version of the code works, but it is somewhat inefficient because it executes as follows:

- When saleAmount is at least $1000, the first Boolean test is true, so commissionRate is assigned .08 and the if structure ends.

- When saleAmount is under $1000 but at least $500, the first Boolean test is false but the second one is true, so commissionRate is assigned .06 and the if structure ends.

- The only saleAmount values that reach the third Boolean test are under $500, so the next Boolean test, if(saleAmount <= 499), is always true. When an expression is always true, there is no need to evaluate it. In other words, if saleAmount is not at least $1000 and is also not at least $500, it must by default be less than or equal to $499.

The improved code is as follows:

```
if(saleAmount >= 1000)
    commissionRate = 0.08;
else if(saleAmount >= 500)
    commissionRate = 0.06;
else commissionRate = 0.05;
```

In other words, because this example uses three commission rates, two boundaries should be checked. If there were four rates, there would be three boundaries to check, and so on.

Within a nested if-else, processing is most efficient when the first question asked is the one that is most likely to be true. In other words, if you know that a large number of saleAmount values are over $1000, compare saleAmount to that value first. That way, the logic bypasses the rest of the decisions. If, however, you know that most saleAmounts are small, processing is most efficient when the first decision is if(saleAmount < 500).

Using && and || Appropriately

Beginning programmers often use the && operator when they mean to use ||, and often use || when they should use &&. Part of the problem lies in the way we use the English language. For example, your boss might request, "Display an error message when an employee's hourly pay rate is under $5.65 and when an employee's hourly pay rate is over $60." Because your boss used the word "and" in the request, you might be tempted to write a program statement like the following:

```
if(payRate < 5.65 && payRate > 60)          This expression can never be true.
    Console.WriteLine("Error in pay rate");
```

However, as a single variable, no payRate value can ever be both below 5.65 and over 60 at the same time, so the output statement can never execute, no matter what value payRate has. In this case, you must write the following statement to display the error message under the correct circumstances:

```
if(payRate < 5.65 || payRate > 60)
    Console.WriteLine("Error in pay rate");
```

Similarly, your boss might request, "Output the names of those employees in departments 1 and 2." Because the boss used the word "and" in the request, you might be tempted to write the following:

```
if(department == 1 && department == 2)
    Console.WriteLine("Name is: {0}", name);
```
This expression can never be true.

However, the variable `department` can never contain both a 1 and a 2 at the same time, so no employee name will ever be output, no matter what department the employee is in.

The correct statement is:

```
if(department == 1 || department == 2)
    Console.WriteLine("Name is: {0}", name);
```

Using the ! Operator Correctly

Whenever you use negatives, it is easy to make logical mistakes. For example, suppose that your boss says, "Make sure if the sales code is not 'A' or 'B', the customer gets a 10% discount." You might be tempted to code the following:

```
if(salesCode != 'A' || salesCode != 'B')
    discount = 0.10;
```
This expression can never be true.

However, this logic will result in every customer receiving the 10% discount because every `salesCode` is either not 'A' or not 'B'. For example, if `salesCode` is 'A', then it is not 'B'. The expression `salesCode != 'A' || salesCode != 'B'` is always `true`. The correct statement is either one of the following:

```
if(salesCode != 'A' && salesCode != 'B')
    discount = 0.10;
```

```
if(!(salesCode == 'A' || salesCode == 'B'))
    discount = 0.10;
```

In the first example, if `salesCode` is not 'A' and it also is not 'B', then the discount is applied correctly. In the second example, if `salesCode` is 'A' or 'B', the inner Boolean expression is `true`, and the NOT operator (!) changes the evaluation to `false`, not applying the discount for 'A' or 'B' sales. You also could avoid the confusing negative situation by asking questions in a positive way, as in the following:

```
if(salesCode == 'A' || salesCode == 'B')
    discount = 0;
else
    discount = 0.10;
```

 Watch the video *Avoiding Common Decision Errors*.

TWO TRUTHS & A LIE

Avoiding Common Errors When Making Decisions

1. If you want to display "OK" when userEntry is 12 and when it is 13, then the following is a usable C# statement:

```
if(userEntry == 12 && userEntry == 13)
    Console.WriteLine("OK");
```

2. If you want to display "OK" when userEntry is 20 or when highestScore is at least 70, then the following is a usable C# statement:

```
if(userEntry == 20 || highestScore >= 70)
    Console.WriteLine("OK");
```

3. If you want to display "OK" when userEntry is anything other than 99 or 100, then the following is a usable C# statement:

```
if(userEntry != 99 && userEntry != 100)
    Console.WriteLine("OK");
```

The false statement is #1. If you want to display "OK" when userEntry is 12 and when it is 13, then you want to display it when it is either 12 or 13 because it cannot be both simultaneously. The expression userEntry == 12 && userEntry == 13 can never be true. The correct Boolean expression is userEntry == 12 || userEntry == 13.

Decision-Making Issues in GUI Programs

Making a decision within a method in a GUI application is no different from making one in a console application; you can use if, if...else, and switch statements in the same ways. For example, Figure 4-25 shows a GUI Form that determines a movie patron discount as described in a program earlier in this chapter. Patrons who are under 12 or over 65 and are seeing a G-rated movie receive a discount, and any other combination pays full price. Figure 4-26 contains the Click() method that makes the discount determination based on age and rating after a user clicks the Determine Discount button. The Boolean expression tested in the if statement in this method is identical to the one in the console version of the program in Figure 4-16.

Figure 4-25 The Movie Discount Form

```
private void discountButton_Click(object sender, EventArgs e)
{
    int age;
    char rating;
    const int CHILD_AGE = 12;
    const int SENIOR_AGE = 65;
    age = Convert.ToInt32(textBox1.Text);
    rating = Convert.ToChar(textBox2.Text);
    outputLabel.Text = String.Format("When age is {0} and rating is {1}",
        age, rating);
    if ((age <= CHILD_AGE || age >= SENIOR_AGE) && rating == 'G')
        outputLabel.Text += "\nDiscount applies";
    else
        outputLabel.Text += "\nFull price";
}
```

Figure 4-26 The discountButton_Click() method for the Form in Figure 4-25

Event-driven programs often require fewer coded decisions than console applications. That's because in event-driven programs, some events are determined by the user's actions when the program is running (also called **at runtime**), rather than by the programmer's coding beforehand. You might say that in many situations, a console-based application must act, but an event-driven application has to *react*.

Suppose that you want to write a program in which the user must select whether to receive instructions in English or Spanish. In a console application, you would issue a prompt such as the following:

```
Which language do you prefer? Enter 1 for English or 2 for Spanish >>
```

The program would accept the user's entry, make a decision about it, and take appropriate action. However, in a GUI application, you are more likely to place controls on a Form to get a user's response. For example, you might use two Buttons—one for English and one for Spanish. The user clicks a Button, and an appropriate method executes. No decision is written in the program because a different event is fired from each Button, causing execution of a different Click() method. The interactive environment decides which method is called, so the programmer does not have to code a decision. (Of course, you might alternately place a TextBox on a Form and ask a user to enter a 1 or a 2. In that case, the decision-making process would be identical to that in the console-based program.)

An additional benefit to having the user click a button to select an option is that the user cannot enter an invalid value. For example, if the user enters a letter in response to a prompt for an integer, the program will fail unless you write additional code to handle the mistake. However, if the user has a limited selection of buttons to click, no invalid entry can be made.

TWO TRUTHS & A LIE

Decision-Making Issues in GUI Programs

1. Event-driven programs can contain if, if...else, and switch statements.

2. Event-driven programs often require fewer coded decisions than console applications.

3. Event-driven programs always contain more automatic decisions determined by user-initiated events than programmer-coded decisions.

The false statement is #3. Event-driven programs might have any number of event-caused or programmer-caused decisions. However, event-driven programs can contain user-initiated events.

You Do It

Creating a GUI Application that Uses an Enumeration and a switch *Structure*

In these steps, you create a GUI application for the Chatterbox Diner that allows a user to enter a day and see the special meal offered that day. Creating the program provides experience using an enumeration in a switch structure.

1. Open a new project in Visual Studio, and name it **DailySpecial**.

2. Design a Form like the one in Figure 4-27 that prompts the user for a day number and allows the user to enter it in a TextBox. Name the TextBox **dayBox** and the Button **specialButton**.

Figure 4-27 The Daily Special form

3. Below the Button, add a Label named **outputLabel** and delete its text.

(continues)

(continued)

184

4. Double-click `specialButton` to create a `specialButton_Click()` method shell. Above the method, add an enumeration for the days of the week as follows:

```
enum Day
{
    SUNDAY = 1, MONDAY, TUESDAY, WEDNESDAY,
        THURSDAY, FRIDAY, SATURDAY
}
```

5. Within the method, declare an integer and accept a value from the TextBox, and then declare a `string` to hold the daily special.

```
int day = Convert.ToInt32(dayBox.Text);
string special;
```

6. Add a `switch` structure that lists the daily specials as follows:

```
switch ((Day)day)
{
    case Day.SUNDAY:
        special = "fried chicken";
        break;
    case Day.MONDAY:
        special = "Sorry - closed";
        break;
    case Day.TUESDAY:
    case Day.WEDNESDAY:
    case Day.THURSDAY:
        special = "meat loaf";
        break;
    case Day.FRIDAY:
        special = "fish fry";
        break;
    case Day.SATURDAY:
        special = "liver and onions";
        break;
    default:
        special = "Invalid day";
        break;
}
```

7. Following the completed `case` structure, assign the result to the `Text` property of `outputLabel`:

```
outputLabel.Text = "Today's special is " + special;
```

8. Save, compile, and execute the application. The appropriate special is displayed for each day of the week.

Chapter Summary

- A flowchart is a pictorial tool that helps you understand a program's logic. A decision structure is one that involves choosing between alternative courses of action based on some value within a program.

- The `if` statement makes a single-alternative decision using the keyword `if`, followed by parentheses that contain a Boolean expression. When the expression is true, the statement body executes. The body can be a single statement or a block of statements.

- When you make a dual-alternative decision, you can use an `if-else` statement. You can block multiple statements after an `else` so they all execute when the evaluated expression is `false`.

- The conditional AND operator (`&&`) takes action when two operand Boolean expressions are both `true`. The conditional OR operator (`||`) takes action when at least one of two operand Boolean expressions is `true`. When `&&` and `||` operators are combined within the same Boolean expression without parentheses, the `&&` operators take precedence, meaning their Boolean values are evaluated first.

- The `switch` statement tests a single variable against a series of exact matches.

- The conditional operator is used as an abbreviated version of the `if-else` statement. It requires three expressions separated with a question mark and a colon.

- The NOT operator, which is written as an exclamation point (!), negates the result of any Boolean expression.

- Common errors when making decisions include using the assignment operator instead of the comparison operator, inserting a semicolon after the Boolean expression in an `if` statement, failing to block a set of statements when they should be blocked, and performing a range check incorrectly or inefficiently.

- Making a decision within a method in a GUI application is no different from making one in a console application; you can use `if`, `if…else`, and `switch` statements in the same ways. However, event-driven programs often require fewer coded decisions than console applications because some events are determined by the user's actions when the program is running, rather than by the programmer's coding beforehand.

Key Terms

Pseudocode is a tool that helps programmers plan a program's logic by writing plain English statements.

A **flowchart** is a tool that helps programmers plan a program's logic by writing program steps in diagram form, as a series of shapes connected by arrows.

A **sequence structure** is a unit of program logic in which one step follows another unconditionally.

185

A **decision structure** is a unit of program logic that involves choosing between alternative courses of action based on some value.

An **if statement** is used to make a single-alternative decision.

A **block** is a collection of one or more statements contained within a pair of curly braces.

A **control statement** is the part of a structure that determines whether the subsequent block of statements executes.

K & R style is a way of writing code so that the opening curly brace of a structure is on the same line as the control statement; it is named for Brian Kernighan and Dennis Ritchie, who wrote the first book on the C programming language.

A **nested if** statement is one in which one decision structure is contained within another.

Dual-alternative decisions have two possible outcomes.

An **if-else statement** performs a dual-alternative decision.

The **conditional AND operator** (or simply the **AND operator**) determines whether two expressions are both `true`; it is written using two ampersands (&&).

Truth tables are diagrams used in mathematics and logic to help describe the truth of an entire expression based on the truth of its parts.

Short-circuit evaluation is the C# feature in which parts of an AND or OR expression are evaluated only as far as necessary to determine whether the entire expression is `true` or `false`.

The **conditional OR operator** (or simply the **OR operator**) determines whether at least one of two conditions is `true`; it is written using two pipes (||).

The **Boolean logical AND operator** determines whether two expressions are both `true`; it is written using a single ampersand (&). Unlike the conditional AND operator, it does not use short-circuit evaluation.

The **Boolean logical inclusive OR operator** determines whether at least one of two conditions is `true`; it is written using a single pipe (|). Unlike the conditional OR operator, it does not use short-circuit evaluation.

A **side effect** is an unintended consequence.

Bitwise operators are used to manipulate the individual bits of values.

The **switch structure** tests a single variable against a series of exact matches.

The keyword **switch** starts a `switch` structure.

The **switch expression** is a condition in a `switch` statement enclosed in parentheses.

The keyword **case** in a `switch` structure is followed by one of the possible values that might equal the `switch` expression.

A **case label** identifies a course of action in a `switch` structure.

The **governing type** of a `switch` statement is established by the `switch` expression and can be sbyte, byte, short, ushort, int, uint, long, ulong, char, string, or enum.

The keyword **break** optionally terminates a `switch` structure at the end of each `case`.

The keyword **default** optionally is used prior to any action that should occur if the test expression in a `switch` structure does not match any `case`.

The **conditional operator** is used as an abbreviated version of the `if-else` statement; it requires three expressions separated by a question mark and a colon.

A **ternary** operator requires three arguments.

The **NOT operator** (!) negates the result of any Boolean expression.

A **range check** is a series of `if` statements that determine whether a value falls within a specified range.

At runtime is a phrase that means "during the time a program is running."

Review Questions

1. What is the output of the following code segment?

    ```
    int a = 3, b = 4;
    if(a == b)
        Console.Write("Black ");
        Console.WriteLine("White");
    ```

    a. Black   c. Black White
    b. White   d. nothing

2. What is the output of the following code segment?

    ```
    int a = 3, b = 4;
    if(a < b)
    {
        Console.Write("Black ");
        Console.WriteLine("White");
    }
    ```

    a. Black   c. Black White
    b. White   d. nothing

3. What is the output of the following code segment?

```
int a = 3, b = 4;
if(a > b)
   Console.Write("Black ");
else
   Console.WriteLine("White");
```

a. Black

b. White

c. Black White

d. nothing

4. If the following code segment compiles correctly, what do you know about the variable x?

```
if(x) Console.WriteLine("OK");
```

a. x is an integer variable

b. x is a Boolean variable

c. x is greater than 0

d. none of these

5. What is the output of the following code segment?

```
int c = 6, d = 12;
if(c > d);
   Console.Write("Green ");
   Console.WriteLine("Yellow");
```

a. Green

b. Yellow

c. Green Yellow

d. nothing

6. What is the output of the following code segment?

```
int c = 6, d = 12;
if(c < d)
   if(c > 8)
      Console.Write("Green");
   else
      Console.Write("Yellow");
else
   Console.Write("Blue");
```

a. Green

b. Yellow

c. Blue

d. nothing

7. What is the output of the following code segment?

```
int e = 5, f = 10;
if(e < f && f < 0)
   Console.Write("Red ");
else
   Console.Write("Orange");
```

a. Red

b. Orange

c. Red Orange

d. nothing

8. What is the output of the following code segment?

```
int e = 5, f = 10;
if(e < f || f < 0)
    Console.Write("Red ");
else
    Console.Write("Orange");
```

    a. Red   c. Red Orange

    b. Orange   d. nothing

9. Which of the following expressions is equivalent to the following code segment?

```
if(g > h)
    if(g < k)
        Console.Write("Brown");
```

    a. `if(g > h && g < k) Console.Write("Brown");`

    b. `if(g > h && < k) Console.Write("Brown");`

    c. `if(g > h || g < k) Console.Write("Brown");`

    d. two of these

10. Which of the following expressions assigns `true` to a Boolean variable named `isIDValid` when `idNumber` is both greater than 1000 and less than or equal to 9999, or else is equal to 123456?

    a. `isIDValid = (idNumber > 1000 && idNumber <= 9999 && idNumber == 123456)`

    b. `isIDValid = (idNumber > 1000 && idNumber <= 9999 || idNumber == 123456)`

    c. `isIDValid = ((idNumber > 1000 && idNumber <= 9999) || idNumber == 123456)`

    d. two of these

11. Which of the following expressions is equivalent to `a || b && c || d`?

    a. `a && b || c && d`   c. `a || (b && c) || d`

    b. `(a || b) && (c || d)`   d. two of these

12. How many case labels would a `switch` statement require to be equivalent to the following `if` statement?

```
if(v == 1)
    Console.WriteLine("one");
else
    Console.WriteLine("two");
```

    a. zero   c. two

    b. one   d. impossible to tell

13. Falling through a `switch case` is most often prevented by using the _____.

    a. break statement   c. case statement

    b. default statement   d. end statement

14. If the test expression in a `switch` does not match any of the `case` values, and there is no `default` value, then _____.

    a. a compiler error occurs

    b. a run-time error occurs

    c. the program continues with the next executable statement

    d. the expression is incremented and the `case` values are tested again

15. Which of the following is equivalent to the statement `if(m == 0) d = 0 ; else d = 1;`?

    a. `? m == 0 : d = 0, d = 1;`   c. `m == 0 ; d = 0; d = 1?`

    b. `m? d = 0; d = 1;`   d. `m == 0 ? d = 0 : d = 1;`

16. Which of the following C# expressions is equivalent to `a < b && b < c`?

    a. `c > b > a`   c. `!(b <= a) && b < c`

    b. `a < b && c >= b`   d. two of these

17. Which of the following C# expressions means, "If `itemNumber` is not 8 or 9, add TAX to `price`"?

    a. `if(itemNumber != 8 || itemNumber != 9)`
       `price = price + TAX;`

    b. `if(itemNumber != 8 && itemNumber != 9)`
       `price = price + TAX;`

    c. `if(itemNumber != 8 && != 9)`
       `price = price + TAX;`

    d. two of these

18. Which of the following C# expressions means, "If `itemNumber` is 1 or 2 and `quantity` is 12 or more, add TAX to `price`"?

    a. `if(itemNumber = 1 || itemNumber = 2 && quantity >= 12)`
       `price = price + TAX;`

    b. `if(itemNumber == 1 || itemNumber == 2 || quantity >= 12)`
       `price = price + TAX;`

    c. `if(itemNumber == 1 && itemNumber == 2 && quantity >= 12)`
       `price = price + TAX;`

    d. none of these

19. Which of the following C# expressions means, "If itemNumber is 5 and zone is 1 or 3, add TAX to price"?

   a.   `if(itemNumber == 5 && zone == 1 || zone == 3)`
      `price = price + TAX;`

   b.   `if(itemNumber == 5 && (zone == 1 || zone == 3))`
      `price = price + TAX;`

   c.   `if(itemNumber == 5 && (zone == 1 || 3))`
      `price = price + TAX;`

   d.   two of these

20. Which of the following C# expressions results in TAX being added to price if the integer itemNumber is not 100?

   a.   `if(itemNumber != 100)`
      `price = price + TAX;`

   b.   `if(!(itemNumber == 100))`
      `price = price + TAX;`

   c.   `if(itemNumber <100 || itemNumber > 100)`
      `price = price + TAX;`

   d.   all of these

Exercises

Programming Exercises

1.   a. Write a console-based program named **CheckYear** that prompts users to enter their year of birth. If the value entered is greater than the current year, display an error message.

    b. Create a GUI application named **CheckYearGUI** that allows users to enter their year of birth into a TextBox. When the user clicks a button and the value in the TextBox is greater than the current year, display an error message.

2.   a. Write a console-based program named **CheckYear2** that prompts users for their year of birth. If the value entered is greater than the current year or less than 1890, display an error message; otherwise, display a message indicating that the year is valid.

    b. Create a GUI application named **CheckYearGUI2** that allows users to enter their year of birth into a TextBox. When the user clicks a button and the value in the TextBox is greater than the current year or less than 1890, display an error message; otherwise, display a message indicating that the year is valid.

3. a. Write a console-based program named **Twitter** that accepts a user's message and determines whether it is short enough for a social networking service that does not accept messages of more than 140 characters.

   b. Create a GUI application similar to Exercise 3a named **TwitterGUI**.

4. a. Write a console-based program named **Admission** for a college's admissions office. The user enters a numeric high school grade point average (for example, 3.2) and an admission test score. Display the message "Accept" if the student meets either of the following requirements:

   - A grade point average of 3.0 or higher and an admission test score of at least 60

   - A grade point average of less than 3.0 and an admission test score of at least 80

   If the student does not meet either of the qualification criteria, display "Reject".

   b. Create a GUI application named **AdmissionGUI** for the college admissions office described in Exercise 4a.

5. a. The Saffir-Simpson Hurricane Scale classifies hurricanes into five categories numbered 1 through 5. Write a console-based application named **Hurricane** that outputs a hurricane's category based on the user's input of the wind speed. Category 5 hurricanes have sustained winds of at least 157 miles per hour. The minimum sustained wind speeds for categories 4 through 1 are 130, 111, 96, and 74 miles per hour, respectively. Any storm with winds of less than 74 miles per hour is not a hurricane.

   b. Create a GUI application named **HurricaneGUI** that operates like the program described in Exercise 5a.

6. a. Write a console-based application named **IQ** that asks a user to enter an intelligence quotient. If the quotient is a number less than 0 or greater than 200, issue an error message; otherwise, issue an "above average", "average", or "below average" message for scores over, at, or under 100, respectively.

   b. Create a GUI application named **IQGUI** that operates like the program described in Exercise 6a.

7. a. You can create a random number that is at least min but less than max using the following statements:

```
Random ranNumberGenerator = new Random();
int randomNumber;
randomNumber = ranNumberGenerator.Next(min, max);
```

Write a console-based program named **GuessingGame** that generates a random number between 1 and 10. (In other words, min is 1 and max is 10.) Ask a user to guess the random number, then display the random number and a message indicating whether the user's guess was too high, too low, or correct.

b. Create a GUI application named **GuessingGameGUI** that performs the same tasks as the program in Exercise 7a.

8. a. In the game Rock Paper Scissors, two players simultaneously choose one of three options: rock, paper, or scissors. If both players choose the same option, then the result is a tie. However, if they choose differently, the winner is determined as follows:

- Rock beats scissors, because a rock can break a pair of scissors.

- Scissors beats paper, because scissors can cut paper.

- Paper beats rock, because a piece of paper can cover a rock.

Create a console-based game in which the computer randomly chooses rock, paper, or scissors. Let the user enter a character, 'r', 'p', or 's', each representing one of the three choices. Then, determine the winner. Save the application as **RockPaperScissors.cs**.

b. Create a GUI application in which the user can play Rock, Paper, Scissors by clicking one of three buttons. Save the project as **RockPaperScissorsGUI**.

9. a. Create a console-based lottery game application named **Lottery**. Generate three random numbers, each between 1 and 4. Allow the user to guess three numbers. Compare each of the user's guesses to the three random numbers and display a message that includes the user's guess, the randomly determined three-digit number, and the amount of money the user has won as follows:

Matching Numbers	Award ($)
Any one matching	10
Two matching	100
Three matching, not in order	1000
Three matching in exact order	10,000
No matches	0

Make certain that your application accommodates repeating digits. For example, if a user guesses 1, 2, and 3, and the randomly generated digits are 1, 1, and 1, do not give the user credit for three correct guesses—just one.

b. Create a GUI application named **LotteryGUI** that lets the user play the Lottery game described in Exercise 9a.

Debugging Exercises

1. Each of the following files in the Chapter.04 folder of your downloadable student files has syntax and/or logical errors. In each case, determine the problem and fix the program. After you correct the errors, save each file using the same filename preceded with *Fixed*. For example, save DebugFour1.cs as **FixedDebugFour1.cs**.

a. DebugFour1.cs   c. DebugFour3.cs

b. DebugFour2.cs   d. DebugFour4.cs

Case Problems

1. In Chapter 2, you created an interactive application named **GreenvilleRevenue**, and in Chapter 3 you created a GUI version of the application named **GreenvilleRevenueGUI**. The programs prompt a user for the number of contestants entered in this year's and last year's Greenville Idol competition, and then they display the revenue expected for this year's competition if each contestant pays a $25 entrance fee. The programs also display a statement that compares the number of contestants each year. Now, replace that statement with one of the following messages:

   • If the competition has more than twice as many contestants as last year, display "The competition is more than twice as big this year!"

   • If the competition is bigger than last year's but not more than twice as big, display "The competition is bigger than ever!"

   • If the competition is smaller than last year's, display, "A tighter race this year! Come out and cast your vote!"

2. In Chapter 2, you created an interactive application named **MarshallsRevenue**, and in Chapter 3 you created a GUI version of the application named **MarshallsRevenueGUI**. The programs prompt a user for the number of interior and exterior murals scheduled to be painted during the next month by Marshall's Murals. Next, the programs compute the expected revenue for each type of mural when interior murals cost $500 each and exterior murals cost $750 each. The applications also display the total expected revenue and a statement that indicates whether more interior murals are scheduled than exterior ones. Now, modify one or both of the applications to accept a numeric value for the month being scheduled and to modify the pricing as follows:

- Because of uncertain weather conditions, exterior murals cannot be painted in December through February, so change the number of exterior murals to 0 for those months.

- Marshall prefers to paint exterior murals in April, May, September, and October. To encourage business, he charges only $699 for an exterior mural during those months. Murals in other months continue to cost $750.

- Marshall prefers to paint interior murals in July and August, so he charges only $450 for an interior mural during those months. Murals in other months continue to cost $500.

Looping

In this chapter you will:

◎ Learn how to create loops using the `while` statement

◎ Learn how to create loops using the `for` statement

◎ Learn how to create loops using the `do` statement

◎ Use nested loops

◎ Accumulate totals

◎ Understand how to improve loop performance

◎ Learn about looping issues in GUI programs

In the last chapter, you learned how computers make decisions by evaluating Boolean expressions. Looping allows a program to repeat tasks based on the value of a Boolean expression. For example, programs that produce thousands of paychecks or invoices rely on the ability to loop to repeat instructions. Likewise, programs that repeatedly prompt users for a valid credit card number or for the correct answer to a tutorial question run more efficiently with loop structures. In this chapter, you will learn to create loops in C# programs.

Using the while Loop

Computer programs seem smart due to their ability to make decisions; looping makes programs seem powerful. A **loop** is a structure that allows repeated execution of a block of statements. Within a looping structure, a Boolean expression is evaluated. If it is true, a block of statements called the **loop body** executes and the Boolean expression is evaluated again. As long as the expression is true, the statements in the loop body continue to execute and the loop-controlling Boolean expression continues to be reevaluated. When the Boolean evaluation is false, the loop ends. Figure 5-1 shows a diagram of the logic of a loop. One execution of any loop is called an **iteration**.

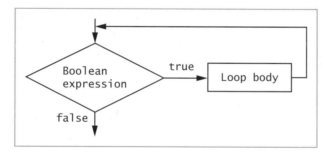

Figure 5-1   Flowchart of a loop structure

You can use a **while loop** to execute a body of statements continuously as long as the loop's test condition continues to be true. A while loop consists of the keyword while, followed by a Boolean expression within parentheses, followed by the body of the loop. The evaluated Boolean expression in a while statement can be either a single Boolean expression or a compound expression that uses ANDs and ORs. The body can be a single statement or any number of statements surrounded by curly braces.

For example, the following code shows an integer declaration followed by a loop that causes the message "Hello" to display (theoretically) forever because there is no code to end the loop. A loop that never ends is called an **infinite loop**. An infinite loop might not actually execute infinitely. All programs run with the help of computer memory and hardware, both of which have finite capacities, so a program with an infinite loop might eventually fail and end. However, any loop that potentially runs forever is called infinite.

```
int number = 1;
while(number > 0)
   Console.WriteLine("Hello");
```

In this loop, the expression `number > 0` evaluates as `true`, and "Hello" is displayed. The expression `number > 0` evaluates as `true` again and "Hello" is displayed again. Because the value of `number` is never altered, the loop runs forever, evaluating the same Boolean expression and repeatedly displaying "Hello" as long as computer memory and hardware allow.

199

Writing an infinite loop is always a bad idea, although even experienced programmers write them by accident. If you ever find yourself in the midst of an infinite loop in a console application, you can break out by holding down the Ctrl key and pressing the C key or the Break (Pause) key. In a GUI program, you can simply close the `Frame` that is hosting the application.

To make a `while` loop end correctly, three separate actions should occur:

- A variable, the **loop control variable**, is initialized (before entering the loop).

- The loop control variable is tested in the `while` expression.

- The body of the `while` statement must take some action that alters the value of the loop control variable (so that the `while` expression eventually evaluates as `false`).

For example, Figure 5-2 shows the logic for a loop that displays "Hello" four times. The variable `number` is initialized to 1 and a constant, `LIMIT`, is initialized to 5. The variable is less than `LIMIT`, and so the loop body executes. The loop body shown in Figure 5-2 contains two statements. The first displays "Hello" and the second adds 1 to `number`. The next time `number` is evaluated, its value is 2, which is still less than `LIMIT`, so the loop body executes again. "Hello" displays a third time and `number` becomes 4, then "Hello" displays a fourth time and `number` becomes 5. Now when the expression `number < LIMIT` evaluates, it is `false`, so the loop ends. If there were any subsequent statements following the `while` loop's closing curly brace, they would execute after the loop was finished.

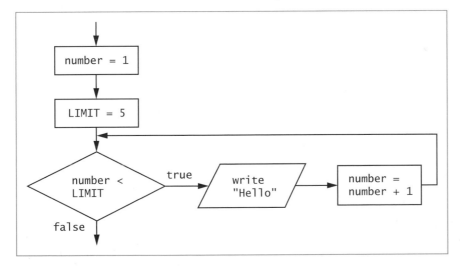

Figure 5-2 Flowchart for the logic of a `while` loop whose body executes four times

Figure 5-3 shows a C# program that uses the same logic as diagrammed in Figure 5-2. After the declarations, the shaded `while` expression compares `number` to `LIMIT`. The two statements that execute each time the Boolean expression is `true` are blocked using a pair of curly braces. Figure 5-4 shows the output.

```
using System;
class FourHellos
{
    static void Main()
    {
        int number = 1;
        const int LIMIT = 5;
        while(number < LIMIT)
        {
            Console.WriteLine("Hello");
            number = number + 1;
        }
    }
}
```

Figure 5-3   A program that contains a `while` loop whose body executes four times

Figure 5-4   Output of `FourHellos` program

Recall from Chapter 2 that you also can use a shortcut operator to increase the value of a variable by 1. Instead of `number = number + 1`, you could achieve the same final result by writing `number++`, `++number`, or `number += 1`. Because counting is such a common feature of loops, you might want to review the difference between the prefix and postfix increment operators. A video called *Using Shortcut Arithmetic Operators* accompanies Chapter 2.

The curly braces surrounding the body of the while loop in Figure 5-3 are important. If they are omitted, the while loop ends at the end of the "Hello" statement. Adding 1 to number would no longer be part of the loop body, so an infinite loop would be created. Even if the statement number = number + 1; was indented under the while statement, it would not be part of the loop without the surrounding curly braces. Figure 5-5 shows the incorrect logic that would result from omitting the curly braces. Many programmers recommend surrounding a loop body with curly braces even when there is only one statement in the body.

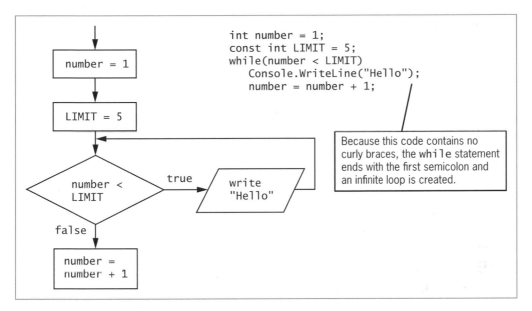

Figure 5-5 Incorrect logic when curly braces are omitted from the loop in the FourHellos program

Also, if a semicolon is mistakenly placed at the end of the partial statement, as in Figure 5-6, then the loop is also infinite. This loop has an **empty body**, or a body with no statements in it. In this case, number is initialized to 1, the Boolean expression number < LIMIT evaluates, and because it is true, the loop body is entered. Because the loop body is empty, ending at the semicolon, no action takes place, and the Boolean expression evaluates again. It is still true (nothing has changed), so the empty body is entered again, and the infinite loop continues. The program can never progress to either the statement that displays "Hello" or the statement that increases the value of number. The fact that these two statements are blocked using curly braces has no effect because of the incorrectly placed semicolon.

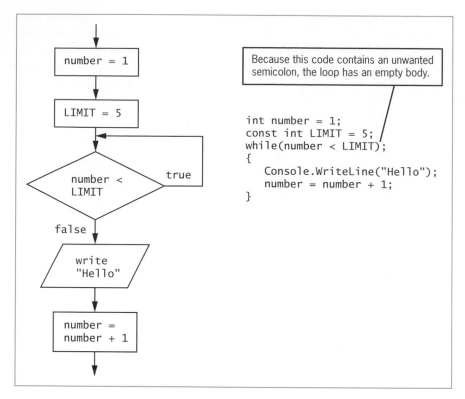

Figure 5-6 Incorrect logic when an unwanted semicolon is mistakenly added to the loop in the FourHellos program

Within a correctly functioning loop's body, you can change the value of the loop control variable in a number of ways. Many loop control variable values are altered by **incrementing**, or adding to them, as in Figures 5-2 and 5-3. Other loops are controlled by reducing, or **decrementing**, a variable and testing whether the value remains greater than some benchmark value. A loop for which the number of iterations is predetermined is called a **definite loop** or **counted loop**. Often, the value of a loop control variable is not altered by arithmetic, but instead is altered by user input. For example, perhaps you want to continue performing some task while the user indicates a desire to continue. In that case, you do not know when you write the program whether the loop will be executed two times, 200 times, or not at all. This type of loop is an **indefinite loop**.

Consider a program that displays a bank balance and asks if the user wants to see what the balance will be after one year of interest has accumulated. Each time the user indicates she wants to continue, an increased balance appears. When the user finally indicates she has had enough, the program ends. The program appears in Figure 5-7, and a typical execution appears in Figure 5-8.

```
using System;
class LoopingBankBal
{
    static void Main()
    {
        double bankBal = 1000;
        const double INT_RATE = 0.04;
        string inputString;
        char response;
        Console.Write("Do you want to see your balance? Y or N ...");
        inputString = Console.ReadLine();
        response = Convert.ToChar(inputString);
        while(response == 'Y')
        {
            Console.WriteLine("Bank balance is {0}", bankBal.ToString("C"));
            bankBal = bankBal + bankBal * INT_RATE;
            Console.Write("Do you want to see next year's balance? Y or N ...");
            inputString = Console.ReadLine();
            response = Convert.ToChar(inputString);
        }
        Console.WriteLine("Have a nice day!");
    }
}
```

Figure 5-7 LoopingBankBal program

Figure 5-8 Typical execution of the LoopingBankBal program

The program shown in Figure 5-7 continues to display bank balances while the response is *Y*. It could also be written to display while the response is not *N*, as in `while(response != 'N')`.... A value such as `'Y'` or `'N'` that a user must supply to stop a loop is a **sentinel value**.

In the program shown in Figure 5-7, the loop control variable is `response`. It is initialized by the first input and tested with `while(response == 'Y')`. If the user types any character other than *Y*, then the loop body never executes; instead, the next statement to execute displays "Have a nice day!". However, if the user enters *Y*, then all five statements within the loop body execute. The current balance is displayed, and the program increases the balance by the interest rate value; this value will not be displayed unless the user requests another loop repetition. Within the loop, the program prompts the user and reads in a new value for `response`. This is the statement that potentially alters the loop control variable. The loop ends with a closing curly brace, and program control returns to the top of the loop, where the Boolean expression is tested again. If the user typed *Y* at the last prompt, then the loop is reentered and the increased `bankBal` value that was calculated during the last loop cycle is displayed.

In C#, character data is case sensitive. If a program tests `response == 'Y'`, a user response of *y* will result in a `false` evaluation. Beware of the pitfall of writing a loop similar to `while(response != 'Y' || response != 'y')`... to test both for uppercase and lowercase versions of the response. Every character is either not 'Y' or not 'y', even 'Y' and 'y'. A correct loop might begin with the following:

`while(response != 'Y' && response != 'y')`...

Watch the video *Using the while Loop*.

TWO TRUTHS & A LIE

Using the while Loop

1. To make a `while` loop that executes correctly, a loop control variable is initialized before entering the loop.

2. To make a `while` loop that executes correctly, the loop control variable is tested in the `while` expression.

3. To make a `while` loop that executes correctly, the body of the `while` statement must never alter the value of the loop control variable.

The false statement is #3. To make a `while` loop that executes correctly, the body of the `while` statement must take some action that alters the value of the loop control variable.

You Do It

Using a `while` Loop

In the next steps, you write a program that continuously prompts the user for a valid ID number until the user enters one. For this application, assume that a valid ID number must be between 1000 and 9999 inclusive.

1. Open a new project named **ValidID**, and enter the beginning of the program by declaring variables for an ID number, the user's input, and constant values for the highest and lowest acceptable ID numbers.

```
using System;
class ValidID
{
    static void Main()
    {
        int idNum;
        string input;
        const int LOW = 1000;
        const int HIGH = 9999;
```

2. Add code to prompt the user for an ID number and to then convert it to an integer.

```
Console.Write("Enter an ID number: ");
input = Console.ReadLine();
idNum = Convert.ToInt32(input);
```

3. Create a loop that continues while the entered ID number is out of range. While the number is invalid, explain valid ID parameters and reprompt the user, converting the input to an integer.

```
while(idNum < LOW || idNum > HIGH)
{
    Console.WriteLine("{0} is an invalid ID number", idNum);
    Console.Write("ID numbers must be ");
    Console.WriteLine("between {0} and {1} inclusive",
        LOW, HIGH);
    Console.Write("Enter an ID number: ");
    input = Console.ReadLine();
    idNum = Convert.ToInt32(input);
}
```

(continues)

(continued)

4. When the user eventually enters a valid ID number, the loop ends. Display a message and add closing curly braces for the `Main()` method and for the class.

```
Console.WriteLine("ID number {0} is valid", idNum);
    }
}
```

5. Save the file, compile the program, and execute it. A typical execution during which the user makes several invalid entries is shown in Figure 5-9.

Figure 5-9 Typical execution of `ValidID` program

Using the for Loop

Each time the `LoopingBankBal` program in Figure 5-7 executes, the user might continue the loop a different number of times, which makes it an indefinite loop. You can use a `while` loop for either definite or indefinite loops. To write either type of `while` loop, you initialize a loop control variable, and as long as its test expression is `true`, you continue to execute the body of the `while` loop. To avoid an infinite loop, the body of the `while` loop must contain a statement that alters the loop control variable.

Because you need definite loops so frequently when you write programs, C# provides a shorthand way to create such a loop. This shorthand structure is called a **for loop**. With a `for` loop, you can indicate the starting value for the loop control variable, the test condition that controls loop entry, and the expression that alters the loop control variable, all in one convenient place.

You begin a for statement with the keyword for followed by a set of parentheses. Within the parentheses are three sections separated by exactly two semicolons. The three sections are usually used for:

- Initializing the loop control variable
- Testing the loop control variable
- Updating the loop control variable

As with an if or a while statement, you can use a single statement as the body of a for loop, or you can use a block of statements enclosed in curly braces. The while and for statements shown in Figure 5-10 produce the same output—the integers 1 through 10.

```
// Declare loop control variable and limit
int x;
const int LIMIT = 10;

// Using a while loop to display 1 through 10
x = 1;
while(x <= LIMIT)
{
    Console.WriteLine(x);
    ++x;
}

// Using a for loop to display 1 through 10
for(x = 1; x <= LIMIT; ++x)
    Console.WriteLine(x);
```

Figure 5-10   Displaying integers 1 through 10 with while and for loops

The amount by which a loop control variable increases or decreases on each cycle through the loop is often called the **step value**. That's because in the BASIC programming language, the keyword STEP was actually used in for loops.

Within the parentheses of the for statement shown in Figure 5-10, the initialization section prior to the first semicolon sets a variable named x to 1. The program executes this statement once, no matter how many times the body of the for loop eventually executes.

After the initialization expression executes, program control passes to the middle, or test, section of the for statement. If the Boolean expression found there evaluates to true, then the body of the for loop is entered. In the program segment shown in Figure 5-10, x is initialized to 1, so when x <= LIMIT is tested, it evaluates to true and the loop body outputs the value of x.

After the loop body executes, the final one-third of the for expression (the update section) executes, and x increases to 2. Following the third section, program control returns to the second (test) section, where x is compared to LIMIT a second time. Because the value of x is 2, it is still less than or equal to LIMIT, so the body of the for loop executes and the value of x is displayed. Then the third, altering portion of the for statement executes again. The variable x increases to 3, and the for loop continues.

Eventually, when x is *not* less than or equal to LIMIT (after 1 through 10 have been output), the for loop ends, and the program continues with any statements that follow the for loop.

Although the three sections of the for loop are most commonly used for initializing a variable, testing it, and incrementing it, you can also perform other tasks:

- You can initialize more than one variable by placing commas between separate initializations in the first section of the for statement, as in the following:

  ```
  for(g = 0, h = 1; g < 6; ++g)
  ```

- You can declare a new variable within the for statement, as in the following:

  ```
  for(int k = 0; k < 5; ++k)
  ```

  In this example, k is declared to be an int and is initialized to 0. This technique is used frequently when the variable exists only to control the loop and for no other purpose. When a variable is declared inside a loop, as k is in this example, it can be referenced only for the duration of the loop body; then it is **out of scope**, which means it is not usable because it has ceased to exist.

- You can perform more than one test in the middle section of the for statement by evaluating compound conditions, as in the following:

  ```
  for(g = 0; g < 3 && h > 1; ++g)
  ```

- You can perform tasks other than incrementing at the end of the loop's execution, as in the following code that decrements a variable:

  ```
  for(g = 5; g >= 1; --g)
  ```

- You can perform multiple tasks at the end of the loop's execution by separating the actions with commas, as in the following:

  ```
  for(g = 0; g < 5; ++g, ++h)
  ```

- You can leave one or more portions of the for expression empty, although the two semicolons are still required as placeholders to separate the three sections. Usually, you want to use all three sections because the function of the loop is clearer to someone reading your program.

Generally, you should use the for loop in the standard manner, which is a shorthand way of initializing, testing, and altering a variable that controls a definite loop. You will learn about a similar loop, the foreach loop, when you study arrays in the next chapter.

Just as with a decision or a while loop, statements in a for loop body can be blocked. For example, the following loop displays "Hello" and "Goodbye" four times each:

```
const int TIMES = 4;
for(int x = 0; x < TIMES; ++x)
{
    Console.WriteLine("Hello");
    Console.WriteLine("Goodbye");
}
```

Without the curly braces in this code, the for loop would end after the statement that displays "Hello". In other words, "Hello" would be displayed four times, but "Goodbye" would be displayed only once.

Watch the video *Using the for Loop*.

TWO TRUTHS & A LIE

Using the for Loop

1. The following statement displays the numbers 3 through 6:

   ```
   for(int x = 3; x <= 6; ++x)
       Console.WriteLine(x);
   ```

2. The following statement displays the numbers 4 through 9:

   ```
   for(int x = 3; x < 9; ++x)
       Console.WriteLine(x + 1);
   ```

3. The following statement displays the numbers 5 through 12:

   ```
   for(int x = 5; x < 12; ++x)
       Console.WriteLine(x);
   ```

The false statement is #3. That loop only displays the numbers 5 through 11, because when x is 12, the loop body is not entered.

You Do It

Using a for Loop

In the next steps, you write a program that creates a tipping table that restaurant patrons can use to approximate the correct tip for meals. Prices range from $10 to $100, and tipping percentage rates range from 10 percent to 25 percent. The program uses several loops.

1. Open a new file to start a program named **TippingTable**. It begins by declaring variables to use for the price of a dinner, a tip percentage rate, and the amount of the tip.

```
using System;
class TippingTable
{
    static void Main()
    {
        double dinnerPrice = 10.00;
        double tipRate;
        double tip;
```

2. Next, create some constants. Every tip from 10 percent through 25 percent will be computed in 5 percent intervals, so declare those values as LOWRATE, MAXRATE, and TIPSTEP. Tips will be calculated on dinner prices up to $100.00 in $10.00 intervals, so declare those constants too.

```
        const double LOWRATE = 0.10;
        const double MAXRATE = 0.25;
        const double TIPSTEP = 0.05;
        const double MAXDINNER = 100.00;
        const double DINNERSTEP = 10.00;
```

3. To create a heading for the table, display "Price". (For alignment, insert three spaces after the quotes and before the *P* in *Price*.) On the same line, use a loop that displays every tip rate from LOWRATE through MAXRATE in increments of TIPSTEP. In other words, the tip rates are 0.10, 0.15, 0.20, and 0.25. Complete the heading for the table using a WriteLine() statement that advances the cursor to the next line of output and a WriteLine() statement that displays a dashed line.

```
Console.Write("   Price");
for(tipRate = LOWRATE; tipRate <= MAXRATE; tipRate +=
    TIPSTEP)
    Console.Write("{0, 8}",tipRate.ToString("F"));
Console.WriteLine();
Console.WriteLine
("---------------------------------------");
```

(continues)

(continued)

Recall that within a `for` loop, the expression before the first semicolon executes once, the middle expression is tested, the loop body executes, and then the expression to the right of the second semicolon executes. In other words, TIPSTEP is not added to `tipRate` until after the `tipRate` is displayed on each cycle through the loop.

As an alternative to typing 40 dashes in the `WriteLine()` statement, you could use the following loop to display a single dash 40 times. When the 40 dashes were completed, you could use `WriteLine()` to advance the cursor to a new line.

```
const int NUM_DASHES = 40;
for(int x = 0; x < NUM_DASHES; ++x)
    Console.Write("-");
Console.WriteLine();
```

4. Reset `tipRate` to 0.10. You must reset the rate because after the last loop, the rate will have been increased to greater than 0.25.

    ```
    tipRate = LOWRATE;
    ```

5. Create a nested loop that continues while the `dinnerPrice` remains 100.00 (MAXDINNER) or less. Each iteration of this loop displays one row of the tip table. Within this loop, display the `dinnerPrice`, then loop to display four tips while the `tipRate` varies from 0.10 through 0.25. At the end of the loop, increase the `dinnerPrice` by 10.00, reset the `tipRate` to 0.10 so it is ready for the next row, and write a new line to advance the cursor.

    ```
    while(dinnerPrice <= MAXDINNER)
    {
        Console.Write("{0, 8}", dinnerPrice.ToString("C"));
        while(tipRate <= MAXRATE)
        {
            tip = dinnerPrice * tipRate;
            Console.Write("{0, 8}",tip.ToString("F"));
            tipRate += 0.05;
        }
        dinnerPrice += DINNERSTEP;
        tipRate = LOWRATE;
        Console.WriteLine();
    }
    ```

Recall that the {0, 8} format string in the `Write()` statements displays the first argument in fields that are eight characters wide. You learned about format strings in Chapter 2.

6. Add two closing curly braces—one for the `Main()` method and one for the class.

(continues)

(continued)

7. Save the file, compile it, and execute the program. The output looks like Figure 5-11.

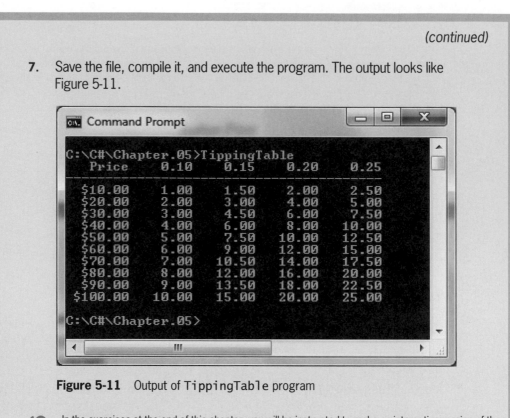

Figure 5-11   Output of `TippingTable` program

 In the exercises at the end of this chapter, you will be instructed to make an interactive version of the `TippingTable` program in which many of the values are input by the user instead of being coded into the program as unnamed constants.

Using the do Loop

With each of the loop statements you have learned about so far, the loop body might execute many times, but it is also possible that the loop will not execute at all. For example, recall the bank balance program that displays compound interest, part of which is shown in Figure 5-12. The loop begins at the shaded line by testing the value of `response`. If the user has not entered *Y*, the loop body never executes. The `while` loop checks a value at the "top" of the loop.

```
Console.Write("Do you want to see your balance? Y or N ...");
inputString = Console.ReadLine();
response = Convert.ToChar(inputString);
while(response == 'Y')
{
    Console.WriteLine("Bank balance is {0}", bankBal.ToString("C"));
    bankBal = bankBal + bankBal * INT_RATE;
    Console.Write("Do you want to see next year's balance? Y or N ...");
    inputString = Console.ReadLine();
    response = Convert.ToChar(inputString);
}
```

Figure 5-12 Part of the bank balance program using a `while` loop

Sometimes you might need a loop body to execute at least one time. If so, you want to write a loop that checks at the "bottom" of the loop after the first iteration. The **do loop** (also called a **do...while loop**) checks the loop-controlling Boolean expression at the bottom of the loop after one repetition has occurred. Figure 5-13 shows a diagram of the structure of a do loop.

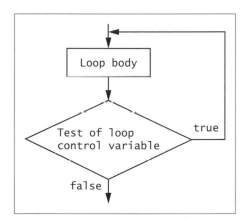

Figure 5-13 Flowchart of a do loop

Figure 5-14 shows the logic for a do loop in a bank balance program, along with the C# code. The loop starts with the keyword do. The body of the loop follows and is contained within curly braces. Within the loop, the next balance is calculated and the user is prompted for a response. The Boolean expression that controls loop execution is written using a `while` statement, placed after the loop body. The `bankBal` variable is output the first time before the user has any option of responding. At the end of the loop, the user is prompted, "Do you want to see next year's balance? Y or N...". Now the user has the option of seeing more balances, but the first view of the balance was unavoidable. The user's response is checked at the bottom of the loop. If it is *Y*, then the loop repeats.

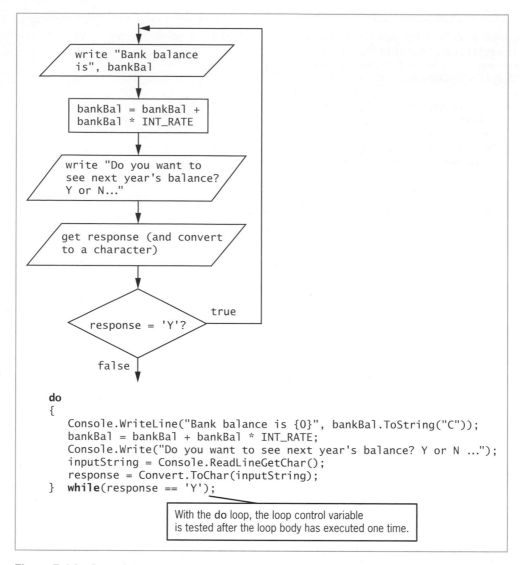

Figure 5-14   Part of the bank balance program using a **do** loop

In a **do** loop, as a matter of style, many programmers prefer to align the **while** expression with the **do** keyword that starts the loop. Others feel that placing the **while** expression on its own line increases the chances that readers might misinterpret the line as the start of its own **while** statement instead of marking the end of a **do** statement.

In any situation where you want to loop, you never are required to use a **do** loop. Within the bank balance example, you could unconditionally display the bank balance once, prompt the user, and then start a **while** loop that might not be entered. However, when a task must be performed at least one time, the **do** loop is convenient.

A while loop is a **pretest loop**—one in which the loop control variable is tested before the loop body executes. The do loop is a **posttest loop**—one in which the loop control variable is tested after the loop body executes.

TWO TRUTHS & A LIE

Using the do Loop

1. The do loop checks the bottom of the loop after one repetition has occurred.

2. The Boolean expression that controls do loop execution is written using a do statement, placed after the loop body.

3. You never are required to use a do loop; you can always substitute one execution of the body statements followed by a while loop.

The false statement is #2. The Boolean expression that controls do loop execution is written using a while statement, placed after the loop body.

You Do It

Using a do Loop

In the next steps, you revise the TippingTable program to use a do loop in place of the while loop.

1. Open the **TippingTable** program, change the class name to **TippingTable2**, and save the file as **TippingTable2**.

2. Cut the while loop clause (while(dinnerPrice <= MAXDINNER)) and replace it with **do**.

3. Paste the while loop clause just after the closing curly brace for the loop and before the final two curly braces in the program, and then add a semicolon.

4. Save, compile, and execute the program. The output is identical to the output in Figure 5-11.

Using Nested Loops

Like if statements, loop statements also can be nested. You can place a while loop within a while loop, a for loop within a for loop, a while loop within a for loop, or any other combination. When loops are nested, each pair contains an **inner loop** and an **outer loop**. The inner loop must be entirely contained within the outer loop; loops can never overlap. Figure 5-15 shows a diagram in which the shaded loop is nested within another loop; the shaded area is the inner loop as well as the body of the outer loop.

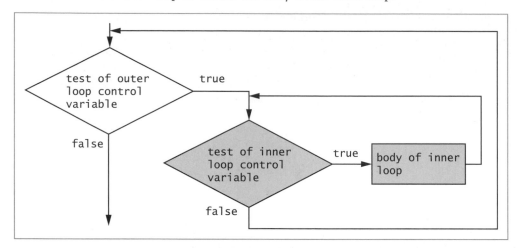

Figure 5-15   Nested loops

Suppose you want to display future bank balances for different years at a variety of interest rates. Figure 5-16 shows an application that contains an outer loop controlled by interest rates (starting with the first shaded statement in the figure) and an inner loop controlled by years (starting with the second shaded statement). The application displays annually compounded interest on $1000 at 4 percent, 6 percent, and 8 percent interest rates for 1 through 5 years. Figure 5-17 shows the output.

```
using System;
class LoopingBankBal2
{
    static void Main()
    {
        double bankBal;
        double rate;
        int year;
        const double START_BAL = 1000;
        const double START_INT = 0.04;
        const double INT_INCREASE = 0.02;
        const double LAST_INT = 0.08;
        const int END_YEAR = 5;
```

Figure 5-16   The LoopingBankBal2 program *(continues)*

(continued)

```
for(rate = START_INT; rate <= LAST_INT; rate += INT_INCREASE)
{
    bankBal = START_BAL;
    Console.WriteLine("Starting bank balance is {0}",
        bankBal.ToString("C"));
    Console.WriteLine("   Interest Rate: {0}",
        rate.ToString("P"));
    for(year = 1; year <= END_YEAR; ++year)
    {
        bankBal = bankBal + bankBal * rate;
        Console.WriteLine("    After year {0}, bank balance is {1}",
            year, bankBal.ToString("C"));
    }
}
}
}
```

Figure 5-16   The LoopingBankBal2 program

Figure 5-17   Output of the LoopingBankBal2 program

When you use a loop within a loop, you should always think of the outer loop as the all-encompassing loop. When you describe the task at hand, you often use the word "each" to refer to the inner loop. For example, if you wanted to output balances for different interest rates each year for 10 years, you could appropriately initialize some constants as follows:

```
const double RATE1 = 0.03;
const double RATE2 = 0.07
const double RATE_INCREASE = 0.01
const int END_YEAR = 10;
```

Then you could use the following nested for loops:

```
for(rate = RATE1; rate <= RATE2; rate += RATE_INCREASE)
   for(year = 1; year <= END_YEAR; ++year)
      Console.WriteLine(bankBal + bankBal * rate);
```

However, if you wanted to display balances for years 1 through 10 for each possible interest rate, you would use the following:

```
for(year = 1; year <= END_YEAR; ++year)
   for(rate = RATE1; rate <= RATE2; rate += RATE_INCREASE)
   Console.WriteLine(bankBal + bankBal * rate);
```

In both of these examples, the same 50 values would be displayed—five different interest rates for 10 years. However, in the first example, balances for years 1 through 10 would be displayed "within" each interest rate, and in the second example, each balance for each interest rate would be displayed "within" each year, 1 through 10. In other words, in the first example, the first 10 amounts displayed would be annual values using a rate of 0.03, and in the second example, the first five amounts displayed would be based on different interest values in the first year.

 Watch the video *Using Nested Loops*.

TWO TRUTHS & A LIE

Using Nested Loops

1. The body of the following loop executes six times:

```
for(a = 1;  a < 4;  ++a)
    for(b = 2;  b < 3;  ++b)
```

2. The body of the following loop executes four times:

```
for(c = 1;  c < 3;  ++c)
    for(d = 1;  d < 3;  ++d)
```

3. The body of the following loop executes 15 times:

```
for(e = 1;  e <= 5;  ++e)
    for(f = 2;  f <= 4;  ++f)
```

The false statement is #1. That loop executes only three times. First, a = 1, and it is less than 4, so the inner loop executes. In the inner loop, b is 2 and it is less than 3, so the loop body executes a second time. Then a becomes 3, and it is still less than 4, so the inner loop executes a third time. Then a becomes 4, and it is no longer less than 4, so the outer loop is done.

Accumulating Totals

Many computer programs display totals. When you receive a credit card or telephone service bill, you are usually provided with individual transaction details, but you are most interested in the total bill. Similarly, some programs total the number of credit hours generated by college students, the gross payroll for all employees of a company, or the total accounts receivable value for an organization. These totals are **accumulated**—that is, they are summed one at a time in a loop.

Figure 5-18 shows an example of an interactive program that accumulates the user's total purchases. The program prompts the user to enter a purchase price or 0 to quit. While the user continues to enter nonzero values, the amounts are added to a total. With each pass through the loop, the total is calculated to be its current amount plus the new purchase amount. After the user enters the loop-terminating 0, the accumulated total can be displayed. Figure 5-19 shows a typical program execution.

```csharp
using System;
class TotalPurchase
{
    static void Main()
    {
        double purchase;
        double total = 0;
        string inputString;
        const double QUIT = 0;
        Console.Write("Enter purchase amount >> ");
        inputString = Console.ReadLine();
        purchase = Convert.ToDouble(inputString);
        while(purchase != QUIT)
        {
            total += purchase;
            Console.Write("Enter next purchase amount, or " +
                QUIT + " to quit >> ");
            inputString = Console.ReadLine();
            purchase = Convert.ToDouble(inputString);
        }
        Console.WriteLine("Your total is {0}", total.ToString("C"));
    }
}
```

Figure 5-18   An application that accumulates total purchases entered by the user

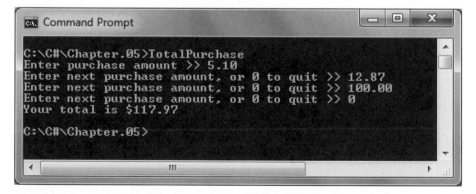

Figure 5-19   Typical execution of the TotalPurchase program

Recall from Chapter 2 that the expression total += purchase uses the shortcut add and assign operator, and that it is equivalent to total = total + purchase. The add and assign operator is most frequently used when a running total is kept.

In the application in Figure 5-18, it is very important that the total variable used for accumulation is set to 0 before the loop begins. When it is not, the program will not compile. When total is not initialized, it might hold any value. The value could be 0 by chance, but it also could be any other value that happens to be located at the memory address of total. (For example, by chance, it could hold 1000 and your total would end up $1000 too high.) An unknown value is known as **garbage**. The C# compiler prevents you from seeing an incorrect total by requiring you to provide a starting value; C# will not use the garbage value that happens to be stored at an uninitialized memory location.

In the application in Figure 5-18, the total variable must be initialized to 0, but the purchase variable is uninitialized. Many programmers would say it makes no sense to initialize this variable because no matter what starting value you provide, the value can be changed by the first input statement before the variable is ever used. As a matter of style, this book generally does not initialize variables if the initialization value is never used; doing so might mislead you into thinking the starting value had some purpose.

TWO TRUTHS & A LIE

Accumulating Totals

1. When totals are accumulated, 1 is added to a variable that represents the total.

2. A variable used to hold a total must be set to 0 before it is used to accumulate a total.

3. The C# compiler will not allow you to accumulate totals in an uninitialized variable.

The false statement is #1. When totals are accumulated, any value might be added to a variable that represents the total. For example, if you total 10 test scores, then each score is added. If you add only 1 to a total variable on each cycle through a loop, then you are counting rather than accumulating a total.

Improving Loop Performance

Whether you decide to use a while, for, or do loop in an application, you can improve loop performance by doing the following:

- Make sure the loop avoids unnecessary operations.

- Consider the order of evaluation for short-circuit operators.

- Make comparisons to 0.

- Employ loop fusion.

- Use prefix incrementing rather than postfix incrementing.

Avoiding Unnecessary Operations

You can improve loop performance by making sure the loop does not include unnecessary operations or statements. For example, suppose that a loop should execute while x is less than the sum of two integers a and b, and that neither a nor b is altered in the loop body. The loop could be written as:

```
while(x < a + b)
    // loop body
```

If this loop executes 1000 times, then the expression a + b is calculated 1000 times. Instead, if you use the following code, the results are the same, but the arithmetic is performed only once:

```
int sum = a + b;
while(x < sum)
    // loop body
```

Of course, if a or b is altered in the loop body, then a new sum must be calculated with every loop iteration. However, if the sum of a and b is fixed prior to the start of the loop, then writing the code the second way is far more efficient.

As another example, suppose you need a temporary variable within a loop to use for some calculation. The loop could be written as follows:

```
while(x < LIMIT)
{
    int tempTotal = a + b;
    // more statements here
}
```

When you declare a variable like tempTotal within a loop, it exists only for the duration of the loop; that is, it exists only until the loop's closing brace. Each time the loop executes, the variable is re-created. A more efficient solution is to declare the variable outside of the loop, as follows:

```
int tempTotal;
while(x < LIMIT)
{
    tempTotal = a + b;
    // more statements here
}
```

It is more efficient to declare this variable outside the loop than to redeclare it on every loop iteration.

Considering the Order of Evaluation of Short-Circuit Operators

In Chapter 4, you learned that the expressions in each part of an AND or OR expression use short-circuit evaluation; that is, they are evaluated only as much as necessary to determine whether the entire expression is true or false. When a loop might execute many times, it becomes increasingly important to consider the number of evaluations that take place.

For example, suppose that a user can request any number of printed copies of a report from 1 to 15, and you want to validate the user's input before proceeding. If you believe that users are far more likely to enter a value that is too high than to enter a negative value, then you want to start a loop that reprompts the user with the following expression:

```
while(requestedNum > 15 || requestedNum < 1)...
```

Because you believe that the first Boolean expression is more likely to be true than the second one, you can eliminate testing the second one on more occasions. The order of the expressions is not very important in a single loop, but if this loop is nested within another loop, then the difference in the number of tests increases. Similarly, the order of the evaluations in `if` statements is more important when the `if` statements are nested within a loop.

Comparing to Zero

Making a comparison to 0 is faster than making a comparison to any other value. Therefore, if your application makes comparison to 0 feasible, you can improve performance by structuring your loops to compare the loop control variable to 0 instead of some other value. For example, a loop based on a variable that ranges from 0 up to 100,000 executes the same number of times as a loop based on a variable that varies from 100,000 down to 0. However, the second loop performs slightly faster. Comparing a value to 0 instead of other values is faster because in a compiled language, condition flags for the comparison are set once, no matter how many times the loop executes. Comparing a value to 0 is faster than comparing to other values, no matter which comparison operator you use—greater than, less than, equal to, and so on.

You can prove that loops that use zero comparisons are faster by writing a test program. An easy way to compare loop execution times is to use C#'s Stopwatch class. You will better understand how this class works after you read Chapter 9, *Using Classes and Objects*, but you can use the class now by making statements similar to the following:

```
Stopwatch sw = Stopwatch.StartNew();
  // Place statements to be timed here
sw.Stop();
```

The first statement creates and starts a `Stopwatch` object for timing events. The object's name is `sw`—you can use any legal C# identifier. The last statement stops the `Stopwatch`. Subsequently, you can use a statement similar to the following to output the object's elapsed time in milliseconds:

```
Console.WriteLine("Time used: {0} ms",sw.Elapsed.TotalMilliseconds);
```

Figure 5-20 contains a program that uses the `Stopwatch` class to test the execution times of two do-nothing loops. (A **do-nothing loop** is one that performs no actions other than looping.) The statement `using System.Diagnostics;` is needed for the `Stopwatch` class. Both loops in the figure execute the same number of times, but one uses a zero comparison and the other does not. Before each loop, a `Stopwatch` object is started, and after each loop repeats 10 million times, the `Stopwatch` is stopped. As the execution in Figure 5-21 shows, there is a small difference in execution time between the two loops—about five milliseconds. The amount of time will vary on different machines, and it will also vary if you run the same program multiple times because you cannot control what other operations your system might need to perform in the background while your C# program is running. The difference in the durations of the two loops would become more pronounced with additional repetitions or the addition of other tasks to the loops.

```
using System;
using System.Diagnostics;
class TimeZeroComparison
{
    static void Main()
    {
        int LOOPS = 10000000;
        Stopwatch sw = Stopwatch.StartNew();
        for(int x = 0; x < LOOPS; ++x);
        sw.Stop();
        Stopwatch sw2 = Stopwatch.StartNew();
        for(int x = LOOPS; x >= 0; --x);
        sw2.Stop();
        Console.WriteLine("Time used comparing to {0}: {1} ms",
            LOOPS, sw.Elapsed.TotalMilliseconds);
        Console.WriteLine("Time used comparing to 0        : {0} ms",
            sw2.Elapsed.TotalMilliseconds);
    }
}
```

Figure 5-20   The TimeZeroComparison program

Figure 5-21   Typical execution of the TimeZeroComparison program

For example, if the loops in the program in Figure 5-20 used the loop control variable to display a count to the user, then they might need to increment the variable, and comparing to zero would not be practical. However, if the purposes of the loops are just to count iterations, you might consider making the loop comparison use 0.

Employing Loop Fusion

Loop fusion is the technique of combining two loops into one. For example, suppose that you want to call two methods 100 times each. You can set a constant named TIMES to 100 and use the following code:

```
for(int x = 0; x < TIMES; ++x)
    method1();
for(int x = 0; x < TIMES; ++x)
    method2();
```

However, you can also use the following code:

```
for(int x = 0; x < TIMES; ++x)
{
    method1();
    method2();
}
```

Fusing loops will not work in every situation; sometimes all the activities for method1() must be finished before those in method2() can begin. However, if the two methods do not depend on each other, fusing the loops can improve performance. Performance issues can be crucial when you write programs for small mobile devices such as phones. On the other hand, if saving a few milliseconds ends up making your code harder to understand, you almost always should err in favor of slower but more readable programs.

Using Prefix Incrementing Rather than Postfix Incrementing

Probably the most common action after the second semicolon in a for statement is to increment the loop control variable. In most textbooks and in many professional programs, the postfix increment operator is used for this purpose, as in the following:

```
for(int x = 0; x < LIMIT; x++)
```

Because incrementing x is a stand-alone statement in the for loop, the result is identical whether you use x++ or ++x. However, using the prefix increment operator produces a faster loop. Consider the program in Figure 5-22. It is similar to the TimeZeroComparison application in Figure 5-20, but instead of comparing loops that count up and down, it compares loops that use prefix and postfix incrementing. Figure 5-23 shows the output of the program.

```
using System;
using System.Diagnostics;
class PrefixPostfixComparison
{
    static void Main()
    {
        int LOOPS = 10000000;
        Stopwatch sw = Stopwatch.StartNew();
        for(int x = 0; x < LOOPS; ++x);
        sw.Stop();
        Stopwatch sw2 = Stopwatch.StartNew();
        for(int x = 0; x < LOOPS; x++);
        sw2.Stop();
        Console.WriteLine("Time with prefix increment: {0} ms",
            sw.Elapsed.TotalMilliseconds);
        Console.WriteLine("Time with postfix increment: {0} ms",
            sw2.Elapsed.TotalMilliseconds);
    }
}
```

Figure 5-22   The PrefixPostfixComparison program

Figure 5-23   Typical execution of the PrefixPostfixComparison program

The program that uses prefix incrementing runs slightly faster than the one that uses postfix incrementing. The difference in duration for the loops is very small, but it would increase if tasks were added to the loop bodies. If you run the PrefixPostfixComparison program multiple times, you will get different results, and occasionally the prefix operator loop might take longer than the postfix loop because other programs are running concurrently on your computer. However, using the prefix operator typically saves a small amount of time. As a professional, you will encounter programmers who insist on using either postfix or prefix increments in their loops. You should follow the conventions established by your organization, but now you have the tools to prove that prefix incrementing is faster.

As you continue to study programming, you will discover many situations in which you can make your programs more efficient. You should always be on the lookout for ways to improve program performance without sacrificing readability.

TWO TRUTHS & A LIE

Improving Loop Performance

1. You can improve loop performance by making sure the loop does not include unnecessary operations or statements.

2. You can improve loop performance by declaring temporary variables outside of a loop instead of continuously redeclaring them.

3. You can improve loop performance by omitting the initialization of the loop control variable.

The false statement is #3. A loop control variable must be initialized for every loop.

Looping Issues in GUI Programs

Using a loop within a method in a GUI application is no different from using one in a console application; you can use while, for, and do statements in the same ways in both types of programs. For example, Figure 5-24 shows a GUI Form that prompts a user to enter a number and then displays "Hello" the corresponding number of times. The image on the left shows the Form when the program starts, and the image on the right shows the output after the user enters a value and clicks the button. Figure 5-25 shows the code in the greetingsButton_Click() method. When a user clicks the greetingsButton, an integer is extracted from the TextBox on the Form. Then a for loop appends "Hello" and a newline character to the Text property of the outputLabel the correct number of times.

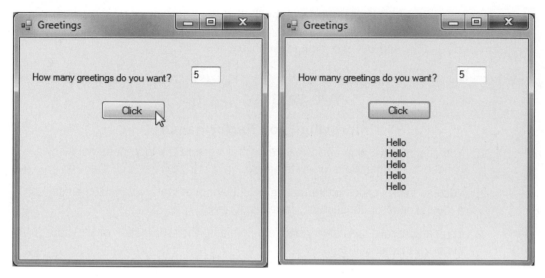

Figure 5-24   The Greetings Form when it starts and after the user enters a number and clicks the button

```
private void greetingsButton_Click(object sender, EventArgs e)
{
   int numGreetings = Convert.ToInt32(greetingsTextBox.Text);
   int count;
   for (count = 0; count < numGreetings; ++count)
      outputLabel.Text += "Hello\n";
}
```

Figure 5-25   The greetingsButton_Click() method in the ManyHellosGUI application

Event-driven programs sometimes require fewer coded loops than their counterpart console applications, because in these programs some events are determined by the user's actions when the program is running, rather than by the programmer's coding beforehand. You can write an event-driven program so that an action continues as long as the user continues to make an appropriate selection. Depending on the application, the sentinel value for this sort of implicit loop might occur when the user clicks a button that indicates "quit," or clicks the close button on the Form that hosts the application.

For example, Figure 5-26 shows a Form that controls a bank balance application similar to the one shown earlier in this chapter in Figure 5-7. The left side of the figure shows the Form when the application starts, and the right side shows the Form after the user has clicked the Yes button three times. Figure 5-27 shows the significant Form class code.

Figure 5-26   The BankBalance Form when it starts and after the user has clicked Yes three times

```
namespace LoopingBankBalGUI
{
    partial class Form1 : Form
    {
        double bankBal = 1000;
        const double INT_RATE = 0.04;
        private void yesButton_Click(object sender, EventArgs e)
        {
            outputLabel.Text += String.Format("Bank balance is {0}\n",
                bankBal.ToString("C"));
            bankBal = bankBal + bankBal * INT_RATE;
        }

        private void noButton_Click(object sender, EventArgs e)
        {
            outputLabel.Text = "Have a nice day!";
        }
    }
}
```

Figure 5-27   Code for the LoopingBankBalGUI program

In the `LoopingBankBalGUI` program, you might also choose to disable the Yes button or make it invisible so that the user cannot select it again after clicking No.

230

No loop is written in the code in Figure 5-27 because a loop body execution is caused automatically each time a user clicks the Yes button on the `Form`. Whenever `yesButton_Click()` executes, the `Text` of the `outputLabel` is appended to include a new line that displays the bank balance, and then the bank balance is increased by the interest rate. It is important that the `bankBal` variable is initialized outside the `yesButton_Click()` method; if it was initialized within the method, the balance would be reset to the original value of $1000 with each new button click. In the application in Figure 5-27, the balances in the `outputLabel` are replaced with "Have a nice day!" when the user indicates no more balances are needed.

Chapter Summary

- You can use a `while` loop to execute a body of statements continuously while a condition continues to be `true`. A `while` loop consists of the keyword `while`, followed by a Boolean expression within parentheses, followed by the body of the loop, which can be a single statement or a block of statements surrounded by curly braces.

- A `for` statement includes loop control variable initialization, the test condition that controls loop entry, and the expression that alters the loop control variable. You begin a `for` statement with the keyword `for`, followed by a set of parentheses. Within the parentheses, the initialization, test, and update sections are separated by exactly two semicolons.

- The `do` loop checks the loop-controlling Boolean expression at the bottom of the loop after one repetition has occurred.

- You can nest any combination of loops.

- In computer programs, totals frequently are accumulated—that is, summed one at a time in a loop.

- You can improve loop performance by making sure the loop does not include unnecessary operations or statements, considering the order of evaluation for short-circuit operators, using comparisons to zero, employing loop fusion, and using prefix incrementing.

- You can use `while`, `for`, and `do` statements in the same ways in console and GUI programs. However, event-driven programs sometimes require fewer coded loops than console applications because some events are determined by the user's actions when the program is running, rather than by the programmer's coding beforehand.

Key Terms

A **loop** is a structure that allows repeated execution of a block of statements.

A **loop body** is the block of statements executed in a loop.

An **iteration** is one execution of any loop.

A **while loop** executes a body of statements continuously while a test condition continues to be **true**; it uses the keyword **while**.

An **infinite loop** is one that (theoretically) never ends.

A **loop control variable** determines whether loop execution will continue.

An **empty body** has no statements in it.

Incrementing a variable means adding a value to it. (Specifically, the term often means to add 1 to a variable.)

Decrementing a variable means subtracting a value from it. (Specifically, the term often means to subtract 1 from a variable.)

In a **definite loop**, the number of iterations is predetermined.

A **counted loop** is a definite loop.

In an **indefinite loop**, the number of iterations is not predetermined.

A **sentinel value** is one that a user must supply to stop a loop.

A **for loop** contains the starting value for the loop control variable, the test condition that controls loop entry, and the expression that alters the loop control variable, all in one statement.

A **step value** is the amount by which a loop control variable is altered, especially in a **for** loop.

Out of scope describes a program component that is not usable because it has ceased to exist.

The **do loop** (also called a **do...while loop**) checks the loop-controlling Boolean expression at the bottom of the loop after one repetition has occurred.

In a **pretest loop**, the loop control variable is tested before the loop body executes.

In a **posttest loop**, the loop control variable is tested after the loop body executes.

An **inner loop** is the loop in a pair of nested loops that is entirely contained within another loop.

An **outer loop** is the loop in a pair of nested loops that contains another loop.

Accumulated totals are computed by adding values one at a time in a loop.

Garbage is a term used to describe an unknown memory value.

A **do-nothing loop** is one that performs no actions other than looping.

Loop fusion is the technique of combining two loops into one.

Review Questions

1. A structure that allows repeated execution of a block of statements is a(n) _____.

    a. sequence   c. loop
    b. selection   d. array

2. The body of a `while` loop can consist of _____.

    a. a single statement
    b. a block of statements within curly braces
    c. either a or b
    d. neither a nor b

3. A loop that never ends is called a(n) _____ loop.

    a. `while`   c. counted
    b. `for`   d. infinite

4. Which of the following is not required of a loop control variable in a correctly working loop?

    a. It is reset to its initial value before the loop ends.
    b. It is initialized before the loop starts.
    c. It is tested.
    d. It is altered in the loop body.

5. A `while` loop with an empty body contains no _____.

    a. loop control variable
    b. statements
    c. curly braces
    d. test within the parentheses of the `while` statement

6. A loop for which you do not know the number of iterations when you write it is a(n) _____.

    a. definite loop   c. counted loop
    b. indefinite loop   d. `for` loop

7. What is the major advantage of using a `for` loop instead of a `while` loop?

    a. With a `for` loop, it is impossible to create an infinite loop.
    b. It is the only way to achieve an indefinite loop.
    c. Unlike with a `while` loop, the execution of multiple statements can depend on the test condition.
    d. The loop control variable is initialized, tested, and altered all in one place.

8. A `for` loop statement must contain _____.

    a. two semicolons
    b. three commas
    c. four dots
    d. five pipes

9. In a `for` statement, the section before the first semicolon executes _____.

    a. once
    b. once prior to each loop iteration
    c. once after each loop iteration
    d. one less time than the initial loop control variable value

10. The three sections of the `for` loop are most commonly used for _____ the loop control variable.

    a. testing, outputting, and incrementing
    b. initializing, testing, and incrementing
    c. incrementing, selecting, and testing
    d. initializing, converting, and outputting

11. Which loop is most convenient to use if the loop body must always execute at least once?

    a. a do loop
    b. a while loop
    c. a for loop
    d. an if loop

12. The loop control variable is checked at the bottom of which kind of loop?

    a. a while loop
    b. a do loop
    c. a for loop
    d. all of the above

13. A `for` loop is an example of a(n) _____ loop.

    a. untested
    b. pretest
    c. posttest
    d. infinite

14. A `while` loop is an example of a(n) _____ loop.

    a. untested
    b. pretest
    c. posttest
    d. infinite

15. When a loop is placed within another loop, the loops are said to be _____.

    a. infinite   c. nested
    b. bubbled   d. overlapping

16. What does the following code segment display?

```
a = 1;
while (a < 5);
{
    Console.Write("{0} ", a);
    ++a;
}
```

    a. 1 2 3 4   c. 4
    b. 1   d. nothing

17. What is the output of the following code segment?

```
s = 1;
while (s < 4)
    ++s;
    Console.Write(" {0}", s);
```

    a. 1   c. 1 2 3 4
    b. 4   d. 2 3 4

18. What is the output of the following code segment?

```
j = 5;
while(j > 0)
{
    Console.Write("{0} ", j);
    j--;
}
```

    a. 0   c. 5 4 3 2 1
    b. 5   d. 5 4 3 2 1 0

19. What does the following code segment display?

```
for(f = 0; f < 3; ++f);
    Console.Write("{0} ", f);
```

    a. 0   c. 3
    b. 0 1 2   d. nothing

20. What does the following code segment display?

```
for(t = 0; t < 3; ++t)
    Console.Write("{0} ", t);
```

    a. 0   c. 0 1 2
    b. 0 1   d. 0 1 2 3

Exercises

Programming Exercises

1.   a. Write a console-based application named **SumFiveDoubles** that allows the user to enter five `doubles` and displays their sum.

  b. Write a console-based application named **SumDoubles** that allows the user to enter any number of `doubles` continuously until the user enters 999. Display the sum of the values entered, not including 999.

2.   Write a console-based application named **EnterLowercaseLetters** that asks the user to type a lowercase letter from the keyboard. If the character entered is a lowercase letter, display "OK"; if it is not a lowercase letter, display an error message. The program continues until the user types '!'.

3.   Write a console-based application named **CreditScores** that continuously prompts a user for consumer credit scores until the user enters a sentinel value. A valid credit score ranges from 300 through 850. When the user enters a valid score, add it to a total; when the user enters an invalid credit score, display an error message. Before the program ends, display the average of the credit scores entered.

4.   The Anderson, Bowman, and Claxton families are running their annual garage sale. Write a console-based application named **GarageSale** that prompts the user for a family initial (*A*, *B*, or *C*). Either uppercase or lowercase initials are valid. While the user does not type *Z*, continue by prompting for the amount of a sale. Keep a running total of the amount earned by each family. After the user types *Z* or *z* for an initial, display each family's total as well as a grand total made at the garage sale.

5.   a. Write a console-based application named **DisplayMultiplicationTable** that displays a table of the products of every combination of two integers from 1 through 10.

  b. Create a GUI application named **DisplayMultiplicationTableGUI** that displays the multiplication table when the user clicks a button.

6.   a. Write a console-based application named **OddNums** that displays all the odd numbers from 1 through 99.

  b. Create a GUI application named **OddNumsGUI** that displays all the odd numbers from 1 through 99 when the user clicks a button.

7.   a. Write a console-based application named **TableOfSquares** that displays every integer value from 1 to 20, along with its squared value.

  b. Create a GUI application named **TableOfSquaresGUI** that displays every integer from 1 to 20, along with its squared value, when the user clicks a button.

8. a. Write a console-based application named **Sum100** that sums the integers from 1 through 100.

   b. Create a GUI application named **Sum100GUI** that sums the integers from 1 through 100. Display the sum when the user clicks a button.

9. a. Write a console-based application named **Perfect** that displays every perfect number from 1 through 1000. A number is perfect if it equals the sum of all the smaller positive integers that divide evenly into it. For example, 6 is perfect because 1, 2, and 3 divide evenly into it and their sum is 6.

   b. Create a GUI application named **PerfectGUI** that displays every perfect number from 1 through 1000 when the user clicks a button.

10. a. In a "You Do It" section of this chapter, you created a tipping table for patrons to use when analyzing their restaurant bills. Now, create a modified program named **TippingTable2** in which each of the following values is obtained from user input:

    • The lowest tipping percentage

    • The highest tipping percentage

    • The lowest possible restaurant bill

    • The highest restaurant bill

    b. Create a GUI application named **TippingTable2GUI** that creates a tipping table after the user clicks a button. Get the lowest and highest tipping percentages and the lowest and highest restaurant bills from TextBox entries. The application should look similar to Figure 5-28.

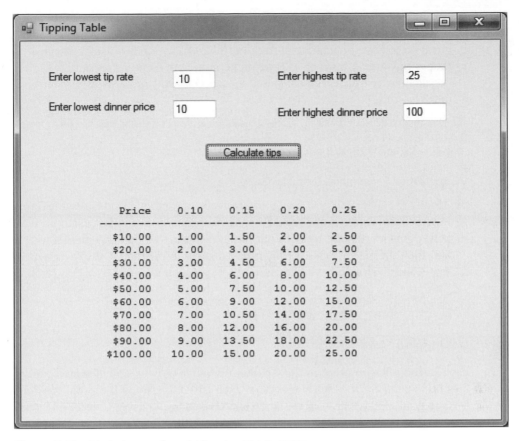

Figure 5-28 Typical execution of TippingTable2GUI program

11. a. Write a console based program named **WebAddress** that asks a user for a business name. Suggest a good Web address by adding "www." to the front of the name, removing all spaces from the name, and adding ".com" to the end of the name. For example, a good Web address for "Acme Plumbing and Supply" is *www.AcmePlumbingandSupply.com*.

    b. Create a GUI application named **WebAddressGUI** that creates a Web address name from a business name, as described in Exercise 11a.

12. a. Write a console-based program named **CountVowels** that accepts a phrase from the user and counts the number of vowels in the phrase. For this exercise, count both uppercase and lowercase vowels, but do not consider "y" to be a vowel.

    b. Create a GUI application named **CountVowelsGUI** that counts vowels, as described in Exercise 12a.

13.   a.   In Chapter 4, you created a console-based program that generates a random number, allows a user to guess it, and displays a message indicating whether the guess is too low, too high, or correct. Now, create a modified program called **GuessingGame2** in which the user can continue to enter values until the correct guess is made. After the user guesses correctly, display the number of guesses made.

Recall that you can generate a random number whose value is at least `min` and less than `max` using the following statements:

```
Random ranNumber = new Random();
int randomNumber;
randomNumber = ranNumber.Next(min, max);
```

b.   Modify the `GuessingGame2` program to create a program called **GuessingGame3** in which the player is criticized for making a "dumb" guess. For example, if the player guesses that the random number is 4 and is told that the guess is too low, and then the player subsequently makes a guess lower than 4, display a message that the user should have known not to make such a low guess.

Debugging Exercises

1.   Each of the following files in the Chapter.05 folder of your downloadable student files has syntax and/or logical errors. In each case, determine the problem and fix the program. After you correct the errors, save each file using the same filename preceded with *Fixed*. For example, save DebugFive1.cs as **FixedDebugFive1.cs**.

a.   DebugFive1.cs   c.   DebugFive3.cs

b.   DebugFive2.cs   d.   DebugFive4.cs

Case Problems

1.   In Chapter 4, you created an interactive application named **GreenvilleRevenue** that prompts a user for the number of contestants entered in this year's and last year's Greenville Idol competition and displays the revenue expected for this year's competition if each contestant pays a $25 entrance fee. The program also displays one of three appropriate statements specified in the case problem in Chapter 4, based on a comparison between the number of contestants this year and last year. Now, modify the program so that the user must enter a number between 0 and 30 inclusive for the number of contestants each year. If the user enters an incorrect number, the program prompts for a valid value.

2.   In Chapter 4, you created an interactive application named **MarshallsRevenue** that prompts a user for the number of interior and exterior murals scheduled to be painted during a month and computes the expected revenue for each type of mural.

The program also prompts the user for the month number and modifies the pricing based on requirements listed in Chapter 4. Now, modify the program so that the user must enter a month value from 1 through 12. If the user enters an incorrect number, the program prompts for a valid value. Also, the user must enter a number between 0 and 30 inclusive for the number of murals of each type; otherwise, the program prompts the user again.

CHAPTER 6

Using Arrays

In this chapter you will:

- ◎ Declare an array and assign values to array elements
- ◎ Access array elements
- ◎ Search an array using a loop
- ◎ Use the `BinarySearch()`, `Sort()`, and `Reverse()` methods
- ◎ Use multidimensional arrays
- ◎ Learn about array issues in GUI programs

Storing values in variables provides programs with flexibility; a program that uses variables to replace constants can manipulate different values each time it executes. When you add loops to your programs, the same variable can hold different values during successive cycles through the loop within the same program execution. This ability makes the program even more flexible. Learning to use the data structure known as an array offers further flexibility. Arrays allow you to store multiple values in adjacent memory locations and access them by varying a value that indicates which of the stored values to use. In this chapter, you will learn to create and manage C# arrays.

Declaring an Array and Assigning Values to Array Elements

Sometimes, storing just one value in memory at a time isn't adequate. For example, a sales manager who supervises 20 employees might want to determine whether each employee has produced sales above or below the average amount. When you enter the first employee's sales figure into a program, you can't determine whether it is above or below average because you won't know the average until you have entered all 20 figures. You might plan to assign 20 sales figures to 20 separate variables, each with a unique name, then sum and average them. However, that process is awkward and unwieldy: You need 20 prompts, 20 input statements using 20 separate storage locations (in other words, 20 separate variable names), and 20 addition statements. This method might work for 20 salespeople, but what if you have 30, 40, or 10,000 salespeople?

A superior approach is to assign the sales value to the same variable in 20 successive iterations through a loop that contains one prompt, one input statement, and one addition statement. Unfortunately, when you enter the sales value for the second employee, that data item replaces the figure for the first employee, and the first employee's value is no longer available to compare to the average of all 20 values. With this approach, when the data-entry loop finishes, the only sales value left in memory is the last one entered.

The best solution to this problem is to create an array. An **array** is a list of data items that all have the same data type and the same name. Each object in an array is an **array element**. You can distinguish each element from the others in an array with a subscript. A **subscript** (also called an **index**) is an integer contained within square brackets that indicates the position of particular array elements.

You declare an array variable with a data type, a pair of square brackets, and an identifier. For example, to declare an array of `double` values to hold sales figures for salespeople, you write the following:

```
double[] sales;
```

In some programming languages, such as C++ and Java, you also can declare an array variable by placing the square brackets after the array name, as in `double sales[];`. This format is illegal in C#.

You can provide any legal identifier you want for an array, but programmers conventionally name arrays like they name variables—starting with a lowercase letter and using uppercase letters to begin subsequent words. Additionally, many programmers observe one of the following conventions to make it more obvious that the name represents a group of items:

- Arrays are often named using a plural noun such as `sales`.

- Arrays are often named by adding a final word that implies a group, such as `salesList`, `salesTable`, or `salesArray`.

After you create an array variable, you still need to create the actual array. Declaring an array and reserving memory space for it are two distinct processes. To reserve memory locations for 20 `sales` objects, you declare the array variable with the following two statements:

```
double[] sales;
sales = new double[20];
```

The keyword **new** is also known as the **new operator**; it is used to create objects. In this case, it creates 20 separate `sales` elements. You also can declare and create an array in one statement, such as the following:

```
double[] sales = new double[20];
```

> You can change the size of an array associated with an identifier, if necessary. For example, if you declare `int[] array;`, you can assign five elements later with `array = new int[5];`; later in the program, you might alter the array size to 100 with `array = new int[100];`. Still later, you could alter it again to be either larger or smaller. Most other programming languages do not provide this capability. If you resize an array in C#, the same identifier refers to a new array in memory and all the values are set to 0.

The statement `double[] sales = new double[20];` reserves 20 memory locations. In C#, an array's elements are numbered beginning with 0, so if an array has 20 elements, you can use any subscript from 0 through 19. In other words, the first `sales` array element is `sales[0]` and the last `sales` element is `sales[19]`. Figure 6-1 shows how the array of 20 sales figures appears in computer memory. The figure assumes that the array begins at memory address 20000. When you instantiate an array, you cannot choose its location in memory any more than you can choose the location of any other variable. However, you do know that after the first array element, the subsequent elements will follow immediately. Because a `double` takes eight bytes of storage, each element of the array is stored in succession at an address that is eight bytes higher than the previous one.

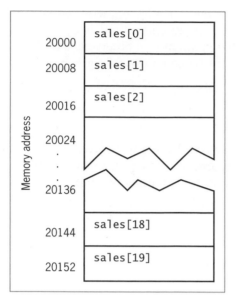

Figure 6-1   An array of 20 `sales` items in memory

In C#, an array subscript must be an integer. For example, no array contains an element with a subscript of 1.5. A subscript can be an integer constant or variable or an expression that evaluates to an integer. For example, if x and y are integers and their sum is at least 0 but less than the size of an array named `array`, then it is legal to refer to `array[x + y]`.

 Some other languages, such as COBOL, BASIC, and Visual Basic, use parentheses rather than square brackets to refer to individual array elements. By using brackets, the creators of C# made it easier for you to distinguish arrays from methods. Like C#, C++ and Java also use brackets surrounding array subscripts.

A common mistake is to forget that the first element in an array is element 0 (sometimes called the zeroth element), especially if you know another programming language in which the first array element is element 1. Making this mistake means you will be "off by one" in your use of any array. If you are "off by one" but still using a valid subscript when accessing an array element, your program will produce incorrect output. If you are "off by one" so that your subscript becomes larger than the highest value allowed, you will cause a program error.

To remember that array elements begin with element 0, it might be helpful to think of the first array element as being "zero elements away from" the beginning of the array, the second element as being "one element away from" the beginning of the array, and so on.

When you work with any individual array element, you treat it no differently than you treat a single variable of the same type. For example, to assign a value to the first `sales` in an array, you use a simple assignment statement, such as the following:

```
sales[0] = 2100.00;
```

To output the value of the last **sales** in a 20-element array, you write:

```
Console.WriteLine(sales[19]);
```

 Watch the video *Declaring Arrays*.

Initializing an Array

In C#, arrays are objects. When you instantiate an array, you are creating a specific instance of a class that derives from, or builds upon, the built-in class named **System.Array**. (In the chapter *Introduction to Inheritance*, you will learn more about deriving classes.)

When you declare arrays or any other objects, the following default values are assigned to the elements:

- Numeric fields are set to 0.

- Character fields are set to '\u0000' or **null**. (You learned about the notation '\u0000' in Chapter 2.)

- **bool** fields are set to **false**.

For example, when you declare an array of five **int**s, each of the elements is initialized to 0.

You can assign nondefault values to array elements at declaration by including a comma-separated list of values enclosed within curly braces. For example, if you want to create an array named **myScores** and store five test scores within the array, you can use any of the following declarations:

```
int[] myScores - new int[5] {100, 76, 88, 100, 90};
int[] myScores = new int[] {100, 76, 88, 100, 90};
int[] myScores = {100, 76, 88, 100, 90};
```

The list of values provided for an array is an **initializer list**. When you initialize an array by providing a size and an initializer list, as in the first example, the stated size and number of list elements must match. However, when you initialize an array with values, you are not required to give the array a size, as shown in the second example; in that case, the size is assigned based on the number of values in the initializing list. The third example shows that when you initialize an array, you do not need to use the keyword **new** and repeat the type; instead, memory is assigned based on the stated array type and the length of the list of provided values. Of these three examples, the first is most explicit, but it requires two changes if the number of elements is altered. The third example requires the least typing, but might not clarify that a new object is being created. Microsoft's documentation prefers the third example because it is most concise, but you should use the form of array initialization that is clearest to you or that is conventional in your organization.

When you use curly braces at the end of a block of code, you do not follow the closing curly brace with a semicolon. However, when you use curly braces to enclose a list of array values, you must complete the statement with a semicolon. Programmers who have used other languages such as C++ might expect that when an initialization list is shorter than the number of declared array elements, the "extra" elements will be set to default values. This is not the case in C#; if you declare a size, then you must list a value for each element.

An array of characters can be assigned to a string. For example, you can write the following:

```
char[] arrayOfLetters = {'h', 'e', 'l', 'l', 'o'};
string word = new string(arrayOfLetters);
```

TWO TRUTHS & A LIE

Declaring an Array and Assigning Values to Array Elements

1. To reserve memory locations for 10 testScore objects, you can use the following statement:

   ```
   int[] testScore = new int[9];
   ```

2. To assign 60 to the last element in a 10-element array named testScore, you can use the following statement:

   ```
   testScore[9] = 60;
   ```

3. The following statement creates an array named purchases and stores four values within the array:

   ```
   double[] purchases = new double [] {23.55, 99.20, 4.67, 9.99};
   ```

The false statement is #1. To reserve memory locations for 10 testScore objects, you must use 10 within the second set of square braces. The 10 elements will use the subscripts 0 through 9.

Accessing Array Elements

If you treat each array element as an individual entity, declaring an array doesn't offer much of an advantage over declaring individual variables. The power of arrays becomes apparent when you use subscripts that are variables rather than constant values.

For example, when you declare an array of five integers, such as the following, you often want to perform the same operation on each array element:

```
int[] myScores = {100, 76, 88, 100, 90};
```

To increase each array element by 3, for example, you can write the following five statements:

```
myScores[0] += 3;
myScores[1] += 3;
myScores[2] += 3;
myScores[3] += 3;
myScores[4] += 3;
```

You can shorten the task by using a variable as a subscript. Then you can use a loop to perform arithmetic on each element in the array. For example, you can use a while loop, as follows:

```
int sub = 0;
while(sub < 5)
{
    myScores[sub] += 3;
    ++sub;
}
```

You also can use a for loop, as follows:

```
for(int sub = 0; sub < 5; ++sub)
    myScores[sub] += 3;
```

In both examples, the variable sub is declared and initialized to 0, then compared to 5. Because it is less than 5, the loop executes and myScores[0] increases by 3. The variable sub is incremented and becomes 1, which is still less than 5, so when the loop executes again, myScores[1] increases by 3, and so on. If the array had 100 elements, individually increasing the array values by 3 would require 95 additional statements, but the only change required using either loop would be to change the limiting value for sub from 5 to 100.

New array users sometimes think there is a permanent connection between a variable used as a subscript and the array with which it is used, but that is not the case. For example, if you vary sub from 0 to 10 to fill an array, you do not need to use sub later when displaying the array elements—either the same variable or a different variable can be used as a subscript elsewhere in the program.

Using the Length Property

When you work with array elements, you must ensure that the subscript you use remains in the range of 0 through one less than the array's length. If you declare an array with five elements and use a subscript that is negative or more than 4, you will receive the error message "IndexOutOfRangeException" when you run the program. (You will learn about the IndexOutOfRangeException in the chapter *Exception Handling*.) This message means the index, or subscript, does not hold a value that legally can access an array element. For example, if you declare an array of five integers, you can display them as follows:

```
int[] myScores = {100, 75, 88, 100, 90};
for(int sub = 0; sub < 5; ++sub)
    Console.WriteLine("{0} ", myScores[sub]);
```

If you modify your program to change the size of the array, you must remember to change the comparison in the for loop as well as every other reference to the array size within the program. Many text editors have a "find and replace" feature that lets you change (for example) all of the 5s in a file, either simultaneously or one by one. However, you must be careful not to change 5s that have nothing to do with the array; for example, do not change the 5 in the score 75 inadvertently—it is the second listed value in the myScores array and has nothing to do with the array size.

A better approach is to use a value that is automatically altered when you declare an array. Because every array automatically derives from the class **System.Array**, you can use the fields and methods that are part of the System.Array class with any array you create. In Chapter 2, you learned that every string has a Length property. Similarly, every array has a **Length property** that is a member of the System.Array class and that automatically holds an array's length. The Length property is always updated to reflect any changes you make to an array's size. The following segment of code displays "Array size is 5" and subsequently displays the array's contents:

```
int[] myScores = {100, 76, 88, 100, 90};
Console.WriteLine("Array size is {0}", myScores.Length);
for(int x = 0; x < myScores.Length; ++x)
   Console.WriteLine(myScores[x]);
```

 An array's Length is a read-only property—you cannot assign it a new value. It is capitalized, as is the convention with all C# property identifiers. You will create property identifiers for your own classes in the chapter *Using Classes and Objects*.

Using foreach

You can easily navigate through arrays using a for or while loop that varies a subscript from 0 through Array.Length - 1. C# also supports a **foreach statement** that you can use to cycle through every array element without using a subscript. With the foreach statement, you provide a temporary **iteration variable** that automatically holds each array value in turn.

For example, the following code displays each element in the payRate array in sequence:

```
double[] payRate = {6.00, 7.35, 8.12, 12.45, 22.22};
foreach(double money in payRate)
   Console.WriteLine("{0}", money.ToString("C"));
```

The variable money is declared as a double within the foreach statement. During the execution of the loop, money holds each payRate value in turn—first, payRate[0], then payRate[1], and so on. As a simple variable, money does not require a subscript, making it easier to work with.

The foreach statement is used only under certain circumstances:

- You typically use foreach only when you want to access every array element. To access only selected array elements, you must manipulate subscripts using some other technique—for example, using a for loop or while loop.

- The foreach iteration variable is read-only—that is, you cannot assign a value to it. If you want to assign a value to array elements, you must use a different type of loop.

Using foreach with Enumerations

The foreach statement can provide a convenient way to display enumeration values. For example, Figure 6-2 shows a program that contains an enumeration for days of the week, and Figure 6-3 shows the output. The foreach block in the Main() method gets and displays each string in the enumeration using the GetNames() method that is built into the Enum class. You will learn more about built-in classes and methods in the coming chapters, but for now you can use the format shown in Figure 6-2 to conveniently work with enumeration values.

```csharp
using System;
class DemoForEachWithEnum
{
    enum Day
    {
        SUNDAY, MONDAY, TUESDAY, WEDNESDAY,
            THURSDAY, FRIDAY, SATURDAY
    }
    static void Main()
    {
        foreach(string day in Enum.GetNames(typeof(Day)))
            Console.WriteLine(day);
    }
}
```

Figure 6-2   DemoForEachWithEnum program

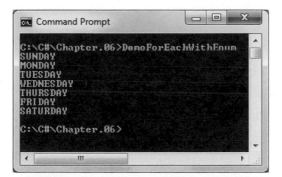

Figure 6-3   Output of DemoForEachWithEnum program

TWO TRUTHS & A LIE

Accessing Array Elements

1. Assume you have declared an array of six `doubles` named `balances`. The following statement displays all the elements:

```
for(int index = 0; index < 6; ++index)
    Console.WriteLine(balances[index]);
```

2. Assume you have declared an array of eight `doubles` named `prices`. The following statement subtracts 2 from each element:

```
for(double pr = 0; pr < 8; ++pr)
    prices[pr] -= 2;
```

3. The following code displays 3:

```
int[] array = {1, 2, 3};
Console.WriteLine(array.Length);
```

The false statement is #2. You can only use an `int` as the subscript to an array, and this example attempts to use a `double`.

 You Do It

Creating and Using an Array

In the next steps, you create a small array to see how it is used. The array will hold salaries for four categories of employees.

1. Open a new file and begin a console-based program named **ArrayDemo1** that demonstrates array use:

```
using System;
class ArrayDemo1
{
    static void Main()
    {
```

2. Declare and create an array that holds four `double` values by typing:

```
double[] payRate = {6.00, 7.35, 8.12, 12.45};
```

(continues)

(continued)

3. To confirm that the four values have been assigned, display them using the following code:

```
for(int x = 0; x < payRate.Length; ++x)
    Console.WriteLine("Pay rate {0} is {1}",
        x, payRate[x].ToString("C"));
```

4. Add the two closing curly brackets that end the Main() method and the ArrayDemo1 class.

5. Save the program, and then compile and run it. The output appears in Figure 6-4.

Figure 6-4 Output of ArrayDemo1 program

Searching an Array Using a Loop

When you want to determine whether a variable holds one of many possible valid values, one option is to use if statements to compare the variable to valid values. For example, suppose that a company manufactures 10 items. When a customer places an order for an item, you need to determine whether the item number is valid. If valid item numbers are sequential, say 101 through 110, then the following simple if statement that uses a logical AND operator can verify the order number and set a Boolean field to true:

```
if(itemOrdered >= 101 && itemOrdered <= 110)
    isValidItem = true;
```

If the valid item numbers are nonsequential, however—for example, 101, 108, 201, 213, 266, 304, and so on—you must code the following deeply nested if statement or a lengthy OR comparison to determine the validity of an item number:

```
if(itemOrdered == 101)
    isValidItem = true;
else if(itemOrdered == 108)
    isValidItem = true;
else if(itemOrdered == 201)
    isValidItem = true;
// and so on
```

Instead of creating a long series of if statements, a more elegant solution to determining whether a value is valid is to compare it to a list of values in an array. For example, you can initialize an array with the valid values by using the following statement:

```
int[] validValues = {101, 108, 201, 213, 266, 304, 311,
    409, 411, 412};
```

You might prefer to declare the validValues array as a constant because, presumably, the valid item numbers should not change during program execution. In C# you must use the keywords static and readonly prior to the constant declaration. To keep these examples simple, all arrays in this chapter are declared as variable arrays.

After the validValues array is declared, you can use either a for loop or a while loop to search whether the itemOrdered variable value matches any of the array entries.

Using a for Loop to Search an Array

One way to determine whether an itemOrdered value equals a value in the validValues array is to use a for statement to loop through the array and set a Boolean variable to true when a match is found:

```
for(int x = 0; x < validValues.Length; ++x)
    if(itemOrdered == validValues[x])
        isValidItem = true;
```

This type of search is called a **sequential search** because each array element is examined in sequence. This simple for loop replaces the long series of if statements. What's more, if a company carries 1000 items instead of 10, then the list of valid items in the array must be altered, but the for statement does not change at all. As an added bonus, if you set up another array as a **parallel array** with the same number of elements and corresponding data, you can use the same subscript to access additional information. For example, if the 10 items your company carries have 10 different prices, then you can set up an array to hold those prices as follows:

```
double[] prices = {0.89, 1.23, 3.50, 0.69…}; // and so on
```

The prices must appear in the same order as their corresponding item numbers in the validValues array. Now the same for loop that finds the valid item number also finds the price, as shown in the program in Figure 6-5. In other words, if the item number is found in the second position in the validValues array, then you can find the correct price in the second position in the prices array. In the program in Figure 6-5, the variable used as a subscript, x, is set to 0 and the Boolean variable isValidItem is false. In the shaded portion of the figure, while the subscript remains smaller than the length of the array of valid item numbers, the subscript is continuously increased so that subsequent array values can be tested. When a match is found between the user's item and an item in the array, `isValidItem` is set to `true` and the price of the item is stored in `itemPrice`. Figure 6-6 shows two typical program executions.

If you initialize parallel arrays, it is convenient to use spacing so that the corresponding values visually align on the screen or printed page.

Although parallel arrays can be very useful, they also can increase the likelihood of mistakes. Any time you make a change to one array, you must remember to make the corresponding change in its parallel array. As you continue to study C#, you will learn superior ways to correlate data items. For example, in the chapter *Using Classes and Objects*, you will learn that you can encapsulate corresponding data items in objects and create arrays of objects.

```csharp
using System;
class FindPriceWithForLoop
{
    static void Main()
    {
        int[] validValues = {101,  108,  201, 213,  266,
            304,  311, 409, 411,  412};
        double[] prices =    {0.89, 1.23, 3.50, 0.69, 5.79,
            3.19, 0.99, 0.89, 1.26, 8.00};
        int itemOrdered;
        double itemPrice = 0;
        bool isValidItem = false;
        Console.Write("Please enter an item ");
        itemOrdered = Convert.ToInt32(Console.ReadLine());
        for(int x = 0; x < validValues.Length; ++x)
        {
            if(itemOrdered == validValues[x])
            {
                isValidItem = true;
                itemPrice = prices[x];
            }
        }
        if(isValidItem)
            Console.WriteLine("Price is {0}", itemPrice);
        else
            Console.WriteLine("Sorry - item not found");
    }
}
```

Figure 6-5   The FindPriceWithForLoop program

Figure 6-6   Two typical executions of the FindPriceWithForLoop program

In the fourth statement of the Main() method in Figure 6-5, itemPrice is set to 0. Setting this variable is required because its value is later altered only if an item number match is found in the validValues array. When C# determines that a variable's value is only set depending on an if statement, C# will not allow you to display the variable because the compiler assumes that the if statement's Boolean expression could have been false and the variable might not have been set to a valid value.

Improving a Loop's Efficiency

In an array that has many possible matches of a search value, the most efficient strategy is to place the most common items first so they are matched immediately. For example, if item 311 is ordered most often, place 311 first in the validValues array and its price ($0.99) first in the prices array. However, it might be more convenient for people to view the item numbers in ascending numerical order. In many business applications, your first consideration is how easily users can read, understand, and modify your programs. However, in other applications, such as programming for mobile devices, speed and memory considerations are more important. You should follow the recommendations of your instructors or supervisors.

Other efficiency improvements are possible with the code shown in Figure 6-5. In the program, you compare every itemOrdered with each of the 10 validValues. Even when an itemOrdered is equivalent to the first value in the validValues array (101), you always make nine additional cycles through the array. On each of these nine additional iterations, the comparison between itemOrdered and validValues[x] is always false. As soon as a match for an itemOrdered is found, the most efficient action is to break out of the for loop early. An easy way to accomplish this task is to set x to a high value within the block of statements executed when a match is found. Then, after a match, the for loop will not execute again because the limiting comparison (x < validValues.Length) will have been surpassed. Figure 6-7 shows this approach.

```
for(int x = 0; x < validValues.Length; ++x)
{
   if(itemOrdered == validValues[x])
   {
      isValidItem = true;
      itemPrice = prices[x];
      x = validValues.Length;
         // break out of loop when you find a match
   }
}
```

Figure 6-7 Loop with forced early exit

In the code segment in Figure 6-7, instead of the statement that sets x to validValues.
Length when a match is found, you could remove that statement and change the comparison
in the middle section of the for statement to a compound statement, as follows:

for(int x = 0; x < validValues.Length && !isValidItem; ++x)...

As another alternative, you could remove the statement that sets x to validValues.Length
and place a break statement within the loop in its place. A break statement exits the current
code block immediately. Some programmers disapprove of exiting a for loop early, whether
by setting a variable's value or by using a break statement. They argue that programs are
easier to debug and maintain if each program segment has only one entry and one exit point.
If you (or your instructor) agree with this philosophy, then you can select an approach that
uses a while statement, as described next.

Using a while Loop to Search an Array

As an alternative to using a for loop to search an array, you can use a while loop to search
for a match. Using this approach, you set a subscript to 0 and, while the itemOrdered is not
equal to a value in the array, increase the subscript and keep looking. You search only while
the subscript remains lower than the number of elements in the array. If the subscript
increases to match validValues.Length, then you never found a match in the array. If the
loop ends before the subscript reaches validValues.Length, then you found a match and
the correct price can be assigned to the itemPrice variable. Figure 6-8 shows a program
that uses this approach.

```csharp
using System;
class FindPriceWithWhileLoop
{
   static void Main()
   {
      int x;
      string inputString;
      int itemOrdered;
      double itemPrice = 0;
      bool isValidItem = false;
      int[] validValues = {101,  108,  201, 213, 266,
         304,  311,  409,  411,  412};
      double[] prices =    {0.89, 1.23, 3.50, 0.69, 5.79,
         3.19,  0.99, 0.89, 1.26, 8.00};
      Console.Write("Enter item number ");
      inputString = Console.ReadLine();
      itemOrdered = Convert.ToInt32(inputString);
      x = 0;
      while(x < validValues.Length &&
         itemOrdered != validValues[x])
            ++x;
      if(x != validValues.Length)
      {
         isValidItem = true;
         itemPrice = prices[x];
      }
      if(isValidItem)
         Console.WriteLine("Item {0} sells for {1}",
            itemOrdered, itemPrice.ToString("C"));
      else
         Console.WriteLine("No such item as {0}",
            itemOrdered);
   }
}
```

Figure 6-8 The FindPriceWithWhileLoop program that searches with a while loop

In the application in Figure 6-8, the variable used as a subscript, x, is set to 0 and the Boolean variable isValidItem is false. In the shaded portion of the figure, while the subscript remains smaller than the length of the array of valid item numbers, and while the user's requested item does not match a valid item, the subscript is increased so that subsequent array values can be tested. The while loop ends when a match is found or the array tests have been exhausted, whichever comes first. When the loop ends, if x is not equal to the size of the array, then a valid item has been found and its price can be retrieved from the prices array. Figure 6-9 shows two executions of the program. In the first execution, a match is found; in the second, an invalid item number is entered, so no match is found.

Command Prompt

```
C:\C#\Chapter.06>FindPriceWithWhileLoop
Enter item number 409
Item 409 sells for $0.89

C:\C#\Chapter.06>FindPriceWithWhileLoop
Enter item number 410
No such item as 410

C:\C#\Chapter.06>
```

Figure 6-9 Two executions of the FindPriceWithWhileLoop application

 Watch the video *Searching an Array.*

Searching an Array for a Range Match

Searching an array for an exact match is not always practical. For example, suppose your mail-order company gives customer discounts based on the quantity of items ordered. Perhaps no discount is given for any order of up to a dozen items, but increasing discounts are available for orders of increasing quantities, as shown in Figure 6-10.

Total Quantity Ordered	Discount (%)
1 to 12	None
13 to 49	10
50 to 99	14
100 to 199	18
200 or more	20

Figure 6-10 Discount table for a mail-order company

One awkward, impractical option is to create a single array to store the discount rates. You could use a variable named numOfItems as a subscript to the array, but the array would need hundreds of entries, such as the following:

```
double[] discounts = {0, 0, 0, 0, 0, 0, 0, 0, 0, 0,
    0, 0, 0, 0.10, 0.10, 0.10 …}; // and so on
```

When numOfItems is 3, for example, then discounts[numOfItems] or discounts[3] is 0. When numOfItems is 14, then discounts[numOfItems] or discounts[14] is 0.10. Because a customer might order thousands of items, the array would need to be ridiculously large.

Notice that 13 zeroes are listed in the discount array in this example. The first array element has a 0 subscript (and a 0 discount for 0 items). The next 12 discounts (1 through 12 items) also have 0 discounts.

A better option is to create parallel arrays. One array will hold the five discount rates, and the other array will hold five discount range limits. Then you can perform a **range match** by determining the pair of limiting values between which a customer's order falls. The Total Quantity Ordered column in Figure 6-10 shows five ranges. If you use only the first figure in each range, then you can create an array that holds five low limits:

```
int[] discountRangeLowLimits = {1, 13, 50, 100, 200};
```

A parallel array will hold the five discount rates:

```
double[] discounts = {0, 0.10, 0.14, 0.18, 0.20};
```

Then, starting at the last discountRangeLowLimits array element, for any numOfItems greater than or equal to discountRangeLowLimits[4], the appropriate discount is discounts[4]. In other words, for any numOfItems less than discountRangeLowLimits[4], you should decrement the subscript and look in a lower range. Figure 6-11 shows the code.

```
// Assume numOfItems is a declared integer for which a user
// has input a value
int[] discountRangeLowLimits = {1,   13,   50,  100,  200};
double[] discounts =           {0, 0.10, 0.14, 0.18, 0.20};
double customerDiscount;
int sub = discountRangeLowLimits.Length - 1;
while(sub >= 0 && numOfItems < discountRangeLowLimits[sub])
   --sub;
customerDiscount = discounts[sub];
```

Figure 6-11 Searching an array of range limits

As an alternate approach to the range-checking logic in Figure 6-11, you can choose to create an array that contains the upper limit of each range, such as the following:

```
int[] discountRangeUpperLimits = {12, 49, 99, 199, 9999999};
```

Then the logic can be written to compare numOfItems to each range limit until the correct range is located, as follows:

```
int sub = 0;
while(sub < discountRangeUpperLimits.Length && numOfItems >
   discountRangeUpperLimits[sub])
   ++sub;
customerDiscount = discounts[sub];
```

In this example, sub is initialized to 0. While it remains within array bounds, and while numOfItems is more than each upper-range limit, sub is increased. In other words, if numOfItems is 3, the while expression is false on the first loop iteration, the loop ends, sub remains 0, and the customer discount is the first discount. However, if numOfItems is 30, then the while expression is true on the first loop iteration, sub becomes 1, the while expression is false on the second iteration, and the second discount is used. In this example, the last discountRangeUpperLimits array value is 9999999. This very high value was used with the assumption that no numOfItems would ever exceed it. As with many issues in programming, multiple correct approaches frequently exist for the same problem.

TWO TRUTHS & A LIE

Searching an Array Using a Loop

1. A parallel array has the same number of elements as another array, and corresponding data.

2. When you search an array for an exact match in a parallel array, you must perform a loop as many times as there are elements in the arrays.

3. One practical solution to creating an array with which to perform a range check is to design the array to hold the lowest value in each range.

The false statement is #2. When you search an array for an exact match in a parallel array, you can perform a loop as many times as there are elements in the arrays, but once a match is found, the additional loop iterations are unnecessary. Terminating the loop cycles as soon as a match is found is the most efficient approach.

Using the BinarySearch(), Sort(), and Reverse() Methods

You have already learned that because every array in C# is derived from the System.Array class, you can use the Length property. Additionally, the System.Array class contains a variety of useful, built-in methods that can search, sort, and manipulate array elements. (You already have used many built-in C# methods such as WriteLine() and ReadLine(). You will learn to write your own methods in the next chapter.)

Using the BinarySearch() Method

The **BinarySearch() method** finds a requested value in a sorted array. Instead of employing the logic you used to find a match in the last section, you can take advantage of this built-in method to locate a value within an array, as long as the array items are organized in ascending order. A **binary search** is one in which a sorted list of objects is split in half repeatedly as the search gets closer and closer to a match. Perhaps you have played a guessing game, trying to guess a number from 1 to 100. If you asked, "Is it less than 50?", then continued to narrow your guesses upon hearing each subsequent answer, then you have performed a binary search.

Figure 6-12 shows a program that declares an array of integer idNumbers arranged in ascending order. The program prompts a user for a value, converts it to an integer, and passes the array and the entered value to the BinarySearch() method in the shaded statement. The method returns −1 if the value is not found in the array; otherwise, it returns the array position of the sought value. Figure 6-13 shows two executions of this program.

The BinarySearch() method takes two arguments—the array name and the value for which to search. In Chapter 1 you learned that arguments represent information that a method needs to perform its task. When methods require multiple arguments, they are separated by commas. For example, when you have used the Console.WriteLine() method, you have passed a format string and values to be displayed, all separated by commas.

```
using System;
class BinarySearchDemo          These values must be sorted in ascending
{                               order for the BinarySearch ( )
                                method to work correctly.
    static void Main()
    {

    int[] idNumbers = {122, 167, 204, 219, 345};
    int x;
    string entryString;
    int entryId;
    Console.Write("Enter an Employee ID ");
    entryString = Console.ReadLine();
    entryId = Convert.ToInt32(entryString);
    x = Array.BinarySearch(idNumbers, entryId);
    if(x < 0)
       Console.WriteLine("ID {0} not found", entryId);
    else
       Console.WriteLine("ID {0} found at position {1} ",
          entryId, x);
    }
}
```

Figure 6-12   BinarySearchDemo program

Figure 6-13   Two executions of the BinarySearchDemo program

When you use the following statement, you send a string to the Write() method:

Console.Write("Enter an Employee ID ");

When you use the following statement, you get a value back from the ReadLine() method:

entryString = Console.ReadLine();

In Figure 6-12, the following single statement both sends a value to a method and gets a value back:

x = Array.BinarySearch(idNumbers, entryId);

The statement calls the method that performs the search, returning a −1 or the position where entryId was found; that value is then stored in x. This single line of code is easier to write, less prone to error, and easier to understand than writing a loop to cycle through the idNumbers array looking for a match. Still, it is worthwhile to understand how to perform the search without the BinarySearch() method, as you learned while studying parallel arrays. You will need to use that technique under the following conditions, when the BinarySearch() method proves inadequate:

- If your array items are not arranged in ascending order, the BinarySearch() method does not work correctly.

- If your array holds duplicate values and you want to find all of them, the BinarySearch() method doesn't work—it can return only one value, so it returns the position of the first matching value it finds (which is not necessarily the first instance of the value in the array).

- If you want to find a range match rather than an exact match, the BinarySearch() method does not work.

Using the Sort() Method

The **Sort() method** arranges array items in ascending order. Ascending order is lowest to highest; it works numerically for number types and alphabetically for characters and strings.

To use the method, you pass the array name to `Array.Sort()`, and the element positions within the array are rearranged appropriately. Figure 6-14 shows a program that sorts an array of strings; Figure 6-15 shows its execution.

```
using System;
class SortArray
{
    static void Main()
    {
        string[] names = {"Olive", "Patty",
            "Richard", "Ned", "Mindy"};
        int x;
        Array.Sort(names);
        for(x = 0; x < names.Length; ++x)
            Console.WriteLine(names[x]);
    }
}
```

Figure 6-14   SortArray program

C:\C#\Chapter.06>SortArray
Mindy
Ned
Olive
Patty
Richard

C:\C#\Chapter.06>

Figure 6-15   Execution of SortArray program

Because the `BinarySearch()` method requires that array elements be sorted in order, the `Sort()` method is often used in conjunction with it.

 The `Array.Sort()` method provides a good example of encapsulation—you can use the method without understanding how it works internally. The method actually uses an algorithm named Quicksort. You will learn how to implement this algorithm yourself as you continue to study programming.

Using the Reverse() Method

The **Reverse() method** reverses the order of items in an array. In other words, for any array, the element that starts in position 0 is relocated to position `Length – 1`, the element that starts in position 1 is relocated to position `Length – 2`, and so on until the element that starts in position Length − 1 is relocated to position 0. The Reverse() method does not sort array elements; it only rearranges their positions to the opposite order.

You call the Reverse() method the same way you call the Sort() method—you simply pass the array name to the method. Figure 6-16 shows a program that uses Reverse() with an array of strings, and Figure 6-17 shows its execution.

When you Reverse() an array that contains an odd number of elements, the middle element will remain in its original location.

```
using System;
class ReverseArray
{
    static void Main()
    {
        string[] names = {"Zach", "Rose", "Wendy", "Marcia"};
        int x;
        Array.Reverse(names);
        for(x = 0; x < names.Length; ++x)
            Console.WriteLine(names[x]);
    }
}
```

Figure 6-16 ReverseArray program

Figure 6-17 Execution of ReverseArray program

TWO TRUTHS & A LIE

**Using the `BinarySearch()`, `Sort()`,
and `Reverse()` Methods**

1. When you use the `BinarySearch()` method with an array, the array items must first be organized in ascending order.

2. The `Array.Sort()` and `Array.Reverse()` methods are similar in that both require a single argument.

3. The `Array.Sort()` and `Array.Reverse()` methods are different in that one places items in ascending order and the other places them in descending order.

The false statement is #3. The `Array.Sort()` method places items in ascending order, but the `Array.Reverse()` method simply reverses the existing order of any array whether it was presorted or not.

 You Do It

Using the `Sort()` and `Reverse()` Methods

In the next steps, you create an array of integers and use the `Sort()` and `Reverse()` methods to manipulate it.

1. Open a new file and type the beginning of a program named **ArrayDemo2** that includes an array of eight integer test scores, an integer you will use as a subscript, and a string that will hold user-entered data.

```
using System;
class ArrayDemo2
{
    static void Main()
    {
        int[] scores = new int[8];
        int x;
        string inputString;
```

2. Add a loop that prompts the user, accepts a test score, converts the score to an integer, and stores it as the appropriate element of the `scores` array.

(continues)

(continued)

```
for(x = 0; x < scores.Length; ++x)
{
    Console.Write("Enter your score on test {0} ", x + 1);
    inputString = Console.ReadLine();
    scores[x] = Convert.ToInt32(inputString);
}
```

The program displays `x + 1` with each `score[x]` because, although array elements are numbered starting with 0, people usually count items starting with 1.

3. Add a statement that creates a dashed line to visually separate the input from the output. Display "Scores in original order:", then use a loop to display each score in a field that is six characters wide.

```
Console.WriteLine("\n--------------------------------");
Console.WriteLine("Scores in original order:");
for(x = 0; x < scores.Length; ++x)
    Console.Write("{0, 6}", scores[x]);
```

You learned to set display field sizes when you learned about format strings in Chapter 2.

4. Add another dashed line for visual separation, then pass the `scores` array to the `Array.Sort()` method. Display "Scores in sorted order:", then use a loop to display each of the newly sorted scores.

```
Console.WriteLine("\n--------------------------------");
Array.Sort(scores);
Console.WriteLine("Scores in sorted order:");
for(x = 0; x < scores.Length; ++x)
    Console.Write("{0, 6}", scores[x]);
```

5. Add one more dashed line, reverse the array elements by passing `scores` to the `Array.Reverse()` method, display "Scores in reverse order:", and show the rearranged scores.

```
Console.WriteLine("\n--------------------------------");
Array.Reverse(scores);
Console.WriteLine("Scores in reverse order:");
for(x = 0; x < scores.Length; ++x)
    Console.Write("{0, 6}", scores[x]);
```

6. Add two closing curly braces—one for the `Main()` method and one for the class.

(continues)

(continued)

7. Save the file, and then compile and execute the program. Figure 6-18 shows a typical execution of the program. The user-entered scores are not in order, but after the call to the Sort() method, they appear in ascending order. After the call to the Reverse() method, they appear in descending order.

```
C:\C#\Chapter.06>ArrayDemo2
Enter your score on test 1 75
Enter your score on test 2 82
Enter your score on test 3 100
Enter your score on test 4 90
Enter your score on test 5 92
Enter your score on test 6 78
Enter your score on test 7 95
Enter your score on test 8 89

_____
Scores in original order:
    75     82    100     90     92     78     95     89
_____
Scores in sorted order:
    75     78     82     89     90     92     95    100
_____
Scores in reverse order:
   100     95     92     90     89     82     78     75
C:\C#\Chapter.06>
```

Figure 6-18   Typical execution of `ArrayDemo2` program

Using Multidimensional Arrays

When you declare an array such as `double[] sales = new double[20];`, you can envision the declared integers as a column of numbers in memory, as shown at the beginning of this chapter in Figure 6-1. In other words, you can picture the 20 declared numbers stacked one on top of the next. An array that you can picture as a column of values, and whose elements you can access using a single subscript, is a **one-dimensional** or **single-dimensional array**. In other words, you can think of the single dimension of a single-dimensional array as the height of the array.

C# also supports **multidimensional arrays**—those that require multiple subscripts to access the array elements. The most commonly used multidimensional arrays are two-dimensional arrays that are rectangular. **Two-dimensional arrays** have two or more columns of values for each row, as shown in Figure 6-19. You can think of the two dimensions of a two-dimensional array as height and width.

sales[0, 0]	sales[0, 1]	sales[0, 2]	sales[0, 3]
sales[1, 0]	sales[1, 1]	sales[1, 2]	sales[1, 3]
sales[2, 0]	sales[2, 1]	sales[2, 2]	sales[2, 3]

Figure 6-19   View of a rectangular, two-dimensional array in memory

The array in Figure 6-19 is a rectangular array. In a **rectangular array**, each row has the same number of columns. You must use two subscripts when you access an element in a two-dimensional array. When mathematicians use a two-dimensional array, they often call it a **matrix** or a **table**; you might have used a two-dimensional array called a spreadsheet. You might want to create a `sales` array with two dimensions as shown in Figure 6-19 if, for example, each row represented a category of items sold, and each column represented a salesperson who sold them.

When you declare a one-dimensional array, you type a single, empty set of square brackets after the array type, and you use a single subscript in a set of square brackets when reserving memory. To declare a two-dimensional array, you type a comma in the square brackets after the array type, and you use two subscripts, separated by a comma in brackets, when reserving memory. For example, the array in Figure 6-19 can be declared as the following, creating an array named `sales` that holds three rows and four columns:

```
double[ , ] sales = new double[3, 4];
```

When you declare a two-dimensional array, spaces surrounding the comma within the square brackets are optional.

Just as with a one-dimensional array, if you do not provide values for the elements in a two-dimensional numerical array, the values are set to the default value for the data type (for example, zero for numeric data). You can assign other values to the array elements later. For example, the following statement assigns the value 14.00 to the element of the `sales` array that is in the first column of the first row:

```
sales[0, 0] = 14.00;
```

Alternatively, you can initialize a two-dimensional array by assigning values when it is created. For example, the following code assigns values to `sales` upon declaration:

```
double[ , ] sales = {{14.00, 15.00, 16.00, 17.00},
                     {21.99, 34.55, 67.88, 31.99},
                     {12.03, 55.55, 32.89,  1.17}};
```

The `sales` array contains three rows and four columns. You contain the entire set of values within a pair of curly braces. The first row of the array holds the four `double`s 14.00, 15.00, 16.00 and 17.00. Notice that these four values are placed within their own inner set of curly braces to indicate that they constitute one row, or the first row, which is row 0. The row and its curly braces are separated from the next row with a comma. The next four values in their own set of braces make up the second row (row 1), which you reference with the subscript 1, and the last four values constitute the third row (row 2).

When you refer to an element in a two-dimensional array, the first value within the brackets following the array name always refers to the row; the second value, after the comma, refers to the column. As examples, the value of sales[0, 0] is 14.00, the value of sales[0, 1] is 15.00, the value of sales[1, 0] is 21.99, and the value of sales[2, 3] is 1.17. You do not need to place each row of values that initializes a two-dimensional array on its own line. However, doing so makes the positions of values easier to understand.

As an example of how useful two-dimensional arrays can be, assume that you own an apartment building with four floors—a basement, which you refer to as floor zero, and three other floors numbered one, two, and three. In addition, each of the floors has studio (with no bedroom), one-, and two-bedroom apartments. The monthly rent for each type of apartment is different, and the rent is higher for apartments with more bedrooms. Figure 6-20 shows the rental amounts.

Floor	Zero Bedrooms	One Bedroom	Two Bedrooms
0	400	450	510
1	500	560	630
2	625	676	740
3	1000	1250	1600

Figure 6-20 Rents charged (in dollars)

To determine a tenant's rent, you need to know two pieces of information about the apartment: the floor and the number of bedrooms. Within a C# program, you can declare an array of rents using the following code:

```
int[ , ] rents = { {400, 450, 510},
                   {500, 560, 630},
                   {625, 676, 740},
                   {1000, 1250, 1600} };
```

Assume that you declare two integers to hold the floor number and bedroom count, as in the following statement:

```
int floor, bedrooms;
```

Then any tenant's rent can be referred to as rents[floor, bedrooms].

Figure 6-21 shows a complete program that uses a rectangular, two-dimensional array to hold rent values. Figure 6-22 shows a typical execution.

```
using System;
class RentFinder
{
    static void Main()
    {
        int[ , ] rents = { {400, 450, 510},
                           {500, 560, 630},
                           {625, 676, 740},
                           {1000, 1250, 1600} };
        int floor;
        int bedrooms;
        string inputString;
        Console.Write("Enter the floor on which you want to live ");
        inputString = Console.ReadLine();
        floor = Convert.ToInt32(inputString);
        Console.Write("Enter the number of bedrooms you need ");
        inputString = Console.ReadLine();
        bedrooms = Convert.ToInt32(inputString);
        Console.WriteLine("The rent is {0}",
            rents[floor, bedrooms]);
    }
}
```

Figure 6-21   The RentFinder program

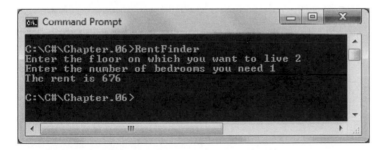

Figure 6-22   Typical execution of the RentFinder program

   Watch the video *Using a Two-Dimensional Array*.

C# supports arrays with more than two dimensions. For example, as in the program in Figure 6-21, if you own a multistory apartment building with different numbers of bedrooms available in apartments on each floor, you can use a two-dimensional array to store the rental fees. If you own several apartment buildings, you might want to employ a third dimension to store the building number. Suppose you want to store rents for four buildings that have three floors each and that each hold two types of apartments. Figure 6-23 shows how you might define such an array.

```
int[ , , ] rents = { { {400, 500}, {450, 550}, {500, 550}},
                     { {510, 610}, {710, 810}, {910, 1010}},
                     { {525, 625}, {725, 825}, {925, 1025}},
                     { {850, 950}, {1050, 1150}, {1250, 1350}}};
```

Figure 6-23   A three-dimensional array definition

The empty brackets that follow the data type contain two commas, showing that the array supports three dimensions. A set of curly braces surrounds all the data. Four inner sets of braces surround the data for each floor. In this example, each row of values represents a building (0 through 3). Then 12 sets of innermost brackets surround the values for each floor—first a zero-bedroom apartment and then a one-bedroom apartment.

Using the three-dimensional array in Figure 6-23, an expression such as rents[building, floor, bedrooms] refers to a specific rent value for a building whose number is stored in the building variable and whose floor and bedroom numbers are stored in the floor and bedrooms variables. Specifically, rents[3, 1, 0] refers to a studio (zero-bedroom) apartment on the first floor of building 3 ($1050 in Figure 6-23). When you are programming in C#, you can use four, five, or more dimensions in an array. As long as you can keep track of the order of the variables needed as subscripts, and as long as you don't exhaust your computer's memory, C# lets you create arrays of any size.

Using Jagged Arrays

C# also supports jagged arrays. A **jagged array** is a one-dimensional array in which each element is another array. The major difference between jagged and rectangular arrays is that in jagged arrays, each row can be a different length.

For example, consider an application in which you want to store train ticket prices for each stop along five different routes. Suppose some of the routes have as many as 10 stops and others have as few as two. Each of the five routes could be represented by a row in a multidimensional array. Then you would have two logical choices for the columns:

- You could create a rectangular, two-dimensional array, allowing 10 columns for each row. In some of the rows, as many as eight of the columns would be empty, because some routes have only two stops.

- You could create a jagged two-dimensional array, allowing a different number of columns for each row. Figure 6-24 shows how you could implement this option.

```
double [][] tickets = {
    new double[] {5.50, 6.75, 7.95, 9.00, 12.00,
        13.00, 14.50, 17.00, 19.00, 20.25},
    new double[] {5.00, 6.00},
    new double[] {7.50, 9.00, 9.95, 12.00, 13.00, 14.00},
    new double[] {3.50, 6.45, 9.95, 10.00, 12.75},
    new double[] {15.00, 16.00} };
```

Figure 6-24 A jagged, two-dimensional array

Two square brackets are used following the data type of the array in Figure 6-24. This notation declares a jagged array that is composed of five separate one-dimensional arrays. Within the jagged array, each row needs its own new operator and data type. To refer to a jagged array element, you use two sets of brackets after the array name—for example, tickets[route][stop]. In Figure 6-24, the value of tickets[0][0] is 5.50, the value of tickets[0][1] is 6.75, and the value of tickets[0][2] is 7.95. The value of tickets[1][0] is 5.00, and the value of tickets[1][1] is 6.00. Referring to tickets[1][2] is invalid because there is no column 2 in the second row (that is, there are only two stops, not three, on the second train route).

TWO TRUTHS & A LIE

Using Multidimensional Arrays

1. A rectangular array has the same number of columns as rows.

2. The following array contains two rows and three columns:

   ```
   int[ , ] departments = {{12, 54, 16},
                           {22, 44, 47}};
   ```

3. A jagged array is a one-dimensional array in which each element is another array.

The false statement is #1. In a rectangular array, each row has the same number of columns, but the numbers of rows and columns are not required to be the same.

Array Issues in GUI Programs

The major unusual consideration when using an array in a GUI program is that if the array values change based on user input, the array must be stored outside any method that reacts to the user's event. For example, consider an application that accumulates contribution totals for a fund-raising drive competition between four departments in a company. The left side of

Figure 6-25 shows a Form into which a user types a department number and a contribution amount. The user clicks OK, then enters the next contribution amount. When the user clicks the Done button, a summary of contributions appears, as shown in the right half of Figure 6-25.

Figure 6-25   The Form for the CountContributions program as the user enters values and after the user clicks Done

Figure 6-26 shows the code needed to implement the application. An array named total is declared outside of any methods. The okButton_Click() method accepts a department number and contribution amount from the user. It then adds the contribution into the array element that corresponds to the department and clears the text boxes so they are empty prior to the next entry. The total array must be declared outside of the okButton_Click() method; if it was inside the method, it would be redeclared and all its elements would be reset to 0 with each button click. The doneButton_Click() method displays the array's contents.

```
double[] total = { 0, 0, 0, 0 };
private void okButton_Click(object sender, EventArgs e)
{
    int dept;
    double contribution;
    dept = Convert.ToInt32(deptTextbox.Text);
    contribution = Convert.ToDouble(contributionTextbox.Text);
    --dept;
    total[dept] += contribution;
    deptTextbox.Text = "";
    contributionTextbox.Text = "";
}

private void doneButton_Click(object sender, EventArgs e)
{
    outputLabel.Text = "Dept     Total";
    for (int x = 0; x < total.Length; ++x)
        outputLabel.Text +=
            String.Format("\n    {0}{1, 10}", x + 1, total[x].ToString("C"));
}
```

Figure 6-26   Code that declares array and two methods needed for the `CountContributions` application

TWO TRUTHS & A LIE

Array Issues in GUI Programs

1. A GUI program can contain declarations for any number of arrays of any data type.

2. If a method reacts to a user-initiated event, it cannot contain an array declaration.

3. If a method reacts to a user-initiated event and the method contains an array declaration, the array will be redeclared with each event occurrence.

The false statement is #2. If a method reacts to a user-initiated event, it can contain an array. The only problem is that the array will be redeclared with each new event, so it cannot store data that must persist over a number of events.

Chapter Summary

- An array is a list of data items, all of which have the same type and the same name, but are distinguished from each other using a subscript or index. You declare an array variable by inserting a pair of square brackets after the type, and reserve memory for an array by using the keyword new. Any array's elements are numbered 0 through one less than the array's length. In C#, arrays are objects that derive from a class named System.Array. An array's fields are initialized to default values. To initialize an array to nondefault values, you use a list of values that are separated by commas and enclosed within curly braces.

- Arrays are most powerful when variable subscripts are used to process array elements. Any array subscript must remain in the range of 0 through length - 1. The Length property automatically holds an array's length. You can use the foreach statement to cycle through every array element without using subscripts.

- When you want to determine whether a variable holds one of many possible valid values, you can compare the variable to a list of values in an array. You can set up a parallel array to access additional information.

- The BinarySearch() method finds a requested value in a sorted array. The method returns −1 if the value is not found in the array; otherwise, it returns the array position of the sought value. You cannot use the BinarySearch() method if your array items are not arranged in ascending order, if the array holds duplicate values and you want to find all of them, or if you want to find a range match rather than an exact match. The Sort() method arranges array items in ascending order. The Reverse() method reverses the order of items in an array.

- C# supports multidimensional arrays—those that require multiple subscripts to access the array elements. The most commonly used multidimensional arrays are two-dimensional arrays that are rectangular. Two-dimensional arrays have two or more columns of values for each row. In a rectangular array, each row has the same number of columns. C# also supports jagged arrays, which are arrays of arrays.

- The major unusual consideration when using an array in a GUI program is that if the array values change based on user input, the array must be stored outside any method that reacts to the user's event.

Key Terms

An **array** is a list of data items that all have the same data type and the same name, but are distinguished from each other by a subscript or index.

Each object in an array is an **array element**.

A **subscript** (also called an **index**) is an integer contained within square brackets that indicates the position of one of an array's elements.

The keyword **new** is also known as the **new operator**; it is used to create objects.

An **initializer list** is the list of values provided for an array.

The class **System.Array** defines fields and methods that belong to every array.

The **Length property** is a member of the System.Array class that automatically holds an array's length.

The **foreach statement** is used to cycle through every array element without using a subscript.

A temporary **iteration variable** holds each array value in turn in a foreach statement.

A **sequential search** is conducted by examining a list in sequence.

A **parallel array** has the same number of elements as another array, and corresponding data.

A **range match** determines the pair of limiting values between which a value falls.

The **BinarySearch() method** finds a requested value in a sorted array.

A **binary search** is an algorithm that attempts to find an item in a list by splitting the sorted list of objects in half repeatedly as the search gets closer to a match.

The **Sort() method** arranges array items in ascending order.

The **Reverse() method** reverses the order of items in an array.

A **one-dimensional** or **single-dimensional array** is an array whose elements you can access using a single subscript.

Multidimensional arrays require multiple subscripts to access the array elements.

Two-dimensional arrays have two or more columns of values for each row.

In a **rectangular array**, each row has the same number of columns.

Matrix and **table** are alternate names used to describe a two-dimensional array.

A **jagged array** is a one-dimensional array in which each element is another array.

Review Questions

1. In an array, every element has the same _____.

   a. subscript
   b. data type

   c. memory location
   d. all of the above

2. The operator used to create objects is _____.

   a. =
   b. +=

   c. new
   d. create

3. Which of the following correctly declares an array of six integers?

   a. `int array[6];`   c. `int[6] array;`

   b. `int[] array = 6;`   d. `int[] array = new int[6];`

4. The value placed within square brackets after an array name is _____.

   a. a subscript   c. always an integer

   b. an index   d. all of these

5. If you define an array to contain 10 elements, then the highest array subscript you can use is _____.

   a. 11   c. 9

   b. 10   d. 8

6. Initializing an array is _____ in C#.

   a. required   c. difficult

   b. optional   d. prohibited

7. When you declare an array of six `double` elements but provide no initialization values, the value of the first element is _____.

   a. 0.0   c. 5.0

   b. 1.0   d. unknown

8. Which of the following correctly declares an array of four integers?

   a. `int[] ages = new int[4] {20, 30, 40, 50};`

   b. `int[] ages = new int[] {20, 30, 40, 50};`

   c. `int[] ages = {20, 30, 40, 50};`

   d. all of these

9. When an `ages` array is correctly initialized using the values {20, 30, 40, 50}, as in Question 8, then the value of `ages[1]` is _____.

   a. 0   c. 30

   b. 20   d. undefined

10. When an `ages` array is correctly initialized using the values {20, 30, 40, 50}, as in Question 8, then the value of `ages[4]` is _____.

   a. 0   c. 50

   b. 4   d. undefined

11. When you declare an array as `int[] temperature = {0, 32, 50, 90, 212, 451};`, the value of `temperature.Length` is _____.

    a. 5   c. 7
    b. 6   d. unknown

12. Which of the following doubles every value in a 10-element integer array named `amount`?

    a. `for(int x = 9; x >= 0; --x) amount[x] *= 2;`
    b. `foreach(int number in amount) number *= 2;`
    c. both of these
    d. neither of these

13. Which of the following adds 10 to every value in a 16-element integer array named `points`?

    a. `for(int sub = 0; sub > 15; ++sub) points[sub] += 10;`
    b. `foreach(int sub in points) points += 10;`
    c. both of these
    d. neither of these

14. Two arrays that store related information in corresponding element positions are _____.

    a. analogous arrays   c. relative arrays
    b. polymorphic arrays   d. parallel arrays

15. Assume an array is defined as `int[] nums = {2, 3, 4, 5};`. Which of the following would display the values in the array in reverse?

    a. `for(int x = 4; x > 0; --x) Console.Write(nums[x]);`
    b. `for(int x = 3; x >= 0; --x) Console.Write(nums[x]);`
    c. `for(int x = 3; x > 0; --x) Console.Write(nums[x]);`
    d. `for(int x = 4; x >= 0; --x) Console.Write(nums[x]);`

16. Assume an array is defined as `int[] nums = {7, 15, 23, 5};`. Which of the following would place the values in the array in descending numeric order?

    a. `Array.Sort(nums);`
    b. `Array.Reverse(nums);`
    c. `Array.Sort(nums); Array.Reverse(nums);`
    d. `Array.Reverse(nums); Array.Sort(nums);`

17. Which of the following traits do the BinarySearch() and Sort() methods have in common?

    a. Both methods take a single argument that must be an array.

    b. Both methods belong to the System.Array class.

    c. The array that each method uses must be in ascending order.

    d. They both operate on arrays made up of simple data types but not class objects.

18. If you use the BinarySearch() method and the object you seek is not found in the array, _____.

    a. an error message is displayed   c. the value false is returned

    b. a zero is returned   d. a negative value is returned

19. The BinarySearch() method is inadequate when _____.

    a. array items are in ascending order

    b. the array holds duplicate values and you want to find them all

    c. you want to find an exact match for a value

    d. array items are not numeric

20. Which of the following declares an integer array that contains eight rows and five columns?

    a. `int[8, 5] num = new int[ , ];`

    b. `int [8][5] num = new int[];`

    c. `int [ , ] num = new int[5, 8];`

    d. `int [ , ] num = new int[8, 5];`

Exercises

Programming Exercises

1. Write a program named **IntArrayDemo** that stores an array of 10 integers. Until the user enters a sentinel value, allow the user three options: (1) to view the list in order from the first to last position, (2) to view the list in order from the last to first position, or (3) to choose a specific position to view.

2. Write a program named **TipsList** that accepts seven double values representing tips earned by a waiter each day during the week. Display each of the values along with a message that indicates how far it is from the average.

3. Write a program named **ScoresComparison** that allows a user to input four integer quiz scores ranging from 0 through 100. If no score is lower than any

previous score, display a message that congratulates the user on making improvement and then display the scores in the order they were entered. If every score is lower than the previous one, display the scores in the order they were entered, display an appropriate message about the scores' descent, and then display the scores in the more desirable reverse order. If the scores neither increase nor decrease consistently, display an appropriate message along with the scores.

4. Write a program named **CheckZips** that is used by a package delivery service to check delivery areas. The program contains an array that holds the 10 zip codes of areas to which the company makes deliveries. Prompt a user to enter a zip code and display a message indicating whether the zip code is in the company's delivery area.

5. Write a program called **DeliveryCharges** for the package delivery service in Exercise 4. The program should again use an array that holds the 10 zip codes of areas to which the company makes deliveries. Create a parallel array containing 10 delivery charges that differ for each zip code. Prompt a user to enter a zip code and then display either a message indicating the price of delivery to that zip code or a message indicating that the company does not deliver to the requested zip code.

6. The Chat-A-While phone company provides service to six area codes and charges the per-minute rates for phone calls shown in Figure 6-27. Write a program named **ChatAWhile** that allows a user to enter an area code and the length of time for a call in minutes, and then display the total cost of the call.

Area Code	Per-Minute Rate ($)
262	0.07
414	0.10
608	0.05
715	0.16
815	0.24
920	0.14

Figure 6-27   Per-minute phone call rates

7. The Whippet Bus Company charges prices for tickets based on distance traveled, as shown in Figure 6-28. Write a program named **WhippetBus** that allows a user to enter a trip distance. The output is the ticket price.

Distance (miles)	Ticket Price ($)
0 – 99	25.00
100 – 299	40.00
300 – 499	55.00
500 and farther	70.00

Figure 6-28　Bus ticket prices

8.　a.　Write a program named **PizzaPrices** that prompts the user to make a choice for a pizza size—*S*, *M*, *L*, or *X*—and then displays the price as $6.99, $8.99, $12.50, or $15.00, respectively.

　　b.　Create a program named **PizzaPrices2** that modifies the PizzaPrices program so that the following discounts apply: no discount for one pizza, 10 percent for two pizzas, 15 percent for three or four pizzas, and 20 percent for five or more pizzas. Display a full accounting of the transaction, similar to that shown in Figure 6-29.

Figure 6-29　Typical execution of PizzaPrices2 program as a command-line application and as a GUI application

9.　Write a program named **Commission** that computes commissions for automobile salespeople based on the value of a car sold. Salespeople receive 5 percent of the sale price for any car sold for up to and including $15,000; 7 percent for any car over $15,000 up to and including $24,000; and 10 percent of the sale price of any car over $24,000. Write a program that allows a user to enter a car price. The output is the salesperson's commission.

10. In Chapter 5, you wrote a **GarageSale** application for the Anderson, Bowman, and Claxton families. The program prompts the user for a family initial (an uppercase or lowercase *A*, *B*, or *C*). The program continues while the user does not type *Z*, and it displays each family's total sales as well as the grand total made at the garage sale. Now, modify the program to use arrays to store the family names, allowed initials, and accumulated sales values.

11. Create a game similar to Hangman named **GuessAWord** in which a player guesses letters to try to replicate a hidden word. Store at least eight words in an array, and randomly select one to be the hidden word. (The statements needed to generate a random number are shown in the Exercises in the *Decision Making* and *Looping* chapters.) Initially, display the hidden word using asterisks to represent each letter. Allow the user to guess letters to replace the asterisks in the hidden word until the user completes the entire word. If the user guesses a letter that is not in the hidden word, display an appropriate message. If the user guesses a letter that appears multiple times in the hidden word, make sure that each correct letter is placed. Figure 6-30 shows typical games in progress in a console-based application and in a GUI application. In the GUI application, the user has successfully guessed *a*, *c*, and *t*, and is about to guess *r*. *Hint:* If you create the GUI version of the game, you might want to include a Start button that selects the random word and performs other start-up tasks before you reveal the game interface. After the start-up tasks are complete, you can remove the Start button from the form.

Figure 6-30 Typical executions of console-based and GUI GuessAWord programs

Debugging Exercises

1. Each of the following files in the Chapter.06 folder of your downloadable student files has syntax and/or logical errors. In each case, determine the problem and fix the program. After you correct the errors, save each file using the same filename preceded with *Fixed*. For example, DebugSix01.cs will become FixedDebugSix01.cs.

   a. DebugSix01.cs
   b. DebugSix02.cs

   c. DebugSix03.cs
   d. DebugSix04.cs

Case Problems

1. In previous chapters, you created applications for the Greenville Idol competition. Now, modify the version of the **GreenvilleRevenue** program created in Chapter 5 so that after the user enters the number of contestants in this year's competition, the user is prompted for the appropriate number of contestant names and a code for each contestant that indicates the type of talent: *S* for singing, *D* for dancing, *M* for playing a musical instrument, or *O* for other. Make sure that all entered codes are valid, or reprompt the user. After contestant data entry is complete, display a count of each type of talent. Then, continuously prompt the user for a talent code until the user enters a sentinel value. With each code entry, display a list of the contestants with that code, or display a message that the code is not valid and reprompt the user.

2. In previous chapters, you created applications for Marshall's Murals. Now, modify the version of the **MarshallsRevenue** program created in Chapter 5 so that after mural data entry is complete, the user is prompted for the appropriate number of customer names for both the interior and exterior murals and a code for each that indicates the mural style: *L* for landscape, *S* for seascape, *A* for abstract, *C* for children's, or *O* for other. When a code is invalid, reprompt the user for a valid code continuously. After data entry is complete, display a count of each type of mural. Then, continuously prompt the user for a mural style code until the user enters a sentinel value. With each code entry, display a list of all the customers with that code and whether their mural is interior or exterior. If the requested code is invalid, display an appropriate message and reprompt the user.

Using Methods

In this chapter you will:

◎ Learn about methods and implementation hiding

◎ Write methods with no parameters and no return value

◎ Write methods that require a single argument

◎ Write methods that require multiple arguments

◎ Write a method that returns a value

◎ Pass array values to a method

◎ Learn some alternate ways to write a `Main()` method header

◎ Learn about issues using methods in GUI programs

In the first chapters of this book, you learned to create C# programs containing Main() methods that declare variables, accept input, perform arithmetic, and produce output. You learned to add decisions, loops, and arrays to your programs. As your programs grow in complexity, their Main() methods will contain many additional statements. Rather than creating increasingly long Main() methods, most programmers prefer to modularize their programs, placing instructions in smaller "packages" called methods. In this chapter, you learn to create many types of C# methods. You will understand how to send data to these methods and receive information back from them.

284

Understanding Methods and Implementation Hiding

A **method** is an encapsulated series of statements that carry out a task. Any class can contain an unlimited number of methods. So far, you have written console-based applications that contain a Main() method, but no others. You also have created GUI applications with a Click() method. Frequently, the methods you have written have **invoked**, or **called**, other methods; that is, your program used a method's name and the method executed to perform a task for the class. For example, you have created many programs that call the WriteLine() and ReadLine() methods. These methods are prewritten; you only had to call them to have them work.

For example, consider the simple HelloClass program shown in Figure 7-1. The Main() method contains a statement that calls the Console.WriteLine() method. You can identify method names because they always are followed by a set of parentheses. Depending on the method, there might be an argument within the parentheses. You first encountered the term *argument* in Chapter 1. An argument is the data that appears between the parentheses in a method call. The call to the WriteLine() method within the HelloClass program in Figure 7-1 contains the string argument "Hello". The simplest methods you can invoke don't require any arguments.

 Methods are similar to the procedures, functions, and subroutines used in other programming languages.

```
using System;
class HelloClass
{
    static void Main()
    {
        Console.WriteLine("Hello");
    }
}
```

Figure 7-1   The HelloClass program

In the HelloClass program in Figure 7-1, Main() is a **calling method**—one that calls another. The WriteLine() method is a **called method**.

Understanding Implementation Hiding

When you call the WriteLine() method within the HelloClass program in Figure 7-1, you use a method that has already been created for you. Because the creators of C# knew you would often want to write a message to the output screen, they created a method you could call to accomplish that task. This method takes care of all the hardware details of producing a message on the output device; you simply call the method and pass the desired message to it. The WriteLine() method provides an example of **implementation hiding**, which means keeping the details of a method's operations hidden. For example, when you make a dental appointment, you do not need to know how the appointment is actually recorded at the dental office—perhaps it is written in a book, marked on a large chalkboard, or entered into a computerized database. The implementation details are of no concern to you as a client, and if the dental office changes its methods from one year to the next, the change does not affect your use of the appointment-making method. Your only concern is the way you **interface** or interact with the dental office, not how the office tracks appointments. In the same way that you are a client of the dental practice, a method that uses another is a **client** of that method.

Hidden implementation methods often are said to exist in a black box. A **black box** is any device you can use without knowing how it works internally. The same is true with well-written program methods; the invoking program or method must know the name of the method it is using and what type of information to send it, but the program does not need to know how the method works. Later, you might substitute a new, improved method for the old one, and if the interface to the method does not change, you won't need to make any changes in programs that invoke the method. The creators of C# were able to anticipate many of the methods that would be necessary for your programs; you will continue to use many of these methods throughout this book. However, your programs often will require custom methods that the creators of C# could not have expected. In this chapter, you will learn to write your own custom methods.

To more easily incorporate methods into a program, it is common practice to store methods (or groups of associated methods) in their own classes and files. Then you can add the methods into any application that uses them. The resulting compound program is called a **multifile assembly**. As you learn more about C#, you might prefer to take this approach with your own programs. For simplicity, example methods in this book are contained in the same file as any other methods that use them.

TWO TRUTHS & A LIE

Understanding Methods and Implementation Hiding

1. A method is an encapsulated series of statements that carry out a task.

2. Any class can contain an unlimited number of methods.

3. All the methods that will be used by your programs have been written for you and stored in files.

The false statement is #3. As you write programs, you will want to write many of your own custom methods.

Writing Methods with No Parameters and No Return Value

The output of the program in Figure 7-1 is simply the word "Hello". Suppose you want to add three more lines of output to display a standard welcoming message when users execute your program. Of course, you can add three new `WriteLine()` statements to the existing program, but you also can create a method to display the three new lines.

Creating a method instead of adding three lines to the existing program is useful for two major reasons:

- If you add a method call instead of three new lines, the `Main()` method will remain short and easy to follow. The `Main()` method will contain just one new statement that calls a method rather than three separate `WriteLine()` statements.

- More importantly, a method is easily *reusable*. After you create the welcoming method, you can use it in any program, and you can allow other programmers to use it in their programs. In other words, you do the work once, and then you can use the method many times.

 When you place code in a callable method instead of repeating the same code at several points in a program, you are avoiding **code bloat**—a colorful term that describes unnecessarily long or repetitive statements.

Figure 7-2 shows the parts of a C# method. A method must include:

- A **method declaration**, which is also known as a **method header** or **method definition**

- An opening curly brace

- A **method body**, which is a block of statements that carry out the method's work
- A closing curly brace

The method declaration defines the rules for using the method. It contains:

- Optional declared accessibility
- An optional static modifier
- The return type for the method
- The method name, or identifier
- An opening parenthesis
- An optional list of method parameters (separated with commas if there is more than one parameter)
- A closing parenthesis

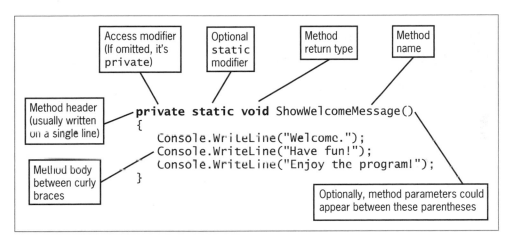

Figure 7-2   The ShowWelcomeMessage() method

An Introduction to Accessibility

The optional declared **accessibility** for a method sets limits as to how other methods can use your method; accessibility can be any of the levels described in Table 7-1. The two levels you will use most frequently, public and private access, are shaded in the table. You will learn about protected access and what it means to derive types in the chapter *Introduction to Inheritance*.

- **Public access** is established by including a public modifier in the member declaration. This modifier allows access to a method from other classes.
- **Private access** is established by including a private modifier in the member declaration or by omitting any accessibility modifier. This modifier limits method access to the class that contains the method.

Declared accessibility	Can methods contained in the same class access this method?	Can derived classes access this method?	Can assemblies or projects that contain this class access this method?	Can any class access this method?
public	Yes	Yes	Yes	Yes
protected internal	Yes	Yes	Yes	No
protected	Yes	Yes	No	No
internal	Yes	No	Yes	No
private	Yes	No	No	No

Table 7-1   Summary of method accessibility

If you do not provide an accessibility modifier for a method, it is `private` by default. The `Main()` method headers that you have seen in all of the examples in this book have no access modifier, so they are `private` by default. You could explicitly add the keyword `private` to the method headers in any of the programs you have seen so far in this book, and you would notice no difference in execution: The methods still would be `private`. Actually, you could also substitute the `public` keyword in the `Main()` method headers without noticing any execution differences either—it's just that other classes could have called the public `Main()` methods by using the appropriate class name and a dot before the method name. When you use a method's complete name, including its class, you are using its **fully qualified** name. When you use `Console.WriteLine()` or `Console.ReadLine()`, you are using fully qualified method names. Because the classes you write can use the `Console` class methods `WriteLine()` and `ReadLine()`, you know those methods must not be private.

In Chapter 3, you learned to create simple GUI applications, and you learned how to automatically generate a `Click()` method for a button; the generated method header started with the keyword `private`. For example, a private method named `button1_Click()` cannot be used by any other class. If you changed the method's access specifier to `public`, it could be used by another class, but you probably would have no reason to do so. As you study C#, you will learn how to decide which access modifier to choose for each method you write. For now, unless you want a method to be accessible by outside classes, you should use the `private` access modifier with the method. This book uses no modifiers with `Main()` methods because Visual Studio does not create them in its automatically generated code, but this book uses appropriate access modifiers with other methods.

An Introduction to the Optional `static` Modifier

You can declare a method to be **static** or **nonstatic**. If you use the keyword modifier `static`, you indicate that a method can be called without referring to an object. Instead, you refer to the class. For example, if you have a class named `PayrollApplication` that contains a static method named `DeductUnionDues()`, you can call the method using the class name, a dot, and the method name, as in the following:

```
PayrollApplication.DeductUnionDues();
```

If you call the method from another method in the same class, you *can* use the class name as a prefix, although this approach is neither required nor conventional. In other words, within a method in the `PayrollApplication` class, you can simply write the following method call:

```
DeductUnionDues();
```

If you do not indicate that a method is `static`, it is nonstatic by default and can only be used in conjunction with an object. Static methods cannot call nonstatic methods without using an object. (However, nonstatic methods can call static ones.) When you begin to create your own class objects in the chapter *Using Classes and Objects*, you will write many nonstatic methods and your understanding of the terms *static* and *nonstatic* will become clearer. As you work through this chapter, you will learn why each method is created to be static or nonstatic. Do not worry if you do not completely understand this chapter's references to nonstatic methods that require an object—the concept is explored in Chapter 9.

An Introduction to Return Types

Every method has a **return type**, indicating what kind of value the method will return to any other method that calls it. If a method does not return a value, its return type is `void`. A method's return type is known more succinctly as a **method's type**. Later in this chapter, you will create methods with return types such as `int` or `double` that return values of the corresponding type; such methods can be called *value-returning methods*. For now, the methods discussed are `void` methods that do not return a value.

When a method's return type is `void`, most C# programmers do not end the method with a `return` statement. However, you can end a `void` method with the following statement that indicates nothing is returned:

```
return;
```

Understanding the Method Identifier

Every method has a name that must be a legal C# identifier; that is, it must not contain spaces and must begin with a letter of the alphabet or an underscore. By convention, many programmers start method names with a verb because methods cause actions. Examples of conventional method names include `DeductTax()` and `DisplayNetPay()`.

Every method name is followed by a set of parentheses. Sometimes these parentheses contain parameters, but in the simplest methods, the parentheses are empty. A **parameter to a method** is a variable that holds data passed to a method when it is called. The terms *argument* and *parameter* are closely related. An argument is data in a method call, and a parameter receives an argument's value when the method executes.

The parentheses that follow a method name can hold one parameter or multiple parameters separated with commas. The contents within the parentheses are known as the **parameter list**.

Placing a Method in a Class

In summary, the first methods you write in console-based applications will be `private`, `static`, and `void` and will have empty parameter lists. Therefore, you can write the `ShowWelcomeMessage()` method as it is shown in Figure 7-2. According to its declaration, the method is `private` and `static`. It returns nothing, so the return type is `void`. Its identifier is `ShowWelcomeMessage`, and it receives nothing, so the parentheses are empty. The method body, consisting of three `WriteLine()` statements, appears within curly braces.

By convention, programmers indent the statements in a method body, which makes the method header and its braces stand out. When you write a method using the Visual Studio editor, the method statements are indented for you automatically. You can place as many statements as you want within a method body.

You can place a method in its own file, as you will learn in the next section. You also can place a method within the file of a program that will use it, but you cannot place a method within any other method. Figure 7-3 shows the two locations where you can place the `ShowWelcomeMessage()` method within the `HelloClass` program file—before the `Main()` method header or after the `Main()` method's closing brace.

```
using System;
class HelloClass
{
    // The ShowWelcomeMessage() method could go here
    static void Main()
    {
        Console.WriteLine("Hello");
    }
    // Alternatively, the ShowWelcomeMessage() method could go here
    // But it cannot go in both places
}
```

Figure 7-3 Placement of a method

To make the `Main()` method call the `ShowWelcomeMessage()` method, you simply use the `ShowWelcomeMessage()` method's name as a statement within the body of the `Main()` method. Figure 7-4 shows the complete program with the method call shaded, and Figure 7-5 shows the output.

```
using System;
class HelloClass
{
    static void Main()
    {
        ShowWelcomeMessage();
        Console.WriteLine("Hello");
    }
    private static void ShowWelcomeMessage()
    {
        Console.WriteLine("Welcome.");
        Console.WriteLine("Have fun!");
        Console.WriteLine("Enjoy the program!");
    }
}
```

Figure 7-4 HelloClass program with Main() method calling the
ShowWelcomeMessage() method

The ShowWelcomeMessage() method in the HelloClass class is static, and therefore it can
be called without creating an object from the Main() method, which is also static.

Figure 7-5 Output of HelloClass program

When the Main() method executes, it calls the ShowWelcomeMessage() method, so the three
lines that make up the welcome message appear first in the output in Figure 7-5. Then, after
the method is done, the Main() method displays *Hello*.

Each of two different classes can have its own method named ShowWelcomeMessage(). Such a
method in the second class would be entirely distinct from the identically named method
in the first class. The complete name of this method is HelloClass.ShowWelcomeMessage(),
but you do not need to use the complete name when calling the method within the class.

If another class named SomeOtherClass had a public static method with the same name, the class could call the method using the following statement:

SomeOtherClass.ShowWelcomeMessage();

Declaring Variables and Constants in a Method

You can write any statements you need within a method, including variable and constant declarations. When a variable is declared within a method, it is known only from that point to the end of the method; programmers say the variable is *in scope* until the end of its method. A program element's **scope** is the segment of code in which it can be used. Programmers also say that the variable is **local** to the method.

A locally declared variable is not known to other methods or usable in them, and if another method contains a variable with the same name, the two variables are completely distinct. For example, Figure 7-6 shows a program containing two methods—Main() and MethodWithItsOwnA()—that each declare a variable named a. The variable in each method is completely distinct from the other and holds its own value, as shown in Figure 7-7. If you declared a variable named b in the Main() method and then tried to use b in MethodWithItsOwnA(), you would generate a compiler error. If you declared a variable named c in MethodWithItsOwnA() and tried to use it in Main(), you would generate another compiler error.

```
using System;
class LocalVariableDemo
{
    static void Main()
    {
        int a = 12;
        Console.WriteLine("In Main() a is {0}", a);
        MethodWithItsOwnA();
        Console.WriteLine("In Main() a is {0}", a);
    }
    private static void MethodWithItsOwnA()
    {
        int a = 354;
        Console.WriteLine("In method a is {0}", a);
    }
}
```

Figure 7-6   The LocalVariableDemo program

Figure 7-7 Execution of the LocalVariableDemo program

 Watch the video *Using Methods*.

TWO TRUTHS & A LIE

Writing Methods with No Parameters and No Return Value

1. A method header must contain declared accessibility.

2. A method header must contain a return type.

3. A method header must contain an identifier.

The false statement is #1. Declaring accessibility in a method header is optional. If you do not use an access modifier, the method is private by default.

You Do It

Calling a Method

294

In this section, you write a program in which a Main() method calls another method that displays a company's logo.

1. Open a new program named **DemoLogo** and enter the statement that uses the System namespace. Then type the class header for the DemoLogo class and the class-opening curly brace.

    ```
    using System;
    class DemoLogo
    {
    ```

2. Type the Main() method for the DemoLogo class. This method displays a line, then calls the DisplayCompanyLogo() method.

    ```
    static void Main()
    {
        Console.Write("Our company is ");
        DisplayCompanyLogo();
    }
    ```

3. Add a method that displays a two-line logo for a company.

    ```
    private static void DisplayCompanyLogo()
    {
        Console.WriteLine("See Sharp Optical");
        Console.WriteLine("We prize your eyes");
    }
    ```

4. Add the closing curly brace for the class (}), and then save the file.

5. Compile and execute the program. The output should look like Figure 7-8.

```
Command Prompt

C:\C#\Chapter.07>DemoLogo
Our company is See Sharp Optical
We prize your eyes

C:\C#\Chapter.07>
```

Figure 7-8   Output of the DemoLogo program

(continues)

(continued)

6. Remove the keyword `static` from the `DisplayCompanyLogo()` method, and then save and compile the program. An error message appears, as shown in Figure 7-9. The message indicates that an object reference is required for the nonstatic `DisplayCompanyLogo()` method. The error occurs because the `Main()` method is `static`; therefore, without declaring an object, it can only call other `static` methods. Remember that you will learn to create objects in Chapter 9, and then you can create the types of methods that do not use the keyword `static`. For now, replace the keyword `static` in the `DisplayCompanyLogo()` method header, and compile and execute the program again.

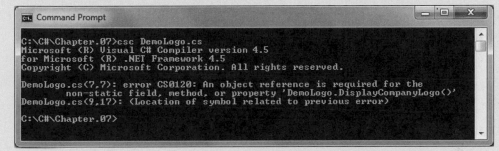

Figure 7-9 Error message when calling a nonstatic method from a static method

7. Remove the keyword `private` from the header of the `DisplayCompanyLogo()` method. Save and compile the program, and then execute it. The execution is successful because the `private` keyword is optional. Replace the `private` keyword, and save the program.

Writing Methods That Require a Single Argument

Some methods require additional information. If a method could not receive arguments, then you would have to write an infinite number of methods to cover every possible situation. For example, when you make a dental appointment, you do not need to employ a different method for every date of the year at every possible time of day. Rather, you can supply the date and time as information to the method, and no matter what date and time you supply, the method is carried out correctly. If you design a method to compute an employee's paycheck, it makes sense that you can write a method named ComputePaycheck() and supply it with an hourly pay rate rather than having to develop methods with names like ComputePaycheckAtSevenDollarsAnHour(), ComputePaycheckAtEightDollarsAnHour(), and so on.

You already have used methods to which you supplied a wide variety of parameters. At any call, the Console.WriteLine() method can receive any one of an infinite number of strings as a parameter—"Hello", "Goodbye", and so on. No matter what message you send to the WriteLine() method, the message is displayed correctly.

When you write the declaration for a method that accepts a parameter, you need to include the following items within the method declaration parentheses:

- The type of the parameter
- A local identifier (name) for the parameter

For example, consider a method named DisplaySalesTax(), which computes and displays a tax as 7 percent of a selling price. The method header for a usable DisplaySalesTax() method could be the following:

```
static void DisplaySalesTax(double saleAmount)
```

You can think of the parentheses in a method declaration as a funnel into the method—data parameters listed there are "dropping in" to the method.

The parameter double saleAmount within the parentheses indicates that the DisplaySalesTax() method will receive a value of type double. Within the method, the value will be known as saleAmount. Figure 7-10 shows a complete method.

```
private static void DisplaySalesTax(double saleAmount)
{
    double tax;
    const double RATE = 0.07;
    tax = saleAmount * RATE;
    Console.WriteLine("The tax on {0} is {1}",
        saleAmount, tax.ToString("C"));
}
```

Figure 7-10 The DisplaySalesTax() method

Within the DisplaySalesTax() method, you must use the format string and ToString() method if you want figures to display to exactly two decimal positions. You learned how to display values to a fixed number of decimal places in Chapter 2; recall that using the fixed format with no number defaults to two decimal places.

You create the DisplaySalesTax() method as a void method (has a void return type) because you do not need it to return any value to any method that uses it—its only function is to receive the saleAmount value, multiply it by 0.07, and then display the result. You create it as a static method because you do not want to create an object with which to use it; you want the static Main() method to be able to call it directly.

Within a program, you can call the DisplaySalesTax() method by using the method's name, and, within parentheses, an argument that is either a constant value or a variable. Thus, both of the following calls to the DisplaySalesTax() method invoke it correctly:

```
double myPurchase = 12.99;
DisplaySalesTax(12.99);
DisplaySalesTax(myPurchase);
```

You can call the DisplaySalesTax() method any number of times, with a different constant or variable argument each time. The value of each of these arguments becomes known as saleAmount within the method. The identifier saleAmount holds any double value passed into the method. Interestingly, if the argument in the method call is a variable, it might possess the same identifier as saleAmount or a different one, such as myPurchase. The identifier saleAmount is simply the name the value "goes by" while being used within the method, no matter what name it goes by in the calling program. That is, the variable saleAmount is a local variable to the DisplaySalesTax() method, as are variables and constants declared within a method. The variable saleAmount is also an example of a **formal parameter**, a parameter within a method header that accepts a value. In contrast, arguments within a method *call* often are referred to as **actual parameters**. For example, in the statement DisplaySalesTax(myPurchase);, myPurchase is an actual parameter.

The variable saleAmount is a formal parameter, and it also is an example of a *value parameter*, or a parameter that receives a copy of the value passed to it. You will learn more about value parameters and other types of parameters in the next chapter.

The DisplaySalesTax() method employs implementation hiding. That is, if a programmer changes the way in which the tax value is calculated—for example, by coding one of the following—programs that use the DisplaySalesTax() method will not be affected and will not need to be modified:

```
tax = saleAmount * 7 / 100;
tax = 0.07 * saleAmount;
tax = RATE * saleAmount;
```

Each of these statements computes tax as 7 percent of saleAmount. No matter how the tax is calculated, a calling program passes a value into the DisplaySalesTax() method, and a calculated result appears on the screen.

Figure 7-11 shows a complete program called UseTaxMethod. It uses the DisplaySalesTax() method twice, first with a variable argument, and then with a constant argument. The program's output appears in Figure 7-12.

```
using System;
class UseTaxMethod
{
    static void Main()
    {
        double myPurchase = 12.99;
        DisplaySalesTax(myPurchase);
        DisplaySalesTax(35.67);
    }
    private static void DisplaySalesTax(double saleAmount)
    {
        double tax;
        const double RATE = 0.07;
        tax = saleAmount * RATE;
        Console.WriteLine("The tax on {0} is {1}",
            saleAmount.ToString("C"), tax.ToString("C"));
    }
}
```

Figure 7-11   Complete program using the `DisplaySalesTax()` method two times

Figure 7-12   Output of the `UseTaxMethod` program

An argument type in a method call can match the method's parameter type exactly, but it can use a different data type if the argument can be converted automatically to the parameter type. Recall from Chapter 2 that C# supports the following automatic conversions:

- From sbyte to short, int, long, float, double, or decimal
- From byte to short, ushort, int, uint, long, ulong, float, double, or decimal
- From short to int, long, float, double, or decimal
- From ushort to int, uint, long, ulong, float, double, or decimal
- From int to long, float, double, or decimal
- From uint to long, ulong, float, double, or decimal
- From long to float, double, or decimal

- From ulong to float, double, or decimal

- From char to ushort, int, uint, long, ulong, float, double, or decimal

- From float to double

As an example, a method with the header private static void DisplaySalesTax(double saleAmount) can work with the following method call that uses an integer argument because integers are promoted automatically to doubles:

```
DisplaySalesTax(100);
```

Now that you have seen how to write methods that accept an argument, you might guess that when you write Console.WriteLine("Hello");, the header for the called method is similar to public static void WriteLine(string s). You might not know the parameter name the creators of C# have chosen, but you do know the method's return type, name, and parameter type. (If you use the IntelliSense feature of Visual Studio, you can discover the parameter name. See Appendix C for more details.)

Watch the video *Arguments and Parameters*.

TWO TRUTHS & A LIE

Writing Methods That Require a Single Argument

1. When you write the declaration for a method that accepts a parameter, you need to include the parameter's data type within the method header.

2. When you write the declaration for a method that accepts a parameter, you need to include the identifier of the argument that will be sent to the method within the method header.

3. When you write the declaration for a method that accepts a parameter, you need to include a local identifier for the parameter within the method header.

The false statement is #2. When you write the definition for a method, you include the data type and a local parameter name within the parentheses of the method header, but you do not include the name of any argument that will be sent from a calling method. After all, the method might be invoked any number of times with any number of different arguments.

Writing Methods That Require Multiple Arguments

A method can require more than one argument. You can pass multiple arguments to a method by listing the arguments within the call to the method and separating them with commas. For example, rather than creating a DisplaySalesTax() method that multiplies an amount by 0.07, you might prefer to create a more flexible method to which you can pass two values—the value on which the tax is calculated and the tax percentage by which it should be multiplied. Figure 7-13 shows a method that uses two such arguments.

```
private static void DisplaySalesTax(double saleAmount, double taxRate)
{
    double tax;
    tax = saleAmount * taxRate;
    Console.WriteLine("The tax on {0} at {1} is {2}",
        saleAmount.ToString("C"),
        taxRate.ToString("P"), tax.ToString("C"));
}
```

Figure 7-13　The DisplaySalesTax() method that takes two arguments

In Figure 7-13, two parameters (saleAmount and taxRate) appear within the parentheses in the method header. A comma separates the parameters, and each parameter requires its own named type (in this case, both parameters are of type double) and an identifier. A declaration for a method that receives two or more arguments must list the type for each parameter separately, even if the parameters have the *same* type.

When you pass values to the method in a statement such as DisplaySalesTax(myPurchase, localRate);, the first value passed will be referenced as saleAmount within the method, and the second value passed will be referenced as taxRate. Therefore, it is very important that arguments be passed to a method in the correct order. The following call results in output stating that "The tax on $200.00 at 10.00% is $20.00":

DisplaySalesTax(200.00, 0.10);

However, the following call results in output stating that "The tax on $0.10 at 10.00% is $20.00", which is clearly incorrect.

DisplaySalesTax(0.10, 200.00);

 If two method parameters are of the same type—for example, two doubles—passing arguments to a method in the wrong order results in a logical error. For example, if you pass values to DisplaySalesTax() in the wrong order, the multiplication works but the output description is incorrect. However, if a method expects parameters of diverse types, then passing arguments in reverse order constitutes a syntax error, and the program will not compile.

You can write a method to take any number of parameters in any order. When you call the method, however, the arguments you send to it must match (in both number and type) the parameters listed in the method declaration, with the following exceptions:

- The type of an argument does not need to match the parameter list exactly if the argument can be promoted to the parameter type. For example, an `int` argument can be passed to a `double` parameter.

- The number of arguments does not need to match the number in the parameter list when you use *default arguments*. You will learn about default arguments in Chapter 8.

Thus, a method to compute and display an automobile salesperson's commission might require arguments such as a string for the salesperson's name, an integer value of a sold car, a `double` percentage commission rate, and a character code for the vehicle type. The correct method will execute only when all arguments of the correct types are sent in the correct order.

TWO TRUTHS & A LIE

Writing Methods That Require Multiple Arguments

1. The following is a usable C# method header:

   ```
   private static void MyMethod(double amt, sum)
   ```

2. The following is a usable C# method header:

   ```
   private static void MyMethod2(int x, double y)
   ```

3. The following is a usable C# method header:

   ```
   static void MyMethod3(int id, string name, double rate)
   ```

The false statement is #1. In a method header, each parameter must have a data type, even if the data types for all the parameters are the same. The header in #3 does not contain an accessibility indicator, but that is optional.

Writing a Method that Returns a Value

A method can return, at most, one value to a method that calls it. The return type for a method can be any type used in the C# programming language, which includes the basic built-in types `int`, `double`, `char`, and so on. You can also use a class type as the return type for a method, including any type built into the C# language and others that you will learn to create in Chapter 9. Of course, a method also can return nothing, in which case the return type is `void`.

You have used a return value from the ReadLine() method when writing a statement such as inputString = Console.ReadLine();. Because the ReadLine() method call can be assigned to a string, its return type is string.

For example, a method that returns true or false depending on whether an employee worked overtime hours might be defined as:

```
private static bool IsOvertimeEarned()
```

This method returns a bool value; in other words, the method's type is bool.

As another example, a method that prompts a user for an integer test score and returns it might be defined as:

```
private static int GetScore()
```

Suppose that you want to create a method to accept the hours an employee worked and the hourly pay rate, and to return a calculated gross pay value. The header for this method could be:

```
private static double CalcPay(double hours, double rate)
```

Figure 7-14 shows this method.

```
private static double CalcPay(double hours, double rate)
{
    double gross;
    gross = hours * rate;
    return gross;
}
```

Figure 7-14   The CalcPay() method

Notice the return statement, which is the last statement within the method. A **return statement** causes a value to be sent back to the calling method; in the CalcPay() method, the value stored in gross is sent back to any method that calls the CalcPay() method. Also notice the type double that precedes the method name in the method header. The data type used in a method's return statement must be the same as the return type declared in the method's header or the program will not compile.

If a method returns a value and you call the method, you typically will want to use the returned value, although you are not required to use it. For example, when you invoke the CalcPay() method, you might want to assign the value to a double variable named grossPay, as in the following statement:

```
grossPay = CalcPay(myHours, myRate);
```

The CalcPay() method returns a double, so it is appropriate to assign the returned value to a double variable. Figure 7-15 shows a program that uses the CalcPay() method in the shaded statement, and Figure 7-16 shows the output.

```
using System;
class UseCalcPay
{
    static void Main()
    {
        double myHours = 37.5;
        double myRate = 12.75;
        double grossPay;
        grossPay = CalcPay(myHours, myRate);
        Console.WriteLine("I worked {0} hours at {1} per hour",
            myHours, myRate);
        Console.WriteLine("My gross pay is {0}",
            grossPay.ToString("C"));
    }
    private static double CalcPay(double hours, double rate)
    {
        double gross;
        gross = hours * rate;
        return gross;
    }
}
```

Figure 7-15   Program using the CalcPay() method

Figure 7-16   Output of UseCalcPay program

Instead of storing a method's returned value in a variable, you can use it directly, as in either of the following statements:

```
Console.WriteLine("My gross pay is {0}",
    CalcPay(myHours, myRate).ToString("C"));
```

```
double tax = CalcPay(myHours, myRate) * TAX_RATE;
```

In the first statement, the call to the CalcPay() method is made within the WriteLine() method call. In the second, CalcPay()'s returned value is used in an arithmetic statement. Because CalcPay() returns a double, you can use the method call CalcPay() in the same way you would use any `double` value. The method call `CalcPay()` has a `double` data type in the same way a `double` variable does.

As an additional example, suppose that you have a method named `GetPrice()` that accepts an item number and returns its price. The header is as follows:

```
private static double GetPrice(int itemNumber)
```

Further suppose that you want to ask the user to enter an item number from the keyboard so you can pass it to the `GetPrice()` method. You can get the value from the user, store it in a string, convert the string to an integer, pass the integer to the `GetPrice()` method, and store the returned value in a variable named `price` in four or five separate statements. Or you can write the following:

```
price = GetPrice(Convert.ToInt32(Console.ReadLine()));
```

This statement contains a method call to `ReadLine()` within a method call to `Convert.ToInt32()`, within a method call to `GetPrice()`. When method calls are placed inside other method calls, the calls are **nested method calls**. When you write a statement with three nested method calls like the previous statement, the innermost method executes first. Its return value is then used as an argument to the intermediate method, and its return value is used as an argument to the outer method. There is no limit to how "deep" you can go with nested method calls.

Writing a Method that Returns a Boolean Value

When a method returns a value that is type `bool`, the method call can be used anywhere you can use a Boolean expression. For example, suppose you have written a method named `isPreferredCustomer()` that returns a Boolean value indicating whether a customer is a preferred customer who qualifies for a discount. Then you can write an `if` statement such as the following:

```
if(isPreferredCustomer())
   price = price - DISCOUNT;
```

In Chapter 4 you learned about side effects and how they affect compound Boolean expressions. When you use Boolean methods, you must be especially careful not to cause unintended side effects. For example, consider the following `if` statement, in which the intention is to set a delivery fee to 0 if both the `isPreferredCustomer()` and `isLocalCustomer()` methods return true:

```
if(isPreferredCustomer() && isLocalCustomer())
   deliveryFee = 0;
```

If the `isLocalCustomer()` method should perform some desired task—for example, displaying a message about the customer's status or applying a local customer discount to the price—then you might achieve the desired results. Because of short-circuit evaluation, if the `isPreferredCustomer()` method returns `false`, the `isLocalCustomer()` method never executes. If that is your intention, then using methods in this way is fine, but always consider any unintended side effects.

Analyzing a Built-in Method

C# provides you with many prewritten methods. For example, you have seen `Console.WriteLine()` and `Console.ReadLine()` methods used in programs throughout this book. In Chapter 2, you learned about C#'s arithmetic operators, such as + and *, and you learned that C# provides no exponential operator. Instead, to raise a number to a power, you can use the built-in `Pow()` method. For example, to raise 2 to the third power (2 * 2 * 2) and store the answer in the variable `result`, you can write a program that includes the following statement:

```
double result = Math.Pow(2.0, 3.0);
```

From this statement, you know the following about the `Pow()` method:

- It is in the `Math` class because the class name and a dot precede the method call.

- It is `public` because you can write a program that uses it.

- It is `static` because it is used with its class name and a dot, without any object.

- It accepts two `double` parameters.

- It returns a `double` or a type that can be promoted automatically to a `double` (such as an `int`) because its answer is stored in a `double`.

Although you know many facts about the `Pow()` method, you do not know how its instructions are carried out internally. In good object-oriented style, its implementation is hidden.

TWO TRUTHS & A LIE

Writing a Method that Returns a Value

1. A method can return, at most, one value to a method that calls it.

2. The data type used in a method's `return` statement must be the same as the return type declared in the method's header.

3. If a method returns a value and you call the method, you must store the value in a variable that has the same data type as the method's parameter.

The false statement is #3. If a method returns a value and you call the method, you typically will want to use the returned value, but you are not required to use it. Furthermore, if you do assign the returned value to a storage variable, that variable does not have to match any parameter's value. Instead, the storage variable needs to be capable of accepting the method's returned type.

You Do It

Writing a Method that Receives Parameters and Returns a Value

Next, you write a method named CalcPhoneCallPrice() that both receives parameters and returns a value. The purpose of the method is to accept the length of a phone call in minutes and the rate charged per minute, and to then calculate the price of a call, assuming each call includes a 25-cent connection charge in addition to the per-minute charge. After writing the CalcPhoneCallPrice() method, you write a Main() method that calls the CalcPhoneCallPrice() method using four different sets of data as arguments.

1. Start a program named **PhoneCall** by typing a using statement, class header, and opening brace:

```
using System;
class PhoneCall
{
```

2. Type the following CalcPhoneCallPrice() method. The method is declared as static because it will be called by a static Main() method without creating an object. The method receives an integer and a double as parameters. The fee for a call is calculated as 0.25 plus the minutes times the rate per minute. The method returns the phone call fee to the calling method.

```
private static double CalcPhoneCallPrice(int minutes,
    double rate)
{
    const double BASE_FEE = 0.25;
    double callFee;
    callFee = BASE_FEE + minutes * rate;
    return callFee;
}
```

3. Add the Main() method header for the PhoneCall class. Begin the method by declaring two arrays; one contains two call lengths and the other contains two rates. You will use all the possible combinations of call lengths and rates to test the CalcPhoneCallPrice() method. Also, declare a double named priceOfCall that will hold the result of a calculated call price.

```
static void Main()
{
    int[] callLengths = {2, 5};
    double[] rates = { 0.03, 0.12};
    double priceOfCall;
```

(continues)

(continued)

4. Add a statement that displays column headings under which you can list combinations of call lengths, rates, and prices. The three column headings are right-aligned, each in a field 10 characters wide.

```
Console.WriteLine("{0, 10}{1, 10}{2, 10}",
    "Minutes", "Rate", "Price");
```

5. Add a pair of nested loops that pass each `callLength` and each `rate` to the `CalcPhoneCallPrice()` method in turn. As each pair is passed, the result is stored in the `priceOfCall` variable, and the details are displayed. Using the nested loops allows you to pass each combination of call time and rate so that multiple possibilities for the values can be tested conveniently.

```
for(int x = 0; x < callLengths.Length; ++x)
    for(int y = 0; y < rates.Length; ++y)
    {
        priceOfCall = CalcPhoneCallPrice(callLengths[x],
            rates[y]);
        Console.WriteLine("{0, 10}{1, 10}{2, 10}",
            callLengths[x], rates[y],
            priceOfCall.ToString("C"));
    }
```

6. Add a closing curly brace for the `Main()` method and another for the `PhoneCall` class.

7. Save the file, and then compile and run the program. The output looks like Figure 7-17. It shows how a single method can produce a variety of results when you use different values for the arguments.

Figure 7-17 Output of the PhoneCall program

Passing Array Values to a Method

Passing an array element to a method and passing an array to a method require different approaches.

Passing a Single Array Element to a Method

In the chapter *Using Arrays*, you learned that you can declare an array to create a list of elements, and that you can use any individual array element in the same manner as you would use any single variable of the same type. That is, suppose you declare an integer array as follows:

```
int[] someNums = new int[12];
```

You can subsequently output someNums[0] or add 1 to someNums[1], just as you would for any integer. Similarly, you can pass a single array element to a method in exactly the same manner as you would pass a variable.

Consider the program shown in Figure 7-18. This program creates and uses an array of four integers. Figure 7-19 shows the program's execution.

```csharp
using System;
class PassArrayElement
{
   static void Main()
   {
      int[] someNums = {10, 12, 22, 35};
      int x;
      Console.Write("\nAt beginning of Main() method...");
      for(x = 0; x < someNums.Length; ++x)
         Console.Write("{0,6}", someNums[x]);
      Console.WriteLine();
      for(x = 0; x < someNums.Length; ++x)
         MethodGetsOneInt(someNums[x]);
      Console.Write("At end of Main() method..........");
      for(x = 0; x < someNums.Length; ++x)
         Console.Write("{0,6}", someNums[x]);
   }
   private static void MethodGetsOneInt(int oneVal)
   {
      Console.Write("In MethodGetsOneInt() {0}", oneVal);
      oneVal = 999;
      Console.WriteLine("    After change {0}", oneVal);
   }
}
```

Figure 7-18 PassArrayElement program

Figure 7-19 Output of the `PassArrayElement` program

As you can see in Figure 7-19, the program displays the four original values, then passes each to the `MethodGetsOneInt()` method, where it is displayed and then changed to 999. After the method executes four times, the `Main()` method displays the four values again, showing that they are unchanged by the assignments within `MethodGetsOneInt()`. The `oneVal` variable is local to the `MethodGetsOneInt()` method; therefore, any changes to variables passed into the method are not permanent and are not reflected in the array declared in the `Main()` program. Each time the `MethodGetsOneInt()` method executes, its `oneVal` parameter holds only a copy of the array element passed into the method, and the `oneVal` variable exists only while the `MethodGetsOneInt()` method is executing.

Passing an Array to a Method

Instead of passing a single array element to a method, you can pass an entire array. You indicate that a method parameter must be an array by placing square brackets after the data type in the method's parameter list. When you pass an array to a method, changes you make to array elements within the method are reflected in the original array that was sent to the method. Arrays, like all objects but unlike built-in types such as `double` and `int`, are **passed by reference**. That is, when a simple built-in type is passed to a method, the method receives a copy of the value at a new memory address, but when an array is passed to a method, the method receives the actual memory address of the array and has access to the actual values in the array elements. You already have seen that methods can alter arrays passed to them. When you use the `Sort()` and `Reverse()` methods, the methods change the array parameter contents.

The program shown in Figure 7-20 creates an array of four integers. After the integers are displayed, the entire array is passed to a method named `MethodGetsArray()` in the shaded statement. Within the method header, the parameter is declared as an array by using square brackets after the parameter data type. Within the method, the numbers are output, which shows that they retain their values from `Main()` upon entering the method, but then the value 888 is assigned to each number. Even though MethodGetsArray() is a void method (meaning that nothing is returned to the Main() method), when the program displays the array for the second time within the Main() method, all of the values have been changed to 888, as you can see in Figure 7-21. Because arrays are passed by reference, the MethodGetsArray() method "knows" the address of the array declared in Main() and makes its changes directly to the original array that was declared in the Main() method.

```
using System;
class PassEntireArray
{
   static void Main()
   {
      int[] someNums = {10, 12, 22, 35};
      int x;
      Console.Write("\nAt beginning of Main() method...");
      for(x = 0; x < someNums.Length; ++x)
         Console.Write("{0, 6}", someNums[x]);
      Console.WriteLine();
      MethodGetsArray(someNums);
      Console.Write("At end of Main() method..........");
      for(x = 0; x < someNums.Length; ++x)
         Console.Write("{0, 6}", someNums[x]);
   }
   private static void MethodGetsArray(int[] vals)
   {
      int x;
      Console.Write("In MethodGetsArray() ");
      for(x = 0; x < vals.Length; ++x)
         Console.Write(" {0}", vals[x]);
      Console.WriteLine();
      for(x = 0; x < vals.Length; ++x)
         vals[x] = 888;
      Console.Write("After change");
      for(x = 0; x < vals.Length; ++x)
         Console.Write(" {0}", vals[x]);
      Console.WriteLine();
   }
}
```

Figure 7-20   The PassEntireArray program

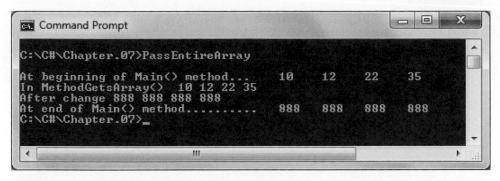

Figure 7-21 Output of the PassEntireArray program

Notice that you do not insert a number within the square brackets of the array definition in the method parameter list. Inserting a number causes a compiler error. It makes sense that the brackets are empty because a method that receives an array gets its starting address, not a number of elements.

 You can create and pass an unnamed array to a method in a single step. For example, you can write the following:

```
MethodThatAcceptsArray(new int[] {45, 67, 89});
```

You can pass a multidimensional array to a method by indicating the appropriate number of dimensions after the data type in the method header. For example, the following method headers accept two-dimensional arrays of ints and doubles, respectively:

```
private static void displayScores(int[,] scoresArray)
private static boolean areAllPricesHigh(double[,] prices)
```

With jagged arrays, you can insert the appropriate number of square brackets after the data type in the method header. For example, the following method headers accept jagged arrays of ints and doubles, respectively:

```
private static void displayIDs(int[][] idArray)
private static double computeTotal(double[][] prices)
```

With methods that accept multidimensional arrays as parameters (whether jagged or not), notice that the brackets that define the array in each method header are empty. Like any other array passed to a method, inserting numbers into the brackets for a jagged array is not necessary because each passed array name is a starting memory address. The way you manipulate subscripts within the method determines how rows and columns are accessed.

The size of each dimension of a multidimensional array can be accessed using the `GetLength()` method. For example, `scoresArray.GetLength(0)` returns the value of the first dimension of `scoresArray`.

Watch the video *Passing Arrays to Methods*.

TWO TRUTHS & A LIE

Passing Array Values to a Method

1. You indicate that a method parameter can be an array element by placing a data type and identifier in the method's parameter list.

2. You indicate that a method parameter must be an array by placing parentheses after the data type in the method's parameter list.

3. Arrays are passed by reference; that is, the method receives the actual memory address of the array and has access to the actual values in the array elements.

The false statement is #2. You indicate that a method parameter must be an array by placing square brackets after the data type in the method's parameter list.

Alternate Ways to Write a `Main()` Method Header

Throughout this book, you have written `Main()` methods with the following header:

```
static void Main()
```

Using the return type `void` and listing nothing between the parentheses that follow `Main` is just one way to write a `Main()` method header in a program. However, it is the first way listed in the C# documentation, and it is the convention used in this book. This section describes alternatives because you might see different `Main()` method headers in other books or in programs written by others.

Writing a `Main()` Method with a Parameter List

An alternate way to write a `Main()` method header is as follows:

```
static void Main(string[] args)
```

The phrase string[] args is a parameter to the Main() method. The variable args represents an array of strings that you can pass to Main(). Although you can use any identifier, args is conventional. In particular, Java programmers might prefer the C# version of Main() that includes the string[] args parameter because their convention is to write main methods with the same parameter.

Use this format for the Main() method header if you need to access command-line arguments passed in to your application. For example, the program in Figure 7-22 displays an args array that is a parameter to its Main() method. Figure 7-23 shows how a program might be executed from the command line using arguments to Main().

```csharp
using System;
class DisplayArgs
{
    static void Main(string[] args)
    {
        for(int x = 0; x < args.Length; ++x)
            Console.WriteLine("Argument {0} is {1}", x, args[x]);
    }
}
```

Figure 7-22 A Main() method with a string[] args parameter

Figure 7-23 Executing the DisplayArgs program with arguments

Even if you do not need access to command-line arguments, you can still use the version of the Main() method header that references them. You should use this version if your instructor or supervisor indicates you should follow this convention.

Writing a `Main()` Method with an Integer Return Type

Some programmers prefer to write `Main()` method headers that have a return type of `int` instead of `void`. If you use this form, the last statement in the `Main()` method must be a return statement that returns an integer. By convention, a return value of 0 means that an application ended without error. The value might be used by your operating system or another program that uses your program. In particular, C++ programmers might prefer the version of `Main()` that returns an `int` because conventionally they write their main methods with an `int` return type.

Even if you do not need to use a return value from a `Main()` method, you can still use the version of the `Main()` method header that includes a return value. You should use this version if your instructor or supervisor indicates you should follow this convention.

Writing a `Main()` Method with `public` Access

Some programmers prefer to write `Main()` method headers with `public` access rather than `private`, which is the default access when no specifier is listed. In particular, Java programmers might prefer using `public` because the style is conventional for them. If a class's `Main()` method is `public`, it can be called from another class by using its fully qualified name. Because you rarely want to do this, C# programmers often omit the `Main()` method's access specifier, making it `private`.

TWO TRUTHS & A LIE

Alternate Ways to Write a `Main()` Method Header

1. In C#, a `Main()` method header can be written `public static void Main()`.

2. In C#, a `Main()` method header can be written `static void Main(string[] args)`.

3. In C#, a `Main()` method header can be written `static int main(string args)`.

The false statement is #3. In C#, a `Main()` method header can be written as shown in either of the first two examples. Statement #3 is wrong because `Main()` must be capitalized and string must be followed by a pair of square brackets.

Issues Using Methods in GUI Programs

You can call methods from other methods in a GUI application in the same way you can in a console application. Some special considerations when creating GUI applications include the following:

- Understanding methods that are automatically generated in the visual environment

- Appreciating scope in a GUI program

- Creating methods to be nonstatic when associated with a Form

Understanding Methods that are Automatically Generated in the Visual Environment

When you create GUI applications using the IDE, many methods are generated automatically. For example, when you place a Button named okButton on a Form in the IDE and double-click it, a method is generated with the following header:

```
private void okButton_Click(object sender, EventArgs e)
```

The method is private, which means it can only be used within its class, and it is void, meaning it does not return a value. You could change the access specifier to public and the method would still work, but usually you would have no reason to make such a change. If you change the return type (void), the program will not compile.

The format of the method name okButton_Click() is conventional for automatically created event handling methods. The name includes the control name, an underscore, and the event that causes the method to execute—in this case, a Click event. Although the C# convention is to begin method names with an uppercase letter, event-handling method names like okButton_Click() begin with a lowercase letter to echo the format of the control's name.

The parameters received by the okButton_Click() method arrive automatically when a user clicks the okButton. The parameter sender is the object that generated the event that caused the method to execute, and the parameter e contains information about the type of event. Figure 7-24 shows a Click() method in a GUI application that displays the ToString() values of these two parameters.

```
private void okButton_Click(object sender, EventArgs e)
{
   label1.Text = sender.ToString();
   label2.Text = e.ToString();
}
```

Figure 7-24 The okButton_Click() method in the ClickParameterDemo program

Figure 7-25 shows the output after the button is clicked. The object that generated the event is the button that contains the text "OK" and the type of event was generated by a mouse. You have seen many Click() methods in earlier chapters that had the same parameters, but you did not use them. As with any other method, you never are required to use the parameters passed in.

Figure 7-25   Output generated by the okButton_Click() method in Figure 7-24

Appreciating Scope in A GUI Program

When you create event-handling methods in a GUI application, you must constantly be aware of which variables and constants are needed by multiple methods. When you declare a variable or constant within a method, it is local to that method. If a variable or constant is needed by multiple event-handling methods—for example, by two different Click() methods—then the variables or constants in question must be defined outside the methods (but within the Form class) so that both Click() methods have access to them. When you write other methods, you can decide what arguments to pass in, but automatically generated event-handling methods have predefined sets of parameters, so you cannot be as flexible in using them as you can with other methods you write. In Chapter 9, *Using Classes and Objects*, you see many examples of variables declared within a class but outside methods; such variables are called *fields*.

Creating Methods to be Nonstatic when Associated with a Form

In Chapter 1, you learned that the keyword static is used with Main() methods in console applications because the method is associated with its containing class and not with an object. When you create a GUI application and generate a method, such as a Click() method associated with a Button on a Form, the keyword static does not appear in the method header because the method is associated with an object—the Form from which the method-invoking events are sent. When you execute a GUI program using a Form, the program creates a Form object, and the methods associated with it are nonstatic. In the chapter *Using Classes and Objects*, you will learn much more about the differences between static and nonstatic methods. For now, omit the word static when you create methods that are intended to be called by other nonstatic methods in your GUI applications. For example, if you create a Click() method that responds to button clicks, it will be nonstatic by default because it is associated with an object that is a Form.

TWO TRUTHS & A LIE

Issues Using Methods in GUI Programs

1. An advantage to using the IDE to create GUI programs is that many methods you need are generated automatically.

2. As with any other methods, when you create a Click() method associated with a button in a GUI application, you do not need to reference the parameters within the method body.

3. If you want a Click() method to add two variables, you must pass them in as parameters.

The false statement is #3. Automatically generated event-handling methods have predefined sets of parameters, so you cannot be as flexible in using them as you can with other methods you write.

Chapter Summary

- A method is a series of statements that carry out a task. Any class can contain an unlimited number of methods. Object-oriented programs hide their methods' implementations; a client method uses an interface to work with the method.

- You write methods to make programs easier to understand and so that you can easily reuse them. In C#, a method must include a method declaration, an opening curly brace, a method body, and a closing curly brace. The method declaration defines the rules for using the method; it contains an optional declared accessibility, an optional static modifier, a return type for the method, an identifier, and an optional list of method parameters between parentheses.

- Some methods require passed-in information. The data items sent in method calls are arguments. The items received by a method are parameters. When you write the declaration for a method that can receive a parameter, you need to include the type of parameter and a local identifier for it within the method declaration parentheses. A variable declared in a method header is a formal parameter, and an argument within a method call is an actual parameter.

- You can pass multiple arguments to a method by listing the arguments within the parentheses in the call to the method and separating them with commas. You can write a method to take any number of parameters in any order. When you call the method, however, the arguments you send to it must match in both number and type (allowing for type conversion) with the nondefault parameters listed in the method declaration.

- The return type for a method defines the type of value sent back to the calling method. It can be any type used in the C# programming language, which includes the basic built-in types int, double, char, and so on, as well as class types (including class types you create). A method also can return nothing, in which case the return type is void.

- You can pass an array as a parameter to a method. You indicate that a method parameter is an array by placing square brackets after the data type in the method's parameter list. Arrays, like all objects but unlike built-in types, are passed by reference; that is, the method receives the actual memory address of the array and has access to the actual values in the array elements.

- You might see different Main() method headers in other books or in programs written by others. Some programmers include an array of strings as a parameter to Main(), some programmers return an int from the Main() method, and some programmers give Main() methods public access.

- Special considerations exist for methods when you create GUI applications. You must understand the automatically generated methods in the visual environment, appreciate the differences in scope in GUI programs, and understand that many methods must be nonstatic when associated with a Form.

Key Terms

A **method** is an encapsulated series of statements that carry out a task.

Methods are **invoked**, or **called**, by other methods.

A **calling method** calls another method.

A **called method** is invoked by another method.

Implementation hiding means keeping the details of a method's operations hidden.

To **interface** with a system is to interact with it.

A **client** is a method that uses another method.

A **black box** is any device you can use without knowing how it works internally.

A **multifile assembly** is a group of files containing methods that work together to create an application.

Code bloat is a term that describes unnecessarily long or repetitive program statements.

A **method declaration** is a **method header** or **method definition**.

A **method body** is a block of statements that carry out a method's work.

Accessibility for a method is a declaration that sets limits as to whether and how other methods can use it.

Public access is a level of method accessibility that allows unlimited access to a method.

Private access is a level of method accessibility that limits method access to the containing class.

A **fully qualified** name is one that includes the class name.

A **static** method can be called without referring to an object. It can be called using its class name, a dot, and the method name. Within its class, a static method can be called by just using its name.

A **nonstatic** method requires an object reference.

A **return type** indicates what kind of value a method will return to any other method that calls it.

A **method's type** is its return type.

A **parameter to a method** is a variable that holds data passed to a method when it is called.

A **parameter list** consists of the data types and parameter names that appear between parentheses in a method header. The list might hold only one item.

A variable's **scope** is the segment of program code where it can be used.

A **local** variable is one that is declared in the current method.

A **formal parameter** is a parameter within a method header that accepts a value.

Actual parameters are arguments within a method call.

A **return statement** causes a value to be sent back from a method to its calling method.

Nested method calls are method calls placed inside other method calls.

When data is **passed by reference** to a method, the method receives the memory address of the argument passed to it.

Review Questions

1. At most, a class can contain _____ method(s).

   a. 0

   b. 1

   c. 2

   d. any number of

2. Which of the following is a good reason for creating methods within a program?

    a.   Methods are easily reusable.

    b.   Because all methods must be stored in the same class, they are easy to find.

    c.   The Main() method becomes more detailed.

    d.   All of these are true.

3. In C#, a method must include all of the following *except* a _____.

    a.   return type   c.   body

    b.   access modifier   d.   closing curly brace

4. A method declaration might contain _____.

    a.   declared accessibility   c.   multiple return types

    b.   a nonstatic modifier   d.   parameters separated by dots

5. Every method declaration must contain _____.

    a.   a statement of purpose   c.   the static modifier

    b.   declared accessibility   d.   a return type

6. If you want to create a method that other methods can access without limitations, you declare the method to be _____.

    a.   unlimited   c.   shared

    b.   public   d.   unrestricted

7. If you use the keyword modifier static in a method header, you indicate that the method _____.

    a.   cannot be copied

    b.   can be called only once

    c.   cannot require parameters

    d.   can be called without referring to an object

8. A method's type is also its _____.

    a.   return type   c.   parameter type

    b.   accessibility   d.   scope

9. When you use a method, you do not need to know how it operates internally. This feature is called _____.

    a.   scope management   c.   implementation hiding

    b.   selective ignorance   d.   privacy

10. When you write the method declaration for a method that can receive a parameter, you need to include all of the following items *except* _____.

   a. a pair of parentheses
   b. the type of the parameter
   c. a local name for the parameter
   d. an initial value for the parameter

11. Suppose you have declared a variable as int myAge = 21;.
    Which of the following is a legal call to a method with the declaration
    private static void AMethod(int num)?

   a. AMethod(int 55);
   b. AMethod(myAge);
   c. AMethod(int myAge);
   d. AMethod();

12. Suppose you have declared a method named
    private static void CalculatePay(double rate). When a method calls the
    CalculatePay() method, the calling method _____.

   a. must contain a declared double named rate
   b. might contain a declared double named rate
   c. cannot contain a declared double named rate
   d. cannot contain any declared double variables

13. In the method call PrintTheData(double salary);, salary is the _____ parameter.

   a. formal
   b. actual
   c. proposed
   d. preferred

14. A program contains the method call PrintTheData(salary);. In the method definition, the name of the formal parameter must be _____.

   a. salary
   b. any legal identifier other than salary
   c. any legal identifier
   d. omitted

15. What is a correct declaration for a method that receives two double arguments and calculates and displays the difference between them?

   a. private static void CalcDifference(double price1, price2)
   b. private static void CalcDifference(double price1, double price2)
   c. Both of these are correct.
   d. None of these are correct.

16. What is a correct declaration for a method that receives two **double** arguments and sums them?

    a.   `private static void CalcSum(double firstValue, double secondValue)`

    b.   `private static void CalcSum(double price1, double price2)`

    c.   Both of these are correct.

    d.   None of these are correct.

17. A method is declared as `private static double CalcPay(int hoursWorked)`. Suppose you write a `Main()` method in the same class that contains the declarations `int hours = 35;` and `double pay;`. Which of the following represents a correct way to call the `CalcPay()` method from the `Main()` method?

    a.   `hours = CalcPay();`

    b.   `hours = Main.CalcPay();`

    c.   `pay = CalcPay(hoursWorked);`

    d.   `pay = CalcPay(hours);`

18. Suppose the value of `isRateOK()` is `true` and the value of `isQuantityOK()` is `false`. When you evaluate the expression `isRateOK() || isQuantityOK()`, which of the following is true?

    a.   Only the method `isRateOK()` executes.

    b.   Only the method `isQuantityOK()` executes.

    c.   Both methods execute.

    d.   Neither method executes.

19. Suppose the value of `isRateOK()` is `true` and the value of `isQuantityOK()` is `false`. When you evaluate the expression `isRateOK() && isQuantityOK()`, which of the following is true?

    a.   Only the method `isRateOK()` executes.

    b.   Only the method `isQuantityOK()` executes.

    c.   Both methods execute.

    d.   Neither method executes.

20. When an array is passed to a method, the method has access to the array's memory address. This means an array is passed by _____.

    a.   reference   c.   alias

    b.   value   d.   orientation

Exercises

Programming Exercises

1. Create a C# statement that uses each of the following built-in methods you have used in previous chapters, then make an intelligent guess about the return type and parameter list for the method used in each statement you created.

    a. `Console.WriteLine()`

    b. `String.Equals()`

    c. `String.Compare()`

    d. `Convert.ToInt32()`

    e. `Convert.ToChar()`

    f. `Array.Sort()`

2. a. Create a console-based program named **Memo** whose `Main()` method uses several `WriteLine()` calls to display a memo to your boss. Use the company name "C# Software Developers" at least three times in the memo. Each time you want to display the company name, call a method named `DisplayCompanyName()` that displays the name as part of the memo.

    b. Create a GUI version of the `Memo` program named **MemoGUI**. When the user clicks a button, display the memo, getting the company name from the `DisplayCompanyName()` method.

3. a. Create a console-based program named **SidingEstimate** whose `Main()` method holds values for the length and depth of a house and accepts values in feet for these variables from a user. Within the class, create a method that accepts the variables and then computes the cost of siding a house as length times width times $5. Return the cost to the `Main()` method and display it.

    b. Create a GUI application named **SidingEstimateGUI** that accepts a house's dimensions from a user and contains the methods described in Exercise 3a. When the user clicks a button, display the results.

4. a. Create a console-based application named **ConvertInchesToCm** whose `Main()` method prompts a user for a number of inches, passes the value to a method that converts the value to centimeters, and then returns the value to the `Main()` method where it is displayed. An inch is 2.54 centimeters.

    b. Create a GUI application named **ConvertInchesToCmGUI** that uses a method like the one described in Exercise 4a. The program converts inches to centimeters when the user clicks a button.

5. a. Create a console-based program named **FormLetter** whose Main() method contains an array of at least six strings with sentences that encourage sales, such as "Buy it today" and "You won't regret your purchase." The program randomly selects three of the sentences and passes them to a method that generates a customer sales letter. The letter contains a greeting followed by the selected phrases.

   b. Create an application named **FormLetterGUI** that is similar to the application described in Exercise 5a, except that the letter is composed when the user clicks a button.

6. a. Create a console-based application named **Multiplication** whose Main() method asks the user to input an integer and then calls a method named MultiplicationTable(), which displays the results of multiplying the integer by each of the numbers 2 through 10.

   b. Create a GUI application named **MultiplicationGUI** that calls the MultiplicationTable() method described in Exercise 6a after the user enters an integer into a TextBox and clicks a Button.

7. In Chapter 4, you wrote a program named Admission for a college admissions office in which the user enters a numeric high school grade point average and an admission test score. The program displays "Accept" or "Reject" based on those values. Now, create a modified program named **AdmissionModularized** in which the grade point average and test score are passed to a method that returns a string containing "Accept" or "Reject".

8. In Chapter 5, you wrote a program named CountVowels that accepts a phrase from the user and counts the number of vowels in the phrase. Now, create a modified program named **CountVowelsModularized** in which the phrase is passed to a method that returns the number of vowels.

9. In Chapter 6, you wrote an application named Commission that computes commissions for automobile salespeople based on the value of the car sold. Now, create a modified application named **CommissionModularized** in which a method accepts the car price and returns the commission rate.

10. a. Create a console-based application named **Desks** that computes the price of a desk and whose Main() method calls the following methods:

   - A method to accept the number of drawers in the desk as input from the keyboard. This method returns the number of drawers to the Main() method.

   - A method to accept as input and return the type of wood—'m' for mahogany, 'o' for oak, or 'p' for pine.

   - A method that accepts the number of drawers and wood type, and calculates the cost of the desk based on the following:

- Pine desks are $100.

- Oak desks are $140.

- All other woods are $180.

- A $30 surcharge is added for each drawer.

- This method returns the cost to the `Main()` method.

- A method to display all the details and the final price.

   b. Create a GUI application named **DesksGUI** that accepts desk order data from TextBoxes and whose button's `Click()` method calls all the methods described in Exercise 10a.

11. Create either a console-based or GUI program named **FlexibleArrayMethod** that declares at least three integer arrays of different sizes. In turn, pass each array to a method that displays all the integers in each array and their sum.

 Debugging Exercises

1. Each of the following files in the Chapter.07 folder of your downloadable student files has syntax and/or logical errors. In each case, determine the problem and fix the program. After you correct the errors, save each file using the same filename preceded with *Fixed*. For example, DebugSeven1.cs will become FixedDebugSeven1.cs.

   a. DebugSeven1.cs   c. DebugSeven3.cs
   b. DebugSeven2.cs   d. DebugSeven4.cs

 Case Problems

1. In Chapter 6, you continued to modify the **GreenvilleRevenue** program. Now, modify the program so that the major functions appear in the following individual methods:

- A method that gets and returns a valid number of contestants and is called twice—once for last year's number of contestants and one for this year's value

- A method that accepts the number of contestants this year and last year, and displays one of the three messages that describes the relationship between the two contestant values

- A method that fills the array of competitors and their talent codes

- A method that continuously prompts for talent codes and displays contestants with the corresponding talent until a sentinel value is entered

2. In previous chapters, you continued to modify the **MarshallsRevenue** program. Now, modify the program so that the major functions appear in the following individual methods:

    • A method that prompts for and returns the month

    • A method that prompts for and returns the number of murals scheduled and is called twice—once for interior murals and once for exterior murals

    • A method that accepts the number of interior and exterior murals scheduled, accepts the month they are scheduled, displays the interior and exterior prices, and then returns the total expected revenue

    • A method that fills an array with customer names and mural codes and is called twice—once to fill the array of interior murals and once to fill the array of exterior murals

    • A method that continuously prompts for mural codes and displays jobs of the corresponding type until a sentinel value is entered

Advanced Method Concepts

In this chapter you will:

◎ Learn about parameter types and review mandatory value parameters

◎ Use `ref` parameters, `out` parameters, and parameter arrays

◎ Overload methods

◎ Learn how to avoid ambiguous methods

◎ Use optional parameters

In the last chapter you learned to call methods, pass arguments to them, and receive values from them. In this chapter you will expand your method-handling skills to include more sophisticated techniques, including using reference, output, and optional parameters and overloading methods. Understanding how to manipulate methods is crucial when you are working on large, professional, real-world projects. With methods, you can coordinate your work with that of other programmers.

Understanding Parameter Types

In C#, you can write methods with several kinds of formal parameters listed within the parentheses in the method header. Parameters can be mandatory or optional. When you use a **mandatory parameter**, an argument for it is required in every method call.

The four types of mandatory parameters are:

- Value parameters, when they are declared *without* default values

- Reference parameters, which are declared with the ref modifier

- Output parameters, which are declared with the out modifier

- Parameter arrays, which are declared with the params modifier

C# includes only one type of optional parameter:

- Value parameters, when they are declared *with* default values

Using Mandatory Value Parameters

So far, all of the method parameters you have created have been mandatory, and all except arrays have been value parameters. When you use a **value parameter** in a method header, you indicate the parameter's type and name, and the method receives a copy of the value passed to it. A variable that is used as an argument to a method with a value parameter must have a value assigned to it. If it does not, the program will not compile.

The value of a method's value parameter is stored at a different memory address than the variable used as the argument in the method call. In other words, the actual parameter (the argument in the calling method) and the formal parameter (the parameter in the method header) refer to two separate memory locations, and the called method receives a copy of the sent value. Changes to value parameters never affect the original arguments in calling methods.

 A popular advertising campaign declares, "What happens in Vegas, stays in Vegas." The same is true of value parameters within a method—changes to them do not persist outside the method.

Figure 8-1 shows a program that declares a variable named x; the figure assumes that x is stored at memory address 2000. The value 4 is assigned to x and then displayed. Then x is passed to a method that accepts a value parameter. The method declares its own local parameter named x, which receives the value 4. This local variable is at a different memory address; for example, assume that it is 8800. The method assigns a new value, 777, to the local variable and displays it. When control returns to the Main() method, the value of x is accessed from memory location 2000 and remains 4.

```
using System;
class ParameterDemo1
{
    static void Main()
    {
        int x= 4;
        Console.WriteLine("In Main x is {0}", x);
        DisplayValueParameter(x);
        Console.WriteLine("In Main x is {0}", x);
    }
    private static void DisplayValueParameter(int x)
    {
        x = 777;
        Console.WriteLine("In method, x is {0}", x);
    }
}
```

Memory address 2000; x is 4

Memory address 8800; x is 4 when it is passed into method

Memory address 8800; x is 777

Figure 8-1 Program calling a method with a value parameter

Changing the value of x within the DisplayValueParameter() method has no effect on x in the Main() method. Even though both methods contain a variable named x, they represent two separate variables, each with its own memory location. Programmers say that a value parameter is used for "in" parameter passing—values for "in" parameters go into a method, but modifications to them do not come "out." In the program in Figure 8-1, it makes no difference whether you use the name x as the Main() method's actual parameter or use some other name. In either case, the parameter received by the DisplayValueParameter() method occupies a separate memory location. Figure 8-2 shows the output of the program in Figure 8-1.

```
C:\C#\Chapter.08>ParameterDemo1
In Main x is 4
In method, x is 777
In Main x is 4

C:\C#\Chapter.08>_
```

Figure 8-2 Output of the ParameterDemo1 program

TWO TRUTHS & A LIE

Understanding Parameter Types

1. When they are declared without default values, value parameters are optional parameters.

2. Reference and output parameters, which are declared with the `ref` and `out` modifiers, respectively, are mandatory parameters.

3. Value parameters are optional parameters when they are declared with default values.

The false statement is #1. When they are declared without default values, value parameters are mandatory parameters.

Using Reference Parameters, Output Parameters, and Parameter Arrays

On occasion, you might want a method to be able to alter a value you pass to it. In that case, you can use a reference parameter, an output parameter, or a parameter array. Each **reference parameter**, **output parameter**, and **parameter array** represents a memory address that is passed to a method, allowing the method to alter the original variable. Reference parameters, output parameters, and parameter arrays differ as follows:

- When you declare a reference parameter in a method header, the argument used to call the method must have been assigned a value.

- When you declare an output parameter, the argument used in the call need not contain an original, assigned value. However, an output parameter must be assigned a value before the method ends.

- When you declare a parameter array, the argument used in the call need not contain any original, assigned values, and the parameter array need not be assigned any values within the method.

Reference parameters, output parameters, and parameter arrays do not occupy their own memory locations. Rather, they act as **aliases**, or pseudonyms (other names), for the same memory location occupied by the values passed to them. You use the keyword `ref` as a modifier to indicate a reference parameter, the keyword `out` as a modifier to indicate an output parameter, and the keyword `params` to indicate a parameter array.

> Using an alias for a variable is similar to using an alias for a person. Jane Doe might be known as "Ms. Doe" at work but "Sissy" at home. Both names refer to the same person.

Using a ref Parameter

Figure 8-3 shows a Main() method that calls a DisplayReferenceParameter() method. The Main() method declares a variable, displays its value, and then passes the variable to the DisplayReferenceParameter() method. The modifier ref precedes both the variable name in the method call and the parameter declaration in the method header. The method's parameter number refers to the memory address of x, making number an alias for x. When DisplayReferenceParameter() changes the value of number, the change persists in the x variable within Main(). Figure 8-4 shows the output of the program.

```
using System;
class ParameterDemo2
{
    static void Main()
    {
        int x = 4;
        Console.WriteLine ("In Main x is {0}", x);
        DisplayReferenceParameter(ref x);
        Console.WriteLine ("In Main x is {0}", x);
    }
    private static void DisplayReferenceParameter(ref int number)
    {
        number = 888;
        Console.WriteLine ("In  method, number is {0}",
            number);
    }
}
```

Memory
address
2000; x is 4

Memory address
2000 – number
is another name
for x

Memory address 2000
now holds 888 both in the
method and in Main()
after the method is done

Figure 8-3 Program calling a method with a reference parameter

Figure 8-4 Output of the ParameterDemo2 program

In the header for the `DisplayReferenceParameter()` method, it makes no difference whether you use the same name as the `Main()` method's passed variable (x) or some other name, such as `number`. In either case, the passed and received variables occupy the same memory location—the address of one is the address of the other.

Using an `out` Parameter

When you use a reference parameter, any passed variable must have an assigned value. Using an output parameter is convenient when the passed variable doesn't have a value yet. For example, the program in Figure 8-5 uses `InputMethod()` to obtain values for two parameters. The arguments that are sent in the shaded statement get their values from the method, so it makes sense to provide them with no values going in. Instead, they acquire values in the method and retain the values coming out. Figure 8-6 shows a typical execution of the program.

```
using System;
class InputMethodDemo
{                                        Notice the
                                         keyword out.
    static void Main()
    {
        int first, second;
        InputMethod(out first, out second);
        Console.WriteLine("After InputMethod first is {0}", first);
        Console.WriteLine("and second is {0}", second);
    }
    private static void InputMethod(out int one, out int two)
    {
        string s1, s2;
        Console.Write("Enter first integer ");
        s1 = Console.ReadLine();                    Notice the
        Console.Write("Enter second integer ");     keyword out.
        s2 = Console.ReadLine();
        one = Convert.ToInt32(s1);
        two = Convert.ToInt32(s2);
    }
}
```

Figure 8-5   The `InputMethodDemo` program

Figure 8-6   Output of the `InputMethodDemo` program

In summary, when you need a method to alter a single value, you have two options:

- You can send an argument to a method that accepts a value parameter, alter the local version of the variable within the method, return the altered value, and assign the return value to the original variable back in the calling method.

- You can send an argument to a method that accepts a reference or output parameter and alter the value at the original memory location within the method.

A major advantage to using reference or output parameters exists when you want a method to change multiple variables. A method can have only a single return type and can return only one value at most. By using reference or output parameters to a method, you can change multiple values.

However, a major disadvantage to using reference and output parameters is that they allow multiple methods to have access to the same data, weakening the "black box" paradigm that is so important to object-oriented methodology. You should never use ref or out parameters to avoid having to return a value, but you should understand them so you can use them if required.

Watch the video *Using ref and out Parameters*.

As with simple parameters, you can use out or ref when passing an array to a method. You do so when you want to declare the array in the calling method, but use the new operator to allocate memory for it in the called method.

Using the `TryParse()` Methods

In Chapter 2, you learned two ways to convert a string to a number—you can use a Convert class method or a Parse() method. For example, each of the following statements accepts a string and converts it to an integer named score:

```
int score = Convert.ToInt32(Console.ReadLine());
int score = int.Parse(Console.ReadLine(());
```

With either of these statements, if the value accepted by ReadLine() cannot be converted to an integer (for example, because it contains a decimal point or an alphabetic character), the program abruptly stops running. Consider the simple program in Figure 8-7. The program prompts the user for a score and displays it. Figure 8-8 shows two executions of the program. In the first execution, the user enters a valid integer and everything goes smoothly. In the second execution, the user enters alphabetic characters, the program stops, and a series of error messages is displayed.

```
using System;
class ConversionWithParse
{
    static void Main()
    {
        string entryString;
        int score;
        Console.Write("Enter your test score >> ");
        entryString = Console.ReadLine();
        score = int.Parse(entryString);
        Console.WriteLine("You entered {0}", score);
    }
}
```

Figure 8-7   The ConversionWithParse program

Figure 8-8   Two typical executions of the ConversionWithParse program

The messages in Figure 8-8 indicate that the program contains an unhandled exception because *Input string was not in a correct format*. An exception is a program error; you will learn much more about exceptions in Chapter 11, *Exception Handling*. For now, however, you can handle data conversion exceptions by using a version of the TryParse() method with an out parameter. C#'s TryParse() methods convert a string to the correct data type and store the result in a passed variable if possible. If conversion is not possible, the methods assign 0 to the variable.

Figure 8-9 contains a program that uses the int.TryParse() method to convert entryString to an integer that is assigned to score. The only differences from the program in Figure 8-7 are the shaded change to the class name and the shaded call to the int.TryParse() method. The TryParse() method accepts two parameters: the string to be converted and the variable where the result is stored. The keyword out is required with the second parameter because the method receives its address and changes the value. Figure 8-10 shows two typical executions of the ConversionWithTryParse program. When the user's input cannot be converted correctly, the out parameter is assigned 0. Whether the user's input is in the correct format or not, the program continues and displays output instead of error messages.

```
using System;
class ConversionWithTryParse
{
    static void Main()
    {
        string entryString;
        int score;
        Console.Write("Enter your test score >> ");
        entryString = Console.ReadLine();
        int.TryParse(entryString, out score);
        Console.WriteLine("You entered {0}", score);
    }
}
```

Figure 8-9   The ConversionWithTryParse program

Figure 8-10   Two typical executions of the ConversionWithTryParse program

The TryParse() methods require the receiving variable to be an out parameter because the method can return only one value. The TryParse() methods return a Boolean value that indicates whether the conversion was successful. Suppose that you do not want a score to be assigned 0 if the conversion fails, because 0 is a legitimate score. Instead, you want to assign a −1 if the conversion fails. In that case you can use a statement similar to the following:

```
if(!int.TryParse(entryString, out score))
    score = -1;
```

In this example, if `entryString`'s conversion is successful, `score` holds the converted value; otherwise, `score` holds −1. Alternatively, you might consider code that includes a loop that continues until the entered value is in the correct format, such as the following:

```
Console.Write("Enter your test score >> ");
entryString = Console.ReadLine();
while(!int.TryParse(entryString, out score))
{
    Console.WriteLine("Input data was not formatted correctly");
    Console.Write("Please enter score again >> ");
}
```

In this example, the loop continues until the `TryParse()` method returns `true`.

C# also provides `char.TryParse()`, `double.TryParse()`, and `decimal.TryParse()` methods that work in the same way—each converts a first parameter string and assigns its value to the second parameter variable, returning `true` or `false` based on the success of the conversion.

Using Parameter Arrays

When you don't know how many arguments of the same data type might eventually be sent to a method, you can declare a parameter array—a local array declared within the method header using the keyword `params`. Such a method accepts any number of arguments that are all the same type.

For example, a method with the following header accepts an array of strings:

```
private static void DisplayStrings(params string[] people)
```

In the call to this method, you can use one, two, or any other number of strings as actual parameters; within the method, they will be treated as an array.

When a method header uses the `params` keyword, the following two restrictions apply:

- Only one `params` keyword is permitted in a method declaration.

- If a method declares multiple parameters, the `params`-qualified parameter must be the last one in the list.

Figure 8-11 shows a program that calls `DisplayStrings()` three times—once with one string argument, once with three string arguments, and once with an array of strings. In each case, the method works correctly, treating the passed strings as an array and displaying them appropriately. Figure 8-12 shows the output.

```
using System;
class ParamsDemo
{
    static void Main()
    {
        string[] names = {"Mark", "Paulette", "Carol", "James"};
        DisplayStrings("Ginger");
        DisplayStrings("George", "Maria", "Thomas");
        DisplayStrings(names);
    }
    private static void DisplayStrings(params string[] people)
    {
        foreach(string person in people)
            Console.Write("{0} ", person);
        Console.WriteLine("\n--------------");
    }
}
```

Figure 8-11   The ParamsDemo program

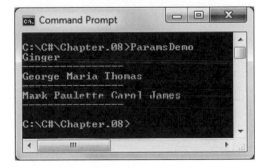

Figure 8-12   Output of the ParamsDemo program

You could create an even more flexible method by using a method header such as
Display(params Object[] things). Then the passed parameters could be any type—strings,
integers, other classes, and so on. The method could be implemented as follows:

```
private static void Display(params Object[] things)
{
    foreach(Object obj in things)
        Console.Write("{0} ", obj);
    Console.WriteLine("\n--------------");
}
```

All data types are Objects; you will learn more about the Object class in the chapters *Using
Classes and Objects* and *Introduction to Inheritance*.

TWO TRUTHS & A LIE

Using Reference Parameters, Output Parameters, and Parameter Arrays

1. Both reference and output parameters represent memory addresses that are passed to a method, allowing the method to alter the original variables.

2. When you declare a reference parameter in a method header, the parameter must not have been assigned a value.

3. When you use an output parameter, it need not contain an original, assigned value when the method is called, but it must receive a value before the method ends.

The false statement is #2. When you declare a reference parameter in a method header, the parameter must have been assigned a value.

You Do It

Using Reference Parameters

You use reference parameters when you want a method to have access to the memory address of arguments in a calling method. For example, suppose that you have two values and you want to exchange them (or swap them), making each equal to the value of the other. Because you want to change two values, a method that accepts copies of arguments will not work—a method can return one value at most. Therefore, you can use reference parameters to provide your method with the actual addresses of the values you want to change.

1. Open your editor and begin a program named **SwapProgram** as follows:
   ```
   using System;
   class SwapProgram
   {
       static void Main()
       {
   ```

2. Declare two integers and display their values. Call the Swap() method and pass in the addresses of the two variables to swap. Because the parameters already have assigned values, and because you want to alter

(continues)

(continued)

those values in Main(), you can use reference parameters. After the method call, display the two values again. Add the closing curly brace for the Main() method.

```csharp
int first = 34, second = 712;
Console.Write("Before swap first is {0}", first);
Console.WriteLine(" and second is {0}", second);
Swap(ref first, ref second);
Console.Write("After swap first is {0}", first);
Console.WriteLine(" and second is {0}", second);
}
```

3. Create the Swap() method as shown. You can swap two values by storing the first value in a temporary variable, then assigning the second value to the first variable. At this point, both variables hold the value originally held by the second variable. When you assign the temporary variable's value to the second variable, the two values are reversed.

```csharp
private static void Swap(ref int one, ref int two)
{
    int temp;
    temp = one;
    one = two;
    two = temp;
}
```

4. Add the closing curly brace for the class. Save the program, and then compile and execute it. Figure 8-13 shows the output.

Figure 8-13 Output of the SwapProgram program

You might want to use a module like Swap() as part of a larger program in which you verify, for example, that a higher value is displayed before a lower one; you would include the call to Swap() as part of a decision whose body executes only when a first value is less than a second one.

Overloading Methods

Overloading involves using one term to indicate diverse meanings. When you use the English language, you frequently overload words. When you say "open the door," "open your eyes," and "open a computer file," you describe three very different actions that use different methods and produce different results. However, anyone who speaks English fluently has no trouble comprehending your meaning because the verb "open" is understood in the context of the noun that follows it.

Some C# operators are overloaded. For example, a + between two numeric values indicates addition, but a single + to the left of a value means the value is positive. The + sign has different meanings based on the arguments used with it. In the chapter *Using Classes and Objects*, you will learn how to overload operators to make them mean what you want with your own classes.

When you overload a C# method, you write multiple methods with a shared name but different parameter lists. A method's name and parameter list constitute the method's **signature**.

The compiler understands which method to use based on the arguments you use in a method call. For example, suppose that you create a method to display a string surrounded by a border. The method receives a string and uses the string Length property to determine how many asterisks to use to construct a border around the string. Figure 8-14 shows a program that contains the method.

```csharp
using System;
class BorderDemo1
{
   static void Main()
   {
      DisplayWithBorder("Ed");
      DisplayWithBorder("Theodore");
      DisplayWithBorder("Jennifer Ann");
   }
   private static void DisplayWithBorder(string word)
   {
      const int EXTRA_STARS = 4;
      const string SYMBOL = "*";
      int size = word.Length + EXTRA_STARS;
      int x;
      for(x = 0; x < size; ++x)
         Console.Write(SYMBOL);
      Console.WriteLine();
      Console.WriteLine(SYMBOL + " " + word + " " + SYMBOL);
      for(x = 0; x < size; ++x)
         Console.Write(SYMBOL);
      Console.WriteLine("\n\n");
   }
}
```

Figure 8-14   The BorderDemo1 program

When the `Main()` method calls the `DisplayWithBorder()` method in the program in Figure 8-14 and passes a `string` value, the method calculates a size as the length of the string plus 4, and then draws that many symbols on a single line. The method then displays a symbol, a space, the string, another space, and another symbol on the next line. The method ends by again displaying a row of symbols and some blank lines. Figure 8-15 shows the output.

Figure 8-15 Output of the `BorderDemo1` program

Suppose that you are so pleased with the output of the `DisplayWithBorder()` method that you want to use something similar to display your company's weekly sales goal figure. The problem is that the weekly sales goal amount is stored as an integer, and so it cannot be passed to the existing method. You can take one of several approaches:

- You can convert the integer sales goal to a `string` and use the existing method. This is an acceptable approach, but it requires that you remember to write an extra step in any program in which you display an integer using the border.

- You can create a new method with a unique name such as `DisplayWithBorderUsingInt()` and use it to accept an integer parameter. The drawback to this approach is that you must remember different method names when you use different data types.

- You can overload the `DisplayWithBorder()` method. Overloading methods involves writing multiple methods with the same name, but with different parameter types. For example, in addition to the `DisplayWithBorder()` method shown in Figure 8-14, you could use the method shown in Figure 8-16.

```
private static void DisplayWithBorder(int number)
{
    const int EXTRA_STARS = 4;
    const string SYMBOL = "*";
    int size = EXTRA_STARS + 1;
    int leftOver = number;
    int x;
    while(leftOver >= 10)
    {
        leftOver = leftOver / 10;
        ++size;
    }
    for(x = 0; x < size; ++x)
        Console.Write(SYMBOL);
    Console.WriteLine();
    Console.WriteLine(SYMBOL + " " + number + " " + SYMBOL);
    for(x = 0; x < size; ++x)
        Console.Write(SYMBOL);
    Console.WriteLine("\n\n");
}
```

Figure 8-16   The DisplayWithBorder() method with an integer parameter

In the version of the DisplayWithBorder() method in Figure 8-16, the parameter is an int. To determine how many asterisks to display, the method discovers the number of digits in the parameter by repeatedly dividing by 10. For example, when the argument to the method is 456, leftOver is initialized to 456. Because it is at least 10, it is divided by 10, giving 45, and size is increased to 2. Then 45 is divided by 10, giving 4, and size is increased to 3. Because 4 is not at least 10, the loop ends, and the program has determined that the parameter contains three digits. The rest of the method executes like the original version that accepts a string parameter.

 The DisplayWithBorder() method does not quite work correctly if a negative integer is passed to it because the negative sign occupies an additional display space. To rectify the problem, you could modify the method to add an extra symbol to the border when a negative argument is passed in, or you could force all negative numbers to be their positive equivalent.

If both versions of DisplayWithBorder() are included in a program and you call the method using a string, as in DisplayWithBorder("Ed"), the first version of the method shown in Figure 8-14 executes. If you use an integer as the argument in the call to DisplayWithBorder(), as in DisplayWithBorder(456), then the method shown in Figure 8-16 executes. Figure 8-17 shows a program that demonstrates several method calls, and Figure 8-18 shows the output.

```
using System;
class BorderDemo2
{
   static void Main()
   {
      DisplayWithBorder("Ed");
      DisplayWithBorder(3);
      DisplayWithBorder(456);
      DisplayWithBorder(897654);
      DisplayWithBorder("Veronica");
   }
   private static void DisplayWithBorder(string word)
   {
      const int EXTRA_STARS = 4;
      const string SYMBOL = "*";
      int size = word.Length + EXTRA_STARS;
      int x;
      for(x = 0; x < size; ++x)
         Console.Write(SYMBOL);
      Console.WriteLine();
      Console.WriteLine(SYMBOL + " " + word + " " + SYMBOL);
      for(x = 0; x < size; ++x)
         Console.Write(SYMBOL);
      Console.WriteLine("\n\n");
   }
   private static void DisplayWithBorder(int number)
   {
      const int EXTRA_STARS = 4;
      const string SYMBOL = "*";
      int size = EXTRA_STARS + 1;
      int leftOver = number;
      int x;
      while(leftOver >= 10)
      {
         leftOver = leftOver / 10;
         ++size;
      }
      for(x = 0; x < size; ++x)
         Console.Write(SYMBOL);
      Console.WriteLine();
      Console.WriteLine(SYMBOL + " " + number + " " + SYMBOL);
      for(x = 0; x < size; ++x)
         Console.Write(SYMBOL);
      Console.WriteLine("\n\n");
   }
}
```

Figure 8-17   The BorderDemo2 program

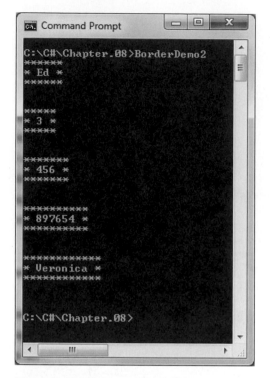

Figure 8-18   Output of the `BorderDemo2` program

Methods are overloaded correctly when they have the same identifier but their parameter lists are different. Parameter lists differ when the number and order of types within the lists are unique. For example, you could write several methods with the same identifier and one method could accept an `int`, another two `int`s, and another three `int`s. A fourth method could accept an `int` followed by a `double`, and another could accept a `double` followed by an `int`. Yet another version could accept no parameters. The parameter identifiers in overloaded methods do not matter, and neither do the return types of the methods. Only the method identifier and parameter list types cause a method to be overloaded.

Instead of overloading methods, you can choose to use methods with different names to accept the diverse data types, and you can place a decision within your program to determine which version of the method to call. However, it is more convenient to use one method name and then let the compiler determine which method to use. Overloading a method also makes it more convenient for other programmers to use your method in the future. Usually you do not create overloaded methods so that a single program can use all the versions. More often, you create overloaded methods so different programs can use the version most appropriate to the task at hand. Frequently, you create overloaded methods in your classes not because you need them immediately, but because you know client programs might need multiple versions in the future, and it is easier for programmers to remember one reasonable name for tasks that are functionally identical except for parameter types.

In this book you have seen the Console.WriteLine() method used with a string parameter, a numeric parameter, and with no parameter. You have also seen it used with several parameters when you use a format string along with several variables. Therefore, you know Console.WriteLine() is an overloaded method.

Understanding Overload Resolution

When a method call could execute multiple overloaded method versions, C# determines which method to execute using a process called **overload resolution**. For example, suppose that you create a method with the following declaration:

```
private static void MyMethod(double d)
```

You can call this method using a double argument, as in the following:

```
MyMethod(2.5);
```

You can also call this method using an int argument, as in the following:

```
MyMethod(4);
```

The call that uses the int argument works because an int can automatically be promoted to a double. In Chapter 2 you learned that when an int is promoted to a double, the process is called an *implicit conversion* or *implicit cast*.

Suppose that you create overloaded methods with the following declarations:

```
private static void MyMethod(double d)
private static void MyMethod(int i)
```

If you then call MyMethod() using an integer argument, both methods are **applicable methods**. That means either method on its own could accept a call that uses an int. However, if both methods exist in the same class (making them overloaded), the second version will execute because it is a better match for the method call. The rules that determine which method version to call are known as **betterness rules**.

Betterness rules are similar to the implicit conversion rules you learned in Chapter 2. For example, although an int could be accepted by a method that accepts an int, a float, or a double, an int is the best match. If no method version with an int parameter exists, then a float is a better match than a double. Table 8-1 shows the betterness rules for several data types.

Data Type	Conversions Are Better in This Order
byte	short, ushort, int, uint, long, ulong, float, double, decimal
sbyte	short, int, long, float, double, decimal
short	int, long, float, double, decimal
ushort	int, uint, long, ulong, float, double, decimal
int	long, float, double, decimal
uint	long, ulong, float, double, decimal
long	float, double, decimal
ulong	float, double, decimal
float	double
char	ushort, int, uint, long, ulong, float, double, decimal

Table 8-1   Betterness rules for data type conversion

Discovering Built-In Overloaded Methods

When you use the IDE to create programs, Visual Studio's IntelliSense features provide information about methods you are using. For example, Figure 8-19 shows the IDE just after the programmer has typed the opening parenthesis to the Convert.ToInt32() method. Notice the drop-down list that indicates Convert.ToInt32(bool value) is just 1 of 19 overloaded versions of the method. You can click the nodes to scroll through the rest of the list and see that other versions accept bool, byte, char, and so on. When retrieving an entry from a TextBox on a Form, your intention is to use the Convert. ToInt32(string value) version of the method, but many overloaded versions are available for your convenience. C# could have included multiple methods with different names such as ConvertBool.ToInt32() and ConvertString.ToInt32(), but having a single method with the name Convert.ToInt32() that takes many different argument types makes it easier for you to remember the method name and to use it. As you work with the IDE, you will examine many such methods.

Figure 8-19   Examining the overloaded versions of `Convert.ToInt32()`

TWO TRUTHS & A LIE

Overloading Methods

1. The following methods are overloaded:

    ```
    private static void MethodA(int a)
    private static void MethodA(double b)
    ```

2. The following methods are overloaded:

    ```
    private static void MethodC(int c)
    private static void MethodD(int c)
    ```

3. The following methods are overloaded:

    ```
    private static void MethodE(int e)
    private static void MethodE(int e, int f)
    ```

The false answer is #2. Overloaded methods must have the same name, but different parameter lists.

You Do It

Overloading Methods

In the next steps, you overload methods that correctly triple a parameter that might be an integer or a string.

1. Start a new program named **OverloadedTriples**, and create a method that triples and displays an integer parameter as follows:

```
private static void Triple(int num)
{
    const int MULT_FACTOR = 3;
    Console.WriteLine("{0} times {1} is {2}\n",
        num, MULT_FACTOR, num * MULT_FACTOR);
}
```

2. Create a second method with the same name that takes a string parameter. Assume you want to define tripling a message as displaying it three times, separated by tabs.

```
private static void Triple(string message)
{
    Console.WriteLine("{0}\t{0}\t{0}\n", message);
}
```

3. Position your cursor at the top of the file and add a `using` statement, class header, and opening curly brace so the overloaded `Triple()` methods will be contained in a class named `OverloadedTriples`.

```
using System;
class OverloadedTriples
{
```

4. Position your cursor at the bottom of the file and add the closing curly brace for the `OverloadedTriples` class.

5. Position your cursor after the opening curly brace for the class. On a new line, insert a `Main()` method that declares an integer and a string and, in turn, passes each to the appropriate `Triple()` method.

```
static void Main()
{
    int num = 20;
    string message = "Go team!";
    Triple(num);
    Triple(message);
}
```

6. Save the file, and then compile and execute the program. Figure 8-20 shows the output. Even though the same method name is used in the two method calls, the appropriate overloaded method executes each time.

(continues)

Figure 8-20   Output of the `OverloadedTriples` program

Avoiding Ambiguous Methods

When you overload a method, you run the risk of creating **ambiguous** methods—a situation in which the compiler cannot determine which method to use. Every time you call a method, the compiler decides whether a suitable method exists; if so, the method executes, and if not, you receive an error message.

For example, suppose that you write two versions of a simple method, as in the program in Figure 8-21. The class contains two versions of a method named `SimpleMethod()`—one that takes a `double` and an `int`, and one that takes an `int` and a `double`.

```
using System;
class AmbiguousMethods
{
    static void Main()
    {
        int iNum = 20;
        double dNum = 4.5;
        SimpleMethod(iNum, dNum);   // calls first version
        SimpleMethod(dNum, iNum);   // calls second version
        SimpleMethod(iNum, iNum);   // error! Call is ambiguous.
    }
    private static void SimpleMethod(int i, double d)
    {
        Console.WriteLine("Method receives int and double");
    }
    private static void SimpleMethod(double d, int i)
    {
        Console.WriteLine("Method receives double and int");
    }
}
```

Figure 8-21   Program containing an ambiguous method call

In the `Main()` method in Figure 8-21, a call to `SimpleMethod()` with an integer argument first and a `double` argument second executes the first version of the method, and a call to `SimpleMethod()` with a `double` argument first and an integer argument second executes the second version of the method. With each of these calls, the compiler can find an exact match for the arguments you send. However, if you call `SimpleMethod()` using two integer arguments, as in the shaded statement, an ambiguous situation arises because there is no exact match for the method call. Because the first integer could be promoted to a `double` (matching the second version of the overloaded method), or the second integer could be promoted to a `double` (matching the first version), the compiler does not know which version of `SimpleMethod()` to use, and the program will not compile or execute. Figure 8-22 shows the error message that is generated.

Figure 8-22   Error message generated by an ambiguous method call

An overloaded method is not ambiguous on its own—it becomes ambiguous only if you create an ambiguous situation. A program with potentially ambiguous methods will run without problems if you make no ambiguous method calls. For example, if you remove the shaded statement from Figure 8-21 that calls `SimpleMethod()` using two integer arguments, the program compiles and executes.

 If you remove one of the versions of `SimpleMethod()` from the program in Figure 8-21, then the method call that uses two integer arguments would work, because one of the integers could be promoted to a `double`. However, then one of the other method calls would fail.

Methods can be overloaded correctly by providing different parameter lists for methods with the same name. Methods with identical names that have identical parameter lists but different return types are not overloaded—they are illegal. For example, the following two methods cannot coexist within a class:

```
private static int AMethod(int x)
private static void AMethod(int x)
```

The compiler determines which of several versions of a method to call based on parameter lists. When the method call `AMethod(17);` is made, the compiler will not know which method to execute because both possibilities take an integer argument. Similarly, the following method could not coexist with either of the previous versions:

```
private static void MethodA(int someNumber)
```

Even though this method uses a different local identifier for the parameter, its parameter list—a single integer—is still the same to the compiler.

351

 Watch the video *Overloading Methods*.

TWO TRUTHS & A LIE

Avoiding Ambiguous Methods

1. The following methods are potentially ambiguous:

   ```
   private static int Method1(int g)
   private static int Method1(int g, int h)
   ```

2. The following methods are potentially ambiguous:

   ```
   private static double Method2(int j)
   private static void Method2(int k)
   ```

3. The following methods are potentially ambiguous:

   ```
   private static void Method3(string m)
   private static string Method3(string n)
   ```

The false answer is #1. Those methods are not ambiguous because they have different parameter lists. Their matching return types do not cause ambiguity.

Using Optional Parameters

Sometimes it is useful to create a method that allows one or more arguments to be omitted from the method call. An **optional parameter** to a method is one for which a default value is automatically supplied if you do not explicitly send one as an argument. You make a parameter optional by providing a value for it in the method declaration. Only value parameters can be given default values; ref, out, and array parameters cannot have default values. Any optional parameters in a parameter list must appear to the right of the mandatory parameters.

For example, suppose that you write a method that calculates either the area of a square or the volume of a cube, depending on whether two or three arguments are sent to it. Figure 8-23 shows such a method; notice the shaded default value provided for the third parameter. When you want a cube's volume, you can pass three arguments to the method: length, width, and height. When you want a square's area, you pass only two parameters, and a default value of 1 is used for the height. In this example, the height is a default parameter and is optional; the length and width, which are not provided with default values, are mandatory parameters. That is, at least two arguments must be sent to the DisplaySize() method, but three can be sent. In the program in Figure 8-23, calling DisplaySize(4, 6) has the same effect as calling DisplaySize(4, 6, 1). Figure 8-24 shows the execution of the OptionalParameterDemo program.

```
using System;
class OptionalParameterDemo
{
    static void Main()
    {
        Console.Write("Using 2 arguments: ");
        DisplaySize(4, 6);
        Console.Write("Using 3 arguments: ");
        DisplaySize(4, 6, 8);
    }
    private static void DisplaySize(int length, int width, int height = 1)
    {
        int area = length * width * height;
        Console.WriteLine("Size is {0}", area);
    }
}
```

Figure 8-23   The OptionalParameterDemo class

Figure 8-24   Execution of the OptionalParameterDemo program

If you assign a default value to any variable in a method's parameter list, then all parameters to the right of that parameter must also have default values. Table 8-2 shows some examples of valid and invalid method declarations.

Method Declaration	Explanation
`private static void M1(int a, int b, int c, int d = 10)`	Valid. The first three parameters are mandatory and the last one is optional.
`private static void M2(int a, int b = 3, int c)`	Invalid. Because b has a default value, c must also have one.
`private static void M3(int a = 3, int b = 4, int c = 5)`	Valid. All parameters are optional.
`private static void M4(int a, int b, int c)`	Valid. All parameters are mandatory.
`private static void M5(int a = 4, int b, int c = 8)`	Invalid. Because a has a default value, both b and c must have default values.

Table 8-2   Examples of valid and invalid optional parameter method declarations

When you call a method that contains default parameters, you can always choose to provide a value for every parameter. However, if you omit an argument when you call a method that has default parameters, then you must do one of the following:

- You must leave out all unnamed arguments to the right of the last argument you use.

- You can name arguments.

Leaving Out Unnamed Arguments

When calling a method with optional parameters (and using unnamed arguments), you must leave out any arguments to the right of the last one used. In other words, once an argument is left out, you must leave out all the arguments that would otherwise follow.

For example, assume you have declared a method as follows:

```
private static void Method1(int a, char b, int c = 22, double d = 33.2)
```

Table 8-3 shows some legal and illegal calls to this method.

Call to Method1()	Explanation
Method1(1, 'A', 3, 4.4);	Valid. The four arguments are assigned to the four parameters.
Method1(1, 'K', 9);	Valid. The three arguments are assigned to a, b, and c in the method, and the default value of 33.2 is used for d.
Method1(5, 'D');	Valid. The two arguments are assigned to a and b in the method, and the default values of 22 and 33.2 are used for c and d, respectively.
Method1(1);	Invalid. Method1() requires at least two arguments for the first two parameters.
Method1();	Invalid. Method1() requires at least two arguments for the first two parameters.
Method1(3, 18.5);	Invalid. The first argument, 3, can be assigned to a, but the second argument must be type char.
Method1(4, 'R', 55.5);	Invalid. The first argument, 4, can be assigned to a, and the second argument, 'R', can be assigned to b, but the third argument must be type int. When arguments are unnamed, you cannot "skip" parameter c, use its default value, and assign 55.5 to parameter d.

Table 8-3   Examples of legal and illegal calls to Method1()

Using Named Arguments

You can leave out optional arguments in a method call if you pass the remaining arguments by name. A **named argument** is a method argument that is preceded with the name of the method's parameter to which it will be assigned. Named arguments can appear in any order, but they must appear after all the unnamed arguments have been listed. Each unnamed argument is also known as a **positional argument**. You name an argument using its parameter name and a colon before the value.

For example, assume you have declared a method as follows:

```
private static void Method2(int a, char b, int c = 22, double d = 33.2)
```

Table 8-4 shows some legal and illegal calls to this method.

Call to Method2()	Explanation
Method2(1, 'A');	Valid. The two arguments are assigned to a and b in the method, and the default values of 22 and 33.2 are used for c and d, respectively.
Method2(2, 'E', 3);	Valid. The three arguments are assigned to a, b, and c. The default value 33.2 is used for d.
Method2(2, 'E', c : 3);	Valid. This call is identical to the one above.
Method2(1, 'K', d : 88.8);	Valid. The first two arguments are assigned to a and b. The default value 22 is used for c. The named value 88.8 is used for d.
Method2(d : 2.1, b : 'A', c : 88, a: 12);	Valid. All the arguments are assigned to parameters whether they are listed in order or not.
Method2(5, 'S', d : 7.4, c: 9);	Valid. The first two arguments are assigned to a and b. Even though the values for c and d are not listed in order, they are assigned correctly.
Method2(d : 11.1, 6, 'P');	Invalid. This call contains an unnamed argument after the first named argument. Named arguments must appear after all unnamed arguments.

Table 8-4   Examples of legal and illegal calls to Method2()

Advantages to Using Named Arguments

Optional parameters can provide a convenient shortcut to writing multiple overloaded versions of a method. For example, suppose that you want to create a method that adds your signature to business letters. Usually, you want the signature to be "Sincerely, James O'Hara". However, occasionally you want to change the name to a more casual "Jim". You could write two method versions, as shown on the top in Figure 8-25, or you could write one version, as shown on the bottom. With both versions, you can call Closing() with or without an argument. The version with the optional parameter is less work when you write the method. It is also less work if you later want to modify the method—for example, to change "Sincerely," to "Best wishes," or some other closing.

Overloaded implementations of Closing()

```
private static void Closing()
{
    Console.WriteLine("Sincerely,");
    Console.WriteLine("James O'Hara");
}
private static void Closing(string name)
{
    Console.WriteLine("Sincerely,");
    Console.WriteLine(name);
}
```

Single implementation of Closing() with optional parameter

```
private static void Closing(string name = "James O'Hara")
{
    Console.WriteLine("Sincerely,");
    Console.WriteLine(name);
}
```

Figure 8-25   Two ways to implement Closing() to accept a name parameter or not

Another advantage to using named parameters is to make your programs more self-documenting. Programs that are **self-documenting** provide built-in explanations that make the code clearer to readers and therefore easier for others to modify in the future. For example, suppose that you encounter the following method call:

```
DisplayEmployeeData(empNumber, true);
```

From the method call, it is not clear what `true` means. Perhaps it means that only certain parts of the record should be displayed, or that the employee is a current employee, or that the employee's salary should be hidden from view. The following method call makes your intentions clearer:

```
DisplayEmployeeData(empNumber, shouldHideSalary : true);
```

Of course, a program comment adjacent to the statement could also provide clarity.

Disadvantages to Using Named Arguments

A major disadvantage to using named arguments is that the calling method becomes linked to details within the method. When the calling method must know parameter names within the called method, an important principle of programming—method implementation hiding—is compromised. If the parameter name in the called method is changed in the future, the client method also will have to change.

Another possible disadvantage to using named arguments occurs when a named parameter value is an expression instead of a constant. Suppose that a payroll program contains two methods used in paycheck calculations. The first method, shown in Figure 8-26, accepts three parameters—hours, rate, and bonus. A gross pay value is calculated by multiplying hours by rate, and a bonus value is assigned based on the number of hours worked. The second method sums its gross and bonus parameters. The intention is that an employee who works 40 hours at $10 per hour receives $400 gross pay, plus a $100 bonus, for a total of $500.

```
private static double ComputeGross(double hours, double rate, out double bonus)
{
    double gross = hours * rate;
    if(hours >= 40)
        bonus = 100;
    else
        bonus = 50;
    return gross;
}
private static double ComputeTotalPay(double gross, double bonus)
{
    double total = gross + bonus;
    return total;
}
```

Figure 8-26   Two payroll program methods

Figure 8-27 shows the Main() method of a program that assigns 40 to hours and 10.00 to rate. Then, the method calls the ComputeTotalPay() method by passing it the result of ComputeGross() and the value of bonus that is set within ComputeGross(). Figure 8-28 shows that the employee's total pay is correctly calculated as $500.

```
static void Main()
{
    double hours = 40;
    double rate = 10.00;
    double bonus = 0;
    double totalPay;
    totalPay = ComputeTotalPay(ComputeGross(hours, rate, out bonus),
        bonus);
    Console.WriteLine("Total pay is {0}", totalPay);
}
```

Figure 8-27   A Main() method that calls ComputeTotalPay() using positional arguments

Figure 8-28   Execution of the `Main()` method in Figure 8-27

Figure 8-29 shows a `Main()` method that calls `ComputeTotalPay()` using named arguments. The only difference from the program in Figure 8-27 is the shaded method call that uses named arguments. In this case, the bonus value sent to `ComputeTotalPay()` is 0, and then `ComputeGross()` is called to alter the bonus. However, the bonus alteration is too late and the program output is incorrect, as shown in Figure 8-30.

```
static void Main()
{
    double hours = 40;
    double rate = 10.00;
    double bonus = 0;
    double totalPay;
    totalPay = ComputeTotalPay(bonus: bonus,
        gross: ComputeGross(hours, rate, out bonus));
    Console.WriteLine("Total pay is {0}", totalPay);
}
```

Figure 8-29   A `Main()` method that calls `ComputeTotalPay()` using named arguments

Figure 8-30   Execution of the `Main()` method in Figure 8-29

In Chapter 4, you learned that when you combine operands in a Boolean expression using `&&` or `||`, you risk side effects because of short-circuit evaluation. The situation with named arguments is similar. When a named argument is an expression, there can be unintended consequences.

Overload Resolution with Named and Optional Arguments

Named and optional arguments affect overload resolution. The rules for betterness on argument conversions are applied only for arguments that are given explicitly; in other words, omitted optional arguments are ignored for betterness purposes. For example, suppose that you have the following methods:

```
private static void AMethod(int a, double b = 2.2)
private static void AMethod(int a, char b = 'H')
```

Both are applicable methods when a call is made using an integer argument; in other words, if either method existed alone, the call `AMethod(12)` would work. When the two methods coexist, however, neither is "better." Because C# cannot determine which one is better, the code will not compile.

If two signatures are equally good, the one that does not omit optional parameters is considered better. For example, suppose that you have two methods as follows:

```
private static void BMethod(int a)
private static void BMethod(int a, char b = 'B')
```

If either method existed alone, the call `BMethod(12)` would work, but when the two coexist, the first version is better because no optional parameters are omitted in the call.

 Watch the video *Using Optional Method Parameters*.

TWO TRUTHS & A LIE

Using Optional Parameters

1. An optional parameter to a method is one for which an argument can be a value parameter, a `ref` parameter, or an `out` parameter.

2. You make a parameter optional by providing a value for it in the method declaration.

3. If you assign a default value to any variable in a method's parameter list, then all parameters to the right of that parameter must also have default values.

The false statement is #1. An optional parameter to a method is one for which a default value is automatically supplied if you do not explicitly send one as an argument.

Chapter Summary

- Method parameters can be mandatory or optional. The mandatory parameters are reference parameters, which are declared with the `ref` modifier; output parameters, which are declared with the `out` modifier; and parameter arrays, which are declared with the `params` modifier. Value parameters can be mandatory or optional.

- When you overload a C# method, you write multiple methods with a shared name but different parameter lists. The compiler understands your meaning based on the combination of arguments you use with the method. When a method call could execute multiple overloaded method versions, C# determines which method to execute using a process called overload resolution.

- When you overload a method, you run the risk of creating an ambiguous situation—one in which the compiler cannot determine which method to use. Methods can be overloaded correctly by providing different parameter lists for methods with the same name.

- An optional parameter to a method is one for which a default value is automatically supplied if you do not explicitly send one as an argument. You make a parameter optional by providing a value for it in the method declaration. When calling a method with optional parameters, you must leave out all unnamed arguments to the right of the last one used, or you can name arguments.

Key Terms

Mandatory parameters are method parameters for which an argument is required in every method call.

A **value parameter** in a method header receives a copy of the value passed to it.

A **reference parameter** in a method header receives the parameter's address; a variable sent to a reference parameter is required to have been assigned a value before it is used in the method call.

An **output parameter** in a method header receives the parameter's address; a variable sent to an output parameter is not required to have been assigned a value before it is used in the method call.

A **parameter array** is a local array declared within a method header that can accept any number of arguments of the same type.

Aliases are alternate names or pseudonyms.

Overloading involves using one term to indicate diverse meanings. When you overload a C# method, you write multiple methods with the same name but different parameter lists.

A method's **signature** is composed of its name and parameter list.

Overload resolution is the process of determining which of multiple applicable methods is the best match for a method call.

Applicable methods are all the methods that could be used by a method call if the method was not overloaded.

Betterness rules are the rules that determine the best overloaded method to execute based on the arguments in a method call.

Ambiguous methods are overloaded methods from which the compiler cannot determine which one to use.

An **optional parameter** to a method is one for which a default value is automatically supplied if you do not explicitly send one as an argument; a parameter is optional when it is given a value in the method declaration.

A **named argument** is a method argument that is preceded with the name of the method's parameter to which it will be assigned.

A **positional argument** is an unnamed method argument that is assigned to a parameter list based on its position in the method call.

Self-documenting describes programs that provide built-in explanations to make the code clearer to readers and therefore easier for others to modify in the future.

Review Questions

1. A mandatory parameter _____.

    a.   is any argument sent to a method
    b.   is preceded by the keyword man
    c.   requires an argument to be sent from a method call
    d.   All of the above are true.

2. Which is *not* a type of method parameter in C#?

    a.   value   c.   forensic
    b.   reference   d.   output

3. Which type of method parameter receives the address of the variable passed in?

    a.   a value parameter   c.   an output parameter
    b.   a reference parameter   d.   two of the above

4. When you declare a value parameter, you precede its name with _____.

    a.   nothing   c.   the keyword val and a data type
    b.   a data type   d.   the keyword ref and its data type

5. Assume that you declare a variable as int x = 100; and correctly pass it to a method with the declaration private static void IncreaseValue(ref int x). There is a single statement within the IncreaseValue() method: x = x + 25;. Back in the Main() method, after the method call, what is the value of x?

a. 100
b. 125
c. It is impossible to tell.
d. The program will not run.

6. Assume that you declare a variable as int x = 100; and correctly pass it to a method with the declaration private static void IncreaseValue(int x). There is a single statement within the IncreaseValue() method: x = x + 25;. Back in the Main() method, after the method call, what is the value of x?

a. 100
b. 125
c. It is impossible to tell.
d. The program will not run.

7. Which of the following is a difference between a reference parameter and an output parameter?

a. A reference parameter receives a memory address; an output parameter does not.
b. A reference parameter occupies a unique memory address; an output parameter does not.
c. A reference parameter requires an initial value; an output parameter does not.
d. A reference parameter does not require an initial value; an output parameter does.

8. A parameter array _____.

a. is declared using the keyword params
b. can accept any number of arguments of the same data type
c. Both of these are true.
d. Neither of these is true.

9. Assume that you have declared a method with the following header:
private static void DisplayScores(params int[] scores)
Which of the following method calls is valid?

a. DisplayScores(20);
b. DisplayScores(20, 33);
c. DisplayScores(20, 30, 90);
d. All of the above are valid.

10. Correctly overloaded methods must have the same _____.

a. return type
b. identifier
c. parameter list
d. All of the above.

11. Methods are ambiguous when they _____.

   a. are overloaded

   b. are written in a confusing manner

   c. are indistinguishable to the compiler

   d. have the same parameter type as their return type

12. Which of the following pairs of method declarations represent correctly overloaded methods?

   a. `private static void MethodA(int a)`
   `private static void MethodA(int b, double c)`

   b. `private static void MethodB(double d)`
   `private static void MethodB()`

   c. `private static double MethodC(int e)`
   `private static double MethodD(int f)`

   d. Two of these are correctly overloaded methods.

13. Which of the following pairs of method declarations represent correctly overloaded methods?

   a. `private static void Method(int a)`
   `private static void Method(int b)`

   b. `private static void Method(double d)`
   `private static int Method()`

   c. `private static double Method(int e)`
   `private static int Method(int f)`

   d. Two of these are correctly overloaded methods.

14. The process of determining which overloaded version of a method to execute is overload _____.

   a. confusion   c. revolution

   b. infusion   d. resolution

15. When one of a method's parameters is optional, it means that _____.

   a. no arguments are required in a call to the method

   b. a default value will be assigned to the parameter if no argument is sent for it

   c. a default value will override any argument value sent to it

   d. you are not required to use the parameter within the method body

16. Which of the following is an illegal method declaration?

    a. `private static void CreateStatement(int acctNum,`
       `double balance = 0.0)`

    b. `private static void CreateStatement(int acctNum = 0,`
       `double balance)`

    c. `private static void CreateStatement(int acctNum = 0, balance = 0)`

    d. All of these are legal.

17. Assume you have declared a method as follows:
    `private static double ComputeBill(int acct, double price,`
    `double discount = 0)`
    Which of the following is a legal method call?

    a. `ComputeBill();`

    b. `ComputeBill(1001);`

    c. `ComputeBill(1001, 200.00);`

    d. None of the above is legal.

18. Assume you have declared a method as follows:
    `private static double CalculateDiscount(int acct = 0,`
    `double price = 0, double discount = 0)`
    Which of the following is a legal method call?

    a. `CalculateDiscount();`

    b. `CalculateDiscount(200.00);`

    c. `CalculateDiscount(3000.00. 0.02);`

    d. None of the above is legal.

19. Assume you have declared a method as follows:
    `private static double DisplayData(string name = "XX",`
    `double amount = 10.0)`
    Which of the following is an illegal method call?

    a. `DisplayData(name : "Albert");`

    b. `DisplayData(amount : 200, name : "Albert");`

    c. `DisplayData(amount : 900.00);`

    d. All of these are legal.

20. Suppose that you have declared an integer array named `scores` and you make the following method call:

    `TotalScores(scores, num : 1);`

    Of the following overloaded method definitions, which would execute?

    a. `private static void TotalScores(int[] scores)`

    b. `private static void TotalScores(int[] scores, int num)`

    c. `private static void TotalScores(int[] scores, int num = 10, int code = 10)`

    d. The program would not compile.

Exercises

 Programming Exercises

1. a. Create a program named **Reverse3** whose `Main()` method declares three integers named `firstInt`, `middleInt`, and `lastInt`. Assign values to the variables, display them, and then pass them to a method that accepts them as reference variables, places the first value in the `lastInt` variable, and places the last value in the `firstInt` variable. In the `Main()` method, display the three variables again, demonstrating that their positions have been reversed.

   b. Create a new program named **Reverse4**, which contains a method that reverses the positions of four variables. Write a `Main()` method that demonstrates the method works correctly.

   c. Create an application named **Reverse4GUI** that accepts four integers from text boxes. When the user clicks a button, the application calls a method that reverses the positions of the variables. If any of the values cannot be converted, substitute 0.

2. Create a program named **IntegerStatistics** whose `Main()` method declares an array of 10 integers. Call a method to interactively fill the array with any number of values up to 10 until a sentinel value is entered. If an entry is not an integer, keep prompting the user to enter it. Call a second method that accepts `out` parameters for the highest value in the array, lowest value in the array, sum of the values in the array, and arithmetic average. In the `Main()` method, display all the statistics.

3. Create a program for Potsie's Pottery named **FlexibleOrder** that accepts a user's choice from the options in the accompanying table. Allow the user to enter either an integer item number or a string description. Pass the user's entry to one of two overloaded `GetDetails()` methods and then display the returned string. The method version that accepts an integer looks up the description and price and returns a string with all the order details. The version that accepts a string

description looks up the item number and price and returns a string with all the order details. The methods return an appropriate message if the item is not found.

Item number	Description	Price
112	plate	16.95
123	cup	10.95
134	bowl	14.25
213	vase	21.95
224	planter	45.99
235	statue	89.99

4. Create a program named **Auction** that allows a user to enter an amount bid on an item. Include three overloaded methods that accept an integer, double, or string bid. Each method should display the bid and indicate whether it is over the minimum acceptable bid of $10. If the bid is a string, accept it only if one of the following is true: it is numeric and preceded with a dollar sign, or it is numeric and followed by the word *dollars*. Otherwise, display a message that indicates the format was incorrect.

5. Create a program named **TaxCalculation** that includes two overloaded methods—one that accepts a price and a tax rate expressed as doubles (for example, 79.95 and 0.06, where 0.06 represents 6%), and one that accepts a price as a double and a tax rate as an integer (for example, 79.95 and 6, where 6 also represents 6%). Include a Main() method to demonstrate that each method calculates the same tax amount appropriately.

6. Write a program named **InputMethodDemo2** that eliminates the repetitive code in the InputMethod() in the InputMethodDemo program in Figure 8-5. Rewrite the program so the InputMethod() contains only two statements:

```
one = DataEntry("first");
two = DataEntry("second");
```

7. Write a program named **Averages** that includes a method that accepts any number of numeric parameters, displays them, and displays their average. Demonstrate that the method works correctly when passed one, two, or three numbers, or an array of numbers.

8. Write a program named **Desks2** that modifies the Desks program you created in Chapter 7 so that all the methods are void methods and receive ref or out parameters as appropriate.

9. Write a program named **SortNames** that includes a method that accepts any number of names and sorts them in alphabetical order. Demonstrate that the program works correctly when the method is called with one, two, five, and ten names.

10. Write a program named **Movie** that contains a method that accepts and displays two parameters: a string name of a movie and an integer running time in minutes. Provide a default value for the minutes so that if you call the method without an integer argument, minutes is set to 90. Write a Main() method that proves you can call the movie method with only a string argument as well as with a string and an integer.

11. a. In the card game War, a deck of playing cards is divided between two players. Each player exposes a card; the player whose card has the higher value wins possession of both exposed cards. Create a console-based computerized game of War named **WarCardGame** in which a standard 52-card deck is randomly divided between two players, one of which is the computer. Reveal one card for the computer and one card for the player at a time. Award two points for the player whose card has the higher value. (For this game the king is the highest card, followed by the queen and jack, then the numbers 10 down to 2, and finally the ace.) If the computer and player expose cards with equal values in the same turn, award one point to each. At the end of the game, all 52 cards should have been played only once, and the sum of the player's and computer's score will be 52.

Use an array of 52 integers to store unique values for each card. Write a method named FillDeck() that places 52 unique values into this array. Write another method named SelectCard() that you call twice on each deal to select a unique card for each player, with no repetition of cards in 26 deals. (To pause the play between each dealt hand, use a call to ReadLine().)

The left side of Figure 8-31 shows the start of a typical program execution. (*Caution:* This is a difficult exercise!)

Figure 8-31 Start of typical execution of console-based and GUI WarCardGame programs

b. Create a GUI version of the War card game described in Exercise 11a and name it **WarCardGameGUI**. Let the user click a button to deal the cards, then make that button invisible and expose a Play button. Each time the user clicks Play, a pair of cards is revealed. To keep the Frame size reasonable, you might want to erase the output label's contents every four hands or so. The right side of Figure 8-31 shows a typical game in progress.

Debugging Exercises

1. Each of the following files in the Chapter.08 folder of your downloadable student files has syntax and/or logical errors. In each case, determine the problem and fix the program. After you correct the errors, save each file using the same filename preceded with *Fixed*. For example, DebugEight1.cs will become FixedDebugEight1.cs.

   a. DebugEight1.cs   c. DebugEight3.cs
   b. DebugEight2.cs   d. DebugEight4.cs

Case Problems

1. In Chapter 7, you modified the **GreenvilleRevenue** program to include a number of methods. Now modify every data entry statement to use a TryParse() method to ensure that each piece of data is the correct type. Any invalid user entries should generate an appropriate message, and the user should be required to reenter the data.

2. In Chapter 7, you modified the **MarshallsRevenue** program to include a number of methods. Now modify every data entry statement to use a TryParse() method to ensure that each piece of data is the correct type. Any invalid user entries should generate an appropriate message, and the user should be required to reenter the data.

CHAPTER 9

Using Classes and Objects

(Screen shots are used with permission from Microsoft.)

In this chapter you will:

◎ Learn about class concepts

◎ Create classes from which objects can be instantiated

◎ Create objects

◎ Create properties, including auto-implemented properties

◎ Learn more about using `public` and `private` access modifiers

◎ Learn about the `this` reference

◎ Write and use constructors

◎ Use object initializers

◎ Overload operators

◎ Declare an array of objects and use the `Sort()` and `BinarySearch()` methods with them

◎ Write destructors

◎ Understand GUI application objects

Much of your understanding of the world comes from your ability to categorize objects and events into classes. As a young child, you learned the concept of "animal" long before you knew the word. Your first encounter with an animal might have been with the family dog, a neighbor's cat, or a goat at a petting zoo. As you developed speech, you might have used the same term for all of these creatures, gleefully shouting "Doggie!" as your parents pointed out cows, horses, and sheep in picture books or along the roadside on drives in the country. As you grew more sophisticated, you learned to distinguish dogs from cows; still later, you learned to distinguish breeds. Your understanding of the class "animal" helps you see the similarities between dogs and cows, and your understanding of the class "dog" helps you see the similarities between a Great Dane and a Chihuahua. Understanding classes gives you a framework for categorizing new experiences. You might not know the term "okapi," but when you learn it's an animal, you begin to develop a concept of what an okapi might be like.

Classes are also the basic building blocks of object-oriented programming. You already understand that differences exist among the `Double`, `Int32`, and `Float` classes, yet you also know that items belonging to these classes possess similarities—they are all data types, you can perform arithmetic with all of them, they all can be converted to strings, and so on. Understanding classes enables you to see similarities in objects and increases your understanding of the programming process. In this chapter, you will discover how C# handles classes, learn to create your own classes, and learn to construct objects that are members of those classes.

Understanding Class Concepts

When you write programs in C#, you create two types of classes:

- *Classes that are only application programs with a* `Main()` *method.* These classes can contain other methods that the `Main()` method calls. You have been creating these classes throughout this book.

- *Classes from which you instantiate objects.* To **instantiate** an object is to create a tangible example. An object is an **instantiation** of a class or an **instance** of a class. A class that is created to be a model for object instantiations can contain a `Main()` method, but it is not required. This chapter explores the nuances of such classes.

When you think in an object-oriented manner, everything is an object, and every object is an instance or example of a class. You can think of any inanimate physical item as an object— your desk, your computer, and your house are all called "objects" in everyday conversation. You can think of living things as objects, too—your houseplant, your pet fish, and your sister are objects. Events also are objects—for example, the stock purchase you made, the mortgage closing you attended, or a graduation party in your honor.

Every object is an instance of a more general class. Your desk is a specific instance of the class that includes all desks, and your pet fish is an instance of the class that contains all fish. In part, the concept of a class is useful because it provides you with knowledge about objects.

Objects receive their attributes from classes; so, for example, if you invite me to a graduation party, I automatically know many things about the object. I assume that there will be a starting time, a number of guests, and some refreshments. I understand your party because of my previous knowledge of the Party class. I don't necessarily know the number of guests or the date or time of this particular party, but I understand that because all parties have a date and time, then this one must as well. Similarly, even though every stock purchase is unique, each must have a dollar amount and a number of shares. All objects have predictable attributes because they are instances of certain classes.

The data components of a class that differ for each object are stored in **instance variables**. Instance variables also are called **fields** to help distinguish them from other variables you might use. The set of contents of an object's instance variables also are known as its **state**. For example, the current state of a particular party is 8 p.m. and Friday; the state of a particular stock purchase is $10 and five shares.

In addition to their attributes, objects have methods associated with them, and every object that is an instance of the same class possesses the same methods. Methods associated with objects are **instance methods**. For example, two Party objects might possess the identifiers myGraduationParty and yourAnniversaryParty that both have access to an IssueInvitations() method. The method might operate in the same way for both Party objects, but use data appropriate to the specific object. When you program in C#, you frequently create classes from which objects will be instantiated (or other programmers create them for you). You also write applications to use the objects, along with their data and methods. Often, you will write programs that use classes created by others; similarly, you might create a class that other programmers will use to instantiate objects within their own programs. A program or class that instantiates objects of another prewritten class is a **class client** or **class user**.

TWO TRUTHS & A LIE

Understanding Class Concepts

1. C# classes always contain a Main() method.

2. An object is an instantiation of a class.

3. The data components of a class often are its instance variables.

The false statement is #1. C# applications always contain a Main() method, but some classes do not if they are not meant to be run as programs.

Creating a Class from Which Objects Can Be Instantiated

When you create a class, you must assign a name to it and determine what data and methods will be part of the class. For example, suppose that you decide to create a class named `Employee`. One instance variable of `Employee` might be an employee number, and one necessary method might display a welcome message to new employees. To begin, you create a **class header** or **class definition** that starts the class. It contains three parts:

1. An optional access modifier

2. The keyword `class`

3. Any legal identifier you choose for the name of your class; because each class represents a type of object, class names are usually singular nouns.

You will learn about other optional components that can be added to a class definition as you continue to study C#.

For example, one usable header for an `Employee` class is `internal class Employee`. The keyword `internal` is an example of a **class access modifier**. You can declare a class using any of the modifiers in Table 9-1.

Class Access Modifier	Description
`public`	Access to the class is not limited.
`protected`	Access to the class is limited to the class and to any classes derived from the class. (You will learn about deriving classes in the chapter *Introduction to Inheritance*.)
`internal`	Access is limited to the assembly to which the class belongs. (An **assembly** is a group of code modules compiled together to create an executable program. The .exe files you create after compiling a C# program are assemblies.)
`private`	Access is limited to another class to which the class belongs. In other words, a class should be `private` if it is contained within another class, and the containing class is the only one that should have access to it.

Table 9-1   Class access modifiers

When you declare a class using a namespace, you only can declare it to be `public` or `internal`.

If you do not explicitly include an access specifier, class access is `internal` by default. Because most classes you create will have `internal` access, typing an access specifier is often unnecessary.

In addition to the class header, classes you create must have a class body enclosed between curly braces. Figure 9-1 shows a shell for an `Employee` class.

```
class Employee
{
    // Instance variables and methods go here
}
```

Figure 9-1   `Employee` class shell

Creating Instance Variables and Methods

When you create a class, you define both its attributes and its methods. You declare the class's instance variables within the curly braces using the same syntax you use to declare other variables—you provide a type and an identifier. For example, within the `Employee` class, you can declare an integer ID number, and when you create `Employee` objects, each will have its own `idNumber`. You can define the ID number simply as `int idNumber;`. However, programmers frequently include an access modifier for each of the class fields and declare the `idNumber` as `private int idNumber;`. Figure 9-2 shows an `Employee` class that contains the `private idNumber` field.

```
class Employee
{
    private int idNumber;
}
```

Figure 9-2   `Employee` class containing `idNumber` field

The allowable field modifiers are `new`, `public`, `protected`, `internal`, `private`, `static`, `readonly`, and `volatile`. If you do not provide an access specifier for a class field, its access is `private` and nonstatic by default. Most class fields are nonstatic and `private`, which means that no other class can access the field's values, and only nonstatic methods of the same class will be allowed to set, get, or otherwise use the field. Using `private` fields within classes is an example of **information hiding**, a feature found in all object-oriented languages.

You see cases of information hiding in real-life objects every day. For instance, you cannot see into your automobile's gas tank to determine how full it is. Instead, you use a gauge on the dashboard to provide you with the necessary information. Similarly, data fields are frequently `private` in object-oriented programming, but their contents are accessed through `public` methods. The `private` data of a class should be changed or manipulated only by its own methods, not by methods that belong to other classes. A benefit of making data items `private` is the ability to control their values. A method that sets a variable's value can use decisions to ensure that the value falls within a specified range. For example, perhaps an Employee's salary should not be below the federal minimum wage, or perhaps a department number should not be negative or greater than 10.

In contrast to a class's private data fields, most instance methods are not usually private; they are public. The resulting private data/public method arrangement provides a means to control outside access to your data—only a class's nonprivate methods can be used to access a class's private data. The situation is similar to having a "public" receptionist who controls the messages passed in and out of your private office. The way in which the nonprivate methods are written controls how you will use the private data.

For example, an Employee class that contains an idNumber might need a method to display the employee's welcoming message to company clients. A reasonable name for this method is WelcomeMessage(), and its declaration is public void WelcomeMessage(), because it will have public access and return nothing. Figure 9-3 shows the Employee class with the addition of the WelcomeMessage() method.

```
class Employee
{
    private int idNumber;
    public void WelcomeMessage()
    {
        Console.WriteLine("Welcome from Employee #{0}", idNumber);
        Console.WriteLine("How can I help you?");
    }
}
```

Figure 9-3   Employee class with idNumber field and WelcomeMessage() method

Notice that the WelcomeMessage() method does not employ the static modifier, unlike many other methods you have created. The keyword static is used for class-wide methods, but not for instance methods that "belong" to objects. If you are creating a program with a Main() method that you will execute to perform some task, then many of your methods will be static. You can call the static methods from Main() without creating an object. However, if you are creating a class from which objects will be instantiated, most methods will probably be nonstatic, as you will be associating the methods with individual objects and their data. Each time the WelcomeMessage() instance method is used in the class in Figure 9-3, it will display an idNumber for a specific object. In other words, the method will work appropriately for each object instance, so it is not static.

In Chapter 7, you learned that when you create a Form, you sometimes include nonstatic variable declarations outside of any methods—for example, if two Click() methods must access the same data. Now you can understand that such variables are nonstatic because they are associated with an object—the Form that is being defined.

The `Employee` class in Figure 9-3 is not a program that will run; it contains no `Main()` method. Rather, it simply describes what `Employee` objects will have (an `idNumber`) and be able to do (display a greeting) when you write a program that contains one or more `Employee` objects.

A class can contain fields that are objects of other classes. For example, you might create a class named `Date` that contains a month, day, and year, and add two `Date` fields to an `Employee` class to hold the `Employee`'s birth date and hire date. You might also create a `BusinessOffice` class and declare `Employee` objects within it. Using an object within another object is known as **composition**. The relationship created is also called a **has-a relationship** because one class "has an" instance of another.

Watch the video *Creating a Class*.

TWO TRUTHS & A LIE

Creating a Class from Which Objects Can Be Instantiated

1. A class header always contains the keyword `class`.

2. When you create a class, you define both its attributes and its methods.

3. Most class fields and methods are `private`.

The false statement is #3. Most class fields are `private`, but most class methods are `public`.

Creating Objects

Declaring a class does not create any actual objects. A class is just an abstract description of what an object will be like if any objects are ever actually instantiated. Just as you might understand all the characteristics of an item you intend to manufacture long before the first item rolls off the assembly line, you can create a class with fields and methods before you instantiate any objects that are occurrences of that class.

You can think of a class declaration as similar to a blueprint for building a new house or a recipe for baking a cake. In other words, it is a plan that exists before any objects are created.

Defining an object is similar to defining a simple variable that is a built-in data type; in each case, you use a data type and an identifier. For example, you might define an integer as `int someValue;` and you might define an `Employee` as `Employee myAssistant;`, where `myAssistant` could be any legal identifier you choose to represent an `Employee`.

Every object name is a reference—that is, it holds a computer memory location where the fields for the object reside. The memory location holds the values for the object.

When you declare an integer as `int myInteger;`, you notify the compiler that an integer named `myInteger` will exist, and computer memory automatically is reserved for it at the same time—the exact amount of computer memory depends on the declared data type. When you declare the `myAssistant` instance of the `Employee` class, you are notifying the compiler that you will use the identifier `myAssistant`. However, you are not yet setting aside computer memory in which the `Employee` named `myAssistant` can be stored—that is done only for the built-in, predefined types. To allocate the needed memory and instantiate the object, you must use the `new` operator. You used the `new` operator earlier in this book when you learned to set aside memory for an array.

Defining an `Employee` object named `myAssistant` requires two steps—you must declare a reference to the object and then you must use the statement that actually sets aside enough memory to hold `myAssistant`:

```
Employee myAssistant;
myAssistant = new Employee();
```

You also can declare and reserve memory for `myAssistant` in one statement, as in the following:

```
Employee myAssistant = new Employee();
```

In this statement, `Employee` is the object's type (as well as its class), and `myAssistant` is the name of the object. The equal sign is the assignment operator, so a value is being assigned to `myAssistant`. The `new` operator is allocating a new, unused portion of computer memory for `myAssistant`. The value being assigned to `myAssistant` is a memory address at which the value will be located. You need not be concerned with the actual memory address—when you refer to `myAssistant`, the compiler will locate it at the appropriate address for you.

Because the identifiers for objects are references to their memory addresses, you can call any class a **reference type**—in other words, a type that refers to a specific memory location. A reference type is a type that holds an address, as opposed to the predefined types such as `int`, `double`, and `char`, which are **value types**.

You also can use the `new` operator for simple data types. For example, to declare an integer variable `x`, you can write the following:

```
int x = new int();
```

However, programmers usually use the simpler form:

```
int x;
```

With the first form, `x` is initialized to 0. With the second form, `x` holds no usable starting value.

In the statement `Employee myAssistant = new Employee();`, the last portion of the statement after the `new` operator, `Employee()`, looks suspiciously like a method name with its parentheses. In fact, it is the name of a method that constructs an `Employee` object. `Employee()` is a constructor. You will write your own constructors later in this chapter. For now, note that when you don't write a constructor for a class, C# writes one for you, and the name of the constructor is always the same as the name of the class whose objects it constructs.

Later in this chapter you will learn that the automatically generated constructor for a class is a *default constructor*, which means it takes no parameters. Programmers sometimes erroneously equate the terms *automatically generated* and *default*. The automatically created constructor for a class is an *example* of a default constructor, but you also can explicitly create your own default constructor.

After an object has been instantiated, its nonstatic public members can be accessed using the object's identifier, a dot, and the nonstatic public member's identifier. For example, if you declare an `Employee` named `myAssistant`, you can access `myAssistant`'s `WelcomeMessage()` method with the following statement:

`myAssistant.WelcomeMessage();`

An object such as `myAssistant` that uses an instance method is an **invoking object**. The statement `myAssistant.WelcomeMessage()` would be illegal if `WelcomeMessage()` was a `static` method. The method can be used appropriately with each unique `Employee` object only because it is nonstatic.

A program that declares `myAssistant` cannot access `myAssistant`'s `idNumber` directly; the only way a program can access the `private` data is by using one of the object's `public` methods. Because the `WelcomeMessage()` method is part of the same class as `idNumber`, and because `WelcomeMessage()` is `public`, a client method (for example, a `Main()` method in a program) can use the method. Figure 9-4 shows a class named `CreateEmployee` whose `Main()` method declares an `Employee` and displays the `Employee`'s welcome message. Figure 9-5 shows the execution of the program.

```
using System;
class CreateEmployee
{
    static void Main()
    {
        Employee myAssistant = new Employee();
        myAssistant.WelcomeMessage();
    }
}
```

Figure 9-4 The `CreateEmployee` program

Figure 9-5   Output of the `CreateEmployee` program

In the output in Figure 9-5, the `Employee`'s ID number is 0. By default, all unassigned numeric fields in an object are initialized to 0. When you compile the program in Figure 9-4, you receive a warning message:

```
Field 'Employee.idNumber' is never assigned to, and will always have its
default value 0.
```

Of course, usually you want to provide a different value for each `Employee`'s `idNumber` field. One way to accomplish this is to create properties, which you will do later in this chapter.

Passing Objects to Methods

A class represents a data type, and you can pass objects to methods just as you can pass simple data types. For example, the program in Figure 9-6 shows how `string` and `Employee` objects can be passed to a `DisplayEmployeeData()` method. Each `Employee` is assigned to the `emp` parameter within the method. Figure 9-7 shows the program's output.

```csharp
using System;
class CreateTwoEmployees
{
   static void Main()
   {
      Employee aWorker = new Employee();
      Employee anotherWorker = new Employee();
      DisplayEmployeeData("First", aWorker);
      DisplayEmployeeData("Second", anotherWorker);
   }
   static void DisplayEmployeeData(string order, Employee emp)
   {
      Console.WriteLine("\n{0} employee's message:", order);
      emp.WelcomeMessage();
   }
}
```

Figure 9-6   The `CreateTwoEmployees` program

Figure 9-7 Output of the CreateTwoEmployees program

When you pass an object to a method, you pass a reference. Therefore, any change made to an object parameter in a method also affects the object used as an argument in the calling method.

In Figure 9-6, notice that the DisplayEmployeeData() method is internal. Because the method accepts an Employee parameter, it must be no more accessible than the Employee class, which is also internal. This restriction preserves the security provided for the Employee class's nonpublic members. The program would also work if you made both the DisplayEmployeeData() method and the Employee class public.

TWO TRUTHS & A LIE

Creating Objects

1. Declaring a class creates one object of a new data type.

2. After you declare a class, you must use the new operator to allocate memory for an object of that class and to instantiate it.

3. After an object has been instantiated, its public members can be accessed using the object's identifier, a dot, and a method call.

The false statement is #1. Declaring a class does not create any actual objects; the declaration only describes what an object of that class will be.

Creating Properties

Frequently, methods you call with an object are used to alter the states of its fields. For example, you might want to set or change the date or time of a party. In the Employee class, you could write a method such as SetIdNumber() to set an employee's idNumber field as follows:

379

```
public void SetIdNumber(int number)
{
    idNumber = number;
}
```

Then, after you instantiate an Employee object named myAssistant, you could call the method with a statement like the following:

```
myAssistant.SetIdNumber(785);
```

Although this technique would work, and might be used in other programming languages, C# programmers more often create properties to perform similar tasks. A **property** is a member of a class that provides access to a field of a class; properties define how fields will be set and retrieved. C# programmers refer to properties as "smart fields" because they provide a combination of the best features of private fields and public methods:

- Like public methods, they protect private data from outside access.

- Like fields, their names are used in the same way simple variable names are used. When you create properties, the syntax in your client programs becomes more natural and easier to understand.

Properties have **accessors** that specify the statements that execute when a class's fields are accessed. Specifically, properties contain **set accessors** for setting an object's fields and **get accessors** for retrieving the stored values. Figure 9-8 shows an Employee class in which a property named IdNumber has been defined in the shaded area.

```
class Employee
{
    private int idNumber;
    public int IdNumber
    {
        get
        {
            return idNumber;
        }
        set
        {
            idNumber = value;
        }
    }
    public void WelcomeMessage()
    {
        Console.WriteLine("Welcome from Employee #{0}", IdNumber);
        Console.WriteLine("How can I help you?");
    }
}
```

Figure 9-8 Employee class with defined property

A property declaration resembles a variable declaration; it contains an access modifier, a data type, and an identifier. It also resembles a method in that it is followed by curly braces that contain statements. By convention, a property identifier is the same as the field it manipulates, except the first letter is capitalized. The field that supports a property is its **backing field**. Be careful with capitalization of properties. For example, within a get accessor for IdNumber, if you return the property (IdNumber) instead of the backing field (idNumber), you initiate an infinite loop—the property continuously accesses itself.

The IdNumber property in Figure 9-8 contains both get and set accessors defined between curly braces; a property declaration can contain a get accessor, a set accessor, or both. When a property has a set accessor, programmers say the property can be "written to." When it has a get accessor, programmers say the property can be "read from." When a property has only a get accessor (and not a set accessor), it is a **read-only property**. In C#, the get and set accessors often are called the **getter** and the **setter**, respectively.

In the WelcomeMessage() method in Figure 9-8, the IdNumber property is displayed. Alternatively, this method could continue to use the idNumber field (as in Figure 9-3) because the method is a member of the same class as the field. Programmers are divided on whether a method of a class should use a field or a property to access its own methods. One popular position is that if get and set accessors are well-designed, they should be used everywhere, even within the class. Sometimes, you want a field to be read-only, so you do not create a set accessor. In such a case, you can use the field (with the lowercase initial by convention) within class methods.

Throughout this book you have seen keywords displayed in boldface in the program figures. The words get, set, and value are not C# keywords—for example, you could declare a variable named get within a C# program. However, within a property, get, set, and value have special meanings and are not allowed to be declared as identifiers there. In the Visual Studio Integrated Development Environment, these three words appear in blue within properties, but in black elsewhere. Identifiers that act like keywords in specific circumstances are **contextual keywords**. C# has six contextual keywords: get, set, value, partial, where, and yield.

Each accessor in a property looks like a method, except no parentheses are included in the identifier. A set accessor acts like a method that accepts a parameter and assigns it to a variable. However, it is not a method and you do not use parentheses with it. A get accessor returns the value of the field associated with the property, but you do not code a return type; the return type of a get accessor is implicitly the type of the property in which it is contained.

When you use set and get accessors in a method, you do not use the words *set* or *get*. Instead, to set a value, you use the assignment operator (=), and to get a value, you simply use the property name. For example, if you declare an Employee named myChef, you can assign an IdNumber as simply as you would a variable, as in the following:

```
Employee myChef = new Employee();
myChef.IdNumber = 2345;
```

In the second statement, the IdNumber property is set to 2345. The value to the right of the equal sign is sent to the set accessor as an implicit parameter named value. (An **implicit parameter** is one that is undeclared and that gets its value automatically.) In the statement myChef.IdNumber = 2345;, the constant 2345 is sent to the set accessor, where it becomes the value of value. Within the set accessor, value is assigned to the class field idNumber. The idNumber field could not have been set directly from Main() because it is private; however, the IdNumber property can be set through its set accessor because the property is public.

Writing a get accessor allows you to use a property like you would a simple variable. For example, a declared Employee's ID number can be displayed with the following:

```
Console.WriteLine("ID number is {0}", myChef.IdNumber);
```

The expression myChef.idNumber (using the field name that starts with a lowercase *i*) would not be allowed in a client program because idNumber is private; however, the public get accessor of the property allows myChef.IdNumber to be displayed. Figure 9-9 shows a complete application that uses the Employee class with accessors defined in Figure 9-8. Figure 9-10 shows the output.

```
using System;
class CreateEmployee2
{
    static void Main()
    {
        Employee myChef = new Employee();
        myChef.IdNumber = 2345;
        Console.WriteLine("ID number is {0}",
            myChef.IdNumber);
        myChef.WelcomeMessage();
    }
}
```

Figure 9-9   The CreateEmployee2 application that uses the Employee class containing a property

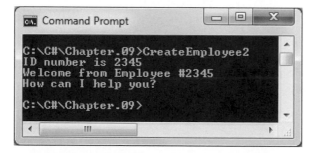

Figure 9-10   Output of the CreateEmployee2 application

At this point, declaring `get` and `set` accessors that do nothing except retrieve a value from a field or assign a value to one might seem like a lot of work for very little payoff. After all, if a class field was `public` instead of `private`, you would just use it directly and avoid the work of creating the property. However, it is conventional (and consistent with object-oriented principles) to make class fields `private` and allow accessors to manipulate them only as you deem appropriate. Keeping data hidden is an important feature of object-oriented programming, as is controlling how data values are set and used. Additionally, you can customize accessors to suit the restrictions you want to impose on how some class fields are retrieved and accessed. For example, you could write a `set` accessor that restricts ID numbers within the `Employee` class as follows:

```
set
{
    if(value < 500)
        idNumber = value;
    else
        idNumber = 500;
}
```

This `set` accessor would ensure that an `Employee idNumber` would never be greater than 500. If clients had direct access to a `private idNumber` field, you could not control what values could be assigned there, but when you write a custom `set` accessor for your class, you gain full control over the allowed data values.

A minor inconvenience when using properties is that a property cannot be passed to a method as a `ref` or `out` parameter. For example, if `IdNumber` is an `Employee` property and `myChef` is an `Employee` object, the following statement does not compile:

```
int.TryParse(Console.ReadLine(), out myChef.IdNumber);
```

Instead, to use `TryParse()` to interactively get an `IdNumber` value, you must use a temporary variable, as in the following example:

```
int temp;
int.TryParse(Console.ReadLine() out temp);
myChef.IdNumber = temp;
```

Using Auto-Implemented Properties

Although you can include any number of custom statements within the `get` and `set` accessors in a property, the most frequent scenario is that a `set` accessor simply assigns a value to the appropriate class field, and the `get` accessor simply returns the field value. Because the code in `get` and `set` accessors frequently is standard as well as brief, programmers sometimes take one of several shorthand approaches to writing properties.

For example, instead of writing an `IdNumber` property using 11 code lines as in Figure 9-8, a programmer might write the property on five lines, as follows:

```
public int IdNumber
{
    get{return idNumber;}
    set{idNumber = value;}
}
```

This format does not eliminate any of the characters in the original version of the property; it only eliminates some of the white space, placing each accessor on a single line.

Other programmers choose an even more condensed form and write the entire property on one line as:

```
public int IdNumber {get{return idNumber;} set{idNumber = value;}}
```

An even more concise format was introduced in C# 3.0. In this and newer versions of C#, you can write a property as follows:

```
public int IdNumber {get; set;}
```

A property written in this format is an **auto-implemented property**. The property's implementation (its set of working statements) is created for you automatically with the assumptions that the `set` accessor should simply assign a value to the appropriate field, and the `get` accessor should simply return the field. You cannot use an auto-implemented property if you need to include customized statements within one of your accessors (such as placing restrictions on an assigned value), and you can only declare an auto-implemented property when you use both `get` and `set`. Auto-implemented properties are sometimes called **automatic properties**.

When you create an auto-implemented property, you should not declare the backing field that corresponds to the property. The corresponding backing field is generated by the compiler and has an internal name that would not match the field's name if you had coded the field yourself. If you also declare a field for the property and do not refer to it explicitly, you will receive a warning that your field is never used because your field and the property's field refer to separate memory addresses. You can avoid the warning by using the declared field, but that can lead to potential confusion and errors. For example, Figure 9-11 shows an `Employee` class in which no specialized code is needed for the properties associated with the ID number and salary. In this class, the fields are not declared explicitly; only auto-implemented properties are declared. The figure also contains a short program that uses the class, and Figure 9-12 shows the output. Auto-implemented properties provide a convenient shortcut when you need both `get` and `set` abilities without specialized statements.

```
using System;
class CreateEmployee3
{
    static void Main()
    {
        Employee aWorker = new Employee();
        aWorker.IdNumber = 3872;
        aWorker.Salary = 22.11;
        Console.WriteLine("Employee #{0} makes {1}",
            aWorker.IdNumber, aWorker.Salary.ToString("C"));
    }
}
class Employee
{
    public int IdNumber {get; set;}
    public double Salary {get; set;}
}
```

Figure 9-11 An Employee class with no declared fields and auto-implemented properties, and a program that uses them

Figure 9-12 Output of the CreateEmployee3 application

If you want to create a read-only property using auto-implemented accessors, you can make the set accessor private, as in the following:

```
public int IdNumber {get; private set;}
```

Using this technique, the IdNumber property cannot be set by any statement in another class. However, it could be assigned a value by methods within its own class. You also might want to create a property that outside classes could set but not retrieve, as follows:

```
public int IdNumber {private get; set;}
```

 Watch the video *Creating Properties*.

TWO TRUTHS & A LIE

Creating Properties

1. A property is a member of a class that defines how fields will be set and retrieved.

2. Properties contain set accessors for retrieving an object's fields and get accessors for setting the stored values.

3. You can create auto-implemented properties when you want a field's set accessor to assign a value to the appropriate class field, and a field's get accessor simply to return the field value.

The false statement is #2. Properties contain set accessors for setting an object's fields and get accessors for retrieving the stored values.

You Do It

Creating a Class and Objects

In this section, you create a Student class and instantiate objects from it. This class contains an ID number, last name, and grade point average for the Student. It also contains properties that get and set each of these fields. You also pass each Student object to a method.

1. Open a new file in your text editor. Begin the Student class by declaring the class name, inserting an opening curly brace, and declaring three private fields that will hold an ID number, last name, and grade point average, as follows:

```
class Student
{
    private int idNumber;
    private string lastName;
    private double gradePointAverage;
```

2. Add two constants that represent the highest and lowest possible values for a grade point average.

```
public const double HIGHEST_GPA = 4.0;
public const double LOWEST_GPA = 0.0;
```

(continues)

(continued)

3. Add two properties that get and set `idNumber` and `lastName`. By convention, properties have an identifier that is the same as the field they service, except they start with a capital letter.

```
public int IdNumber
{
    get
    {
        return idNumber;
    }
    set
    {
        idNumber = value;
    }
}
public string LastName
{
    get
    {
        return lastName;
    }
    set
    {
        lastName = value;
    }
}
```

4. Add the following `set` accessor in the property for the `gradePointAverage` field. It sets limits on the value assigned, assigning 0 if the value is out of range.

```
public double GradePointAverage
{
    get
    {
        return gradePointAverage;
    }
    set
    {
        if(value >= LOWEST_GPA && value <= HIGHEST_GPA)
            gradePointAverage = value;
        else
            gradePointAverage = LOWEST_GPA;
    }
}
```

5. Add a closing curly brace for the class. Save the file as **CreateStudents.cs**.

(continues)

(continued)

6. At the top of the file, begin a program that creates two Student objects, assigns some values, and displays the Students.

```
using System;
class CreateStudents
{
```

7. Add a Main() method that declares two Students. Assign field values, including one "illegal" value—a grade point average that is too high.

```
static void Main()
{
    Student first = new Student();
    Student second = new Student();
    first.IdNumber = 123;
    first.LastName = "Anderson";
    first.GradePointAverage = 3.5;
    second.IdNumber = 789;
    second.LastName = "Daniels";
    second.GradePointAverage = 4.1;
```

8. Instead of creating similar WriteLine() statements to display the two Students, call a method with each Student. You will create the method to accept a Student argument in the next step. Add a closing curly brace for the Main() method.

```
    Display(first);
    Display(second);
}
```

9. Write the Display() method so that the passed-in Student's IdNumber, LastName, and GradePointAverage are displayed and aligned. Add a closing curly brace for the class.

```
static void Display(Student stu)
{
    Console.WriteLine("{0,5}   {1,-10}{2,6}",
        stu.IdNumber, stu.LastName,
        stu.GradePointAverage.ToString("F1"));
}
}
```

Recall that field contents are left-aligned when you use a minus sign before the field size. Also recall that the "F1" argument to the ToString() method causes the value to be displayed to one decimal place.

(continues)

(continued)

10. Save the file, and then compile and execute the program. Figure 9-13 shows the output. Each `Student` has unique data values and uses the same `Display()` method. Notice how the second `Student`'s grade point average was forced to 0 by the `set` accessor in the property for the field.

Figure 9-13   Output of the `CreateStudents` program

Using Auto-Implemented Properties

When a property's `get` accessor simply returns the corresponding field's value, and its `set` accessor simply assigns a value to the appropriate field, you can reduce the code in your classes by using auto-implemented properties. In the `Student` class, both `IdNumber` and `LastName` are candidates for this shortcut, so you can replace the full versions of these properties with their auto-implemented versions. The `GradePointAverage` property cannot take advantage of auto-implementation because additional code is required for the property to fulfill its intended function.

1. Open the file that contains the `Student` class if it is not still open on your screen. Remove the properties for `IdNumber` and `LastName` and replace them with these auto-implemented versions:

```
public int IdNumber {get; set;}
public string LastName {get; set;}
```

2. Remove the declarations for the fields `idNumber` and `lastName`.

3. Save the file, and then recompile and execute it. The output is the same as when the program used the original version of the `Student` class in Figure 9-13.

More About `public` and `private` Access Modifiers

Most of the time, class data fields are `private` and class methods are `public`. This technique ensures that data will be used and changed only in the ways provided in your accessors. Novice programmers might make a data field `public` to avoid having to create a property containing `get` and `set` accessors. However, doing so violates a basic principle of object-oriented programming. Data should be hidden when at all possible, and access to it should be controlled by well-designed accessors.

Although private fields and public methods and accessors are the norm, occasionally you need to create public fields or private methods. Consider the Carpet class shown in Figure 9-14. Although it contains several private data fields, this class also contains one public constant field (shaded). Following the three public property declarations, one private method is defined (also shaded).

```
class Carpet
{
    public const string MOTTO = "Our carpets are quality-made";
    private int length;
    private int width;
    private int area;
    public int Length
    {
        get
        {
            return length;
        }
        set
        {
            length = value;
            CalcArea();
        }
    }
    public int Width
    {
        get
        {
            return width;
        }
        set
        {
            width = value;
            CalcArea();
        }
    }
    public int Area
    {
        get
        {
            return area;
        }
    }
    private void CalcArea()
    {
        area = Length * Width;
    }
}
```

Figure 9-14   The Carpet class

When you create `Carpet` objects from the class in Figure 9-14, each `Carpet` will have its own `length`, `width`, and `area`, but all `Carpet` objects will have the same `MOTTO`. The field `MOTTO` is preceded by the keyword `const`, meaning `MOTTO` is constant. That is, no program can change its value. Making a constant `public` does not violate information hiding in the way that making an object's data fields `public` would, because programs that use this class cannot change the constant's value.

When you define a named constant within a class, it is always `static`, even though you cannot use the keyword `static` as a modifier. In other words, the field belongs to the entire class, not to any particular instance of the class. When you create a `static` field, only one copy is stored for the entire class, no matter how many objects you instantiate. When you use a constant field in a client class, you use the class name and a dot rather than an object name, as in `Carpet.MOTTO`. Some built-in C# classes contain useful named constants, such as `Math.PI`, which contains the value of pi. You do not create a `Math` object to use `PI`; therefore, you know it is `static`.

 Throughout this book, you have been using `static` to describe the `Main()` method of a class. You do not need to create an object of any class that contains a `Main()` method to be able to use `Main()`.

Figure 9-15 shows a program that instantiates and uses a `Carpet` object, and Figure 9-16 shows the results when the program executes. Notice that, although the output statements require an object to use the `Width`, `Length`, and `Area` properties, `MOTTO` is referenced using the class name only.

```
using System;
class TestCarpet
{
    static void Main()
    {
        Carpet aRug = new Carpet();
        aRug.Width = 12;
        aRug.Length = 14;
        Console.Write("The {0} X {1} carpet ", aRug.Width, aRug.Length);
        Console.WriteLine("has an area of {0}", aRug.Area);
        Console.WriteLine("Our motto is: {0}", Carpet.MOTTO);
    }
}
```

Figure 9-15 The `TestCarpet` class

Figure 9-16 Output of the TestCarpet program

The Carpet class contains one private method named CalcArea(). As you examine the code in the TestCarpet class in Figure 9-15, notice that Width and Length are set using an assignment operator, but Area is not. The TestCarpet class can make assignments to Width and Length because these properties are public. However, you would not want a client program to assign a value to Area because the assigned value might not agree with the Width and Length values. Therefore, the Area property is a read-only property—it does not contain a set accessor, and no assignments by clients are allowed. Instead, whenever the Width or Length properties are set, the private CalcArea() method is called from the accessor. The CalcArea() method is defined as private because there is no reason for a client class like TestCarpet to call CalcArea(). Programmers probably create private methods more frequently than they create public data fields. Some programmers feel that the best style is to use public methods that are nothing but a list of method calls with descriptive names. Then, the methods that actually do the work are all private.

TWO TRUTHS & A LIE

More About public and private Access Modifiers

1. Good object-oriented techniques require that data should usually be hidden and access to it should be controlled by well-designed accessors.

2. Although private fields, methods, and accessors are the norm, occasionally you need to create public versions of them.

3. When you define a named constant within a class, it is always static; that is, the field belongs to the entire class, not to any particular instance of the class.

The false statement is #2. Although private fields and public methods and accessors are the norm, occasionally you need to create public fields or private methods.

Understanding the this Reference

When you create a class, only one copy of the class code is stored in computer memory. However, you might eventually create thousands of objects from the class. When you create each object, you provide storage for each of the object's instance variables. For example,

Figure 9-17 shows part of a Book class that contains three fields, a property for the title field, and an advertising message method. When you declare several Book objects, as in the following statements, each Book object requires separate memory locations for its title, numPages, and price:

```
Book myBook = new Book();
Book yourBook = new Book();
```

```
class Book
{
    private string title;
    private int numPages;
    private double price;
    public string Title
    {
        get
        {
            return title;
        }
        set
        {
            title = value;
        }
    }
    public void AdvertisingMessage()
    {
        Console.WriteLine("Buy it now: {0}", Title);
    }
}
```

Figure 9-17   Partially developed Book class

 When you compile the Book class, you receive warnings that the numPages and price fields are never used. The omission was purposeful for this demonstration program.

In this example, storing a single Book object requires allocating storage space for three separate fields; the storage requirements for Book objects used by a library or retail bookstore would be far more considerable, but necessary—each Book must be able to "hold" its own data, including publisher, date published, author, ISBN, and so on. Each nonstatic field is called an *instance variable* precisely because separate values are stored for each instance. If each Book object also required its own copy of each property and method contained in the class, the storage requirements would multiply. It makes sense that each Book needs space to store its unique title and other data, but because every Book uses the same methods, storing multiple copies of methods is wasteful and unnecessary.

Fortunately, each Book object does not need to store its own copy of each property and method. Whether you make the method call myBook.AdvertisingMessage() or yourBook.

AdvertisingMessage(), you access the same AdvertisingMessage() method. However, there must be a difference between the two method calls, because each displays a different title in its message. The difference lies in an implicit, or invisible, reference that is passed to every instance method and property accessor. The implicitly passed reference is the **this reference**. The this reference is the address of the invoking object. When you call the method myBook.AdvertisingMessage(), you automatically pass the this reference to the method so that it knows which instance of Book to use. Only nonstatic methods receive a this reference. The this reference is aptly named. When you execute a nonstatic method such as myBook.AdvertisingMessage(), you might ask yourself which object's data will be used in the method. The answer is *"This* object's (myBook's) data."

You can explicitly refer to the this reference within an instance method or property, as shown in Figure 9-18. When you refer to Title (or title) within a Book class method or accessor, you are referring to the title field of "this" Book—the Book whose name you used in the method call—perhaps myBook or yourBook. Using the shaded keywords in Figure 9-18 is not required; the version of the methods shown in Figure 9-17 (where this was implied but not written explicitly) works just as well. Figure 9-19 shows an application that uses the Book class, and Figure 9-20 shows the output.

```
class Book
{
    private string title;
    private int numPages;
    private double price;
    public string Title
    {
      get
      {
         return this.title;
      }
      set
      {
         this.title = value;
      }
    }
    public void AdvertisingMessage()
    {
       Console.WriteLine("Buy it now: {0}", this.Title);
    }
}
```

Figure 9-18   Book class with methods explicitly using this references

```
using System;
class CreateTwoBooks
{
    static void Main()
    {
        Book myBook = new Book();
        Book yourBook = new Book();
        myBook.Title = "Silas Marner";
        yourBook.Title = "The Time Traveler's Wife";
        myBook.AdvertisingMessage();
        yourBook.AdvertisingMessage();
    }
}
```

Figure 9-19 Program that declares two Book objects

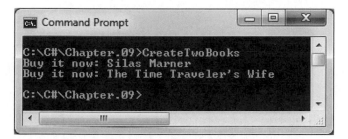

Figure 9-20 Output of the CreateTwoBooks program

The Book class in Figure 9-18 worked without adding the explicit references to this. However, you should be aware that the this reference is always there, working behind the scenes, even if you do not code it. Sometimes, you may want to include the this reference within a method for clarity, so the reader has no doubt when you are referring to a class instance variable.

On occasion, you might need to explicitly code the this reference. For example, consider the abbreviated Book class in Figure 9-21. The programmer has chosen the same identifier for a field and a parameter to a method that uses the field. To distinguish between the two, the field must be referenced as this.price within the method that has a parameter with the same name. All references to price (without using this) in the SetPriceAndTax() method in Figure 9-21 are references to the local parameter. If the method included the statement price = price;, the parameter's value would be assigned to itself and the class's field would never be set.

```
            class Book
            {
                private double price;
                private double tax;
                private double price;
                public void SetPriceAndTax(double price)
                {
                    const double TAX_RATE = 0.07;
                    this.price = price;
                    tax = price * TAX_RATE;
                }
            }
```

The field price is this.price within the method.

The parameter price is just price within the method.

Figure 9-21   Book class that must explicitly use the this reference

Watch the video *Understanding the this Reference.*

TWO TRUTHS & A LIE

Understanding the this Reference

1. An implicit, or invisible, this reference is passed to every instance method and property accessor in a class; instance methods and properties are nonstatic.

2. You can explicitly refer to the this reference within an instance method or property.

3. Although the this reference exists in every instance method, you can never refer to it within a method.

The false statement is #3. Sometimes, you may want to include the this reference within a method for clarity, so the reader has no doubt when you are referring to a class instance variable.

Understanding Constructors

When you create a class such as Employee and instantiate an object with a statement such as Employee aWorker = new Employee();, you are actually calling a method named Employee() that is provided by C#. A **constructor** is a method that instantiates (creates an instance of) an object. If you do not write a constructor for a class, then each class you create is automatically supplied with a `public` constructor with no parameters. A constructor without parameters is a class's **default constructor**. (The term *default constructor* is not just used for a class's automatically supplied constructor; it is used for any constructor that takes no parameters. You will learn to create constructors with parameters in the next section.)

The automatically created constructor named `Employee()` establishes one `Employee` with the identifier `aWorker`, and provides the following initial values to the `Employee`'s data fields:

- Numeric fields are set to 0 (zero).

- Character fields are set to '\0'.

- Boolean fields are set to `false`.

- References, such as `string` fields or any other object fields, are set to `null` (or empty).

The value of an object initialized with a default constructor is known as the **default value of the object**. If you do not want an `Employee`'s fields to hold these default values, or if you want to perform additional tasks when you create an `Employee`, you can write your own constructor to replace the automatically supplied version. Any constructor you write must have the same name as its class, and constructors cannot have a return type. For example, if you create an `Employee` class that contains a `Salary` property, and you want every new `Employee` object to have a salary of 300.00, you could write the constructor for the `Employee` class as follows:

```
Employee()
{
    Salary = 300.00;
}
```

Assuming a `Salary` property has been defined for the `salary` field, any instantiated `Employee` will have a default `salary` value of 300.00.

You can write any statement in a constructor. For example, you can perform arithmetic or display a message. However, the most common constructor task is to initialize fields. If you create a class in which one or more fields are never assigned a value, the compiler will issue a warning that the fields in question will hold default values.

Passing Parameters to Constructors

You can create a constructor to ensure that all objects of a class are initialized with the same values in their data fields. Alternatively, you might create objects initialized with unique field values by writing constructors to which you pass one or more parameters. You then can use the parameter values to set properties or fields for individual object instantiations.

For example, consider an `Employee` class with two data fields, a constructor, and an auto-implemented property, as shown in Figure 9-22. Its constructor assigns 9.99 to each potentially instantiated `Employee`'s `PayRate`. Any time an `Employee` object is created using a statement such as `Employee partTimeWorker = new Employee();`, even if no other data-assigning methods are ever used, you are ensured that the `Employee`'s `PayRate` holds a default value.

```
class Employee
{
    private int idNumber;
    private string name;
    public Employee()
    {
        PayRate = 9.99;
    }
    public double PayRate {get; set;}
    //  Other class members can go here
}
```

Figure 9-22 Employee class with a parameterless constructor

The constructor in Figure 9-22 is a **parameterless constructor**—one that takes no arguments. In other words, it is a default constructor. As an alternative, you might choose to create Employees with different initial PayRate values for each Employee. To accomplish this task, you can pass a pay rate to the constructor. Figure 9-23 shows an Employee constructor that receives a parameter. An integer is passed to the constructor using a statement such as the following:

```
Employee partTimeWorker = new Employee(12.50);
```

When the constructor executes, the double used as the actual parameter within the method call is passed to Employee() and assigned to the Employee's PayRate.

```
public Employee(double rate)
{
    PayRate = rate;
}
```

Figure 9-23 Employee constructor with parameter

Overloading Constructors

C# automatically provides a default constructor for your classes. As soon as you create your own constructor, whether it has parameters or not, you no longer have access to the automatically created version. However, if you want a class to have both parameter and parameterless versions of a constructor, you can create them. Like any other C# methods, constructors can be overloaded. You can write as many constructors for a class as you want, as long as their parameter lists do not cause ambiguity. A class can contain only one parameterless constructor: the default constructor, which can be the automatically provided one or one that you write. If you wrote multiple parameterless constructors, they would be ambiguous. If you create any number of constructors but do not create a parameterless version, then the class does not have a default constructor.

For example, the Employee class in Figure 9-24 contains four constructors. The Main() method within the CreateSomeEmployees class in Figure 9-25 shows how different types of Employees might be instantiated. Notice that one version of the Employee constructor—the one that supports a character parameter—doesn't even use the parameter; sometimes you might create a constructor with a specific parameter type simply to force that constructor to be the version that executes. The output of the CreateSomeEmployees program is shown in Figure 9-26.

```
class Employee
{
    public int IdNumber {get; set;}

    public double Salary {get; set;}
    public Employee()          ──────  This parameterless constructor
    {                                   is the class's default constructor.
        IdNumber = 999;
        Salary = 0;
    }
    public Employee(int empId)
    {
        IdNumber = empId;
        Salary = 0;
    }
    public Employee(int empId, double sal)
    {
        IdNumber = empId;
        Salary = sal;
    }
    public Employee(char code)
    {
        IdNumber = 111;
        Salary = 100000;
    }
}
```

Figure 9-24 Employee class with four constructors

```
using System;
class CreateSomeEmployees
{
    static void Main()
    {
        Employee aWorker = new Employee();
        Employee anotherWorker = new Employee(234);
        Employee theBoss = new Employee('A');
        Console.WriteLine("{0,4}{1,14}", aWorker.IdNumber,
            aWorker.Salary.ToString("C"));
        Console.WriteLine("{0,4}{1,14}", anotherWorker.IdNumber,
            anotherWorker.Salary.ToString("C"));
        Console.WriteLine("{0,4}{1,14}", theBoss.IdNumber,
            theBoss.Salary.ToString("C"));
    }
}
```

Figure 9-25 The CreateSomeEmployees program

Figure 9-26 Output of the CreateSomeEmployees program

Most likely, a single application would not use all four constructors of the Employee class. More likely, each application that uses the class would use only one or two constructors. You create a class with multiple constructors to provide flexibility for your clients. For example, some clients might choose to construct Employee objects with just ID numbers, and others might prefer to construct them with ID numbers and salaries.

Using Constructor Initializers

The Employee class in Figure 9-24 contains four constructors, and each constructor initializes the same two fields. In a fully developed class used by a company, many more fields would be initialized, creating a lot of duplicated code. Besides the original extra work of writing the repetitive statements in these constructors, even more work will be required when the class is modified in the future. For example, if your organization institutes a new employee ID number format that requires a specific number of digits, then each constructor will have to be modified, requiring extra work. In addition, one or more of the constructor versions that must be modified might be overlooked, introducing errors into the programs that are clients of the class.

As an alternative to repeating code in the constructors, you can use a constructor initializer. A **constructor initializer** is a clause that indicates another instance of a class constructor should be executed before any statements in the current constructor body. Figure 9-27 shows a new version of the Employee class using constructor initializers in three of the four overloaded constructor versions.

```
class Employee
{
    public int IdNumber {get; set;}
    public double Salary {get; set;}
    public Employee() : this(999, 0)
    {
    }
    public Employee(int empId) : this(empId, 0)
    {
    }
    public Employee(int empId, double sal)
    {
        IdNumber = empId;
        Salary = sal;
    }
    public Employee(char code) : this(111, 100000)
    {
    }
}
```

Figure 9-27 Employee class with constructor initializers

In the three shaded clauses in Figure 9-27, the this reference is used to mean "the constructor for this object being constructed." For example, when a client calls the parameterless Employee constructor, 999 and 0 are passed to the two-parameter constructor. There, they become empId and sal, parameters that are assigned to the IdNumber and Salary properties. If statements were written within the parameterless constructor, they would then execute; however, in this class, additional statements are not necessary. Similarly, if a client uses the constructor version that accepts only an ID number, that parameter and a 0 for salary are passed to the two-parameter constructor. The only time just one version of the constructor executes is when a client uses both an ID number and a salary as constructor arguments. In the future, if additional statements need to be added to the class (for example, a decision that ensures an ID number was at least five digits at construction), the decision would be added only to the two-parameter version of the constructor, and all the other versions could use it.

Using the readonly Modifier in a Constructor

You have already learned that when you use the const modifier with a variable, you must assign a value at declaration and the value cannot be changed. The readonly modifier is similar to const in that it is used to assign a constant value that cannot be changed, but when you use readonly with a field you can assign a value either at declaration or within a constructor. This means that different constructor versions can assign different values to a readonly field. Additionally, a const field must be assigned its value when a program is compiled, but a readonly field can be assigned a value at runtime. For example, a readonly field's value might be retrieved from user input or from the operating system.

TWO TRUTHS & A LIE

Understanding Constructors

1. Every class you create is automatically supplied with a public constructor with no parameters.

2. If you write a constructor for a class, you do not have a default constructor for the class.

3. Any constructor you write must have the same name as its class, and constructors cannot have a return type.

The false statement is #2. If you write a parameterless constructor for a class, it becomes the default constructor, and you lose the automatically supplied version. If you write only constructors that require parameters, then the class no longer contains a default constructor.

 You Do It

Adding Overloaded Constructors To a Class

In these steps, you add overloaded constructors to the Student class.

1. Open the file that contains the Student class if it is not still open on your screen. Just before the closing curly brace for the Student class, add the following constructor. It takes three parameters and assigns them to the appropriate fields:

(continues)

(continued)

```
public Student(int id, string name, double gpa)
{
    IdNumber = id;
    LastName = name;
    GradePointAverage = gpa;
}
```

2. Add a second parameterless constructor. It calls the first constructor, passing 0 for the ID number, "XXX" for the name, and 0.0 for the grade point average. Its body is empty.

```
public Student() : this(0, "XXX", 0.0)
{
}
```

3. Change the name of the CreateStudents class to **CreateStudents2**.

4. After the existing declarations of the Student objects, add two more declarations. With one, use three arguments, but with the other, do not use any.

```
Student third = new Student(456, "Marco", 2.4);
Student fourth = new Student();
```

5. At the end of the Main() method, just after the two existing calls to the Display() method, add two more calls using the new objects:

```
Display(third);
Display(fourth);
```

6. Save the file, and then compile and execute it. The output looks like Figure 9-28. All four objects are displayed. The first two have had values assigned to them after declaration, but the third and fourth ones obtained their values from their constructors.

Figure 9-28   Output of CreateStudents2 program

Using Object Initializers

An **object initializer** allows you to assign values to any accessible members or properties of a class at the time of instantiation without calling a constructor with parameters. For example, assuming an `Employee` class has been created with a public `IdNumber` property and a parameterless constructor, you can write an object initializer as follows:

```
Employee aWorker = new Employee {IdNumber = 101};
```

In this statement, 101 is assigned to the `aWorker` object's `IdNumber` property. The assignment is made within a pair of curly braces; no parentheses are used with the class name. When this statement executes, the parameterless, default constructor for the class is executed first, and then the object initializer assignment is made.

For example, Figure 9-29 shows an `Employee` class that contains properties for `IdNumber` and `Salary` and a default constructor that assigns a value to `Salary`. For demonstration purposes, the constructor displays the current object's ID number and salary. The figure also shows a program that instantiates one `Employee` object and displays its value, and Figure 9-30 shows the output. When the object is created in the shaded statement, the constructor executes, assigns 99.99 to `Salary`, and displays the first line of output, showing `IdNumber` is still 0. After the object is constructed in the `Main()` method, the next output line is displayed, showing that the assignment of the ID number occurred after construction.

```
using System;
class DemoObjectInitializer
{
    static void Main()
    {
        Employee aWorker = new Employee {IdNumber = 101};
        Console.WriteLine("Employee #{0} exists. Salary is {1}.",
            aWorker.IdNumber, aWorker.Salary);
    }
}
class Employee
{
    public int IdNumber {get; set;}
    public double Salary {get; set;}
    public Employee()
    {
        Salary = 99.99;
        Console.WriteLine("Employee #{0} created. Salary is {1}.",
            IdNumber, Salary);
    }
}
```

Figure 9-29   The DemoObjectInitializer program

Figure 9-30 Output of the `DemoObjectInitializer` program

To use object initializers, a class must have a default constructor. That is, you either must not create any constructors or you must create one that requires no parameters.

Multiple assignments can be made with an object initializer by separating them with commas, as in the following:

```
Employee myAssistant = new Employee {IdNumber = 202, Salary = 25.00};
```

This single code line has the same results as the following three statements:

```
Employee myAssistant = new Employee();
myAssistant.IdNumber = 202;
myAssistant.Salary = 25.00;
```

Using object initializers allows you to create multiple objects with different initial assignments without having to provide multiple constructors to cover every possible situation. Additionally, using object initializers allows you to create objects with different starting values for different properties of the same data type. For example, consider a class like the `Box` class in Figure 9-31 that contains multiple properties of the same type. The constructor sets the `Height`, `Width`, and `Depth` properties to 1. You could write a constructor that accepts an integer parameter to be assigned to `Height` (using the default value 1 for the other dimensions), but then you could not write an additional overloaded constructor that accepts an integer parameter to be assigned to `Width` because the constructors would be ambiguous. However, by using object initializers, you can create objects to which you assign the properties you want. Figure 9-32 shows a program that declares three `Box` objects, each with a different assigned dimension, and Figure 9-33 shows the output, which demonstrates that each property was assigned appropriately.

406

```
class Box
{
   public int Height {get; set;}
   public int Width {get; set;}
   public int Depth {get; set;}
   public Box()
   {
      Height = 1;
      Width = 1;
      Depth = 1;
   }
}
```

Figure 9-31   The Box class

```
using System;
class DemoObjectInitializer2
{
   static void Main()
   {
      Box box1 = new Box {Height = 3};
      Box box2 = new Box {Width = 15};
      Box box3 = new Box {Depth = 268};
      DisplayDimensions(1, box1);
      DisplayDimensions(2, box2);
      DisplayDimensions(3, box3);
   }
   static void DisplayDimensions(int num, Box box)
   {
      Console.WriteLine("Box {0}: Height: {1} Width: {2} Depth: {3}",
         num, box.Height, box.Width, box.Depth);
   }
}
```

Figure 9-32   The DemoObjectInitializer2 program

Figure 9-33   Output of the DemoObjectInitializer2 program

Object initializers have additional uses in LINQ statements. You will learn about LINQ in the chapter *Data Queries and LINQ*.

TWO TRUTHS & A LIE

Using Object Initializers

Assume that a working program contains the following object initializer:

Invoice oneBill = new Invoice {Amount = 0};

1. You know that the Invoice class contains a default constructor.

2. You know that Amount is public.

3. You know that the Invoice class contains a single property.

The false statement is #3. The Invoice class might have any number of properties. However, only one is being initialized in this statement.

Overloading Operators

C# operators are the symbols you use to perform operations on objects. You have used many operators, including arithmetic operators (such as + and) and logical operators (such as == and <). Separate actions can result from what seems to be the same operation or command. This occurs frequently in all computer programming languages, not just object-oriented languages. For example, in most programming languages and applications such as spreadsheets and databases, the + operator has a variety of meanings. A few of them include:

- Alone before a value (called *unary form*), + indicates a positive value, as in the expression +7.

- Between two integers (called *binary form*), + indicates integer addition, as in the expression 5 + 9.

- Between two floating-point numbers (also called binary form), + indicates floating-point addition, as in the expression 6.4 + 2.1.

- Between two strings, + indicates concatenation, as in the expression "Hello, " + "there".

Expressing a value as positive is a different operation from using the + operator to perform arithmetic or concatenate strings, so + is overloaded several times in that it can take one or two arguments and have a different meaning in each case. It also can take different operand types—you use a + to add two ints, two doubles, an int and a double, and a variety of other combinations. Each use results in different actions behind the scenes.

Just as it is convenient to use a + between both integers and doubles to add them, it also can be convenient to use a + between objects, such as Employees or Books, to add them. To be able to use arithmetic symbols with your own objects, you must overload the symbols.

C# operators are classified as unary or binary, depending on whether they take one or two arguments, respectively. The rules for overloading are shown in the following list.

- The overloadable unary operators are:

  `+ - ! ~ ++ -- true false`

- The overloadable binary operators are:

  `+ - * / % & | ^ == != > < >= <=`

- You cannot overload the following operators:

  `= && || ?? ?: checked unchecked new typeof as is`

- You cannot overload an operator for a built-in data type. For example, you cannot change the meaning of + between two ints.

- When a binary operator is overloaded and it has a corresponding assignment operator, it is also overloaded. For example, if you overload +, then += is automatically overloaded too.

- Some operators must be overloaded in pairs. For example, when you overload ==, you also must overload !=, and when you overload >, you also must overload <.

When you overload ==, you also receive warnings about methods in the Object class. You will learn about this class in the chapter *Introduction to Inheritance*; you should not attempt to overload == until you have studied that chapter.

You have used many, but not all, of the operators listed above. If you want to include an overloaded operator in a class, you must decide what the operator will mean in your class. When you do, you write statements in a method to carry out your meaning. The method has a return type and arguments just like other methods, but its identifier is required to be named operator followed by the operator being overloaded—for example, operator+() or operator*().

For example, suppose that you create a Book class in which each object has a title, number of pages, and a price. Further assume that, as a publisher, you have decided to "add" Books together. That is, you want to take two existing Books and combine them into one. Assume that you want the new book to have the following characteristics:

- The new title is a combination of the old titles, joined by the word "and."

- The number of pages in the new book is equal to the sum of the pages in the original Books.

- Instead of charging twice as much for a new Book, you have decided to charge the price of the more expensive of the two original Books, plus $10.

A different publisher might have decided that "adding Books" means something different—for example, an added Book might have a fixed new price of $29.99. The statements you write in your `operator+()` method depend on how you define adding for your class. You could write an ordinary method to perform these tasks, but you could also overload the + operator to mean "add two Books." Figure 9-34 shows a Book class that has properties for each field and a shaded `operator+()` method.

```
class Book
{
    public Book(string title, int pages, double price)
    {
        Title = title;
        NumPages = pages;
        Price = price;
    }
    public static Book operator+(Book first, Book second)
    {
        const double EXTRA = 10.00;
        string newTitle = first.Title + " and " +
            second.Title;
        int newPages = first.NumPages + second.NumPages;
        double newPrice;
        if(first.Price > second.Price)
            newPrice = first.Price + EXTRA;
        else
            newPrice = second.Price + EXTRA;
        return(new Book(newTitle, newPages, newPrice));
    }
    public string Title {get; set;}

    public int NumPages {get; set;}

    public double Price {get; set;}
}
```

Figure 9-34 Book class with overloaded + operator

The `operator+()` method in Figure 9-34 is declared to be `public` (so that class clients can use it) and `static` (which is required). The method is `static` because it does not receive a `this` reference to any object; instead, the two objects to be added are both parameters to the method.

The return type is Book because the addition of two Books is defined to be a new Book with different values from either of the originals. You could overload the + operator so that when two Books are added they return some other type, but it is most common to make the addition of two objects result in an "answer" of the same type.

The two parameters in the `operator+()` method in the Book class are both Books. Therefore, when you eventually call this method, the data types on both sides of the + sign will be Books. For example, you could write other methods that add a Book and an Employee, or a Book and a double.

Within the `operator+()` method, the statements perform the following tasks:

- A constant is declared to hold the extra price used in creating a new Book from two existing ones.

- A new string is created and assigned the first parameter Book's title, plus the `string` " and ", plus the second parameter Book's title.

- A new integer is declared and assigned the sum of the number of pages in each of the parameter Books.

- A new `double` is declared and assigned the value of the more expensive original Book plus $10.00.

- Within the `return` statement, a new anonymous Book is created (an anonymous object is one without an identifier) using the new title, page number, and price, and is returned to the calling method. (Instead of an anonymous Book, it would have been perfectly acceptable to use two statements—the first one creating a named Book with the same arguments, and the second one returning the named Book.)

Figure 9-35 shows a client program that can use the + operator in the Book class. It first declares three Books; then, in the shaded statement, it adds two Books together and assigns the result to the third. When book1 and book2 are added, the `operator+()` method is called. The returned Book is assigned to book3, which is then displayed. Figure 9-36 shows the results.

```
using System;
class AddBooks
{
    static void Main()
    {
        Book book1 = new Book("Silas Marner", 350, 15.95);
        Book book2 = new Book("Moby Dick", 250, 16.00);
        Book book3;
        book3 = book1 + book2;
        Console.WriteLine("The new book is \"{0}\"", book3.Title);
        Console.WriteLine("It has {0} pages and costs {1}",
            book3.NumPages, book3.Price.ToString("C"));
    }
}
```

Figure 9-35   The AddBooks program

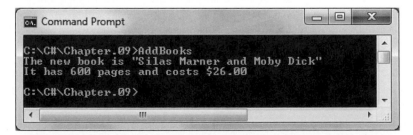

Figure 9-36   Output of the AddBooks program

In the Book class, it took many statements to overload the operator; however, in the client class, just typing a + between objects allows a programmer to use the objects and operator intuitively. You could write any statements you wanted within the operator method. However, for clarity, you should write statements that intuitively have the same meaning as the common use of the operator. For example, although you could overload the operator*() method to display a Book's title and price instead of performing multiplication, it would be a bad programming technique.

Because each addition operation returns a Book, it is possible to chain addition in a statement such as collection = book1 + book2 + book3;, assuming that all the variables have been declared to be Book objects. In this example, book1 and book2 would be added, returning a temporary Book. Then the temporary Book and book3 would be added, returning a different temporary Book that would be assigned to collection.

When you overload an operator, at least one argument to the method must be a member of the containing class. In other words, within the Book class, you can overload operator*() to multiply a Book by an integer, but you cannot overload operator*() to multiply a double by an integer.

When you overload a unary operator, the method takes a single argument. For example, suppose that you want to use a negative sign with a Book to make its price negative. You could use the operator in a statement such as the following:

returnedBook = -purchasedBook;

The operator-() method header might appear as follows:

public static Book operator-(Book aBook)

In this example, the minus sign is understood to cause unary negation instead of binary subtraction because the method accepts only one parameter, which is a Book. The method also returns a Book, which is an altered version of the parameter. Figure 9-37 shows a method that overloads the minus sign for a Book object. The method accepts a Book parameter, changes the price to its negative value, and returns the altered Book object to the calling method.

```
public static Book operator-(Book aBook)
{
    aBook.Price = -aBookPrice;
    return aBook;
}
```

Figure 9-37 An operator-() method for a Book

 Watch the video *Overloading Operators*.

TWO TRUTHS & A LIE

Overloading Operators

1. All C# operators can be overloaded.

2. You cannot overload an operator for a built-in data type.

3. Some operators must be overloaded in pairs.

The false statement is #1. You cannot overload the following operators: = && || ?? ?: checked unchecked new typeof as is

---

Declaring an Array of Objects

Just as you can declare arrays of integers or doubles, you can declare arrays that hold elements of any type, including objects. Remember that object names are references. When you create an array from a value type, such as int or char, the array holds the actual values. When you create an array from a reference type, such as a class you create, the array holds the memory addresses of the objects. In other words, the array "refers to" the objects instead of containing the objects.

You can create an array of references to seven Employee objects as follows:

```
Employee[] empArray = new Employee[7];
```

This statement reserves enough computer memory for the references to seven Employee objects named empArray[0] through empArray[6]. It does not actually construct those Employees; all the references are initialized to null. To create objects for the array, you must call the Employee() constructor seven times.

If the Employee class contains a default constructor, you can use the following loop to call the constructor seven times:

```
for(int x = 0; x < empArray.Length; ++x)
   empArray[x] = new Employee();
```

As x varies from 0 through 6, each of the seven empArray objects is constructed.

If you want to use a nondefault constructor, you must provide appropriate arguments. For example, if the Employee class contains a constructor with an int parameter, you can write the following:

```
Employee[] empArray = {new Employee(123),
   new Employee(234), new Employee(345)};
```

To use a method that belongs to an object that is part of an array, you insert the appropriate subscript notation after the array name and before the dot-method. For example, to set all seven Employee IdNumber properties to 999, you can write the following:

```
for(int x = 0; x < empArray.Length; ++x)
    empArray[x].IdNumber = 999;
```

Using the Sort() and BinarySearch() Methods with Arrays of Objects

In the chapter *Using Arrays*, you learned about using the System.Array class's built-in BinarySearch() and Sort() methods with simple data types such as int, double, and string. The Sort() method accepts an array parameter and arranges its elements in descending order. The BinarySearch() method accepts a sorted array and a value that it attempts to match in the array.

A complication arises when you consider searching or sorting arrays of objects you create. When you create and sort an array of simple data items, there is only one type of value to consider, and the order is based on the Unicode value of that item. The classes that support simple data items each contain a method named **CompareTo()**, which provides the details of how the basic data types compare to each other. In other words, they define comparisons such as "*2* is more than *1*" and "*B* is more than *A*." The Sort() and BinarySearch() methods use the CompareTo() method for the current type of data being sorted. In other words, Sort() uses the Int32 version of CompareTo() when sorting integers and the Char version of CompareTo() when sorting characters.

You learned about the built-in data type class names in Chapter 2; they are summarized in Table 2-1.

You have been using the String class (and its string alias) throughout this book. The class also contains a CompareTo() method that you first used in Chapter 2.

When you create a class in which comparisons will be made between objects, you must tell the compiler which field to use when making those comparisons. For example, you logically might sort an organization's Employee objects by ID number, salary, department number, last name, hire date, or any field contained in the class. To tell C# which field to use for placing Employee objects in order, you must create an interface.

An **interface** is a data type, like a class. It is a collection of abstract methods (and perhaps other members) that can be used by any class, as long as the class provides a definition to override the interface's do-nothing, or abstract, method definitions. Unlike a class, an interface cannot contain instance fields, and you cannot create objects from them.

A class that implements an interface must override the interface's methods. When a method **overrides** another, it takes precedence over the method, hiding the original version. In other words, the methods in an interface are empty, and any class that uses them must contain a new version that provides the details. Interfaces define named behaviors that classes must implement, so that all classes can use the same method names but use them appropriately for the class. In this way, interfaces provide for polymorphism—the ability of different objects to use the same method names but act appropriately based on the context.

When a method overrides another, it has the same signature as the method it overrides. When methods are overloaded, they have different signatures. You will learn more about overriding methods and abstract methods and classes in the next chapter.

C# supports many interfaces. You can identify an interface name by its initial letter *I*. For example, C# contains an **IComparable interface**, which contains the definition for the CompareTo() method that compares one object to another and returns an integer. Figure 9-38 shows the definition of IComparable. The CompareTo() method accepts a parameter Object, but does not contain any statements; you must provide an implementation for this method in classes you create if you want the objects to be comparable. In other words, you must determine the meanings of *greater than*, *less than*, and *equal to* for the class.

```
interface IComparable
{
    int CompareTo(Object o);
}
```

Figure 9-38   The IComparable interface

When you create a class whose instances will likely be compared by clients:

- You must include a single colon and the interface name IComparable after the class name.

- You must write a method that contains the following header:

  ```
  int IComparable.CompareTo(Object o)
  ```

Object is a class—the most generic of all classes. Every Employee object you create is not only an Employee, but also an Object. By using the type Object as a parameter, the CompareTo() method can accept anything. You will learn more about the Object class in the next chapter.

To work correctly in methods such as BinarySearch() and Sort(), the CompareTo() method you create for your class must return an integer value. Table 9-2 shows the return values that every version of CompareTo() should provide.

Return Value	Meaning
Negative	This instance is less than the compared object.
Zero	This instance is equal to the compared object.
Positive	This instance is greater than the compared object.

Table 9-2   Return values of `IComparable.CompareTo()` method

When you create a class that contains an `IComparable.CompareTo()` method, the method is an instance method and receives a `this` reference to the object used to call it. A second object is passed to the method; within the method, you first must convert, or cast, the passed object to the same type as the calling object's class, and then compare the corresponding fields you want from the `this` object and the passed object. For example, Figure 9-39 shows an `Employee` class that contains a shaded `CompareTo()` method and compares `Employee` objects based on the contents of their `idNumber` fields.

```
class Employee : IComparable
{
    public int IdNumber {get; set;}
    public double Salary {get; set;}

    int IComparable.CompareTo(Object o)
    {
        int returnVal;
        Employee temp = (Employee)o;
        if(this.IdNumber > temp.IdNumber)
            returnVal = 1;
        else
            if(this.IdNumber < temp.IdNumber)
                returnVal = -1;
            else
                returnVal = 0;
        return returnVal;
    }
}
```

Figure 9-39   `Employee` class using `IComparable` interface

The `Employee` class in Figure 9-39 uses a colon and `IComparable` in its class header to indicate an interface. The shaded method is an instance method; that is, it "belongs" to an `Employee` object. When another `Employee` is passed in as `Object o`, it is cast as an `Employee` and stored in the `temp` variable. The `idNumber` values of the `this` `Employee` and the passed `Employee` are compared, and one of three integer values is returned.

For example, if you declare two Employee objects named worker1 and worker2, you can use the following statement:

```
int answer = worker1.CompareTo(worker2);
```

Within the CompareTo() method in the Employee class, worker1 would be "this" Employee—the controlling Employee in the method. The temp Employee would be worker2. If, for example, worker1 had a higher ID number than worker2, the value of answer would be 1.

Figure 9-40 shows a program that uses the Employee class. The program declares an array of five Employee objects with different ID numbers and salaries; the ID numbers are purposely out of order to demonstrate that the Sort() method works correctly. The program also declares a seekEmp object with an ID number of 222. The program sorts the array, displays the sorted elements, then finds the array element that matches the seekEmp object. Figure 9-41 shows the program execution.

```csharp
using System;
class ComparableEmployeeArray
{
    static void Main()
    {
        Employee[] empArray = new Employee[5];
        int x;
        for(x = 0; x < empArray.Length; ++x)
            empArray[x] = new Employee();
        empArray[0].IdNumber = 333;
        empArray[1].IdNumber = 444;
        empArray[2].IdNumber = 555;
        empArray[3].IdNumber = 111;
        empArray[4].IdNumber = 222;
        Employee seekEmp = new Employee();
        seekEmp.IdNumber = 222;
        Array.Sort(empArray);
        Console.WriteLine("Sorted employees:");
        for(x = 0; x < empArray.Length; ++x)
          Console.WriteLine("Employee #{0}: {1} {2}",
              x, empArray[x].IdNumber,
              empArray[x].Salary.ToString("C"));
        x = Array.BinarySearch(empArray, seekEmp);
        Console.WriteLine("Employee #{0} was found at position {1}",
            seekEmp.IdNumber, x);
    }
}
```

Figure 9-40 ComparableEmployeeArray program

Command Prompt

```
C:\C#\Chapter.09>ComparableEmployeeArray
Sorted employees:
Employee #0: 111 $0.00
Employee #1: 222 $0.00
Employee #2: 333 $0.00
Employee #3: 444 $0.00
Employee #4: 555 $0.00
Employee #222 was found at position 1

C:\C#\Chapter.09>
```

Figure 9-41 Output of the `ComparableEmployeeArray` program

Notice that the `seekEmp` object matches the `Employee` in the second array position based on the `idNumber` only—not the salary—because the `CompareTo()` method in the `Employee` class uses only `idNumber` values and not salaries to make comparisons. You *could* have written code that requires both the `idNumber` and `salary` values to match before returning a positive number.

TWO TRUTHS & A LIE

Declaring an Array of Objects

Assume that a working program contains the following array declaration:

`BankAccount[] acctArray = new BankAccount[500];`

1. This statement reserves enough computer memory for 500 `BankAccount` objects.

2. This statement constructs 500 `BankAccount` objects.

3. The valid subscripts for `acctArray` are 0 through 499.

The false statement is #2. This statement declares 500 BankAccount objects but does not actually construct those objects; to do so, you must call the 500 individual constructors.

 You Do It

Creating an Array of Objects

In the next steps, you create an array of `Student` objects. You prompt the user for data to fill the array, and you sort the array by student ID number before displaying all the data.

(continues)

(continued)

1. Open the **CreateStudents2** program and immediately save it as **CreateStudents3**. Change the class name to `CreateStudents3`.

2. Delete all the existing statements in the `Main()` method, leaving the opening and closing curly braces. Between the braces, declare an array of eight `Student` objects. Also declare a variable to use as an array subscript and declare three variables that will temporarily hold a user's input data before `Student` objects are constructed.

```
Student[] students = new Student[8];
int x;
int id;
string name;
double gpa;
```

3. In a loop, call a `GetData()` method (which you will write shortly). Send the method `out` arguments so that you can retrieve values for variables that will hold an ID number, name, and grade point average. Then, in turn, send these three values to the `Student` constructor for each of the eight `Student` objects.

```
for(x = 0; x < students.Length; ++x)
{
   GetData(out id, out name, out gpa);
   students[x] = new Student(id, name, gpa);
}
```

4. Call the `Array.Sort()` method, sending it the student array. Then, one object at a time in a loop, call the `Display()` method that you wrote in the last set of steps.

```
Array.Sort(students);
Console.WriteLine("Sorted List:");
for(x = 0; x < students.Length; ++x)
   Display(students[x]);
```

5. Write the `GetData()` method. Its parameters are `out` parameters so that their values will be known to the calling method. The method simply prompts the user for each data item, reads it, and converts it to the appropriate type, if necessary.

```
static void GetData(out int id, out string name,
   out double gpa)
   {
      string inString;
      Console.Write("Please enter student ID number >> ");
      inString = Console.ReadLine();
```

(continues)

(continued)

```
        int.TryParse(inString, out id);
        Console.Write("Please enter last name for " +
            "student {0} >> ", id);
        name = Console.ReadLine();
        Console.Write("Please enter grade point average >> ");
        inString = Console.ReadLine();
        double.TryParse(inString, out gpa);
    }
```

6. After the header for the `Student` class, add a colon and `IComparable` so that objects of the class can be sorted:

```
public class Student : IComparable
```

7. Just before the closing curly brace for the `Student` class, add the `IComparable.CompareTo()` method that is required for the objects of the class to be sortable. The method will sort `Student` objects based on their ID numbers, so it returns 1, –1, or 0 based on `IdNumber` property comparisons. The method accepts an object that is cast to a `Student` object. If the `IdNumber` of the controlling `Student` object is greater than the argument's `IdNumber`, then the return value is set to 1. If the `IdNumber` of the controlling `Student` object is less than the argument's `IdNumber`, then the return value is –1. Otherwise, the return value is 0.

```
int IComparable.CompareTo(Object o)
{
    int returnVal;
    Student temp = (Student)o;
    if(this.IdNumber > temp.IdNumber)
        returnVal = 1;
    else
        if(this.IdNumber < temp.IdNumber)
            returnVal = -1;
        else
            returnVal = 0;
    return returnVal;
}
```

8. Save the file, and then compile and execute it. When prompted, enter any student IDs, names, and grade point averages you choose. The objects will be sorted and displayed in `idNumber` order. Figure 9-42 shows a typical execution.

(continues)

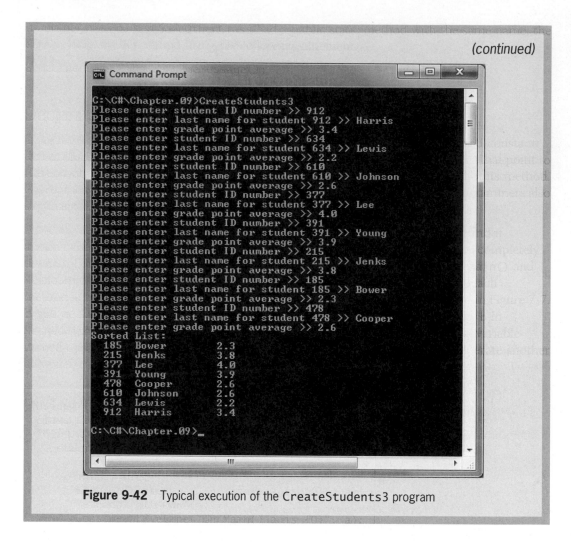

Figure 9-42   Typical execution of the CreateStudents3 program

Understanding Destructors

A **destructor** contains the actions you require when an instance of a class is destroyed. Most often, an instance of a class is destroyed when it goes out of scope. As with constructors, if you do not explicitly create a destructor for a class, C# automatically provides one.

To explicitly declare a destructor, you use an identifier that consists of a tilde (~) followed by the class name. You cannot provide any parameters to a destructor; it must have an empty argument list. As a consequence, destructors cannot be overloaded; a class can have one destructor at most. Like a constructor, a destructor has no return type.

Figure 9-43 shows an Employee class that contains only one field (idNumber), a property, a constructor, and a (shaded) destructor. When you execute the Main() method in the DemoEmployeeDestructor class in Figure 9-44, you instantiate two Employee objects, each with its own idNumber value. When the Main() method ends, the two Employee objects go out of scope, and the destructor for each object is called. Figure 9-45 shows the output.

```
class Employee
{
    public int idNumber {get; set;}
    public Employee(int empID)
    {
        IdNumber = empID;
        Console.WriteLine("Employee object {0} created", IdNumber);
    }
    ~Employee()
    {
        Console.WriteLine("Employee object {0} destroyed!", IdNumber);
    }
}
```

Figure 9-43   Employee class with destructor

```
using System;
class DemoEmployeeDestructor
{
    static void Main()
    {
        Employee aWorker = new Employee(101);
        Employee anotherWorker = new Employee(202);
    }
}
```

Figure 9-44   DemoEmployeeDestructor program

Figure 9-45   Output of DemoEmployeeDestructor program

The program in Figure 9-44 never explicitly calls the `Employee` class destructor, yet you can see from the output that the destructor executes twice. Destructors are invoked automatically; you cannot explicitly call one. Interestingly, the last object created is the first object destroyed; the same relationship would hold true no matter how many objects the program instantiated.

An instance of a class becomes eligible for destruction when it is no longer possible for any code to use it—that is, when it goes out of scope. The actual execution of an object's destructor might occur at any time after the object becomes eligible for destruction.

For now, you have little reason to create a destructor except to demonstrate how it is called automatically. Later, when you write more sophisticated C# programs that work with files, databases, or large quantities of computer memory, you might want to perform specific clean-up or close-down tasks when an object goes out of scope. Then you will place appropriate instructions within a destructor.

TWO TRUTHS & A LIE

Understanding Destructors

1. To explicitly declare a destructor, you use an identifier that consists of a tilde (~) followed by the class name.

2. You cannot provide any parameters to a destructor; it must have an empty argument list.

3. The return type for a destructor is always `void`.

The false statement is #3. Like a constructor, a destructor has no return type.

Understanding GUI Application Objects

The objects you have been using in GUI applications, such as `Forms`, `Buttons`, and `Labels`, are objects just like others you have studied in this chapter. That is, they encapsulate properties and methods. When you start a Windows Forms application in the IDE and drag a `Button` onto a `Form`, a statement is automatically created to instantiate a `Button` object.

Figure 9-46 shows a new GUI application that a programmer started simply by dragging one `Button` onto a `Form`.

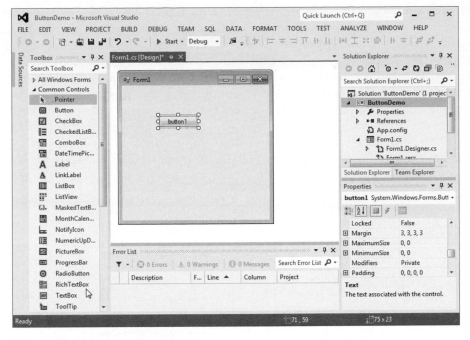

Figure 9-46 A Button on a Form

If you click on Form1.Designer.cs in the Solution Explorer, you can display the code where the Button is declared. See Figure 9-47.

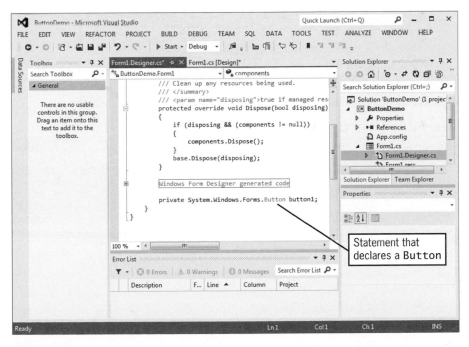

Figure 9-47 The automatically generated statement that declares button1

If you right-click `button1` in the code and select Find All References from the menu that appears, a list of every reference to `button1` in the project is displayed in the Find Symbol Results area at the bottom of the IDE. You can double-click each entry in the list in turn to locate all the places where code has been generated for `button1`. For example, several instances of `button1` are in a method named `InitializeComponent()`, as shown in Figure 9-48. The first reference to `button1` calls its constructor. You can also see how the `Button`'s `Name`, `Location`, `Size`, and other properties are set. You could have written these statements yourself, especially now that you know more about objects and how they are constructed, but it is easier to develop an application visually by dragging a `Button` onto a `Form` and allowing the IDE to create these statements for you.

Figure 9-48   Some automatically generated `button1` references in the IDE

In Figure 9-48, the `this` reference preceding each occurrence of `button1` refers to the class (`Form1`) that contains these statements.

Now that you understand how to create properties in your own classes, you can understand the properties of GUI objects and how they were created for your use.

Chapter Summary

- Application classes contain a `Main()` method. You also can create classes from which you instantiate objects; these classes need not have a `Main()` method. The data components of a class are its instance variables (or fields) and methods. A program or class that instantiates objects of another prewritten class is a class client or class user.

- When you create a class, you must assign a name to it and determine what data and methods will be part of the class. A class header or class definition contains an optional access modifier, the keyword `class`, and an identifier. A class body is enclosed between curly braces. When you create a class, you usually declare instance variables to be `private` and instance methods to be `public`.

- When you create an object that is an instance of a class, you supply a type and an identifier, and you allocate computer memory for that object using the `new` operator. After an object has been instantiated, its `public` methods can be accessed using the object's identifier, a dot, and a method call. You can pass objects to methods just as you can pass simple data types.

- A property is a member of a class that provides access to a field. Properties have `set` accessors for setting an object's fields and `get` accessors for retrieving the stored values. As a shortcut, you can create an auto-implemented property when a field's `set` accessor should simply assign a value to the appropriate field, and when its `get` accessor should simply return the field.

- In most classes, fields are `private` and methods are `public`. This technique ensures that data will be used and changed only in the ways provided in the class's accessors. Occasionally, however, you need to create `public` fields or `private` methods.

- The `this` reference is passed to every instance method and property accessor in a class. You can explicitly refer to the `this` reference within an instance method or property, but usually you are not required to do so.

- A constructor is a method that instantiates an object. If you do not write a constructor, then each class is automatically supplied with a `public` constructor with no parameters. You can write your own constructor to replace the automatically supplied version. Any constructor you write must have the same name as its class, and constructors cannot have a return type. You can overload constructors and pass arguments to a constructor.

- An object initializer allows you to assign values to any accessible members or properties of a class at the time of instantiation without calling a constructor with parameters. Using object initializers allows you to create multiple objects with different initial assignments without having to provide multiple constructors to cover every possible situation. Additionally, using object initializers allows you to create objects with different starting values for different properties of the same data type.

- You can overload an operator by writing a method whose identifier is `operator`, followed by the operator being overloaded—for example, `operator+()` or `operator*()`. When you overload an operator, you should write statements that intuitively have the same meaning as the common use of the operator.

- You can declare arrays of references to objects. After doing so, you must call a constructor to instantiate each object. To use a method that belongs to an object that is part of an array, you insert the appropriate subscript notation after the array name and before the dot-method. The IComparable interface contains the definition for the CompareTo() method; you override this method to tell the compiler how to compare objects.

- A destructor contains the actions you require when an instance of a class is destroyed. If you do not explicitly create a destructor for a class, C# automatically provides one. To explicitly declare a destructor, you use an identifier that consists of a tilde (~) followed by the class name. You cannot provide any parameters to a destructor; a class can have one destructor at most.

- GUI objects such as Forms, Buttons, and Labels are typical C# objects that encapsulate properties and methods. When you start a Windows Forms application and drag a component onto a Form, statements are automatically created by the IDE to instantiate the object and assign values to some of its properties.

Key Terms

To **instantiate** an object is to create it.

An **instantiation** of a class is a created object.

An **instance** of a class is one object, or one instantiation.

The **instance variables** of a class are the data components that exist separately for each instantiation.

Fields are instance variables within a class.

An object's **state** is the set of contents of its fields.

Instance methods are methods that are used with object instantiations.

A **class client** or **class user** is a program or class that instantiates objects of another prewritten class.

A **class header** or **class definition** describes a class; it contains an optional access modifier, the keyword class, and any legal identifier for the name of the class.

A **class access modifier** describes access to a class.

The **public** class access modifier means access to the class is not limited.

The **protected** class access modifier means access to the class is limited to the class and to any classes derived from the class.

The **internal** class access modifier means access is limited to the assembly to which the class belongs.

The **private** class access modifier means access is limited to another class to which the class belongs. In other words, a class can be `private` if it is contained within another class, and only the containing class should have access to the `private` class.

An **assembly** is a group of code modules compiled together to create an executable program.

Information hiding is a feature found in all object-oriented languages, in which a class's data is private and changed or manipulated only by its own methods.

Composition is the technique of using an object within another object.

The relationship created using composition is called a **has-a relationship** because one class "has an" instance of another.

A **reference type** is a type that holds a memory address.

Value types hold a value; they are predefined types such as `int`, `double`, and `char`.

An **invoking object** is an object that calls an instance method.

A **property** is a member of a class that provides access to a field of a class; properties define how fields will be set and retrieved.

Accessors in properties specify how a class's fields are accessed.

An object's fields are assigned by **set accessors** that allow use of the assignment operator with a property name.

An object's fields are accessed by **get accessors** that allow retrieval of a field value by using a property name.

A **backing field** is a field that has a property coded for it.

A **read-only property** has only a `get` accessor, and not a `set` accessor.

The **getter** is another term for a class property's `get` accessor.

The **setter** is another term for a class property's `set` accessor.

Contextual keywords are identifiers that act like keywords in specific circumstances.

An **implicit parameter** is undeclared and gets its value automatically.

An **auto-implemented property** is one in which the code within the accessors is created automatically. The only action in the `set` accessor is to assign a value to the associated field, and the only action in the `get` accessor is to return the associated field value.

Automatic properties are auto-implemented properties.

The **this reference** is the reference to an object that is implicitly passed to an instance method of its class.

A **constructor** is a method that instantiates (creates an instance of) an object.

A **default constructor** is a parameterless constructor.

The **default value of an object** is the value initialized with a default constructor.

A **parameterless constructor** is one that takes no arguments.

A **constructor initializer** is a clause that indicates another instance of a class constructor should be executed before any statements in the current constructor body.

An **object initializer** allows you to assign values to any accessible members or properties of a class at the time of instantiation without calling a constructor with parameters.

The `CompareTo()` method of the `IComparable` interface compares one object to another and returns an integer.

An **interface** is a collection of abstract methods (and perhaps other members) that can be used by any class, as long as the class provides a definition to override the interface's do-nothing, or abstract, method definitions.

When a method **overrides** another, it takes precedence over the method, hiding the original version.

The `IComparable` **interface** contains the definition for the `CompareTo()` method.

A **destructor** contains the actions required when an instance of a class is destroyed.

Review Questions

1. An object is a(n) _____ of a class.

    a. child

    b. institution

    c. instantiation

    d. relative

2. A class header or class definition can contain all of the following *except* _____.

    a. an optional access modifier

    b. the keyword `class`

    c. an identifier

    d. initial field values

3. Most fields in a class are created with the _____ modifier.

    a. `public`

    b. `protected`

    c. `new`

    d. `private`

4. Most methods in a class are created with the _____ modifier.

    a. `public`

    b. `protected`

    c. `new`

    d. `private`

5. Instance methods that belong to individual objects are _____ static methods.

    a. always   c. occasionally

    b. usually   d. never

6. To allocate memory for an object instantiation, you must use the _____ operator.

    a. `mem`   c. `new`

    b. `alloc`   d. `instant`

7. Assume that you have created a class named `MyClass`. The header of the `MyClass` constructor can be _____.

    a. `public void MyClass()`

    b. `public MyClassConstructor()`

    c. Either of these can be the constructor header.

    d. Neither of these can be the constructor header.

8. Assume that you have created a class named `MyClass`. The header of the `MyClass` constructor can be _____.

    a. `public MyClass()`

    b. `public MyClass (double d)`

    c. Either of these can be the constructor header.

    d. Neither of these can be the constructor header.

9. Assume that you have created a class named `DemoCar`. Within the `Main()` method of this class, you instantiate a `Car` object named `myCar` and the following statement executes correctly:

```
Console.WriteLine("The Car gets {0} miles per gallon",
    myCar.ComputeMpg());
```

Within the `Car` class, the `ComputeMpg()` method can be _____.

    a. `public` and `static`   c. `private` and `static`

    b. `public` and nonstatic   d. `private` and nonstatic

10. Assume that you have created a class named `TermPaper` that contains a character field named `letterGrade`. You also have created a property for the field. Which of the following cannot be true?

    a. The property name is `letterGrade`.

    b. The property is read-only.

    c. The property contains a `set` accessor that does not allow a grade lower than 'C'.

    d. The property does not contain a `get` accessor.

11. A `this` reference is _____.

    a. implicitly passed to nonstatic methods

    b. implicitly passed to `static` methods

    c. explicitly passed to nonstatic methods

    d. explicitly passed to `static` methods

12. When you use an instance variable within a class's nonstatic methods, you _____ explicitly refer to the method's `this` reference.

    a. must

    b. can

    c. cannot

    d. should (even though it is not required)

13. A class's default constructor _____.

    a. sets numeric fields to 0   c. both of these

    b. is parameterless   d. none of these

14. Assume that you have created a class named `Chair` with a constructor defined as `Chair(int height)`. Which of the following overloaded constructors could coexist with the `Chair` constructor without ambiguity?

    a. `Chair(int legs)`   c. both of these

    b. `Chair(int height, int legs)`   d. none of these

15. Which of the following statements correctly instantiates a `House` object if the `House` class contains a single constructor with the declaration `House(int bedrooms, double price)`?

    a. `House myHouse = new House();`

    b. `House myHouse = new House(3, 125000.00);`

    c. `House myHouse = House(4, 200,000.00);`

    d. two of these

16. You explicitly call a destructor _____.

    a. when you are finished using an object

    b. when an object goes out of scope

    c. when a class is destroyed

    d. You cannot explicitly call a destructor.

17. In a program that creates five object instances of a class, the constructor
    executes _____ time(s) and the destructor executes _____ time(s).

    a. one; one   c. five; one
    b. one; five   d. five; five

18. Suppose that you declare a class named `Furniture` that contains a `string` field
    named `woodType` and a conventionally named property with a `get` accessor. When
    you declare an array of 200 `Furniture` objects named `myChairs`, which of the
    following accesses the last `Furniture` object's wood type?

    a. `Furniture.Get(woodType[199])`
    b. `myChairs[199].WoodType()`
    c. `myChairs.WoodType[199]`
    d. `myChairs[199].WoodType`

19. A collection of methods that can be used by any class, as long as the class provides
    a definition to override the collection's abstract definitions, is _____.

    a. a superclass   c. a perimeter
    b. a polymorph   d. an interface

20. When you create a class and want to include the capability to compare its objects
    so they can use the `Array.Sort()` or `Array.BinarySearch()` method, you
    must _____.

    a. include at least one numeric field within the class
    b. write a `CompareTo()` method for the class
    c. be careful not to override the existing `IComparable.CompareTo()` method
    d. Two of these are true.

Exercises

 Programming Exercises

1. Create an application named **TestFlight** that instantiates and displays a `Flight`
   object. The `Flight` class contains fields for an airline name (a string), flight number
   (an integer), row (an integer), and seat (a single letter).

2. Create an application named **TestClassifiedAd** that instantiates and displays a
   `ClassifiedAd` object. A `ClassifiedAd` has fields for a category (for example, "Used
   Cars"), a number of words, and a price. Include properties that contain `get` and `set`
   accessors for the category and number of words, but only a `get` accessor for the
   price. The price is calculated at nine cents per word.

3. Create an application named **SalesTransactionDemo** that declares several SalesTransaction objects and displays their values and their sum. The SalesTransaction class contains fields for a salesperson name, sales amount, and commission and a readonly field that stores the commission rate. Include three constructors for the class. One constructor accepts values for the name, sales amount, and rate, and when the sales value is set, the constructor computes the commission as sales value times commission rate. The second constructor accepts a name and sales amount, but sets the commission rate to 0. The third constructor accepts a name and sets all the other fields to 0. An overloaded + operator adds the sales values for two SalesTransaction objects.

4. Create a program named **DemoSquares** that instantiates an array of 10 Square objects with sides that have values of 1 through 10 and that displays the values for each Square. The Square class contains fields for area and the length of a side, and a constructor that requires a parameter for the length of one side of a Square. The constructor assigns its parameter to the length of the Square's side field and calls a private method that computes the area field. Also include read-only properties to get a Square's side and area.

5. Create an application named **CarDemo** that declares at least two Car objects and demonstrates how they can be incremented using an overloaded ++ operator. Create a Car class that contains a model and a value for miles per gallon. Include two overloaded constructors. One accepts parameters for the model and miles per gallon; the other accepts a model and sets the miles per gallon to 20. Overload a ++ operator that increases the miles per gallon value by 1. The CarDemo application creates at least one Car using each constructor and displays the Car values both before and after incrementation. (In some other languages, notably C++, you can write two methods to overload ++ as a prefix and postfix operator. However, when you overload either the ++ or -- operator in C#, the operator can be used either before or after the object, but the same method executes either way, and there is no difference in the results.)

6. a. Create a program named **TaxPayerDemo** that declares an array of 10 Taxpayer objects. Prompt the user for data for each object and display the 10 objects. Data fields for Taxpayer objects include the Social Security number (use a string for the type, but do not use dashes within the Social Security number), the yearly gross income, and the income tax owed. Include a property with get and set accessors for the first two data fields, but make the tax owed a read-only property. The tax should be calculated whenever the income is set. Assume that the tax rate is 15 percent for incomes under $30,000 and 28 percent for incomes that are $30,000 or higher.

    b. Create a program named **TaxPayerDemo2** so that after the 10 Taxpayer objects are displayed, they are sorted in order by the amount of tax owed and displayed again. Modify the Taxpayer class so its objects are comparable to each other based on tax owed.

7. Create an application named **LunchDemo** that declares several Lunch objects and includes a display method to which you can pass different numbers of Lunch objects in successive method calls. The Lunch class contains auto-implemented properties for an entrée, side dish, and drink.

8. a. Create a program named **SchoolsDemo** that allows a user to enter data about five School objects and then displays the School objects in order of enrollment size from smallest to largest. The School class contains fields for the School name and number of students enrolled and properties for each field. Also, include an IComparable.CompareTo() method so that School objects can be sorted by enrollment.

   b. Create a program named **SchoolMinEnroll** that modifies the SchoolsDemo program created in Exercise 8a so that after the School objects are displayed in order, the program prompts the user to enter a minimum enrollment figure. Display all School objects that have an enrollment at least as large as the entered value.

9. a. Create a program named **FriendList** that declares an array of eight Friend objects and prompts the user to enter data about the friends. Display the Friend objects in alphabetical order by first name. The Friend class includes auto-implemented properties for the Friend's name, phone number, and three integers that together represent the Friend's birthday—month, day, and year.

   b. Create a **FriendBirthday** program that modifies the FriendList program created in Exercise 9a so that after the list of Friend objects is displayed, the program prompts the user for a specific Friend's name and the program returns the Friend's phone number and birthday. Display an appropriate message if the friend requested by the user is not found.

   c. Create a program named **AllFriendsInSameMonth** that modifies the program in Exercise 9b so that after the requested Friend's birthday is displayed, the program also displays a list of every Friend who has a birthday in the same month.

10. a. Write a program named **DemoJobs** for Harold's Home Services. The program should instantiate several Job objects and demonstrate their methods. The Job class contains four data fields—description (for example, "wash windows"), time in hours to complete (for example, 3.5), per-hour rate charged (for example, $25.00), and total fee (hourly rate times hours). Include properties to get and set each field except the total fee—that field will be read-only, and its value is calculated each time either the hourly fee or the number of hours is set. Overload the + operator so that two Jobs can be added. The sum of two Jobs is a new Job containing the descriptions of both original Jobs (joined by "and"), the sum of the time in hours for the original Jobs, and the average of the hourly rate for the original Jobs.

b. Harold has realized that his method for computing the fee for combined jobs is not fair. For example, consider the following:

- His fee for painting a house is $100 per hour. If a job takes 10 hours, he earns $1000.

- His fee for dog walking is $10 per hour. If a job takes 1 hour, he earns $10.

- If he combines the two jobs and works a total of 11 hours, he earns only the average rate of $55 per hour, or $605.

Devise an improved, weighted method for calculating Harold's fees for combined Jobs and include it in the overloaded `operator+()` method. Write a program named **DemoJobs2** that demonstrates all the methods in the class work correctly.

11. a. Write a **FractionDemo** program that instantiates several `Fraction` objects and demonstrates that their methods work correctly. Create a `Fraction` class with fields that hold a whole number, a numerator, and a denominator. In addition:

- Create properties for each field. The `set` accessor for the denominator should not allow a 0 value; the value defaults to 1.

- Add three constructors. One takes three parameters for a whole number, numerator, and denominator. Another accepts two parameters for the numerator and denominator; when this constructor is used, the whole number value is 0. The last constructor is parameterless; it sets the whole number and numerator to 0 and the denominator to 1. (After construction, `Fractions` do not have to be reduced to proper form. For example, even though 3/9 could be reduced to 1/3, your constructors do not have to perform this task.)

- Add a `Reduce()` method that reduces a `Fraction` if it is in improper form. For example, 2/4 should be reduced to 1/2.

- Add an `operator+()` method that adds two `Fractions`. To add two fractions, first eliminate any whole number part of the value. For example, 2 1/4 becomes 9/4 and 1 3/5 becomes 8/5. Find a common denominator and convert the fractions to it. For example, when adding 9/4 and 8/5, you can convert them to 45/20 and 32/20. Then you can add the numerators, giving 77/20. Finally, call the `Reduce()` method to reduce the result, restoring any whole number value so the fractional part of the number is less than 1. For example, 77/20 becomes 3 17/20.

- Include a function that returns a `string` that contains a `Fraction` in the usual display format—the whole number, a space, the numerator, a slash (/), and a denominator. When the whole number is 0, just the `Fraction` part of the value should be displayed (for example, 1/2 instead of 0 1/2). If the numerator is 0, just the whole number should be displayed (for example, 2 instead of 2 0/3).

b. Add an `operator*()` method to the `Fraction` class created in Exercise 11a so that it correctly multiplies two `Fractions`. The result should be in proper, reduced format. Demonstrate that the method works correctly in a program named **FractionDemo2**.

c. Write a program named **FractionDemo3** that includes an array of four `Fractions`. Prompt the user for values for each. Display every possible combination of addition results and every possible combination of multiplication results for each `Fraction` pair (that is, each type will have 16 results).

Debugging Exercises

1. Each of the following files in the Chapter.09 folder of your downloadable student files has syntax and/or logical errors. In each case, determine the problem and fix the program. After you correct the errors, save each file using the same filename preceded with *Fixed*. For example, DebugNine1.cs will become FixedDebugNine1.cs.

   a. DebugNine1.cs   c. DebugNine3.cs
   b. DebugNine2.cs   d. DebugNine4.cs

Case Problems

1. In previous chapters, you have created programs for the Greenville Idol competition. Now create a `Contestant` class with the following characteristics:

   - The `Contestant` class contains public static arrays that hold talent codes and descriptions. Recall that the talent categories are *Singing, Dancing, Musical instrument*, and *Other*.

   - The class contains an auto-implemented property that holds a contestant's name.

   - The class contains fields for a talent code and description. The `set` accessor for the code assigns a code only if it is valid. Otherwise, it assigns *I* for *Invalid*. The talent description is a read-only property that is assigned a value when the code is set.

   Modify the **GreenvilleRevenue** program so that it uses the `Contestant` class and performs the following tasks:

   - The program prompts the user for the number of contestants in this year's competition; the number must be between 0 and 30. The program continues to prompt the user until a valid value is entered.

   - The expected revenue is calculated and displayed. The revenue is $25 per contestant.

- The program prompts the user for names and talent codes for each contestant entered. Along with the prompt for a talent code, display a list of the valid categories.

- After data entry is complete, the program displays the valid talent categories and then continuously prompts the user for talent codes and displays the names of all contestants in the category. Appropriate messages are displayed if the entered code is not a character or a valid code.

2. In previous chapters, you have created programs for Marshall's Murals. Now create a Mural class with the following characteristics:

- The Mural class contains public static arrays that hold mural codes and descriptions. Recall that the mural categories are *Landscape*, *Seascape*, *Abstract*, *Children's*, and *Other*.

- The class contains an auto-implemented property that holds a mural customer's name.

- The class contains fields for a mural code and description. The set accessor for the code assigns a code only if it is valid. Otherwise, it assigns *I* for *Invalid*. The mural description is a read-only property that is assigned a value when the code is set.

Modify the **MarshallsRevenue** program so that it uses the Mural class and performs the following tasks:

- The program prompts the user for the month, the number of interior murals scheduled, and the number of exterior murals scheduled. In each case, the program continues to prompt the user until valid entries are made.

- The expected revenue is calculated and displayed. Recall that exterior murals cannot be painted in December through February. Also recall that exterior murals are $750 in all months except April, May, September, and October, when they are $699. Interior murals are $500 except during July and August, when they are $450.

- The program prompts the user for names and mural codes for interior and exterior murals. Along with the prompt for a mural code, display a list of the valid categories.

- After data entry is complete, the program displays the valid mural categories and then continuously prompts the user for codes and displays the names of all customers ordering murals in the category. Appropriate messages are displayed if the entered code is not a character or a valid code.

Introduction to Inheritance

In this chapter you will:

- ◎ Learn about inheritance
- ◎ Extend classes
- ◎ Use the `protected` access specifier
- ◎ Override base class members
- ◎ Understand how a derived class object "is an" instance of the base class
- ◎ Learn about the `Object` class
- ◎ Work with base class constructors
- ◎ Create and use abstract classes
- ◎ Create and use interfaces
- ◎ Use extension methods
- ◎ Recognize inheritance in GUI applications and understand the benefits of inheritance

Understanding classes helps you organize objects. Understanding inheritance helps you organize them more precisely. If you have never heard of a Braford, for example, you would have a hard time forming a picture of one in your mind. When you learn that a Braford is an animal, you gain some understanding of what it must be like. That understanding grows when you learn it is a mammal, and the understanding is almost complete when you learn it is a cow. When you learn that a Braford is a cow, you understand it has many characteristics that are common to all cows. To identify a Braford, you must learn only relatively minor details—its color or markings, for example. Most of a Braford's characteristics, however, derive from its membership in a particular hierarchy of classes: animal, mammal, and cow.

All object-oriented programming languages make use of inheritance for the same reasons—to organize the objects used by programs, and to make new objects easier to understand based on your knowledge of their inherited traits. In this chapter, you will learn to make use of inheritance with your C# objects.

Understanding Inheritance

Inheritance is the principle that you can apply your knowledge of a general category to more specific objects. You are familiar with the concept of inheritance from all sorts of situations. When you use the term *inheritance*, you might think of genetic inheritance. You know from biology that your blood type and eye color are the products of inherited genes. You can say that many other facts about you (your attributes) are inherited. Similarly, you often can attribute your behaviors to inheritance; for example, the way you handle money might be similar to the way your grandmother handles it, and your gait might be the same as your father's—so your methods are inherited, too.

You also might choose to own plants and animals based on their inherited attributes. You plant impatiens next to your house because they thrive in the shade; you adopt a poodle because you know poodles don't shed. Every plant and pet has slightly different characteristics, but within a species, you can count on many consistent inherited attributes and behaviors. In other words, you can reuse the knowledge you gain about general categories and apply it to more specific categories. Similarly, the classes you create in object-oriented programming languages can inherit data and methods from existing classes. When you create a class by making it inherit from another class, you are provided with data fields and methods automatically; you can reuse fields and methods that are already written and tested.

You already know how to create classes and how to instantiate objects from those classes. For example, consider the Employee class in Figure 10-1. The class contains two data fields, empNum and empSal, as well as properties that contain accessors for each field and a method that creates an Employee greeting.

```
class Employee
{
   private int empNum;
   private double empSal;
   public int EmpNum
   {
      get
      {
         return empNum;
      }
      set
      {
         empNum = value;
      }
   }
   public double EmpSal
   {
      get
      {
         return empSal;
      }
      set
      {
         empSal = value;
      }
   }
   public string GetGreeting()
   {
      string greeting = "Hello. I am employee #" + EmpNum;
      return greeting;
   }
}
```

Figure 10-1   The Employee class

After you create the Employee class, you can create specific Employee objects, as in the
following:

```
Employee receptionist = new Employee();
Employee deliveryPerson = new Employee();
```

These Employee objects can eventually possess different numbers and salaries, but because
they are Employee objects, you know that each possesses *some* number and salary.

Suppose that you hire a new type of Employee who earns a commission as well as a salary. You
can create a class with a name such as CommissionEmployee, and provide this class with three
fields (empNum, empSal, and commissionRate), three properties (with accessors to get and set
each of the three fields), and a greeting method. However, this work would duplicate much of
the work that you already have done for the Employee class. The wise and efficient alternative
is to create the class CommissionEmployee so it inherits all the attributes and methods of

Employee. Then, you can add just the single field and property with two accessors that are additions within `CommissionEmployee` objects. Figure 10-2 depicts these relationships.

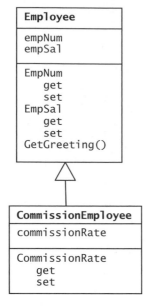

Figure 10-2 `CommissionEmployee` inherits from `Employee`

In class diagrams, the convention is to provide three sections for the class name, its data, and its methods, respectively. The upward-pointing arrow between the classes in Figure 10-2 indicates that the class on the bottom inherits from the one on the top. Using an arrow in this way is conventional in **Unified Modeling Language (UML) diagrams**, which are graphical tools that programmers and analysts use to describe systems.

When you use inheritance to create the `CommissionEmployee` class, you acquire the following benefits:

- You save time, because you need not re-create the `Employee` fields, properties, and methods.

- You reduce the chance of errors, because the `Employee` properties and methods have already been used and tested.

- You make it easier for anyone who has used the `Employee` class to understand the `CommissionEmployee` class because such users can concentrate on the new features only.

The ability to use inheritance makes programs easier to write, easier to understand, and less prone to errors. Imagine that besides `CommissionEmployee`, you want to create several other specific `Employee` classes (perhaps `PartTimeEmployee`, including a field for hours worked, or `DismissedEmployee`, including a reason for dismissal). By using inheritance, you can develop each new class correctly and more quickly.

In part, the concept of class inheritance is useful because it makes class code reusable. However, you do not use inheritance simply to save work. When properly used, inheritance always involves a general-to-specific relationship.

Understanding Inheritance Terminology

A class that is used as a basis for inheritance, like Employee, is called a **base class**. When you create a class that inherits from a base class (such as CommissionEmployee), it is a **derived class** or **extended class**. When presented with two classes that have a parent-child relationship, you can tell which class is the base class and which is the derived class by using the two classes in a sentence with the phrase "is a." A derived class always "is a" case or instance of the more general base class. For example, a Tree class may be a base class to an Evergreen class. Every Evergreen "is a" Tree; however, it is not true that every Tree is an Evergreen. Thus, Tree is the base class and Evergreen is the derived class. Similarly, a CommissionEmployee "is an" Employee—not always the other way around—so Employee is the base class and CommissionEmployee is derived.

You can use the terms **superclass** and **subclass** as synonyms for base class and derived class. Thus, Evergreen can be called a subclass of the Tree superclass. You also can use the terms **parent class** and **child class**. A CommissionEmployee is a child to the Employee parent. Use the pair of terms with which you are most comfortable; all of these terms will be used interchangeably in this book.

As an alternative way to discover which of two classes is the base class and which is the derived class, you can try saying the two class names together (although this technique might not work with every superclass-subclass pair). When people say their names together in the English language, they state the more specific name before the all-encompassing family name, such as "Ginny Kroening." Similarly, with classes, the order that "makes more sense" is the child-parent order. Thus, because "Evergreen Tree" makes more sense than "Tree Evergreen," you can deduce that Evergreen is the child class. It also is convenient to think of a derived class as building upon its base class by providing the "adjectives" or additional descriptive terms for the "noun." Frequently, the names of derived classes are formed in this way, as in CommissionEmployee.

Finally, you usually can distinguish base classes from their derived classes by size. A derived class is larger than a base class, in the sense that it usually has additional fields and methods. A derived class description may look small, but any subclass contains all the fields and methods of its superclass as well as its own more specific fields and methods. Do not think of a subclass as a "subset" of another class—in other words, possessing only parts of its superclass. In fact, a derived class contains everything in the superclass, plus any new attributes and methods.

A derived class can be further extended. In other words, a subclass can have a child of its own. For example, after you create a Tree class and derive Evergreen, you might derive a Spruce class from Evergreen. Similarly, a Poodle class might derive from Dog, Dog from

DomesticPet, and DomesticPet from Animal. The entire list of parent classes from which a child class is derived constitutes the **ancestors** of the subclass.

After you create the Spruce class, you might be ready to create Spruce objects. For example, you might create theTreeInMyBackYard, or you might create an array of 1000 Spruce objects for a tree farm.

Inheritance is **transitive**, which means a child inherits all the members of all its ancestors. In other words, when you declare a Spruce object, it contains all the attributes and methods of both an Evergreen and a Tree. As you work with C#, you will encounter many examples of such transitive chains of inheritance.

When you create your own transitive inheritance chains, you want to place fields and methods at their most general level. In other words, a method named Grow() rightfully belongs in a Tree class, whereas LeavesTurnColor() does not, because the method applies to only some of the Tree child classes. Similarly, a LeavesTurnColor() method would be better located in a Deciduous class than separately within the Oak or Maple child class.

TWO TRUTHS & A LIE

Understanding Inheritance

1. When you use inheritance to create a class, you save time because you can copy and paste fields, properties, and methods that have already been created for the original class.

2. When you use inheritance to create a class, you reduce the chance of errors because the original class's properties and methods have already been used and tested.

3. When you use inheritance to create a class, you make it easier for anyone who has used the original class to understand the new class because such users can concentrate on the new features.

The false statement is #1. When you use inheritance to create a class, you save time because you need not re-create fields, properties, and methods that have already been created for the original class. You do not copy these class members; you inherit them.

Extending Classes

When you create a class that is an extension or child of another class, you use a single colon between the derived class name and its base class name. For example, the following class header creates a subclass-superclass relationship between CommissionEmployee and Employee.

```
class CommissionEmployee : Employee
```

Each CommissionEmployee object automatically contains the fields and methods of the base class; you then can add new fields and methods to the new derived class. Figure 10-3 shows a CommissionEmployee class.

```
class CommissionEmployee : Employee
{
    private double commissionRate;
    public double CommissionRate
    {
        get
        {
            return commissionRate;
        }
        set
        {
            commissionRate = value;
        }
    }
}
```

Figure 10-3 The CommissionEmployee class

Although you see only one field defined in the CommissionEmployee class in Figure 10-3, it contains three fields: empNum and empSal, inherited from Employee, and commissionRate, which is defined within the CommissionEmployee class. Similarly, the CommissionEmployee class contains three properties and a method—two properties and the method are inherited from Employee, and one property is defined within CommissionEmployee itself. When you write a program that instantiates an object using the following statement, then you can use any of the next statements to set field values for the salesperson:

```
CommissionEmployee salesperson = new CommissionEmployee();
salesperson.EmpNum = 234;
salesperson.EmpSal = Convert.ToDouble(Console.ReadLine());
salesperson.CommissionRate = 0.07;
```

The salesperson object has access to all three set accessors (two from its parent and one from its own class) because it is both a CommissionEmployee and an Employee. Similarly, the object has access to three get accessors and the GetGreeting() method. Figure 10-4 shows a Main() method that declares Employee and CommissionEmployee objects and shows all the properties and methods that can be used with each. Figure 10-5 shows the program output.

```
using System;
class DemoEmployees
{
    static void Main()
    {
        Employee clerk = new Employee();
        CommissionEmployee salesperson = new CommissionEmployee();
        clerk.EmpNum = 123;
        clerk.EmpSal = 30000.00;
        salesperson.EmpNum = 234;
        salesperson.EmpSal = 20000;
        salesperson.CommissionRate = 0.07;
        Console.WriteLine("\n" + clerk.GetGreeting());
        Console.WriteLine("Clerk #{0} salary: {1} per year",
            clerk.EmpNum,
            clerk.EmpSal.ToString("C"));
        Console.WriteLine("\n" + salesperson.GetGreeting());
        Console.WriteLine("Salesperson #{0} salary: {1} per year",
            salesperson.EmpNum,
            salesperson.EmpSal.ToString("C"));
        Console.WriteLine("...plus {0} commission on all sales",
            salesperson.CommissionRate.ToString("P"));
    }
}
```

Figure 10-4   The DemoEmployees class that declares Employee and CommissionEmployee objects

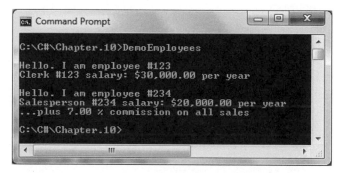

Figure 10-5   Output of the DemoEmployees program

Inheritance works only in one direction: A child inherits from a parent—not the other way around. If a program instantiates an Employee object as in the following statement, the Employee object does *not* have access to the CommissionEmployee properties or methods.

```
Employee clerk = new Employee();
clerk.CommissionRate = 0.1;
```

Don't Do It
This statement is invalid— Employee objects don't have a CommissionRate.

Employee is the parent class, and clerk is an object of the parent class. It makes sense that a parent class object does not have access to its child's data and methods. When you create the parent class, you do not know how many future child classes might be created, or what their data or methods might look like. In addition, child classes are more specific. A HeartSurgeon class and an Obstetrician class are children of a Doctor class. You do not expect all members of the general parent class Doctor to have the HeartSurgeon's RepairValve() method or the Obstetrician's DeliverBaby() method. However, HeartSurgeon and Obstetrician objects have access to the more general Doctor methods TakeBloodPressure() and BillPatients(). As with doctors, it is convenient to think of derived classes as *specialists*. That is, their fields and methods are more specialized than those of the base class.

 Watch the video *Inheritance*.

TWO TRUTHS & A LIE

Extending Classes

1. The following class header indicates that Dog is a subclass of Pet:
   ```
   public class Pet : Dog
   ```

2. If class X has four fields and class Y derives from it, then class Y also contains at least four fields.

3. Inheritance works only in one direction: A child inherits from a parent—not the other way around.

The false statement is #1. The following class header indicates that Dog is a subclass of Pet:
public class Dog : Pet

You Do It

In this section, you create a working example of inheritance. You create this example in four parts:

1. You create a general Loan class that holds data pertaining to a bank loan—a loan number, a customer name, and the amount borrowed.

2. After you create the general Loan class, you write a program to instantiate and use a Loan object.

3. You create a more specific CarLoan derived class that inherits the attributes of the Loan class but adds information about the automobile that serves as collateral for the loan.

4. You modify the Loan demonstration program to add a CarLoan object and demonstrate its use.

Creating the Loan Class and a Program that Uses it

1. Open a new project named **DemoLoan**, and then enter the following first few lines for a Loan class. The class contains three auto-implemented properties for the loan number, the last name of the customer, and the value of the loan.

```
class Loan
{
    public int LoanNumber {get; set;}
    public string LastName {get; set;}
    public double LoanAmount {get; set;}
}
```

2. At the top of the file, enter the following code to add a DemoLoan class that contains a Main() method. The class declares a Loan object and shows how to set each field and display the results.

```
using System;
class DemoLoan
{
    static void Main()
    {
        Loan aLoan = new Loan();
        aLoan.LoanNumber = 2239;
        aLoan.LastName = "Mitchell";
        aLoan.LoanAmount = 1000.00;
```

(continues)

(continued)

```
        Console.WriteLine("Loan #{0} for {1} is for {2}",
            aLoan.LoanNumber, aLoan.LastName,
            aLoan.LoanAmount.ToString("C2"));
    }
}
```

3. Save the file, and then compile and execute the program. The output looks like Figure 10-6. There is nothing unusual about this class or how it operates; it is similar to many you saw in the last chapter before you learned about inheritance.

Figure 10-6 Output of the DemoLoan program

Extending a Class

Next, you create a class named CarLoan. A CarLoan "is a" type of Loan. As such, it has all the attributes of a Loan, but it also has the year and make of the car that the customer is using as collateral for the loan. Therefore, CarLoan is a subclass of Loan.

1. Save the DemoLoan file as **DemoCarLoan**. Change the DemoLoan class name to DemoCarLoan. Begin the definition of the CarLoan class after the closing curly brace for the Loan class. CarLoan extends Loan and contains two properties that hold the year and make of the car.

```
class CarLoan : Loan
{
    public int Year {get; set;}
    public string Make {get; set;}
}
```

2. Within the Main() method of the DemoCarLoan class, just after the declaration of the Loan object, declare a CarLoan as follows:

```
CarLoan aCarLoan = new CarLoan();
```

(continues)

(continued)

3. After the three property assignments for the `Loan` object, insert five assignment statements for the `CarLoan` object.

    ```
    aCarLoan.LoanNumber = 3358;
    aCarLoan.LastName = "Jansen";
    aCarLoan.LoanAmount = 20000.00;
    aCarLoan.Make = "Ford";
    aCarLoan.Year = 2005;
    ```

4. Following the `WriteLine()` statement that displays the `Loan` object data, insert two `WriteLine()` statements that display the `CarLoan` object's data.

    ```
    Console.WriteLine("Loan #{0} for {1} is for {2}",
        aCarLoan.LoanNumber, aCarLoan.LastName,
        aCarLoan.LoanAmount.ToString("C2"));
    Console.WriteLine("    Loan #{0} is for a {1} {2}",
        aCarLoan.LoanNumber, aCarLoan.Year,
        aCarLoan.Make);
    ```

5. Save the program, and then compile and execute it. The output looks like Figure 10-7. The `CarLoan` object correctly uses its own fields and properties as well as those of the parent `Loan` class.

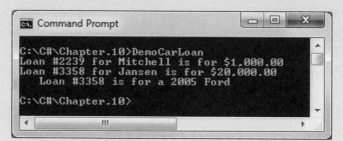

Figure 10-7   Output of the `DemoCarLoan` program

Using the protected Access Specifier

The `Employee` class in Figure 10-1 is a typical C# class in that its data fields are `private` and its properties and methods are `public`. In the chapter *Using Classes and Objects*, you learned that this scheme provides for information hiding—protecting your `private` data from alteration by methods outside the data's own class. When a program is a client of the `Employee` class (that is, it instantiates an `Employee` object), the client cannot alter the data in any `private` field directly. For example, when you write a `Main()` method that creates an `Employee` named `clerk`, you cannot change the `Employee`'s `empNum` or `empSal` directly using a statement such as `clerk.empNum = 2222;`. Instead, you must use the `public EmpNum` property to set the `empNum` field of the `clerk` object.

When you use information hiding, you are assured that your data will be altered only by the properties and methods you choose and only in ways that you can control. If outside classes could alter an Employee's private fields, then the fields could be assigned values that the Employee class couldn't control. In such a case, the principle of information hiding would be destroyed, causing the behavior of the object to be unpredictable.

Any derived class you create, such as CommissionEmployee, inherits all the data and methods of its base class. However, even though a child of Employee has empNum and empSal fields, the CommissionEmployee methods cannot alter or use those private fields directly. If a new class could simply extend your Employee class and "get to" its data fields without "going through the proper channels," then information hiding would not be operating.

On some occasions, you do want to access parent class data from a child class. For example, suppose that the Employee class EmpSal property set accessor has been written so that no Employee's salary is ever set to less than 15000, as follows:

```
set
{
   double MINIMUM = 15000;
   if(value < MINIMUM)
      empSal = MINIMUM;
   else
      empSal = value;
}
```

Also assume that a CommissionEmployee draws commission only and no regular salary; that is, when you set a CommissionEmployee's commissionRate field, the empSal should become 0. You would write the CommissionEmployee class CommissionRate property set accessor as follows:

```
set
{
   commissionRate = value;
   EmpSal = 0;
}
```

Using this implementation, when you create a CommissionEmployee object and set its CommissionRate, 0 is sent to the set accessor for the Employee class EmpSal property. Because the value of the salary is less than 15000, the salary is forced to 15000 in the Employee class set accessor, even though you want it to be 0.

A possible alternative would be to rewrite the set accessor for the CommissionRate property in the CommissionEmployee class using the field empSal instead of the property EmpSal, as follows:

```
set
{
   commissionRate = value;
   empSal = 0;
}
```

In this set accessor, you bypass the parent class's EmpSal set accessor and directly use the empSal field. However, when you include this accessor in a program and compile it, you receive an error message: "Employee.empSal is inaccessible due to its protection level". In other words, Employee.empSal is private, and no other class can access it, even a child class of Employee. So, in summary:

- Using the public set accessor in the parent class does not work because of the minimum salary requirement.

- Using the private field in the parent class does not work because it is inaccessible.

- Making the parent class field public would work, but doing so would violate the principle of information hiding.

Fortunately, there is a fourth option. The solution is to create the empSal field using the specifier **protected**, which provides you with an intermediate level of security between public and private access. A **protected** data field or method can be used within its own class or in any classes extended from that class, but it cannot be used by "outside" classes. In other words, protected members can be used "within the family"—by a class and its descendents.

 Some sources say that private, public, and protected are *access specifiers*, while other class designations, such as static, are *access modifiers*. However, Microsoft developers, who created C#, use the terms interchangeably in their documentation.

Figure 10-8 shows how you can declare empSal as protected within the Employee class so that it becomes legal to access it directly within the CommissionRate set accessor of the CommissionEmployee derived class. Figure 10-9 shows a program that instantiates a CommissionEmployee object, and Figure 10-10 shows the output. Notice that the CommissionEmployee's salary initially is set to 20000 in the program, but the salary becomes 0 when the CommissionRate is set later.

```
class Employee
{
    private int empNum;
    protected double empSal;

    public int EmpNum
    {
        get
        {
            return empNum;
        }
        set
        {
            empNum = value;
        }
    }
}
```

Figure 10-8 The Employee class with a protected field and the CommissionEmployee class *(continues)*

(continued)

```csharp
   public double EmpSal
   {
      get
      {
         return empSal;
      }
      set
      {
         double MINIMUM = 15000;
         if(value < MINIMUM)
            empSal = MINIMUM;
         else
            empSal = value;
      }
   }
   public string GetGreeting()
   {
      string greeting = "Hello. I am employee #" + EmpNum;
      return greeting;
   }
}
class CommissionEmployee : Employee
{
   private double commissionRate;
   public double CommissionRate
   {
      get
      {
         return commissionRate;
      }
      set
      {
         commissionRate = value;
         empSal = 0;
      }
   }
}
```

The protected empSal field is accessible in the child class.

Figure 10-8   The Employee class with a protected field and the
CommissionEmployee class

```
using System;
class DemoSalesperson
{
    static void Main()
    {
        CommissionEmployee salesperson = new CommissionEmployee();
        salesperson.EmpNum = 345;
        salesperson.EmpSal = 20000;
        salesperson.CommissionRate = 0.07;
        Console.WriteLine("Salesperson #{0} makes {1} per year",
            salesperson.EmpNum,
            salesperson.EmpSal.ToString("C"));
        Console.WriteLine("...plus {0} commission on all sales",
            salesperson.CommissionRate.ToString("P"));
    }
}
```

Figure 10-9 The DemoSalesperson program

Figure 10-10 Output of the DemoSalesperson program

If you set the salesperson's CommissionRate first in the DemoSalesperson program, then set EmpSal to a nonzero value, empSal will not be reduced to 0. If your intention is to always create CommissionEmployees with salaries of 0, then the EmpSal property should also be overridden in the derived class.

Using the **protected** access specifier for a field can be convenient, and it also slightly improves program performance by using a field directly instead of "going through" property accessors. Also, using the **protected** access specifier is occasionally necessary. However, **protected** data members should be used sparingly. Whenever possible, the principle of information hiding should be observed, and even child classes should have to go through accessors to "get to" their parent's private data. When child classes are allowed direct access to a parent's fields, the likelihood of future errors increases. Classes that depend on field names from parent classes are said to be **fragile** because they are prone to errors—that is, they are easy to "break."

TWO TRUTHS & A LIE

Using the protected Access Specifier

1. A child class does not possess the private members of its parent.

2. A child class cannot use the private members of its parent.

3. A child class can use the protected members of its parent, but outside classes cannot.

The false statement is #1. A child class possesses the private members of its parent, but cannot use them directly.

Overriding Base Class Members

When you create a derived class by extending an existing class, the new derived class contains data and methods that were defined in the original base class. Sometimes, the superclass fields, properties, and methods are not entirely appropriate for the subclass objects. Using the same method or property name to indicate different implementations is called polymorphism. The word *polymorphism* means "many forms"—in programming, it means that many forms of action take place, even though you use the same method name. The specific method executed depends on the object.

 You first learned the term *polymorphism* in Chapter 1.

Everyday cases provide many examples of polymorphism:

- Although both are musical instruments and have a Play() method, a guitar is played differently than a drum.

- Although both are vehicles and have an Operate() method, a bicycle is operated differently than a truck.

- Although both are schools and have a SatisfyGraduationRequirements() method, a preschool's requirements are different from those of a college.

You understand each of these methods based on the context in which it is used. In a similar way, C# understands your use of the same method name based on the type of object associated with it.

For example, suppose that you have created a Student class as shown in Figure 10-11. Students have names, credits for which they are enrolled, and tuition amounts. You can set a Student's name and credits by using the set accessors in the Name and Credits properties, but you cannot set a Student's tuition directly because there is no set accessor for the Tuition property. Instead, tuition is calculated based on a standard RATE (of $55.75) for each credit that the Student takes.

In Figure 10-11, the Student fields that hold credits and tuition are declared as protected because a child class will use them.

```
class Student
{
    private const double RATE = 55.75;
    private string name;
    protected int credits;
    protected double tuition;
    public string Name
    {
        get
        {
            return name;
        }
        set
        {
            name = value;
        }
    }
    public virtual int Credits
    {
        get
        {
            return credits;
        }
        set
        {
            credits = value;
            tuition = credits * RATE;
        }
    }
    public double Tuition
    {
        get
        {
            return tuition;
        }
    }
}
```

Figure 10-11   The Student class

In Figure 10-11, Credits is declared to be virtual (see shading). A **virtual method** (or property) is one that can be overridden by a method with the same signature in a child class. Suppose that you derive a subclass from Student called ScholarshipStudent, as shown in Figure 10-12. A ScholarshipStudent has a name, credits, and tuition, but the tuition is not calculated in the same way as it is for a Student; instead, tuition for a ScholarshipStudent should be set to 0. You want to use the Credits property to set a ScholarshipStudent's credits, but you want the property to behave differently than the parent class Student's Credits property. As a child of Student, a ScholarshipStudent possesses all the attributes, properties, and methods of a Student, but its Credits property behaves differently.

```
class ScholarshipStudent : Student
{
    public override int Credits
    {
        set
        {
            credits = value;
            tuition = 0;
        }
    }
}
```

Figure 10-12   The ScholarshipStudent class

In C#, you can use either new or override when defining a derived class member that has the same name as a base class member. When you write a statement such as ScholarshipStudent s1 = new ScholarshipStudent();, you won't notice the difference. However, if you use new when defining the derived class Credits property and write a statement such as Student s2 = new ScholarshipStudent(); (using Student as the type), then s2.Credits accesses the base class property. On the other hand, if you use override when defining Credits in the derived class, then s2.Credits uses the derived class property.

In the child ScholarshipStudent class in Figure 10-12, the Credits property is declared with the override modifier (see shading) because it has the same header (that is, the same signature—the same name and parameter list) as a property in its parent class. The Credits property overrides and **hides** its counterpart in the parent class. (You could do the same thing with methods.) If you omit override, the program will still operate correctly, but you will receive a warning that you are hiding an inherited member with the same name in the base class. Using the keyword override eliminates the warning and makes your intentions clear. When you use the Name property with a ScholarshipStudent object, a program uses the parent class property Name; it is not hidden. However, when you use Credits to set a value for a ScholarshipStudent object, the program uses the new, overriding property from its own class.

If `credits` and `tuition` had been declared as `private` within the `Student` class, then `ScholarshipStudent` would not be able to use them.

You are not required to override a virtual method in a derived class; a derived class can simply use the base class version. A base class member that is not hidden by the derived class is **visible** in the derived class.

Figure 10-13 shows a program that uses `Student` and `ScholarshipStudent` objects. Even though each object assigns the `Credits` property with the same number of credit hours (in the two shaded statements), the calculated `tuition` values are different because each object uses a different version of the `Credits` property. Figure 10-14 shows the execution of the program.

```
using System;
class DemoStudents
{
    static void Main()
    {
        Student payingStudent = new Student();
        ScholarshipStudent freeStudent = new ScholarshipStudent();
        payingStudent.Name = "Megan";
        payingStudent.Credits = 15;
        freeStudent.Name = "Luke";
        freeStudent.Credits = 15;
        Console.WriteLine("{0}'s tuition is {1}",
            payingStudent.Name,
            payingStudent.Tuition.ToString("C"));
        Console.WriteLine("{0}'s tuition is {1}",
            freeStudent.Name,
            freeStudent.Tuition.ToString("C"));
    }
}
```

Figure 10-13   The DemoStudents program

Figure 10-14   Output of the DemoStudents program

If a base class and a derived class have methods with the same names but different parameter lists, then the derived class method does not override the base class method; instead, it overloads the base class method. For example, if a base class contains a method with the header `public void Display()`, and its child contains a method with the header `public void Display(string s)`, then the child class would have access to both methods. (You learned about overloading methods in the chapter *Advanced Method Concepts*.)

Accessing Base Class Methods and Properties from a Derived Class

When a derived class contains a method or property that overrides a parent class method or property, you might have occasion to use the parent class version within the subclass. If so, you can use the keyword `base` to access the parent class method or property.

For example, recall the `GetGreeting()` method that appears in the `Employee` class in Figure 10-8. If its child, `CommissionEmployee`, also contains a `GetGreeting()` method, as shown in Figure 10-15, then within the `CommissionEmployee` class you can call `base.GetGreeting()` to access the base class version of the method. Figure 10-16 shows an application that uses the method with a `CommissionEmployee` object. Figure 10-17 shows the output.

```
class CommissionEmployee : Employee
{
    private double commissionRate;
    public double CommissionRate
    {
        get
        {
            return commissionRate;
        }
        set
        {
            commissionRate = value;
            empSal = 0;
        }
    }
    new public string GetGreeting()
    {
        string greeting = base.GetGreeting();
        greeting += "\nI work on commission.";
        return greeting;
    }
}
```

Figure 10-15   The `CommissionEmployee` class with a `GetGreeting()` method

```
using System;
class DemoSalesperson2
{
    static void Main()
    {
        CommissionEmployee salesperson = new CommissionEmployee();
        salesperson.EmpNum = 345;
        Console.WriteLine(salesperson.GetGreeting());
    }
}
```

Figure 10-16   The DemoSalesperson2 program

Figure 10-17   Output of the DemoSalesperson2 program

In Figure 10-15, the child class method uses the keyword new to eliminate a compiler warning. Then, within the GetGreeting() method, the parent's version is called. The returned string is stored in the greeting variable, and then an "I work on commission." statement is added to it before the complete message is returned to the calling program. By overriding the base class method in the child class, the duplicate typing to create the first part of the message was eliminated. Additionally, if the first part of the message is altered in the future, it will be altered in only one place—in the base class.

   Watch the video *Handling Methods and Inheritance.*

TWO TRUTHS & A LIE

Overriding Base Class Members

1. When you override a parent class method in a child class, the methods have the same name.

2. When you override a parent class method in a child class, the methods have the same parameter list.

3. When you override a parent class method in a child class and then use the child class method, the parent class method executes first, followed by the child class method.

The false statement is #3. When you override a parent class method in a child class and then use the child class method, the child class method executes instead of the parent class version.

You Do It

In the previous sections, you created Loan and CarLoan classes and objects. Suppose that the bank adopts new rules as follows:

- No regular loan will be made for less than $5000.

- No car loan will be made for any car older than model year 2006.

- Although Loans might have larger loan numbers, CarLoans will have loan numbers that are no more than three digits. If a larger loan number is provided, the program will use only the last three digits for the loan number.

Using Base Class Members in a Derived Class

1. Open the DemoCarLoan file and immediately save it as **DemoCarLoan2**. Also change the class name from DemoCarLoan to **DemoCarLoan2**.

2. Within the Loan class, add a new constant that represents the minimum loan value:

```
public const double MINIMUM_LOAN = 5000;
```

(continues)

(continued)

3. Add a field for the `loanAmount` because the `LoanAmount` property will need to use it:

    ```
    protected double loanAmount;
    ```

    The field is protected so that `CarLoan` objects will be able to access it as well as `Loan` objects.

4. Replace the auto-implemented property for `LoanAmount` in the `Loan` class with standard `get` and `set` accessors as follows. This change ensures that no loan is made for less than the minimum allowed value.

    ```
    public double LoanAmount
    {
        set
        {
            if(value < MINIMUM_LOAN)
                loanAmount = MINIMUM_LOAN;
            else
                loanAmount = value;
        }
        get
        {
            return loanAmount;
        }
    }
    ```

5. Within the `CarLoan` class, add two new constants to hold the earliest year for which car loans will be given and the lowest allowed loan number:

    ```
    private const int EARLIEST_YEAR = 2006;
    private const int LOWEST_INVALID_NUM = 1000;
    ```

6. Also within the `CarLoan` class, add a field for the year of the car and replace the existing auto-implemented `Year` property with one that contains coded `get` and `set` accessors. The `Year` property `set` accessor not only sets the `year` field, it sets `loanAmount` to 0 when a car's year is less than 2006.

    ```
    private int year;
    public int Year
    {
        set
        {
            if(value < EARLIEST_YEAR)
            {
                year = value;
                loanAmount = 0;
            }
    ```

(continues)

(continued)

```
      else
         year = value;
   }
   get
   {
      return year;
   }
}
```

If `loanAmount` was `private` in the parent `Loan` class, you would not be able to set its value in the child `CarLoan` class, as you do here. You could use the `public` property `LoanAmount` to set the value, but the parent class `set` accessor would force the value to 5000.

7. Suppose that unique rules apply for issuing loan numbers for cars. Within the `CarLoan` class, just before the closing curly brace, change the inherited `LoanNumber` property to accommodate the new rules. If a car loan number is three digits or fewer, pass it on to the base class property. If not, obtain the last three digits by calculating the remainder when the loan number is divided by 1000, and pass the new number to the base class property. Add the following property after the definition of the `Make` property.

```
public new int LoanNumber
{
   get
   {
      return base.LoanNumber;
   }
   set
   {
      if(value < LOWEST_INVALID_NUM)
         base.LoanNumber = value;
      else
         base.LoanNumber = value % LOWEST_INVALID_NUM;
   }
}
```

If you did not use the keyword `base` to access the `LoanNumber` property within the `CarLoan` class, you would be telling this version of the `LoanNumber` property to call itself. Although the program would compile, it would run continuously in an infinite loop until it ran out of memory and issued an error message.

(continues)

461

(continued)

 A method that calls itself is a **recursive** method. Recursive methods are sometimes useful, but they require specialized code to avoid infinite loops, and are not appropriate in this case.

8. Save the file. Compile it and correct any errors. When you execute the program, the output looks like Figure 10-18. Compare the output to Figure 10-7. Notice that the $1000 bank loan has been forced to $5000. Also notice that the car loan number has been shortened to three digits and the value of the loan is $0 because of the age of the car.

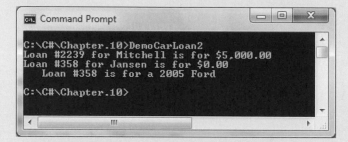

Figure 10-18   Output of the DemoCarLoan2 program

9. Change the assigned values within the DemoCarLoan2 class to combinations of early and late years and valid and invalid loan numbers. After each change, save the program, compile and execute it, and confirm that the program operates as expected.

Understanding Implicit Reference Conversions

Every derived class object "is a" specific instance of both the derived class and the base class. In other words, myCar "is a" Car as well as a Vehicle, and myDog "is a" Dog as well as a Mammal. You can assign a derived class object to an object of any of its superclass types. When you do, C# makes an **implicit conversion** from derived class to base class.

You have already learned that C# also makes implicit conversions when casting one data type to another. For example, in the statement double money = 10;, the value 10 is implicitly converted (or cast) to a double. When a derived class object is assigned to its ancestor's data type, the conversion can more specifically be called an **implicit reference conversion**. This term is more accurate because it emphasizes the difference between numerical conversions and reference objects. When you assign a derived class object to a base class type, the object is treated as though it had only the characteristics defined in the base class and not those added in the child class definition.

For example, when a CommissionEmployee class inherits from Employee, an object of either type can be passed to a method that accepts an Employee parameter. In Figure 10-19, an Employee is passed to DisplayGreeting() in the first shaded statement, and a CommissionEmployee is passed in the second shaded statement. Each is referred to as emp within the method, and each is used correctly, as shown in Figure 10-20.

```
using System;
class DemoSalesperson3
{
    static void Main()
    {
        Employee clerk = new Employee();
        CommissionEmployee salesperson = new CommissionEmployee();
        clerk.EmpNum = 234;
        salesperson.EmpNum = 345;
        DisplayGreeting(clerk);
        DisplayGreeting(salesperson);
    }
    public static void DisplayGreeting(Employee emp)
    {
        Console.WriteLine("Hi there from #" + emp.EmpNum);
        Console.WriteLine(emp.GetGreeting());
    }
}
```

Figure 10-19 The DemoSalesperson3 program

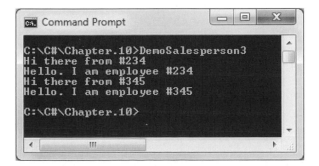

Figure 10-20 Output of the DemoSalesperson3 program

You cannot use both new and override on the same member because they have mutually exclusive meanings. Using new creates a new member with the same name and causes the original member to become hidden. Using override extends the implementation for an inherited member.

TWO TRUTHS & A LIE

Understanding How a Derived Class Object "is an" Instance of the Base Class

1. You can assign a derived class object to an object of any of its superclass types.

2. You can assign a base class object to an object of any of its derived types.

3. An implicit conversion from one type to another is an automatic conversion.

The false statement is #2. You can assign a derived class object to an object of any of its superclass types, but not the other way around.

Using the Object Class

Every class you create in C# derives from a single class named System.Object. In other words, the **object** (or Object) class type in the System namespace is the ultimate base class, or **root class**, for all other types. When you create a class such as Employee, you usually use the header class Employee, which implicitly, or automatically, descends from the Object class. Alternatively, you could use the header class Employee : Object to explicitly show the name of the base class, but it would be extremely unusual to see such a format in a C# program.

The keyword object is an alias for the System.Object class. You can use the lowercase and uppercase versions of the class interchangeably. The fact that object is an alias for System.Object should not surprise you. You already know, for example, that int is an alias for Int32 and that double is an alias for Double.

Because every class descends from Object, every object "is an" Object. As proof, you can write a method that accepts an argument of type Object; it will accept arguments of any type. Figure 10-21 shows a program that declares three objects using classes created earlier in this chapter—a Student, a ScholarshipStudent, and an Employee. Even though these types possess different attributes and methods (and one type, Employee, has nothing in common with the other two), each type can serve as an argument to the DisplayObjectMessage() because each type "is an" Object. Figure 10-22 shows the execution of the program.

```
using System;
class DiverseObjects
{
    static void Main()
    {
        Student payingStudent = new Student();
        ScholarshipStudent freeStudent = new ScholarshipStudent();
        Employee clerk = new Employee();
        Console.Write("Using Student: ");
        DisplayObjectMessage(payingStudent);
        Console.Write("Using ScholarshipStudent: ");
        DisplayObjectMessage(freeStudent);
        Console.Write("Using Employee: ");
        DisplayObjectMessage(clerk);
    }
    public static void DisplayObjectMessage(Object o)
    {
        Console.WriteLine("Method successfully called");
    }
}
```

Figure 10-21 The DiverseObjects program

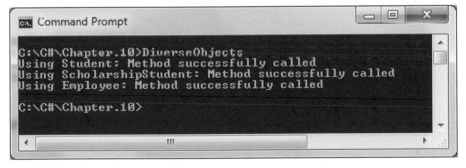

Figure 10-22 Output of the DiverseObjects program

When you create any child class, it inherits all the methods of all of its ancestors. Because all classes inherit from the `Object` class, all classes inherit the `Object` class methods. The `Object` class contains a constructor, a destructor, and four `public` instance methods, as summarized in Table 10-1.

Method	Explanation
Equals()	Determines whether two Object instances are equal
GetHashCode()	Gets a unique code for each object; useful in certain sorting and data management tasks
GetType()	Returns the type, or class, of an object
ToString()	Returns a String that represents the object

Table 10-1 The four public instance methods of the Object class

The Object class contains other nonpublic and noninstance (static) methods in addition to the four methods listed in Table 10-1. The C# documentation provides more details on these methods.

Using the Object Class's GetType() Method

The GetType() method returns an object's type, or class. For example, if you have created an Employee object named someWorker, then the following statement displays Employee:

Console.WriteLine(someWorker.GetType());

If an object's class is defined in a namespace, then GetType() returns a string composed of the namespace, a dot, and the class name.

Using the Object Class's ToString() Method

The Object class methods are not very useful as they stand. For example, when you use the Object class's ToString() method with an object you create, it simply returns a string that holds the name of the class, just as GetType() does. That is, if someWorker is an Employee, then the following statement displays Employee:

Console.WriteLine(someWorker.ToString());

When you create a class such as Employee, you often want to override the Object class's ToString() method with your own, more useful version—perhaps one that returns an Employee's ID number, name, or combination of the two. Of course, you could create a differently named method to do the same thing—perhaps GetEmployeeIdentification() or ConvertEmployeeToString(). However, by naming your class method ToString(), you make the class easier for others to understand and use. Programmers know the ToString() method works with every object; when they use it with your objects, you can provide a useful set of information. A class's ToString() method is often a useful debugging aid.

For example, you might create an `Employee` class `ToString()` method, as shown in Figure 10-23. This method assumes that `EmpNum` and `Name` are `Employee` properties with `get` accessors. The returned `string` will have a value such as "Employee: 234 Johnson".

```
public override string ToString()
{
    return(getType() + ": " + EmpNum + " " + Name);
}
```

Figure 10-23   An `Employee` class `ToString()` method

You have been using an overloaded version of the `ToString()` method since Chapter 2. There, you learned that you can format numeric output when you pass a string such as "F3" or "C2" to the `ToString()` method.

Using the `Object` Class's `Equals()` Method

The `Equals()` method compares objects for reference equality. **Reference equality** occurs when two reference type objects refer to the same object. The `Equals()` method returns `true` if two `Object`s have the same memory address—that is, if one object is a reference to the other and both are literally the same object. For example, you might write the following:

`if oneObject.Equals(anotherObject)…`

Like the `ToString()` method, this method might not be useful to you in its original form. For example, you might prefer to think of two `Employee` objects at unique memory addresses as equal if their ID numbers or first and last names are equal. You might want to override the `Equals()` method for any class you create if you anticipate that class clients will want to compare objects based on any of their field values.

If you overload the `Equals()` method, it should meet the following requirements by convention:

- Its header should be as follows (you can use any identifier for the `Object` parameter):

  `public override bool Equals(Object o)`

- It should return `false` if the argument is `null`.

- It should return `true` if an object is compared to itself.

- It should return `true` only if both of the following are true:

  `oneObject.Equals(anotherObject)`
  `anotherObject.Equals(oneObject)`

- If `oneObject.Equals(anotherObject)` returns `true` and `oneObject.Equals(aThirdObject)` returns `true`, then `anotherObject.Equals(aThirdObject)` should also be `true`.

You first used the Equals() method to compare String objects in Chapter 2. When you use Equals() with Strings, you use the String class's Equals() method that compares String contents as opposed to String addresses. In other words, the Object class's Equals() method has already been overridden in the String class.

When you create an Equals() method to override the one in the Object class, the parameter must be an Object. For example, if you consider Employee objects equal when the EmpNum properties are equal, then an Employee class Equals() method might be created as follows:

```
public override bool Equals(Object e)
{
   bool isEqual;
   Employee temp = (Employee)e;
   if(EmpNum == temp.EmpNum)
     isEqual = true;
   else
     isEqual = false;
   return isEqual;
}
```

In the shaded statement in the method, the Object parameter is cast to an Employee so the Employee's EmpNum can be compared. If you did not perform the cast and tried to make the comparison with o.EmpNum, the method would not compile because an Object does not have an EmpNum property.

An even better alternative is to ensure that compared objects are the same type before making any other decisions. For example, the Equals() method in Figure 10-24 uses the GetType() method with both the this object and the parameter before proceeding. If compared objects are not the same type, then the Equals() method should return false.

```
public override bool Equals(Object e)
{
   bool isEqual;
   if(this.GetType() != e.GetType())
      isEqual = false;
   else
   {
      Employee temp = (Employee)e;
      if(EmpNum == temp.EmpNum)
         isEqual = true;
      else
         isEqual = false;
   }
   return isEqual;
}
```

Figure 10-24   An Equals() method for the Employee class

Using the `Object` Class's `GetHashCode()` Method

When you override the `Equals()` method, you should also override the `GetHashCode()` method, because `Equals()` uses `GetHashCode()` and two objects considered equal should have the same hash code. A **hash code** is a number that should uniquely identify an object; you might use hash codes in some advanced C# applications. For example, Figure 10-25 shows an application that declares two `Employee`s from a class in which the `GetHashCode()` method has not been overridden. The output in Figure 10-26 shows a unique number for each object. (The number, however, is meaningless to you.) If you choose to override the `GetHashCode()` method, you should write this method so it returns a unique integer for every object—an `Employee` number, for example.

A hash code is sometimes called a "fingerprint" for an object because it uniquely identifies the object. In C#, the default implementation of the `GetHashCode()` method does not guarantee unique return values for different objects. However, if `GetHashCode()` is explicitly implemented in a derived class, it must return a unique hash code.

In cooking, hash is a dish that is created by combining ingredients. The term *hash code* derives from the fact that the code is sometimes created by mixing some of an object's data.

```
using System;
class TestHashCode
{
    static void Main()
    {
        Employee first = new Employee();
        Employee second = new Fmployee();
        Console.WriteLine(first.GetHashCode());
        Console.WriteLine(second.GetHashCode());
    }
}
```

Figure 10-25   The `TestHashCode` program

Figure 10-26   Output of the `TestHashCode` program

Although you can write an Equals() method for a class without overriding GetHashCode(), you receive a warning message. Additionally, if you overload == or != for a class, you will receive warning messages if you do not also override both the Equals() and GetHashCode() methods.

TWO TRUTHS & A LIE

Using the Object Class

1. The Object class contains a method named GetType() that returns an object's type, or class.

2. If you do not override the ToString() method for a class, it returns the value of the first string declared within the class, if any.

3. The Object class's Equals() method returns true if two Objects have the same memory address—that is, if one object is a reference to the other and both are literally the same object.

The false statement is #2. If you do not override the ToString() method for a class, it returns a string that holds the name of the class.

Working with Base Class Constructors

When you create any object, you call a constructor that has the same name as the class itself. Consider the following example:

```
SomeClass anObject = new SomeClass();
```

When you instantiate an object that is a member of a derived class, you call both the constructor for the base class and the constructor for the extended, derived class. When you create any derived class object, the base class constructor must execute first; only then does the derived class constructor execute. When you create any object, you always implicitly call the Object constructor because all classes are derived from Object. So, when you create a base class and a derived class, and instantiate a derived class object, you call three constructors: one from the Object class, one from the base class, and one from the derived class.

In the examples of inheritance you have seen so far in this chapter, each class contained default constructors, so their execution was transparent. However, you should realize that when you create a subclass instance, both the base and derived constructors execute. For example, consider the abbreviated Employee and CommissionEmployee classes in Figure 10-27. Employee contains just two fields and a constructor; CommissionEmployee descends from Employee and contains a constructor as well. The DemoSalesperson4 program in Figure 10-28 contains just one statement; it instantiates a CommissionEmployee. The output in Figure 10-29 shows that this one statement causes both constructors to execute.

```
class Employee
{
    private int empNum;
    protected double empSal;
    public Employee()
    {
        Console.WriteLine("Employee constructed");
    }
}
class CommissionEmployee : Employee
{
    private double commissionRate;
    public CommissionEmployee()
    {
        Console.WriteLine("CommissionEmployee constructed");
    }
}
```

Figure 10-27 The Employee and CommissionEmployee classes with parameterless constructors

```
using System;
class DemoSalesperson4
{
    static void Main()
    {
        CommissionEmployee salesperson = new CommissionEmployee();
    }
}
```

Figure 10-28 The DemoSalesperson4 program

Figure 10-29 Output of the DemoSalesperson4 program

Of course, most constructors perform many more tasks than displaying a message to inform you that they exist. When constructors initialize variables, you usually want the base class constructor to initialize the data fields that originate in the base class. The derived class constructor needs to initialize only the data fields that are specific to the derived class.

Using Base Class Constructors That Require Arguments

When you create a class and do not provide a constructor, C# automatically supplies one that never requires arguments. When you write your own constructor for a class, you replace the automatically supplied version. Depending on your needs, the constructor you create for a class might require arguments. When you use a class as a base class and the class only has constructors that require arguments, you must make sure that any derived classes provide arguments so that one of the base class constructors can execute.

When all base class constructors require arguments, you must include a constructor for each derived class you create. Your derived class constructor can contain any number of statements; however, within the header of the constructor, you must provide values for any arguments required by the base class constructor that you use. Even if you have no other reason for creating a derived class constructor, you must write the derived class constructor so it can call its parent's constructor.

The header for a derived class constructor that calls a base class constructor includes a colon, the keyword base, and a list of arguments within parentheses. The keyword **base** always refers to the superclass of the class in which you use it. Although it seems that you should be able to use the base class constructor name to call the base class constructor, C# does not allow you to do so—you must use the keyword base.

For example, if you create an Employee class with a constructor that requires two arguments—an integer and a string—and you create a CommissionEmployee class that is a subclass of Employee, then the following code shows a valid constructor for CommissionEmployee:

```
public CommissionEmployee() : base(1234, "XXXX")
{
    // Other statements can go here
}
```

In this example, the CommissionEmployee constructor requires no arguments, but it passes two arguments to its base class constructor. Every CommissionEmployee instantiation passes 1234 and "XXXX" to the Employee constructor. A different CommissionEmployee constructor might require arguments; then it could pass the appropriate arguments on to the base class constructor, as in the following example:

```
public CommissionEmployee(int id, string name) : base(id, name)
{
    // Other statements can go here
}
```

Yet another CommissionEmployee constructor might require that some arguments be passed to the base class constructor, and that some be used within CommissionEmployee. Consider the following example:

```
public CommissionEmployee(int id, string name, double rate) :
   base(id, name) // two parameters passed to base constructor
{
     CommissionRate = rate;
     // rate is used within child constructor
     // Other statements can go here
}
```

473

 Watch the video *Constructors and Inheritance*.

TWO TRUTHS & A LIE

Working with Base Class Constructors

1. When you create any derived class object, the base class constructor executes first, followed by the derived class constructor.

2. When a base class constructor requires arguments, you must include a constructor for each derived class you create.

3. When a derived class's constructor requires arguments, all of the arguments must be passed to the base class constructor.

The false statement is #3. When a derived class's constructor requires arguments, all of the arguments might be needed in the derived class, or perhaps all must be passed to the base class constructor. It also might be possible that some arguments are passed to the base class constructor and others are used within the derived class constructor.

You Do It

Adding Constructors to Base and Derived Classes

When a base class contains only constructors that require parameters, then any derived classes must provide for the base class constructor. In the next steps, you add constructors to the Loan and CarLoan classes and demonstrate that they work as expected.

1. Open the DemoCarLoan2 program and change the class name to **DemoCarLoan3**. Save the file as **DemoCarLoan3**.

2. In the Loan class, just after the declaration of the loanAmount field, add a constructor that requires values for all the Loan's properties:

```
public Loan(int num, string name, double amount)
{
    LoanNumber = num;
    LastName = name;
    LoanAmount = amount;
}
```

3. In the CarLoan class, just after the declaration of the year field, add a constructor that takes five parameters. It passes three of the parameters to the base class constructor and uses the other two to assign values to the properties that are unique to the child class.

```
public CarLoan(int num, string name, double amount,
    int year, string make) : base(num, name, amount)
{
    Year = year;
    Make = make;
}
```

4. In the Main() method of the DemoCarLoan3 class, remove the existing declarations for aLoan and aCarLoan and replace them with two declarations that use the arguments passed to the constructors.

```
Loan aLoan = new Loan(333, "Hanson", 7000.00);
CarLoan aCarLoan = new CarLoan(444, "Carlisle", 30000.00,
    2011, "BMW");
```

5. Remove the eight statements that assigned values to Loan and CarLoan, but retain the Console.WriteLine() statements that display the values.

6. Save the program, and then compile and execute it. The output looks like Figure 10-30. Both constructors work as expected. The CarLoan

(continues)

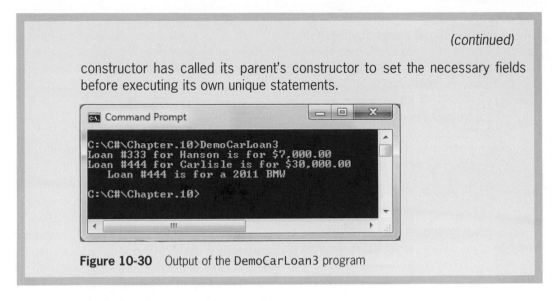

constructor has called its parent's constructor to set the necessary fields before executing its own unique statements.

Figure 10-30   Output of the DemoCarLoan3 program

Creating and Using Abstract Classes

Creating classes is easier after you understand the concept of inheritance. When you create a child class, it inherits all the general attributes you need; you must create only the new, more specific attributes required by the child class. For example, a `Painter` and a `Sculptor` are more specific than an `Artist`. They inherit all the general attributes of `Artists`, but you must add the attributes and methods that are specific to `Painter` and `Sculptor`.

Another way to think about a superclass is to notice that it contains the features shared by its subclasses. The derived classes are more specific examples of the base class type; they add features to the shared, general features. Conversely, when you examine a derived class, you notice that its parent is more general.

Sometimes you create a parent class to be so general that you never intend to create any specific instances of the class. For example, you might never create "just" an `Artist`; each `Artist` is more specifically a `Painter`, `Sculptor`, `Illustrator`, and so on. A class that you create only to extend from, but not to instantiate from, is an abstract class. An **abstract class** is one from which you cannot create concrete objects, but from which you can inherit. You use the keyword `abstract` when you declare an abstract class. If you attempt to instantiate an object from an abstract class, you will receive a compiler error message.

Nonabstract classes from which objects *can* be instantiated are called **concrete** classes.

Abstract classes are like regular classes in that they can contain data fields and methods. The difference is that you cannot create instances of abstract classes by using the `new` operator. Rather, you create abstract classes simply to provide a base class from which other objects may be derived.

Abstract classes usually contain abstract methods, although methods are not required. An **abstract method** has no method statements; any class derived from a class that contains an abstract method must override the abstract method by providing a body (an implementation) for it. (Alternatively, the derived class can declare the method to be abstract; in that case, the derived class's children must implement the method.) You can create an `abstract` class with no `abstract` methods, but you cannot create an `abstract` method outside of an `abstract` class.

 A method that is declared `virtual` is not required to be overridden in a child class, but a method declared `abstract` must be overridden.

When you create an abstract method, you provide the keyword `abstract` and the intended method type, name, and parameters, but you do not provide statements within the method; you do not even supply curly braces. When you create a derived class that inherits an abstract method from a parent, you must use the keyword **override** in the method header and provide the actions, or implementation, for the inherited method within the derived class. In other words, you are required to code a derived class method to override any empty base class methods that are inherited.

For example, suppose that you want to create classes to represent different animals. You can create a generic, abstract class named `Animal` so you can provide generic data fields, such as the animal's name, only once. An `Animal` is generic, but each specific `Animal`, such as `Dog` or `Cat`, makes a unique sound. If you code an abstract `Speak()` method in the abstract `Animal` class, then you require all future `Animal` derived classes to override the `Speak()` method and provide an implementation that is specific to the derived class. Figure 10-31 shows an abstract `Animal` class that contains a data field for the name, a constructor that assigns a name, a `Name` property, and an abstract `Speak()` method.

```
abstract class Animal
{
    private string name;
    public Animal(string name)
    {
        this.name = name;
    }

    public string Name
    {
        get
        {
            return name;
        }
    }
    public abstract string Speak();
}
```

Figure 10-31   The `Animal` class

The Animal class in Figure 10-31 is declared to be abstract. (The keyword is shaded.) You cannot place a statement such as Animal myPet = new Animal("Murphy"); within a program, because the program will not compile. Because Animal is an abstract class, no Animal objects can exist.

You create an abstract class like Animal so that you can extend it. For example, you can create Dog and Cat classes as shown in Figure 10-32. Because the Animal class contains a constructor that requires a string argument, both Dog and Cat must contain constructors that provide string arguments for their base class.

```
class Dog : Animal
{
    public Dog(string name) : base(name)
    {
    }
    public override string Speak()
    {
        return "woof";
    }
}
class Cat : Animal
{
    public Cat(string name) : base(name)
    {
    }
    public override string Speak()
    {
        return "meow";
    }
}
```

Figure 10-32   The Dog and Cat classes

If a method that should be overridden in a child class has its own implementation, you declare the base class method to be virtual. If it does not have its own implementation, you declare the base class and the method to be abstract.

The Dog and Cat constructors perform no tasks other than passing out the name to the Animal constructor. The overriding Speak() methods within Dog and Cat are required because the abstract parent Animal class contains an abstract Speak() method. The keyword override (shaded) is required in the method header. You can code any statements you want within the Dog and Cat class Speak() methods, but the Speak() methods must exist.

Figure 10-33 shows a program that implements Dog and Cat objects. Figure 10-34 shows the output, in which Speak() operates correctly for each animal type.

```
using System;
class DemoAnimals
{
   static void Main()
   {
      Dog spot = new Dog("Spot");
      Cat puff = new Cat("Puff");
      Console.WriteLine(spot.Name + " says " + spot.Speak());
      Console.WriteLine(puff.Name + " says " + puff.Speak());
   }
}
```

Figure 10-33   The DemoAnimals program

Figure 10-34   Output of the DemoAnimals program

Figure 10-35 shows an alternate way to create the DemoAnimals program. In this version the Dog and Cat objects are passed to a method that accepts an Animal parameter. The output is the same as in Figure 10-34. The Name property and Speak() method operate polymorphically, acting appropriately for each object type.

```
using System;
class DemoAnimals2
{
   static void Main()
   {
      Dog spot = new Dog("Spot");
      Cat puff = new Cat("Puff");
      DisplayAnimal(spot);
      DisplayAnimal(puff);
   }
   public static void DisplayAnimal(Animal creature)
   {
      Console.WriteLine(creature.Name + " says " + creature.Speak());
   }
}
```

Figure 10-35   The DemoAnimals2 program

TWO TRUTHS & A LIE

Creating and Using Abstract Classes

1. An abstract class is one from which you cannot create concrete objects.

2. Unlike regular classes, abstract classes cannot contain methods.

3. When a base class contains an abstract method, the descendents of the base class must override the abstract method or declare the overriding method to be abstract.

The false statement is #2. Abstract classes are like regular classes in that they can contain data fields and methods. The difference is that you cannot create instances of abstract classes by using the new operator. Rather, you create abstract classes simply to provide a base class from which other objects may be derived.

Creating and Using Interfaces

Some object-oriented programming languages, notably C++, allow a subclass to inherit from more than one parent class. For example, you might create an `Employee` class that contains data fields pertaining to each employee in your organization. You also might create a `Product` class that holds information about each product your organization manufactures. When you create a `Patent` class for each product for which your company holds a patent, you might want to include product information as well as information about the employee who was responsible for the invention. In this situation, it would be convenient to inherit fields and methods from both the `Product` and `Employee` classes. The ability to inherit from more than one class is called **multiple inheritance**.

Multiple inheritance is a difficult concept, and programmers encounter many problems when they use it. For example, variables and methods in the parent classes may have identical names, creating a conflict when the child class uses one of the names. Additionally, as you already have learned, a child class constructor must call its parent class constructor. When two or more parents exist, this becomes a more complicated task: To which class should `base` refer when a child class has multiple parents?

For all of these reasons, multiple inheritance is prohibited in C#. However, C# does provide an alternative to multiple inheritance, known as an interface. Much like an abstract class, an **interface** is a collection of methods (and perhaps other members) that can be used by any class as long as the class provides a definition to override the interface's abstract definitions. Within an abstract class, some methods can be abstract, while others need not be. Within an interface, all methods are abstract.

You first learned about interfaces in the chapter *Using Classes and Objects* when you used the `IComparable` interface.

You create an interface much as you create an abstract class definition, except that you use the keyword `interface` instead of `abstract class`. For example, suppose that you create an `IWorkable` interface as shown in Figure 10-36. For simplicity, the `IWorkable` interface contains a single method named `Work()`.

Although not required, in C# it is customary to start interface names with an uppercase "I". Other languages follow different conventions. Interface names frequently end with "able".

```
public interface IWorkable
{
    string Work();
}
```

Figure 10-36   The `IWorkable` interface

When any class implements `IWorkable`, it must also include a `Work()` method that returns a `string`. Figure 10-37 shows two classes that implement `IWorkable`: the `Employee` class and the `Animal` class. Because each implements `IWorkable`, each must declare a `Work()` method. The `Employee` class implements `Work()` to return the "I do my job" `string`. The abstract `Animal` class defines `Work()` as an abstract method, meaning that descendents of `Animal` must implement `Work()`. Figure 10-37 also shows two child classes of `Animal`: `Dog` and `Cat`. Note how `Work()` is defined differently for each.

```
class Employee : IWorkable
{
   public Employee(string name)
   {
      Name = name;
   }
   public string Name {get; set;}
   public string Work()
   {
      return "I do my job";
   }
}
abstract class Animal : IWorkable
{
   public Animal(string name)
   {
      Name = name;
   }
   public string Name {get; set;}

   public abstract string Work();
}
class Dog : Animal
{
   public Dog(string name) : base(name)
   {
   }
   public override string Work()
   {
      return "I watch the house";
   }
}
class Cat : Animal
{
   public Cat(string name) : base(name)
   {
   }
   public override string Work()
   {
      return "I catch mice";
   }
}
```

Figure 10-37   The Employee, Animal, Cat, and Dog classes with the
IWorkable interface

When you create a program that instantiates an Employee, a Dog, or a Cat, as in
the DemoWorking program in Figure 10-38, each object type knows how to "Work()"
appropriately. Figure 10-39 shows the output.

```
using System;
class DemoWorking
{
    static void Main()
    {
        Employee bob = new Employee("Bob");
        Dog spot = new Dog("Spot");
        Cat puff = new Cat("Puff");
        Console.WriteLine(bob.Name + " says " + bob.Work());
        Console.WriteLine(spot.Name + " says " + spot.Work());
        Console.WriteLine(puff.Name + " says " + puff.Work());
    }
}
```

Figure 10-38 The DemoWorking program

Figure 10-39 Output of the DemoWorking program

Abstract classes and interfaces are similar in that you cannot instantiate concrete objects from either one. Abstract classes differ from interfaces in that abstract classes can contain nonabstract methods, but all methods within an interface must be abstract. A class can inherit from only one base class (whether abstract or not), but it can implement any number of interfaces. For example, if you want to create a Child that inherits from a Parent class and implements two interfaces, IWorkable and IPlayable, you would define the class name and list the base class and interfaces separated by commas:

```
class Child : Parent, IWorkable, IPlayable
```

You implement an existing interface because you want a class to be able to use a method that already exists in other applications. For example, suppose that you have created a Payroll application that uses the Work() method in the interface class. Also suppose that you create a new class named BusDriver. If BusDriver implements the IWorkable interface, then

`BusDriver` objects can be used by the existing `Payroll` program. As another example, suppose that you have written a game program that uses an `IAttackable` interface with methods that determine how and when an object can attack. When you create new classes such as `MarsAlien`, `Vampire`, and `CivilWarSoldier`, and each implements the interface, you can define how each one attacks and how each type of object can be added to the game.

You can think of an interface as a contract. A class that implements an interface must abide by the rules of the contract.

Beginning programmers sometimes find it difficult to decide when to create an abstract base class and when to create an interface. You can follow these guidelines:

- Typically, you create an abstract class when you want to provide some data or methods that derived classes can inherit, but you want the subclasses to override some specific methods that you declare to be `abstract`.

- You create an interface when you want derived classes to override every method.

- Use a base class when the class you want to create "is a" subtype of another class; use an interface when the class you want to create will act like the interface.

Interfaces provide you with a way to exhibit polymorphic behavior. If diverse classes implement the same interface in unique ways, then you can treat each class type in the same way using the same language. When various classes use the same interface, you know the names of the methods that are available with those classes, and C# classes adopt a more uniform functionality; this consistency helps you to understand new classes you encounter more easily. If you know, for example, the method names contained in the `IWorkable` interface, and you see that a class implements `IWorkable`, you have a head start in understanding how the class functions.

Now that you understand how to construct your own interfaces, you will benefit from rereading the section describing the `IComparable` interface in the chapter *Using Classes and Objects*.

> ## TWO TRUTHS & A LIE
> ### Creating and Using Interfaces
>
> 1. An interface is a collection of methods (and perhaps other members) that can be used by any class as long as the class provides a definition to override the interface's abstract definitions.
>
> 2. Abstract classes and interfaces differ in that all methods in abstract classes must be abstract, but interfaces can contain nonabstract methods.
>
> 3. A class can inherit from only one base class, but it can implement any number of interfaces.

> The false statement is #2. Abstract classes and interfaces are similar in that you cannot instantiate concrete objects from either one. However, they differ in that abstract classes can contain nonabstract methods, but all methods within an interface must be abstract.

Using Extension Methods

When you write a C# program, sometimes you might wish a class had an additional method that would be useful to you. If you created the original class, you have two options:

- You could revise the existing class, including the new useful method.

- You could derive a child class from the existing class and provide it with a new method.

Sometimes, however, classes you use were created by others, and you might not be allowed to either revise or extend them. Of course, you could create an entirely new class that includes your new method, but that would duplicate a lot of the work already done when the first class was created. In these cases, the best option is to write an extension method. **Extension methods** are methods you can write to add to any type. Extension methods were introduced in C# 3.0.

Programmers sometimes define classes as sealed within the class header, as in `sealed class InventoryItem`. A **sealed class** cannot be extended. For example, the built-in `String` class is a sealed class.

For example, you have used the prewritten `Int32` class throughout this book to declare integers. Suppose that you work for a company that frequently uses customer account numbers, and that the company has decided to add an extra digit to each account number. For simplicity, assume that all account numbers are two digits and that the new, third digit should be the rightmost digit in the sum of the first two digits. You could handle this problem by creating a class named AccountNumber, including a method to produce the extra digit, and redefining every instance of a customer's account number in your applications as an AccountNumber object. However, if you already have many applications that define the account number as an integer, you might prefer to create an extension method that extends the Int32 class.

In Chapter 2 you learned that each C# intrinsic type, such as int, is an alias for a class in the System namespace, such as Int32.

When organizations append extra digits to account numbers, the extra digits are called check digits. **Check digits** help assure that all the digits in account numbers and other numbers are entered correctly. Check digits are calculated using different formulas. If a digit used to calculate the check digit is incorrect, then the resulting check digit is probably incorrect as well.

Figure 10-40 contains a method that extends the Int32 class. The first parameter in an extension method specifies the type extended and must begin with the keyword this. For example, the first (and in this case, only) parameter in the AddCheckDigit() method is this int num, as shown in the shaded portion of the figure. Extension methods must be static methods. Within the AddCheckDigit() method in Figure 10-40, the first digit is extracted from the two-digit account number by dividing by 10 and taking the resulting whole number, and the second digit is extracted by taking the remainder. Those two digits are added, and the last digit of that sum is returned from the method. For example, if 49 is passed into the method, first becomes 4, second becomes 9, and third becomes the last digit of 13, or 3. Then the original number (49) is multiplied by 10 and added to the third digit, resulting in 493.

```
public static int AddCheckDigit(this int num)
{
    int first = num / 10;
    int second = num % 10;
    int third = (first + second) % 10;
    int result = num * 10 + third;
    return result;
}
```

Figure 10-40 The AddCheckDigit() extension method

An extension method is static and must be stored in a static class. For example, the DemoExtensionMethod program in Figure 10-41 shows an application that is declared static in the first shaded statement and uses the extension method in the second shaded statement. The static method AddCheckDigit() is used as if it were an instance method of the Int32 class; in other words, it is attached to an Int32 object with a dot, just as instance methods are when used with objects. No arguments are passed to the AddCheckDigit() method explicitly from the DemoExtensionMethod class. The parameter in the method is implied, just as these references are always implied in instance methods. Figure 10-42 shows the execution of the program.

```
using System;
static class DemoExtensionMethod
{
   static void Main()
   {
      int acctNum = 49;
      int revisedAcctNum = acctNum.AddCheckDigit();
      Console.WriteLine("Original account number was {0}",
         acctNum);
      Console.WriteLine("Revised account number is {0}",
         revisedAcctNum);
   }
   public static int AddCheckDigit(this int num)
   {
      int first = num / 10;
      int second = num % 10;
      int third = (first + second) % 10;
      int result = num * 10 + third;
      return result;
   }
}
```

Figure 10-41   The DemoExtensionMethod application

Figure 10-42   Execution of the DemoExtensionMethod application

You can create extension methods for your own classes in the same way one was created for the Int32 class in this example. Just like other outside methods, and unlike ordinary class instance methods, extension methods cannot access any private members of classes they extend. Furthermore, if a class contains an instance method with the same signature as an extension method, the instance method takes priority and will be the one that executes.

TWO TRUTHS & A LIE

Using Extension Methods

1. The first parameter in an extension method specifies the type extended and must be preceded by the keyword `this`.

2. Extension methods must be static methods.

3. When you write an extension method, it must be stored within the class to which it refers, along with the class's other instance methods.

The false statement is #3. Although you use an extension method like an instance method, any extension method you write must be stored in a static class.

Recognizing Inheritance in GUI Applications and Recapping the Benefits of Inheritance

When you create a Windows Forms application using Visual Studio's IDE, you automatically use inheritance. Every `Form` you create is a descendent of the `Form` class. Figure 10-43 shows a just-started project in which the programmer has double-clicked the automatically generated `Form` to expose the code. You can see that the automatically generated `Form1` class extends `Form`.

488

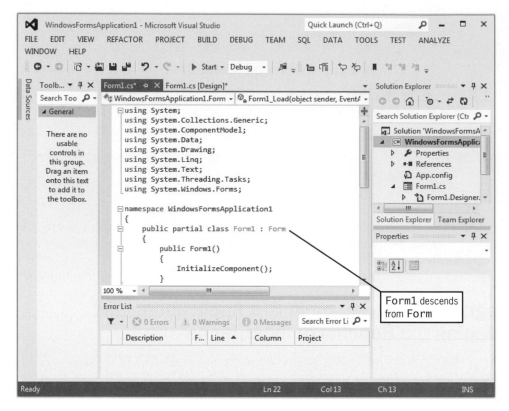

Figure 10-43   Automatically generated `Form` code in the IDE

The `Form` class descends from the `Object` class like all other C# classes, but not directly. It is six generations removed from the `Object` class in the following line of descent:

- `Object`
- `MarshalByRefObject`
- `Component`
- `Control`
- `ScrollableControl`
- `ContainerControl`
- `Form`

Other GUI objects such as `Label`s and `Button`s follow similar lengthy ancestry lines. You might guess that certain universal properties of GUI controls such as `Text` and `Visible` are inherited from ancestors. You will learn more about these hierarchies in the chapter *Using Controls*, but even though you have worked with only a few controls so far, you can understand the benefits inheritance provides.

When an automobile company designs a new car model, it does not build every component from scratch. The car might include a new feature—for example, some model contained the first air bag—but many of a new car's features are simply modifications of existing features. The manufacturer might create a larger gas tank or a more comfortable seat, but these new features still possess many of the properties of their predecessors from older models. Most features of new car models are not even modified; instead, existing components, such as air filters and windshield wipers, are included on the new model without any changes.

Similarly, you can create powerful computer programs more easily if many of their components are used either "as is" or with slight modifications. Inheritance does not enable you to write any programs that you could not write if inheritance did not exist; you *could* create every part of a program from scratch, but reusing existing classes and interfaces makes your job easier.

You already have used many "as is" classes, such as `Console`, `Int32`, and `String`. Using these classes made it easier to write programs than if you had to invent the classes yourself. Now that you have learned about inheritance, you can extend existing classes as well as just use them. When you create a useful, extendable base class, you and other future programmers gain several advantages:

- Derived class creators save development time because much of the code that is needed for the class already has been written.

- Derived class creators save testing time because the base class code already has been tested and probably used in a variety of situations. In other words, the base class code is reliable.

- Programmers who create or use new derived classes already understand how the base class works, so the time it takes to learn the new class features is reduced.

- When you create a derived class in C#, the base class source code is not changed. Thus, the base class maintains its integrity.

 Classes that are not intended to be instantiated and that contain only `static` members are declared as `static` classes. You cannot extend `static` classes. For example, `System.Console` is a static class.

When you think about classes, you need to think about the commonalities between them, and then you can create base classes from which to inherit. You might even be rewarded professionally when you see your own superclasses extended by others in the future.

489

> ## TWO TRUTHS & A LIE
>
> ### Recognizing Inheritance in GUI Applications and Recapping the Benefits of Inheritance
>
> 1. Inheritance enables you to create powerful computer programs more easily.
>
> 2. Without inheritance, you *could* create every part of a program from scratch, but reusing existing classes and interfaces makes your job easier.
>
> 3. Inheritance is frequently inefficient because base class code is seldom reliable when extended to a derived class.
>
> The false statement is #3. Derived class creators save testing time because the base class code has already been tested and probably used in a variety of situations. In other words, the base class code is reliable.

Chapter Summary

- The classes you create in object-oriented programming languages can inherit data and methods from existing classes. The ability to use inheritance makes programs easier to write, easier to understand, and less prone to errors. A class that is used as a basis for inheritance is called a base class, superclass, or parent class. When you create a class that inherits from a base class, it is called a derived class, extended class, subclass, or child class.

- When you create a class that is an extension or child of another class, you use a single colon between the derived class name and its base class name. The child class inherits all the methods and fields of its parent. Inheritance works only in one direction—a child inherits from a parent, but not the other way around.

- If you could use private data outside of its class, the principle of information hiding would be destroyed. On some occasions, however, you want to access parent class data from a derived class. For those occasions, you declare parent class fields using the keyword `protected`, which provides you with an intermediate level of security between `public` and `private` access.

- When you declare a child class method with the same name and parameter list as a method within its parent class, you override the parent class method and allow your class objects to exhibit polymorphic behavior. You can use the keyword `new` or `override` with the derived class method. When a derived class overrides a parent class member but you want to access the parent class version, you can use the keyword `base`.

- Every derived class object "is a" specific instance of both the derived class and the base class. Therefore, you can assign a derived class object to an object of any of its base class types. When you do so, C# makes an implicit conversion from derived class to base class.

- Every class you create in C# derives from a single class named `System.Object`. Because all classes inherit from the `Object` class, all classes inherit the four `Object` class `public` instance methods: `Equals()`, `GetHashCode()`, `GetType()`, and `ToString()`.

- When you instantiate an object that is a member of a subclass, the base class constructor executes first; only then does the derived class constructor execute.

- An abstract class is one from which you cannot create concrete objects, but from which you can inherit. Usually, abstract classes contain abstract methods; an abstract method has no method statements. Any class derived from a class that contains an abstract method must override the abstract method by providing a body (an implementation) for it.

- An interface provides an alternative to multiple inheritance. Much like an abstract class, an interface is a collection of methods (and perhaps other members) that can be used by any class as long as the class provides a definition to override the interface's abstract definitions. Within an abstract class, some methods can be abstract, while others need not be. Within an interface, all methods are abstract. A class can inherit from only one abstract base class, but it can implement any number of interfaces.

- Extension methods are methods you can write to add to any type. They are static methods, but they operate like instance methods. Their parameter lists begin with the keyword `this` and the data type being extended.

- Every GUI object you create descends from ancestors. You can create powerful computer programs more easily using inheritance because it saves development and testing time.

Key Terms

Inheritance is the application of your knowledge of a general category to more specific objects.

Unified Modeling Language (UML) diagrams are graphical tools that programmers and analysts use to describe systems.

A **base class** is a class that is used as a basis for inheritance.

A **derived class** or **extended class** is one that has inherited from a base class.

A **superclass** is a base class.

A **subclass** is a derived class.

A **parent class** is a base class.

A **child class** is a derived class.

The **ancestors** of a derived class are all the superclasses from which the subclass is derived.

Transitive describes the feature of inheritance in which a child inherits all the members of all its ancestors.

The keyword **protected** provides an intermediate level of security between `public` and `private` access. A `protected` data field or method can be used within its own class or in any classes extended from that class, but it cannot be used by "outside" classes.

Fragile describes classes that depend on field names from parent classes because they are prone to errors—that is, they are easy to "break."

A **virtual method** is one whose behavior is determined by the implementation in a child class.

To **hide** a parent class member is to override it in a derived class.

Visible describes a base class member that is not hidden by a derived class.

Recursive describes a method that calls itself.

An **implicit conversion** occurs when a type is automatically converted to another upon assignment.

An **implicit reference conversion** occurs when a derived class object is assigned to its ancestor's data type.

The **object** (or `Object`) class type in the `System` namespace is the root base class for all other types.

A **root class** is the ultimate or first base class in a hierarchal ancestry tree.

Reference equality occurs when two reference type objects refer to the same object.

A **hash code** is a number that should uniquely identify an object.

The keyword **base** always refers to the superclass of the class in which you use it.

An **abstract class** is one from which you cannot create concrete objects, but from which you can inherit.

Concrete classes are nonabstract classes from which objects can be instantiated.

An **abstract method** has no method statements; any class derived from a class that contains an abstract method must override the abstract method by providing a body (an implementation) for it.

The keyword **override** is used in method headers when you create a derived class that inherits an abstract method from a parent.

Multiple inheritance is the ability to inherit from more than one class.

An **interface** is a collection of abstract methods (and perhaps other members) that can be used by any class as long as the class provides a definition to override the interface's abstract definitions.

Extension methods are static methods that act like instance methods. You can write extension methods to add to any type.

A **sealed class** cannot be extended.

A **check digit** is a digit calculated from a formula and appended to a number to help verify the accuracy of the other digits in the number.

Review Questions

1. Specific types of objects assume features of more general classes through _____.

   a. polymorphism
   b. encapsulation
   c. inheritance
   d. structure

2. Which of the following is *not* a benefit of using inheritance when creating a new class?

   a. You save time, because you need not create fields and methods that already exist in a parent class.
   b. You reduce the chance of errors, because the parent class methods have already been used and tested.
   c. You make it easier for anyone who has used the parent class to understand the new class because the programmer can concentrate on the new features.
   d. You save computer memory because when you create objects of the new class, storage is not required for parent class fields.

3. A child class is also called a(n) _____.

   a. extended class
   b. base class
   c. superclass
   d. delineated class

4. Assuming that the following classes are well named, which of the following is a parent class of House?

   a. Apartment
   b. Building
   c. Victorian
   d. myHouse

5. A derived class usually contains _____ than its parent.

   a. more fields and methods
   b. the same number of fields but fewer methods
   c. fewer fields but more methods
   d. fewer fields and methods

6. When you create a class that is an extension or child of another class, you use a(n) _____ between the derived class name and its base class name.

    a. ampersand   c. dot

    b. colon   d. hyphen

7. A base class named `Garden` contains a private field `width` and a property `public int Width` that contains `get` and `set` accessors. A child class named `VegetableGarden` does not contain a `Width` property. When you write a class in which you declare an object as follows, what statement can you use to access the `VegetableGarden`'s `width`?

    `VegetableGarden myGarden = new VegetableGarden();`

    a. `myGarden.Width`

    b. `myGarden.base.Width`

    c. `VegetableGarden.Width`

    d. You cannot use `Width` with a `VegetableGarden` object.

8. When a parent class contains a `private` data field, the field is _____ the child class.

    a. hidden in   c. directly accessible in

    b. not a member of   d. `public in`

9. When a base class and a derived class contain a method with the same name and parameter list, and you call the method using a derived class object, _____.

    a. you receive an error message

    b. the base class version overrides the derived class version

    c. the derived class version overrides the base class version

    d. both method versions execute

10. Which of the following is an English-language form of polymorphism?

    a. seeing a therapist and seeing the point

    b. moving friends with a compelling story and moving friends to a new apartment

    c. both of these

    d. neither of these

11. When base and derived classes contain a method with the same name and parameter list, you can use the base class method within the derived class by using the keyword _____ before the method name.

    a. `new`   c. `base`

    b. `override`   d. `super`

12. In a program that declares a derived class object, you _____ assign it to an object of its base class type.

   a. can
   b. cannot
   c. must
   d. should not

13. The root base class for all other class types is _____.

   a. Base
   b. Super
   c. Parent
   d. Object

14. All of the following are `Object` class methods *except* _____.

   a. `ToString()`
   b. `Equals()`
   c. `Print()`
   d. `GetHashCode()`

15. When you create any derived class object, _____.

   a. the base class and derived class constructors execute simultaneously
   b. the base class constructor must execute first, and then the derived class constructor executes
   c. the derived class constructor must execute first, and then the base class constructor executes
   d. neither the base class constructor nor the derived class constructor executes

16. When a base class constructor requires arguments, then each derived class _____.

   a. must include a constructor
   b. must include a constructor that requires arguments
   c. must include two or more constructors
   d. must not include a constructor

17. When you create an abstract class, _____.

   a. you can inherit from it
   b. you can create concrete objects from it
   c. Both of these are true.
   d. None of these is true.

18. When you create an abstract method, you provide _____.

   a. the keyword `abstract`
   b. curly braces
   c. method statements
   d. all of these

19.   Within an interface, _____.

    a.   no methods can be abstract

    b.   some methods might be abstract

    c.   some, but not all, methods must be abstract

    d.   all methods must be abstract

20.   Abstract classes and interfaces are similar in that _____.

    a.   you can instantiate concrete objects from both

    b.   you cannot instantiate concrete objects from either one

    c.   all methods in both must be abstract

    d.   neither can contain nonabstract methods

Exercises

Programming Exercises

1.   Create an application class named **BillDemo** that instantiates objects of two classes named Bill and OverdueBill, and that demonstrates all their methods. The Bill class includes auto-implemented properties for the name of the company or person to whom the bill is owed and for the amount due. Also, include a ToString() method that overrides the Object class's ToString() method and returns a string that contains the name of the class (using GetType()) and the Bill's data field values. Create a child class named OverdueBill that includes an auto-implemented property that holds the number of days the bill is overdue.

2.   Create an application class named **PhotoDemo** that demonstrates the methods of three related classes for a company that develops photographs. Create a class named Photo that includes fields for width and height in inches and properties for each field. Include a protected price field, and set it to $3.99 for an 8-inch by 10-inch photo, $5.99 for a 10-inch by 12-inch photo, and $9.99 for any other size (because custom cutting is required). The price field requires a get accessor, but no set accessor. Also include a ToString() method that returns a string constructed from the return value of the object's GetType() method and the values of the fields. Derive two subclasses—MattedPhoto and FramedPhoto. The MattedPhoto class includes a string field to hold a color, and the FramedPhoto class includes two string fields that hold the frame's material (such as *silver*) and style (such as *modern*). The price for a MattedPhoto increases by $10 over its base cost, and the price for a FramedPhoto increases by $25 over its base cost. Each subclass should include a ToString() method that overrides the parent class version.

3. a. Create an application named **OrderDemo** that declares and uses Order objects. The Order class performs order processing of a single item that sells for $19.95 each. The class has four variable fields that hold an order number, customer name, quantity ordered, and total price. Create a constructor that requires parameters for all the fields except total price. Include public get and set accessors for each field except the total price field; that field is calculated as quantity ordered times unit price (19.95) whenever the quantity is set, so it needs only a get accessor. Also create the following for the class:

   - An Equals() method that determines two Orders are equal if they have the same order number

   - A GetHashCode() method that returns the order number

   - A ToString() method that returns a string containing all order information

   The OrderDemo application declares a few Order objects and sets their values. Make sure to create at least two orders with the same order number. Display the string from the ToString() method for each order. Write a method that compares two orders at a time and displays a message if they are equal. Send the Orders you created to the method two at a time and display the results.

   b. Using the Order class you created in Exercise 3a, write a new application named **OrderDemo2** that creates an array of five Orders. Prompt the user for values for each Order. Do not allow duplicate order numbers; force the user to reenter the order when a duplicate order number is entered. When five valid orders have been entered, display them all, plus a total of all orders.

   c. Create a ShippedOrder class that derives from Order. A ShippedOrder has a $4.00 shipping fee (no matter how many items are ordered). Override any methods in the parent class as necessary. Write a new application named **OrderDemo3** that creates an array of five ShippedOrders. Prompt the user for values for each, and do not allow duplicate order numbers—force the user to reenter the order when a duplicate order number is entered. When five valid orders have been entered, display them all, plus a total of all orders.

   d. Make any necessary modifications to the ShippedOrder class so that it can be sorted by order number. Modify the OrderDemo3 application so the displayed orders have been sorted. Save the application as **OrderDemo4**.

4. a. Create an application named **BookDemo** that declares and demonstrates objects of the Book class and its descendents. The Book class includes auto-implemented properties for the International Standard Book Number (ISBN), title, author, and price. (An ISBN is a unique number assigned to each published book.) Create a child class named TextBook that includes a grade level and a CoffeeTableBook child class that contains no additional fields or properties. In the child classes, override the accessor that sets a Book's price so

that TextBooks must be priced between $20.00 and $80.00, inclusive, and CoffeeTableBooks must be priced between $35.00 and $100.00, inclusive. Be sure to use valid and invalid values when testing the child class properties.

b. In the Book class you created in Exercise 4a, overload the Object class Equals() method to consider two Books equal if they have the same ISBN. Create a program that declares three Books; two should have the same ISBN and one should have a different one. Demonstrate that the Equals() method works correctly to compare the Books. Save the program as **BookDemo2**.

c. Write an application that declares two Book objects and uses an extension method named DisplayTitleAndAuthor() with each. The method displays a Book's title, the word "by", and the author's name. Save the program as **BookDemo3**.

5. a. Create an application named **CustomerDemo** that prompts a user for data for five Customer objects, sorts them in ID number order, and displays all their data as well as a grand total of the amounts owed by all customers. The Customer class includes auto-implemented properties for a customer ID number, name, and balance due. Override the ToString() method to return all the details for a customer.

b. Using the Customer class as a base, derive a **CreditCustomer** class. A CreditCustomer contains all the data of a Customer, plus a field to hold a monthly interest rate. Create a program named **CustomerDemo2** that contains an array of five CreditCustomer objects. Prompt the user for all the necessary data. Override the parent class ToString() method to include the child class's additional data. Sort all the records in ID number order and display them with a total amount owed from all CreditCustomers.

c. Write an application named **CustomerDemo3** that uses an extension method for the CreditCustomer class. The method computes and returns a CreditCustomer's monthly payment due (1/24 of the balance). The application should allow the user to enter data for five CreditCustomers and then display all the data for each.

6. Create an application named **ShapesDemo** that creates several objects that descend from an abstract class called GeometricFigure. Each GeometricFigure includes a height, a width, and an area. Provide get and set accessors for each field except area; the area is computed and is read-only. Include an abstract method called ComputeArea() that computes the area of the GeometricFigure. Create three additional classes:

- A Rectangle is a GeometricFigure whose area is determined by multiplying width by height.

- A Square is a Rectangle in which the width and height are the same. Provide a constructor that accepts both height and width, forcing them to be equal if they are not. Provide a second constructor that accepts just one dimension and uses it for both height and width. The `Square` class uses the `Rectangle`'s `ComputeArea()` method.

- A `Triangle` is a `GeometricFigure` whose area is determined by multiplying the width by half the height.

In the `ShapesDemo` class, after each object is created, pass it to a method that accepts a `GeometricFigure` argument in which the figure's data is displayed. Change some dimensions of some of the figures and pass each to the display method again.

7. Create an application named **RecoveringDemo** that declares objects of three types: `Patient`, `Upholsterer`, and `FootballPlayer`. Create an interface named `IRecoverable` that contains a single method named `Recover()`. Create the classes named `Patient`, `Upholsterer`, and `FootballPlayer` so that each implements `IRecoverable`. Create each class's `Recover()` method to display an appropriate message. For example, the `Patient`'s `Recover()` method might display "I am getting better."

8. Create an application named **TurningDemo** that creates instances of four classes: `Page`, `Corner`, `Pancake`, and `Leaf`. Create an interface named `ITurnable` that contains a single method named `Turn()`. The classes named `Page`, `Corner`, `Pancake`, and `Leaf` implement `ITurnable`. Create each class's `Turn()` method to display an appropriate message. For example, the `Page`'s `Turn()` method might display "You turn a page in a book."

9. Write a program named **SalespersonDemo** that instantiates objects using classes named `RealEstateSalesperson` and `GirlScout`. Demonstrate that each object can use a `SalesSpeech()` method appropriately. Also, use a `MakeSale()` method two or three times with each object and display the final contents of each object's data fields. First, create an abstract class named `Salesperson`. Fields include first and last names; the `Salesperson` constructor requires both these values. Include properties for the fields. Include a method that returns a string that holds the `Salesperson`'s full name—the first and last names separated by a space. Then perform the following tasks:

- Create two child classes of `Salesperson`: `RealEstateSalesperson` and `GirlScout`. The `RealEstateSalesperson` class contains fields for total value sold in dollars and total commission earned (both of which are initialized to 0), and a commission rate field required by the class constructor. The `GirlScout` class includes a field to hold the number of boxes of cookies sold, which is initialized to 0. Include properties for every field.

- Create an interface named `ISellable` that contains two methods: `SalesSpeech()` and `MakeSale()`. In each `RealEstateSalesperson` and `GirlScout` class, implement `SalesSpeech()` to display an appropriate one- or two-sentence sales speech that the objects of the class could use.

In the RealEstateSalesperson class, implement the MakeSale() method to accept an integer dollar value for a house, add the value to the RealEstateSalesperson's total value sold, and compute the total commission earned. In the GirlScout class, implement the MakeSale() method to accept an integer representing the number of boxes of cookies sold and add it to the total field.

Debugging Exercises

1. Each of the following files in the Chapter.10 folder of your downloadable student files has syntax and/or logical errors. In each case, determine the problem and fix the program. After you correct the errors, save each file using the same filename preceded with *Fixed*. For example, DebugTen01.cs will become FixedDebugTen01.cs.

   a. DebugTen01.cs   c. DebugTen03.cs
   b. DebugTen02.cs   d. DebugTen04.cs

Case Problems

1. In Chapter 9, you created a Contestant class for the Greenville Idol competition. The class includes a contestant's name, talent code, and talent description. The competition has become so popular that separate contests with differing entry fees have been established for children, teenagers, and adults. Modify the Contestant class to contain a field that holds the entry fee for each category, and add get and set accessors.

   Extend the Contestant class to create three subclasses: ChildContestant, TeenContestant, and AdultContestant. Child contestants are 12 years old and younger, and their entry fee is $15. Teen contestants are between 13 and 17 years old inclusive, and their entry fee is $20. Adult contestants are 18 years old and older, and their entry fee is $30. In each subclass, set the entry fee field to the correct value and override the ToString() method to return a string that includes all the contestant data, including the age category and the entry fee.

   Modify the **GreenvilleRevenue** program so that it performs the following tasks:

   - The program prompts the user for the number of contestants in this year's competition, which must be between 0 and 30. The program continues to prompt the user until a valid value is entered.

   - The program prompts the user for names, ages, and talent codes for the contestants entered. Along with the prompt for a talent code, display a list of valid categories. Based on the age entered for each contestant, create an object of the correct type (adult, teen, or child), and store it in an array of Contestant objects.

- After data entry is complete, display the total expected revenue, which is the sum of the entry fees for the contestants.

- After data entry is complete, display the valid talent categories and then continuously prompt the user for talent codes and display all the data for all the contestants in each category. Display an appropriate message if the entered code is not a character or a valid code.

2. In Chapter 9, you created a Mural class for Marshall's Murals. The class holds a customer's name, a mural code, and a description. Now, add a field to the Mural class that holds a price. Extend the Mural class to create subclasses named InteriorMural and ExteriorMural, and place statements that determine a mural's price within these classes. (A mural's price depends on the month, as described in the case problem in Chapter 9.) Also create ToString() methods for these subclasses that return a string containing all the pertinent data for a mural.

   Modify the **MarshallsRevenue** program so that it performs the following tasks:

   - The program prompts the user for the month, the number of interior murals scheduled, and the number of exterior murals scheduled. In each case, the program continues to prompt the user until valid entries are made.

   - The program prompts the user for customer names and mural codes for interior and exterior murals. Along with the prompt for a mural code, display a list of valid categories.

   - After data entry is complete, display the total revenue of interior murals, exterior murals, and all murals.

   - After data entry is complete, the program displays the valid mural categories and then continuously prompts the user for codes and uses the ToString() method to display all the details for the murals in each category. Appropriate messages are displayed if the entered code is not a character or a valid code.

CHAPTER 11

Exception Handling

In this chapter you will:

◎ Learn about exceptions, the `Exception` class, and generating `SystemException`s

◎ Learn about traditional and object-oriented error-handling methods

◎ Use the `Exception` class's `ToString()` method and `Message` property

◎ Catch multiple exceptions

◎ Examine the structure of the `TryParse()` methods

◎ Use the `finally` block

◎ Handle exceptions thrown from outside methods

◎ Trace `Exception` objects through the call stack

◎ Create your own `Exception` classes

◎ Rethrow `Exception`s

While visiting Web sites, you have probably seen an unexpected and cryptic message that announces an error and then shuts down your browser immediately. Perhaps something similar has happened to you while using a piece of application software. Certainly, if you have worked your way through all of the programming exercises in this book, you have encountered such errors while running your own programs. A program that just stops is aggravating, especially when you lose data and the error message seems to indicate that the program "knows" what is causing the problem. You might grumble, "If the program knows what is wrong, why doesn't it just fix the problem?" In this chapter, you will learn how to handle these unexpected error conditions so your programs can be more user-friendly than those that simply shut down in the face of errors.

Understanding Exceptions

An **exception** is any error condition or unexpected behavior in an executing program. Exceptions are caused by errors in program logic or insufficient system resources. The programs you write can generate many types of potential exceptions, including when:

- Your program asks for user input, but the user enters invalid data.

- The program attempts to divide an integer by zero.

- You attempt to access an array with a subscript that is too large or too small.

- You calculate a value that is too large for the answer's variable type.

These errors are called exceptions because presumably they are not usual occurrences; they are "exceptional." The object-oriented techniques used to manage such errors make up the group of methods known as **exception handling**. If you do not handle an exception, the running program terminates abruptly.

Managing exceptions involves an oxymoron; you must expect the unexpected.

Errors you discover when compiling a program are not exceptions; only execution-time (also called *runtime*) errors are called exceptions.

In C#, all exceptions are objects that are instances of the Exception class or one of its derived classes. An exception condition generates an object that encapsulates information about the error. Like all other classes in the C# programming language, the Exception class is a descendent of the Object class. The Exception class has several descendent classes of its own, many with unusual names such as CodeDomSerializerException, SUDSParserException, and SoapException. Others have names that are more easily understood, such as IOException (for input and output errors), InvalidPrinterException (for when a user requests an invalid printer), and PathTooLongException (used when the path to a file contains more characters than a system allows). C# has more than 100 defined Exception subclasses; Table 11-1 lists just a few to give you an idea of the wide variety of circumstances they cover.

Class	Description
System.ArgumentException	Thrown when one of the arguments provided to a method is not valid
System.ArithmeticException	Thrown for errors in an arithmetic, casting, or conversion operation
System.ArrayTypeMismatchException	Thrown when an attempt is made to store an element of the wrong type within an array
System.Data.OperationAbortedException	Thrown when an ongoing operation is aborted by the user
System.Drawing.Printing. InvalidPrinterException	Thrown when you try to access a printer using printer settings that are not valid
System.FormatException	Thrown when the format of an argument does not meet the parameter specifications of the invoked method
System.IndexOutOfRangeException	Thrown when an attempt is made to access an element of an array with an index that is outside the bounds of the array; this class cannot be inherited
System.InvalidCastException	Thrown for an invalid casting or explicit conversion
System.InvalidOperationException	Thrown when a method call is invalid for the object's current state
System.IO.InvalidDataException	Thrown when a data stream is in an invalid format
System.IO.IOException	Thrown when an I/O error occurs
System.MemberAccessException	Thrown when an attempt to access a class member fails
System.NotImplementedException	Thrown when a requested method or operation is not implemented
System.NullReferenceException	Thrown when there is an attempt to dereference a null object reference
System.OperationCanceledException	Thrown in a thread upon cancellation of an operation that the thread was executing
System.OutOfMemoryException	Thrown when there is not enough memory to continue the execution of a program
System.RankException	Thrown when an array with the wrong number of dimensions is passed to a method
System.StackOverflowException	Thrown when the execution stack overflows because it contains too many nested method calls; this class cannot be inherited

Table 11-1   Selected C# Exception subclasses

Table 11-1 uses the term *thrown*, which is explained later in this chapter.

Most exceptions you will use derive from three classes:

- The predefined Common Language Runtime exception classes derived from SystemException

- The user-defined application exception classes you derive from ApplicationException

- The Exception class, which is the parent of SystemException and ApplicationException

Microsoft previously advised that you should create your own custom exceptions from the ApplicationException class. They have revised their thinking because in practice, they have not found the approach to be of significant value. For updates, visit *http://msdn.microsoft.com*.

Purposely Generating a SystemException

You can deliberately generate a SystemException by forcing a program to contain an error. As an example, in every programming language, it is illegal to divide an integer by zero because the operation is mathematically undefined. Consider the simple MilesPerGallon program in Figure 11-1, which prompts a user for two values and divides the first by the second. If the user enters nonzero integers, the program runs correctly and without incident. However, if the user enters 0 when prompted to enter gallons, division by 0 takes place and an error is generated. Figure 11-2 shows two executions of the program.

When you divide a floating-point value by 0 in C#, no exception occurs. Instead, C# assigns the special value Infinity to the result. Because floats and doubles are imprecise, dividing them by 0.000000… to an infinite number of decimal places approaches infinity mathematically.

```
using System;
class MilesPerGallon
{
    static void Main()
    {
        int milesDriven;
        int gallonsOfGas;
        int mpg;
        Console.Write("Enter miles driven ");
        milesDriven = Convert.ToInt32(Console.ReadLine());
        Console.Write("Enter gallons of gas purchased ");
        gallonsOfGas = Convert.ToInt32(Console.ReadLine());
        mpg = milesDriven / gallonsOfGas;
        Console.WriteLine("You got {0} miles per gallon", mpg);
    }
}
```

Figure 11-1   The MilesPerGallon program

```
C:\C#\Chapter.11>MilesPerGallon
Enter miles driven 300
Enter gallons of gas purchased 12
You got 25 miles per gallon

C:\C#\Chapter.11>MilesPerGallon
Enter miles driven 300
Enter gallons of gas purchased 0

Unhandled Exception: System.DivideByZeroException: Attempted to divide by zero.
    at MilesPerGallon.Main<>

C:\C#\Chapter.11>
```

Figure 11-2   Two executions of the `MilesPerGallon` program

When the user enters a 0 for gallons in the `MilesPerGallon` program, a dialog box reports that the application has stopped working and needs to close. Because this error is intentional for demonstration purposes, you can ignore the message by clicking the Close program button in the lower-right corner of the dialog box.

In the first execution of the `MilesPerGallon` program in Figure 11-2, the user entered two usable integers, and division was carried out successfully. However, in the second execution, the user entered 0 for gallons of gas, and the error message indicates that an unhandled exception named `System.DivideByZeroException` was created. The message gives further information ("Attempted to divide by zero."), and shows the method where the exception occurred—in `MilesPerGallon.Main()`.

The `DivideByZeroException` object was generated automatically by C#. It is an instance of the `DivideByZeroException` class that has four ancestors. It is a child of the `ArithmeticException` class, which descends from the `SystemException` class. The `SystemException` class derives from the `Exception` class, which is a child of the `Object` class.

Just because an exception occurs and an `Exception` object is created, you don't necessarily have to deal with it. In the `MilesPerGallon` class, you simply let the offending program terminate; that's why the error message in Figure 11-2 indicates that the `Exception` is "Unhandled." However, the termination of the program is abrupt and unforgiving. When a program divides two numbers, or even performs a more trivial task like playing a game, the user might be annoyed if the program ends abruptly. If the program is used for air-traffic control or to monitor a patient's vital statistics during surgery, an abrupt conclusion could be disastrous. Object-oriented error-handling techniques provide more elegant solutions than simply shutting down.

Programs that can handle exceptions appropriately are said to be more fault tolerant and robust than those that do not. **Fault-tolerant** applications are designed so that they continue to operate, possibly at a reduced level, when some part of the system fails. **Robustness** represents the degree to which a system is resilient to stress, maintaining correct functioning.

With exception handling, a program can continue after dealing with a problem. This is especially important in mission-critical applications. The term **mission critical** refers to any process that is crucial to an organization.

Watch the video *System Exceptions*.

508

You Do It

Purposely Causing Exceptions

C# generates SystemExceptions automatically under many circumstances. In the next steps, you purposely generate a SystemException by executing a program that provides multiple opportunities for Exceptions.

1. Start a new project named **ExceptionsOnPurpose**, and type the following program, which allows you to generate several different Exceptions.

```
using System;
class ExceptionsOnPurpose
{
    static void Main()
    {
        int answer;
        int result;
        int zero = 0;
```

(continues)

(continued)

```
        Console.Write("Enter an integer >> ");
        answer = Convert.ToInt32(Console.ReadLine());
        result = answer / zero;
        Console.WriteLine("The answer is " + answer);
    }
}
```

 You would never write a program that purposely divides by zero; you do so here to demonstrate C#'s exception-generating capabilities.

2. You cannot divide by the unnamed constant 0, nor can you change the variable `zero` to a named constant. In either case, the program will not compile because the compiler determines that division by zero will occur. As a variable, the compiler "trusts" that a legitimate value will be provided for `zero` before division occurs (although in this case, the trust was not warranted). Save the program, and compile it.

3. Execute the program several times using different input values and observe the results. Two windows appear with each execution. The first reports that Windows is collecting more information about the problem. This window is soon replaced with the one shown in Figure 11-3, which repeats that ExceptionsOnPurpose.exe has stopped working. If you were executing a professional application, you might be notified of a solution. Because you created this exception on purpose, just click the **Close program** button.

Figure 11-3   The error report window generated by an unhandled exception

(continues)

(continued)

Figure 11-4 shows three executions of the program during which the user typed the following:

- **seven**—This generates a System.FormatException, which occurs when the program tries to convert the input value to an integer, because letters are not allowed in integers.

- **7.7**—This also generates a System.FormatException because the decimal point is not allowed in an integer.

- **7**—This does not generate a System.FormatException, but instead causes a System.DivideByZeroException when the result is calculated.

Figure 11-4   Error messages generated by successive executions of the ExceptionsOnPurpose program

Understanding Traditional and Object-Oriented Error-Handling Methods

Programmers had to deal with error conditions long before object-oriented methods were conceived. For example, dividing by zero is an avoidable error for which programmers always have had to plan. If you simply check a variable's value with an `if` statement before attempting to divide it into another number, you can prevent the creation of an `Exception` object. For example, the following code uses a traditional `if` statement to check a variable to prevent division by zero.

```
if(gallonsOfGas != 0)
   mpg = milesDriven / gallonsOfGas;
else
   mpg = 0;
```

This code successfully prevents division by zero, but it does not really "handle an exception" because no `Exception` class object is created. The example code illustrates a perfectly legal and reasonable method of preventing division by zero, and it represents the most efficient method of handling the error if you think it will be a frequent problem. Because a program that contains this code does not have to instantiate an `Exception` object every time the user enters a 0 for the value of `gallonsOfGas`, the program saves time and computer memory. (Programmers say this program has little "overhead.") On the other hand, if you think dividing by zero will be infrequent—that is, the *exception* to the rule—then the decision will execute many times when it is not needed. In other words, if a user enters 0 for `gallonsOfGas` in only one case out of 1,000, then the `if` statement is executed unnecessarily 999 times. In that case, it is more efficient to eliminate the `if` test and instantiate an `Exception` object when needed.

The creators of C# define "infrequent" as an event that happens less than 30 percent of the time. That is, if you think an error will occur in less than 30 percent of all program executions, create an exception; if you think the error will occur more often, use traditional error checking. Of course, your boss or instructor might prefer a different percentage.

Exception handling is critical in operations that are prone to failure. For example, after you open a file, it might not exit, or when you attempt to connect to a remote server, the connection might be down.

Another advantage to using exception handling instead of decision making to control errors is that when a program's main logic is interrupted by a series of `if` statements and decisions that might detect errors, the program can become more complicated and difficult to understand. The object-oriented approach to error handling separates a program's main tasks from code that deals with rare exceptions.

Programmers use the phrase "sunny day case" to describe a scenario in which everything goes well and no errors occur.

Understanding Object-Oriented Exception-Handling Methods

Object-oriented exception handling uses three unique terms: *try*, *throw*, and *catch*.

- You "try" a procedure that may not complete correctly.

- A method that detects an error condition "throws" an exception.
- The block of code that processes the error "catches" the exception.

When you write a block of code in which something can go wrong, you can place the code in a **try block**, which consists of the following elements:

- The keyword try
- A pair of curly braces containing statements that might cause exceptions

You must code at least one catch block or finally block immediately following a try block. (You will learn about finally blocks later in this chapter.) Each **catch block** can "catch" one type of exception—that is, an Exception object or an object of one of its child classes. Programmers sometimes refer to a catch block as a *catch clause*. You create a catch block by typing the following elements:

- The keyword catch
- Parentheses containing an Exception type and, optionally, a name for an instance of the Exception type
- A pair of curly braces containing statements that deal with the error condition

Figure 11-5 shows the general format of a try...catch pair. The placeholder XxxException in the catch block represents the Exception class or any of its more specific subclasses. The placeholder XxxException is the data type of the anExceptionInstance object. A catch block looks a lot like a method named catch(), which takes an argument that is an instance of XxxException. However, it is not a method; it can catch only one object, it has no return type, and you can't call it directly.

As XxxException implies, Exception classes typically are created using Exception as the second half of the name, as in SystemException and ApplicationException. The compiler does not require this naming convention, but the convention does make Exception descendents easier to identify.

```
try
{
    // Any number of statements;
    // some might cause an exception
}
catch(XxxException anExceptionInstance)
{
    // Do something about it
}
// Statements here execute whether there was an exception or not
```

Figure 11-5   General form of a `try...catch` pair

You can place any number of statements in a `try` block, including those you know will never throw an exception. However, if any one of the statements you place within a `try` block does throw an exception, then the statements in the `catch` block will execute. If no exception occurs within the `try` block, then the `catch` block does not execute. Either way, the statements following the `catch` block execute normally.

For example, Figure 11-6 contains a program in which the statements that prompt for, accept, and use `gallonsOfGas` are encased in a `try` block. Figure 11-7 shows two executions of the program. In the first execution, a usable value is entered for `gallonsOfGas` and the program operates normally, bypassing the `catch` block. In the second execution, however, the user enters 0 for `gallonsOfGas`. When division is attempted, an `Exception` object is automatically created and thrown. The `catch` block catches the `Exception`, where it becomes known as `e`. (The shaded arrow in Figure 11-6 extends from where the exception is created and thrown to where it is caught.) The statements in the `catch` block set `mpg` to 0 and display a message. Whether the `catch` block executes or not, the final `WriteLine()` statement that follows the `catch` block's closing curly brace executes.

514

```
using System;
class MilesPerGallon2
{
    static void Main( )
    {
        int milesDriven;
        int gallonsOfGas;
        int mpg;
        try
        {
            Console.Write("Enter miles driven ");
            milesDriven = Convert.ToInt32(Console.ReadLine( ));
            Console.Write("Enter gallons of gas purchased ");
            gallonsOfGas = Convert.ToInt32(Console.ReadLine( ));
            mpg = milesDriven / gallonsOfGas;
        }

        catch(Exception e)
        {
            mpg = 0;
            Console.WriteLine("You attempted to divide by zero!");
        }
        Console.WriteLine("You got {0} miles per gallon", mpg);
    }
}
```

Figure 11-6   The MilesPerGallon2 program

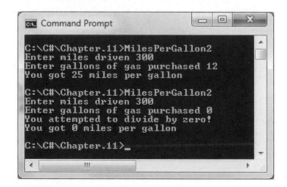

Figure 11-7   Two executions of the MilesPerGallon2 program

When you compile the program in Figure 11-6, you receive a warning that e is declared but never used. You can declare a variable to hold the thrown Exception object, but you do not want to use it in this example, so you can safely ignore the warning. If you do not want to use the caught Exception object within a catch block, then you do not have to provide an instance name for it. For example, in Figure 11-6, the catch clause could begin as follows:

```
catch(Exception)
```

In later examples in this chapter, the Exception object will be used to provide information. In those cases, it is required to have an identifier.

In the MilesPerGallon2 program, you could catch a more specific DivideByZeroException object instead of catching an Exception object. You will employ this technique later in the chapter. If you are working on a professional project, Microsoft recommends that you never use the general Exception class in a catch block.

In the application in Figure 11-6, the source of the exception and the catch block reside in the same method. Later in this chapter, you will learn that exceptions and their corresponding catch blocks frequently reside in separate methods.

Watch the video *Throwing and Catching Exceptions*.

TWO TRUTHS & A LIE

Understanding Traditional and Object-Oriented Error-Handling Methods

1. Before object-oriented methods were conceived, programmers had no way of handling unexpected conditions.

2. Using object-oriented techniques, when you write a block of code in which something can go wrong, you can place the code in a try block.

3. If a catch block executes, then an Exception must have been thrown.

The false statement is #1. Programmers had to deal with error conditions long before object-oriented methods were conceived.

You Do It

Handling Exceptions

You can handle exceptions by placing them in a `try` block and then catching any exceptions that are thrown from it.

1. Open the **ExceptionsOnPurpose** program if it is not still open. Change the class name to `ExceptionsOnPurpose2`, and immediately save the project as **ExceptionsOnPurpose2**.

2. In the `Main()` method, after the three variable declarations, enclose the next three statements in a `try` block as follows:

```
try
{
    Console.Write("Enter an integer >> ");
    answer = Convert.ToInt32(Console.ReadLine());
    result = answer / zero;
}
```

3. Following the `try` block (but before the statement that displays the answer), add a `catch` block that catches any thrown `Exception` object and displays its `Message` property:

```
catch(Exception e)
{
    Console.WriteLine(e.Message);
}
```

4. Save the program and compile it. You should receive a compiler error indicating that `answer` is an unassigned local variable. This error occurs at the last line of the program where `answer` is displayed. In the first version of this program, no such message appeared. However, now that the assignment to `answer` is within the `try` block, the compiler understands that an exception might be thrown, terminating the block before a valid value is assigned to `answer`. To eliminate this problem, initialize `answer` at its declaration:

```
int answer = 0;
```

5. Compile and execute the program again. Figure 11-8 shows three executions. The values typed by the user are the same as in Figure 11-4 in the previous "You Do It" section. However, the results are different in several significant ways:

(continues)

(continued)

- No error message window appears (as in Figure 11-3).
- The error messages displayed are cleaner and "friendlier" than the automatically generated versions in Figure 11-4.
- The program ends normally in each case, with the answer value displayed in a user-friendly manner.

Figure 11-8 Error messages generated by successive executions of the ExceptionsOnPurpose2 program

Using the Exception Class's ToString() Method and Message Property

When the MilesPerGallon2 program displays the error message ("You attempted to divide by zero!"), you actually cannot confirm from the message that division by zero was the source of the error. In reality, any Exception type generated within the try block of the program would be caught by the catch block in the method because the argument in the catch block is a general Exception, which is the parent class to all the Exception subtypes.

Instead of writing your own message, you can use the ToString() method that every Exception object inherits from the Object class. The Exception class overrides ToString() to provide a descriptive error message so a user can receive precise information about the nature of any Exception that is thrown. For example, Figure 11-9 shows a MilesPerGallon3 program. The shaded areas show the only changes from the MilesPerGallon2 program: the name of the class and the message that is displayed when an Exception is thrown. In this example, the ToString() method is used with the caught Exception e. Figure 11-10 shows an execution of the program in which the user enters 0 for gallonsOfGas.

You learned about overriding the Object class ToString() method in the chapter *Introduction to Inheritance*.

```
using System;
class MilesPerGallon3
{
    static void Main()
    {
        int milesDriven;
        int gallonsOfGas;
        int mpg;
        try
        {
            Console.Write("Enter miles driven ");
            milesDriven = Convert.ToInt32(Console.ReadLine());
            Console.Write("Enter gallons of gas purchased ");
            gallonsOfGas = Convert.ToInt32(Console.ReadLine());
            mpg = milesDriven / gallonsOfGas;
        }
        catch(Exception e)
        {
            mpg = 0;
            Console.WriteLine(e.ToString());
        }
        Console.WriteLine("You got {0} miles per gallon", mpg);
    }
}
```

Figure 11-9 The MilesPerGallon3 program

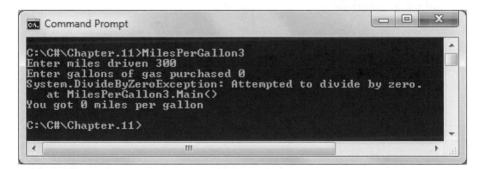

Figure 11-10 Execution of the MilesPerGallon3 program

The error message displayed in Figure 11-10 ("System.DivideByZeroException: Attempted to divide by zero.") is the same message that appeared in Figure 11-2 when you provided no exception handling. Therefore, you can assume that the operating system uses the same ToString() method you can use when displaying information about an Exception object. In the program in which you provided no exception handling, execution simply stopped; in this one, execution continues and the final output statement is displayed whether the user's input was usable or not. Programmers would say this new version of the program ended more "elegantly."

The Exception class also contains a read-only property named Message that contains useful information about an Exception object. For example, the program in Figure 11-11 contains just two shaded changes from the MilesPerGallon3 program: the class name and the use of the Message property in the statement that displays the error message in the catch block. The program produces the output shown in Figure 11-12. The value of e.Message is a string that is identical to the second part of the value returned by the ToString() method. You can guess that the DivideByZeroException class's ToString() method used in MilesPerGallon3 constructs its string from two parts: the return value of the getType() method (that indicates the name of the class) and the return value from the Message property.

```
using System;
class MilesPerGallon4
{
    static void Main()
    {
        int milesDriven;
        int gallonsOfGas;
        int mpg;
        try
        {
            Console.Write("Enter miles driven ");
            milesDriven = Convert.ToInt32(Console.ReadLine());
            Console.Write("Enter gallons of gas purchased ");
            gallonsOfGas = Convert.ToInt32(Console.ReadLine());
            mpg = milesDriven / gallonsOfGas;
        }
        catch(Exception e)
        {
            mpg = 0;
            Console.WriteLine(e.Message);
        }
        Console.WriteLine("You got {0} miles per gallon", mpg);
    }
}
```

Figure 11-11   The MilesPerGallon4 program

520

Figure 11-12 Execution of the MilesPerGallon4 program

TWO TRUTHS & A LIE

Using the Exception Class's ToString() Method and Message Property

1. Any Exception type generated within a try block in a program will be caught by a catch block that has an Exception type argument.

2. The Exception class overrides the Object class Description() method to provide a descriptive error message so a user can receive precise information about the nature of any Exception object that is thrown.

3. The Exception class contains a property named Message that contains useful information about an Exception.

The false statement is #2. The Exception class overrides the Object class ToString() method to provide a descriptive error message so a user can receive precise information about the nature of any Exception that is thrown.

Catching Multiple Exceptions

You can place as many statements as you need within a try block, and you can include as many catch blocks as you want to handle different Exception types. When a try block contains more than one statement, only the first error-generating statement throws an exception. As soon as the exception occurs, the logic transfers to the catch block, which leaves the rest of the statements in the try block unexecuted.

The set of **catch** blocks should cover all possible exceptions that the code in the **try** block might encounter. If an exception is thrown without a matching **catch** block, the program will terminate abruptly.

When an **Exception** object is thrown and multiple **catch** blocks are present, the **catch** blocks are examined in sequence until a match is found. The matching **catch** block then executes, and each remaining **catch** block is bypassed.

For example, consider the program in Figure 11-13. The **Main()** method in the **TwoErrors** class potentially throws two types of **Exceptions**—a **DivideByZeroException** and an **IndexOutOfRangeException**. (An **IndexOutOfRangeException** occurs when an array subscript is not within the allowed range. In the **TwoErrors** program, the array has only three elements, but 13 is used as a subscript.)

```
using System;
class TwoErrors
{
    static void Main( )
    {
        int num = 13, denom = 0, result;
        int[ ] array = {22, 33, 44};
        try
        {
            result = num / denom;
            result = array[num];
        }
        catch(DivideByZeroException error)
        {
            Console.WriteLine("In first catch block: ");
            Console.WriteLine(error.Message);
        }
        catch(IndexOutOfRangeException error)
        {
            Console.WriteLine("In second catch block: ");
            Console.WriteLine(error.Message);
        }
    }
}
```

Figure 11-13 The TwoErrors program with two catch blocks

The TwoErrors class declares three integers and an integer array with three elements. In the Main() method, the try block executes, and at the first statement within the try block, an exception occurs because the denom in the division problem is zero. The try block is abandoned and control transfers to the first catch block. Integer division by zero causes a DivideByZeroException, and because the first catch block receives that type of Exception, the message "In first catch block" appears along with the Message value of the Exception object. In this example, the second try statement is never attempted, and the second catch block is skipped. Figure 11-14 shows the output.

Figure 11-14   Output of the TwoErrors program

If you reverse the two statements within the try block in the TwoErrors program, the process changes. If you use the try block in Figure 11-15, division by zero does not take place because the invalid array access throws an exception first.

```
using System;
class TwoErrors2
{
    static void Main( )
    {
        int num = 13, denom = 0, result;
        int[ ] array = {22, 33, 44};
        try
        {
            result = array[num];
            result = num / denom;
        }
        catch(DivideByZeroException error)
        {
            Console.WriteLine("In first catch block: ");
            Console.WriteLine(error.Message);
        }
        catch(IndexOutOfRangeException error)
        {
            Console.WriteLine("In second catch block: ");
            Console.WriteLine(error.Message);
        }
    }
}
```

Figure 11-15   The TwoErrors2 program

The first statement within the try block in Figure 11-15 attempts to access element 13 of a three-element array, so the program throws an IndexOutOfRangeException. The try block is abandoned, and the first catch block is examined and found unsuitable because the Exception object is of the wrong type—it is not a DivideByZeroException object. The program logic proceeds to the second catch block, whose IndexOutOfRangeException argument type is a match for the thrown Exception type. The message "In second catch block" and the Exception's Message value are therefore displayed. Figure 11-16 shows the output.

Command Prompt

```
C:\C#\Chapter.11>TwoErrors2
In second catch block:
Index was outside the bounds of the array.

C:\C#\Chapter.11>
```

Figure 11-16   Output of the `TwoErrors2` program

Sometimes you want to execute the same code, no matter which `Exception` type occurs. For example, in each version of the `TwoErrors` program, each of the two `catch` blocks displays a unique message. Instead, you might want both the `DivideByZeroException catch` block and the `IndexOutOfRangeException catch` block to use the thrown `Exception`'s `Message` field. Because `DivideByZeroExceptions` and `IndexOutOfRangeExceptions` both are subclasses of `Exception`, you can rewrite the `TwoErrors` class as shown in Figure 11-17 and include only one `Exception catch` block that catches any type of `Exception`.

```csharp
using System;
class TwoErrors3
{
    static void Main()
    {
        int num = 13, denom = 0, result;
        int[] array = {22, 33, 44};
        try
        {
            result = array[num];
            result = num / denom;
        }
        catch(Exception error)
        {
            Console.WriteLine(error.Message);
        }
    }
}
```

Figure 11-17   The `TwoErrors3` class with one `catch` block

As an alternative to using a single `catch` block for multiple `Exception` types that require the same action, as in Figure 11-17, you could create the class to have separate `catch` blocks, each of which calls the same method that contains the desired action.

The `catch` block in Figure 11-17 accepts a more generic `Exception` type than might be thrown by either statement in the `try` block, so the generic `catch` block can act as a "catch-all" block. That is, when either a division arithmetic error or an array error occurs, the thrown error is "promoted" to an Exception error in the catch block. Through inheritance, DivideByZeroExceptions and IndexOutOfRangeExceptions are Exceptions.

 As stated earlier, Microsoft recommends that a catch block should not handle general Exceptions. They say that if you cannot predict all possible causes of an exception, you should allow the application to terminate instead of handling the exception. Otherwise, it is easier for malicious code to exploit the resulting application state.

Although a block of code can throw any number of Exception types, many developers believe that it is poor style for a block or method to throw more than three or four types. If it does, one of the following conditions might be true:

- Perhaps the code block or method is trying to accomplish too many diverse tasks and should be broken up into smaller blocks or methods.

- Perhaps the Exception types thrown are too specific and should be generalized, as they are in the TwoErrors3 program in Figure 11-17.

When you list multiple catch blocks following a try block, you must be careful that some catch blocks don't become unreachable. **Unreachable** blocks contain statements that can never execute under any circumstances because the program logic "can't get there." Programmers also call unreachable code **dead code**.

For example, if successive catch blocks catch an Exception and a DivideByZeroException, then even DivideByZeroExceptions will be caught by the Exception catch. The DivideByZeroException catch block is unreachable because the more general Exception catch block is in its way, and therefore the class will not compile.

TWO TRUTHS & A LIE

Catching Multiple Exceptions

1. If you try more than one statement in a block, each error-generating statement throws an Exception.
2. You can write catch blocks that catch multiple Exception types.
3. When you list multiple catch blocks following a try block, you must be careful that some catch blocks don't become unreachable.

The false statement is #1. If you try more than one statement in a block, only the first error-generating statement throws an Exception.

You Do It

Catching Multiple Exception Types

In this section, you instigate multiple outcomes by providing multiple `catch` blocks for code in a `try` block.

1. Open the **ExceptionsOnPurpose2** program if it is not still open. Change the class name to `ExceptionsOnPurpose3`, and immediately save the project as **ExceptionsOnPurpose3**.

2. Replace the existing generic `catch` block with two `catch` blocks. (The statement that displays the answer still follows these `catch` blocks.) The first catches any `FormatException` and displays a short message. The second catches a `DivideByZeroException` and displays a much longer message.

```
catch(FormatException e)
{
    Console.WriteLine("You did not enter an integer");
}
catch(DivideByZeroException e)
{
    Console.WriteLine("This is not your fault.");
    Console.WriteLine("You entered the integer correctly.");
    Console.WriteLine("The program divides by zero.");
}
```

3. Save the program and compile it. When you execute the program and enter a value that is not an integer, the first `catch` block executes. When you enter an integer so that the program can proceed to the statement that divides by 0, the second `catch` block executes. Figure 11-18 shows two typical executions of the program.

(continues)

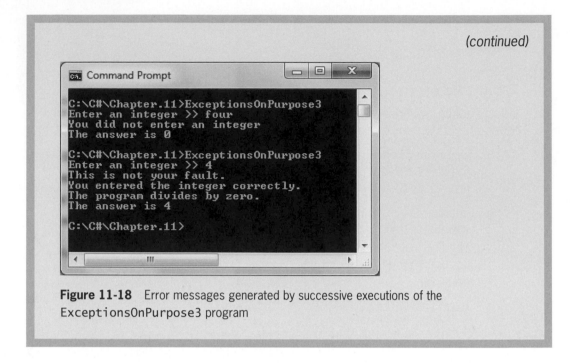

(continued)

Figure 11-18   Error messages generated by successive executions of the ExceptionsOnPurpose3 program

Examining the Structure of the `TryParse()` Methods

In Chapter 8, you learned about the `TryParse()` methods that you can use to convert string data to another data type, such as `int`, `double`, or `bool`, without fear of generating an exception. A typical `TryParse()` statement might be as follows:

```
if(!int.TryParse(inputString, out number)
    number = DEFAULT_VALUE;
```

This statement uses the `int` version of the method. The first argument is the string that you want to convert to a number, and the second argument is an `out` parameter that receives the result if the conversion is successful, or 0 if it is not. Each of the `TryParse()` methods returns a Boolean value that indicates whether the conversion was successful. In the preceding example, the variable `number` is assigned a constant `DEFAULT_VALUE` if the method returns `false`.

Suppose that no `TryParse()` method existed to convert a string to an integer safely. Using what you have learned so far in this chapter, you could now write your own method. The method handles the exception it might generate so that when a client uses the method, the client doesn't have to be concerned with exception handling. Figure 11-19 shows a usable method.

```
public static bool TryParse(string inputString, out int number)
{
    bool wasSuccessful = true;
    try
    {
        number = Convert.ToInt32(inputString);
    }
    catch(FormatException e)
    {
        wasSuccessful = false;
        number = 0;
    }
    return wasSuccessful;
}
```

Figure 11-19   A possible TryParse() method version

The TryParse() method in Figure 11-19 is public so that other classes can use it and static so that no object of its class needs to be instantiated. The method accepts a string and an out parameter that can hold the string's converted value. A bool variable named wasSuccessful is set to true and then conversion is attempted. If the Convert.ToInt32() method works correctly, the variable number accepts the converted value. However, if a FormatException object is thrown, wasSuccessful is set to false and 0 is assigned to number. Whether an exception is thrown or not, the value of wasSuccessful is returned.

The creators of C# wrote code similar to that in Figure 11-19 when they created the TryParse() method for the Integer class. They may have included some differences –for example, they probably gave their variables different identifiers, and they might have reversed the positions of the statements in the catch block that set the Boolean value and the integer value, but the basic structure of the method must be similar. If no TryParse() method existed, you could write one for yourself, but the method is a convenience that already exists. As you continue to study programming, you might develop a method that would be convenient for others, and you might be rewarded in seeing your method used by other developers.

Your downloadable Student Data Files contain a program named TestTryParse.cs that can be used to test the TryParse() method.

TWO TRUTHS & A LIE

Examining the Structure of the `TryParse()` Methods

1. The `TryParse()` method uses an out parameter.

2. The `TryParse()` method employs exception handling.

3. The `TryParse()` method must be used within a `try` block.

The false statement is #3. The `TryParse()` method contains a `try` block, but you don't need to use the method in a `try` block because it handles its own exception.

Using the `finally` Block

When you have actions to perform at the end of a `try...catch` sequence, you can use a **`finally` block**, which executes whether the `try` block identifies any exceptions or not. Typically, you use the `finally` block to perform clean-up tasks that must occur, regardless of whether any errors occurred or were caught. Figure 11-20 shows the format of a `try...catch` sequence that uses a `finally` block.

```
try
{
    // Statements that might cause an Exception
}
catch(SomeException anExceptionInstance)
{
    // What to do about it
}
finally
{
    // Statements here execute
    // whether an Exception occurred or not
}
```

Figure 11-20   General form of a `try...catch` block with a `finally` block

At first glance, it seems as though the `finally` block serves no purpose. When a `try` block works without error, control passes to the statements that come after the `catch` block. Additionally, if the `try` code fails and throws an `Exception` object that is caught, then the `catch` block executes and control again passes to any statements that are coded after the `catch` block. Therefore, it seems as though the statements after the `catch` block always execute, so there is no need to place any statements within a special `finally` block. However, statements after the `catch` block might never execute for at least two reasons:

- An `Exception` for which you did not plan might occur, terminating the program.
- The `try` or `catch` block might contain a statement that terminates the application.

You can terminate an application with a statement such as `Environment.Exit(0);`. The `Environment.Exit()` method is part of the `System` namespace. It terminates a program and passes the argument (which can be any integer) to the operating system. You also might exit a `catch` block with a `break` statement or a `return` statement. You encountered `break` statements when you learned about the `switch` statement, and you learned about `return` statements when you studied methods.

The possibility exists that a `try` block might throw an `Exception` for which you did not provide a `catch`. After all, exceptions occur all the time without your handling them, as you saw in the first `MilesPerGallon` program at the beginning of this chapter. In case of an unhandled exception, program execution stops immediately, sending the error to the operating system for handling and abandoning the current method. Likewise, if the `try` block contains an exit statement, execution stops immediately. When you include a `finally` block, you are assured that its enclosed statements will execute before the program is abandoned, even if the method concludes prematurely.

For example, the `finally` block is used frequently with file input and output to ensure that open files are closed. You will learn more about writing to and reading from data files in a later chapter. For now, however, consider the format shown in Figure 11-21, which represents part of the logic for a typical file-handling program. The `catch` block was written to catch an `IOException`, which is the type of `Exception` automatically generated if there is a problem opening a file, reading data from a file, or writing to a file.

```
try
{
    // Open the file
    // Read the file
    // Place the file data in an array
    // Calculate an average from the data
    // Display the average
}
catch(IOException e)
{
    // Issue an error message
    // Exit
}
finally
{
    // If the file is open, close it
}
```

Figure 11-21   Format of code that tries reading a file and handles an exception

The pseudocode in Figure 11-21 handles any file problems. However, because the application uses an array (see the statement "Place the file data in an array") and performs division (see the statement "Calculate an average…"), an uncaught exception could occur even though the file opened successfully. In such an event, you would want to close the file before proceeding. By using the `finally` block, you ensure that the file is closed, because the code in the `finally` block executes before the uncaught exception returns control to the operating system. The code in the `finally` block executes no matter which of the following outcomes of the `try` block occurs:

- The `try` ends normally.

- The `try` ends abnormally and the `catch` executes.

- The `try` ends abnormally and the `catch` does not execute. For example, an exception might cause the method to abandon prematurely—perhaps the array is not large enough to hold the data, or calculating the average results in division by 0. These exceptions do not allow the `try` block to finish, nor do they cause the `catch` block to execute.

If an application might throw several types of exceptions, you can try some code, catch the possible exception, try some more code, catch the possible exception, and so on. Usually, however, the superior approach is to try all the statements that might throw exceptions, then include all the needed `catch` blocks and an optional `finally` block. This is the approach shown in Figure 11-21, and it usually results in logic that is easier to follow.

You often can avoid using a `finally` block, but you would need repetitious code. For example, instead of using the `finally` block in the pseudocode in Figure 11-21, you could insert the statement "If the file is open, close it" as both the last statement in the `try` block and the second-to-last statement in the `catch` block, just before the program exits. However, writing code just once in a `finally` block is clearer and less prone to error.

Java and C++ provide `try` and `catch` blocks. Java also provides a `finally` block, but C++ does not.

Many well-designed programs that try code do not include `catch` blocks; instead, they contain only `try-finally` pairs. The `finally` block is used to release resources that other applications might be waiting for, such as database connections.

TWO TRUTHS & A LIE

Using the `finally` Block

1. When a `finally` block follows a `try` block, it executes whether the `try` block identifies any `Exceptions` or not.

2. Typically, you use a `finally` block to perform clean-up tasks that must occur after an `Exception` has been thrown and caught.

3. Statements that follow a `try...catch` pair might never execute because an unplanned `Exception` might occur, or the `try` or `catch` block might contain a statement that quits the application.

The false statement is #2. Typically, you use a `finally` block to perform clean-up tasks that must occur, regardless of whether any errors occurred or were caught.

Handling Exceptions Thrown from Outside Methods

An advantage of using object-oriented exception-handling techniques is the ability to deal with exceptions appropriately as you decide how to handle them. When methods from other classes throw exceptions, the methods don't have to catch them; instead, your calling program can catch them, and you can decide what to do.

For example, suppose that you prompt a user to enter a value at the console and then call the `Convert.ToInt32()` method to convert the input to an integer with a statement such as the following:

```
int answer = Convert.ToInt32(Console.ReadLine());
```

If the user enters a noninteger value, a `FormatException` is generated from the `Convert.ToInt32()` method, but it is not caught and handled there. Instead, your program can catch the exception and you can take appropriate action for your specific application. For example, you might want to force the user to reenter a value, but a different program might force the value to a default value or display an error message and terminate the program. This flexibility is an advantage when you need to create specific reactions to thrown exceptions. In many cases, you want a method to check for errors, but you do not want to require the method to handle an error if it finds one. Just as a police officer can deal with a speeding driver differently depending on circumstances, you can react to exceptions specifically for your current purposes.

When you design classes containing methods that have statements that might throw exceptions, you most frequently should create the methods so they throw the Exception object but do not handle it. Handling an exception usually should be left to the client—the program that uses your class—so the exception can be handled in an appropriate way for the application.

For example, consider the very brief PriceList class in Figure 11-22. The class contains a list of prices and a single method that displays one price based on a parameter subscript value. Because the DisplayPrice() method uses an array, an IndexOutOfRangeException might be thrown. However, the DisplayPrice() method does not handle the potential exception.

```
class PriceList
{
    private static double[] price = {15.99, 27.88, 34.56, 45.89};
    public static void DisplayPrice(int item)
    {
        Console.WriteLine("The price is " +
            price[item].ToString("C"));
    }
}
```

Figure 11-22   The PriceList class

Figure 11-23 shows an application that uses the DisplayPrice() method. It calls the method in a try block and handles an IndexOutOfRangeException by displaying a price of $0. Figure 11-24 shows the output when a user enters an invalid item number.

```
using System;
class PriceListApplication1
{
    static void Main()
    {
        int item;
        try
        {
            Console.Write("Enter an item number >> ");
            item = Convert.ToInt32(Console.ReadLine());
            PriceList.DisplayPrice(item);
        }
        catch(IndexOutOfRangeException e)
        {
            Console.WriteLine(e.Message + " The price is $0");
        }
    }
}
```

Figure 11-23   The PriceListApplication1 program

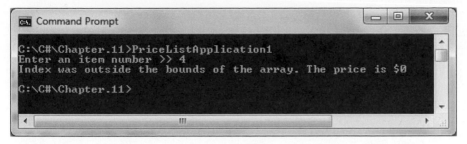

Figure 11-24 Output of the `PriceListApplication1` program when a user enters an invalid item number

Figure 11-25 shows a different application that uses the same `PriceList` class, but handles the exception differently. In this case, the programmer wanted the user to keep responding until a correct entry was made. If an `IndexOutOfRangeException` is thrown from the `try` block, the `try` block is abandoned, `isGoodItem` is not set to `true`, and the `catch` block executes. Because `isGoodItem` remains `false`, the `while` loop continues to execute. Only when the first three statements in the `try` block are successful does the last statement execute, changing `isGoodItem` to `true` and ending the loop repetitions. Because the `DisplayPrice()` method in the `PriceList` class was written to throw an `Exception` but not handle it, the programmer of `PriceListApplication2` could handle the `Exception` in a totally different manner from the way it was handled in `PriceListApplication1`. Figure 11-26 shows a typical execution of this program.

```
using System;
class PriceListApplication2
{
    static void Main()
    {
        int item = 0;
        bool isGoodItem = false;
        while(!isGoodItem)
        {
            try
            {
                Console.Write("Enter an item number >> "");
                item = Convert.ToInt32(Console.ReadLine());
                PriceList.DisplayPrice(item);
                isGoodItem = true;
            }
        }
```

Figure 11-25 The `PriceListApplication2` program *(continues)*

(continued)

```
        catch(IndexOutOfRangeException e)
        {
           Console.WriteLine("You must enter a number less " +
              "than 4");
           Console.WriteLine("Please reenter item number ");
        }
     }
     Console.WriteLine("Thank you");
   }
}
```

Figure 11-25   The PriceListApplication2 program

Figure 11-26   Output of the PriceListApplication2 program when a user enters an invalid item number several times

> **TWO TRUTHS & A LIE**
>
> ## Handling Exceptions Thrown from Outside Methods
>
> 1. When methods from other classes throw exceptions, the methods don't have to catch them; instead, your calling program can catch them, and you can decide what to do.
>
> 2. Often, you don't want a method to handle its own exception; in many cases, you want the method to check for errors, but you do not want to require a method to handle an error if it finds one.
>
> 3. When you design classes containing methods that have statements that might throw exceptions, you almost always should make sure your class handles each exception appropriately.
>
> The false statement is #3. When you design classes containing methods that have statements that might throw Exceptions, you most frequently should create the methods so they throw the exception but do not handle it.

Tracing Exception Objects Through the Call Stack

When one method calls another, the computer's operating system must keep track of where the method call came from, and program control must return to the calling method when the called method is complete. For example, if MethodA() calls MethodB(), the operating system has to "remember" to return to MethodA() when MethodB() ends. Similarly, if MethodB() calls MethodC(), then while MethodC() is executing, the computer needs to "remember" that it will return to MethodB() and eventually to MethodA(). The memory location where the computer stores the list of locations to which the system must return is known as the **call stack**.

If a method throws an exception and does not catch it, then the exception is thrown to the next method "up" the call stack; in other words, it is thrown to the method that called the offending method. Consider this sequence of events:

1. MethodA() calls MethodB().
2. MethodB() calls MethodC().
3. MethodC() throws an Exception.
4. C# looks first for a catch block in MethodC().

5. If none exists, then C# looks for the same thing in MethodB().

6. If MethodB() does not have a catch block for the Exception, then C# looks to MethodA().

7. If MethodA() doesn't catch the Exception, then the program terminates and the operating system displays an error message.

This system of passing an exception through the chain of calling methods is called **propagating the exception**. It has great advantages because it allows your methods to handle exceptions more appropriately. However, a program that uses several classes makes it difficult for the programmer to locate the original source of an exception.

You already have used the Message property to obtain information about an Exception object. The StackTrace property is another useful Exception property. When you catch an Exception, you can display the value of StackTrace to provide a list of methods in the call stack so you can determine the location where the Exception object was created.

The StackTrace property can be a useful debugging tool. When your program stops abruptly, it is helpful to discover the method in which the exception occurred. Often, you do not want to display a StackTrace property in a finished program; the typical user has no interest in the cryptic messages that would appear. However, while you are developing a program, using StackTrace can help you diagnose problems.

A Case Study: Using StackTrace

As an example of when StackTrace can be useful, consider the Tax class in Figure 11-27. Suppose that your company has created or purchased this class to make it easy to calculate tax rates on products sold. For simplicity, assume that only two tax rates are in effect—6 percent for sales of $20 or less and 7 percent for sales over $20. The Tax class would be useful for anyone who wrote a program involving product sales, except for one flaw: in the shaded statement, the subscript is erroneously set to 2 instead of 1 for the higher tax rate. If this subscript is used with the taxRate array in the next statement, it will be out of bounds.

```
class Tax
{
    private static double[] taxRate = {0.06, 0.07};
    private static double CUTOFF = 20.00;
    public static double DetermineTaxRate(double price)
    {
        int subscript;
        double rate;
        if(price <= CUTOFF)
            subscript = 0;
        else
            subscript = 2;
        rate = taxRate[subscript];
        return rate;
    }
}
```

> **Don't Do It**
> This mistake is intentional.

Figure 11-27 The Tax class

Assume that your company has also created a revised `PriceList` class, as shown in Figure 11-28. This class is similar to the one in Figure 11-22, except that it includes a tax calculation and calls the `DetermineTaxRate()` method in the shaded statement.

```
class PriceList
{
    private static double[] price = {15.99, 27.88, 34.56, 45.89};
    public static void DisplayPrice(int item)
    {
        double tax;
        double total;
        double pr;
        pr = price[item];
        tax = pr * Tax.DetermineTaxRate(pr);
        total = pr + tax;
        Console.WriteLine("The total price is " +
            total.ToString("C"));
    }
}
```

Figure 11-28 The `PriceList` class that includes a call to the `Tax` class method `DetermineTaxRate()`

Suppose that you write the application shown in Figure 11-29. Your application is similar to the price list applications created earlier in this chapter, including a call to `PriceList.DisplayPrice()`. As in `PriceListApplication1` and `PriceListApplication2`, your new program tries the data entry and display statement and then catches an exception. When you run the program using what you know to be a good item number, as in Figure 11-30, you are surprised to see the shaded "Error!" message you have coded in the catch block. In the earlier examples that used PriceList.DisplayPrice(), using an item number 1 would have resulted in a successful program execution.

```csharp
using System;
class PriceListApplication3
{
    static void Main()
    {
        int item;
        try
        {
            Console.Write("Enter an item number >> ");
            item = Convert.ToInt32(Console.ReadLine());
            PriceList.DisplayPrice(item);
        }
        catch(Exception e)
        {
            Console.WriteLine("Error!");
        }
    }
}
```

Figure 11-29   The PriceListApplication3 class

When you compile the program in Figure 11-29, you receive a warning that variable e is declared but never used. If you omit the name e from the catch block, the application will execute identically.

Figure 11-30   Execution of the PriceListApplication3 program when a user enters 1 for the item number

To attempt to discover what caused the "Error!" message, you can replace the statement that writes it as follows:

```csharp
Console.WriteLine(e.Message);
```

When the statement to display e.Message is added to the price list program, a warning that e is never used no longer appears when the program is compiled.

However, when you execute the program with this modification, you receive the output in Figure 11-31, indicating that the index is out of the bounds of the array. You are puzzled because you know 1 is a valid item number for the price array, and it should not be considered out of bounds.

Figure 11-31   Execution of the modified price list application in which e.Message is displayed in the catch block

Finally, you decide to replace the WriteLine() argument in the catch block statement with a StackTrace call, as follows:

```
Console.WriteLine(e.StackTrace);
```

The output is shown in Figure 11-32. You can see from the list of methods that the error in your application came from PriceList.DisplayPrice(), which in turn came from Tax.DetermineTaxRate(). You might have not even considered that the Tax class could have been the source of the problem. If you work in a small organization, you can look at the code yourself and fix it. If you work in a larger organization or you purchased the class from an outside vendor, you can contact the programmer who created the class for assistance.

Figure 11-32   Execution of the modified price list application in which e.StackTrace is displayed in the catch block

The classes in this example were small to help you easily follow the discussion. However, a real-world application might have many more classes that contain many more methods, and so using StackTrace would become increasingly beneficial. In a large system of programs, you might find it useful to locate StackTrace calls strategically throughout the programs while testing them, and then remove them or comment them out when the programs are complete.

 Watch the video *Tracing Exceptions Through the Call Stack*.

TWO TRUTHS & A LIE

Tracing Exception Objects Through the Call Stack

1. The memory location where the computer stores the list of locations to which the system must return after a series of method calls is known as the stack trace.

2. If a method throws an exception and does not catch it, then the exception is thrown to the method that called the offending method.

3. When you catch an Exception object, you can output the value of StackTrace to display a list of methods in the call stack so you can determine the location of the error.

The false statement is #1. The memory location where the computer stores the list of locations to which the system must return after a series of method calls is known as the call stack.

Creating Your Own Exception Classes

C# provides more than 100 categories of Exceptions that you can throw in your programs. However, C#'s creators could not predict every condition that might be an exception in the programs you write. For example, you might want to declare an Exception when your bank balance is negative or when an outside party attempts to access your e-mail account. Most organizations have specific rules for exceptional data, such as "an employee number must not exceed three digits" or "an hourly salary must not be less than the legal minimum wage." Of course, you can handle these potential error situations with if statements, but you also can create your own Exception subclasses.

To create your own Exception type from which you can instantiate throwable objects, you can extend the ApplicationException class, which is a subclass of Exception, or you can extend `Exception`. As you saw earlier in the chapter, Microsoft's advice on this matter has changed over time. Although you might see extensions of `ApplicationException` in classes written by others, the current advice is simply to derive your own classes from `Exception`. Either approach will produce workable programs.

Figure 11-33 shows a `NegativeBalanceException` class that extends `Exception`. This class passes an appropriate `string` message to its parent's constructor. If you create an `Exception` object and display its `Message` property, you will see the message "Error in the application." When the `NegativeBalanceException` constructor passes the string "Bank balance is negative." to its parent's constructor, the `Message` property will hold this more descriptive message. The C# documentation recommends that you create all `Exception` subclass messages to be grammatically correct, complete sentences ending in a period.

```
class NegativeBalanceException : Exception
{
    private static string msg = "Bank balance is negative. ";
    public NegativeBalanceException() : base(msg)
    {
    }
}
```

Figure 11-33 The `NegativeBalanceException` class

When you create a `BankAccount` class like the one shown in Figure 11-34, you can create the `Balance` property set accessor to throw a `NegativeBalanceException` when a client attempts to set the balance to be negative.

Instead of creating the **nbe** object in the `Balance` property in Figure 11-34, you could code the following statement, which creates and throws an anonymous `NegativeBalanceException` in a single step:

```
throw(new NegativeBalanceException());
```

Figure 11-35 shows a program that attempts to set a `BankAccount` balance to a negative value in the shaded statement. When the `BankAccount` class's `Balance` set accessor throws the `NegativeBalanceException`, the `catch` block in the `TryBankAccount` program executes, displaying both the `NegativeBalanceException` `Message` and the value of `StackTrace`. Figure 11-36 shows the output.

```
class BankAccount
{
   private double balance;
   public int AccountNum {get; set;}
   public double Balance
   {
      get
      {
         return balance;
      }
      set
      {
         if(value < 0)
         {
            NegativeBalanceException nbe =
               new NegativeBalanceException();
            throw(nbe);
         }
         balance = value;
      }
   }
}
```

Figure 11-34 The BankAccount class

```
using System;
class TryBankAccount
{
   static void Main()
   {
      BankAccount acct = new BankAccount();
      try
      {
         acct.AccountNum = 1234;
         acct.Balance = -1000;
      }
      catch(NegativeBalanceException e)
      {
         Console.WriteLine(e.Message);
         Console.WriteLine(e.StackTrace);
      }
   }
}
```

Figure 11-35 The TryBankAccount program

Figure 11-36 Output of the `TryBankAccount` program

In the error message in Figure 11-36, notice that the `set` accessor for the `Balance` property is known internally as `set_Balance`. You can guess that the `set` accessor for the `AccountNum` property is known as `set_AccountNum`.

The `StackTrace` begins at the point where an `Exception` is thrown, not where it is instantiated. This consideration makes a difference when you create an `Exception` in a class and throw it from multiple methods.

`Exception`s can be particularly useful when you throw them from constructors. Constructors do not have a return type, so they have no other way to send information back to the calling method.

In C#, you can't throw an object unless it is an `Exception` or a descendent of the `Exception` class. In other words, you cannot throw a **double** or a **BankAccount**. However, you can throw any type of `Exception` at any time, not just `Exception`s of your own creation. For example, within any program you can code any of the following:

```
throw(new ApplicationException());
throw(new IndexOutOfRangeException());
throw(new Exception());
```

Of course, you should not throw an `IndexOutOfRangeException` when you encounter division by 0 or data of an incorrect type; you should use it only when an index (subscript) is too high or too low. However, if a built-in `Exception` type is appropriate and suits your needs, you should use it. You should not create an excessive number of special `Exception` types for your classes, especially if the C# development environment already contains an `Exception` type that accurately describes the error. Extra `Exception` types add a level of complexity for other programmers who will use your classes. Nevertheless, when appropriate, creating a specialized `Exception` class is an elegant way for you to take care of error situations. `Exception`s allow you to separate your error code from the usual, nonexceptional sequence of events and allow for errors to be passed up the stack and traced.

TWO TRUTHS & A LIE

Creating Your Own Exception Classes

1. To create your own Exception types whose objects you can throw, you can extend the ApplicationException class or the Exception class.

2. In C#, you can throw any object that you create if it is appropriate for the application.

3. You can throw any type of Exception at any time—both those that are already created as part of C# and those of your own creation.

The false statement is #2. In C#, you can't throw an object unless it is an Exception or a descendent of the Exception class.

Rethrowing an Exception

When you write a method that catches an exception, your method does not have to handle it. Instead, you might choose to **rethrow the exception** to the method that called your method. Then you can let the calling method handle the problem.

Within a catch block, you can rethrow an unnamed exception that was caught by using the keyword throw with no object after it. For example, Figure 11-37 shows a class that contains four methods. In this program, the following sequence of events takes place:

1. The Main() method calls MethodA().

2. MethodA() calls MethodB().

3. MethodB() calls MethodC().

4. MethodC() throws an Exception.

5. When MethodB() catches the Exception, it does not handle the Exception; instead, it throws the Exception back to MethodA().

6. MethodA() catches the Exception, but does not handle it either. Instead, MethodA() throws the Exception back to the Main() method.

7. The Exception is caught in the Main() method, where the message that was created in MethodC() is finally displayed.

Figure 11-38 shows the execution of the program.

```
using System;
class ReThrowDemo
{
   static void Main()
   {
      try
      {
         Console.WriteLine("Trying in Main() method");
         MethodA();
      }
      catch(Exception ae)
      {
         Console.WriteLine("Caught in Main() method --\n   {0}",
            ae.Message);
      }
      Console.WriteLine("Main() method is done");
   }
   private static void MethodA()
   {
      try
      {
         Console.WriteLine("Trying in method A");
         MethodB();
      }
      catch(Exception)
      {
         Console.WriteLine("Caught in method A");
         throw;
      }
   }
   private static void MethodB()
   {
      try
      {
         Console.WriteLine("Trying in method B");
         MethodC();
      }
      catch(Exception)
      {
         Console.WriteLine("Caught in method B");
         throw;
      }
   }
   private static void MethodC()
   {
      Console.WriteLine("In method C");
      throw(new Exception("This came from method C"));
   }
}
```

Figure 11-37   The ReThrowDemo program

Figure 11-38 Execution of the ReThrowDemo program

If you name the Exception argument in a catch block (for example, catch(Exception e)), then you should use that identifier when you use a throw statement in the block (for example, throw e;).

TWO TRUTHS & A LIE

Rethrowing an Exception

1. When you write a method that catches an exception, your method must handle it.

2. When a method catches an exception, you can rethrow it to a calling method.

3. Within a catch block, you can rethrow an unnamed caught Exception object by using the keyword throw with no object after it.

The false statement is #1. When you write a method that catches an Exception, your method does not have to handle the Exception.

Chapter Summary

- An exception is any error condition or unexpected behavior in an executing program. In C#, all exceptions are objects that are instances of the Exception class or one of its derived classes. Most exceptions you will use are derived from three classes: SystemException, ApplicationException, and their parent Exception. You can purposely generate a SystemException by forcing a program to contain an error. Although you are not required to handle exceptions, you can use object-oriented techniques to provide elegant error-handling solutions.

- When you think an error will occur frequently, the most efficient approach is to handle the error in the traditional way, with `if` statements. If an error will occur infrequently, instantiating an `Exception` object when needed is more efficient. In object-oriented terminology, you "try" a procedure that may not complete correctly. A method that detects an error condition or exception "throws" an exception, and the block of code that processes the error "catches" the exception. You must include at least one `catch` block or `finally` block immediately following a `try` block.

- Every `Exception` object contains a `ToString()` method and a `Message` property that contains useful information about the `Exception`.

- You can place as many statements as you need within a `try` block, and you can catch as many different exceptions as you want. If you try more than one statement, only the first error-generating statement throws an exception. When multiple `catch` blocks are present, they are examined in sequence until a match is found for the `Exception` type that occurred. When you list multiple `catch` blocks after a `try` block, you must be careful about their order, or some `catch` blocks might become unreachable.

- The `TryParse()` methods that you can use to convert strings to other data types without causing exceptions use exception-handling techniques internally.

- A `finally` block performs actions at the end of a `try...catch` sequence, whether an exception was thrown or not.

- Exceptions do not have to be caught by the methods that generate them. Instead, a program that calls a method that throws an exception can catch and handle it. Often, this approach produces the best software design.

- If a method throws an exception and does not catch it, then the `Exception` object is thrown to the calling method. When you catch an `Exception` object, you can display the value of the `StackTrace` property, which provides a list of methods in the call stack, allowing you to determine the location where the error occurred.

- To create your own `Exception` classes from which you create throwable objects, you can extend the `ApplicationException` class or the `Exception` class. The current advice is to extend `Exception`.

- When you write a method that catches an exception, your method does not have to handle it. Instead, you might choose to rethrow the exception to the method that called your method and let that method handle it.

Key Terms

An **exception** is any error condition or unexpected behavior in an executing program.

Exception handling is the set of object-oriented techniques used to manage unexpected errors in an executing program.

Fault-tolerant applications are designed so that they continue to operate, possibly at a reduced level, when some part of the system fails.

Robustness represents the degree to which a system is resilient to stress, maintaining correct functioning even in the presence of errors.

The term **mission critical** refers to any process that is crucial to an organization.

A **try block** contains code that might create exceptions you want to handle.

A **catch block** can catch one type of Exception.

Unreachable blocks contain statements that can never execute under any circumstances because the program logic "can't get there."

Dead code is unreachable code.

A **finally block** can follow a try block; code within a finally block executes whether the try block identifies any Exceptions or not.

The **call stack** is the memory location where the computer stores the list of locations to which the system must return after method calls.

Propagating an exception is the act of transmitting it unchanged through the call stack.

To **rethrow an exception** is to throw a caught exception to a calling method instead of handling it within the method that generated it.

Review Questions

1. Any error condition or unexpected behavior in an executing program is known as an _____.

    a. exception   c. exclusion

    b. anomaly   d. omission

2. Which of the following is *not* treated as a C# Exception?

    a. Your program asks the user to input a number, but the user enters a character.

    b. You attempt to execute a C# program, but the C# compiler has not been installed.

    c. You attempt to access an array with a subscript that is too large.

    d. You calculate a value that is too large for the answer's variable type.

3. Most exceptions you will use derive from three classes: _____.

    a. Object, ObjectException, and ObjectApplicationException

    b. Exception, SystemException, and ApplicationException

    c. FormatException, ApplicationException, and IOException

    d. SystemException, IOException, and FormatException

4. Exception objects can be _____.

   a. generated automatically by C#   c. both of these

   b. created by a program   d. none of these

5. When a program creates an Exception object, you _____.

   a. must handle it

   b. can handle it

   c. must not handle it

   d. none of these; programs cannot create Exceptions

6. If you do not use object-oriented techniques, _____.

   a. there are no error situations

   b. you cannot manage error situations

   c. you can manage error situations, but with great difficulty

   d. you can manage error situations

7. In object-oriented terminology, you _____ a procedure that may not complete correctly.

   a. circumvent   c. catch

   b. attempt   d. try

8. In object-oriented terminology, a method that detects an error condition _____ an exception.

   a. throws   c. tries

   b. catches   d. unearths

9. When you write a block of code in which something can go wrong, and you want to throw an exception if it does, you place the code in a _____ block.

   a. catch   c. system

   b. blind   d. try

10. A catch block executes when its try block _____.

    a. completes

    b. throws any Exception object

    c. throws an Exception of an acceptable type

    d. completes without throwing anything

11. Which of the following catch blocks will catch any Exception object?

    a. catch(Any e) {}
    b. catch(Exception e) {}
    c. catch(e) {}
    d. All of the above will catch any Exception.

12. Which of the following is valid within a catch block with the header catch(Exception error)?

    a. Console.WriteLine(error.ToString());
    b. Console.WriteLine(error.Message);
    c. return(error.ToString());
    d. two of these

13. You can place _____ statement(s) within a try block.

    a. zero
    b. one
    c. two
    d. any number of

14. How many catch blocks might follow a try block within the same method?

    a. only one
    b. any number as long as it is greater than zero
    c. any number as long as it is greater than one
    d. any number, including zero or one

15. Consider the following try block. If x is 15, what is the value of a when this code completes?

```
try
{
   a = 99;
   if(x > 10)
      throw(new Exception());
   a = 0;
   ++a;
}
```

    a. 0
    b. 1
    c. 99
    d. undefined

16. Consider the following `catch` blocks. The variable b has been initialized to 0. If a `DivideByZeroException` occurs in a `try` block just before this `catch` block, what is the value of b when this code completes?

```
catch(DivideByZeroException e)
{
    ++b;
}
catch(Exception e)
{
    ++b;
}
```

a. 0   c. 2

b. 1   d. 3

17. Consider the following `catch` blocks. The variable c has been initialized to 0. If an `IndexOutOfRangeException` occurs in a `try` block just before this `catch` block, what is the value of c when this code completes?

```
catch(IndexOutOfRangeException e)
{
    ++c;
}
catch(Exception e)
{
    ++c;
}
finally
{
    ++c;
}
```

a. 0   c. 2

b. 1   d. 3

18. If your program throws an `IndexOutOfRangeException` and the only available `catch` block catches an `Exception`, _____.

a. an `IndexOutOfRangeException` catch block is generated automatically

b. the `Exception` catch block executes

c. the `Exception` catch block is bypassed

d. the `IndexOutOfRangeException` is thrown to the operating system

19. When you design your own classes that might cause exceptions, and other classes will use your classes as clients, you should usually create your methods to _____.

a. neither throw nor handle exceptions

b. throw exceptions but not handle them

c. handle exceptions but not throw them

d. both throw and handle exceptions

20. When you create an `Exception` subclass of your own, you should extend the _____ class.

a. `SystemException`

b. `PersonalException`

c. `OverloadedException`

d. `Exception`

Exercises

Programming Exercises

1. Write a program named **SubscriptValidation** in which you declare an array of 10 integers and store values in the array. Write a `try` block in which you place a loop that prompts the user for a subscript value and displays the value stored in the corresponding array position. Create a `catch` block that catches any `IndexOutOfRangeException` and displays an appropriate error message.

2. `ArgumentException` is an existing class that derives from `Exception`; you use it when one or more of a method's arguments do not fall within an expected range. Create an application for Midtown College named **CollegeApplication** containing variables that can hold a student's name, high school grade point average, and entrance examination score. Within the class, create a method that accepts parameters for the student's grade point average and test score and returns true or false indicating whether the student is accepted to the college. A student is accepted when his grade point average is at least 2.5 and his test score is at least 75. If the grade point average is not between 0.0 and 4.0 inclusive or the test score is not between 0 and 100 inclusive, throw an `ArgumentException` from the method. In the `Main()` method, continuously prompt the user for student data. Call the method that determines college acceptance, and then display an appropriate message based on the returned value.

3. Create a program named **FindSquareRoot** that finds the square root of a user's input value. The `Math` class contains a static method named `Sqrt()` that accepts a `double` and returns the parameter's square root. If the user's entry cannot be

converted to a double, display an appropriate message and set the square root value to 0. Otherwise, test the input number's value. If it is negative, throw a new ApplicationException to which you pass the message "Number can't be negative." and again set sqrt to 0. If the input value is a double and not negative, pass it to the Math.Sqrt() method, and display the returned value.

4.   a.   Create a program named **InvoiceExceptionDemo** that attempts to create several valid and invalid Invoice objects. Immediately after each instantiation attempt, handle any thrown exceptions by displaying an error message. Create an Invoice class with three fields for an ID number, balance due, and day due. The Invoice constructor requires values for each field. Upon construction, throw an ArgumentException if the ID number is less than 100 or more than 999, or if the day due is not between 1 and 31 inclusive.

   b.   Add get properties for each field in the Invoice class created in Exercise 4a. Then, write an application named **InvoiceExceptionDemo2** that creates an array of five Invoices. Prompt the user for values for each field of each Invoice. If the user enters improper or invalid data for any field, set the ID number to 999, the balance to 0, and the due day to 1. At the end of the program, display all the entered, and possibly corrected, records.

5.   a.   Create a program named **BookExceptionDemo** for the Peterman Publishing Company. The company has decided that no published book should cost more than 10 cents per page. Create a BookException class whose constructor requires three arguments: a string Book title, a double price, and an int number of pages. Create an error message that is passed to the Exception class constructor for the Message property when a Book does not meet the price-to-pages ratio. For example, an error message might be:

```
For Goodnight Moon, ratio is invalid.
...Price is $12.99 for 25 pages.
```

   Create a Book class that contains fields for title, author, price, and number of pages. Include properties for each field. Throw a BookException if a client program tries to construct a Book object for which the price is more than 10 cents per page. Create a program that creates at least four Book objects—some where the ratio is acceptable and others where it is not. Catch any thrown exceptions and display the BookException Message.

   b.   Using the Book class created in Exercise 5a, write an application named **BookExceptionDemo2** that creates an array of five Books. Prompt the user for values for each Book. To handle any exceptions that are thrown because of improper or invalid data entered by the user, set the Book's price to the maximum 10 cents per page. At the end of the program, display all the entered, and possibly corrected, records.

6. Create a GUI application named **ExceptionHandlingDemoGUI** that prompts a user to enter an integer. When the user clicks a button, try to convert the user's entry to an integer using the ConvertToInt32() method, and display a message indicating whether the user was successful.

7. In Chapter 6, you created a game named GuessAWord in which a player guesses letters to try to replicate a hidden word. Now create a modified version of the program named **GuessAWordWithExceptionHandling** that throws and catches an exception when the user enters a guess that is not a letter of the alphabet. Create a NonLetterException class that descends from Exception. The Message string for your new class should indicate the nonletter character that caused the Exception's creation. When a NonLetterException is thrown and caught, the message should be displayed.

Debugging Exercises

1. Each of the following files in the Chapter.11 folder of your downloadable student files has syntax and/or logical errors. In each case, determine the problem and fix the program. After you correct the errors, save each file using the same filename preceded with *Fixed*. For example, DebugEleven1.cs will become FixedDebugEleven1.cs.

    a. DebugEleven1.cs   c. DebugEleven3.cs

    b. DebugEleven2.cs   d. DebugEleven4.cs

Case Problems

1. Modify the **GreenvilleRevenue** program created in the previous chapter so that it performs the following tasks:

    • The program prompts the user for the number of contestants in this year's competition; the number must be between 0 and 30. Use exception-handling techniques to ensure a valid value.

    • The program prompts the user for talent codes. Use exception-handling techniques to ensure a valid code.

    • After data entry is complete, the program prompts the user for codes so the user can view lists of appropriate contestants. Use exception-handling techniques for the code verification.

2. Modify the **MarshallsRevenue** program created in the previous chapter so that it performs the following tasks:

- Modify the program to use exception-handling techniques to ensure valid values for the month, the number of interior murals scheduled, and the number of exterior murals scheduled. In each case, the program continues to prompt the user until valid entries are made.

- Modify the program to use exception-handling techniques to ensure valid mural codes for the scheduled jobs.

- After data entry is complete, the program continuously prompts the user for codes and displays associated jobs. Use exception-handling techniques to verify valid codes.

Throughout this book, you have created both console and GUI applications. Your GUI applications have used only a few Controls—Forms, Labels, TextBoxes, and Buttons.

If you have been creating mostly console applications while learning the concepts in this book, you might want to review the chapter *Using GUI Objects and the Visual Studio IDE*. That chapter provides instruction in the basic procedures used to create GUI applications and describes Visual Studio Help.

When using programs or visiting Internet sites, you have encountered and used many other interactive **widgets**—elements of graphical interfaces that allow you to interact with programs—such as scroll bars, check boxes, and radio buttons. C# has many classes that represent these GUI objects, and the Visual Studio IDE makes it easy to add them to your programs. In this chapter, you will learn to incorporate some of the most common and useful widgets into your programs. Additionally, you will see how these components work in general so you can use other widgets that are not covered in this book or that become available to programmers in future releases of C#.

GUI components are referred to as *widgets*, which some sources claim is a combination of the terms *window* and *gadgets*. Originally, "widget" comes from the 1924 play "Beggar on Horseback," by George Kaufman and Marc Connelly. In the play, a young composer gets engaged to the daughter of a rich businessman, and foresees spending his life doing pointless work in a bureaucratic big business that manufactures widgets, which represent a useless item whose purpose is never explained.

Understanding Controls

When you design a Form, you can place Buttons and other controls on the Form surface. The **Control** class provides the definitions for these GUI objects. Control objects such as Forms and Buttons, like all other objects in C#, ultimately derive from the Object class. Figure 12-1 shows where the Control class fits into the inheritance hierarchy.

```
System.Object
    System.MarshalByRefObject
        System.ComponentModel.Component
            System.Windows.Forms.Control
                26 Derived classes
```

Figure 12-1 The Control class inheritance hierarchy

Figure 12-1 shows that all Controls are Objects, of course. They are also all MarshalByRefObjects. (A MarshalByRefObject is one you can instantiate on a remote computer so that you can manipulate a reference to the object rather than a local copy of the object.) Controls also descend from Component. (The **Component** class provides containment and cleanup for other objects—inheriting from Component allows Controls to be contained in objects such as Forms, and provides for disposal of Controls when they are destroyed. The Control class adds visual representation to Components.) The Control class implements very basic functionality required by classes that appear to the user—in other words, the GUI objects the user sees on the screen. This class handles user input through the keyboard and pointing devices as well as message routing and security. It defines the bounds of a Control by determining its position and size.

Table 12-1 shows the 26 direct descendents of Control and some commonly used descendents of those classes. It does not show all the descendents that exist; rather, it shows only the descendents covered previously or in this chapter. For example, the ButtonBase class is the parent of Button, a class you have used throughout this book. In this chapter, you will use two other ButtonBase children—CheckBox and RadioButton. This chapter cannot cover every Control that has been invented; however, after you learn to use some Controls, you will find that others work in much the same way. You also can read more about them in the Visual Studio Help documentation.

Class	Commonly used descendents
Microsoft.WindowsCE.Forms.DocumentList	
System.Windows.Forms.AxHost	
System.Windows.Forms.ButtonBase	Button, CheckBox, RadioButton
System.Windows.Forms.DataGrid	
System.Windows.Forms.DataGridView	
System.Windows.Forms.DateTimePicker	
System.Windows.Forms.GroupBox	
System.Windows.Forms.Integration.ElementHost	
System.Windows.Forms.Label	LinkLabel
System.Windows.Forms.ListControl	ListBox, ComboBox, CheckedListBox
System.Windows.Forms.ListView	
System.Windows.Forms.MdiClient	
System.Windows.Forms.MonthCalendar	
System.Windows.Forms.PictureBox	
System.Windows.Forms.PrintPreviewControl	
System.Windows.Forms.ProgressBar	
System.Windows.Forms.ScrollableControl	
System.Windows.Forms.ScrollBar	
System.Windows.Forms.Splitter	
System.Windows.Forms.StatusBar	

Table 12-1 Classes derived from System.Windows.Forms.Control *(continues)*

(continued)

Class	Commonly used descendents
System.Windows.Forms.TabControl	
System.Windows.Forms.TextBoxBase	TextBox
System.Windows.Forms.ToolBar	
System.Windows.Forms.TrackBar	
System.Windows.Forms.TreeView	
System.Windows.Forms.WebBrowserBase	

Table 12-1   Classes derived from System.Windows.Forms.Control

Because Controls are all relatives, they share many of the same attributes. Each Control has more than 80 public properties and 20 protected properties. For example, each Control has a Font and a ForeColor that dictate how its text is displayed, and each Control has a Width and Height. Table 12-2 shows just some of the public properties associated with Controls in general; reading through them will give you an idea of the Control attributes that you can change.

Property	Description
AllowDrop	Gets or sets a value indicating whether the control can accept data that the user drags onto it
Anchor	Gets or sets the edges of the container to which a control is bound and determines how a control is resized with its parent
BackColor	Gets or sets the background color for the control
BackgroundImage	Gets or sets the background image displayed in the control
Bottom	Gets the distance, in pixels, between the bottom edge of the control and the top edge of its container's client area
Bounds	Gets or sets the size and location of the control, including its nonclient elements, in pixels, relative to the parent control
CanFocus	Gets a value indicating whether the control can receive focus
CanSelect	Gets a value indicating whether the control can be selected
Capture	Gets or sets a value indicating whether the control has captured the mouse
Container	Gets the IContainer that contains the Component (inherited from Component)
ContainsFocus	Gets a value indicating whether the control or one of its child controls currently has the input focus

Table 12-2   Selected public Control properties (continues)

(continued)

Property	Description
Cursor	Gets or sets the cursor that is displayed when the mouse pointer is over the control
Disposing	Gets a value indicating whether the base Control class is in the process of disposing
Dock	Gets or sets which control borders are docked to their parent control and determines how a control is resized with its parent
Enabled	Gets or sets a value indicating whether the control can respond to user interaction
Focused	Gets a value indicating whether the control has input focus
Font	Gets or sets the font of the text displayed by the control
ForeColor	Gets or sets the foreground color of the control
HasChildren	Gets a value indicating whether the control contains one or more child controls
Height	Gets or sets the height of the control
IsDisposed	Gets a value indicating whether the control has been disposed of
Left	Gets or sets the distance, in pixels, between the left edge of the control and the left edge of its container's client area
Location	Gets or sets the coordinates of the upper-left corner of the control relative to the upper-left corner of its container
Margin	Gets or sets the space between controls
ModifierKeys	Gets a value indicating which of the modifier keys (Shift, Ctrl, and Alt) is in a pressed state
MouseButtons	Gets a value indicating which of the mouse buttons is in a pressed state
MousePosition	Gets the position of the mouse cursor in screen coordinates
Name	Gets or sets the name of the control
Parent	Gets or sets the parent container of the control
Right	Gets the distance, in pixels, between the right edge of the control and the left edge of its container's client area
Size	Gets or sets the height and width of the control
TabIndex	Gets or sets the tab order of the control within its container
TabStop	Gets or sets a value indicating whether the user can give focus to the control using the Tab key
Text	Gets or sets the text associated with this control

Table 12-2 Selected public Control properties (continues)

(continued)

Property	Description
Top	Gets or sets the distance, in pixels, between the top edge of the control and the top edge of its container's client area
TopLevelControl	Gets the parent control that is not parented by another Windows Forms control; typically, this is the outermost Form in which the control is contained
Visible	Gets or sets a value indicating whether the control and all its parent controls are displayed
Width	Gets or sets the width of the control

Table 12-2 Selected public Control properties

The description of each property in Table 12-2 indicates whether the property is read-only; such properties only get values and do not set them.

You have altered Label, TextBox, and Button properties such as Text and Visible using the Properties window in Visual Studio. All the other Controls you learn about in this chapter can be manipulated in the same way.

A project can contain multiple Forms, each with its own Controls. You will learn how to add more Forms to a project in the "You Do It" exercises later in this chapter.

TWO TRUTHS & A LIE

Understanding Controls

1. The Control class implements basic functionality required by GUI objects that a user sees on the screen.

2. Most Controls have Font and ForeColor properties.

3. Every Control has Width and Height properties.

The false statement is #2. Every Control has Font and ForeColor properties.

Examining the IDE's Automatically Generated Code

Figure 12-2 shows a Form created in the IDE. The following actions have been performed:

1. A new Windows Forms project has been started and given the name FormWithALabelAndAButton.

2. A Label has been dragged onto Form1. Using the Properties window in the IDE, the Label's Text property has been changed to "Click the button", and its Font has been changed to Georgia, Bold, and size 16.

3. A Button has been dragged onto Form1. The Button's Text property has been changed to "OK" and its Name has been changed to okButton.

Figure 12-2 A Form generated by the FormWithALabelAndAButton program

When you open the Form1.Designer.cs file in Visual Studio, you can see two lines of code generated within it as follows:

```
private System.Windows.Forms.Label label1;
private System.Windows.Forms.Button okButton;
```

These lines appear under a gray box that contains *Windows Form Designer generated code*, and they declare the Label and Button objects using the default identifier label1 and the programmer-created identifier okButton.

You can expand the code generated by the Form Designer by clicking the + in the **method node** to the left of the gray box that contains *Windows Form Designer generated code*, or you can double-click the gray box. As partially shown in Figure 12-3, the gray box is replaced by the expanded code that it represents, and more than 30 automatically generated statements are revealed. (In the code in the figure, every instance of this means "this Form".)

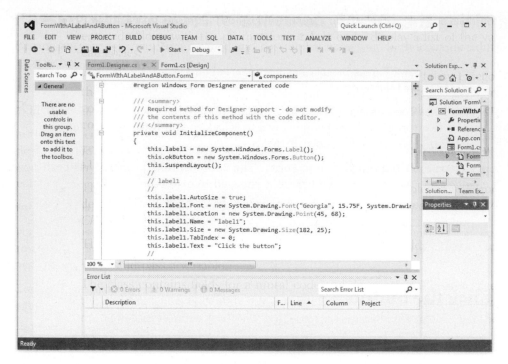

Figure 12-3   Some of the code in the InitializeComponent() method for FormWithALabelAndAButton

So much code is automatically generated by Visual Studio that it can be hard to find what you want. To locate a line of code, click EDIT on the main menu in the IDE, click Find and Replace, click Find, type a key phrase to search for, and click the Find Next button.

Do not be intimidated by the amount of code automatically generated by the IDE. Based on what you have learned so far in this book, you can easily make sense of most of it.

- After the InitializeComponent() method header and opening brace, the next two statements call the constructor for each object that the programmer dragged onto the Form:

```
this.label1 = new System.Windows.Forms.Label();
this.okButton = new System.Windows.Forms.Button();
```

- The next statement is a method call as follows:

```
this.SuspendLayout();
```

SuspendLayout() is a method that prevents conflicts when you are placing Controls on a form. Its counterparts are ResumeLayout() and PerformLayout(), which appear at the bottom of the method. If you remove these method calls from small applications, you won't notice the difference. However, in large applications, suspending the layout logic while you adjust the appearance of components improves performance.

- Comments that start with forward slashes serve to separate the label1 code from other code in the method. Following the label1 comment lines, seven statements set properties of the Label as follows:

```
this.label1.AutoSize = true;
this.label1.Font = new System.Drawing.Font("Georgia",
    15.75F, System.Drawing.FontStyle.Bold,
    System.Drawing.GraphicsUnit.Point, ((byte)(0)));
this.label1.Location = new System.Drawing.Point(45, 68);
this.label1.Name = "label1";
this.label1.Size = new System.Drawing.Size(182, 25);
this.label1.TabIndex = 0;
this.label1.Text = "Click the button";
```

You can see that the Font, Location, Name, Size, and Text have been assigned values based on the programmer's choices in the IDE. The TabIndex for label1 is 0 by default; TabIndex values determine the order in which Controls receive focus when the user presses the Tab key. This property is typically more useful for selectable items like Buttons.

- Although not visible in Figure 12-3, the next set of statements defines the properties of the Button on the Form. Notice that the TabIndex for the Button is set to 1 because it was dragged onto the Form after the Label. Additional Controls would receive consecutive TabIndex values.

```
this.okButton.Location = new System.Drawing.Point(95, 120);
this.okButton.Name = "okButton";
this.okButton.Size = new System.Drawing.Size(75, 23);
this.okButton.TabIndex = 1;
this.okButton.Text = "OK";
this.okButton.UseVisualStyleBackColor = true;
```

- The InitializeComponent() method ends with statements that set the properties of the Form, such as its drawing size and text, and that add the Label and Button to the Form:

```
// Form1
//
this.AutoScaleDimensions = new System.Drawing.SizeF(6F, 13F);
this.AutoScaleMode = System.Windows.Forms.AutoScaleMode.Font;
this.ClientSize = new System.Drawing.Size(284, 262);
this.Controls.Add(this.okButton);
this.Controls.Add(this.label1);
this.Name = "Form1";
this.Text = "Form1";
this.ResumeLayout(false);
this.PerformLayout();
```

Although the property settings for the Label and Button include identifiers for the Controls (for example, this.label1.Name or this.okButton.Text), the property settings for the Form itself use only the reference this. That's because the statements are part of the Form1 class.

In this chapter, you will learn about several additional Controls. When designing a Form, you usually will use the drag-and-drop design features in the IDE instead of typing code statements. However, this chapter also teaches you about the code behind these actions so you can troubleshoot problems in projects and write usable statements when necessary.

 Watch the video *Examining the IDE Code.*

TWO TRUTHS & A LIE

Examining the IDE's Automatically Generated Code

1. By using the Visual Studio Designer, you save time and eliminate many chances for error.

2. When you use the Visual Studio IDE to drag a Label onto a Form, no constructor call is needed for the Label.

3. You can use the Visual Studio IDE to set properties for a Label such as Font, Location, Size, and Text.

The false statement is #2. When you use the Visual Studio IDE to drag a Label onto a Form, you do not have to write a constructor call, but one is generated for you.

Setting a Control's Font

You use the **Font** class to change the appearance of printed text on your Forms. When designing a Label, Button, or other Control on a Form, it is easiest to select a Font from the Properties list. After you place a Control on a Form in the IDE, you can select the ellipsis (three dots) that follows the current Font property name in the Properties list. (See Figure 12-4.) This selection displays a Font window in which you can choose a Font name, size, style, and other effects. (See Figure 12-5.)

Figure 12-4 Clicking the ellipsis following the Font property

Figure 12-5 The Font window

However, if you wanted to change a Font later in a program—for example, after a user clicks a button—you might want to create your own instance of the Font class. As another example, suppose you want to create multiple controls that use the same Font. In that case, it makes sense to declare a named instance of the Font class. For example, you can declare the following Font:

```
System.Drawing.Font bigFont = new
    System.Drawing.Font("Courier New", 16.5f);
```

This version of the Font constructor requires two arguments—a string and a float. The string you pass to the Font constructor is the name of the font. If you use a font name that does not exist in your system, the font defaults to Microsoft Sans Serif. The second value is a float that represents the font size. Notice that you must use an *F* (or an *f*) following the Font size value constant when it contains a decimal point to ensure that the constant will be recognized as a float and not a double. (If you use an int as the font size, you do not need the *f* because the int will automatically be cast to a float.) An alternative would be to instantiate a float constant or variable and use its name as an argument to the Font constructor.

In Chapter 2, you learned to use an *f* following a floating-point constant to indicate the float type. Recall that a numeric constant with digits to the right of the decimal point is a double by default.

After a Font object named bigFont is instantiated, you can code statements similar to the following:

```
this.label1.Font = bigFont;
this.okButton.Font = bigFont;
```

If you want to change the properties of several objects at once in the IDE, you can drag your mouse around them to create a temporary group, and then change the property for all of them with one entry in the Properties list.

The Font class includes a number of overloaded constructors.

You also can create a Font using three arguments, adding a FontStyle, as in the following example:

```
Font aFancyFont = new Font("Arial", 24, FontStyle.Italic);
```

Table 12-3 lists the available FontStyles. You can combine multiple styles using the pipe (|), which is also called the **logical OR operator**. For example, the following code creates a Font that is bold and underlined:

```
Font boldAndUnderlined = new Font("Helvetica",
    10, FontStyle.Bold | FontStyle.Underline);
```

Member Name	Description
Bold	Bold text
Italic	Italic text
Regular	Normal text
Strikeout	Text with a line through the middle
Underline	Underlined text

Table 12-3   FontStyle enumeration

Instead of instantiating a named Font object, you can create and assign an anonymous Font in one step. In other words, an identifier is not provided for the Font, as in this example:

```
this.label1.Font = new
    System.Drawing.Font("Courier New", 12.5F);
```

If you don't provide an identifier for a Font, you can't reuse it. You will have to create it again to use it with additional Controls.

TWO TRUTHS & A LIE

Setting a Control's Font

1. You use the Font class to change the appearance of printed text on Controls in your Forms.

2. When designing a Control on a Form, you must select a Font from the Properties list in the IDE.

3. The Font class includes several overloaded constructors.

The false statement is #2. When designing a Label or other Control on a Form, it is easiest to select a Font from the Properties list, but you also can create your own instance of the Font class.

Using a LinkLabel

A **LinkLabel** is similar to a Label; it is a child of Label. Therefore, you can use it like a Label, but it provides the additional capability to link the user to other sources, such as Web pages or files. Table 12-4 summarizes the properties and lists the default event method for a LinkLabel. The **default event** for a Control is:

- The method whose shell is automatically created when you double-click the Control while designing a project in the IDE

- The method that you are most likely to alter when you use the Control

- The event that users most likely expect to generate when they encounter the Control in a working application

With many Controls, including a LinkLabel, a mouse click by the user triggers the default event. When designing a program, you can double-click a Control in the IDE to generate a method shell, and then write any necessary statements within the shell.

Property or Method	Description
ActiveLinkColor	The color of the link when it is clicked
LinkColor	The original color of links before they have been visited; usually blue by default
LinkVisited	If true, the link's color is changed to the VisitedLinkColor
VisitedLinkColor	The color of a link after it has been visited; usually purple by default
LinkClicked()	Default event that is generated when the link is clicked by the user

Table 12-4 Commonly used LinkLabel properties and default event

The default event for many Controls, such as Buttons and LinkLabels, occurs when the user clicks the Control. However, the default event for a Form is the Load() method. In other words, if you double-click a Form in the IDE, you generate this method. In it, you can place statements that execute as soon as a Form is loaded.

When you create a LinkLabel, it appears as underlined text. The text is blue by default, but you can change the color in the LinkLabel Properties list in the IDE. When you pass the mouse pointer over a LinkLabel, the pointer changes to a hand; you have seen similar behavior while using hyperlinks in Web pages. When a user clicks a LinkLabel, it generates a click event, just as clicking a Button does. When a click event is fired from a LinkLabel, a LinkClicked() method is executed, similar to how clicking a Button can execute a Click() method.

You can create a program so that a user generates an event by clicking many types of objects. For example, for a Label named label1, you could write statements in a label1_Click() method. However, users do not usually expect to click Labels; they do expect to click LinkLabels.

When you double-click a Label, the automatically generated method name ends with Click(), but when you double-click a LinkLabel, the corresponding method ends with Clicked().

Figure 12-6 shows a Form onto which two LinkLabels have been dragged from the Toolbox in the IDE. The Text properties of the LinkLabels have been changed to "Course Technology Website" and "Read Our Policy".

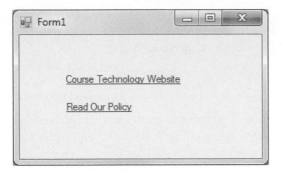

Figure 12-6 A Form with two LinkLabels

If you double-click a LinkLabel in the IDE, a method shell is created for you in the format xxx_LinkClicked(), where xxx is the value of the Name property assigned to the LinkLabel. (This corresponds to what happens when you double-click a Button in the IDE.) For example, Figure 12-7 shows the two generated methods for the Form in Figure 12-6 when the default LinkLabel identifiers linkLabel1 and linkLabel2 are used. In Figure 12-7, all the code was automatically generated except for the two shaded lines. The programmer added those lines to indicate which actions should occur when a user clicks the corresponding LinkLabel in a running application.

```
public partial class Form1 : Form
{
    public Form1()
    {
        InitializeComponent();
    }

    private void linkLabel1_LinkClicked(object sender,
        LinkLabelLinkClickedEventArgs e)
    {
        System.Diagnostics.Process.Start("IExplore",
            "http://www.course.com");
    }

    private void linkLabel2_LinkClicked(object sender,
        LinkLabelLinkClickedEventArgs e)
    {
        System.Diagnostics.Process.Start
            (@"C:\C#\Chapter.12\Policy.txt");
    }
}
```

Figure 12-7 Two LinkClicked() methods

In each of the LinkClicked() methods in Figure 12-7, the programmer has added a call to System.Diagnostics.Process.Start(). This method allows you to run other programs within an application. The Start() method has two overloaded versions:

- When you use one string argument, you open the named file.

- When you use two arguments, you open an application and provide its needed arguments.

In the linkLabel1_LinkClicked() method, the two arguments open Internet Explorer ("IExplore") and pass it the address of the Course Technology Web site. If an Internet connection is active, control transfers to the Web site.

In the linkLabel2_LinkClicked() method, only one argument is provided. It opens a file stored on the local disk. The correct application opens based on the default application for the file. For example, Notepad is the default application for a file with a .txt extension. Alternatively, you could code the following, which explicitly names Notepad as the application:

```
System.Diagnostics.Process.Start("Notepad",
  @"C:\C#\Chapter.12\Policy.txt");
```

 In the linkLabel2_LinkClicked() method, an at sign (@) appears in front of the filename to be opened. This symbol indicates that all characters in the string should be interpreted literally. Therefore, the backslashes in the path are not interpreted as escape sequence characters.

The LinkVisited property can be set to true when you determine that a user has clicked a link, as shown in Figure 12-8. This setting indicates that the link should be displayed in a different color so the user can see the link has been visited. By default, the visited link color is purple, but you can change this setting in the Properties list for the LinkLabel.

```
private void linkLabel1_LinkClicked(object sender,
  LinkLabelLinkClickedEventArgs e)
{
   System.Diagnostics.Process.Start("IExplore",
      "http://www.course.com");
   linkLabel1.LinkVisited = true;
}
```

Figure 12-8 Setting the LinkVisited property

TWO TRUTHS & A LIE

Using a LinkLabel

1. A LinkLabel is a child class of Label and it provides the additional capability to link the user to other sources.

2. The default event for a Control is the method whose shell is automatically created when you double-click the Control while designing a project in the IDE. Users most likely expect to generate this event when they encounter the Control in a working application.

3. When you create a LinkLabel, it appears as italicized underlined text, and when you pass the mouse pointer over a LinkLabel, the pointer changes to an hourglass.

The false statement is #3. When you create a LinkLabel, it appears as underlined text, and when you pass the mouse pointer over a LinkLabel, the pointer changes to a hand.

Adding Color to a Form

The **Color** class contains a wide variety of predefined Colors that you can use with your Controls (see Table 12-5).

 C# also allows you to create custom colors. If no color in Table 12-5 suits your needs, search for "custom color" in the Visual Studio Help to obtain more information.

AliceBlue	DeepPink	Lime	RosyBrown
AntiqueWhite	DeepSkyBlue	LimeGreen	RoyalBlue
Aqua	DimGray	Linen	SaddleBrown
Aquamarine	DodgerBlue	Magenta	Salmon
Azure	Firebrick	Maroon	SandyBrown
Beige	FloralWhite	MediumAquamarine	SeaGreen
Bisque	ForestGreen	MediumBlue	SeaShell
Black	Fuchsia	MediumOrchid	Sienna

Table 12-5　Color properties *(continues)*

(continued)

BlanchedAlmond	Gainsboro	MediumPurple	Silver
Blue	GhostWhite	MediumSeaGreen	SkyBlue
BlueViolet	Gold	MediumSlateBlue	SlateBlue
Brown	Goldenrod	MediumSpringGreen	SlateGray
BurlyWood	Gray	MediumTurquoise	Snow
CadetBlue	Green	MediumVioletRed	SpringGreen
Chartreuse	GreenYellow	MidnightBlue	SteelBlue
Chocolate	Honeydew	MintCream	Tan
Coral	HotPink	MistyRose	Teal
CornflowerBlue	IndianRed	Moccasin	Thistle
Cornsilk	Indigo	NavajoWhite	Tomato
Crimson	Ivory	Navy	Transparent
Cyan	Khaki	OldLace	Turquoise
DarkBlue	Lavender	Olive	Violet
DarkCyan	LavenderBlush	OliveDrab	Wheat
DarkGoldenrod	LawnGreen	Orange	White
DarkGray	LemonChiffon	OrangeRed	WhiteSmoke
DarkGreen	LightBlue	Orchid	Yellow
DarkKhaki	LightCoral	PaleGoldenrod	YellowGreen
DarkMagenta	LightCyan	PaleGreen	
DarkOliveGreen	LightGoldenrodYellow	PaleTurquoise	
DarkOrange	LightGray	PaleVioletRed	
DarkOrchid	LightGreen	PapayaWhip	
DarkRed	LightPink	PeachPuff	
DarkSalmon	LightSalmon	Peru	
DarkSeaGreen	LightSeaGreen	Pink	
DarkSlateBlue	LightSkyBlue	Plum	
DarkSlateGray	LightSlateGray	PowderBlue	
DarkTurquoise	LightSteelBlue	Purple	
DarkViolet	LightYellow	Red	

Table 12-5   Color properties

When you are designing a Form, you can choose colors from a list next to the BackColor and ForeColor properties in the IDE's Properties list. The statements created will be similar to the following:

```
this.label1.BackColor = System.Drawing.Color.Blue;
this.label1.ForeColor = System.Drawing.Color.Gold;
```

If you add using System.Drawing; at the top of your file, you can eliminate the references in the preceding lines and refer to the colors simply as Color.Blue and Color.Gold.

For professional-looking results when you prepare a resume or most other business documents, experts recommend that you only use one or two fonts and colors, even though your word-processing program allows many such selections. The same is true when you design interactive GUI applications. Although many fonts and colors are available, you probably should stick with a few choices in a single project.

TWO TRUTHS & A LIE

Adding Color to a Form

1. Because the choice of colors in C# is limited, you are required to create custom colors for many GUI applications.

2. When you are designing a Form, color choices appear in a list next to the BackColor and ForeColor properties in the IDE's Properties list.

3. The complete name of the color pink in C# is System.Drawing.Color.Pink.

The false statement is #1. The Color class contains a wide variety of predefined Colors that you can use with your Controls.

 You Do It

Adding Labels to a Form and Changing their Properties

In the next steps, you begin to create an application for Bailey's Bed and Breakfast. The main Form allows the user to select one of two suites and discover the amenities and price associated with each choice. You will start by placing two Labels on a Form and setting several of their properties.

(continues)

(continued)

The screen images in the next steps represent a typical Visual Studio environment. Based on the version of Visual Studio you are using and the options selected during your installation, your screen might look different.

1. Open Microsoft Visual Studio. Select **New Project** and **Windows Forms Application**. Near the bottom of the New Project window, click in the **Name** text box and replace the default name with **BedAndBreakfast**. Make sure that the Location field contains the folder where you want to store the project. See Figure 12-9.

Figure 12-9 The New Project window for the `BedAndBreakfast` application

2. Click **OK**. The design screen opens. The blank Form in the center of the screen has an empty title bar. Click the Form. The lower-right corner of the screen contains a Properties window that lists the Form's properties. (If you do not see the Properties window, you can click **VIEW** on the main menu, and then click **Properties Window**.) In the Properties list, click the **Name** property and change the Name of the Form to **BaileysForm**. Click the **Text** property and change it to **Bailey's Bed and Breakfast**.

(continues)

(continued)

3. From the Toolbox at the left of the screen, drag a `Label` onto the `Form`. Change the `Name` of `label1` to **welcomeLabel** and change the `Text` property to **Welcome to Bailey's**. Drag and resize the `Label` so it is close to the position of the `Label` in Figure 12-10. (If you prefer to set the `Label`'s `Location` property manually in the Properties list, the `Location` should be **60, 30**.)

If you do not see the Toolbox, click the **Toolbox tab** at the left side of the screen and pin it to the screen by clicking the pushpin. Alternatively, you can select **VIEW** from the main menu, and then click **Toolbox**.

Figure 12-10   A `Label` placed on the `Form` in the `BedAndBreakfast` project

(continues)

(continued)

4. Locate the Font property in the Properties list. Currently, it lists the default font: Microsoft Sans Serif, 8.25 pt. Notice the ellipsis (three dots) at the right of the Font property name. (You might have to click in the Property to see the button.) Click the ellipsis to display the Font dialog box. Make selections to change the font to **Microsoft Sans Serif**, **18 point**, and **Bold**. Click **OK**. When you enlarge the Font for the Label, it is too close to the right edge of the Form. Drag the Label to change its Location property to approximately **20, 30**, or type the new Location value in the Properties window.

5. Drag a second Label onto the Form beneath the first one, and then set its Name property to rateLabel and its Text property to **Check our rates**. Change its Location to approximately **80, 80** and its Font to **Microsoft Sans Serif, 12 point, Regular**.

6. Save the project, click **DEBUG** on the menu bar, and click **Start Without Debugging**, or use the shortcut keys listed in the menu. The Form appears, as shown in Figure 12-11.

Figure 12-11   The BedAndBreakfast Form with two Labels

7. Dismiss the Form by clicking the **Close** button in its upper-right corner.

(continues)

(continued)

Examining the Code Generated by the IDE

In the next steps, you examine the code generated by the IDE for the following reasons:

- To gain an understanding of the types of statements created by the IDE.

- To lose any intimidation you might have about the code that is generated. You will recognize many of the C# statements from what you have already learned in this book.

1. Click **VIEW** on the menu bar, and then click **Code** (or press the shortcut key displayed on the drop-down menu) to view the code. As shown in Figure 12-12, you see several `using` statements, the `BedAndBreakfast` namespace header, the `BaileysForm` class header, and the constructor for `BaileysForm` that calls the `InitializeComponent()` method.

```
Form1.cs    Form1.cs [Design]
BedAndBreakfast.BaileysForm    BaileysForm()

        using System.Collections.Generic;
        using System.ComponentModel;
        using System.Data;
        using System.Drawing;
        using System.Linq;
        using System.Text;
        using System.Threading.Tasks;
        using System.Windows.Forms;

namespace BedAndBreakfast
{
    public partial class BaileysForm : Form
    {
        public BaileysForm()
        {
            InitializeComponent();
        }
    }
}

100 %
```

Figure 12-12   The Form1.cs code

(continues)

(continued)

2. In the Solution Explorer at the right side of the screen, double-click the **Form1.Designer.cs** filename. Scroll to the gray rectangle that contains **Windows Form Designer generated code** and click the node to its left to expose the hidden code. (You can drag the bottom and side borders of the code window to expose more of the code, or you can scroll to see all of it.) As Figure 12-13 shows, `welcomeLabel`, `rateLabel`, and `BaileysForm` have been declared and assigned the attributes you provided for them.

```
Form1.Designer.cs  ⊕ ✕ Form1.cs        Form1.cs [Design]
🏷 BedAndBreakfast.BaileysForm                                    ▾  🏷 component
⊟              private void InitializeComponent()
               {
                   this.welcomeLabel = new System.Windows.Forms.Label();
                   this.rateLabel = new System.Windows.Forms.Label();
                   this.SuspendLayout();
                   //
                   // welcomeLabel
                   //
                   this.welcomeLabel.AutoSize = true;
                   this.welcomeLabel.Font = new System.Drawing.Font("Microsoft Sans Serif'
                   this.welcomeLabel.Location = new System.Drawing.Point(20, 30);
                   this.welcomeLabel.Name = "welcomeLabel";
                   this.welcomeLabel.Size = new System.Drawing.Size(248, 29);
                   this.welcomeLabel.TabIndex = 0;
                   this.welcomeLabel.Text = "Welcome to Bailey\'s";
                   //
                   // rateLabel
                   //
                   this.rateLabel.AutoSize = true;
                   this.rateLabel.Font = new System.Drawing.Font("Microsoft Sans Serif", 1
                   this.rateLabel.Location = new System.Drawing.Point(80, 80);
                   this.rateLabel.Name = "rateLabel";
                   this.rateLabel.Size = new System.Drawing.Size(121, 20);
                   this.rateLabel.TabIndex = 1;
                   this.rateLabel.Text = "Check our rates";
                   //
                   // BaileysForm
                   //
                   this.AutoScaleDimensions = new System.Drawing.SizeF(6F, 13F);
                   this.AutoScaleMode = System.Windows.Forms.AutoScaleMode.Font;
                   this.ClientSize = new System.Drawing.Size(284, 262);
                   this.Controls.Add(this.rateLabel);
                   this.Controls.Add(this.welcomeLabel);
                   this.Name = "BaileysForm";
                   this.Text = "Bailey\'s Bed and Breakfast";
                   this.ResumeLayout(false);
                   this.PerformLayout();

               }
```

These statements continue as you scroll to the right.

Figure 12-13 Part of the Form1.Designer.cs code

(continues)

(continued)

3. Next, change the BackColor property of the Bailey's Bed and Breakfast Form. Click the **Form1.cs[Design]** tab and click the **Form**, or click the list box of components at the top of the Properties window and select **BaileysForm**. In the Properties list, click the BackColor property to see its list of choices. Choose the **Custom** tab and select **Yellow** in the third row of available colors. Click the **Form**, notice the color change, and then view the code in the Form1. Designer.cs file. Locate the statement that changes the BackColor of the Form to Yellow. As you continue to design Forms, periodically check the code to confirm your changes and better learn C#.

4. Save the project.

5. If you want to take a break at this point, close Visual Studio. You return to this project in the "You Do It" section at the end of this chapter.

Using CheckBox and RadioButton Objects

CheckBox and RadioButton widgets allow users to select an option by clicking a small square or circle beside a label. Like Button, both classes descend from ButtonBase. When a Form contains multiple **CheckBoxes**, any number of them can be checked or unchecked at the same time. **RadioButtons** differ in that only one RadioButton in a group can be selected at a time—selecting any RadioButton automatically deselects the others.

Table 12-6 contains commonly used CheckBox and RadioButton properties and the default event for which a method shell is generated when you double-click a CheckBox or RadioButton in the IDE.

Property or Method	Description
Checked	Indicates whether the CheckBox or RadioButton is checked
Text	The text displayed to the right of the CheckBox or RadioButton
CheckedChanged()	Default event that is generated when the Checked property changes

Table 12-6 Commonly used CheckBox and RadioButton properties and default event

If you precede a letter with an ampersand (&) in the Text property value of a ButtonBase object, that letter acts as an access key. For example, if a Button's text is defined as &Press, then typing Alt+P has the same effect as clicking the Button. Access keys are also called hot keys.

 You can place multiple groups of RadioButtons on a Form by using a GroupBox or Panel. You will learn more about GroupBoxes and Panels later in this chapter.

Figure 12-14 shows an example of a Form that contains several Labels, four CheckBox objects, and three RadioButton objects. It makes sense for the pizza topping choices to be displayed using CheckBoxes because a user might select multiple toppings. However, options for delivery, pick-up, and dining in the restaurant are mutually exclusive, so they are presented using RadioButton objects.

Figure 12-14   A Form with Labels, CheckBoxes, and RadioButtons

When you add CheckBox and RadioButton objects to a form, they automatically are named using the same conventions you have seen with Buttons and Labels. That is, the first CheckBox without an explicitly assigned name is checkBox1 by default, the second is named checkBox2, and so on. Using the Properties list, you can assign more meaningful names such as sausageCheckBox and pepperoniCheckBox. Naming objects appropriately makes your code more understandable to others, and makes your programming job easier.

Both CheckBox and RadioButton objects have a Checked property whose value is true or false. For example, if you create a CheckBox named sausageCheckBox and you want to add $1.00 to a pizzaPrice value when the user checks the box, you can write the following:

```
if(sausageCheckBox.Checked)
    pizzaPrice = pizzaPrice + 1.00;
```

 The Checked property is a read/write property. That is, you can assign a value to it as well as access its value.

The default method that executes when a user clicks either a CheckBox or RadioButton is xxx_CheckedChanged(), where xxx represents the name of the invoking object. For example, suppose that the total price of a pizza should be altered based on a user's CheckBox selections. In this example, the base price for a pizza is $12.00, and $1.25 is added for each selected topping. You can declare constants for the BASE_PRICE and TOPPING_PRICE of a pizza and declare a variable that is initialized to the pizza base price as follows:

```
private const double BASE_PRICE = 12.00;
private const double TOPPING_PRICE = 1.25;
private double price = BASE_PRICE;
```

Figure 12-15 shows some of the code you would add to the Form.cs file for the application. The sausageCheckBox_CheckedChanged() method changes the pizza price. The shaded statements in the method were written by a programmer; the unshaded statements were generated by the IDE. If a change occurs because the sausageCheckBox was checked, then the TOPPING_PRICE is added to the price. If the change to the checkBox was to uncheck it, the TOPPING_PRICE is subtracted from the price. Either way, the Text property of a Label named outputLabel is changed to reflect the new price. Figure 12-16 shows the Form after the user has checked a box and then unchecked it.

```
    private void sausageCheckBox_CheckedChanged(object sender, EventArgs e)
    {
        if (sausageCheckBox.Checked)
            price += TOPPING_PRICE;
        else
            price -= TOPPING_PRICE;
        outputLabel.Text = "Total is " + price.ToString("C");
    }
```

Figure 12-15   The sausageCheckBox_CheckedChanged() method

Figure 12-16 Typical execution of the `PizzaOrder` program after code is added for `CheckBox`es

In a similar fashion, you can add appropriate code for `RadioButton` objects. For example, assume that a $2.00 delivery charge is in effect, but there is no extra charge for customers who pick up a pizza or dine in. The code for `deliverRadioButton_CheckedChanged()` appears in Figure 12-17. When the user selects the `deliverRadioButton`, $2.00 is added to the total. When the user selects either of the other `RadioButton`s, the `deliverRadioButton` becomes unchecked and the $2.00 charge is removed from the total.

```
private void deliverRadioButton_CheckedChanged(object sender, EventArgs e)
{
    const double DELIVERY_CHARGE = 2.00;
    if (deliverRadioButton.Checked)
        price += DELIVERY_CHARGE;
    else
        price -= DELIVERY_CHARGE;
    outputLabel.Text = "Total is " + price.ToString("C");
}
```

Figure 12-17 The `deliverRadioButton_CheckedChanged()` method

The entire pizza-order application can be found in the downloadable student files.

When an application starts, sometimes you want a specific `CheckBox` or `RadioButton` to be selected by default. If so, you can set the `Control`'s `Checked` property to true in the Properties list in the IDE.

Watch the video *CheckBoxes and RadioButtons.*

TWO TRUTHS & A LIE

Using `CheckBox` and `RadioButton` Objects

1. CheckBox objects are GUI widgets that the user can click to select or deselect an option; when a `Form` contains multiple `CheckBoxes`, any number of them can be checked or unchecked at the same time.

2. `RadioButtons` are similar to `CheckBoxes`, except that when they are placed on a `Form`, only one `RadioButton` can be selected at a time—selecting any `RadioButton` automatically deselects the others.

3. The default event for a `CheckBox` is `CheckBoxChanged()`, and the default event for a `RadioButton` is `RadioButtonChanged()`.

The false statement is #3. The default event for both CheckBox and RadioButton objects is CheckedChanged().

Adding a `PictureBox` to a `Form`

A **PictureBox** is a `Control` in which you can display graphics from a bitmap, icon, JPEG, GIF, or other image file type. Just as with a `Button` or a `Label`, you can easily drag a `PictureBox` `Control` onto a `Form` in the Visual Studio IDE. Table 12-7 shows the common properties and default event for a `PictureBox`.

Property or Method	Description
`Image`	Sets the image that appears in the `PictureBox`
`SizeMode`	Controls the size and position of the image in the `PictureBox`; values are `Normal`, `StretchImage` (which resizes the image to fit the `PictureBox`), `AutoSize` (which resizes the `PictureBox` to fit the image), and `CenterImage` (which centers the image in the `PictureBox`)
`Click()`	Default event that is generated when the user clicks the `PictureBox`

Table 12-7   Commonly used `PictureBox` properties and default event

Figure 12-18 shows a new project in the IDE. The following tasks have been completed:

- A project was started.
- The Form Text property was changed to "Save Money".
- The Form BackColor property was changed to White.
- A Label was dragged onto the Form, and its Text and Font were changed.
- A PictureBox was dragged onto the Form.

Figure 12-18 The IDE with a Form that contains a PictureBox

In Figure 12-18, in the Properties list at the right of the screen, the Image property is set to *none*. If you click the button with the ellipsis, a Select Resource window appears, as shown on the left in Figure 12-19. When you click the Import button, you can browse for stored images. When you select one, you see a preview in the Select Resource window, as shown on the right in Figure 12-19.

Figure 12-19   The Select Resource window before and after an image is selected

After you click OK, the image appears in the `PictureBox`, as in Figure 12-20. (You can resize the `PictureBox` so the image displays clearly.)

Figure 12-20   The `SaveMoney Frame` with an inserted image

If you examine the generated code, you can find the statements that instantiate a `PictureBox` (named `pictureBox1` by default) and statements that set its properties, such as `Size` and `Location`.

TWO TRUTHS & A LIE

Adding a PictureBox to a Form

1. A PictureBox is a Control in which you can display graphics from a bitmap, icon, JPEG, GIF, or other image file type.

2. The default event for a PictureBox is LoadImage().

3. The Image property of a PictureBox holds the name of a file where a picture is stored.

The false statement is #2. The default event for a PictureBox is Click().

Adding ListBox, CheckedListBox, and ComboBox Controls to a Form

ListBox, CheckedListBox, and ComboBox objects all allow users to select choices from a list. The three classes descend from ListControl. Of course, they are also Controls and so inherit properties such as Text and BackColor from the Control class. Other properties are more specific to list-type objects. Table 12-8 describes some commonly used ListBox properties.

Property or Method	Description
Items	The collection of items in the ListBox; frequently, these are strings, but they can also be other types of objects
MultiColumn	Indicates whether display can be in multiple columns
SelectedIndex	Returns the index of the selected item. If no item has been selected, the value is −1. Otherwise, it is a value from 0 through $n-1$, where n is the number of items in the ListBox.
SelectedIndices	Returns a collection of all the selected indices (when SelectionMode is more than One)
SelectedItem	Returns a reference to the selected item
SelectedItems	Returns a collection of the selected items (when SelectionMode is more than One)
SelectionMode	Determines how many items can be selected (see Table 12-9)
Sorted	Sorts the items when set to true
SelectedIndexChanged()	Default event that is generated when the selected index changes

Table 12-8   Commonly used ListBox properties and default event

Figure 12-21 shows a typical ListBox on a Form. The **ListBox Control** enables you to display a list of items that the user can select by clicking. After you drag a ListBox onto a Form, you can select its Items property and type a list into a String Collection Editor, as shown on the left in Figure 12-21.

Figure 12-21   The String Collection Editor filling a ListBox and the completed ListBox on a Form

Assuming the Name property of the ListBox is majorListBox, the following code is generated in the InitializeComponent() method when you fill the String Collection Editor with the strings in Figure 12-21:

```
this.majorListBox.Items.AddRange(new object[] {
    "Accounting",
    "Biology",
    "Chemistry",
    "English",
    "Math",
    "Psychology"});
```

Objects added to a ListBox are not required to be strings. For example, you could add a collection of Employee or Student objects. The value returned by each added object's ToString() method is displayed in the ListBox. After the user selects an object, you can cast the ListBox's SelectedItem to the appropriate type and access the object's other properties. The Chapter.12 folder of your student files contains a project named AddRangeObjectsDemo that illustrates this technique.

With a ListBox, you allow the user to make a single selection or multiple selections by setting the SelectionMode property appropriately. For example, when the SelectionMode property is set to One, the user can make only a single selection from the ListBox. When the SelectionMode is set to MultiExtended, pressing Shift and clicking the mouse or pressing Shift and one of the arrow keys (up, down, left, or right) extends the selection to span from the previously selected item to the current item. Pressing Ctrl and clicking the mouse selects or deselects an item in the list. Table 12-9 lists the possible `SelectionMode` values.

 When the `SelectionMode` property is set to `SelectionMode.MultiSimple`, click the mouse or press the spacebar to select or deselect an item in the list.

Member Name	Description
MultiExtended	Multiple items can be selected, and the user can press the Shift, Ctrl, and arrow keys to make selections.
MultiSimple	Multiple items can be selected.
None	No items can be selected.
One	Only one item can be selected.

Table 12-9 `SelectionMode` enumeration list

For example, within a `Form`'s `Load()` method (the one that executes when a `Form` is first loaded), you could add the following:

```
this.majorListBox.SelectionMode =
    System.Windows.Forms.SelectionMode.MultiExtended;
```

As the example in Figure 12-22 shows, when you size a `ListBox` so that all the items cannot be displayed at the same time, a scroll bar is provided automatically on the side. The `ListBox` also provides the Boolean `MultiColumn` property, which you can set to display items in columns instead of a straight vertical list. This approach allows the control to display more items and avoids the need for the user to scroll down to an item. See Figure 12-23.

Figure 12-22 A `ListBox` with a scroll bar

Figure 12-23 A multicolumn ListBox

The SelectedItem property of a ListBox contains a reference to the item a user has selected. For example, you can modify a label's Text property in the majorListBox_SelectedIndexChanged() method with a statement such as the following:

```
private void majorListBox_SelectedIndexChanged
    (object sender, EventArgs e)
{
    majorLabel.Text = "You selected " + majorListBox.SelectedItem;
}
```

The SelectedItem is appended to the label. Figure 12-24 shows a typical result.

 With this code, the user's selection is appended to the text. If the user continues to make selections, the Text for label2 will continue to grow longer. Depending on your application, you might prefer to replace the Text for the label instead of adding to it.

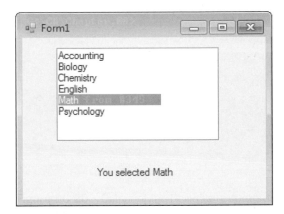

Figure 12-24 The MajorListDemo application after a user has chosen *Math*

The Items.Count property of a ListBox object holds the number of items in the ListBox. The GetSelected() method accepts an integer argument representing the position of an item in the list. The method returns `true` if an item is selected and `false` if it is not. Therefore, code like the following could be used to count the number of selections a user makes from majorListBox:

```
int count = 0;
for(int x = 0; x < majorListBox.Items.Count; ++x)
    if(majorListBox.GetSelected(x))
        ++count;
```

 Recall that the first position in an array is position 0. The same is true in a `ListBox`.

Alternatively, you can use a `ListBox`'s `SelectedItems` property; it contains the items selected in a list. The following code assigns the number of selections a user makes from the majorListBox to count:

```
count = majorListBox.SelectedItems.Count;
```

The `SetSelected()` method can be used to set a `ListBox` item to be automatically selected. For example, the following statement causes the first item in majorListBox to be the selected one:

```
majorListBox.SetSelected(0, true);
```

A **ComboBox** is similar to a `ListBox`, except that it displays an additional editing field to allow the user to select from the list or to enter new text. The default `ComboBox` displays an editing field with a hidden list box. The application in Figure 12-25 contains a `ComboBox` for selecting an airline. A **CheckedListBox** is also similar to a `ListBox`, with check boxes appearing to the left of each desired item. The application in Figure 12-25 uses a `CheckedListBox` for flight options.

Figure 12-25   The `FlightDemo` application after the user has made some selections

---

TWO TRUTHS & A LIE

Adding ListBox, CheckedListBox, and ComboBox Controls to a Form

1. With a ListBox Control, the user can select only one option at a time.

2. A ComboBox is similar to a ListBox, except that it displays an additional editing field that allows users to select from the list or to enter new text.

3. A CheckedListBox is similar to a ListBox, with check boxes appearing to the left of each desired item.

The false statement is #1. With a ListBox, you allow the user to make a single selection or multiple selections by setting the SelectionMode property appropriately.

Adding MonthCalendar and DateTimePicker Controls to a Form

The **MonthCalendar** and **DateTimePicker** Controls allow you to retrieve date and time information. Figure 12-26 shows a MonthCalendar that has been placed on a Form. The current date is contained in a rectangle by default, and the date that the user clicked is shaded. Controls at the top of the calendar allow the user to go forward or back one month at a time. Table 12-10 describes common MonthCalendar properties and the default event.

Figure 12-26 Typical execution of the MonthCalendarDemo application

Property or Method	Description
MaxDate	Sets the last day that can be selected (the default is 12/31/9998)
MaxSelectionCount	Sets the maximum number of dates that can be selected at once (the default is 7)
MinDate	Sets the first day that can be selected (the default is 1/1/1753)
MonthlyBoldedDates	An array of dates that appear in boldface in the calendar (for example, holidays)
SelectionEnd	The last of a range of dates selected by the user
SelectionRange	The dates selected by the user
SelectionStart	The first of a range of dates selected by the user
ShowToday	If true, the date is displayed in text at the bottom of the calendar
ShowTodayCircle	If true, today's date is circled (the "circle" appears as a square)
DateChanged()	Default event that is generated when the user selects a date

Table 12-10   Commonly used MonthCalendar properties and default event

Several useful methods can be applied to the SelectionStart and SelectionEnd properties of MonthCalendar, including the following:

- ToShortDateString(), which displays the date in the format of 2/16/2014

- ToLongDateString(), which displays the date in the format of Sunday, February 16, 2014

- AddDays(), which takes a double argument and adds a specified number of days to the date

- AddMonths(), which takes an int argument and adds a specified number of months to the date

- AddYears(), which takes an int argument and adds a specified number of years to the date

The format in which dates are displayed depends on the operating system's regional settings. For example, using United Kingdom settings, the short string format would use the day first, followed by the month, as in 16/02/2012. The examples in the list above assume United States settings.

The AddDays() method accepts a double argument because you can add fractional days to SelectionStart and SelectionEnd.

SelectionStart and SelectionEnd are structures of the DateTime type. The chapter *Files and Streams* contains additional information about using DateTime objects to determine when files were created, modified, or accessed.

Many business and financial applications use AddDays(), AddMonths(), and AddYears() to calculate dates for events, such as payment for a bill (perhaps due in 10 days from an order) or scheduling a salesperson's callback to a customer (perhaps two months after initial contact). The default event for `MonthCalendar` is `DateChanged()`. For example, Figure 12-27 shows a method that executes when the user clicks a `MonthCalendar` named `calendar`. A `string` is created from the literal text "You selected " and the start of the user's selection is converted to a short `string`. The message is placed on a `Label` that has been named `messageLabel`. Figure 12-28 shows the output when the user selects May 29, 2014. The date that is 10 days in the future is correctly calculated as June 8.

```
private void monthCalendar1_DateChanged(object sender, DateRangeEventArgs e)
{
    const int DAYS_TO_ADD = 10;
    string newDate = "You selected " +
        monthCalendar1.SelectionStart.ToShortDateString();
    messageLabel.Text = newDate + "\nTen days ahead is " +
        monthCalendar1.SelectionStart.AddDays(DAYS_TO_ADD).ToShortDateString();
}
```

Figure 12-27   The `MonthCalendarDemo` application `monthCalendar1_DateChanged()` method

Figure 12-28   Typical execution of `MonthCalendarDemo`

If you set the `MinDate` value to the `MonthCalendar`'s `TodayDate` property, the user cannot select a date before the date you select. For example, you cannot make appointments or schedule deliveries to happen in the past, so you might code the following:

```
monthCalendar1.MinDate = monthCalendar1.TodayDate;
```

Conversely, you might want to prevent users from selecting a date in the future—for example, if the user is entering the date he placed an outstanding order. In that case, you could code a statement similar to the following:

```
monthCalendar1.MaxDate = monthCalendar1.TodayDate;
```

The `DateTimePicker Control` displays a month calendar when the down arrow is selected. For example, Figure 12-29 shows a `DateTimePicker` before and after the user clicks the down arrow.

Figure 12-29   The DateTimePicker Control

When you use the `CustomFormat` property, the date displayed in a `DateTimePicker Control` is more customizable than the one in a `MonthCalendar`. Table 12-11 describes some commonly used `DateTimePicker` properties and the default event.

Property or Method	Description
CalendarForeColor	Sets the calendar text color
CalendarMonthBackground	Sets the calendar background color
CustomFormat	A string value that uses codes to set a custom date and time format. For example, to display the date and time as 02/16/2011 12:00 PM - Wednesday, set this property to "MM'/'dd'/'yyyy hh':'mm tt - dddd". See the C# documentation for a complete set of format string characters.
Format	Sets the format for the date or time. Options are Long (for example, Wednesday, February 16, 2011), Short (2/16/2011), and Time (for example, 3:15:01 PM). You can also create a CustomFormat.
Value	The data selected by the user
ValueChanged()	Default event that is generated when the Value property changes

Table 12-11   Commonly used DateTimePicker properties and default event

Working with a Form's Layout

When you place Controls on a Form in the IDE, you can drag them to any location to achieve the effect you want.

When you drag multiple Controls onto a Form, blue **snap lines** appear and help you align new Controls with others already in place. Figure 12-30 shows two snap lines that you can use to align a second label below the first one. Snap lines also appear when you place a control closer to the edge of a container than is recommended.

Figure 12-30 Snap lines in the Visual Studio Designer

You also can use the Location property in a Control's Properties list to specify a location. With either technique, code like the following is generated:

```
this.label1.Location = new System.Drawing.Point(23, 19);
```

Several other properties can help you to manage the appearance of a Form (or other ContainerControl). For example, setting the **Anchor property** causes a Control to remain at a fixed distance from the side of a container when the user resizes it. Figure 12-31 shows the Properties window for a Label that has been placed on a Form. The Anchor property has a drop-down window that lets you select or deselect the sides to which the label should be anchored. For most Controls, the default setting for Anchor is Top, Left.

Figure 12-31   Selecting an Anchor property

Figure 12-32 shows a Form with two Labels. On the Form, label1 has been anchored to the top left and label2 has been anchored to the bottom right. The left side of the figure shows the Form as it first appears to the user, and the right side shows the Form after the user has resized it. Notice that in the resized Form, label1 is still the same distance from the top left as it originally was, and label2 is still the same distance from the bottom right as it originally was. Anchoring is useful when users expect a specific control to always be in the same general location in a container.

Figure 12-32   A Form with two Labels anchored to opposite corners

Setting the **Dock property** attaches a Control to the side of a container so that the Control stretches when the container's size is adjusted. Figure 12-33 shows the drop-down Dock Properties window for a Button. You can select any region in the window. Figure 12-34 shows a Button docked to the bottom of a Form before and after the Form has been resized.

Figure 12-33   The Dock Properties window

Figure 12-34 A Form with a docked Button

A Form also has a **MinimumSize property** and a **MaximumSize property**. Each has two values—Width and Height. If you set these properties, the user cannot make the Form smaller or larger than you have specified. If you do not want the user to be able to adjust a Form's size at all, set the MinimumSize and MaximumSize properties to be equal.

Understanding GroupBoxes and Panels

Many types of ContainerControls are available to hold Controls. For example, you can use a **GroupBox** or **Panel** to group related Controls on a Form. When you move a GroupBox or Panel, all its Controls are moved as a group. To create either of these Controls, you drag it from the Toolbox in the IDE, and then drag the Controls you want on top of it. GroupBoxes can display a caption, but Panels cannot. Panels can include a scroll bar that the user can manipulate to view Controls; GroupBoxes do not have scroll bars. You can anchor or dock Controls inside a GroupBox or Panel, and you can anchor or dock a GroupBox or Panel inside a Form. Doing this provides Control groups that can be arranged easily.

If you place several GroupBox Controls on a Form and several RadioButtons in each GroupBox, then a user can select one RadioButton from each GroupBox instead of being able to select just one RadioButton on a Form. In other words, each GroupBox operates independently.

TWO TRUTHS & A LIE

Working with a Form's Layout

1. Setting the Anchor property causes a Control to remain at a fixed distance from the side of a container when the user resizes it.

2. Setting the Dock property attaches a Control to the side of a container so that the Control's size does not change when the container's size is adjusted.

3. The GroupBox and Panel controls are ContainerControls.

The false statement is #2. Setting the Dock property attaches a Control to the side of a container so that the Control stretches when the container's size is adjusted.

Adding a MenuStrip to a Form

Many programs you use in a Windows environment contain a **menu strip**, which is a horizontal list of general options that appears under the title bar of a Form or Window. When you click an item in a menu strip, you might initiate an action. More frequently, you see a list box that contains more specific options. Each of these might initiate an action or lead to another menu. For example, the Visual Studio IDE contains a horizontal main menu strip that begins with the options FILE, EDIT, and VIEW. You have used word-processing, spreadsheet, and game programs with similar menus.

You can add a **MenuStrip** Control object to any Form you create. Using the Visual Studio IDE, you can add a MenuStrip to a Form by dragging it from the Toolbox onto the Form. This creates a menu bar horizontally across the top of the Form, just below the title bar. The strip extends across the width of the Form and contains a "Type Here" text box. When you click the text box, you can enter a menu item. New text boxes appear below and to the right of the first one, as shown in Figure 12-35. Each time you add a menu item, new boxes are created so you can see where your next options will go.

If you do not see a MenuStrip in your Toolbox, click the Menus & Toolbars group to expose it.

Figure 12-35 A Form with a MenuStrip

You can click the MenuStrip icon at the bottom of the design screen to view and change the properties for the MenuStrip. For example, you might want to change the Font or BackColor for the MenuStrip.

The left side of Figure 12-36 shows a MenuStrip in which the programmer has typed *Font*, and beneath it, *Large* and *Small*. New boxes are available to the right of Font and beneath Small. The right side of the figure shows that the programmer continued by entering *Color* and three choices beneath it.

Figure 12-36 A Form that contains a MenuStrip as the programmer makes entries

If you create each main menu item with an ampersand (&) in front of a unique letter, then the user can press Alt and the letter to activate the menu choice, besides clicking it with the mouse. For example, if two choices were Green and Gray, you might want to type &Green and G&ray so the user could type Alt+G to select Green and Alt+R to select Gray.

When you double-click an entry in the MenuStrip, a Click() method is generated. For example, if you click *Large* under Font in a menu, the method generated is largeToolStripMenuItem_Click(), as follows:

```
private void largeToolStripMenuItem_Click
    (object sender, EventArgs e)
{
}
```

As with all the other controls you have learned about, you can write any code statements within the method. For example, suppose that a Label named helloLabel has been dragged onto the Form. If choosing the *Large* menu option should result in a larger font for the label, you might code the method as follows:

```
private void largeToolStripMenuItem_Click
  (object sender, EventArgs e)
{
    helloLabel.Font = new Font("Courier New", 34);
}
```

With the addition of this method, the Form operates as shown in Figure 12-37. If the Label appears in a small font and the user clicks the *Large* menu option, the font changes.

Figure 12-37 Executing the MenuStripDemo program

You can work with the other menu items in this program in an exercise at the end of this chapter.

If possible, your main menu selections should be single words. That way, a user will not mistakenly think that a single menu item represents multiple items. Also, users expect menu options to appear in conventional order. For example, users expect the far-left option on the main menu to be File, and they expect the Exit option to appear under File. Similarly, if an application contains a Help option, users expect to find it at the right side of the main menu. You should follow these conventions when designing your own main menus.

Main menu entries typically use mixed case, although Microsoft did not follow this convention in the current version of Visual Studio.

Watch the video *Using a MenuStrip*.

TWO TRUTHS & A LIE

Adding a MenuStrip to a Form

1. When you click an item in a menu strip, the most common result is to initiate an action.

2. When you drag a MenuStrip Control object onto a Form using the Visual Studio IDE, the MenuStrip is added horizontally across the top of the Form, just below the title bar.

3. The default event for MenuStrip is Click().

The false statement is #1. When you click an item in a menu strip, you might initiate an action. More frequently, you see a list box that contains more specific options.

Using Other Controls

If you examine the Visual Studio IDE or search through the Visual Studio documentation, you will find many other Controls that are not covered in this chapter. If you click PROJECT on the main menu and click Add New Item, you can add extra Forms, Files, Controls, and other elements to your project. New controls and containers will be developed in the future, and you might even design new controls of your own. Still, all controls will contain properties and methods, and your solid foundation in C# will prepare you to use new controls effectively.

You Do It

Adding CheckBoxes to a Form

In the next steps, you add two CheckBoxes to the BedAndBreakfast Form. These controls allow the user to select an available room and view information about it.

1. Open the BedAndBreakfast project in Visual Studio, if it is not still open on your screen.

2. In the Design view of the Bed and Breakfast project in the Visual Studio IDE, drag a CheckBox onto the Form below the "Check our rates" Label. (See Figure 12-38 for its approximate placement.) Change the Text property of the CheckBox to **BelleAire Suite**. Change the Name of the property to **belleAireCheckBox**. Drag a second CheckBox onto the Form beneath the first one. Change its Text property to **Lincoln Room** and its Name to **lincolnCheckBox**.

Figure 12-38 The BedAndBreakfast Form with two CheckBoxes

3. Next, you will create two new Forms: one that appears when the user selects the BelleAire CheckBox and one that appears when the user selects the Lincoln CheckBox. Click **PROJECT** on the menu bar, and then click **Add New Item**. In the Add New Item window, click **Windows Form**. In the Name text box at the bottom of the window, type **BelleAireForm**. See Figure 12-39.

(continues)

(continued)

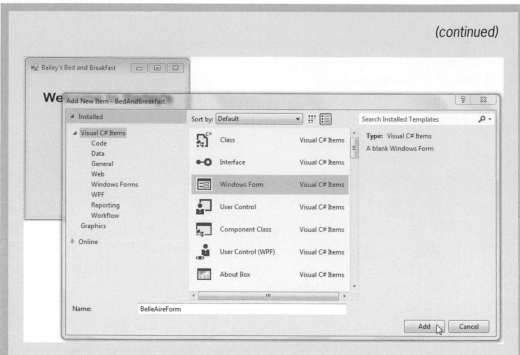

Figure 12-39   The Add New Item window

4. Click the **Add** button. A new Form is added to the project, and its Name and Text (title bar) properties contain *BelleAireForm*. Save the project (and continue to do so periodically).

5. Change the BackColor property of the Form to Yellow to match the color of BaileysForm.

6. Drag a Label onto the Form. Change the Name of the Label to **belleAireDescriptionLabel**. Change the Text property of the Label to contain the following: **The BelleAire suite has two bedrooms, two baths, and a private balcony**. Click the arrow on the text property to type the long label message on two lines. Adjust the size and position of the Label to resemble Figure 12-40. Drag a second Label onto the Form, name it **belleAirePriceLabel**, and type the price as the Text property: **$199.95 per night**.

(continues)

(continued)

Figure 12-40   The BelleAireForm with two Labels

7. Select the **Pointer** tool from the Toolbox at the left of the screen. Drag it to encompass both Labels. In the Properties list, select the **Font** property to change the Font for both Controls at once. Choose a suitable Font. Figure 12-41 shows **9-point Bold Papyrus**; you might choose a different font. Adjust the positions of the Labels if necessary to achieve a pleasing effect.

Figure 12-41   Font changed for the Labels

(continues)

(continued)

8. Click the **Form1.cs[Design]** tab at the top of the Designer screen to view the Bailey's Bed and Breakfast Form. Double-click the **BelleAire Suite CheckBox**. The program code (the method shell for the default event of a CheckBox) appears in the IDE main window. Within the belleAireCheckBox_CheckedChanged() method, add an if statement that determines whether the BelleAire CheckBox is checked. If it is checked, create a new instance of BelleAireForm and display it.

```
private void belleAireCheckBox_CheckedChanged(object sender,
   EventArgs e)
{
    if (belleAireCheckBox.Checked)
    {
        BelleAireForm belleAireForm = new BelleAireForm();
        belleAireForm.ShowDialog();
    }
}
```

When a new Frame (or other Windows class) is instantiated, it is not visible by default. ShowDialog() shows the window and disables all other windows in the application. The user must dismiss the new Frame before proceeding. A secondary window that takes control of a program is a **modal window**; the user must deal with this window before proceeding.

9. Save and then execute the program by selecting **DEBUG** from the main menu, and then select **Start Without Debugging**. The main Bed and Breakfast Form appears. Click the **BelleAire Suite CheckBox**. The BelleAire Form appears. Dismiss the Form. Click the **Lincoln Room CheckBox**. Nothing happens because you have not yet written event code for this CheckBox. When you uncheck and then check the **BelleAire Suite CheckBox** again, the BelleAire form reappears. Dismiss the BelleAire Form.

10. When you dismiss the BelleAire Form, the BelleAire CheckBox remains checked. To see it appear as unchecked after its Form is dismissed, dismiss the program's main form (Bailey's Bed and Breakfast) to end the program. Then, add a third statement within the if block in the CheckedChanged() message as follows:

```
belleAireCheckBox.Checked = false;
```

That way, whenever the CheckedChanged() method executes because the belleAireCheckBox was checked, it will become unchecked. Save the

(continues)

(continued)

project, and then execute it again. When you select the BelleAire CheckBox, view the Form, and dismiss it, the CheckBox appears unchecked and is ready to check again. Dismiss the BedAndBreakfast Form.

11. Click **PROJECT** on the menu bar, and then click **Add New Item**. Click **Windows Form** and enter its Name: **LincolnForm**. When the new Form appears, its Name and Text properties will have been set to **LincolnForm**. Change the Text property to **Lincoln Room**. Then add two Labels to the Form and provide appropriate Name properties for them. Change the Text on the first Label to **Return to the 1850s in this lovely room with private bath**. The second should be **$110 per night**. Change the Form's BackColor property to **White**. Change the Font to match the Font you chose for the BelleAire Form. See Figure 12-42.

Figure 12-42   The LincolnForm

12. From the Toolbox, drag a PictureBox onto the Form. Select its **Image** property. A dialog box allows you to select a resource. Click **Local resource**, and then click the **Import** button to browse for an image. Find the AbeLincoln file in the Chapter.12 folder of your downloadable student files, and double-click it. After the image appears in the Select Resource dialog box, click **OK**. The selected image appears in the PictureBox. Adjust the size of the Form and the sizes and positions of the labels and picture box so that the picture is fully visible and everything looks attractive on the Form. See Figure 12-43.

(continues)

610

(continued)

Figure 12-43 The LincolnForm with an Image in a PictureBox

 The AbeLincoln file was obtained at *www.free-graphics.com*. You can visit the site and download other images to use in your own applications. You should also search the Web for "free clip art" and similar phrases.

13. In the Solution Explorer, double-click **Form1.cs** or click the **Form1.cs[Design]** tab at the top of the design screen. On the Bed and Breakfast Form, double-click the Lincoln Room CheckBox, and add the following if statement to the lincolnCheckBox_CheckedChanged() method:

```
private void lincolnCheckBox_CheckedChanged(object sender,
    EventArgs e)
{
    if (lincolnCheckBox.Checked)
    {
        LincolnForm lincolnForm = new LincolnForm();
        lincolnForm.ShowDialog();
        lincolnCheckBox.Checked = false;
    }
}
```

14. Save the project and then execute it. When the Bed and Breakfast Form appears, click either CheckBox—the appropriate informational Form appears. Close it and then click the other CheckBox. Again, the appropriate Form appears.

15. Close all forms.

(continues)

(continued)

Adding RadioButtons to a Form

Next you add more Controls to the Bed and Breakfast Form. You generally use RadioButtons when a user must select from mutually exclusive options.

1. In the Design view of the main Form in the BedAndBreakfast project, add a Button near the bottom of the Form. Change the Button's Name property to **mealButton** and the Button's Text to **Click for meal options**. Adjust the size of the Button so that its text is fully visible.

2. From the main menu, select **PROJECT**, click **Add New Item**, and click **Windows Form**. Name the Form **BreakfastOptionForm** and click **Add**. On the new Form, make the following changes:

   - Set the Form's BackColor to **Yellow**.

   - Drag a Label onto the Form. Name it appropriately and set its Text to **Select your breakfast option**.

   - Drag three RadioButtons onto the Form. Set their respective Text properties to **Continental**, **Full**, and **Deluxe**. Set their respective Names to **contBreakfastButton**, **fullBreakfastButton**, and **deluxeBreakfastButton**.

   - Select an appropriate font for the Label and RadioButtons.

   - Drag a Label onto the Form, and then set its Text to **Price:** and its Name to **priceLabel**. Make the Font property a little larger than for the other Form components.

   See Figure 12-44 for approximate placement of all these Controls.

   (continues)

(continued)

Figure 12-44 Developing the BreakfastOptionForm

3. Double-click the title bar of the BreakfastOptionForm to generate a method named BreakfastOptionForm_Load(). Within this method, you can type statements that execute each time the Form is created. Add the following statements within the BreakfastOptionForm class, which declare three constants representing prices for different breakfast options. Within the BreakfastOptionForm_Load() method, set the priceLabel Text to the lowest price by default when the Form loads.

```
public partial class BreakfastOptionForm : Form
{
    private const double CONT_BREAKFAST_PRICE = 6.00;
    private const double FULL_BREAKFAST_PRICE = 9.95;
    private const double DELUXE_BREAKFAST_PRICE = 16.50;
    public BreakfastOptionForm()
    {
        InitializeComponent();
    }

    private void BreakfastOptionForm_Load
      (object sender, EventArgs e)
    {
        priceLabel.Text = "Price: " +
            CONT_BREAKFAST_PRICE .ToString("C");
    }
}
```

(continues)

(continued)

4. Return to the Design view for the BreakfastOptionForm and double-click the **contBreakfastButton RadioButton**. When you see the generated CheckedChanged() method, add a statement that sets priceLabel to the continental breakfast price when the user makes that selection:

```
private void contBreakfastButton_CheckedChanged
    (object sender, EventArgs e)
{
    priceLabel.Text = "Price: " +
        CONT_BREAKFAST_PRICE.ToString("C");
}
```

5. Return to the Design view for the BreakfastOptionForm, double-click the **fullBreakfastButton RadioButton**, and add a statement to the generated method that sets the priceLabel to the full breakfast price when the user makes that selection:

```
private void fullBreakfastButton_CheckedChanged
    (object sender, EventArgs e)
{
    priceLabel.Text = "Price: " +
        FULL_BREAKFAST_PRICE.ToString("C");
}
```

6. Return to the Design view for the BreakfastOptionForm, double-click the **deluxeBreakfastButton RadioButton**, and add a statement to the generated method that sets the priceLabel to the deluxe breakfast price when the user makes that selection:

```
private void deluxeBreakfastButton_CheckedChanged
    (object sender, EventArgs e)
{
    priceLabel.Text = "Price: " +
        DELUXE_BREAKFAST_PRICE.ToString("C");
}
```

7. In the Solution Explorer, double-click the **Form1.cs file** to view the original Form. Double-click the **mealButton Button**. When the Click() method is generated, add the following code so that the BreakfastOptionForm is loaded when a user clicks the Button.

(continues)

(continued)

```
private void mealButton_Click(object sender,
   EventArgs e)
{
   BreakfastOptionForm breakfastForm = new
      BreakfastOptionForm();
   breakfastForm.ShowDialog();
}
```

8. Save the project and execute it. When the BedAndBreakfast Form appears, confirm that the BelleAire Suite and Lincoln Room CheckBoxes still work correctly, displaying their information Forms when they are clicked. Then click the **Click for meal options** Button. By default, the Continental breakfast option is chosen, as shown in Figure 12-45, so the price is $6.00. Click the other RadioButton options to confirm that each correctly changes the breakfast price.

Figure 12-45   The BreakfastOptionForm with Continental breakfast RadioButton selected

9. Dismiss all the Forms and close Visual Studio.

Chapter Summary

- The Control class provides definitions for GUI objects such as Forms and Buttons. There are 26 direct descendents of Control and additional descendents of those classes. Each Control has more than 80 public properties and 20 protected ones. For example, each Control has a Font and a ForeColor that dictate how its text is displayed, and each Control has a Width and Height.

- When you design GUI applications using the Visual Studio IDE, much of the code is automatically generated.

- You use the Font class to change the appearance of printed text on your Forms. When designing a Label, Button, or other Control on a Form, it is easiest to select a Font from the Properties list. The Font class includes a number of overloaded constructors.

- A LinkLabel is similar to a Label; it is a child of Label, but it provides the additional capability to link the user to other sources, such as Web pages or files.

- The Color class contains a wide variety of predefined Colors that you can use with your Controls.

- CheckBox objects are GUI widgets the user can click to select or deselect an option. When a Form contains multiple CheckBoxes, any number of them can be checked or unchecked at the same time. RadioButtons are similar to CheckBoxes, except that when they are placed on a Form, only one RadioButton can be selected at a time—selecting any RadioButton automatically deselects the others. CheckBox and RadioButton objects both have a Checked property whose value is true or false.

- A PictureBox is a Control in which you can display graphics from a bitmap, icon, JPEG, GIF, or other image file type. Just as with a Button or a Label, you can easily add a PictureBox by dragging its Control onto the Form in the Visual Studio IDE.

- ListBox, ComboBox, and CheckedListBox objects descend from ListControl. The ListBox Control enables you to display a list of items that the user can select by clicking. With a ListBox, you allow the user to make a single selection or multiple selections by setting the SelectionMode property appropriately. A ComboBox is similar to a ListBox, except that it displays an additional editing field to allow the user to select from the list or to enter new text. A CheckedListBox is also similar to a ListBox, with check boxes appearing to the left of each desired item.

- The MonthCalendar and DateTimePicker Controls allow you to retrieve date and time information.

- When you place Controls on a Form in the IDE, you can drag them to any location to achieve the effect you want. When you drag multiple Controls onto a Form, blue snap lines appear and help you align new Controls with others already in place. You also can use the Location property in the Properties list to specify a location. The Anchor and Dock properties help you determine a Control's size and position in the Form. A Form also has a MinimumSize property and a MaximumSize property. Each has two values—Width and Height. Many types of ContainerControls are available to hold Controls. For example,

615

you can use a GroupBox or Panel to group related Controls on a Form. When you move a GroupBox or Panel, all its Controls are moved as a group.

- Many programs you use in a Windows environment contain a menu strip, which is a horizontal list of general options that appears under the title bar of a Form or Window. When you click an item in a menu strip, you might initiate an action. More frequently, you see a list box that contains more specific options. Each of these might initiate an action or lead to another menu. You can add a MenuStrip Control object to any Form you create.

- If you examine the Visual Studio IDE or search through the Visual Studio documentation, you will find many other Controls you can use. If you click PROJECT on the main menu and click Add New Item, you can add extra Forms, Files, Controls, and other elements to a project.

Key Terms

Widgets are interactive controls such as labels, scroll bars, check boxes, and radio buttons.

The **Control** class provides the definitions for GUI objects.

The **Component** class provides containment and cleanup for other objects.

In Visual Studio, a **method node** is a small box that appears to the left of code; you use it to expand or collapse code.

The **Font** class is used to change the appearance of printed text on Forms.

The **logical OR operator** is the pipe (|).

A **LinkLabel** is similar to a Label, but it provides the additional capability to link the user to other sources, such as Web pages or files.

The **default event** for a Control is the one generated when you double-click the Control while designing it in the IDE. The default event is the method you are most likely to alter when you use the Control, as well as the event that users most likely expect to generate when they encounter the Control in a working application.

The **Color** class contains a wide variety of predefined colors to use with Controls.

CheckBox objects are GUI widgets the user can click to select or deselect an option. When a Form contains multiple CheckBoxes, any number of them can be checked or unchecked at the same time.

RadioButtons are similar to CheckBoxes, except that when they are placed on a Form, only one RadioButton can be selected at a time—selecting any RadioButton automatically deselects the others.

A **PictureBox** is a Control in which you can display graphics from a bitmap, icon, JPEG, GIF, or other image file type.

The **ListBox** Control enables you to display a list of items that the user can select by clicking.

A **ComboBox** is similar to a ListBox, except that it displays an additional editing field that allows a user to select from the list or enter new text.

A **CheckedListBox** is also similar to a ListBox, with check boxes appearing to the left of each desired item.

The **MonthCalendar** and **DateTimePicker** Controls allow you to retrieve date and time information.

Snap lines appear in a design environment to help you align new Controls with others already in place.

The **Anchor property** for a Control causes it to remain at a fixed distance from the side of a container when the user resizes it.

The **Dock property** for a Control attaches it to the side of a container so that the Control stretches when the container's size is adjusted.

The **MinimumSize property** and **MaximumSize property** of a Control define the limits of the sizes to which users can adjust the Control. Each property has two values: Width and Height.

A **GroupBox** or **Panel** can be used to group related Controls on a Form.

A **menu strip** is a horizontal list of general options that appears under the title bar of a Form or Window.

A **MenuStrip** Control is an object on a Form that contains a menu strip.

A **modal window** is a secondary window that takes control from a primary window. A user must deal with a modal window before proceeding.

Review Questions

1. Labels, Buttons, and CheckBoxes are all _____.

    a. GUI objects   c. widgets
    b. Controls   d. all of these

2. All Control objects descend from _____.

    a. Form   c. ButtonBase
    b. Component   d. all of these

3. Which of the following is most like a RadioButton?

    a. ListControl   c. PictureBox
    b. CheckedListBox   d. Button

4.   Which of the following is not a commonly used `Control` property?

  a.   `BackColor`   c.   `Location`

  b.   `Language`   d.   `Size`

5.   The `Control` you frequently use to provide descriptive text for another `Control` object is a _____.

  a.   `Form`   c.   `CheckBox`

  b.   `Label`   d.   `MessageBox`

6.   Which of the following creates a `Label` named `firstLabel`?

  a.   `firstLabel = new firstLabel();`

  b.   `Label = new firstLabel();`

  c.   `Label firstLabel = new Label();`

  d.   `Label firstLabel = Label();`

7.   The property that determines what the user reads on a `Label` is the _____ property.

  a.   `Text`   c.   `Phrase`

  b.   `Label`   d.   `Setting`

8.   Which of the following correctly creates a `Font`?

  a.   `Font myFont = new Font("Arial", 14F, FontStyle.Bold);`

  b.   `Font myFont = new Font("Courier", 13.6);`

  c.   `myFont = Font new Font("TimesRoman", FontStyle.Italic);`

  d.   `Font myFont = Font(20, "Helvetica", Underlined);`

9.   The default event for a `Control` is the one that _____.

  a.   occurs automatically whether a user manipulates the `Control` or not

  b.   is generated when you double-click the `Control` while designing it in the IDE

  c.   requires no parameters

  d.   occurs when a user clicks the `Control` with a mouse

10. Assume that you have created a `Label` named `myLabel`. Which of the following sets `myLabel`'s background color to green?

  a.   `myLabel = BackColor.System.Drawing.Color.Green;`

  b.   `myLabel.BackColor = System.Drawing.Color.Green;`

  c.   `myLabel.Green = System.DrawingColor;`

  d.   `myLabel.Background = new Color.Green;`

11. What is one difference between CheckBox and RadioButton objects?

    a. RadioButtons descend from ButtonBase; CheckBoxes do not.
    b. Only one RadioButton can be selected at a time.
    c. Only one CheckBox can appear on a Form at a time.
    d. RadioButtons cannot be placed in a GroupBox; CheckBoxes can.

12. The Checked property of a RadioButton can hold the values _____.

    a. true and false   c. 0 and 1
    b. Checked and Unchecked   d. Yes, No, and Undetermined

13. The Control in which you can display a bitmap or JPEG image is a(n) _____.

    a. DisplayModule   c. BitmapControl
    b. ImageHolder   d. PictureBox

14. ListBox, ComboBox, and CheckedListBox objects all descend from which family?

    a. ListControl   c. ButtonBase
    b. List   d. ListBase

15. Which of the following properties is associated with a ListBox but not a Button?

    a. BackColor   c. Location
    b. SelectedItem   d. IsSelected

16. With a ListBox you can allow the user to choose _____.

    a. only a single option   c. either of these
    b. multiple selections   d. none of these

17. You can add items to a ListBox by using the _____ method.

    a. AddList()   c. List()
    b. Append()   d. AddRange()

18. A ListBox's SelectedItem property contains _____.

    a. the position of the currently selected item
    b. the value of the currently selected item
    c. a Boolean value indicating whether an item is currently selected
    d. a count of the number of currently selected items

19. When you create a ListBox, by default its SelectionMode is _____.

    a. Simple   c. One
    b. MultiExtended   d. false

20. A horizontal list of general options that appears under the title bar of a Form or Window is a _____.

   a. task bar

   c. menu strip

   b. subtitle bar

   d. list box

Exercises

Programming Exercises

1. Create a project named **DayNight**. Include a Form that contains two Buttons, one labeled Day and one labeled Night. Add a Label telling the user to click a button. When the user clicks Day, change the BackColor of the Form to Yellow; when the user clicks Night, change the BackColor of the Form to DarkBlue.

2. Create a project named **FiveColors**. Its Form contains at least five Button objects, each labeled with a color. When the user clicks a Button, change the BackColor of the Form appropriately.

3. Create a project named **FiveColors2**. Its Form contains at least five RadioButton objects, each labeled with a color. When the user clicks a RadioButton, change the BackColor of the Form appropriately.

4. Create a project named **MyTunes**. Its Form contains a ListBox with the titles of at least eight songs available to purchase. Provide directions that tell users they can choose as many songs as they want by holding down the Ctrl key while making selections. When the user clicks a Button to indicate the choices are final, display the total price, which is $0.99 per song. If the user selects or deselects items and clicks the button again, make sure the total is updated correctly.

5. Create a project named **FontSelector**. Its Form contains two ListBoxes—one contains at least four Font names and the other contains at least four Font sizes. Let the first item in each list be the default selection if the user fails to make a selection. Allow only one selection per ListBox. After the user clicks a Button, display "Hello" in the selected Font and size.

6. Create a project named **ClearlyWindows** that contains a Form for the Clearly It's Windows company. Allow the user to choose a window style (casement, awning, double-hung, or single-hung) and a number of windows (1 through 25). After the user makes selections, display the total price, which is $199 for a casement window, $175 for an awning window, $200 for double-hung, and $169 for single-hung. Use the Controls that you think are best for each function. Label items appropriately and use fonts and colors to achieve an attractive design.

7. Create a project named **Restaurant** that contains a Form that allows the user to choose one item from at least three options in each of the following categories— appetizer, entrée, and dessert. Assign a different price to each selection and display

the total when the user clicks a Button. Use the Controls that you think are best for each function. Label items appropriately and use fonts and colors to achieve an attractive design.

8. Create a project named **CarDealer** that contains a Form for an automobile dealer. Include options for at least three car models. After users make a selection, proceed to a new Form that contains information about the selected model. Use the Controls that you decide are best for each function. Label items on the Form appropriately and use fonts and colors to achieve an attractive design.

9. Create a project named **AnnualBudget** that includes a Form with two LinkLabels. One opens a spreadsheet for viewing, and the other visits your favorite Web site. Include Labels on the Form to explain each link. You can create a spreadsheet with a few numbers that represent an annual budget, or you can use the AnnualBudget. xls file in the Chapter.12 folder of the downloadable student files.

10. Create a project named **NinasCookieSource** that includes a Form for a company named The Cookie Source. Allow the user to select from at least three types of cookies, each with a different price per dozen. Allow the user to select 1/2, 1, 2, or 3 dozen cookies. Adjust the final displayed price as the user chooses cookie types and quantities. Also allow the user to select an order date from a MonthCalendar. Assuming that shipping takes three days, display the estimated arrival date for the order. Include as many labels as necessary so the user understands how to use the Form.

11. Create a project named **MenuStripDemo2** that is based on the MenuStripDemo project in the Chapter.12 folder of your downloadable student files (see Figure 12-37). Add appropriate functionality to the currently unprogrammed menu options (*Small* in the Font menu and the three options in the Color menu). Add at least three other menu options to the program, either vertically, horizontally, or both.

12. Create a project named **LetsMakeADeal**. In this game, three prizes of varying value are assigned randomly to be hidden behind three "doors" that you can implement as Buttons. For example, the prizes might be a new car, a big-screen TV, and a live goat. The player chooses a Button, and then one of the two other prizes is revealed; the one revealed is never the most desirable prize. The user then has the option of changing the original selection to the remaining unseen choice. For example, consider these two game scenarios:

- Suppose that the most valuable prize is randomly assigned to the first button. If the user chooses the first button, reveal either of the other two prizes and ask the user if he wants to change his selection.

- Suppose that the most valuable prize is assigned to the first button, but the user chooses the second button. Reveal the third prize so that the most valuable prize's location is still hidden, and then ask the user whether he wants to change the selection.

After the user has chosen to retain his original selection or make a change, reveal what he has won.

Debugging Exercises

1. Each of the following projects in the Chapter.12 folder of your downloadable student files has syntax and/or logical errors. Immediately save the four project folders with their new names before starting to correct their errors. After you correct the errors, save each project using the same name preceded with *Fixed*. For example, DebugTwelve1 will become FixedDebugTwelve1.

   a. DebugTwelve1   c. DebugTwelve3
   b. DebugTwelve2   d. DebugTwelve4

Case Problems

1. Throughout this book, you have created programs for the Greenville Idol competition. Now, create an interactive advertisement named **GreenvilleAdvertisement** that can be used to recruit contestants. Include at least three Controls that you studied in this chapter, and use at least two different Fonts and two different Colors.

2. Throughout this book, you have created programs for Marshall's Murals. Now, create an interactive advertisement named **MarshallsAdvertisement** that can be used to advertise the available murals. Include at least three Controls that you studied in this chapter, and use at least two different Fonts and two different Colors.

Handling Events

In this chapter you will:

◎ Learn about event handling

◎ Learn about delegates

◎ Declare your own events and handlers and use the built-in `EventHandler`

◎ Handle `Control` component events

◎ Handle mouse and keyboard events

◎ Manage multiple `Control`s

◎ Learn how to continue your exploration of `Control`s and events

Throughout this book, you have learned how to create interactive GUI programs in which a user can manipulate a variety of Controls. You have worked with several Controls that respond to a user-initiated event, such as a mouse click, and you have provided actions for Control default events. In this chapter, you will expand your understanding of the event-handling process. You will learn more about the object that triggers an event and the object that captures and responds to that event. You also will learn about delegates—objects that act as intermediaries in transferring messages from senders to receivers. You will create delegates and manage interactive events. You will learn to manage multiple events for a single Control and to manage multiple Controls for a project.

Event Handling

In C#, an **event** is a reaction to an occurrence in a program; an event transpires when something interesting happens to an object. When you create a class, you decide exactly what is considered "interesting." For example, when you create a Form, you might decide to respond to a user clicking a Button but ignore a user who clicks a Label—clicking the Label is not "interesting" to the Form.

A program uses an event to notify a client when something happens to an object. Events are used frequently in GUI programs—for example, a program is notified when the user clicks a Button or chooses an option from a ListBox. In addition, you can use events with ordinary classes that do not represent GUI controls. When an object's client might want to know about any changes that occur in the object, events enable the object to signal the client.

The actions that occur during the execution of a program occur **at runtime**. The expression *at runtime* is used to distinguish execution-time activities from those that occur during development time and compile time. Events are runtime occurrences.

You have learned that when a user interacts with a GUI object, an event is generated that causes the program to perform a task. GUI programs are **event driven**—an event such as a button click "drives" the program to perform a task. Programmers also say that an action like a button click **raises an event**, **fires an event**, or **triggers an event**. A method that performs a task in response to an event is an **event handler**.

For example, Figure 13-1 shows a Form that contains a Label and a Button. The following changes are the only ones that have been made to the default Form in the IDE:

- The Size property of the Form has been adjusted to 500, 120.

- A Label has been dragged onto the Form, its Name property has been set to helloLabel, its Text property has been set to "Hello", and its Font has been increased to 9.

- A Button has been dragged onto the Form, its Name property has been set to changeButton, and its Text property has been set to "Change Label".

Figure 13-1   A Form with a Label and a Button

If you double-click the button on the form in the IDE, you generate the following empty method in the program code:

```
private void changeButton_Click(object sender, EventArgs e)
{
}
```

The changeButton_Click() method is an event handler. Conventionally, event handlers are named using the identifier of the Control (in this case, changeButton), an underscore, and the name of the event type (in this case, Click). You can create your own methods to handle events and provide any names for them, but the names should follow these conventions.

Suppose that when a user clicks the button, you want the text on the label to change from "Hello" to "Goodbye". You can write the following code within the event handler:

```
private void changeButton_Click(object sender, EventArgs e)
{
    helloLabel.Text = "Goodbye";
}
```

Then, when you run the application and click the button, the output appears as shown in Figure 13-2.

Figure 13-2   Output of the EventDemo application after the user clicks the button

The event-handler method is also known as an **event receiver**. The control that generates an event is an **event sender**. The first parameter in the list for the event receiver method is an object named sender; it is a reference to the object that generated the event. For example, if you code the event handler as follows, the output appears as in Figure 13-3.

```
private void changeButton_Click(object sender, EventArgs e)
{
    helloLabel.Text = sender.ToString();
}
```

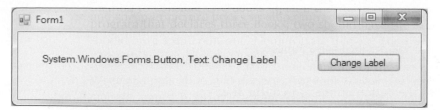

Figure 13-3 The EventDemo application modified to display sender information

The label in Figure 13-3 shows that the sender of the event is an instance of System.Windows.Forms.Button, whose Text property is "Change Label".

The second parameter in the event-handler parameter list is a reference to an event arguments object of type EventArgs; in this method, the EventArgs argument is named e. **EventArgs** is a C# class designed for holding event information. If you change the code in the event handler to the following, and then run the program and click the button, you see the output in Figure 13-4.

```
private void changeButton_Click(object sender, EventArgs e)
{
    helloLabel.Text = e.ToString();
}
```

Figure 13-4 The EventDemo application modified to display EventArgs information

In Figure 13-4, you can see that the e object is a MouseEventArgs object. That makes sense, because the user used the mouse to click the Button.

When you open the Designer.cs file in the IDE, you can examine all the code generated for the application that creates the Form shown in Figure 13-4. Expanding the code generated by the Windows Form Designer lets you see comments as well as statements that set the Controls' properties. For example, the code generated for changeButton appears in Figure 13-5. You can recognize that such features as the button's Location, Name, and Size have been set.

```
//
// changeButton
//
this.changeButton.Location = new System.Drawing.Point(359, 24);
this.changeButton.Name = "changeButton";
this.changeButton.Size = new System.Drawing.Size(101, 23);
this.changeButton.TabIndex = 1;
this.changeButton.Text = "Change Label";
this.changeButton.UseVisualStyleBackColor = true;
this.changeButton.Click += new
    System.EventHandler(this.changeButton_Click);
```

Figure 13-5   Code involving `changeButton` generated by Visual Studio

The code generated in Design mode in the IDE is not meant to be altered by typing. You should modify `Control` properties through the Properties window in the IDE, not by typing in the Designer.cs file.

The most unusual statement in the section of `changeButton` code is shaded in Figure 13-5. This statement concerns the **Click event**, which is generated when `changeButton` is clicked by a user. The statement is necessary because `changeButton` does not automatically "know" what method will handle its events—C# and all other .NET languages allow you to choose your own names for event-handling methods for events generated by GUI objects. In other words, the event-handling method is not required to be named `changeButton_Click()`. You *could* create your program so that when the user clicks the button, the event-handling method is named `calculatePayroll()`, `changeLabel()`, or any other identifier for a method you could then write. Of course, you do not want to make such a change; using the name `changeButton_Click()` for the method that executes when `changeButton` is clicked is the clearest approach. The shaded statement indicates that, for this program, the method named `changeButton_Click()` is the receiver for `changeButton`'s `Click` event. Programmers say the shaded method creates a delegate, or more specifically, a composed delegate. The delegate's type is `EventHandler`, and it takes a reference to the `changeButton_Click()` method. That method is the one that will react when a user clicks the button. You will learn about delegates in the next two sections of this chapter.

Connecting an event to its resulting actions is called **event wiring**.

628

Understanding Delegates

A **delegate** is an object that contains a reference to a method; object-oriented programmers would say that a delegate encapsulates a method. In government, a delegate is a representative that you authorize to make choices for you. For example, you select a delegate to a presidential nominating convention. When human delegates arrive at a convention, they are free to make last-minute choices based on current conditions. Similarly, C# delegates provide a way for a program to take alternative courses that are not determined until runtime. When you write a method, you don't always know which actions will occur at runtime, so you give your delegates authority to run the correct methods.

In Chapter 1, you learned that encapsulation is a basic feature of object-oriented programming. Recall that encapsulation is the technique of packaging an object's attributes and methods into a cohesive unit that can then be used as an undivided entity.

After you have instantiated a C# delegate, you can pass this object to a method, which then can call the method referenced within the delegate. In other words, a delegate provides a way to pass a reference to a method as an argument to another method. For example, if del is a delegate that contains a reference to the method M1(), you can pass del to a new method named MyMethod(). Alternatively, you could create a delegate named del that contains a reference to a method named M2() and then pass this version to MyMethod(). When you write MyMethod(), you don't have to know whether it will call M1() or M2(); you only need to know that it will call whatever method is referenced within del.

A C# delegate is similar to a function pointer in C++. A function pointer is a variable that holds a method's memory address. In the C++ programming language, you pass a method's address to another method using a pointer variable. Java does not allow function pointers because they are dangerous—if the program alters the address, you might inadvertently execute the wrong method. C# provides a compromise between the dangers of C++ pointers and the Java ban on passing functions. Delegates allow flexible method calls, but they remain secure because you cannot alter the method addresses.

You declare a delegate using the keyword `delegate`, followed by an ordinary method declaration that includes a return type, method name, and argument list. For example, by entering the following statement, you can declare a delegate named `GreetingDelegate()`, which accepts a `string` argument and returns nothing:

```
delegate void GreetingDelegate(string s);
```

The `GreetingDelegate` can encapsulate any method as long as it has a `void` return type and a single `string` parameter. Any delegate can encapsulate any method that has the same return type and parameter list as the delegate. If you declare the delegate and then write a method with the same return type and parameter list, you can assign an instance of the delegate to represent it. For example, the following `Hello()` method is a `void` method that takes a `string` parameter:

```
public static void Hello(string s)
{
    Console.WriteLine("Hello, {0}!", s);
}
```

Because the `Hello()` method matches the `GreetingDelegate` definition, you can assign a reference to the `Hello()` method to a new instance of `GreetingDelegate`, as follows:

```
GreetingDelegate myDel = new GreetingDelegate(Hello);
```

Once the reference to the `Hello()` method is encapsulated in the delegate `myDel`, each of the following statements will result in the same output: "Hello, Kim!".

```
Hello("Kim");
myDel("Kim");
```

In this example, the ability to use the delegate `myDel` does not seem to provide any benefits over using a regular method call to `Hello()`. If you have a program in which you pass the delegate to a method, however, the method becomes more flexible; you gain the ability to send a reference to an appropriate method you want to execute at the time.

For example, Figure 13-6 shows a `Greeting` class that contains `Hello()` and `Goodbye()` methods. The `Main()` method declares two delegates named `firstDel` and `secondDel`. One is instantiated using the `Hello()` method, and the other is instantiated using the `Goodbye()` method. When the `Main()` method calls `GreetMethod()` two times, it passes a different method and string each time. Figure 13-7 shows the output.

```
using System;
delegate void GreetingDelegate(string s);
class Greeting
{
    public static void Hello(string s)
    {
        Console.WriteLine("Hello, {0}!", s);
    }
```

Figure 13-6 The `Greeting` program *(continues)*

(continued)

```
    public static void Goodbye(string s)
    {
        Console.WriteLine("Goodbye, {0}!", s);
    }
    static void Main()
    {
        GreetingDelegate firstDel, secondDel;
        firstDel = new GreetingDelegate(Hello);
        secondDel = new GreetingDelegate(Goodbye);
        GreetMethod(firstDel, "Cathy");
        GreetMethod(secondDel, "Bob");
    }
    public static void GreetMethod
      (GreetingDelegate gd, string name)
    {
        Console.WriteLine("The greeting is:");
        gd(name);
    }
}
```

Figure 13-6   The Greeting program

Figure 13-7   Output of the Greeting program

Creating Composed Delegates

You can assign one delegate to another using the = operator. You also can use the + and +=
operators to combine delegates into a **composed delegate** that calls the delegates from which it
is built. As an example, assume that you declare three delegates named del1, del2, and del3,
and that you assign a reference to the method M1() to del1 and a reference to method M2() to
del2. When the statement del3 = del1 + del2; executes, del3 becomes a delegate that executes
both M1() and M2(), in that order. Only delegates with the same parameter list can be composed,
and the delegates used must have a void return type. Additionally, you can use the – and –=
operators to remove a delegate from a composed delegate. A composed delegate is a collection
of delegates. The += and –= operators add and remove items from the collection.

Figure 13-8 shows a program that contains a composed delegate. This program contains only two changes from the Greeting program in Figure 13-6: the class name (Greeting2) and the shaded statement that creates the composed delegate. The delegate firstDel now executes two methods, Hello() and Goodbye(), whereas secondDel still executes only Goodbye(). Figure 13-9 shows the output; "Cathy" is used with two methods, but "Bob" is used with only one.

```csharp
using System;
delegate void GreetingDelegate(string s);
class Greeting2
{
    public static void Hello(string s)
    {
        Console.WriteLine("Hello, {0}!", s);
    }
    public static void Goodbye(string s)
    {
        Console.WriteLine("Goodbye, {0}!", s);
    }
    static void Main()
    {
        GreetingDelegate firstDel, secondDel;
        firstDel = new GreetingDelegate(Hello);
        secondDel = new GreetingDelegate(Goodbye);
        firstDel += secondDel;
        GreetMethod(firstDel, "Cathy");
        GreetMethod(secondDel, "Bob");
    }
    public static void GreetMethod
      (GreetingDelegate gd, string name)
    {
        Console.WriteLine("The greeting is:");
        gd(name);
    }
}
```

Figure 13-8   The Greeting2 program

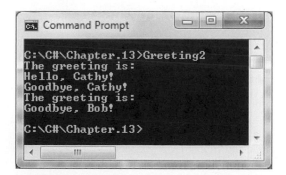

Figure 13-9   Output of the Greeting2 program

Watch the video *Event Handling*.

TWO TRUTHS & A LIE

Understanding Delegates

1. A delegate is an object that contains a reference to a method.

2. Once you have created a delegate, it can encapsulate any method with the same identifier as the delegate.

3. A composed delegate can be created using the += operator; it calls the delegates from which it is built.

The false statement is #2. Once you have created a delegate, it can encapsulate any method with the same return type and parameter list as the delegate.

You Do It

Creating Delegates

To demonstrate how delegates work, you create two delegate instances in the next steps and assign different method references to them.

1. Open a new project named **DiscountDelegateDemo**. Type the necessary `using` statement, and then create a delegate that encapsulates a `void` method that accepts a `double` argument:

```
using System;
delegate void DiscountDelegate(ref double saleAmount);
```

2. Begin creating a `Discount` class that contains a `StandardDiscount()` method. The method accepts a reference parameter that represents an amount of a sale. If the sale amount is at least $1,000, a discount of 5 percent is calculated and subtracted from the sale amount. If the sale amount is not at least $1,000, nothing is subtracted.

(continues)

(continued)

```
class DiscountDelegateDemo
{
   public static void StandardDiscount(ref double saleAmount)
   {
      const double DISCOUNT_RATE = 0.05;
      const double CUTOFF = 1000.00;
      double discount;
      if(saleAmount >= CUTOFF)
         discount = saleAmount * DISCOUNT_RATE;
      else
         discount = 0;
      saleAmount -= discount;
   }
```

3. Add a `PreferredDiscount()` method. The method also accepts a reference parameter that represents the amount of a sale and calculates a discount of 10 percent on every sale.

```
public static void PreferredDiscount(ref double saleAmount)
{
   const double SPECIAL_DISCOUNT = 0.10;
   double discount = saleAmount * SPECIAL_DISCOUNT;
   saleAmount -= discount;
}
```

4. Start a `Main()` method that declares variables whose values (a sale amount and a code) will be supplied by the user. Declare two `DiscountDelegate` objects named `firstDel` and `secondDel`. Assign a reference to the `StandardDiscount()` method to one `DiscountDelegate` object and a reference to the `PreferredDiscount()` method to the other `DiscountDelegate` object.

```
static void Main()
{
   double saleAmount;
   char code;
   DiscountDelegate firstDel, secondDel;
   firstDel = new DiscountDelegate(StandardDiscount);
   secondDel = new DiscountDelegate(PreferredDiscount);
```

5. Continue the `Main()` method with prompts to the user to enter a sale amount and a code indicating whether the standard or preferred discount should apply. Then, depending on the code, use the appropriate delegate to calculate the correct new value for `saleAmount`. Display the value and add closing curly braces for the `Main()` method and the class.

(continues)

(continued)

```
          Console.Write("Enter amount of sale ");
          saleAmount = Convert.ToDouble(Console.ReadLine());
          Console.Write("Enter S for standard discount, " +
             "or P for preferred discount ");
          code = Convert.ToChar(Console.ReadLine());
          if(code == 'S')
             firstDel(ref saleAmount);
          else
             secondDel(ref saleAmount);
          Console.WriteLine("New sale amount is {0}",
             saleAmount.ToString("C2"));
       }
    }
```

6. Save the file, and then compile and execute it. Figure 13-10 shows the results when the program is executed several times.

Figure 13-10 Sample executions of the `DiscountDelegateDemo` program

Creating a Composed Delegate

When you compose delegates, you can invoke multiple method calls using a single statement. In the next steps, you create a composed delegate to demonstrate how composition works.

(continues)

(continued)

1. Open the **DiscountDelegateDemo** file, and immediately save it as **DiscountDelegateDemo2**.

2. Within the `Main()` method, add a third `DiscountDelegate` object to the statement that declares the two existing versions, as follows:

```
DiscountDelegate firstDel, secondDel, thirdDel;
```

3. After the statements that assign values to the existing `DiscountDelegate` objects, add statements that assign the `firstDel` object to `thirdDel` and then add `secondDel` to it through composition.

```
thirdDel = firstDel;
thirdDel += secondDel;
```

4. Change the prompt for the code, as follows, to reflect three options. The standard and preferred discounts remain the same, but the extreme discount (supposedly for special customers) provides both types of discounts, first subtracting 5 percent for any sale equal to or greater than $1,000, and then providing a discount of 10 percent more.

```
Console.Write("Enter S for standard discount, " +
    "P for preferred discount, " +
    "\nor X for eXtreme discount ");
```

5. Change the `if` statement so that if the user does not enter *S* or *P*, then the extreme discount applies.

```
if(code == 'S')
    firstDel(ref saleAmount);
else
    if(code == 'P')
        secondDel(ref saleAmount);
    else
        thirdDel(ref saleAmount);
```

6. Save the program, and then compile and execute it. For reference, Figure 13-11 shows the complete program. Figure 13-12 shows the output when the program is executed several times. When the user enters a sale amount of $1,000 and an *S*, a 5 percent discount is applied. When the user enters a *P* for the same amount, a 10 percent discount is applied. When the user enters *X* with the same amount, a 5 percent discount is applied, followed by a 10 percent discount, which produces a net result of a 14.5 percent discount.

(continues)

(continued)

```
using System;
delegate void DiscountDelegate(ref double saleAmount);
class DiscountDelegateDemo2
{
    public static void StandardDiscount(ref double saleAmount)
    {
        const double DISCOUNT_RATE = 0.05;
        const double CUTOFF = 1000.00;
        double discount;
        if(saleAmount >= CUTOFF)
            discount = saleAmount * DISCOUNT_RATE;
        else
            discount = 0;
        saleAmount -= discount;
    }
    public static void PreferredDiscount(ref double saleAmount)
    {
        const double SPECIAL_DISCOUNT = 0.10;
        double discount = saleAmount * SPECIAL_DISCOUNT;
        saleAmount -= discount;
    }
    static void Main()
    {
        double saleAmount;
        char code;
        DiscountDelegate firstDel, secondDel, thirdDel;
        firstDel = new DiscountDelegate(StandardDiscount);
        secondDel = new DiscountDelegate(PreferredDiscount);
        thirdDel = firstDel;
        thirdDel += secondDel;
        Console.Write("Enter amount of sale ");
        saleAmount = Convert.ToDouble(Console.ReadLine());
        Console.Write("Enter S for standard discount, " +
            "P for preferred discount, " +
            "\nor X for eXtreme discount ");
        code = Convert.ToChar(Console.ReadLine());
        if(code == 'S')
            firstDel(ref saleAmount);
        else
            if(code == 'P')
                secondDel(ref saleAmount);
```

Figure 13-11   The DiscountDelegateDemo2 program *(continues)*

(continues)

(continued)

(continued)

```
        else
            thirdDel(ref saleAmount);
        Console.WriteLine("New sale amount is {0}",
            saleAmount.ToString("C2"));
    }
}
```

Figure 13-11 The DiscountDelegateDemo2 program

Figure 13-12 Three executions of the DiscountDelegateDemo2 program

For static methods like StandardDiscount and PreferredDiscount, a delegate object encapsulates the method to be called. When creating a class that contains instance methods, you create delegate objects that encapsulate both an instance of the class and a method of the instance. You will create this type of delegate in the next section.

Declaring Your Own Events and Handlers and Using the Built-in EventHandler

To declare your own event, you use a delegate. An event provides a way for the clients of a class to dictate methods that should execute when an event occurs. The clients identify methods to execute by associating the delegate with the method that should execute when the event occurs. Just like the event handlers that are automatically created in the IDE, each of your own event handler delegates requires two arguments: the object where the event was initiated (the sender) and an EventArgs argument. You can create an EventArgs object that contains event information, or you can use the EventArgs class static field named Empty, which represents an event that contains no event data. In other words, using the EventArgs.Empty field simply tells the client that an event has occurred, without specifying details. For example, you can declare a delegate event handler named ChangedEventHandler, as follows:

```
public delegate void ChangedEventHandler
    (object sender, EventArgs e);
```

The identifier ChangedEventHandler can be any legal identifier you choose. This delegate defines the set of arguments that will be passed to the method that handles the event. The delegate ChangedEventHandler can be used in a client program that handles events.

For example, Figure 13-13 contains the ChangedEventHandler delegate and a simple Student class that is similar to many classes you already have created. The Student class contains just two data fields and will generate an event when the data in either field changes.

```
public delegate void ChangedEventHandler
    (object sender, EventArgs e);
class Student
{
    private int idNum;
    private double gpa;
    public event ChangedEventHandler Changed;
    public int IdNum
    {
        get
        {
            return idNum;
        }
        set
        {
            idNum = value;
            OnChanged(EventArgs.Empty);
        }
    }
}
```

Figure 13-13   The Student class *(continues)*

(continued)

```
    public double Gpa
    {
        get
        {
            return gpa;
        }
        set
        {
            gpa = value;
            OnChanged(EventArgs.Empty);
        }
    }
    private void OnChanged(EventArgs e)
    {
        Changed(this, e);
    }
}
```

Figure 13-13   The Student class

The class in Figure 13-13 contains fields that hold an ID number and grade point average (GPA) for a Student. The first shaded statement in the figure defines a third Student class attribute—an event named Changed. The declaration for an event looks like a field, but instead of being an int or a double, it is a ChangedEventHandler.

 Events usually are declared as public, but you can use any accessibility modifier.

The Student class event (Changed) looks like an ordinary field. However, you cannot assign values to the event as easily as you can to ordinary data fields. You can take only two actions on an event: You can compose a new delegate onto it using the += operator, and you can remove a delegate from it using the -= operator. For example, to add StudentChanged to the Changed event of a Student object named stu, you would write the following:

stu.Changed += new ChangedEventHandler(StudentChanged);

In the Student class, each set accessor assigns a value to the appropriate class instance field. However, when either the idNum or the gpa changes, the method in the Student class named OnChanged() is also called, using EventArgs.Empty as the argument. The value of EventArgs.Empty is a read-only instance of EventArgs. You can pass it to any method that accepts an EventArgs parameter.

The OnChanged() method calls Changed() using two arguments: a reference to the Student object that was changed and the empty EventArgs object. Calling Changed() is also known as **invoking the event**.

If no client has wired a delegate to the event, the Changed field will be null, rather than referring to the delegate that should be called when the event is invoked. Therefore, programmers often check for null before invoking the event, as in the following example:

```
if(Changed != null)
    Changed(this, e);
```

For simplicity, the example in Figure 13-13 does not bother checking for null.

Figure 13-14 shows an EventListener class that listens for Student events. This class contains a Student object that is assigned a value using the parameter to the EventListener class constructor. The StudentChanged() method is added to the Student's event delegate using the += operator. The StudentChanged() method is the event-handler method that executes in response to a Changed event; it displays a message and Student data.

```
class EventListener
{
    private Student stu;
    public EventListener(Student student)
    {
        stu = student;
        stu.Changed += new ChangedEventHandler
          (StudentChanged);
    }
    private void StudentChanged(object sender, EventArgs e)
    {
        Console.WriteLine("The student has changed.");
        Console.WriteLine("   ID# {0}  GPA {1}",
          stu.IdNum, stu.Gpa);
    }
}
```

Figure 13-14 The EventListener class

Figure 13-15 shows a program that demonstrates the Student and EventListener classes. The program contains a single Main() method, which declares one Student and registers the program to listen for events from the Student class. Then three assignments are made. Because this program is registered to listen for events from the Student, each change in a data field triggers an event. That is, each assignment not only changes the value of the data field, it also executes the StudentChanged() method that displays two lines of explanation. In Figure 13-16, the program output shows that an event occurs three times—once when the ID becomes 2345 (and the GPA is still 0), again when the ID becomes 4567 (and the GPA still has not changed), and a third time when the GPA becomes 3.2.

```
using System;
class DemoStudentEvent
{
    static void Main()
    {
        Student oneStu = new Student();
        EventListener listener = new EventListener(oneStu);
        oneStu.IdNum = 2345;
        oneStu.IdNum = 4567;
        oneStu.Gpa = 3.2;
    }
}
```

Figure 13-15   The DemoStudentEvent program

Figure 13-16   Output of the DemoStudentEvent program

Using the Built-in EventHandler

The C# language allows you to create events using any delegate type. However, the .NET Framework provides guidelines you should follow if you are developing a class that others will use. These guidelines indicate that the delegate type for an event should take exactly two parameters: a parameter indicating the source of the event, and an EventArgs parameter that encapsulates any additional information about the event. For events that do not use additional information, the .NET Framework has already defined an appropriate delegate type named **EventHandler**.

Figure 13-17 shows all the code necessary to demonstrate an EventHandler. Note the following changes from the classes used in the DemoStudentEvent program:

- No delegate is declared explicitly in the Student class.

- In the first statement with shading in the Student class, the event is associated with the built-in delegate EventHandler.

- In the second statement with shading, which appears in the EventListener class, the delegate composition uses EventHandler.

```
using System;
class Student
{
   private int idNum;
   private double gpa;
   public event EventHandler Changed;
   public int IdNum
   {
      get
      {
         return idNum;
      }
      set
      {
         idNum = value;
         OnChanged(EventArgs.Empty);
      }
   }
   public double Gpa
   {
      get
      {
         return gpa;
      }
      set
      {
         gpa = value;
         OnChanged(EventArgs.Empty);
      }
   }
   private void OnChanged(EventArgs e)
   {
      Changed(this, e);
   }
}
class EventListener
{
   private Student stu;
   public EventListener(Student student)
   {
      stu = student;
      stu.Changed += new EventHandler(StudentChanged);
   }
```

Figure 13-17   The Student, EventListener, and DemoStudentEvent2 classes *(continues)*

(continued)

```csharp
    private void StudentChanged(object sender, EventArgs e)
    {
        Console.WriteLine("The student has changed.");
        Console.WriteLine("   ID# {0}   GPA {1}",
          stu.IdNum, stu.Gpa);
    }
}
class DemoStudentEvent2
{
    static void Main()
    {
        Student oneStu = new Student();
        EventListener listener = new EventListener(oneStu);
        oneStu.IdNum = 2345;
        oneStu.IdNum = 4567;
        oneStu.Gpa = 3.2;
    }
}
```

Figure 13-17   The Student, EventListener, and DemoStudentEvent2 classes

When you compile and execute the program in Figure 13-17, the output is identical to that shown in Figure 13-16.

TWO TRUTHS & A LIE

Declaring Your Own Events and Handlers and Using the Built-in EventHandler

1. When an event occurs, any delegate that a client has given or passed to the event is invoked.

2. Built-in event handler delegates have two arguments, but those you create yourself have only one.

3. You can take only two actions on an event field: composing a new delegate onto the field using the += operator, and removing a delegate from the field using the -= operator.

The false statement is #2. Every event handler delegate requires two arguments—the object where the event was initiated (the sender) and an EventArgs argument.

You Do It

Creating a Delegate that Encapsulates Instance Methods

In the next set of steps, you create a simple `BankAccount` class that contains just two data fields: an account number and a balance. It also contains methods to make withdrawals and deposits. An event is generated after any withdrawal or deposit.

1. Open a project named **DemoBankEvent**. Type the `using System;` statement, and then begin a class named `BankAccount`. The class contains an account number, a balance, and an event that executes when an account's balance is adjusted.

```
using System;
class BankAccount
{
    private int acctNum;
    private double balance;
    public event EventHandler BalanceAdjusted;
```

2. Add a constructor that accepts an account number parameter and initializes the balance to 0.

```
public BankAccount(int acct)
{
    acctNum = acct;
    balance = 0;
}
```

3. Add read-only properties for both the account number and the account balance.

```
public int AcctNum
{
    get
    {
        return acctNum;
    }
}
public double Balance
{
    get
    {
        return balance;
    }
}
```

(continues)

644

4. Add two methods. One makes account deposits by adding the parameter to the account balance, and the other makes withdrawals by subtracting the parameter value from the bank balance. Each uses the OnBalanceAdjusted event handler that reacts to all deposit and withdrawal events by displaying the new balance.

```
public void MakeDeposit(double amt)
{
   balance += amt;
   OnBalanceAdjusted(EventArgs.Empty);
}
public void MakeWithdrawal(double amt)
{
   balance -= amt;
   OnBalanceAdjusted(EventArgs.Empty);
}
```

5. Add the OnBalanceAdjusted() method that accepts an EventArgs parameter and calls BalanceAdjusted(), passing it references to the newly adjusted BankAccount object and the EventArgs object. (Earlier in the chapter, you learned that calling a method such as OnBalanceAdjusted() is also known as *invoking the event*.) Include a closing curly brace for the class.

```
public void OnBalanceAdjusted(EventArgs e)
{
   BalanceAdjusted(this, e);
}
}
```

6. Save the file.

Creating an Event Listener

When you write an application that declares a BankAccount, you might want the client program to listen for BankAccount events. To do so, you create an EventListener class.

1. After the closing curly brace of the BankAccount class, type the following EventListener class that contains a BankAccount object. When the EventListener constructor executes, the BankAccount field is initialized with the constructor parameter. Using the += operator, add the BankAccountBalanceAdjusted() method to the event delegate. Next, write the BankAccountBalanceAdjusted() method to display a message and information about the BankAccount.

(continued)

```
class EventListener
{
    private BankAccount acct;
    public EventListener(BankAccount account)
    {
        acct = account;
        acct.BalanceAdjusted += new EventHandler
          (BankAccountBalanceAdjusted);
    }
    private void BankAccountBalanceAdjusted(object sender,
        EventArgs e)
    {
        Console.WriteLine
          ("The account balance has been adjusted.");
        Console.WriteLine("   Account# {0}  balance {1}",
            acct.AcctNum, acct.Balance.ToString("C2"));
    }
}
```

2. Create a class to test the BankAccount and EventListener classes. Below the closing curly brace for the EventListener class, start a DemoBankAccountEvent class that contains a Main() method. Declare an integer to hold the number of transactions that will occur in the demonstration program. Also declare two variables: One can hold a code that indicates whether a transaction is a deposit or withdrawal, and one is the amount of the transaction.

```
class DemoBankAccountEvent
{
    static void Main()
    {
        const int TRANSACTIONS = 5;
        char code;
        double amt;
```

3. Declare a BankAccount object that is assigned an arbitrary account number, and declare an EventListener object so this program is registered to listen for events from the BankAccount. Each change in the BankAccount balance will not only change the balance data field, it will execute the BankAccountBalanceAdjusted() method that displays two lines of explanation.

```
        BankAccount acct = new BankAccount(334455);
        EventListener listener = new EventListener (acct);
```

(continues)

(continued)

4. Add a loop that executes five times (the value of TRANSACTIONS). On each iteration, prompt the user to indicate whether the current transaction is a deposit or withdrawal and to enter the transaction amount. Call the MakeDeposit() or MakeWithdrawal() method accordingly. At the end of the for loop, add a closing curly brace for the Main() method and another one for the class.

```
for(int x = 0; x < TRANSACTIONS; ++x)
{
    Console.Write
        ("Enter D for deposit or W for withdrawal ");
    code = Convert.ToChar(Console.ReadLine());
    Console.Write("Enter dollar amount ");
    amt = Convert.ToDouble(Console.ReadLine());
    if(code == 'D')
        acct.MakeDeposit(amt);
    else
        acct.MakeWithdrawal(amt);
}
}
}
```

5. Save the file, and then compile and execute it. For reference, Figure 13-18 shows a typical execution in which five transactions modify the account. The output shows that an event occurs five times—twice for deposits and three times for withdrawals.

(continues)

(continued)

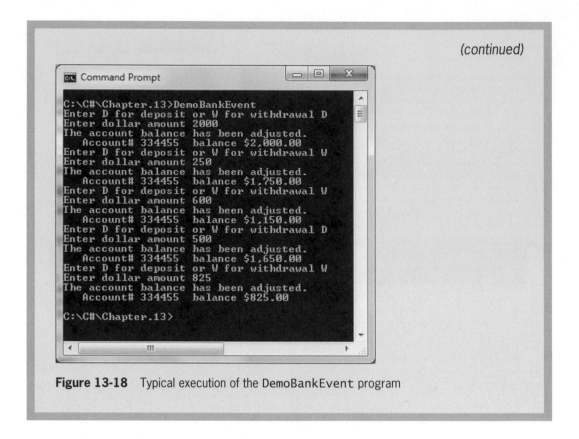

Figure 13-18 Typical execution of the DemoBankEvent program

Handling Control Component Events

Handling events requires understanding several difficult concepts. Fortunately, you most frequently will want to handle events in GUI environments when the user will manipulate Controls, and the good news is that these events have already been defined for you. When you want to handle events generated by GUI Controls, you use the same techniques as when you handle events that are not generated by Controls. The major difference is that when you create your own classes, like Student, you must define both the data fields and events you want to manage. However, existing Control components, like Buttons and ListBoxes, already contain fields and public properties, like Text, as well as events with names, like Click. Table 13-1 lists just some of the more commonly used Control events.

You can consult the Visual Studio Help feature to discover additional Control events as well as more specific events assigned to individual Control child classes.

Event	Description
BackColorChanged	Occurs when the value of the BackColor property has changed
Click	Occurs when a control is clicked
ControlAdded	Occurs when a new control is added
ControlRemoved	Occurs when a control is removed
CursorChanged	Occurs when the Cursor property value has changed
DragDrop	Occurs when a drag-and-drop operation is completed
DragEnter	Occurs when an object is dragged into a control's bounds
DragLeave	Occurs when an object has been dragged into and out of a control's bounds
DragOver	Occurs when an object has been dragged over a control's bounds
EnabledChanged	Occurs when the Enabled property value has changed
Enter	Occurs when a control is entered
FontChanged	Occurs when the Font property value has changed
ForeColorChanged	Occurs when the ForeColor property value has changed
GotFocus	Occurs when a control receives focus
HelpRequested	Occurs when a user requests help for a control
KeyDown	Occurs when a key is pressed while a control has focus; event is followed immediately by KeyPress
KeyPress	Occurs when a key is pressed while a control has focus; event occurs just after KeyDown
KeyUp	Occurs when a key is released while a control has focus
Leave	Occurs when a control is left
LocationChanged	Occurs when the Location property value has changed
LostFocus	Occurs when a control loses focus
MouseDown	Occurs when the mouse pointer hovers over a control and a mouse button is pressed
MouseEnter	Occurs when the mouse pointer enters a control
MouseHover	Occurs when the mouse pointer hovers over a control
MouseLeave	Occurs when the mouse pointer leaves a control
MouseMove	Occurs when the mouse pointer moves over a control

Table 13-1   Some Control class public instance events *(continues)*

(continued)

Event	Description
MouseUp	Occurs when the mouse pointer hovers over a control and a mouse button is released
MouseWheel	Occurs when the mouse wheel moves while a control has focus
Move	Occurs when a control is moved
Resize	Occurs when a control is resized
TextChanged	Occurs when the Text property value has changed
VisibleChanged	Occurs when the Visible property value has changed

Table 13-1 Some Control class public instance events

You have already used the IDE to create some event-handling methods. These methods have been the default events generated when you double-click a Control in the IDE. For example, you have created a Click() method for a Button and a LinkClicked() method for a LinkLabel. A Form can contain any number of Controls that might have events associated with them. Additionally, a single Control might be able to raise any number of events. For example, besides creating a Button's default Click event, you might want to define various actions when the user's mouse rolls over the button. Table 13-1 lists only a few of the many events available with Controls; any Control could conceivably raise many of the available events.

Suppose you want to create a project that takes a different set of actions when the mouse is over a Button than when the mouse is clicked. Figure 13-19 shows a project that has been started in the IDE. The following actions have been taken:

- The Form was resized to 225, 150.
- A Button was dragged onto the Form and its Text was set to "Click me".
- A Label was added to the Form, its Text was set to "Hello", and its Font was increased.

Figure 13-19 Start of the OneButtonTwoEvents project in the IDE

When you double-click the Button on the Form in the IDE, you generate the shell of a Click() method into which you can type a command to change the Label's text and color, as follows:

```
private void button1_Click(object sender, EventArgs e)
{
    label1.Text = "Button was clicked";
    label1.BackColor = Color.CornflowerBlue;
}
```

> Color.CornflowerBlue is one of C#'s predefined Color properties. A complete list appears in Table 12-5 in Chapter 12.

With the Button selected on the design Form, you can click the Events icon in the Properties window at the right side of the screen. The Events icon looks like a lightning bolt. Figure 13-20 shows that the Properties window displays events instead of properties and that the Click event has an associated method.

Figure 13-20   The Properties window displaying events

If you scroll through the Events listed in the Properties window, you can see a wide variety of Event choices. If you scroll down to MouseEnter and double-click, you can view the code for an event handler in the Form1.cs file as follows:

```
private void button1_MouseEnter(object sender, EventArgs e)
{
}
```

When you are viewing events in the Properties window, you can return to the list of properties by clicking the Properties icon. This icon is to the immediate left of the Events icon.

You can type any statements you want within this method. For example:

```
private void button1_MouseEnter(object sender, EventArgs e)
{
    label1.Text = "Go ahead";
    button1.BackColor = Color.Red;
}
```

When you run the program with the two new methods, two different events can occur:

- When you enter the button with the mouse (that is, pass the mouse over it), the Label's Text changes to "Go ahead" and the button turns red, as shown on the left in Figure 13-21.

- After the button is clicked, the Label's Text changes again and the Label becomes blue, as shown on the right in Figure 13-21.

Figure 13-21   The OneButtonTwoEvents program when the mouse enters the button and after the button is clicked

If you examine the code generated by the Windows Form Designer, you will find the following two statements:

```
this.button1.Click += new System.EventHandler(this.button1_Click);
this.button1.MouseEnter += new System.EventHandler(this.button1_MouseEnter);
```

These EventHandler statements are similar to those in the Student class in Figure 13-17. The Click and MouseEnter delegates have been set to handle events appropriately for this application. You could have used the IDE to create these events just by selecting them from the Properties list and writing the action statements you want. The IDE saves you time by automatically entering the needed statement correctly. However, by knowing how to manually create a GUI program that contains events, you gain a greater understanding of how event handling works. This knowledge helps you troubleshoot problems and helps you create your own new events and handlers when necessary.

 Watch the video *Handling Control Component Events.*

TWO TRUTHS & A LIE

Handling Control Component Events

1. The default methods generated when you double-click a Control in the IDE are known as procedures.

2. A Form can contain any number of Controls that might have events associated with them, and a single Control might be able to raise any number of events.

3. You can type any statements you want within an automatically generated event method.

The false statement is #1. The default methods generated when you double-click a Control in the IDE are known as event handlers.

Handling Mouse and Keyboard Events

Users can interact with GUI applications in multiple ways. Certainly the most common tactics are to use a mouse or to type on a keyboard. Mouse and keyboard events are similar in that every mouse or key event-handling method must have two parameters: an object representing the sender and an object that holds information about the event.

Handling Mouse Events

Mouse events include all the actions a user takes with a mouse, including clicking, pointing, and dragging. Mouse events can be handled for any Control through an object of the class MouseEventArgs, which descends from EventArgs. The delegate used to create mouse event handlers is MouseEventHandler. Depending on the event, the type of the second parameter in the event-handling method is EventArgs or MouseEventArgs. Table 13-2 describes several common mouse events, and Table 13-3 lists some properties of the MouseEventArgs class.

Mouse event	Description	Event argument type
MouseClick	Occurs when the user clicks the mouse within the Control's boundaries	MouseEventArgs
MouseDoubleClick	Occurs when the user double-clicks the mouse within the Control's boundaries	MouseEventArgs
MouseEnter	Occurs when the mouse cursor enters the Control's boundaries	EventArgs
MouseLeave	Occurs when the mouse cursor leaves the Control's boundaries	EventArgs
MouseDown	Occurs when a mouse button is pressed while the mouse is within the Control's boundaries	MouseEventArgs
MouseHover	Occurs when the mouse cursor is within the Control's boundaries	MouseEventArgs
MouseMove	Occurs when the mouse is moved while within the Control's boundaries	MouseEventArgs
MouseUp	Occurs when a mouse button is released while the mouse is within the Control's boundaries	MouseEventArgs

Table 13-2 Common mouse events

A MouseDown event can occur without a corresponding MouseUp if the user presses the mouse but switches focus to another control or application before releasing the mouse button.

MouseEventArgs property	Description
Button	Specifies which mouse button triggered the event; the value can be Left, Right, Middle, or none
Clicks	Specifies the number of times the mouse was clicked
X	The x-coordinate where the event occurred on the control that generated the event
Y	The y-coordinate where the event occurred on the control that generated the event

Table 13-3 Properties of the MouseEventArgs class

MouseClick and Click are separate events. The Click event takes an EventArgs parameter, but MouseClick takes a MouseEventArgs parameter. For example, if you define a Click event, you do not have the MouseEventArgs class properties.

Each part of Figure 13-22 contains a Form with a single Label named clickLocationLabel that changes as the user continues to click the mouse on it. The figure shows how the Label changes in response to a series of user clicks. Initially, the Label is empty (that is, the default Text property has been deleted and not replaced), but the following code was added to the Form.cs file:

```
private void Form1_MouseClick(object sender, MouseEventArgs e)
{
    clickLocationLabel.Text += "\nClicked at " + e.X +
        ", " + e.Y;
}
```

Every time the mouse is clicked on the Form, the Label is appended with a new line that contains "Clicked at" and the x- and y-coordinate position where the click occurred on the Form.

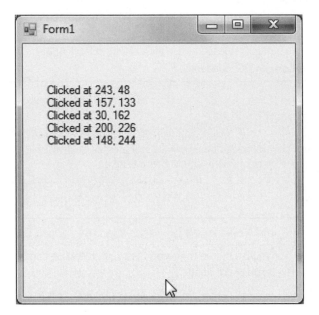

Figure 13-22   A Form that responds to clicks

When the programmer selects the MouseClick() event for Form1 from the Event list in the IDE, the following code is generated in the Designer.cs file. This code instantiates the MouseClick delegate.

```
this.MouseClick += new System.Windows.Forms.MouseEventHandler
    (this.Form1_MouseClicked);
```

Handling Keyboard Events

Keyboard events, also known as **key events**, occur when a user presses and releases keyboard keys. Table 13-4 lists some common keyboard events. Similar to the way mouse events work, every keyboard event-handling method must have two parameters. Depending on the event, the delegate used to create the keyboard event handler is either KeyEventHandler or KeyPressEventHandler, and the type of the second parameter is KeyEventArgs or KeyPressEventArgs.

Keyboard event	Description	Event argument type
KeyDown	Occurs when a key is first pressed	KeyEventArgs
KeyUp	Occurs when a key is released	KeyEventArgs
KeyPress	Occurs when a key is pressed	KeyPressEventArgs

Table 13-4   Keyboard events

Table 13-5 describes KeyEventArgs properties, and Table 13-6 describes KeyPressEventArgs properties. An important difference is that KeyEventArgs objects include data about helper keys or modifier keys that are pressed with another key. For example, if you need to distinguish between a user pressing *A* and pressing Alt+A in your application, then you must use a keyboard event that uses an argument of type KeyEventArgs.

Property	Description
Alt	Indicates whether the Alt key was pressed
Control	Indicates whether the Control (Ctrl) key was pressed
Shift	Indicates whether the Shift key was pressed
KeyCode	Returns the code for the key
KeyData	Returns the key code along with any modifier key
KeyValue	Returns a numeric representation of the key (this number is known as the Windows virtual key code)

Table 13-5   Some properties of KeyEventArgs class

Property	Description
KeyChar	Returns the ASCII character for the key pressed

Table 13-6   A property of KeyPressEventArgs class

For example, suppose that you create a Form with a Label, like the Form in Figure 13-24. From the Properties window for the Form, you can double-click the KeyUp event to generate the shell for a method named Form1_KeyUp(). Suppose you then insert the statements into the method in the Form1.cs file, as shown in Figure 13-23. When the user runs the program and presses and releases a keyboard key, the Label is filled with information about the key. Figure 13-24 shows four executions of this modified program. During the first execution, the user typed *a*. You can see on the form that the KeyCode is "A" (not "a"), but you also can see that the user did not press the Shift key.

```
private void Form1_KeyUp(object sender, KeyEventArgs e)
{
    label1.Text += "Key Code " + e.KeyCode;
    label1.Text += "\nAlt " + e.Alt;
    label1.Text += "\nShift " + e.Shift;
    label1.Text += "\nControl " + e.Control;
    label1.Text += "\nKey Data " + e.KeyData;
    label1.Text += "\nKey Value " + e.KeyValue + "\n\n";
}
```

Figure 13-23   The KeyUp() method

Figure 13-24   Four executions of the KeyDemo program

In the second execution in Figure 13-24, the user held down Shift, pressed *a*, and then released the Shift key. This causes two separate KeyUp events. The first has KeyCode "A" with Shift true, and the second has KeyCode ShiftKey. Notice that the Key values generated after typing *a*, *A*, and Shift are all different.

In the third execution in Figure 13-24, the user pressed the number 1, whose code is D1.

In the final execution, the user pressed Alt+F10 and released the F10 key first. When you view the Form1.Designer.cs file for the KeyDemo program, you see the following automatically created statement, which defines the composed delegate:

```
this.KeyUp += new System.Windows.Forms.KeyEventHandler
    (this.Form1_KeyUp);
```

659

TWO TRUTHS & A LIE

Handling Mouse and Keyboard Events

1. The delegate used to create mouse event handlers is MouseEventHandler.

2. Keyboard events, also known as key events, occur when a user presses and releases keyboard keys.

3. Unlike mouse events, every keyboard event-handling method must be parameterless.

The false statement is #3. Like mouse events, every keyboard event-handling method must have two parameters: an object representing the sender and an object that holds information about the event.

Managing Multiple Controls

When Forms contain multiple Controls, you often want one to have focus. You also might want several actions to have a single, shared consequence. For example, you might want the same action to occur whether the user clicks a button or presses the Enter key, or you might want multiple buttons to generate the same event when they are clicked.

Defining Focus

When users encounter multiple GUI Controls on a Form, usually one Control has **focus**. For example, when a Button has focus, a user expects that clicking the button or pressing the Enter key will raise an event.

TabStop is a Boolean property of a Control that identifies whether the Control will serve as a stopping place—that is, a place that will receive focus—in a sequence of Tab key presses. The default value for TabStop for a Button is true, but the default value for a Label is false because Labels are not expected to be part of a tabbing sequence. TabIndex is a numeric property that indicates the order in which the Control will receive focus when the user presses the Tab key. Programmers typically use small numbers for TabIndex values, beginning with 0. When a Control's TabStop value is true and the Control has the lowest TabIndex of a Form's Controls, it receives focus when the Form is initialized.

Setting the `TabIndex` values of two or more `Control`s to 0 does not cause an error. Only one `Control` will receive focus, however.

Figure 13-25 shows a `Form` that contains three `Button`s and a `Label`. Each `Button` has been associated with a `Click()` event such as the following:

```
private void button1_Click(object sender, EventArgs e)
{
    buttonInfoLabel.Text = "Button 1 selected";
}
```

Each `Button` has been assigned a `TabIndex` value in ascending order. When the application starts, the first `Button` (labeled "1") has focus. Whether the user clicks that button or presses Enter, the message appears as shown on the left in Figure 13-25. In the next part of the figure, the user has pressed Tab and Enter to select `button2`, so it has focus and the `Label`'s `Text` property has changed. Alternatively, the user could have clicked `button2` to achieve the same result. The user could then select either of the other `Button`s by clicking them as usual, or by pressing Tab until the desired button has focus and then pressing Enter.

Figure 13-25   The `FocusDemo` application

Handling Multiple Events with a Single Handler

When a `Form` contains multiple `Control`s, you can create a separate event handler for each `Control`. However, you can also associate the same event handler with multiple `Control`s. For example, suppose you create a `Form` that contains three `Button`s and a `Label`. The buttons have been labeled "A", "B", and "3". Further suppose you want to display one message when the user clicks a letter button and a different message when the user clicks a number button. In the IDE, you can double-click the first `Button` and create an associated method such as the following:

```
private void button1_Click(object sender, EventArgs e)
{
    buttonInfoLabel.Text = "You clicked a letter button";
}
```

If you click the second button so its properties are displayed in the IDE's Properties list, you can click the Events icon to see a list of events associated with the second button. If no Click event has been chosen yet, a list box is available. This list contains all the existing events that have the correct signature to be the event handler for the event. Because the button1_Click() handler can also handle a button2_Click event, you can select it as the event for button2. When you run the program, clicking either button produces the output shown in Figure 13-26.

Figure 13-26   Output of the SingleHandler program after either letter button is clicked

Until you associate an event with the "3" button, nothing happens when the user clicks it. To complete the application that is running in Figure 13-26, you would want to associate an event with the "3" button to modify the Label's Text to "You clicked a number button".

When two or more Controls generate the same event, many programmers prefer to generalize the event method name. For example, if button1 and button2 call the same method when clicked, it makes sense to name the event method letterButton_Click() instead of button1_Click().

Perhaps you have shopped online at a site that offers multiple ways to "buy now." For example, you might click a grocery cart icon, choose "Place order now" from a menu, or click a button. Often, "Place order now" buttons are displayed at several locations on the page. If you want to encourage a user's behavior, you should provide multiple ways to accommodate it.

Watch the video *Managing Multiple Controls*.

662

TWO TRUTHS & A LIE

Managing Multiple Controls

1. The Control TabStop property can be set to true or false; it identifies whether the Control will serve as a stopping place in a sequence of Tab key presses.

2. On a Form with multiple Controls, one Control must have a TabIndex value of 0.

3. When a Form contains multiple Controls, you can associate the same event with all of them.

The false statement is #2. TabIndex is a numeric property that indicates the order in which the Control will receive focus when the user presses the Tab key. Programmers typically use small numbers for TabIndex values, beginning with 0. However, you might choose not to use any TabIndex values, or if you do, you might choose not to start with 0.

Continuing to Learn about Controls and Events

If you examine the Visual Studio IDE, you will discover many additional Controls that contain hundreds of properties and events. No single book or programming course can demonstrate all of them for you. However, if you understand good programming principles and the syntax and structure of C# programs, learning about each new C# feature becomes progressively easier. When you encounter a new control in the IDE, you probably can use it without understanding all the code generated in the background, but when you do understand the background, your knowledge of C# is more complete.

Continue to explore the Help facility in the Visual Studio IDE. Particularly, read the brief tutorials there. Also, you should search the Internet for C# discussion groups. C# is a new, dynamic language, and programmers pose many questions to each other online. Reading these discussions can provide you with valuable information and suggest new approaches to resolving problems.

You Do It

Using TabIndex

In the next steps, you create a Form in the Visual Studio IDE and add four Buttons so you can demonstrate how to manipulate their TabIndex properties.

1. Open the Visual Studio IDE and start a new project. Define it to be a **Windows Forms Application** named **ManyButtons**.

2. Change the Size of the Form to **350, 130**. Change the Text property of Form1 to **Many Buttons**.

3. Drag four Buttons onto the Form and place them so that they are similar to the layout shown in Figure 13-27. Change the Name properties of the buttons to redButton, whiteButton, blueButton, and favoriteButton. Change the Text on the Buttons to **Red**, **White**, **Blue**, and **My favorite color**, respectively. Adjust the size of the last button so its longer Text is fully displayed.

Figure 13-27   Four Buttons on the Many Buttons Form

4. Examine the Properties list for the Red button. The TabIndex is 0. Examine the properties for the White, Blue, and My favorite color buttons. The IDE has set their TabIndex values to 1, 2, and 3, respectively.

5. Click the **Save All** button and then run the program. When the Form appears, the Red button has focus. Press the **Tab** key, and notice that focus changes to the White button. When you press **Tab** again, focus changes to the Blue button. Press **Tab** several more times and observe that the focus rotates among the four Buttons.

6. Dismiss the Form.

(continues)

(continued)

7. Change the TabIndex property of the Blue button to **0**, and change the TabIndex of the Red button to **2**. (The TabIndex of the White button remains 1 and the TabIndex of the My favorite color button remains 3.) Save the program again and then run it. This time, the Blue button begins with focus. When you press Tab, the order in which the Buttons receive focus is Blue, then White, then Red, then My favorite color. (Clicking the Buttons or pressing Enter raises no event because you have not assigned events to the Buttons.)

8. Change the TabIndex property for the Red button back to **0** and the TabIndex property for the Blue button back to **2**. Click the **Save All** button.

Associating One Method with Multiple Events

In the next steps, you add three methods to the Many Buttons Form and cause one of the methods to execute each time the user clicks one of the four Buttons.

1. If it is not still open, open the **ManyButtons** project in the Visual Studio IDE.

2. Double-click the **Red** button on the Form to view the code for the shell of a redButton_Click() method. Between the method's curly braces, insert a statement that will change the Form's background color to red as follows:

this.BackColor = Color.Red;

At first glance, you might think this refers to the Button that is clicked. However, if you examine the redButton_Click() code in the Form1.cs file in the IDE, you will discover that the method is part of the Form1 class. Therefore, this.BackColor refers to the Form's BackColor property.

3. Select the **Form1.cs [Design]** tab and then double-click the **White** button. Add the following code to the whiteButton_Click() method that is generated:

this.BackColor = Color.White;

4. On the Form, double-click the **Blue** button. In its Click() method, add the following statement:

this.BackColor = Color.Blue;

5. On the form, click the **My favorite color** button. In its Properties list, click the **Events** button (the lightning bolt). Select the Click event. From the list box next to the Click event, select one of the three events to correspond to your favorite color of the three.

(continues)

> *(continued)*
>
> When you double-click a component on a Form in Design View, you move to the default method code. By clicking the component, however, you remain in Design View and the correct set of properties appears in the Properties list.

6. Click the **Save All** button and then execute the program. As you click ButtonS, the Form's background color changes appropriately.

7. Dismiss the form and exit Visual Studio.

Chapter Summary

- Programs use events to notify clients when something happens to an object. GUI programs are event driven—an event such as a button click "drives" the program to perform a task. Programmers also say a button click raises an event, fires an event, or triggers an event. A method that performs a task in response to an event is an event handler. The Click event is the event generated when a button is clicked.

- A delegate is an object that contains a reference to a method. C# delegates provide a way for a program to take alternative courses that are not predetermined; a delegate provides a way to pass a reference to a method as an argument to another method. You can assign one delegate to another using the = operator. You also can use the + and += operators to combine delegates into a composed delegate that calls the delegates from which it is built.

- To declare your own event, you use a delegate. A client identifies methods to execute by associating the delegate with the method that should execute when the event occurs. The .NET Framework provides guidelines that the delegate type for an event should take exactly two parameters: a parameter indicating the source of the event, and an EventArgs parameter that encapsulates any additional information about the event. For events that do not use additional information, the .NET Framework has already defined an appropriate type named EventHandler.

- When you use existing Control components like Buttons and ListBoxes, they contain fields and public properties like Text as well as events with names like Click. A Form can contain any number of Controls that might have events associated with them. Additionally, a single control might be able to raise any number of events.

- Every mouse or keyboard event-handling method must have two parameters: an object representing the sender and an object that holds event information. Mouse events include all the actions a user takes with a mouse, including clicking, pointing, and dragging. Mouse events can be handled for any Control through an object of the class MouseEventArgs. The delegate used to create mouse event handlers is MouseEventHandler. Depending on the event, the type of the second parameter is

EventArgs or MouseEventArgs. Keyboard events, also known as key events, occur when a user presses and releases keyboard keys. Depending on the event, the type of the second parameter is KeyEventArgs or KeyPressEventArgs.

- When users encounter multiple GUI Controls on a Form, usually one Control has focus. That is, if the user presses Enter, the Control will raise an event. When a Form contains multiple Controls, you can create a separate event for each Control. However, you can also associate the same event with multiple Controls.

- When you encounter a new control in the IDE, you probably can use it without understanding all the code generated in the background. However, when you learn about the background code, your knowledge of C# is more complete.

Key Terms

An **event** is a reaction to an occurrence in a program.

"At runtime" describes actions that occur during a program's execution.

Event-driven programs contain code that causes an event such as a button click to drive the program to perform a task.

A button click **raises an event**, **fires an event**, or **triggers an event**.

An **event handler** is a method that performs a task in response to an event.

An **event receiver** is another name for an event handler.

An **event sender** is the control that generates an event.

EventArgs is a C# class designed for holding event information.

The **Click event** is the event generated when a Control is clicked.

Event wiring is the act of connecting an event to its resulting actions.

A **delegate** is an object that contains a reference to a method.

A **composed delegate** calls the delegates from which it is built.

Invoking the event occurs when you call an event method.

EventHandler is an appropriate type for events that do not use any information besides the source of the event and the EventArgs parameter.

Key events are keyboard events that occur when a user presses and releases keyboard keys.

Focus is the property of a Control that causes an event to be raised when the user presses Enter.

Review Questions

1. In C#, events are _____.

   a. triggered by actions   c. Boolean objects

   b. handled by catch blocks   d. only used in GUI programs

2. A delegate is an object that contains a reference to a(n) _____.

   a. object   c. method

   b. class   d. Control

3. C# delegates provide a way for a program to _____.

   a. take alternative courses that are not determined until runtime

   b. include multiple methods

   c. include methods from other classes

   d. include multiple Controls that use the same method

4. Which of the following correctly declares a delegate type?

   a. void aDelegate(int num);

   b. delegate void aDelegate(num);

   c. delegate void aDelegate(int num);

   d. delegate aDelegate(int num);

5. If you have declared a delegate instance, you can assign it a reference to a method as long as the method has the same _____ as the delegate.

   a. return type   c. parameter list

   b. identifier   d. two of the above

6. You can combine two delegates to create a(n) _____ delegate.

   a. assembled   c. artificial

   b. classified   d. composed

7. To combine two delegates using the + operator, the delegate objects must _____.

   a. have the same parameter list   c. both of these

   b. have the same return type   d. neither of these

8. In C#, a(n) _____ is triggered when specific changes to an object occur.

   a. delegate   c. notification

   b. event   d. instantiation

9. An event handler delegate requires _____ argument(s).

 a. zero
 b. one
 c. two
 d. at least one

10. In an event-handler method, the sender is the _____.

 a. delegate associated with the event
 b. method called by the event
 c. object where the event was initiated
 d. class containing the method that the event invokes

11. The `EventArgs` class contains a static field named _____.

 a. `Empty`
 b. `Text`
 c. `Location`
 d. `Source`

12. When creating events, you can use a predefined delegate type named _____ that is automatically provided by the .NET Framework.

 a. `EventArgs`
 b. `EventHandler`
 c. `EventType`
 d. `Event`

13. Which of the following is not a predefined `Control` event?

 a. `MouseEnter`
 b. `Click`
 c. `Destroy`
 d. `TextChanged`

14. A single `Control` can raise _____ event(s).

 a. one
 b. two
 c. five
 d. any number of

15. When you create `Forms` with `Controls` that raise events, an advantage to creating the code by hand over using the Visual Studio IDE is _____.

 a. you are less likely to make typing errors
 b. you save a lot of repetitious typing
 c. you are less likely to forget to set a property
 d. you gain a clearer understanding of the C# language

16. When a `Form` contains three `Controls` and one has focus, you can raise an event by _____.

 a. clicking any `Control`
 b. pressing Enter
 c. either of these
 d. none of these

17. The TabStop property of a Control is a(n) _____.

    a. integer value indicating the tab order
    b. Boolean value indicating whether the Control has a position in the tab sequence

    c. string value indicating the name of the method executed when the Control raises an event
    d. delegate name indicating the event raised when the user tabs to the Control

18. The TabIndex property of a Control is a(n) _____.

    a. integer value indicating the tab order
    b. Boolean value indicating whether the Control has a position in the tab sequence
    c. string value indicating the name of the method executed when the Control raises an event
    d. delegate name indicating the event raised when the user tabs to the Control

19. The Control that causes an event is the _____ argument to an event method.

    a. first   c. third
    b. second   d. fourth

20. Which of the following is true?

    a. A single event can be generated from multiple Controls.
    b. Multiple events can be generated from a single Control.
    c. Both of the above are true.
    d. None of the above are true.

Exercises

Programming Exercises

1. Create a project named **DisplayQuotes** with a Form containing three Labels that hold famous quotes of your choice. When the program starts, the background color of the Form and each Label should be black. When the user passes a mouse over a Label, change its BackColor to white, revealing the text of the quote.

2. Create a project named **RecentlyVisitedSites** that contains a Form with a list of three LinkLabels that link to any three Web sites you choose. When a user clicks a LinkLabel, link to that site. When a user's mouse hovers over a LinkLabel, display a brief message that explains the site's purpose. After a user clicks a link, move the

most recently selected link to the top of the list and move the other two links down, making sure to retain the correct explanation with each link.

3. Create a project named **MovieSelector** that contains a Form with a ListBox that lists at least four movies playing at a local theater. When the user places the mouse over the ListBox, display a Label that contains the starting time for all the movies. The Label disappears when the user's mouse leaves the ListBox area. When the user clicks a movie title in the ListBox, display another Label that contains the correct starting time for the selected movie. Also change the BackColor of the Form to a different color for each movie.

4. Locate an animated .gif file on the Web. Create a project named **Animated** with a Form that contains a PictureBox. Display three different messages on a Label—one when the user's mouse is over the PictureBox, one when the mouse is not over the PictureBox, and one when the user clicks the PictureBox.

5. Emma's Custom Embroidery sells shirts with detailed embroidered images. Emma allows users to select the color for a shirt, but she allows only specific embroidery designs with each shirt color. Create a project named **EmmasEmbroidery** that allows a user to choose one of four shirt colors from a ListBox—white, black, red, or blue. When the user selects a shirt color, the program should display a second ListBox that contains the following embroidery design choices:

   - White shirt—peacock, palm tree, or rose

   - Black shirt—race car, star, or moon

   - Red shirt—palm tree or moon

   - Blue shirt—peacock or moon

   After the user selects an embroidery design, the program should display a congratulatory message on a Label indicating that the choice is a good one, and the design ListBox also becomes invisible. If the user makes a new selection from the shirt color ListBox, the congratulatory message is invisible until the user selects a complementary design.

   Hint: You can remove the entire contents of a ListBox using the Items.Clear() method, as in this.listBox1.Items.Clear();.

6. Create a project named **GuessANumber** with a Form that contains a guessing game with five RadioButtons numbered 1 through 5. Randomly choose one of the RadioButtons as the winning button. When the user clicks a RadioButton, display a message indicating whether the user is right.

   Add a Label to the Form that provides a hint. When the user's mouse hovers over the label, notify the user of one RadioButton that is incorrect. After the user makes a selection, disable all the RadioButtons.

You can create a random number that is at least `min` but less than `max` using the following statements:

```
Random ran = new Random();
int randomNumber;
randomNumber = ran.Next(min, max);
```

7. Create a project named **PickLarger** with a Form that contains two randomly generated arrays, each containing 100 numbers. Include two Buttons labeled "1" and "2". Starting with position 0 in each array, ask the user to guess which of the two arrays contains the higher number and to click one of the two buttons to indicate the guess. After each button click, the program displays the values of the two compared numbers, as well as running counts of the number of correct and incorrect guesses. After the user makes a guess, disable the Buttons while the user views the results. After clicking a Next Button, the user can make another guess using the next two array values. If the user makes more than 100 guesses, the program should reset the array subscript to 0 so the comparisons start over, but continue to keep a running score.

Debugging Exercises

1. Each of the following files or projects in the Chapter.13 folder of your downloadable student files has syntax and/or logical errors. Immediately save the two project folders with their new names before starting to correct their errors. After you correct the errors, save each file or project using the same filename preceded with *Fixed*. For example, the file DebugThirteen1.cs will become FixedDebugThirteen1.cs and the project folder for DebugThirteen3 will become FixedDebugThirteen3.

   a. DebugThirteen1.cs   c. DebugThirteen3

   b. DebugThirteen2.cs   d. DebugThirteen4

Case Problems

1. In Chapter 12, you created an interactive advertisement named **GreenvilleAdvertisement** that can be used to recruit contestants for the Greenville Idol competition. Now, modify that program to include at least one handled event using the techniques you learned in this chapter.

2. In Chapter 12, you created an interactive advertisement named **MarshallsAdvertisement** that can be used to advertise the available murals painted by Marshall's Murals. Now, modify that program to include at least one handled event using the techniques you learned in this chapter.

14

Files and Streams

In this chapter you will:

◎ Learn about computer files and the `File` and `Directory` classes

◎ Understand file data organization

◎ Understand streams

◎ Write to and read from a sequential access text file

◎ Search a sequential access text file

◎ Understand serialization and deserialization

In the early chapters of this book, you learned that using variables to store values in computer memory provides programs with flexibility; a program that uses variables to replace constants can manipulate different values each time the program executes. However, when data values in a program are stored in memory, they are lost when the program ends. To retain data values for future use, you must store them in files. In this chapter, you will learn to create and manage files in C#.

Files and the `File` and `Directory` Classes

When data items are stored in a computer system, they can be stored for varying periods of time—temporarily or permanently.

Temporary storage is usually called computer memory or **random access memory** (RAM). When you write a C# program that stores a value in a variable, you are using temporary storage; the value you store is lost when the program ends or the computer loses power. This type of storage is **volatile**.

Permanent storage, on the other hand, is not lost when a computer loses power; it is **nonvolatile**. When you write a program and save it to a disk, you are using permanent storage.

When discussing computer storage, *temporary* and *permanent* refer to volatility, not length of time. For example, a *temporary* variable might exist for several hours in a large program or one that the user forgets to end, but a *permanent* piece of data might be saved and then deleted within a few seconds.

A **computer file** is a collection of data stored on a nonvolatile device in a computer system. Files exist on **permanent storage devices**, such as hard disks, USB drives, reels of magnetic tape, and optical discs, which include CDs and DVDs.

You can categorize files by the way they store data:

- **Text files** contain data that can be read in a text editor because the data has been encoded using a scheme such as ASCII or Unicode. Text files might include facts and figures used by business programs; when they do, they are also called **data files**. The C# source programs you have written are stored in text files.

- **Binary files** contain data that has not been encoded as text. Their contents are in binary format, which means that you cannot understand them by viewing them in a text editor. Examples include images, music, and the compiled program files with an .exe extension that you have created using this book.

Although their contents vary, files have many common characteristics, as follows:

- Each has a name. The name often includes a dot and a file extension that describes the type of the file. For example, .txt is a plain text file, .dat is a data file, and .jpg is an image file in Joint Pictures Expert Group format.

- Each file has a specific time of creation and a time it was last modified.

- Each file occupies space on a section of a storage device; that is, each file has a size. Sizes are measured in bytes. A **byte** is a small unit of storage; for example, in a simple text file, a byte holds only one character. Because a byte is so small, file sizes usually are expressed in **kilobytes** (thousands of bytes), **megabytes** (millions of bytes), or **gigabytes** (billions of bytes).

When you use data, you never directly use the copy that is stored in a file. Instead, you use a copy that is in memory. Especially when data items are stored on a hard disk, their locations might not be clear to you—data just seems to be "in the computer." However, when you work with stored data, you must transfer copies from the storage device into memory. When you copy data from a file on a storage device into RAM, you **read from the file**. When you store data in a computer file on a persistent storage device, you **write to the file**. This means you copy data from RAM to the file.

Because you can erase data from files, some programmers prefer the term *persistent* storage to permanent storage. In other words, you can remove data from a file stored on a device such as a disk drive, so it is not technically permanent. However, the data remains in the file even when the computer loses power, so, unlike RAM, the data persists, or perseveres.

Computer files are the electronic equivalent of paper documents stored in file cabinets. In a physical file cabinet, the easiest way to store a document is to toss it into a drawer without a folder. When storing computer files, this is the equivalent of placing a file in the main or **root directory** of your storage device. However, for better organization, most office clerks place documents in folders; most computer users also organize their files into **folders** or **directories**. Users also can place folders within folders to form a hierarchy. The combination of the disk drive plus the complete hierarchy of directories in which a file resides is its **path**. For example, in the Windows operating system, the following line would be the complete path for a file named Data.txt on the C drive in a folder named Chapter.14 within the C# folder:

```
C:\C#\Chapter.14\Data.txt
```

The terms *directory* and *folder* are used synonymously to mean an entity that is used to organize files. *Directory* is the more general term; the term *folder* came into use in graphical systems. For example, Microsoft began calling directories *folders* with the introduction of Windows 95.

C# provides built-in classes named `File` and `Directory` that contain methods to help you manipulate files and their directories, respectively.

Using the `File` and `Directory` Classes

The **File class** contains methods that allow you to access information about files. Some of the methods are listed in Table 14-1.

Method	Description
Create()	Creates a file
CreateText()	Creates a text file
Delete()	Deletes a file
Exists()	Returns true if the specified file exists
GetCreationTime()	Returns a DateTime object specifying when a file was created
GetLastAccessTime()	Returns a DateTime object specifying when a file was last accessed
GetLastWriteTime()	Returns a DateTime object specifying when a file was last modified
Move()	Moves a file to the specified location

Table 14-1 Selected File class methods

DateTime is a structure that contains data about a date and time. In the chapter *Using Controls*, you used the data from DateTime structures with MonthCalendar and DateTimePicker GUI objects. DateTime values can be expressed using Coordinated Universal Time (UTC), which is the internationally recognized name for Greenwich Mean Time (GMT). By default, DateTime values are expressed using the local time set on your computer. The property DateTime.Now returns the current local time. The property DateTime.UtcNow returns the current UTC time.

The File class is contained in the System.IO namespace. So, to use the File class, you can use its fully qualified name, System.IO.File, or you can add the statement using System.IO; at the top of your file. Figure 14-1 shows a program that includes the using statement and demonstrates several File class methods. The program prompts the user for a filename and then tests the file's existence. If the file exists, the creation time, last access time, and last write time are displayed. If the file does not exist, a message is displayed. Figure 14-2 shows two executions of the program. In the first execution, the user enters a filename that is not found. In the second execution, the file is found and the three significant dates and times are displayed.

The System.IO.FileInfo class also allows you to access information about a file. See the Microsoft documentation at *http://msdn.microsoft.com* for more information.

```
using System;
using System.IO;
class FileStatistics
{
    static void Main()
    {
        string fileName;
        Console.Write("Enter a filename >> ");
        fileName = Console.ReadLine();
        if(File.Exists(fileName))
        {
            Console.WriteLine("File exists");
            Console.WriteLine("File was created " +
                File.GetCreationTime(fileName));
            Console.WriteLine("File was last accessed " +
                File.GetLastAccessTime(fileName));
            Console.WriteLine("File was last written to " +
                File.GetLastWriteTime(fileName));
        }
        else
        {
            Console.WriteLine("File does not exist");
        }
    }
}
```

Figure 14-1   The FileStatistics program

In the FileStatistics program in Figure 14-1, the file must be in the same directory as the program that is running.

Figure 14-2   Two typical executions of the FileStatistics program

The **Directory class** provides you with information about directories or folders. Table 14-2 lists some available methods in the Directory class.

Method	Description
CreateDirectory()	Creates a directory
Delete()	Deletes a directory
Exists()	Returns true if the specified directory exists
GetCreationTime()	Returns a DateTime object specifying when a directory was created
GetDirectories()	Returns a string array that contains the names of the subdirectories in the specified directory
GetFiles()	Returns a string array that contains the names of the files in the specified directory
GetLastAccessTime()	Returns a DateTime object specifying when a directory was last accessed
GetLastWriteTime()	Returns a DateTime object specifying when a directory was last modified
Move()	Moves a directory to the specified location

Table 14-2   Selected Directory class methods

Figure 14-3 contains a program that prompts a user for a directory and then displays a list of the files stored within it. Figure 14-4 shows two typical executions of the program.

```
using System;
using System.IO;
class DirectoryInformation
{
   static void Main()
   {
      string directoryName;
      string[] listOfFiles;
      Console.Write("Enter a folder >> ");
      directoryName = Console.ReadLine();
      if(Directory.Exists(directoryName))
      {
         Console.WriteLine("Directory exists, " +
            "and it contains the following: ");
```

Figure 14-3   The DirectoryInformation program *(continues)*

(*continued*)

```
        listOfFiles = Directory.GetFiles(directoryName);
        for(int x = 0; x < listOfFiles.Length; ++x)
           Console.WriteLine("   {0}", listOfFiles[x]);
     }
     else
     {
        Console.WriteLine("Directory does not exist");
     }
   }
}
```

Figure 14-3 The DirectoryInformation program

Figure 14-4 Two typical executions of the DirectoryInformation program

  Watch the video *File Handling*.

TWO TRUTHS & A LIE

Files and the File and Directory Classes

1. Temporary storage is nonvolatile; permanent storage is volatile.

2. When you write to a file, you copy data from RAM to a permanent storage device.

3. Most computer users organize their files into directories; the complete hierarchy of directories in which a file resides is its path.

The false statement is #1. Temporary storage is volatile; permanent storage is nonvolatile.

Understanding File Data Organization

Most businesses generate and use large quantities of data every day. You can store data in variables within a program, but this type of storage is temporary. When the application ends, the variables no longer exist, and the data is lost. Variables are stored in the computer's main or primary memory (RAM). When you need to retain data for any significant amount of time, you must save the data on a permanent, secondary storage device.

Businesses store data in a relationship known as the **data hierarchy**, as described in Figure 14-5. For most users, the smallest useful piece of data is the character. A **character** is any one of the letters, numbers, or other special symbols (such as punctuation marks and arithmetic symbols) that comprise data. Characters are made up of bits (the zeros and ones that represent computer circuitry), but people who use data do not care whether the internal representation for an 'A' is 01000001 or 10111110; rather, they are concerned with the meaning of 'A'. For example, it might represent a grade in a course, a person's initial, or a company code.

 C# uses Unicode to represent its characters. You first learned about Unicode in Chapter 1. The set of all the characters used to represent data on a particular computer is that computer's **character set**.

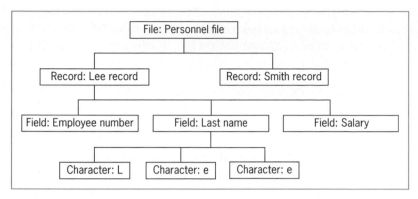

Figure 14-5 Hierarchical relationships of data components

You can think of a character as a unit of information instead of data with a particular appearance. For example, the mathematical character *pi* (π) and the Greek letter *pi* look the same, but have two different Unicode values.

In computer terminology, a character can be any group of bits, and it does not necessarily represent a letter or number. Some characters do not correspond to those in natural language; for example, some "characters" produce a sound or control your display. You also have used the '\n' character to start a new line.

When businesses use data, they group characters into fields. A **field** is a character or group of characters that has some meaning. For example, the characters *T*, *o*, and *m* might represent your first name. Other data fields might represent items such as last name, Social Security number, zip code, and salary.

Fields are grouped together to form records. A **record** is a collection of fields that contain data about an entity. For example, the fields that hold a person's first and last names, Social Security number, zip code, and salary collectively are that person's record. When programming in C#, you have created many classes, such as an `Employee` class or a `Student` class. You can think of the data typically stored in each of these classes as a record. These classes contain individual variables that represent data fields. A business's data records usually represent a person, item, sales transaction, or some other concrete object or event.

Records are grouped to create files. Data files consist of related records. For example, a company's personnel file contains many related records—one record for each company employee. Some files have only a few records; perhaps your professor maintains a file for your class with 25 records—one record for each student. Other files contain thousands or even millions of records. For example, a large insurance company maintains a file of policyholders, and a mail-order catalog company maintains a file of available items.

A data file is a **sequential access file** when each record is read in order of its position in the file. Usually, the records are stored in order based on the value in some field; for example, employees might be stored in Social Security number order, or inventory items might be stored in item number order. The field used to uniquely identify each record in a sequential file is the **key field**. Frequently, records are sorted based on the key field. When records are not used in sequence, the file is used as a **random access file**, in which records can be accessed in any order.

682

Frequently, business data is stored in databases. You will learn about databases in the next chapter.

Before an application can use a data file, it must open the file. A C# application **opens a file** by creating an object and associating a stream of bytes with that object. When you finish using a file, the program should **close the file**—that is, make the file no longer available to your application. Failing to close an input file (a file from which you are reading data) usually does not result in serious consequences; the data still exists in the file. However, if you fail to close an output file (a file to which you are writing data), the data might become inaccessible. You should always close every file you open, and you should close the file as soon as you no longer need it. Leaving a file open for no reason uses computer resources, and your computer's performance will suffer. Also, particularly within a network, another program might be waiting to use the file.

Failing to close an input file for which only one client is allowed access at a time can present consequences for another application. For example, if your program leaves the company's inventory file open after adding a new item, the program that fills orders for customers might fail to work correctly.

Understanding Streams

Whereas people view files as a series of records, with each record containing data fields, C# views files as just a series of bytes. When you perform an input operation in an application, you can picture bytes flowing into your program from an input device through a **stream**, which functions as a pipeline or channel. When you perform output, some bytes flow out of your application through another stream to an output device, as shown in Figure 14-6. A stream is an object, and like all objects, streams have data and methods. The methods allow you to perform actions such as opening, closing, and flushing (clearing) the stream.

Figure 14-6   File streams

When you produce screen output and accept keyboard input, you use the `Console` class, which provides access to several standard streams:

- `Console.In` refers to the standard input stream object, which accepts data from the keyboard.

- `Console.Out` refers to the standard output stream object, which allows a program to produce output on the screen.

- `Console.Error` refers to the standard error stream object, which allows a program to write error messages to the screen.

You have been using `Console.Out` and its `WriteLine()` and `Write()` methods throughout this book. However, you may not have realized it because you do not need to refer explicitly to `Out`, so you have been writing the instruction as `Console.WriteLine()`. Likewise, you have used `Console.In` with the `ReadLine()` and `Read()` methods.

Most streams flow in only one direction; each stream is either an input or output stream. You might open several streams at once within an application. For example, an application that reads a data disk and separates valid records from invalid ones might require three streams. The data arrives via an input stream, and as the program checks the data for invalid values, one output stream writes some records to a file of valid records, and another output stream writes other records to a file of invalid records.

When you read from or write to a file, you use a file processing class instead of `Console`. Many file processing classes are available in C#, including:

- `StreamReader`, for text input from a file

- `StreamWriter`, for text output to a file

- `FileStream` (which is used alone and with both `StreamReader` and `StreamWriter`), for both input from and output to a file

StreamReader and StreamWriter inherit from TextReader and TextWriter, respectively. Console.In and Console.Out are properties of TextReader and TextWriter, respectively.

When you write a program that stores data in a file, you create a `FileStream` object that defines a file's characteristics and abilities. Programmers say `FileStream` **exposes** a stream around a file. Table 14-3 lists some `FileStream` properties.

Property	Description
CanRead	Gets a value indicating whether current FileStream supports reading
CanSeek	Gets a value indicating whether current FileStream supports seeking
CanWrite	Gets a value indicating whether current FileStream supports writing
Length	Gets the length of the FileStream in bytes
Name	Gets the name of the FileStream
Position	Gets or sets the current position of the FileStream

Table 14-3 Selected FileStream properties

The `FileStream` class has 15 overloaded constructors. One that is used frequently includes the filename (which might include the complete path), mode, and type of access. For example, you might construct a `FileStream` object using the following statement:

```
FileStream outFile = new FileStream("SomeText.txt",
    FileMode.Create, FileAccess.Write);
```

In this example, the filename is "SomeText.txt". Because no path is indicated, the file is assumed to be in the current directory. The mode is `Create`, which means a new file will be created even if one with the same name already exists. The access is `Write`, which means you can write data to the file but not read from it.

Another of `FileStream`'s overloaded constructors requires only a filename and mode. If you use this version and the mode is set to `Append`, then the default access is `Write`; otherwise, the access is set to `ReadWrite`.

Table 14-4 describes the available file modes, and Table 14-5 describes the access types.

Member	Description
Append	Opens the file if it exists and seeks the end of the file to append new data
Create	Creates a new file; if the file already exists, it is overwritten
CreateNew	Creates a new file; if the file already exists, an IOException is thrown
Open	Opens an existing file; if the file does not exist, a System.IO.FileNotFoundException is thrown
OpenOrCreate	Opens an existing file; if the file does not exist, it is created
Truncate	Opens an existing file; once opened, the file is truncated so its size is zero bytes

Table 14-4   FileMode enumeration

Member	Description
Read	Data can be read from the file.
ReadWrite	Data can be read from and written to the file.
Write	Data can be written to the file.

Table 14-5   FileAccess enumeration

You can use a FileStream object as an argument to the StreamWriter constructor. Then you use WriteLine() or Write() with the StreamWriter object in much the same way you use it with Console.Out. For example, Figure 14-7 shows an application in which a FileStream object named outFile is created, then associated with a StreamWriter named writer in the first shaded line. The writer object then uses WriteLine() to send a string to the FileStream file instead of sending it to the Console. Figure 14-8 shows a typical execution of the program, and Figure 14-9 shows the file as it appears in Notepad.

```
using System;
using System.IO;
class WriteSomeText
{
   static void Main()
   {
      FileStream outFile = new
         FileStream("SomeText.txt", FileMode.Create,
            FileAccess.Write);
      StreamWriter writer = new StreamWriter(outFile);
      Console.Write("Enter some text >> ");
      string text = Console.ReadLine();
```

Figure 14-7   The WriteSomeText program *(continues)*

(continued)

```
        writer.WriteLine(text);
        // Error occurs if the next two statements are reversed
        writer.Close();
        outFile.Close();
    }
}
```

Figure 14-7 The WriteSomeText program

 Although the WriteSomeText application uses Console.ReadLine() to accept user input, you could also create a GUI Form to accept input. You will create an application that writes to and reads from files using a GUI environment in a "You Do It" exercise at the end of this chapter.

Figure 14-8 Typical execution of the WriteSomeText program

Figure 14-9 File created by the WriteSomeText program

 In most applications that use files, you will want to place all the statements that open, write to, read from, and close files in a try block and then catch any IOExceptions that are thrown. Exception handling is eliminated from many examples in this chapter so that you can concentrate on the details of handling files without extra statements. In the "You Do It" section at the end of this chapter, you will add exception handling to an application.

The classes `BinaryReader` and `BinaryWriter` exist for working with binary files, which can store any of the 256 combinations of bits in any byte instead of just those combinations that form readable text. For example, photographs and music are stored in binary files.

The classes `XmlTextReader` and `XmlTextWriter` exist for working with XML files. **XML** is an abbreviation of eXtensible Markup Language, which is a standard for exchanging data over the Internet.

TWO TRUTHS & A LIE

Understanding Streams

1. When a file is opened in C#, an object is created and a stream is associated with that object.

2. Most streams flow in only one direction; each stream is either an input or output stream.

3. You can open one stream at a time within a C# application.

The false statement is #3. You might open several streams at once within an application.

Writing and Reading a Sequential Access File

Although people think of data files as consisting of records that contain fields, C# uses files only as streams of bytes. Therefore, when you write a program to store a data file, or write a program to retrieve data from an already-created file, you must dictate the form in which the program will handle the file. Additionally, whether you are writing data to a file or reading data from one, you create a `FileStream` object.

Writing Data to a Sequential Access Text File

For example, suppose that you want to store `Employee` data in a file. Assume that an `Employee` contains an ID number, a name, and a salary. You could write stand-alone data for each of the three types to a file, or you could create an `Employee` class that is similar to many you have seen throughout this book. Figure 14-10 shows a typical `Employee` class that contains three fields and properties for each.

```
class Employee
{
    public int EmpNum {get; set;}
    public string Name {get; set;}
    public double Salary {get; set;}
}
```

Figure 14-10   An Employee class

To store Employee data to a persistent storage device, you declare a FileStream object. For example:

```
FileStream outFile = new FileStream(FILENAME,
    FileMode.Create, FileAccess.Write);
```

The object is then passed to the constructor of a StreamWriter object. For example:

```
StreamWriter writer = new StreamWriter(outFile);
```

You can then use the writer object's WriteLine() method to write Employee data to the output stream. You can compose strings to write using text fields and commas. A block of text within a string that represents an entity or field is a **token**. Each comma that separates tokens is a **delimiter**, which is a character used to specify the boundary between data items in text files. Without a delimiter, the process of separating and interpreting tokens is more difficult. For example, suppose you define a delimiter as a comma using the following statement:

```
const string DELIM = ",";
```

Then, when you write data to a file, you can separate the fields with the comma delimiter using a statement such as the following:

```
writer.WriteLine(emp.EmpNum + DELIM + emp.Name + DELIM + emp.Salary);
```

A comma is a commonly used delimiter, but a delimiter can be any character that is not needed as part of the data in a file. A file that contains comma-separated values is often called a **CSV file**. When commas are needed as part of the data, sometimes either the Tab character, the pipe character (|), or a comma within quotation marks is used as a delimiter.

The WriteLine() method ends output with a carriage return. When you use this method to create file output, the automatically appended carriage return becomes the *record delimiter*.

Figure 14-11 contains a complete program that opens a file and continuously prompts the user for Employee data. When all three fields have been entered for an employee, the fields are written to the file, separated by commas. When the user enters the sentinel value 999 for an Employee ID number, the data entry loop ends and the file is closed. Figure 14-12 shows a typical execution, and Figure 14-13 shows the contents of the sequential data file that is created.

```
using System;
using System.IO;
class WriteSequentialFile
{
    static void Main()
    {
        const int END = 999;
        const string DELIM = ",";
        const string FILENAME = "EmployeeData.txt";
        Employee emp = new Employee();
        FileStream outFile = new FileStream(FILENAME,
            FileMode.Create, FileAccess.Write);
        StreamWriter writer = new StreamWriter(outFile);
        Console.Write("Enter employee number or " + END +
            " to quit >> ");
        emp.EmpNum = Convert.ToInt32(Console.ReadLine());
        while(emp.EmpNum != END)
        {
            Console.Write("Enter last name >> ");
            emp.Name = Console.ReadLine();
            Console.Write("Enter salary >> ");
            emp.Salary = Convert.ToDouble(Console.ReadLine());
            writer.WriteLine(emp.EmpNum + DELIM + emp.Name +
                DELIM + emp.Salary);
            Console.Write("Enter next employee number or " +
                END + " to quit >> ");
            emp.EmpNum = Convert.ToInt32(Console.ReadLine());
        }
        writer.Close();
        outFile.Close();
    }
}
```

Figure 14-11   The WriteSequentialFile class

In the WriteSequentialFile class, the delimiter is defined to be a string instead of a char to force the composed argument to WriteLine() to be a string. If the first data field sent to WriteLine() was a string, then DELIM could have been declared as a char.

In the WriteSequentialFile program in Figure 14-11, the constant END is defined to be 999 so it can be used to check for the sentinel value. You first learned to use named constants in Chapter 2. Defining a named constant eliminates using a magic number in a program. The term **magic number** refers to the bad programming practice of hard-coding numbers (unnamed, literal constants) in code without explanation. In most cases, this makes programs harder to read, understand, and maintain.

Figure 14-12   Typical execution of the `WriteSequentialFile` program

Figure 14-13   Contents of file created by the `WriteSequentialFile` program

Reading from a Sequential Access Text File

A program that reads from a sequential access data file contains many similar components to one that writes to a file. For example, a `FileStream` object is created, as in a program that writes a file. However, the access must be `FileAccess.Read` (or `ReadWrite`), as in the following statement:

```
FileStream inFile = new FileStream(FILENAME,
    FileMode.Open, FileAccess.Read);
```

Then, as when data is being written, the `FileStream` object is passed to a `StreamReader` object's constructor, as in the following statement:

```
StreamReader reader = new StreamReader(inFile);
```

After the `StreamReader` has been defined, the `ReadLine()` method can be used to retrieve one line at a time from the data file. For example, the following statement gets one line of data from the file and stores it in a string named `recordIn`:

```
string recordIn = reader.ReadLine();
```

Using ReadLine() assumes a carriage return is the record delimiter, which is true, for example, if the records were created using WriteLine().

If the value of recordIn is null, then no more data exists in the file. Therefore, a loop that begins while(recordIn != null) can be used to control the data entry loop.

After a record (line of data) is read in, the Split() method can be used to separate the data fields into an array of strings. The Split() method is a member of the String class; it takes a character delimiter parameter and separates a string into substrings at each occurrence of the delimiter. For example, the following code splits recordIn into the fields array at each DELIM occurrence. Then the three array elements can be stored as an int, string, and double, respectively.

```
string[] fields;
fields = recordIn.Split(DELIM);
emp.EmpNum = Convert.ToInt32(fields[0]);
emp.Name = fields[1];
emp.Salary = Convert.ToDouble(fields[2]);
```

Figure 14-14 contains a complete ReadSequentialFile application that uses the data file created in Figure 14-12. The records stored in the EmployeeData.txt file are read in one at a time, split into their Employee record components, and displayed. Figure 14-15 shows the output.

```
using System;
using System.IO;
class ReadSequentialFile
{
    static void Main()
    {
        const char DELIM = ',';
        const string FILENAME = "EmployeeData.txt";
        Employee emp = new Employee();
        FileStream inFile = new FileStream(FILENAME,
            FileMode.Open, FileAccess.Read);
        StreamReader reader = new StreamReader(inFile);
        string recordIn;
        string[] fields;
        Console.WriteLine("\n{0,-5}{1,-12}{2,8}\n",
            "Num", "Name", "Salary");
        recordIn = reader.ReadLine();
        while(recordIn != null)
        {
            fields = recordIn.Split(DELIM);
            emp.EmpNum = Convert.ToInt32(fields[0]);
            emp.Name = fields[1];
            emp.Salary = Convert.ToDouble(fields[2]);
```

Figure 14-14 The ReadSequentialFile program *(continues)*

(*continued*)

```
        Console.WriteLine("{0,-5}{1,-12}{2,8}",
            emp.EmpNum, emp.Name, emp.Salary.ToString("C"));
        recordIn = reader.ReadLine();
    }
    reader.Close();
    inFile.Close();
  }
}
```

Figure 14-14 The ReadSequentialFile program

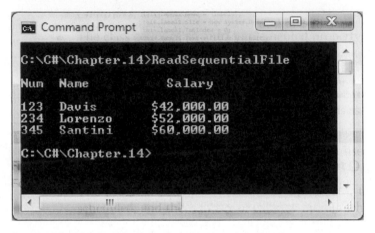

Figure 14-15 Output of the ReadSequentialFile program

 Watch the video *Sequential Access Files.*

TWO TRUTHS & A LIE

Writing and Reading a Sequential Access File

1. Although people think of data files as consisting of records that contain fields, C# uses files only as streams of bytes.

2. A comma is the default C# delimiter.

3. The Split() method can be used to separate data fields into an array of strings based on the placement of the designated delimiter.

The false statement is #2. A delimiter is any character used to specify the boundary between characters in text files. Although a comma is commonly used for this purpose, there is no default C# delimiter, and any character could be used.

 You Do It

Creating a File

In the next steps, you create a file that contains a list of names.

1. Open a new file named **CreateNameFile**, and write the first lines needed for a program that creates a file of names.

    ```
    using System;
    using System.IO;
    class CreateNameFile
    {
    ```

2. Start a Main() method that declares a FileStream you can use to create a file named Names.txt that is open for writing. Also create a StreamWriter to which you associate the file.

    ```
    static void Main()
    {
        FileStream file = new FileStream("Names.txt",
            FileMode.Create, FileAccess.Write);
        StreamWriter writer = new StreamWriter(file);
    ```

    (continues)

(continued)

3. Add an array of names as follows. Each name is padded with spaces to make it 10 characters long so that you can easily demonstrate the `Seek()` method in a later exercise.

```
string[] names = {"Anthony   ",
                  "Belle     ",
                  "Carolyn   ",
                  "David     ",
                  "Edwin     ",
                  "Frannie   ",
                  "Gina      ",
                  "Hannah    ",
                  "Inez      ",
                  "Juan      "};
```

4. Declare a variable to use as an array subscript, then write each name to the output file.

```
int x;
for(x = 0; x < names.Length; ++x)
    writer.WriteLine(names[x]);
```

5. Close the `StreamWriter` and the `FileStream`. Also add two closing curly braces—one for the `Main()` method and one for the class.

```
        writer.Close();
        file.Close();
    }
}
```

6. Save the file, and then compile and execute it. Using My Computer or Windows Explorer, open the newly created **Names.txt** file in a text editor. The file contents appear in Figure 14-16.

(continues)

(continued)

Figure 14-16 File created by the CreateNameFile program

Reading from a File

In the next steps, you read the text from the file created by the CreateNameFile program.

1. Start a new file named **ReadNameFile** as follows:

    ```
    using System;
    using System.IO;
    class ReadNameFile
    {
    ```

2. Start a Main() method that declares a FileStream that uses the same filename as the one created by the CreateNameFile program. Declare the file mode to be Open and the access to be Read. Declare a StreamReader with which to associate the file. Also declare an integer that counts the names read and a string that holds the names.

    ```
    static void Main()
    {
        FileStream file = new FileStream("Names.txt",
            FileMode.Open, FileAccess.Read);
        StreamReader reader = new StreamReader(file);
        int count = 1;
        string name;
    ```

(continues)

(continued)

3. Display a heading and read the first line from the file. While a name is not `null`, display a count and a name, and increment the count.

```
Console.WriteLine("Displaying all names");
name = reader.ReadLine();
while(name != null)
{
   Console.WriteLine("" + count + " " + name);
   name = reader.ReadLine();
   ++count;
}
```

4. Close the `StreamReader` and the `File`, and add closing curly braces for the method and the class.

```
      reader.Close();
      file.Close();
   }
}
```

5. Save the file, and then compile and execute it. The output appears in Figure 14-17.

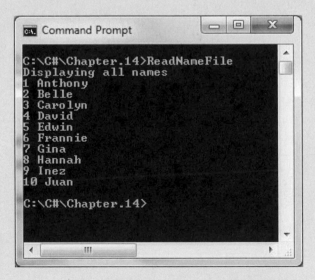

Figure 14-17   Output produced by the `ReadNameFile` program

Searching a Sequential Text File

When you read data from a sequential text file, as in the `ReadSequentialFile` program in Figure 14-14, the program starts at the beginning of the file and reads each record in turn until all the records have been read. Subsequent records are read in order because a file's **file position pointer** holds the byte number of the next byte to be read. For example, if each record in a file is 32 bytes long, then the file position pointer holds 0, 32, 64, and so on in sequence during the execution of the program.

Sometimes it is necessary to process a file multiple times from the beginning during a program's execution. For example, suppose you want to continue to prompt a user for a minimum salary and then search through a file for `Employees` who make at least that salary. You can compare the user's entered minimum with each salary in the data file and list those employees who meet the requirement. However, after one list is produced, the file pointer is at the end of the file and no more records can be read. To reread the file, you could close it and reopen it, but that requires unnecessary overhead. Instead, you can just reposition the file pointer using the `Seek()` method and the `SeekOrigin` enumeration. For example, the following statement repositions the pointer of a file named `inFile` to 0 bytes away from the `Begin` position of the file:

```
inFile.Seek(0, SeekOrigin.Begin);
```

Table 14-6 lists the values in the `SeekOrigin` enumeration that you can use.

Member	Description
Begin	Specifies the beginning of a stream
Current	Specifies the current position of a stream
End	Specifies the end of a stream

Table 14-6   The `SeekOrigin` enumeration

Figure 14-18 contains a program that repeatedly searches a file to produce lists of employees who meet a minimum salary requirement. The shaded portions of the program represent differences from the `ReadSequentialFile` application in Figure 14-14. In this program, each time the user enters a minimum salary that does not equal 999, the file position pointer is set to the beginning of the file, and then each record is read and compared to the minimum. Figure 14-19 shows a typical execution of the program.

```
using System;
using System.IO;
class FindEmployees
{
    static void Main()
    {
        const char DELIM = ',';
        const int END = 999;
        const string FILENAME = "EmployeeData.txt";
        Employee emp = new Employee();
        FileStream inFile = new FileStream(FILENAME,
            FileMode.Open, FileAccess.Read);
        StreamReader reader = new StreamReader(inFile);
        string recordIn;
        string[] fields;
        double minSalary;
        Console.Write("Enter minimum salary to find or " +
            END + " to quit >> ");
        minSalary = Convert.ToDouble(Console.ReadLine());
        while(minSalary != END)
        {
            Console.WriteLine("\n{0,-5}{1,-12}{2,8}\n",
                "Num", "Name", "Salary");
            inFile.Seek(0, SeekOrigin.Begin);
            recordIn = reader.ReadLine();
            while(recordIn != null)
            {
                fields = recordIn.Split(DELIM);
                emp.EmpNum = Convert.ToInt32(fields[0]);
                emp.Name = fields[1];
                emp.Salary = Convert.ToDouble(fields[2]);
                if(emp.Salary >= minSalary)
                    Console.WriteLine("{0,-5}{1,-12}{2,8}",
                        emp.EmpNum, emp.Name,
                            emp.Salary.ToString("C"));
                recordIn = reader.ReadLine();
            }
            Console.Write("\nEnter minimum salary to find or " +
                END + " to quit >> ");
            minSalary = Convert.ToDouble(Console.ReadLine());
        }
        reader.Close();  // Error occurs if
        inFile.Close();  // these two statements are reversed
    }
}
```

Figure 14-18 The FindEmployees program

Figure 14-19 Typical execution of the FindEmployees program

The program in Figure 14-18 is intended to demonstrate using the Seek() method. In a business setting, you might prefer to not leave a file open in one application if other users might be waiting for it. As an alternative, you could load all the records into an array and then search the array for desired records. Problems also exist with this approach because you would have to overestimate the number of records in the file to create an array large enough to hold them.

When you seek beyond the length of the file, you do not cause an error. Instead, the file size grows. In Microsoft Windows NT and later, any data added to the end of a file is set to zero. In Microsoft Windows 98 or earlier, any data added to the end of the file is not set to zero. This means that previously deleted data might become visible to the stream.

TWO TRUTHS & A LIE

Searching a Sequential Text File

1. When you read data from a sequential file, the program starts at the beginning of the file and reads each record in turn until all the records have been read.

2. When you read from a sequential file, its file position pointer holds the number of the record to be read.

3. To reread a file, you can close it and reopen it, or you can reposition the file pointer to the beginning of the file.

The false statement is #2. When you read from a sequential file, its file position pointer holds the byte number of the next byte to be read.

You Do It

Using the Seek() Method

In the next steps, you use the Seek() method to reposition a file pointer so you can access a file from any location. The user will be prompted to enter a number representing a starting point to list the names in the Names.txt file. Names from that point forward will be listed, and then the user will be prompted for another selection.

1. Start a new program named **AccessSomeNames** that demonstrates how to access requested names from the Names.txt file you created in the CreateNameFile application.

```
using System;
using System.IO;
class AccessSomeNames
{
    static void Main()
    {
        FileStream file = new FileStream("Names.txt",
            FileMode.Open, FileAccess.Read);
        StreamReader reader = new StreamReader(file);
```

(continues)

(continued)

2. Declare a constant named END that represents an input value that allows the user to exit the program. Then declare other variables that the program will use.

```
const int END = 999;
int count = 0;
int num;
int size;
string name;
```

3. Read a line from the input file. While names are available, continue to read and count them. Then compute the size of each name by dividing the file length by the number of strings stored in it.

```
name = reader.ReadLine();
while(name != null)
{
    ++count;
    name = reader.ReadLine();
}
size = (int)file.Length / count;
```

4. Prompt the user for the number of the first record to read, and read the value from the Console.

```
Console.Write("\nWith which number do you want to start? >> ");
num = Convert.ToInt32(Console.ReadLine());
```

5. Start a loop that continues as long as the user does not enter the sentinel END value. Within the loop, display the user's number, and then use the Seek() method to position the file pointer at the correct file location. Because users enter numbers starting with 1 and file positions start with 0, you calculate the file position by first subtracting 1 from the user's entry. The calculated record number is then multiplied by the size of each name in the file. For example, if each name is 10 bytes long, then the calculated starting position should be 0, 10, 20, 30, or some other multiple of the name size.

```
while(num != END)
{
    Console.WriteLine("Starting with name " + num +": ");
    file.Seek((num - 1) * size, SeekOrigin.Begin);
```

(continues)

(continued)

6.   Read and write the name at the calculated location. Then, in a nested loop, read and write all the remaining names until the end of the file.

```
name = reader.ReadLine();
Console.WriteLine("   " + name);
while(name != null)
{
    name = reader.ReadLine();
    Console.WriteLine("   " + name);
}
```

7.   Finally, prompt the user for the next starting value for a new list, inform the user how to quit the application, and accept the next input value. Add a closing brace for the outer `while` loop.

```
    Console.WriteLine("\nWith which number do you " +
        "want to start?");
    Console.Write("   (Enter " + END + " to quit) >> ");
    num = Convert.ToInt32(Console.ReadLine());
}
```

8.   Close the `StreamReader` and `File` objects, and add closing braces for the method and the class.

```
        reader.Close();
        file.Close();
    }
}
```

9.   Save the file, and then compile and execute it. Figure 14-20 shows a typical execution during which the user displays three sets of names starting at a different point each time.

(continues)

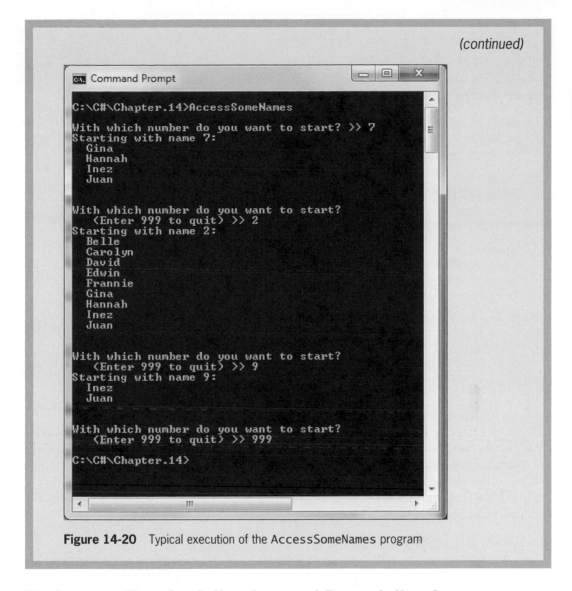

Figure 14-20 Typical execution of the AccessSomeNames program

Understanding Serialization and Deserialization

Writing to a text file allows you to store data for later use. However, writing to a text file does present two disadvantages:

- Data in a text file is easily readable in a text editor such as Notepad. Although this feature is useful to developers when they test programs, it is not a very secure way to store data.

- When a record in a data file contains many fields, it is cumbersome to convert each field to text and combine the fields with delimiters before storing the record on a disk. Similarly, when you read a text file, it is somewhat unwieldy to eliminate the delimiters, split the text into tokens, and convert each token to the proper data type. Writing an entire object to a file at once would be more convenient.

C# provides a technique called serialization that can be used for writing objects to and reading objects from data files. **Serialization** is the process of converting objects into streams of bytes. **Deserialization** is the reverse process; it converts streams of bytes back into objects.

To create a class that can be serialized, you mark it with the [Serializable] attribute, as shown in the shaded statement in Figure 14-21. The Employee class in the figure is identical to the one in Figure 14-10 except for the [Serializable] attribute.

```
[Serializable]
class Employee
{
    public int EmpNum {get; set;}
    public string Name {get; set;}
    public double Salary {get; set;}
}
```

Figure 14-21 The serializable Employee class

Attributes provide a method of associating information with C# code. They are always contained in square brackets. Search for "C# attributes" at *http://msdn.microsoft.com* for more details.

In a class marked with the [Serializable] attribute, every instance variable must also be serializable. By default, all C# simple data types are serializable, including strings. However, if your class contains fields that are more complex data types, you must check the declaration of those classes to ensure they are serializable. By default, array objects are serializable. However, if the array contains references to other objects, such as Dates or Students, those objects must be serializable.

If you create a class and want to be able to write its objects to a file, you can implement the ISerializable interface instead of marking a class with the [Serializable] attribute. When you use this approach, you must write a method named GetObjectData(). Marking the class with the attribute is simpler.

Two namespaces are included in programs that employ serialization:

- System.Runtime.Serialization.Formatters.Binary;

- System.Runtime.Serialization;

When you create a program that writes objects to files, you declare an instance of the BinaryFormatter class with a statement such as the following:

```
BinaryFormatter bFormatter = new BinaryFormatter();
```

Then, after you fill a class object with data, you can write it to the output file stream named `outFile` with a statement such as the following:

```
bFormatter.Serialize(outFile, objectFilledWithData);
```

The `Serialize()` method takes two arguments—a reference to the output file and a reference to a serializable object that might contain any number of data fields. The entire object is written to the data file with this single statement.

Similarly, when you read an object from a data file, you use a statement like the following:

```
objectInstance = (TypeOfObject)bFormatter.Deserialize(inFile);
```

This statement uses the `Deserialize()` method with a `BinaryFormatter` object to read in one object from the file. The object is cast to the appropriate type and can be assigned to an instance of the object. Then you can access individual fields. An entire object is read with this single statement, no matter how many data fields it contains.

Figure 14-22 shows a program that writes `Employee` class objects to a file and later reads them from the file into the program. After the `FileStream` is declared for an output file, a `BinaryFormatter` is declared in the first shaded statement. The user enters an ID number, name, and salary for an `Employee`, and the completed object is written to a file in the second shaded statement. When the user enters 999, the output file is closed.

```
using System;
using System.IO;
using System.Runtime.Serialization.Formatters.Binary;
using System.Runtime.Serialization;
class SerializableDemonstration
{
   static void Main()
   {
      const int END = 999;
      const string FILENAME = "Data.ser";
      Employee emp = new Employee();
      FileStream outFile = new FileStream(FILENAME,
         FileMode.Create, FileAccess.Write);
      BinaryFormatter bFormatter = new BinaryFormatter();
      Console.Write("Enter employee number or " + END +
         " to quit >> ");
      emp.EmpNum = Convert.ToInt32(Console.ReadLine());
      while(emp.EmpNum != END)
      {
         Console.Write("Enter last name >> ");
         emp.Name = Console.ReadLine();
         Console.Write("Enter salary >> ");
         emp.Salary = Convert.ToDouble(Console.ReadLine());
         bFormatter.Serialize(outFile, emp);
```

Figure 14-22   The SerializableDemonstration program *(continues)*

(continued)

```
            Console.Write("Enter employee number or " + END +
               " to quit >> ");
            emp.EmpNum = Convert.ToInt32(Console.ReadLine());
         }
         outFile.Close();
         FileStream inFile = new FileStream(FILENAME,
            FileMode.Open, FileAccess.Read);
         Console.WriteLine("\n{0,-5}{1,-12}{2,8}\n",
            "Num", "Name", "Salary");
         while(inFile.Position < inFile.Length)
         {
            emp = (Employee)bFormatter.Deserialize(inFile);
            Console.WriteLine("{0,-5}{1,-12}{2,8}",
               emp.EmpNum, emp.Name, emp.Salary.ToString("C"));
         }
         inFile.Close();
      }
   }
```

Figure 14-22   The SerializableDemonstration program

After the output file closes in the SerializableDemonstration program in Figure 14-22, it is reopened for reading. A loop is executed while the Position property of the input file is less than its Length property. In other words, the loop executes while there is more data in the file. The last shaded statement in the figure deserializes data from the file and casts it to an Employee object, where the individual fields can be accessed. Figure 14-23 shows a typical execution of the program.

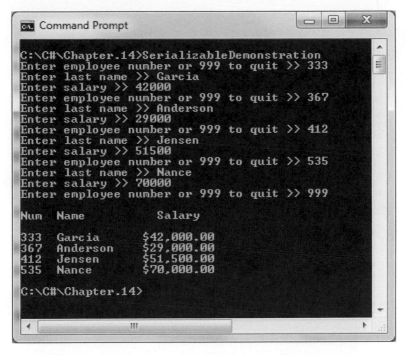

Figure 14-23 Typical execution of the SerializableDemonstration program

The file created by the SerializableDemonstration program is not as easy to read as the text file created by the WriteSequentialFile program discussed earlier in the chapter (in Figure 14-11). Figure 14-24 shows the file contents displayed in Notepad (with some newline characters inserted so the output can fit on this page). If you examine the file carefully, you can discern the string names and some Employee class information, but the rest of the file is not easy to read.

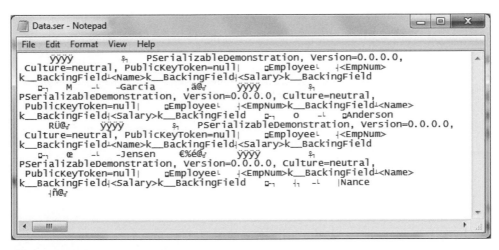

Figure 14-24 Data file created using the SerializableDemonstration program

Watch the video *Understanding Serialization and Deserialization*.

TWO TRUTHS & A LIE

Understanding Serialization and Deserialization

1. An advantage of writing data to a text file is that the data is easily readable in a text editor such as Notepad.

2. Serialization is the process of converting objects into streams of bytes. Deserialization is the reverse process; it converts streams of bytes back into objects.

3. By default, all C# classes are serializable.

The false statement is #3. By default, all C# simple data types are serializable, including strings. However, if your class contains fields that are more complex data types, you must check the declaration of those classes to ensure they are serializable.

You Do It

Creating a Text File in a GUI Environment

The file writing and reading examples in this chapter have used console applications so that you could concentrate on the features of files in the simplest environment. However, you can write and read files in GUI environments as well. In the next steps, you create two applications. The first allows a user to enter invoice records using a `Form` and to store them in a file. The second application allows a user to view stored records using a `Form`.

1. Open the Visual Studio IDE and start a new Windows Forms Application project named **EnterInvoices**.

(continues)

(continued)

2. Create a `Form` like the one shown in Figure 14-25 by making the following changes:

- Change the `Text` property of the `Form` to **Invoice Data**.

- Drag a `Label` onto the `Form` and change its `Text` property to **Enter invoice data**. Increase the `Label`'s `Font` to **12**.

- Drag three more `Labels` onto the `Form` and change their `Text` properties to **Invoice number**, **Last name**, and **Amount**, respectively.

- Drag three `TextBoxes` onto the `Form` next to the three descriptive `Labels`. Change the `Name` properties of the three `TextBoxes` to `invoiceBox`, `nameBox`, and `amountBox`, respectively.

- Drag a `Button` onto the `Form`, change its `Name` to `enterButton`, and change its `Text` to **Enter record**. If necessary, resize `enterButton` so all of its text is visible.

Figure 14-25 Designing the `EnterInvoices` Form

3. View the code for the `Form`. At the start of the class, before the `Form1()` constructor, add the shaded code shown in Figure 14-26. The new code contains statements that perform the following:

- Declare a delimiter that will be used to separate records in the output file.

- Declare a path and filename. You can change the path if you want to store the file in a different location on your system.

(continues)

(continued)

- Declare variables for the number, name, and amount of each invoice.
- Open the file and associate it with a `StreamWriter`.

```
namespace EnterInvoices
{
    public partial class Form1 : Form
    {
        const string DELIM = ",";
        const string FILENAME =
            @"C:\C#\Chapter.14\Invoices.txt";
        int num;
        string name;
        double amount;
        static FileStream outFile = new
            FileStream(FILENAME, FileMode.Create,
            FileAccess.Write);
        StreamWriter writer = new StreamWriter(outFile);
        public Form1()
        {
            InitializeComponent();
        }
```

Figure 14-26   Partial code for the `EnterInvoices` program with typed statements shaded

Remember that placing an at sign (@) in front of a string indicates that its characters should be interpreted literally. The @ sign is used with the filename so that the backslashes in the path will not be interpreted as escape sequence characters.

4. At the top of the file, with the other `using` statements, add the following so that the `FileStream` can be declared:

   `using System.IO;`

5. Click **Save All** (and continue to do so periodically as you work). Return to Design view and double-click the **Enter record** button. As shown in the shaded portions of Figure 14-27, add statements within the method to accept data from each of the three `TextBoxes` and convert each field to the appropriate type. Then write each field to a text file, separated by delimiting commas. Finally, clear the `TextBox` fields to be ready for the user to enter a new set of data.

(continues)

(continued)

```
private void enterButton_Click(object sender, EventArgs e)
{
    num = Convert.ToInt32(invoiceBox.Text);
    name = nameBox.Text;
    amount = Convert.ToDouble(amountBox.Text);
    writer.WriteLine(num + DELIM + name + DELIM + amount);
    invoiceBox.Clear();
    nameBox.Clear();
    amountBox.Clear();
}
```

Figure 14-27   Code for the enterButton_Click() method of the EnterInvoices program

6. Locate the Dispose() method, which executes when the user clicks the Close button to dismiss the Form. A quick way to locate the method in the Visual Studio IDE is to select **EDIT** from the main menu, click **Find and Replace**, click **Quick Find**, and type **Dispose** in the dialog box. (The Look in: setting can be either Entire Solution or Current Project.) The method appears on the screen. Add two statements to close writer and outFile, as shown in the shaded statements in Figure 14-28.

```
protected override void Dispose(bool disposing)
    {
        writer.Close();
        outFile.Close();
        if (disposing && (components != null))
        {
            components.Dispose();
        }
        base.Dispose(disposing);
    }
```

Figure 14-28   The Dispose() method in the EnterInvoices program

7. Click **Save All**. Execute the program. When the Form appears, enter data in each TextBox and then click the **Enter record** button when you finish. The TextBoxes clear in preparation for you to enter another record. Enter at least three records before dismissing the Form. Figure 14-29 shows data entry in progress.

(continues)

(continued)

Figure 14-29 Entering data in the `EnterInvoices` application

Reading Data from a Text File into a Form

In the next steps, you create a `Form` that you can use to read records from a `File`.

1. Open a new Windows project in Visual Studio and name it **ViewInvoices**.

2. Create a `Form` like the one shown in Figure 14-30 by making the following changes:

   - Change the `Text` of `Form1` to **Invoice Data**.

   - Add four `Labels` with the text, font size, and approximate locations shown in Figure 14-30. (You can click the down arrow next to the `Text` property of a component to get a box into which you can type multiline text.)

   - Add a `Button` with the `Text` **View records**. Resize the `Button` if necessary. Name the `Button` `viewButton`.

   - Add three `TextBoxes`. Name them **invoiceBox**, **nameBox**, and **amountBox**, respectively.

(continues)

Figure 14-30 The ViewInvoices Form

3. In the IDE, double-click the **View records** Button to view the code.

4. Add the shaded statements shown in Figure 14-31. They include:

- A using System.IO statement

- Constants for the file delimiter character and the filename (change the path for your file if necessary)

- A string into which whole records can be read before they are split into fields

- An array of strings used to hold the separate, split fields of the entered string

- A FileStream and StreamReader to handle the input file

- Within the viewButton_Click() method, statements to read in a line from the file and split it into three components

(continued)

(continues)

(continued)

714

```csharp
using System;
using System.Collections.Generic;
using System.ComponentModel;
using System.Data;
using System.Drawing;
using System.Linq;
using System.Text;
using System.Windows.Forms;
using System.IO;

namespace ViewInvoices
{
    public partial class Form1 : Form
    {
        const char DELIM = ',';
        const string FILENAME = @"C:\C#\Chapter.14\Invoices.txt";
        string recordIn;
        string[] fields;
        static FileStream file = new FileStream(FILENAME,
            FileMode.Open, FileAccess.Read);
        StreamReader reader = new StreamReader(file);
        public Form1()
        {
            InitializeComponent();
        }

        private void viewButton_Click(object sender, EventArgs e)
        {
            recordIn = reader.ReadLine();
            fields = recordIn.Split(DELIM);
            invoiceBox.Text = fields[0];
            nameBox.Text = fields[1];
            amountBox.Text = fields[2];
        }
    }
}
```

Figure 14-31   Partial code for the `ViewInvoices` application

(continues)

(continued)

5. Add two Close() statements to the Dispose() method in the Form1Designer.cs file, as shown in Figure 14-32.

```
protected override void Dispose(bool disposing)
{
    reader.Close();
    file.Close();
    if (disposing && (components != null))
    {
        components.Dispose();
    }
    base.Dispose(disposing);
}
```

Figure 14-32   The Dispose() method for the ViewInvoices program

6. Save the project and then execute it. When the Form appears, click the Button to view records. You see the data for the first record you entered when you ran the EnterInvoices application; your Form should look like the one in Figure 14-33. Click the Button again to display the next record.

Figure 14-33   Typical execution of the ViewInvoices program

7. Continue to click the Button to view each record. After you view the last record you entered, click the Button again. An unhandled exception is generated, as shown in Figure 14-34, because you attempted to read data past the end of the input file.

(continues)

(continued)

Figure 14-34   Error message window displayed after user attempts to read past the end of the file

8. Click the **Details** button in the `UnhandledException` window to view details of the error. Figure 14-35 shows that a `System.NullReferenceException` was thrown and not handled.

Figure 14-35   Details displayed by the unhandled exception window

(continues)

(continued)

9. Click **Quit** to close the unhandled exception window.

10. To remedy the unhandled `NullReferenceException` problem, you could take any number of actions. Depending on the application, you might want to do one or more of the following:

    - Display a message.

    - Disallow any more button clicks.

    - End the program.

    - Reposition the file pointer to the file's beginning so the user can view the records again.

    For this example, you take the first two actions: display a message and disallow further button clicks. Return to Visual Studio and locate the code for the `viewButton_Click()` method. Add a `try...catch` block, as shown in Figure 14-36. Place all the record-handling code in a `try` block, and if a `NullReferenceException` is thrown, change the `Text` in `label1` and disable the View records `Button`.

```csharp
private void viewButton_Click(object sender, EventArgs e)
{
    try
    {
        recordIn = reader.ReadLine();
        fields = recordIn.Split(DELIM);
        invoiceBox.Text = fields[0];
        nameBox.Text = fields[1];
        amountBox.Text = fields[2];
    }
    catch (NullReferenceException)
    {
        label1.Text = "You have viewed\nall the records";
        viewButton.Enabled = false;
    }
}
```

Figure 14-36 The `viewButton_Click()` method modified to handle an exception

(continues)

(continued)

11. Save the project and then execute it. This time, after you have viewed all the available records, the last record remains on the Form, an appropriate message is displayed, and the button is disabled, as shown in Figure 14-37.

Figure 14-37   The `ViewInvoices Form` after user has viewed the last record

12. Dismiss the `Form`. Close Visual Studio.

Chapter Summary

- A computer file is a collection of information stored on a nonvolatile, permanent storage device in a computer system. When you store data in a computer file on a persistent storage device, you write to the file from random access memory (RAM). When you copy data from a file on a storage device into RAM, you read from the file. Computer users organize their files into folders or directories. The `File` class contains methods that allow you to access information about files. The `Directory` class provides you with information about directories or folders.

- A character can be any one of the letters, numbers, or other special symbols that comprise data. A field is a group of characters that has some meaning. Fields are grouped together to form records. A record is a collection of fields that contain data about an entity. Records are grouped to create files. A data file is a sequential access file when each record is read in order of its position in the file. Usually, the records are stored in order based on the value in a key field. Before an application can use a data file, it must open the file by creating an object and associating a stream of bytes with that object. When you close a file, it is no longer available to your application.

- Bytes flow into and out of applications through streams. When you use the Console class, you have access to several standard streams: Console.In, Console.Out, and Console.Error. When you read from or write to a file, you use a file processing class instead of Console. Many file processing classes are available in C#, including StreamReader for text input from a file, StreamWriter for text output to a file, and FileStream for both input and output. The FileStream class has 15 overloaded constructors.

- You can use a StreamWriter object to write objects to a file using the WriteLine() method. Fields should be separated by a delimiter, which is a character used to specify the boundary between data items in text files. Data can be read from a file using a StreamReader object and the ReadLine() method. If the value of the returned string from ReadLine() is null, then no more data exists in the file. After a record (line of data) is read in, the String class Split() method can be used to separate the data fields into an array of strings.

- When you read data from a sequential file, subsequent records are read in order because a file's position pointer holds the byte number of the next byte to be read. To reread a file, you could close it and reopen it, or you can just reposition the file pointer using the Seek() method and the SeekOrigin enumeration.

- Serialization is the process of converting objects into streams of bytes. Deserialization is the reverse process; it converts streams of bytes back into objects. To create a class that can be serialized, you mark it with the [Serializable] attribute. A serializable object can be written to or read from a data file with a single statement.

Key Terms

Random access memory (RAM) is temporary storage in a computer.

Volatile describes storage in which data is lost when power is interrupted.

Nonvolatile storage is permanent storage; it is not lost when a computer loses power.

A **computer file** is a collection of information stored on a nonvolatile device in a computer system.

Permanent storage devices, such as hard disks, USB drives, reels of magnetic tape, and optical discs, are used to store files.

Text files contain data that can be read in a text editor because the data has been encoded using a scheme such as ASCII or Unicode.

Data files contain facts and figures.

Binary files contain data that has been encoded in binary format.

A **byte** is a small unit of storage; in a simple text file, a byte holds only one character.

A **kilobyte** is approximately one thousand bytes.

A **megabyte** is approximately one million bytes.

A **gigabyte** is approximately one billion bytes.

To **read from a file** is to copy data from a file on a storage device into RAM.

To **write to a file** is to store data in a computer file on a permanent storage device.

Persistent storage is nonvolatile storage.

The **root directory** is the main directory of a storage device.

Folders or **directories** are structures used to organize files on a storage device.

A **path** is composed of the disk drive in which a file resides plus the complete hierarchy of directories.

The `File` **class** contains methods that allow you to access information about files.

The `Directory` **class** provides information about directories or folders.

The **data hierarchy** is the relationship of characters, fields, records, and files.

A **character** is any one of the letters, numbers, or other special symbols (such as punctuation marks) that comprise data.

A **character set** is the group of all the characters used to represent data on a particular computer.

A **field** is a character or group of characters that has some meaning.

A **record** is a collection of fields that contain data about an entity.

A **sequential access file** is a data file in which each record is read in order based on its position in the file; usually the records are stored in order based on the value in some field.

The **key field** is the field used to control the order of records in a sequential file.

A **random access file** is one for which records can be accessed in any order.

Opening a file involves creating an object and associating a stream of bytes with it.

Closing a file means it is no longer available to an application.

A **stream** is a pipeline or channel through which bytes are input from and output to a file.

Programmers say `FileStream` **exposes** a stream around a file.

XML is an abbreviation of eXtensible Markup Language, which is a standard for exchanging data over the Internet.

A **token** is a block of text within a string that represents an entity or field.

A **delimiter** is a character used to specify the boundary between characters in text files.

A **CSV file** is one that contains comma-separated values.

The term **magic number** refers to the bad programming practice of hard-coding numbers in code without explanation.

A file's **file position pointer** holds the byte number of the next byte to be read.

Serialization is the process of converting objects into streams of bytes.

Deserialization is the process of converting streams of bytes back into objects.

Review Questions

1. Random access memory is _____.

    a. persistent   c. permanent
    b. volatile   d. sequential

2. A collection of data stored on a nonvolatile device in a computer system is a(n) _____.

    a. application   c. operating system
    b. computer file   d. memory map

3. Which of the following is not permanent storage?

    a. RAM   c. a USB drive
    b. a hard disk   d. all of these

4. When you store data in a computer file on a persistent storage device, you are _____.

    a. reading   c. writing
    b. directing   d. rooting

5. Which of the following is not a `File` class method?

    a. `Create()`   c. `Exists()`
    b. `Delete()`   d. `End()`

6. In the data hierarchy, a group of characters that has some meaning, such as a last name or ID number, is a _____.

    a. byte   c. file
    b. field   d. record

7. When each record in a file is stored in order based on the value in some field, the file is a(n) _____ file.

    a. random access   c. formatted
    b. application   d. sequential

8. A channel through which data flows between a program and storage is a _____.

    a. path   c. stream
    b. folder   d. directory

9. Which of the following is not part of a `FileStream` constructor?

    a. the file size   c. the filename
    b. the file mode   d. the type of access

10. When a file's mode is `Create`, a new file will be created _____.

    a. even if one with the same name already exists
    b. only if one with the same name does not already exist
    c. only if one with the same name already exists
    d. only if the access is `Read`

11. Which of the following is not a `FileStream` property?

    a. `CanRead`   c. `CanSeek`
    b. `CanExist`   d. `CanWrite`

12. Which of the following is not a file `Access` enumeration?

    a. `Read`   c. `WriteRead`
    b. `Write`   d. `ReadWrite`

13. A character used to specify the boundary between data items in text files is a _____.

    a. sentinel   c. delimiter
    b. stopgap   d. margin

14. Which character can be used to specify a boundary between characters in text files?

    a. a comma   c. either of these
    b. a semicolon   d. neither of these

15. After a StreamReader has been created, the ReadLine() method can be used to _____.

    a. retrieve one line at a time from the file

    b. retrieve one character at a time from the file

    c. store one line at a time in a file

    d. split a string into tokens

16. The argument to the String class Split() method is _____.

    a. void

    b. the number of fields into which to split a record

    c. the character that identifies a new field in a string

    d. a string that can be split into tokens

17. The String class Split() method stores its results in _____.

    a. a string

    b. an array of strings

    c. an appropriate data type for each token

    d. an array of bytes

18. A file's _____ holds the byte number of the next byte to be read.

    a. index indicator   c. header file

    b. position pointer   d. key field

19. The process of converting objects into streams of bytes is _____.

    a. extrication   c. mapping

    b. splitting   d. serialization

20. Which of the following is serializable?

    a. an int   c. a string

    b. an array of ints   d. all of the above

Exercises

 Programming Exercises

1. Create a program named **TestFileAndDirectory** that allows a user to continually enter directory names until the user types "end". If the directory name exists, display a list of the files in it; otherwise, display a message indicating the directory does not exist. If the directory exists and files are listed, prompt the user to enter

one of the filenames. If the file exists, display its creation date and time; otherwise, display a message indicating the file does not exist. Create as many test directories and files as necessary to test your program.

2. Create a program named **FileComparison** that compares two files. First, use a text editor such as Notepad to save your favorite movie quote. Next, copy the file contents and paste them into a word-processing program such as Word. Then, write the file comparison application that displays the sizes of the two files as well as the ratio of their sizes to each other. To discover a file's size, you can create a System.IO.FileInfo object using statements such as the following, where FILE_NAME is a string that contains the name of the file, and size has been declared as an integer:

```
FileInfo fileInfo = new FileInfo(FILE_NAME);
size = wordInfo.Length;
```

3. Using Visual Studio, create a Form like the one shown in Figure 14-38. Specify a directory on your system, and when the Form loads, list the files the directory contains in a CheckedListBox. (You first saw an example of a CheckedListBox in Chapter 12.) Allow the user to click a file's corresponding check box and display the file's creation date and time. (Each time the user checks a new filename, display its creation date in place of the original selection.) Save the project as **TestFileAndDirectory2**. Create as many files as necessary to test your program.

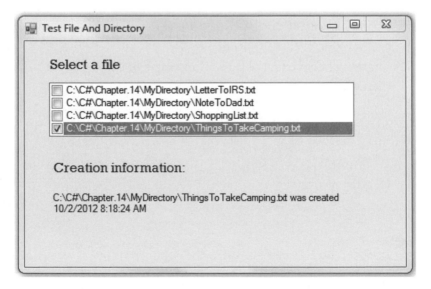

Figure 14-38   Typical execution of the TestFileAndDirectory2 program

4. a. Create a program named **WriteInventoryRecords** that allows you to enter data for items you sell at an online auction site and saves the data to a file. Create an Inventory class that contains fields for item number, description, and asking price.

   b. Create a program named **ReadInventoryRecords** that reads the file created in Exercise 4a and displays each item's data on the screen.

   c. Create a program named **FindInventoryRecords** that prompts the user for an item number, reads the file created in Exercise 4a, and displays data for the specified record.

   d. Create a program named **FindInventoryRecords2** that prompts the user for a minimum selling price, reads the file created in Exercise 4a, and displays all the records containing a price greater than or equal to the entered price.

5. a. Create a program named **CustomizeAForm** that includes a Form for which a user can select options for the background color, size, and title. The Form should look like the one shown in Figure 14-39. Change each feature of the Form as the user makes selections. After the user clicks the "Save form settings" Button, save the color, size, and title as strings to a file and disable the button.

Figure 14-39 The Form in the CustomizeAForm project

   b. Design a program named **RetrieveCustomizedForm** that includes a Form like the one in Figure 14-39, except that instead of saving settings, the Form's Button should retrieve the saved settings. When the user clicks the Button, read the saved settings from the file created in the CustomizeAForm project, and set the Form's color, size, and title appropriately.

726

6. Create a program named **HighScore** containing a Form that hosts a game in which the computer randomly selects one of three letters (A, B, or C) and the user tries to guess which letter was selected. At the start of the game, read in the previous high score from a data file. (Create this file to hold "0" the first time the game is played.) Display the previous high score on the Form to show the player the score to try to beat. Play continues for 10 rounds. As the player makes each guess, show the player's guess and the computer's choice, and award a point if the player correctly guesses the computer's choice. Keep a running count of the number of correct guesses. After 10 rounds, disable the game controls and create a file that holds the new high score, which might be the same as before the game or a new higher number. When the player begins a new game, the high score will be displayed on the Form as the new score to beat.

Debugging Exercises

1. Each of the following files in the Chapter.14 folder of your downloadable student files has syntax and/or logical errors. In each case, determine the problem and fix the program. After you correct the errors, save each file using the same filename preceded with *Fixed*. For example, save DebugFourteen1.cs as **FixedDebugFourteen1.cs**.

    a. DebugFourteen1.cs   c. DebugFourteen3.cs
    b. DebugFourteen2.cs   d. DebugFourteen4.cs

Case Problems

1. In Chapter 11, you created the most recent version of the **GreenvilleRevenue** program, which prompts the user for contestant data for this year's Greenville Idol competition. Now, save all the entered data to a file that is closed when data entry is complete and then reopened and read in, allowing the user to view lists of contestants with requested talent types.

2. In Chapter 11, you created the most recent version of the **MarshallsRevenue** program, which prompts the user for customer data for scheduled mural painting. Now, save all the entered data to a file that is closed when data entry is complete and then reopened and read in, allowing the user to view lists of customer orders for mural types.

Using LINQ to Access Data in C# Programs

In this chapter you will:

- ◎ Understand relational database fundamentals
- ◎ Create databases and table descriptions
- ◎ Create SQL queries
- ◎ Create an Access database
- ◎ Understand implicitly typed variables
- ◎ Understand LINQ
- ◎ Retrieve data from an Access database in C#
- ◎ Use LINQ queries with an Access database table
- ◎ Use LINQ operators to sort and group data

Businesses run by using data. Most businesses would suffer greatly if their data was lost—for example, customers could not be contacted, employees could not be paid, and orders could not be shipped. Well-run businesses do not just possess a lot of data; the data must be organized to be useful. When a business's data is structured in a useful manner, the business can improve its performance. For example, salespeople can track which customers prefer specific products or services, and administrators can identify which employees are the most productive. Businesses can determine which products and services produce the most profit and which should be dropped. Relational databases provide a means to accomplish all these tasks.

In this chapter you will learn about databases. You also will learn about LINQ (pronounced *link*), which is a Visual Studio tool for accessing data stored in databases and other collections, and you will learn how to incorporate LINQ into your C# programs. This chapter is only a brief introduction to these topics. You can buy entire books on database construction and theory and the details of LINQ. This chapter covers only the fundamentals of each topic so you can begin to appreciate how your C# programs have the potential to satisfy important business data needs.

A **collection** is any data structure that holds objects of the same type. Data structures include arrays, lists, queues, and directories. You will learn about other data structures as you continue to study C#.

Understanding Relational Database Fundamentals

As you learned in Chapter 14, data items that are used in computer systems are often stored in a data hierarchy. In the data hierarchy, the smallest usable unit of data is the character, often a letter or number, and characters are grouped together to form fields, such as firstName, lastName, and socialSecurityNumber. Related fields are often grouped together to form records—groups of fields that go together because they represent attributes of some entity, such as an employee, customer, inventory item, or bank account. Files are composed of related records; for example, a file might contain a record for each employee in a company or each account at a bank. Most organizations store many files that contain the data they need to operate their businesses. For example, businesses often need to maintain separate files that contain data about employees, customers, inventory items, and orders. Many organizations use database software to organize the information in these files. A **database** holds a file, or more frequently, a group of files that an organization needs to support its applications. In a database, the files often are called **tables** because you can arrange their contents in rows and columns. Real-life examples of database-like tables abound. For example, consider the listings in a telephone book. Each listing in a city directory might contain four columns, as shown in Figure 15-1—last name, first name, street address, and phone number. Although your local phone directory might not store its data in the rigid columnar format shown in the figure, it could. You can see that each column represents a field and that each row represents one record. You can picture a table within a database in the same way.

Last name	First name	Address	Phone
Abbott	William	123 Oak Lane	490-8920
Ackerman	Kimberly	467 Elm Drive	787-2781
Adams	Stanley	8120 Pine Street	787-0129
Adams	Violet	347 Oak Lane	490-8912
Adams	William	12 Second Street	490-3667

Figure 15-1   A telephone book table

Arrays (stored in memory) and tables (stored in databases) are similar in that both contain rows and columns. When an array has multiple columns, all columns must have the same data type. The same is not true for tables stored in databases.

Sometimes, one record or row in a database table is also called an *entity*; however, many definitions of *entity* exist in database texts. One column (field) can also be called an *attribute*.

Figure 15-1 includes five records, each representing a unique person. It is relatively easy to scan this short list of names to find a person's phone number; of course, telephone books contain many more records. Most people prefer to use a telephone book in which the records are organized as shown—in alphabetical order by last name. However, some telephone book users, such as telemarketers, might prefer to use a book in which the records are organized in telephone-number order. Others, such as door-to-door sales-people, might prefer a telephone book in which the records are organized in street-address order. Computerized databases offer flexibility and convenience for different users due to their ability to sort records in various orders based on the contents of different columns.

Unless you are reading a telephone book for a very small town, a last name alone often is not sufficient to identify a person. In the example in Figure 15-1, three people have the last name *Adams*. For these records, you need to examine the first name before you can determine the correct phone number. In a large city, many people might have the same first and last names; in that case, you might also need to examine the street address to identify a person. As with the telephone book, most computerized database tables require a way to identify each record uniquely, even if it means using multiple columns. A value that uniquely identifies a record is called a **primary key**, or a **key** for short. Key fields often are defined as a single column, but as with the telephone book, keys can be constructed from multiple columns. A key constructed from multiple columns is a **compound key**, also known as a **composite key**.

Telephone books are republished periodically because changes have occurred—new people have moved into the city and become telephone customers, and others have left, canceled service, or changed phone numbers. With computerized database tables, you also need to add, delete, and modify records.

As with telephone books, computerized database tables frequently contain thousands of records, or rows, and each row might contain entries in dozens of columns. Handling and organizing all the data contained in an organization's tables requires sophisticated software. **Database management software**, also known as a **database management system (DBMS)**, is a set of programs that allows users to:

- Create table descriptions.
- Identify keys.
- Add, delete, and update records within a table.
- Arrange records within a table so they are sorted by different fields.
- Write questions that select specific records from a table for viewing.
- Write questions that combine information from multiple tables. This is possible because the database management software establishes and maintains relationships between the columns in the tables. A group of database tables from which you can make these connections is a **relational database**.
- Create reports that allow users to easily interpret your data, and create forms that allow users to view and enter data using an easy-to-manage interactive screen.
- Keep data secure by employing sophisticated security measures.
- View data relationships graphically.

If you have used various word-processing or spreadsheet programs, you know that each version works a little differently, although each carries out the same types of tasks. Like other computer programs, each database management software package operates differently; however, with each, you need to perform the same types of tasks.

 Watch the video *Relational Databases*.

TWO TRUTHS & A LIE

Understanding Relational Database Fundamentals

1. Files are composed of related records, and records are composed of fields.

2. In a database, files often are called tables because you can arrange their contents in rows and columns.

3. Key fields always are defined as a single table column.

The false statement is #3. Key fields often are defined as a single table column, but keys can be constructed from multiple columns. A key constructed from multiple columns is a compound or composite key.

Creating Databases and Table Descriptions

Creating a useful database requires a lot of planning and analysis. You must decide what data will be stored, how that data will be divided between tables, and how the tables will inter-relate. Before you create any tables, you must create the database itself. With most database software packages, creating the database that will hold the tables requires nothing more than providing a name for the database and indicating the physical location, perhaps a hard disk drive, where the database will be stored. When you save a table, one convention recommends you use a name that begins with the prefix "tbl"—for example, tblCustomers. Your databases often become filled with a variety of objects—tables, forms that users can use for data entry, reports that organize the data for viewing, queries that select subsets of data for viewing, and so on. Using naming conventions, such as beginning each table name with a prefix that identifies it as a table, helps you to keep track of the various objects in your system.

When you save a table description, many database management programs suggest a default, generic name such as Table1. Usually, a more descriptive name is more useful as you continue to create objects.

Beginning table names with the "tbl" prefix is part of the **Leszynski naming convention** (LNC). This convention is most popular with Microsoft Access users and Visual Basic programmers. This format is just a convention, and is not required by any database. Your instructor or supervisor might approve of a different convention.

Before you can enter any data into a database table, you must design the table. At minimum, this involves two tasks:

• You must decide what columns your table needs, and provide names for them.

• You must provide a data type for each column.

For example, assume you are designing a customer database table. Figure 15-2 shows some column names and data types you might use.

Column	Data type
customerID	Text
lastName	Text
firstName	Text
streetAddress	Text
balanceOwed	Numeric

Figure 15-2   Customer table description

It is important to think carefully about the original design of a database. After the database has been created and data has been entered, it could be difficult and time consuming to make changes to the structure.

You can see from Figure 15-2 that a table description closely resembles the list of variables that you have used with every program throughout this book. The table description uses just two data types—text and numeric. Text columns can hold any type of characters, including letters, digits, and punctuation; in other words, they hold strings. Numeric columns can hold numbers only. Depending on the database management software you use, you might have many more sophisticated data types at your disposal. For example, some database software divides the numeric data type into several subcategories such as integers (whole number only) and double-precision numbers (numbers that contain decimals). Other options might include special categories for currency numbers (representing dollars and cents), dates, and Boolean columns (representing true or false). At the least, all database software recognizes the distinction between text and numeric data.

Unassigned variables within computer programs might be empty (containing a null value), or might contain unknown or garbage values. Similarly, columns in database tables might also contain null or unknown values. When a field in a database contains a null value, it does not mean that the field holds a 0 or a space; it means that no data has been entered for the field at all. Although "null" and "empty" are used synonymously by many database developers, the terms have slightly different meanings to some programming professionals, such as Visual Basic programmers.

The table description in Figure 15-2 uses one-word column names and camel casing, in the same way that variable names have been defined throughout this book. Many database software packages do not require that data column names be single words without embedded spaces, but many database table designers prefer single-word names because they resemble variable names in programs. In addition, when you write programs that access a database table, the single-word field names can be used "as is," without special syntax to indicate the names that represent a single field. As a further advantage, when you use a single word to label each database column, it is easier to understand whether just one column is being referenced, or several.

Many database management software packages allow you to add a narrative description of each data column in a table. This allows you to make comments that become part of the table. These comments do not affect the way the table operates; they simply serve as documentation for those who are reading a table description. For example, you might want to make a note that `customerID` should consist of five digits, or that `balanceOwed` should not exceed a given limit. Some software allows you to specify that values for a certain column are required; in such cases, the user cannot create a record without providing data for these columns. In addition, you might be able to indicate column value limits—high and low numbers between which the column contents must fall.

Identifying Primary Keys

In most tables you create for a database, you want to identify a column, or possibly a combination of columns, as the table's key column or field, also called the primary key. The primary key in a table is the column that makes each record different from all others. For example, in the customer table in Figure 15-2, the logical choice for a primary key is the `customerID` column—each customer record that is entered into the customer table has a unique value in this column. Many customers might have the same first name or last name (or both), and multiple customers also might have the same street address or balance due. However, each customer possesses a unique ID number. In some database software packages, such as Microsoft Access, you indicate a primary key simply by selecting a column name and clicking a button that is labeled with a key icon. A primary key should be *immutable*, meaning that a value does not change during normal operation. For example, customer IDs typically do not change, but customer balances, addresses, and even names are frequently modified.

Other typical examples of primary keys include:

- A student ID number in a table that contains college student information
- A part number in a table that contains inventory items
- A Social Security number in a table that contains employee information

In each of these examples, the primary key uniquely identifies the row. For example, each student has a unique ID number assigned by the college. Other columns in a student table would not be adequate keys, because many students have the same last name, first name, hometown, or major. Even if a database table contains only one employee named Smith, for example, or only one employee with the job title of Salesperson, those fields are still not good primary key candidates because more Smiths and salespeople could be added later. Analyzing existing data is not a foolproof way to select a good key; you must also consider likely future data.

It is no coincidence that each of the preceding examples of a key is a number, such as a student ID number or item number. Often, assigning a number to each row in a table is the simplest and most efficient method of obtaining a useful key. However, a table's key could be a text field.

Sometimes, several columns could serve as the key. For example, if an employee record contains both a company-assigned employee ID and a Social Security number, then both columns are *candidate keys*— potential primary keys. After you choose a primary key from among candidate keys, the remaining candidate keys become *alternate keys*.

The primary key is important for several reasons:

- You can configure your database software to prevent multiple records from containing the same value in this column, thus avoiding data-entry errors.

- For some applications, you might want to sort your records in this order before displaying or printing them.

- You use this column when setting up relationships between this table and others that will become part of the same database.

In addition, you need to understand the concept of the primary key when you normalize a database. **Normalization** is the process of designing and creating a set of database tables that satisfies users' needs and avoids many potential problems such as data redundancies and anomalies. **Data redundancy** is the unnecessary repetition of data. An **anomaly** is an irregularity in a database's design that causes problems and inconveniences. To keep the examples in this chapter simple, only single database tables are used. However, as you grow proficient in database use and constructions, you will want to create databases with relationships among multiple tables, which requires a more thorough understanding of normalization.

 As an example of data redundancy, consider a table of names and addresses in which many addresses are in the same zip code. Instead of storing the same city and state name with each record, it is more efficient to store only the zip code with each record, and then to associate the table with another table that contains a list of zip codes and the corresponding cities and states.

 Anomalies take many forms. For example, an anomaly occurs when the same data is stored in multiple locations. If a database contains a table of in-stock items and their prices, and another table contains customer orders, including items and prices, then any price changes must be made in multiple locations, increasing the chance for error.

Usually, after you have identified the necessary fields and their data types and identified the primary key, you are ready to save your table description and begin to enter data.

Understanding Database Structure Notation

A shorthand way to describe a table is to use the table name followed by parentheses that contain all the field names, with the primary key underlined. (Some database designers use an asterisk instead of an underline to specify a primary key.) Thus, when a table is named tblStudents and contains columns named idNumber, lastName, firstName, and gradePointAverage, and idNumber is the key, you can reference the table using the following notation:

tblStudents(<u>idNumber</u>, lastName, firstName, gradePointAverage)

Although this shorthand notation does not provide information about data types or range limits on values, it does provide a quick overview of the table's structure. The key does not have to be the first attribute listed in a table reference, but frequently it is.

TWO TRUTHS & A LIE

Creating Databases and Table Descriptions

1. Databases are often filled with multiple objects such as tables, forms, and queries.
2. The primary key in a table is the record that appears first in a sorted list.
3. Data redundancy is the unnecessary repetition of data.

The false statement is #2. The primary key in a table is the column that makes each record different from all others.

Creating SQL Queries

Data tables often contain hundreds or thousands of rows; making sense out of that much information is a daunting task. Frequently, you want to cull subsets of data from a table you have created. For example, you might want to view only those customers with an address in a specific state, only inventory items whose quantity in stock has fallen below the normal reorder point, or only employees who participate in an insurance plan. Besides limiting records, you might also want to limit the columns that you view. For example, student records might contain dozens of fields, but a school administrator might only be interested in looking at names and grade point averages. The questions that cause the database software to extract the appropriate records from a table and specify the fields to be viewed are called queries; a **query** is simply a request using syntax that the database software can understand.

Depending on the software you use, you might create a query by filling in blanks (using a language called **query by example**) or by writing statements similar to those in many programming languages. The most common language that database administrators use to access data in their tables is **Structured Query Language**, or **SQL**. The basic form of the SQL command that retrieves selected records from a table is **SELECT-FROM-WHERE**. The SELECT-FROM-WHERE SQL statement:

- *Selects* the columns you want to view
- *From* a specific table
- *Where* one or more conditions are met

 SQL frequently is pronounced *sequel*, but several SQL product Web sites insist that the official pronunciation is *S-Q-L*. Similarly, some people pronounce GUI as *gooey* and others insist that it should be *G-U-I*. In general, a preferred pronunciation evolves in an organization. The **TLA**, which is a three-letter abbreviation for *three-letter abbreviation*, is the most popular type of abbreviation in technical terminology.

For example, suppose that a customer table named `tblCustomer` contains data about your business customers and that the structure of the table is `tblCustomer(custId, lastName, state)`. Then, a statement such as:

`SELECT custId, lastName FROM tblCustomer WHERE state = "WI"`

would display a new table that contains two columns—`custId` and `lastName`—and only as many rows as needed to hold customers whose state column contains "WI". Besides using = to mean "equal to," you can use the comparison conditions > (greater than), < (less than), >= (greater than or equal to), and <= (less than or equal to). As you have already learned from working with programming variables throughout this book, text field values are always contained within quotes, whereas numeric values are not.

Conventionally, SQL keywords such as SELECT appear entirely in uppercase; this book follows that convention.

In database management systems, a particular way of looking at a database is sometimes called a **view**. Typically, a view arranges records in some order and makes only certain fields visible. The different views provided by database software are virtual; that is, they do not affect the physical organization of the database.

To select all fields for each record in a table, you can use the asterisk as a wildcard; a **wildcard** is a symbol that means "any" or "all." For example, `SELECT * FROM tblCustomer WHERE state = "WI"` would select all columns for every customer whose state is "WI", not just specifically named columns. To select all customers from a table, you can omit the `WHERE` clause in a `SELECT-FROM-WHERE` statement. In other words, `SELECT * FROM tblCustomer` selects all columns for all customers.

You learned about making selections in computer programs much earlier in this book, and you have probably noticed that `SELECT-FROM-WHERE` statements serve the same purpose as programming decisions. As with decision statements in programs, SQL allows you to create compound conditions using `AND` or `OR` operators. In addition, you can precede any condition with a `NOT` operator to achieve a negative result. In summary, Figure 15-3 shows a database table named `tblInventory` with the following structure:

`tblInventory(itemNumber, description, quantityInStock, price)`

The table contains five records. Figure 15-4 lists several typical SQL `SELECT` statements you might use with `tblInventory`, and explains each.

itemNumber	description	quantityInStock	price
144	Pkg 12 party plates	250	$14.99
231	Helium balloons	180	$2.50
267	Paper streamers	68	$1.89
312	Disposable tablecloth	20	$6.99
383	Pkg 20 napkins	315	$2.39

Figure 15-3   The `tblInventory` table

SQL Statement	Explanation
SELECT itemNumber, price FROM tblInventory	Shows only the item number and price for all five records.
SELECT * FROM tblInventory WHERE price > 5.00	Shows all fields from only those records in which price is greater than $5.00—items 144 and 312.
SELECT itemNumber FROM tblInventory WHERE quantityInStock > 200 AND price > 10.00	Shows item number 144—the only record that has a quantity greater than 200 as well as a price greater than $10.00.
SELECT description, price FROM tblInventory WHERE description = "Pkg 20 napkins" OR itemNumber < 200	Shows the description and price fields for the package of 12 party plates and the package of 20 napkins. Each selected record only needs to satisfy one of the two criteria.
SELECT itemNumber FROM tblInventory WHERE NOT price < 14.00	Shows the item number for the only record in which the price is not less than $14.00— item 144.

Figure 15-4 Sample SQL statements and explanations

TWO TRUTHS & A LIE

Creating SQL Queries

1. A query is a question that causes database software to extract appropriate fields and records from a table.

2. The most common language that database administrators use to access data in their tables is Structured Query Language, or SQL.

3. The basic form of the SQL command that retrieves selected records from a table is RETRIEVE-FROM-SELECTION.

The false statement is # 3. The basic form of the SQL command that retrieves selected records from a table is SELECT-FROM-WHERE.

Creating an Access Database

Microsoft Office Access is a relational database that is part of some versions of the Microsoft Office system. It combines the relational Microsoft Jet Database Engine with a GUI user interface and other tools. Access is not the only database on the market, but it is convenient for many users because it comes packaged with some versions of Microsoft Office. Using

Access correctly and efficiently can take some time to learn; at most colleges, you can take at least a two-semester course to learn Access thoroughly. This section introduces you to Access as an example of a typical database.

 Access was the name of an earlier failed Microsoft communications program. The corporation reused the name when it developed its database software in 1992.

 Other popular database packages include Microsoft SQL, MySQL, Borland Paradox, FileMaker Pro, Lotus Approach, Oracle XE, and Sun StarBase.

Figure 15-5 shows the environment in which a database table is designed in Access. Suppose Cartman College wants to keep track of some student data in a database. To keep the example simple, suppose the college wants to store only an ID number, first and last names, and a GPA for each student. In Access, a database developer can type field names for the data that will be stored and can assign an appropriate data type for each field. In Figure 15-5, a tblStudents table is defined, including fields for ID, LastName, FirstName, and GradePointAverage.

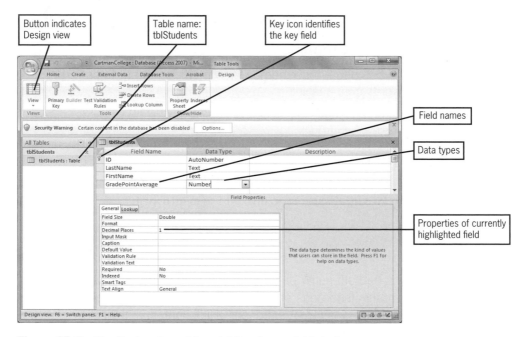

Figure 15-5   The Design view of the tblStudents table in Access

Figure 15-5 shows that the ID field type was chosen to be **AutoNumber**, which means Access will automatically assign consecutive numbers to each new record as it is entered.

After a table's design has been completed, a user can enter data into the table. Figure 15-6 shows the **tblStudents** table in Access's Datasheet view, in which a user can type data the way it would be typed into a spreadsheet. The column headings in the datasheet are provided automatically based on the names that were selected in the Design view.

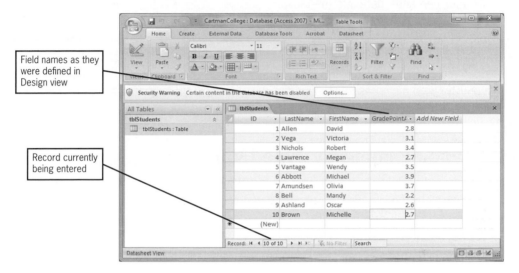

Figure 15-6   The Datasheet view of the **tblStudents** table in Access

In a database actually used by a college, many more fields would be stored for each student and additional tables would be created for courses, faculty, and so on. However, this small database provides enough data to demonstrate using C# to access the stored data.

TWO TRUTHS & A LIE

Creating an Access Database

1. Microsoft Office Access is a relational database that is part of the Microsoft Office system.

2. Access is the only popular commercial database that can be used with C#.

3. In Access, a user designs tables by choosing fields and data types; then the user can enter data into the tables.

The false statement is #2. Access is not the only database on the market, and is not the only one that can be accessed in C#, but it is convenient for many users because it comes packaged with Microsoft Office.

Understanding Implicitly Typed Variables

An **implicitly typed variable** has a data type that is inferred from the expression used to initialize the variable. To create an implicitly typed variable, you use a variable declaration with **var** as the data type. When you use an implicitly typed variable, the C# compiler decides on a data type for you. This process is called **type inference**—an object's set of allowed properties and methods is not fixed when the code is written, but is determined when the program executes.

Using `var` to create implicitly typed variables is also called **duck typing** because it fits the phrase, "If it walks like a duck and quacks like a duck, I would call it a duck." The phrase is attributed to an American writer and poet, James Whitcomb Riley, who lived from 1849 to 1916.

For example, in the following statement, `money` is implicitly typed as a `double` because the value assigned to the variable is a `double`:

```
var money = 1.99;
```

Because `money` is a `double`, you can, for example, perform arithmetic with it. If the declaration had been `var money = "a dollar ninety-nine";`, then `money` would be a string and you could not perform arithmetic with it. The statement `var money = 1.99;` has exactly the same meaning as the following:

```
double money = 1.99;
```

Other examples of assigning values to implicitly typed variables include the following:

- `var age = 30;` has the same meaning as `int age = 30;`

- `var name = "Roxy";` has the same meaning as `string name = "Roxy";`

- `var book = new Book()` has the same meaning as `Book book = new Book();`

- `var emp = new Employee(101, "Smith", 15.00);` has the same meaning as `Employee emp = new Employee(101, "Smith", 15.00);`

Although each of these uses of `var` is a valid C# statement, professional programmers are divided on when `var` should be used. Some think that `var` is acceptable when the data type is obvious from the statement, as in the following examples:

```
var money = 1.99;
var myDog = new Dog();
```

However, `var` should not be used when the type is not obvious, as in the following example:

```
var result = myMethod();
```

Other professionals believe that you should not use `var` even when its implied type is clear, and that you should almost always declare a data type for each program element. They feel that the `var` keyword should be used only in specific situations, such as with LINQ statements.

You have already learned that you can use the `foreach` statement to process array elements. For example, the following code displays each `double` in the `payRate` array:

```
double[] payRate = {6.00, 7.35, 8.12, 12.45, 22.22};
foreach(double money in payRate)
    Console.WriteLine("{0}", money.ToString("C"));
```

In this example, `money` is declared as a `double` and is used as the **iteration variable**—the variable that is used to hold each successive value in the array. Alternatively, you can declare the iteration variable in a `foreach` statement to be an implicitly typed local variable. In this case, the iteration variable's type is inferred from the collection type it uses. For example, the same results can be achieved with the following:

```
double[] payRate = {6.00, 7.35, 8.12, 12.45, 22.22};
foreach(var money in payRate)
    Console.WriteLine("{0}", money.ToString("C"));
```

In this example, `money` is implied to be a `double` because `payRate` is an array of `double`s. In Figure 15-7, the implicitly typed variable `n` is an `int` because `numbers` is an `int` array. Figure 15-8 shows the program's output.

```
using System;
class ImplicitVariableDemo
{
    static void Main()
    {
        int[] numbers = { 6, 4, 2, 1, 8, 3, 7, 5, 2, 0 };
        Console.WriteLine("Numbers List");
        foreach (var n in numbers)
            Console.Write("{0}  ", n);
        Console.WriteLine();
    }
}
```

Figure 15-7 The ImplicitVariableDemo class

```
Command Prompt

C:\C#\Chapter.15>ImplicitVariableDemo
Numbers List
6   4   2   1   8   3   7   5   2   0

C:\C#\Chapter.15>_
```

Figure 15-8 Output of the ImplicitVariableDemo program

When you declare a variable in a program, usually you want to assign a data type rather than using an implicit type. One advantage of a modern programming language like C# is that it is **strongly typed**. When a language is strongly typed, severe restrictions are placed on what data types can be mixed. Strong typing prevents certain errors—for example, the loss of data that might occur if you inadvertently assigned a `double` to an integer. However, you will use implicitly typed variables frequently in LINQ statements, which you will use to access data stored in a database.

 Unlike C#, Visual Basic is considered to be a weakly typed language. If you run a VB program in Visual Studio, you have the option of declaring `Option Strict`, which means that types will be checked.

743

Understanding LINQ

As you have studied C#, you have become comfortable with the ideas of objects and classes. However, businesses operate using data that frequently is stored in relational databases. Applications that tried to bridge the gap between modern languages and traditional databases have been difficult to build and maintain. To reduce the complexity of accessing and integrating data that is stored in databases and other collections, Microsoft Corporation developed the **LINQ** (Language INtegrated Query) Project to provide queries that can be used in C# and Visual Basic.

In older versions of C#, you could access database data by passing an SQL string to a database object (and you still *can* do so). For example, if you want to select all the fields in records in a table named `tblStudents` for which the field `GradePointAverage` is greater than 3.0, you could create a string such as "`SELECT * from tblStudents WHERE GradePointAverage > 3.00`" and pass it to an object of type `OleDbCommand`, which is a built-in type used to access databases. (The "Ole" stands for "Object linking and embedding.") You also would be required to type a few other statements that perform tasks like establishing a connection to the database and opening the database, and the `SELECT` command would then select all the fields for all the records in the table that met the GPA criterion. The drawback to using a string command is that C# does not provide any syntax checking for characters stored within a string. For example, if you misspelled `SELECT` or `GradePointAverage`, the compiler would not issue an error message, but the program would fail when you executed it. Obviously, allowing any spelling is a beneficial feature when you want to store people's names or addresses, but it is a shortcoming when you want to issue a correct command.

LINQ was created to help solve these problems. LINQ provides a set of general-purpose standard operators that allow queries to be constructed using syntax that is easy to understand. This syntax is similar to SQL's, and the compiler can check it for errors. The operators defined in LINQ can be used to query arrays, enumerable classes, XML, relational databases, and other sources. This chapter concentrates on arrays and databases, but the LINQ queries you learn can be used with many types of data.

Some keywords in the LINQ vocabulary include the following:

- **select** indicates what to select.

- **from** indicates the collection or sequence from which data will be drawn.

- **where** indicates conditions for selecting records.

It is no accident that these are the same words you learned about in the discussion of SQL earlier in this chapter.

The operator **where** is a **restriction operator**, or one that places a restriction on which data is added to a collection. The operator **select** is a **projection operator**, or one that projects, or sends off, specific data from a collection.

Figure 15-9 shows an example of LINQ in action. In the first shaded section, an implicitly typed collection, highNums, is constructed from each variable x in the numbers array where the value of x is greater than 3. The foreach loop uses the sequence that is a subset of the original array to display all the records that meet the selection criteria—that is, all the integers greater than 3. Figure 15-10 shows the output.

```
using System;
using System.Linq;
class LinqDemo1
{
  static void Main()
  {
    int[] numbers = { 6, 4, 2, 1, 8, 3, 7, 5, 2, 0 };
    const int CUTOFF = 3;
    var highNums =
          from x in numbers
          where x > CUTOFF
          select x;

    Console.WriteLine("Numbers > " + CUTOFF);
    foreach (var n in highNums)
    {
        Console.Write("{0}  ", n);
    }
    Console.WriteLine();
  }
}
```

Figure 15-9   The LinqDemo1 program

Figure 15-10 Output of the LinqDemo1 application

You can use LINQ with more complicated sequences, such as an array of objects. Figure 15-11 shows a Student class that is similar to many you have seen throughout this book. The class contains three auto-implemented properties and a constructor that requires three parameters. Figure 15-12 provides an example of how LINQ can select specific Students from an array. Figure 15-13 shows this output.

```
class Student
{
    public Student(int num, string name, double avg)
    {
        IdNumber = num;
        Name = name;
        GradePointAverage = avg;
    }
    public int IdNumber {get; set;}
    public string Name {get; set;}
    public double GradePointAverage {get; set;}
}
```

Figure 15-11 The Student class

```
using System;
using System.Linq;
class LinqDemo2
{
    static void Main()
    {
        Student[] stus = {  new Student(1,  "Jones",    3.1),
                            new Student(2,  "Kimball",  2.9),
                            new Student(5,  "Oliver",   2.6),
                            new Student(6,  "Mitchell", 3.0),
                            new Student(8,  "Lee",      4.0),
                            new Student(10, "Cooper",   3.5) };
```

Figure 15-12 The LinqDemo2 program *(continues)*

746

(continued)

```
        const double CUTOFF = 3.0;
        var goodStudents =
            from s in stus
            where s.GradePointAverage > CUTOFF
            select s;

        Console.WriteLine("Students with GPA > " + CUTOFF);
        foreach (var s in goodStudents)
        {
            Console.WriteLine("{0,3} {1,-8} {2,5}", s.IdNumber,
                s.Name, s.GradePointAverage.ToString("F1"));
        }
    }
}
```

Figure 15-12   The LinqDemo2 program

Figure 15-13   Output of the LinqDemo2 program

Although LINQ statements work well to select specific records from an array, you could have used traditional C# statements to achieve the same results. However, few businesses can operate with all their data hard coded and stored in arrays within programs. The true power of LINQ becomes available when you can access an external database.

 Watch the video *An Introduction to LINQ*.

TWO TRUTHS & A LIE

Understanding LINQ

1. An important new feature in the latest version of C# is the ability to access databases.

2. LINQ provides a way to query collections such as arrays, enumerable classes, XML, and relational databases.

3. Some keywords in the LINQ vocabulary include `select`, `from`, and `where`.

The false statement is #1. In older versions of C#, you could access database data by passing an SQL string to a database object (and you still *can* do so in current versions of C#).

Retrieving Data from an Access Database in C#

As with many features of C#, you can write code to access a database table by hand, but you save time and reduce the chance for error by using the built-in tools of the Visual Studio IDE.

Adding a database to a Windows Forms project requires making only a few menu selections and browsing for a stored database. (In the "You Do It" section later in this chapter, you can walk through instructions that add a database to your project.) To add a database table to a Windows Forms project, you can perform two sets of tasks:

- You drag a `DataGridView` object from the IDE's Toolbox onto a `Form`. As Figure 15-14 shows, a `DataGridView` Tasks menu appears from which you can select a project data source. (If you inadvertently dismiss this menu before selecting a data source, you can select Data Source from the Properties list and make the same selections.)

Figure 15-14 Selecting a data source for a project

- You make a few choices and browse for the database file to add to the project. After a few more choices, the empty grid appears (see Figure 15-15). The Solution Explorer window at the right side of the screen shows that the CartmanCollege database has been added to the project. Also note at the bottom of the screen that three objects have been created:

  ○ cartmanCollegeDataSet—A **dataset** is a temporary set of data stored in your project. In other words, changes made to this dataset in the program will not automatically alter the original database.

  ○ tblStudentsBindingSource—A **BindingSource** object establishes a link from a database to your program.

  ○ tblStudentsTableAdapter—A **table adapter** passes data back and forth between the dataset and the BindingSource.

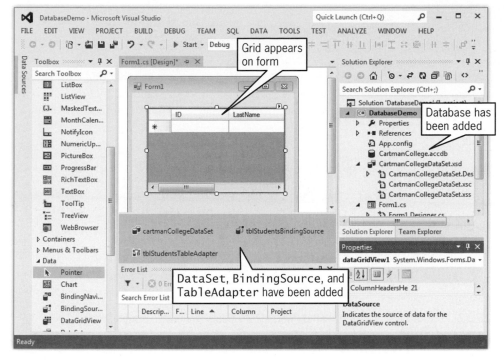

Figure 15-15 The IDE after a database file has been added to the project

After the database table has been added to the project, you can execute the program. The output appears as shown on the left in Figure 15-16. The data from the database appears in the grid, and scroll bars appear so that you can navigate to see the rows and columns that do not fit. If you want to see more columns and rows at a time when the program executes again, you can close the Form, return to the IDE, resize the Form and DataGridView, and execute the program again (see the right side in Figure 15-16).

Figure 15-16 Execution of the DatabaseDemo project

The code for the project that produces Figure 15-16 is stored in your downloadable student files in a project named `DatabaseDemo`.

When you view the code behind the `Form` in Figure 15-16, you can see that one comment and one statement have been added to the `Form1_Load()` method, the method that executes when a Windows application starts and the main form is initialized. Figure 15-17 shows the method.

```
private void Form1_Load(object sender, EventArgs e)
{
    // TODO: This line of code loads data
    // into the 'cartmanCollegeDataSet.tblStudents' table.
    // You can move, or remove it, as needed.

    this.tblStudentsTableAdapter.Fill
      (this.cartmanCollegeDataSet.tblStudents);
}
```

Figure 15-17 The `Form1_Load()` method with automatically generated code after `CartmanCollege` database is added to the `Form`

The line breaks in Figure 15-17 have been altered from the way they appear in Visual Studio to better fit this page.

If you search the code for the project, you will find more than a dozen references to `cartmanCollegeDataSet`. All this code was automatically generated when you added the data to the project and added the table to the `Form`, saving you many chances for error.

The comment in the `Form1_Load()` method indicates that you can move the `Fill()` method statement or delete it. The `Fill()` method fills the table adapter with the data from `tblStudents` in the `cartmanCollegeDataSet`. You do not have to load the data into the viewing grid when the `Form` loads. For example, you could add a button to the `Form` and move the `Fill()` statement to the button's `Click()` method. Then, when the `Form` loads, no data would be visible, but after the user clicks the button, the data fills the table.

TWO TRUTHS & A LIE

Retrieving Data from an Access Database in C#

1. A dataset is another name for a database that your project accesses and alters.

2. A `BindingSource` object establishes a link from a database to a program.

3. A table adapter passes data back and forth between a dataset and the `BindingSource`.

751

The false statement is #1. A dataset is a temporary set of data stored in a project.

 You Do It

Adding a Dataset to a Project

In the next steps, you add a previously created database table to a C# project and retrieve data from the table so you can display it in a `Form`.

1. Your downloadable student files contain a Microsoft Office Access Database file named **HonestRalphsUsedCars**. If Access is installed on your computer, you can open the database file by double-clicking its name. When Access opens, double-click **tblCars : Table** under All Tables. (See Figure 15-18.) Examine the data in the table. The fields are ID, ModelYear, Make, Price, and Color. Ten records have been entered into the table. When you finish examining the records, close Access.

(continues)

(continued)

Figure 15-18   HonestRalphsUsedCars tblCars table in Access

2. Open Visual Studio and start a new Windows Forms Application named **AccessCars**. Change the Text property of the Form to **Honest Ralph's Used Cars**.

3. From the Toolbox at the left of the IDE, drag a DataGridView object onto the Form. Set its Location property to **20, 20**. Select its DataSource property and select **Add Project Data Source**. In the Choose a Data Source Type dialog box, select **Database** and then click **Next**. In the Choose a Database Model dialog box, select **Dataset** and then click **Next**.

4. In the Choose Your Data Connection dialog box, click **New Connection**. In the Add Connection dialog box, select **Microsoft Access Database File** as the Data source, and then click **Browse** to find the file to use. Select **HonestRalphsUsedCars.accdb** from the folder where the file is stored. Then click **OK** and **Next**. A dialog box opens and asks if you want to copy the file into your project. Click **Yes**.

(continues)

(continued)

5. In the Save the Connection String dialog box, make sure that the **Yes** box is checked to save the connection, and click **Next**. In the next window that appears, select both **Tables** and **Views**. Then click the **Finish** button.

6. In the Solution Explorer, confirm that the `HonestRalphsUsedCars` database has been added to the project. Also confirm that the `DataSet`, `BindingSource`, and `TableAdapter` objects have been created. See Figure 15-19.

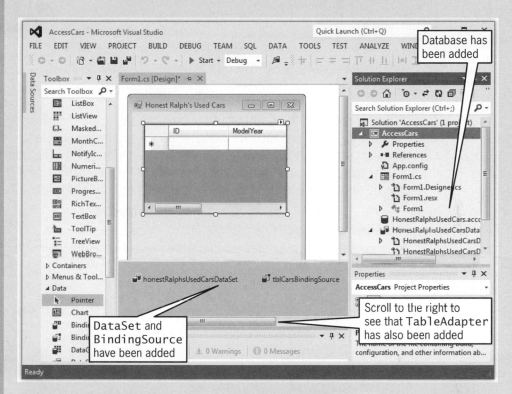

Figure 15-19 The IDE after a database is added to the project

7. Save the project, then click **DEBUG** and **Start Without Debugging**. The data appears in the table grid, as shown on the left side of Figure 15-20. Scroll down and to the right to view all the data. When you finish, dismiss the `Form`.

(continues)

(continued)

Figure 15-20   Honest Ralph's Used Cars data as it appears in the grid and then as it appears in a wider grid

8. In Design view, reposition the grid and widen both the table and the grid so you will be able to see all the records' fields when the program executes. Save the project, then click **DEBUG** and **Start Without Debugging**. The data appears in the table grid, as shown on the right side of Figure 15-20. Use the vertical scroll bar to view the hidden records at the bottom of the list.

9. Dismiss the Form. In the IDE, double-click the Form title bar. The Form1_Load() method appears as follows. (Note that the comment has been divided into three lines and the Fill() method has been divided into two lines so the code fits better on this page.)

```
private void Form1_Load(object sender, EventArgs e)
{
    // TODO: This line of code loads data into the
    // 'honestRalphsUsedCarsDataSet.tblCars' table.
    // You can move, or remove it, as needed.

    this.tblCarsTableAdapter.Fill
        (this.honestRalphsUsedCarsDataSet.tblCars);
}
```

10. Return to Design view. Drag a Button onto the Form. Change its Name property to **recordsButton** and its Text property to **View records**. Adjust the size of the Button so its text is visible. Double-click the Button to generate a recordsButton_Click() method and view its code. Cut the Fill() method call from the Form1_Load() method and paste it into the recordsButton_Click() method. Save the project and then execute the program again. This time the grid is empty when the Form loads, but after you click the button, the grid fills with data.

11. Dismiss the form.

Using LINQ Queries with an Access Database Table

You are not required to use the data grid to view database records. You also are not required to view all the records in the database table or to view all the fields for each record. Instead, you can use a LINQ query to select a collection of data from a table when specific criteria are met. For example, Figure 15-21 shows a showButton_Click() method that could be used to fill a list box with only the last names of students who have a GPA greater than 3.0. The shaded code in the figure is quite similar to the shaded code used with the array in Figure 15-12. Instead of using Console.WriteLine() to display students, this method adds them to a ListBox named outputListBox.

```
private void showButton_Click(object sender, EventArgs e)
{
    const double CUTOFF = 3.0;
    this.tblStudentsTableAdapter.Fill
      (this.cartmanCollegeDataSet.tblStudents);
    var goodStudents =
        from s in this.cartmanCollegeDataSet.tblStudents
        where s.GradePointAverage > CUTOFF
        select s;
    foreach (var s in goodStudents)
        outputListBox.Items.Add(s.LastName);
}
```

Figure 15-21   The showButton_Click() method that uses a ListBox to display the last names of students with high GPAs

The method in Figure 15-21 is part of the project named DatabaseDemo2, which is available in your downloadable student files.

In the example in Figure 15-21, goodStudents is an implicitly typed collection of students with high GPAs. In this case, goodStudents is the following type (where DatabaseDemo2 is the name of the current project):

System.Data.EnumerableRowCollection<DatabaseDemo2.CartmanCollegeDataSet. tblStudentsRow>

This means that goodStudents is a collection of rows from the tblStudents database table. However, it is easier to use var and to have the type inferred than to use this lengthy type name.

Assume that you start a C# Windows Forms project and take the following steps:

- Add the CartmanCollege database tblStudents table to the project.
- Delete the automatically added grid from the Form.

- Drag a button onto the Form. Change its Text property to "Show students with high GPA" and its Name property to showButton.

- Drag a ListBox onto the Form and change its Name property to outputListBox.

- Add the showButton_Click() method from Figure 15-21.

Figure 15-22 shows the results when you execute the program and click the button. Although 10 student records are stored in the table, the figure lists only the last names of the five students who have GPA values over 3.0. You can confirm that these are the correct students by referring back to the complete listing in Figure 15-6.

Figure 15-22   Execution of the program containing the method in Figure 15-21

In the method in Figure 15-21, goodStudents is a collection of student records gathered from the tblStudents table in the CartmanCollege database, as indicated in the from clause. The where clause specifies the condition for selection—a GPA greater than CUTOFF. The select clause indicates what to select—a record. The foreach statement that follows the shaded portion of the method selects each record in the collection, and adds its LastName field to the ListBox. The from-where-select combination is a single statement. Conventionally, its parts are written on separate lines for clarity, but that is not required. However, be careful not to use a semicolon until the entire statement is complete.

As an alternative to the code in Figure 15-21, instead of creating a collection of records, you could create a collection of last names. Figure 15-23 shows an example, in which only last names are selected to be added to the collection (see the first shaded expression in the figure). That is, in this example goodStudents is a collection of strings, and not a collection of records. When each s is added to the ListBox in the second shaded expression, a string is added. In the example in Figure 15-21, you selected records and output each one's last name. In this example, you select last names and output each one. The results are identical to those shown in Figure 15-22.

```
var goodStudents =
    from s in this.cartmanCollegeDataSet.tblStudents
    where s.GradePointAverage > CUTOFF
    select s.LastName;
foreach (var s in goodStudents)
    outputListBox.Items.Add(s);
```

Figure 15-23 Collecting strings from a database table

Figure 15-24 contains a showButton_Click() method from a different application in which a constant GPA cutoff is not used. Instead, the user can enter a cutoff GPA value into a TextBox that has been named gpaTextBox (see the first shaded expression). In this example, a student's GPA must be greater than the user-supplied value to qualify for the list. The last name, a comma, and the first name of each qualifying student (see the last shaded expression in Figure 15-24) are shown in the ListBox. Figure 15-25 shows a typical execution.

```
private void showButton_Click(object sender, EventArgs e)
{
    double minGpa = Convert.ToDouble(gpaTextBox.Text);
    this.tblStudentsTableAdapter.Fill
      (this.cartmanCollegeDataSet.tblStudents);
    var goodStudents =
        from s in this.cartmanCollegeDataSet.tblStudents
        where s.GradePointAverage > minGpa
        select s;
    foreach (var s in goodStudents)
        outputListBox.Items.Add(s.LastName + ", " + s.FirstName);
}
```

Figure 15-24 The showButton_Click() method that displays students with a minimum GPA entered by the user

Figure 15-25   Typical execution of an application containing the showButton_Click() method in Figure 15-24

The method in Figure 15-24 is part of the project named DatabaseDemo3, which is available in your downloadable student files. In the example in Figure 15-24, instead of using a showButton_Click() method, you might prefer to add the code to a gpaTextBox_TextChanged() method so that it executes each time the user enters a new value as a minimum GPA, instead of when the user clicks a button. You might also prefer to add some error checking in case the user enters a nonnumeric value. Error checking was omitted from this example to keep it short.

When you execute an application that contains the method in Figure 15-24, the list of items in the ListBox is appended each time the user clicks the Button. In other words, if a user clicks the button twice without changing the selection criterion, the ListBox contains a second set of the same records. To prevent the list from growing and to see only the students who meet the current criteria, add the following statement near the beginning of the Click() method:

```
outputListBox.Items.Clear();
```

With the inclusion of this statement, the ListBox is emptied before each new group is added to it.

Many other options are available when you use LINQ expressions. For example, you can use AND and OR expressions in your LINQ statements. The following code selects all students with GPAs between 2.5 and 3.0:

```
var someStudents =
    from s in this.cartmanCollegeDataSet.tblStudents
    where s.GradePointAverage > 2.5 && s.GradePointAverage < 3.0
    select s;
```

With text values, you can use StartsWith(), EndsWith(), and Contains(). For example, the following code selects all students whose first name starts with "M".

```
var someStudents =
    from s in this.cartmanCollegeDataSet.tblStudents
    where s.FirstName.StartsWith("M")
    select s;
```

You can use several **aggregate operators**, or operators that produce statistics for groups of data. The aggregate operators include Average(), Count(), Sum(), Max(), and Min(). For example, the method in Figure 15-26 assembles a collection of GradePointAverage values named gpas. Then several aggregate operators are applied to the collection and the results are assigned to Labels. Figure 15-27 shows the output when this method is used with tblStudents. You can confirm the accuracy of these statistics by referring to the complete dataset in Figure 15-6.

```
private void showButton_Click(object sender, EventArgs e)
{
    var gpas =
        from s in this.cartmanCollegeDataSet.tblStudents
            select s.GradePointAverage;
    countLabel.Text = "Count is " + gpas.Count();
    minLabel.Text = "Lowest GPA is " + gpas.Min();
    maxLabel.Text = "Highest GPA is " + gpas.Max();
    avgLabel.Text = "Average of all GPAs is " + gpas.Average();
}
```

Figure 15-26 A method that uses some aggregate operators

The method in Figure 15-26 is part of the project named DatabaseDemo4, which is available in your downloadable student files.

Figure 15-27 Output of the program that uses the method in Figure 15-26

TWO TRUTHS & A LIE

Using LINQ Queries with an Access Database Table

Consider this code:

```
var emps =
    from e in this.abcDataSet.tblEmployees
    where e.YearsOnJob < 10
    select e.IdNumber;
```

1. emps is an implicitly typed collection of ID numbers.

2. emps is a collection of rows from tblEmployees in the abcDataSet.

3. The only data added to emps comes from records in which YearsOnJob is less than 10.

The false statement is #2. In this code, emps is a collection of fields (IdNumbers). Most likely, this means it is a collection of strings or integers—it depends on how IdNumber has been defined in the tblEmployees table.

 You Do It

Querying a Dataset

In the next steps, you write LINQ queries that demonstrate how to access subsets of the data stored in the tblCars table.

1. If it is not still open, open the **AccessCars** project in Visual Studio, and go to Form1.cs[Design] view. Delete the data grid from the Form. Drag a Label and a ListBox onto the Form, as shown in Figure 15-28. Change the Label's Text to **Inexpensive cars**, and choose a larger font for the Label. Change the ListBox name to **inexpensiveCarsBox**. Reduce the width of the Form appropriately.

(continues)

(continued)

Figure 15-28 Adding a `Label` and `ListBox` to the `AccessCars` project

2. Double-click the button on the `Form` and revise the `recordsButton_Click()` method, as shown in the shaded portions of Figure 15-29. The LINQ code selects all the records in the table in which `Price` is less than 20,000 and then adds the ID number, model year, and make of those cars to the `ListBox`.

```
private void recordsButton_Click(object sender, EventArgs e)
{
   const int HIGHPRICE = 20000;
   this.tblCarsTableAdapter.Fill
      (this.honestRalphsUsedCarsDataSet.tblCars);
   var inexpensiveCars =
      from c in this.honestRalphsUsedCarsDataSet.tblCars
      where c.Price < HIGHPRICE
      select c;
   foreach (var c in inexpensiveCars)
      inexpensiveCarsBox.Items.Add
         (c.ID + " - " + c.ModelYear + " " + c.Make);
}
```

Figure 15-29 The modified `recordsButton_Click()` method

(continues)

(continued)

3. Execute the project. When the Form appears, click the Button. The output looks like Figure 15-30. Five cars appear in the list.

Figure 15-30   Execution of the AccessCars project

4. Dismiss the Form.

Allowing the User to Provide Selection Criteria

In the next steps, you provide a TextBox to make the application more flexible. Instead of listing cars priced under $20,000, the user will be able to enter a cutoff price.

1. In the Form1.cs Design view, rearrange and resize the existing components and add a new Label and TextBox, as shown in Figure 15-31. Name the TextBox **priceTextBox**.

(continues)

(continued)

Figure 15-31 A Form with Label and TextBox for data entry

2. Modify the `recordsButton_Click()` method, as shown in the shaded sections of Figure 15-32. Delete the declaration of the constant `HIGHPRICE` and replace it with a statement that accepts entered text from the `TextBox` and uses the `TryParse()` method to convert the user's entry to an `int`. Change the selection criterion from less than the constant `HIGHPRICE` to less than or equal to the value entered by the user. Also, add the price to the output in the `ListBox`, which will make it easier for you to confirm that the correct cars were selected for the `inexpensiveCars` collection.

```
private void recordsButton_Click(object sender, EventArgs e)
{
    int cutoff;
    if (!int.TryParse(priceTextBox.Text, out cutoff))
        cutoff = 0;
    this.tblCarsTableAdapter.Fill
        (this.honestRalphsUsedCarsDataSet.tblCars);
    var inexpensiveCars =
        from c in this.honestRalphsUsedCarsDataSet.tblCars
        where c.Price <= cutoff
        select c;
    foreach (var c in inexpensiveCars)
        inexpensiveCarsBox.Items.Add
            (c.ID + " - " + c.ModelYear + " " + c.Make +
             " $" + c.Price);}
```

Figure 15-32 The recordsButton_Click() method that allows user data entry

(continues)

(continued)

3. Save and execute the program. Depending on the value you type into the TextBox, the output will look similar to Figure 15-33.

Figure 15-33   Typical execution of the application that contains the method in Figure 15-32

4. If you click the button more than once in the current project, the ListBox list is appended rather than replaced. To remedy the problem, dismiss the Form and return to the code. Add the following statement near the beginning of the recordsButton_Click() method, before any items are added to the inexpensiveCarsBox:

   ```
   inexpensiveCarsBox.Items.Clear();
   ```

5. Save and run the application again. If you enter different values and click the Button multiple times, now the list of cars is replaced with each new selection.

6. Dismiss the Form and run the application again, entering a low value such as $3500 for the maximum price in the search. When you click the Button, the ListBox is empty, as it should be, because no cars in the table are priced below that value. However, providing no feedback can confuse or frustrate a user, who might think the application is not working properly. To remedy the problem, you can add a message that appears when no cars meet the search criterion. Just before the closing curly brace of the recordsButton_Click() method, add the following:

(continues)

(continued)

```
if (inexpensiveCars.Count() == 0)
{
    inexpensiveCarsBox.Items.Add("Sorry - there are no cars");
    inexpensiveCarsBox.Items.Add
        ("less than or equal to $" + cutoff);
}
```

This code uses the `Count()` aggregate operator to determine the number of records in the `inexpensiveCars` collection. When the count is 0, the user sees an appropriate message.

7. Save and execute the program. When the entered price is too low, the user sees a message confirming that the program works, but that no records meet the search criterion.

8. Close Visual Studio.

Using LINQ Operators to Sort and Group Data

You can use the **orderby operator** to sort a collection of data based on a field or fields. For example, using the Cartman College dataset, the method in Figure 15-34 produces the output in Figure 15-35. The shaded statement causes the list of students to be ordered by GPA.

```
private void showButton_Click(object sender, EventArgs e)
{
    outputListBox.Items.Add("GPA    LastName");
    var students =
        from s in this.cartmanCollegeDataSet.tblStudents
        orderby s.GradePointAverage
        select s;
    foreach (var s in students)
        outputListBox.Items.Add(" " + s.GradePointAverage + "    " +
            s.LastName);
}
```

Figure 15-34 A method that uses `orderby`

The method in Figure 15-34 is part of the project named `DatabaseDemo5`, which is available in your downloadable student files.

Figure 15-35   Output of the project that uses the method in Figure 15-34

The default order for sorting is ascending—that is, from lowest to highest. You can explicitly indicate an ascending sort by using the following phrase:

```
orderby s.GradePointAverage ascending
```

To view the students in the reverse order, from the highest GPA to the lowest, you would write the following:

```
orderby s.GradePointAverage descending
```

You can use compound conditions for ordering. For example, the following would sort students by last name, and then by first name when last names are the same:

```
orderby s.LastName, s.FirstName
```

Data items also can be grouped; the **group operator** groups data by specified criteria. For example, Figure 15-36 shows a Click() method that groups students by the integer part of the GradePointAverage field. In other words, all students with GPAs between 2 and 3 are in one group, and students with GPAs between 3 and 4 are in another group. (Additional groups would be formed if students had higher or lower GPAs.) The example in Figure 15-36 uses nested foreach loops. In the outer loop, which executes one time for each group, the group Key is displayed as a heading. The Key is not required to be the key field in the database table, although it might be; the Key is the value used to determine the groups, which in this case is determined by the integer part of the GPA. In the inner foreach loop in Figure 15-36, the GPA and last name for each record in the group are added to the ListBox. Figure 15-37 shows the results.

```
private void showButton_Click(object sender, EventArgs e)
{
    var stus = from s in cartmanCollegeDataSet.tblStudents
        group s by (int)s.GradePointAverage;

    foreach (var groupByGpa in stus)
    {
        outputListBox.Items.Add("GPA: " + groupByGpa.Key);
        foreach (var s in groupByGpa)
          outputListBox.Items.Add("   " + s.GradePointAverage +
               "   " + s.LastName);
    }
}
```

Figure 15-36   A method that groups records

The method in Figure 15-36 is part of the project named `DatabaseDemo6`, which is available in your downloadable student files.

Figure 15-37   Output of the application that contains the method in Figure 15-36

When you use the **group** operator, the number of possible values in the criterion determines the number of possible groups. For example, if a company has five departments and you group employees with an expression such as the following, you form five groups:

```
group e by e.Department
```

However, if you use a Boolean expression in the by clause, then only two groups are possible because the by expression has only two possible values—true or false:

```
group e by e.Department == 1
```

That is, every e is part of the group for which e.Department == 1 is true, or the group for which e.Department == 1 is false.

A query body must end with a `select` clause or a `group` clause. Therefore, if you combine orderby and group, orderby must come first and group must come last. For example, to view the students in each GPA category in alphabetical order by last name, you would write the following:

```
var stus = from s in cartmanCollegeDataSet.tblStudents
    orderby s.LastName
    group s by (int)s.GradePointAverage;
```

Many more LINQ operations are available than can be covered in this chapter. More than 50 operators are available, and they can be combined in practically an infinite number of ways. For example, you can insert and delete records from a database. Additionally, a key feature of normalized relational databases is the ability to make relationships between tables. LINQ allows you to join multiple object collections together using a relatively simple syntax that is familiar to those who already know SQL. As you learn more about databases, C#, and LINQ, you will discover many possibilities and learn to create useful applications that access data and provide business clients with powerful ways to view and use their information.

For more good ideas on working with LINQ, see "101 LINQ Samples" at *http://msdn.microsoft.com/en-us/vcsharp/aa336746.aspx*.

Watch the video *Using LINQ with a Database*.

TWO TRUTHS & A LIE

Using LINQ Operators to Sort and Group Data

Consider the following code:

```
var emps =
    from e in this.abcDataSet.tblEmployees
        orderby e.LastName
        group e by e.Department;
```

1. In the collection emps, Brown in Department 1 would come before Adams in Department 3.

2. In the collection emps, Graham in Department 4 would come before Lee in Department 7.

3. In the collection emps, Kimball in Department 5 would come before Thompson in Department 3.

The false statement is #3. Each lower-numbered department group would precede any higher-numbered group. Within the groups, the employees would be in alphabetical order.

You Do It

Grouping Data

In the next steps, you group output records to make them easier for users to view and inspect.

1. Open a new Visual Studio C# project named **CarsGroupByMake**.

2. As shown in Figure 15-38, change the Form's Text property to **Honest Ralph's Used Cars**. Add a Button to the Form, change its Name to **carsButton**, and change its Text property to **View cars**. Add a ListBox to the Form and change its name to **carsListBox**.

(continues)

(continued)

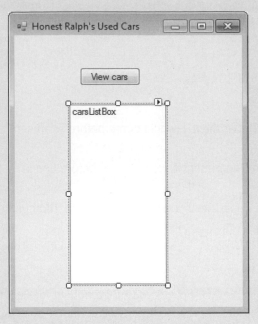

Figure 15-38   Form design for the `CarsGroupByMake` project

3.   Add `HonestRalphsUsedCars.accdb` to the project.

4.   Double-click the `Button` and add the following LINQ query within the automatically generated `Click()` method:

```
var cars =
    from c in this.honestRalphsUsedCarsDataSet.tblCars
    group c by c.Make;
```

This statement groups the cars by the value in each `Make` field.

5.   Following the LINQ query, add a nested `foreach` loop that displays a car make for each group and lists the year and price for each car within each group.

(continues)

770

(continued)

```
foreach (var group in cars)
{
   carsListBox.Items.Add("Make: " + group.Key);
   foreach( var c in group)
      carsListBox.Items.Add("    " + c.ModelYear + " $" + c.Price);
}
```

6. Save and execute the project. Click the Button on the Form. The output appears as shown in Figure 15-39. The year and price for each of the 10 cars in the table is displayed. Each car is grouped with others of the same make, and each group is preceded by a heading that shows the make.

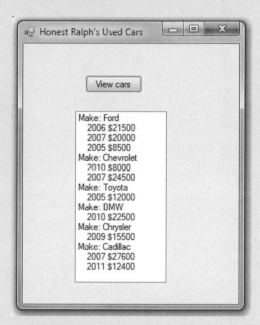

Figure 15-39   Output of the CarsGroupByMake project

7. In Figure 15-39, the order in which cars are listed in each group is inconsistent. For example, the Chevrolets are listed from newest to oldest but the Cadillacs are listed from oldest to newest. To consistently display the cars in each group in order from newest to oldest, insert an orderby clause in the LINQ query as follows:

(continues)

(continued)

```
var cars =
    from c in this.honestRalphsUsedCarsDataSet.tblCars
    orderby c.ModelYear descending
    group c by c.Make;
```

8. Save the project and execute it again. When you click the Button, the output appears as shown in Figure 15-40. The cars are listed in order by model year within each group.

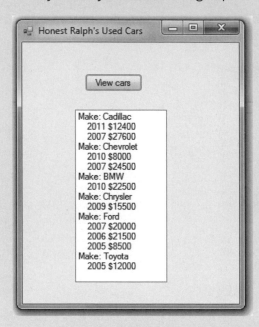

Figure 15-40   Output of the CarsGroupByMake project ordered by ModelYear

9. The output in Figure 15-40 contains only 10 cars in only six different groupings by make. However, if there were more cars, it might be difficult to locate a specific car. To show the Make groups in alphabetical order, add a condition to the sort order specified in the LINQ query, as follows:

```
var cars =
    from c in this.honestRalphsUsedCarsDataSet.tblCars
    orderby c.Make, c.ModelYear descending
    group c by c.Make;
```

(continues)

(continued)

10. Save and execute the program. When you click the Button on the Form, the output appears as shown in Figure 15-41. Each make is listed in alphabetical order and each car is listed in descending model-year order within its Make group.

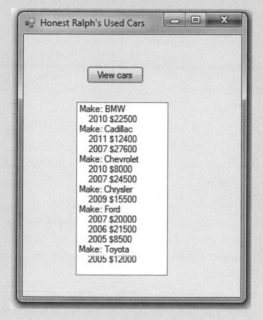

Figure 15-41 Output of the CarsGroupByMake project ordered by ModelYear within alphabetized Make

11. Dismiss the Form and exit Visual Studio.

Chapter Summary

- A database holds a group of files that an organization needs to support its applications. In a database, the files often are called tables because you can arrange their contents in rows and columns. A value that uniquely identifies a record is called a primary key, or a key for short. Database management software, or a database management system, is a set of programs that allows users to create table descriptions; identify keys; add, delete, and update records within a table; arrange records within a table so they are sorted by different fields; write questions that select specific records from a table for viewing; and perform other tasks.

- Creating a useful database requires a lot of planning and analysis. You must decide what data will be stored, how that data will be divided between tables, and how the tables will interrelate. For each table you must decide what columns are needed, provide names for them, and enter data. In most tables you create for a database, you want to identify a primary key, which is the column that makes each record different from all others. A shorthand way to describe a table is to use the table name followed by parentheses that contain all the field names, with the primary key underlined.

- A query is a request to retrieve information from a database using syntax that the database software can understand. The most common language that database administrators use to access data in their tables is Structured Query Language, or SQL. The basic form of the SQL command that retrieves selected records from a table is SELECT-FROM-WHERE.

- Microsoft Office Access is a relational database that is part of the Microsoft Office system. In Access, a database developer can type field names for the data that will be stored and can assign an appropriate data type for each. After a table's design has been completed, a user can enter data into the table.

- An implicitly typed variable has a data type that is inferred from the expression used to initialize the variable. When you use an implicitly typed variable, an object's set of allowed properties and methods is not fixed when the code is written, but is determined when the program executes. Implicitly typed variables are used frequently in LINQ statements, which access data stored in a database.

- The LINQ (Language INtegrated Query) Project provides a set of general-purpose standard operators that allow queries to be constructed using syntax that is easy to understand. This syntax is similar to SQL's, and the compiler can check it for errors. The operators defined in LINQ can be used to query arrays, enumerable classes, XML, relational databases, and other sources. Some keywords in the LINQ vocabulary include `select`, `from`, and `where`.

- To add a database table to a Windows Forms project, you can add a data source to your project and drag a table onto your form. The table's data is bound to the form, and you are supplied with a grid in which you can view the data.

- You can use a LINQ query to select a collection of data from a table when specific criteria are met. You can use AND and OR expressions to limit criteria in your LINQ statements. With text values, you can use `StartsWith()`, `EndsWith()`, and `Contains()`. You can use several aggregate operators, or operators that produce statistics for groups of data, including `Average()`, `Count()`, `Sum()`, `Max()`, and `Min()`.

- You can use the `orderby` operator to sort a collection of data based on a field or fields. Data items also can be grouped. A query body must end with a `select` clause or a `group` clause.

Key Terms

A **collection** is any data structure that holds objects of the same type.

A **database** holds a group of files that an organization needs to support its applications.

Tables are database files. They are called *tables* because their contents are arranged in rows and columns.

A **primary key**, or **key** for short, is a value that uniquely identifies a record.

A **compound key** or **composite key** is constructed from multiple columns.

Database management software, also known as a **database management system (DBMS)**, is a set of programs that allows users to create table descriptions; identify keys; add, delete, and update records within a table; arrange records within a table so they are sorted by different fields; write questions that select specific records from a table for viewing; write questions that combine information from multiple tables; create reports; and keep data secure.

A **relational database** is one in which you can establish and maintain relationships between columns in the tables.

The **Leszynski naming convention** (LNC) is a convention for naming database elements that is popular with Microsoft Access users and Visual Basic programmers.

Normalization is the process of designing and creating a set of database tables that satisfies users' needs and avoids many potential problems such as data redundancies and anomalies.

Data redundancy is the unnecessary repetition of data.

An **anomaly** is an irregularity in the design of a database that causes problems and inconveniences.

A **query** is a request to retrieve information from a database using syntax that the database software can understand.

Query by example is a language that allows you to query relational databases by filling in blanks.

Structured Query Language, or **SQL**, is the most common language that database administrators use to access data in their tables.

SELECT-FROM-WHERE is the basic form of the SQL command that retrieves selected records from a table.

TLA is a three-letter abbreviation for *three-letter abbreviation*; it is the most popular type of abbreviation in technical terminology.

A **view** is a particular way of looking at a database in database management systems.

A **wildcard** is a symbol that means "any" or "all."

Microsoft Office Access is a relational database that is part of the Microsoft Office system.

An **implicitly typed variable** has a data type that is inferred from the expression used to initialize the variable.

The **var** data type creates an implicitly typed variable.

Type inference is the process of implicitly typing a variable; it is also called **duck typing**.

An **iteration variable** is used to hold each successive value in an array.

When a language is **strongly typed**, severe restrictions are placed on what data types can be mixed.

The **LINQ** (Language INtegrated Query) Project provides a set of general-purpose standard operators that allow queries to be constructed in C# using syntax that is easy to understand. This syntax is similar to SQL's, and the compiler can check it for errors.

The LINQ keyword **select** indicates what to select from a collection.

The LINQ keyword **from** indicates the collection or sequence from which data will be drawn.

The LINQ keyword **where** indicates conditions for selecting records.

A **restriction operator** places a restriction on which data is added to a collection.

A **projection operator** is one that projects, or sends off, specific data from a collection.

A **dataset** is a temporary set of data stored in a project.

A **BindingSource** object establishes a link from a database to a program.

A **table adapter** passes data back and forth between a dataset and the BindingSource.

Aggregate operators are operators that produce statistics for groups of data.

The **orderby operator** sorts a collection of data based on a field or fields.

The **group operator** groups data by specified criteria.

Review Questions

1. Files in a database often are called _____.

   a. records   c. catalogs
   b. tables   d. registers

2. A value that uniquely identifies a record is a(n) _____.

   a. source   c. key
   b. ID   d. prime

3. Database management software is a set of programs that allows users to do all of the following *except* _____.

   a. add, delete, and update records within a table

   b. sort records in a table

   c. verify that all entered data is correct

   d. write queries

4. When you design a database table, you must do all of the following *except* _____.

   a. decide how many columns the table needs

   b. decide how many rows the table needs

   c. provide names for the columns

   d. provide a data type for each column

5. Which of the following would *not* be a good candidate for a primary key?

   a. the number of seats on a bus in a table that stores data about a city's fleet of buses

   b. a bus pass number in a table of a city's bus service customers

   c. a bus driver's ID number in a table that stores data about bus drivers

   d. a bus route number in a table that stores bus route data

6. Normalization _____.

   a. is the process of entering data into database tables

   b. is a design process that reduces redundancy and anomalies in databases

   c. is a flaw in database design that results in the repetition of data

   d. is a flaw in database design that causes anomalies

7. Which of the following do you know based on this database notation?

   `tblProducts(itemNum, description, price, quantity)`

   a. The table name is `Products`.

   b. `itemNum` is the key field.

   c. No two descriptions hold the same value.

   d. `price` is a numeric field.

8. A question asked using syntax that database software can understand is a(n) _____.

   a. query

   b. anomaly

   c. request

   d. redundancy

9. The basic form of the SQL command that retrieves selected records from a table is _____.

   a. QUERY-BY-EXAMPLE   c. RETRIEVE-FROM-SOURCE

   b. SELECT-FROM-WHERE   d. STRUCTURED-QUERY-LIST

10. Based on the following SQL statement, you know that _____ will be displayed.

    ```
    SELECT itemNum, price FROM tblProducts WHERE quantity <= 0
    ```

    a. two rows   c. more than two columns

    b. two columns   d. more than two rows

11. Microsoft Office Access is _____.

    a. a spreadsheet as well as a database

    b. no longer used by professional information specialists

    c. part of Visual Studio

    d. a typical database program

12. Which of the following is not true of implicitly typed variables?

    a. Their data types are inferred from the expression used to initialize the variable.

    b. They are declared using var as the data type.

    c. They use a process called type inference.

    d. They use a process called static typing.

13. Which of the following pairs of statements have the same meaning?

    a. `var product = new Product();` and `Product product = new Product();`

    b. `var x = 3;` and `double x = 3.0;`

    c. `var a = 17;` and `var b = 17;`

    d. `var Item();` and `var item = Item();`

14. C# is _____.

    a. strongly typed, like Visual Basic

    b. strongly typed, unlike Visual Basic

    c. weakly typed, like Visual Basic

    d. weakly typed, unlike Visual Basic

15. In _____ you can access database data.

    a. C# 3.0   c. both of the above

    b. older versions of C#   d. none of the above

16. The operators defined in LINQ can be used to query _____.

    a.   arrays   c.   both of these

    b.   relational databases   d.   none of the above

17. Consider the following code. In this example, nums is _____.

```
var nums =
    from n in numbers
    where n > 5
    select n;
```

    a.   an array of integers

    b.   a database

    c.   an implicitly typed collection

    d.   a single record in the collection numbers

18. Consider the following code. In this example, numbers is _____.

```
var nums =
    from n in numbers
    where n > 5
    select n;
```

    a.   an array of integers   c.   a database

    b.   a record in a database   d.   an implicitly typed collection

19. Consider the following code. In this example, x is _____.

```
var cheapProducts =
    from p in this.abcCompany.tblProducts
    where p.Price < MAX
    select p.Description;
foreach (var x in cheapProducts)
    outputListBox.Items.Add(x);
```

    a.   a row in tblProducts   c.   a price

    b.   a column in tblProducts   d.   a description

20. Which of the following is not true of LINQ?

    a.   Average() is an aggregate operator.

    b.   Max() is an aggregate operator.

    c.   You can use the orderby operator to sort data.

    d.   You can use the groupby operator to group data.

Exercises

Programming Exercises

1. Create a program named **LinqDoubles** that holds an array of 15 **doubles**. Prompt the user for and accept a value for the array. Use LINQ statements to sort the values in descending order and display them.

2. Create a program named **EvenAndOdd** that holds an array of eight integers. Prompt the user for and accept a value for each integer. Use LINQ statements to group the integers into two groups (even and odd), and then display each group. Figure 15-42 shows a typical execution.

Figure 15-42   Typical execution of the EvenAndOdd program

3. Create a program named **ShortWords** that contains an array of 15 strings. Prompt the user to enter a maximum string length, and use LINQ statements to display all the strings that are shorter than the value entered by the user. If no strings meet the criterion, display an appropriate message.

4. Create a program named **SplitAlphabet** that contains an array of 20 words of your choice. Use LINQ statements to display separate lists: One shows words that begin with letters in the first half of the alphabet (A through M), and the other list shows words that begin with letters in the second half (N through Z). Display a count of the number of words in each group.

5. Create a Customer class that contains Name, ZipCode, and BalanceDue properties and a constructor that requires data for all three. Create a program named **CustomerQuery** that declares an array of at least 10 Customers and stores appropriate data. Prompt the user for a zip code and display all the data for all the customers in that zip code, or display an appropriate message if no such customers exist.

6. Create a program named **CustomerQuery2** that uses the Customer class created in Exercise 5, declares an array of at least 10 Customers, and stores appropriate data. Display the Customer names and balances alphabetically by name and grouped by zip code. For an example, see Figure 15-43.

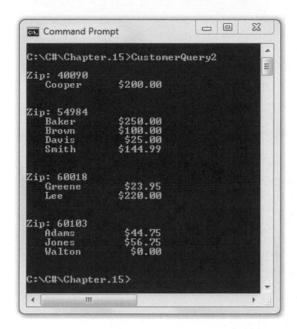

Figure 15-43   Typical execution of the CustomerQuery2 program

7. Create an application named **CarStatistics** that displays statistics about a database table when a user clicks various buttons. Using the HonestRalphsUsedCars database in your downloadable student files, allow the user to click any of three buttons that, respectively, display a count of the records, details about the most expensive car, and details about the least expensive car.

8. Create an application named **CarFinderByMake** that allows a user to display cars of different makes. Use the HonestRalphsUsedCars database in your downloadable student files. Your application should contain four check boxes labeled "Ford", "Chevrolet", "Cadillac", and "All". The user should be able to click any combination of check boxes to see the color, year, make, and price for each car with the desired make. For example, when the user clicks "Cadillac" and "Chevrolet", only those cars are displayed.

9. Create an application named **CarPriceFinder** in which all of the cars in a database are displayed in a checked list box. When the user makes a selection, the car's price is displayed. Use the HonestRalphsUsedCars database in your downloadable student files.

10. Create an application named **MovieFinder** in which the user can select movies to view by entering part of the title or part of the director's name. The user clicks a radio button to choose which type of criterion is used. Then the user can enter all or part of the title's name or director's name into a TextBox. Allow the user to find matches regardless of case. See Figure 15-44 for a typical execution. Use the Movies database in your downloadable student files.

Figure 15-44   Typical execution of the MovieFinder project

11. Create an application named **MovieFinder2** in which the user can enter a year to split a list of movies into those released before the indicated year and those released in the indicated year or afterward. Labels above each list should reflect the user's chosen cutoff year. Each list should be in order by release year. See Figure 15-45 for a typical execution. Use the Movies database in your downloadable student files.

Figure 15-45 Typical execution of the `MovieFinder2` project

Debugging Exercises

1. Each of the following files in the Chapter.15 folder of your downloadable
   student files has syntax and/or logical errors. In each case, determine the problem
   and fix the program. After you correct the errors, save each file using the same
   filename preceded with *Fixed*. For example, save DebugFifteen1.cs as
   FixedDebugFifteen1.cs.

   a. DebugFifteen1.cs

   b. DebugFifteen2.cs

   c. DebugFifteen3.cs

   d. DebugFifteen4.cs

Case Problems

1. Throughout this book, you have developed programs for the Greenville Idol talent competition. Now, create a database of contestant data, or store data in an array if you do not have access to a database software package. Enter names and talent codes for at least 15 contestants. Then, create an interactive program named **GreenvilleLinq** that uses the techniques you learned in this chapter to give the user three options: (1) to view contestants in alphabetical order by name; (2) to view contestants in groups by talent code (S, D, M, or O for Singing, Dancing, Musical instrument, or Other, respectively); or (3) to view contestants with a specific talent.

2. Throughout this book, you have developed programs for Marshall's Murals. Now, create a database of client data, or store data in an array if you do not have access to a database software package. Enter names, mural location (I or E for interior or exterior), and style (L, S, A, C, or O for Landscape, Seascape, Abstract, Children's, or Other, respectively). Then, create an interactive program named **MarshallsLinq** that uses the techniques you learned in this chapter to give the user three options: (1) to view clients in alphabetical order by name; (2) to view clients in groups by location; or (3) to view clients in groups by mural style.

Operator Precedence and Associativity

When an expression contains multiple operators, their **precedence** controls the order in which the individual operators are evaluated. For example, multiplication has a higher precedence than addition, so the expression 2 + 3 * 4 evaluates as 14 because the value of 3 * 4 is calculated before adding 2. Table A-1 summarizes all operators in order of precedence from highest to lowest.

When you use two operators with the same precedence, the **associativity** of the operators controls the order in which the operations are performed:

- Except for the assignment and conditional operators, all binary operators (those that take two arguments) are **left-associative**, meaning that operations are performed from left to right. For example, 5 + 6 + 7 is evaluated first as 5 + 6, or 11; then 7 is added, bringing the value to 18.

- The assignment operators and the conditional operator (?:) are **right-associative**, meaning that operations are performed from right to left. For example, x = y = z is evaluated as y = z first, and then x is set to the result.

- All unary operators (those that take one argument) are right-associative. If b is 5, the value of −++b is determined by evaluating ++b first (6), then taking its negative value (−6).

You can control precedence and associativity by using parentheses. For example, a + b * c first multiplies b by c and then adds the result to a. The expression (a + b) * c, however, forces the sum of a and b to be calculated first; then the result is multiplied by c.

Category	Operators	Associativity
Primary	x.y f(x) a[x] x++ x– – new type of checked unchecked	left
Unary	+ – ! ~ ++x – –x (T)x	right
Multiplicative	* / %	left
Additive	+ –	left
Shift	<< >>	right
Relational and type testing	< > <= >= is as	left
Equality	== !=	left
Logical AND	&	left
Logical XOR	^	left
Logical OR	|	left
Conditional AND	&&	left
Conditional OR	||	left
Conditional	?:	right
Assignment	= *= /= %= += = <<= >>= &= ^= |=	right

Table A-1 Operator precedence

Key Terms

The **precedence** of operators controls the order in which individual operators are evaluated in an expression.

The **associativity** of operators controls the order in which operations of equal precedence are performed in an expression.

With **left-associative** operators, operations are performed from left to right.

With **right-associative** operators, operations are performed from right to left.

APPENDIX B

Understanding Numbering Systems and Computer Codes

The numbering system you know best is the **decimal numbering system**, which is based on 10 digits, 0 through 9. Mathematicians call decimal system numbers *base 10 numbers*. When you use the decimal system to express positive whole numbers, no other symbols are available; if you want to express a value larger than 9, you must resort to using multiple digits from the same pool of 10, placing them in columns.

When you use the decimal system, you analyze a multicolumn number by mentally assigning place values to each column. The value of the rightmost column is 1, the value of the next column to the left is 10, the next column is 100, and so on, multiplying the column value by 10 as you move to the left. There is no limit to the number of columns you can use; you simply keep adding columns to the left as you need to express higher values. For example, Figure B-1 shows how the value 305 is represented in the decimal system. You simply sum the value of the digit in each column after it has been multiplied by the value of its column.

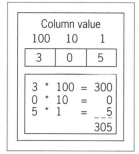

Figure B-1   Representing 305 in the decimal system

The **binary numbering system** works in the same way as the decimal numbering system, except that it uses only two digits, 0 and 1. Mathematicians call these numbers *base 2 numbers*. When you use the binary system, if you want to express a value greater than 1, you must resort to using multiple columns, because no single symbol is available that represents any value other than 0 or 1. However, instead of each new column to the left being 10 times greater than the previous column, when you use the binary system, each new column is only two times the value of the previous column. For example, Figure B-2 shows how the numbers 9 and 305 are represented in the binary system. Notice that in both binary numbers and the decimal system, it is perfectly acceptable—and often necessary—to create numbers with 0 in one or more columns. As with the decimal system, the binary system has no limit to the number of columns; you can use as many as it takes to express a value.

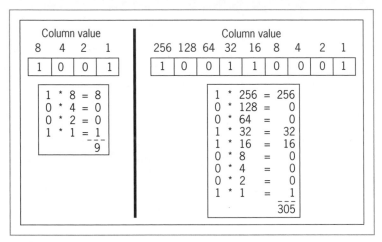

Figure B-2   Representing decimal values 9 and 305 in the binary system

A computer stores every piece of data it uses as a set of 0s and 1s. Each 0 or 1 is known as a **bit**, which is short for binary digit. Every computer uses 0s and 1s because all values in a computer are stored as electronic signals that are either on or off. This two-state system is most easily represented using just two digits.

Computers use a set of binary digits to represent stored characters. If computers used only one binary digit to represent characters, then only two different characters could be represented, because the single bit could be only 0 or 1. If computers used only two digits, then only four characters could be represented—the four codes 00, 01, 10, and 11, which in decimal values are 0, 1, 2, and 3, respectively. Many computers use sets of eight binary digits to represent each character they store, because using eight binary digits provides 256 different combinations. One combination can represent an *A*, another a *B*, still others *a* and *b*, and so on. Two hundred fifty-six combinations are enough so that each capital letter, small letter, digit, and punctuation mark used in English has its own code; even a space has a code. For example, in some computers 01000001 represents the character *A*. The binary number 01000001 has a decimal value of 65, but this numeric value is not important to ordinary computer users; it is simply a code that stands for *A*. The code that uses 01000001 to mean *A* is the **American Standard Code for Information Interchange**, or **ASCII**.

 A set of eight bits is called a **byte**. Half a byte, or four bits, is a **nibble**. You will learn more about bytes later in this appendix.

The ASCII code is not the only computer code; it is typical, and is the one used in most personal computers. The **Extended Binary Coded Decimal Interchange Code**, or **EBCDIC**, is an eight-bit code that is used in IBM mainframe computers. In these computers, the principle is the same—every character is stored as a series of binary digits. However, the actual values used are different. For example, in EBCDIC, an *A* is 11000001, or 193. **Unicode** is another code used by languages such as Java and C#; with this code, 16 bits are used to represent each character. The character *A* in Unicode has the same decimal value (65) as the ASCII *A*, but it is stored as 0000000001000001. Using 16 bits provides many more possible combinations than using only eight bits—65,536 to be exact. Unicode has enough available codes for all English letters and digits and for characters from many international alphabets.

Ordinary computer users seldom think about the numeric codes behind the letters, numbers, and punctuation marks they enter from their keyboards or see displayed on a monitor. However, they see the consequence of the values behind letters when they see data sorted in alphabetical order. When you sort a list of names, *Andrea* comes before *Brian*, and *Caroline* comes after *Brian* because the numeric code for *A* is lower than the code for *B*, and the numeric code for *C* is higher than the code for *B*, no matter whether you are using ASCII, EBCDIC, or Unicode.

Table B-1 shows the decimal and binary values behind the most commonly used characters in the ASCII character set—the letters, numbers, and punctuation marks you can enter from your keyboard using a single key press. Most of the values not included in Table B-1 have a purpose. For example, the decimal value 7 represents a bell—a dinging sound your computer can make, often used to notify you of an error or some other unusual condition. Each binary number in Table B-1 is shown containing two sets of four digits; this convention makes the long eight-digit numbers easier to read.

Decimal number	Binary number	ASCII character	Decimal number	Binary number	ASCII character
32	0010 0000	Space	51	0011 0011	3
33	0010 0001	! Exclamation point	52	0011 0100	4
34	0010 0010	" Quotation mark, or double quote	53	0011 0101	5
35	0010 0011	# Number sign, also called an octothorpe or a pound sign	54	0011 0110	6
36	0010 0100	$ Dollar sign	55	0011 0111	7
37	0010 0101	% Percent	56	0011 1000	8
38	0010 0110	& Ampersand	57	0011 1001	9
39	0010 0111	' Apostrophe, single quote	58	0011 1010	: Colon
40	0010 1000	(Left parenthesis	59	0011 1011	; Semicolon
41	0010 1001	) Right parenthesis	60	0011 1100	< Less-than sign
42	0010 1010	* Asterisk	61	0011 1101	= Equal sign
43	0010 1011	+ Plus sign	62	0011 1110	> Greater-than sign
44	0010 1100	, Comma	63	0011 1111	? Question mark
45	0010 1101	- Hyphen or minus sign	64	0100 0000	@ At sign
46	0010 1110	. Period or decimal point	65	0100 0001	A
47	0010 1111	/ Slash or front slash	66	0100 0010	B
48	0011 0000	0	67	0100 0011	C
49	0011 0001	1	68	0100 0100	D
50	0011 0010	2	69	0100 0101	E

Table B-1 Decimal and binary values for common ASCII characters (*continues*)

(continued)

Decimal number	Binary number	ASCII character	Decimal number	Binary number	ASCII character
70	0100 0110	F	89	0101 1001	Y
71	0100 0111	G	90	0101 1010	Z
72	0100 1000	H	91	0101 1011	[Opening or left bracket
73	0100 1001	I	92	0101 1100	\ Backslash
74	0100 1010	J	93	0101 1101	] Closing or right bracket
75	0100 1011	K	94	0101 1110	^ Caret
76	0100 1100	L	95	0101 1111	_ Underline or underscore
77	0100 1101	M	96	0110 0000	` Grave accent
78	0100 1110	N	97	0110 0001	a
79	0100 1111	O	98	0110 0010	b
80	0101 0000	P	99	0110 0011	c
81	0101 0001	Q	100	0110 0100	d
82	0101 0010	R	101	0110 0101	e
83	0101 0011	S	102	0110 0110	f
84	0101 0100	T	103	0110 0111	g
85	0101 0101	U	104	0110 1000	h
86	0101 0110	V	105	0110 1001	i
87	0101 0111	W	106	0110 1010	j
88	0101 1000	X	107	0110 1011	k

Table B-1 Decimal and binary values for common ASCII characters *(continues)*

(continued)

Decimal number	Binary number	ASCII character	Decimal number	Binary number	ASCII character
108	0110 1100	l	118	0111 0110	v
109	0110 1101	m	119	0111 0111	w
110	0110 1110	n	120	0111 1000	x
111	0110 1111	o	121	0111 1001	y
112	0111 0000	p	122	0111 1010	z
113	0111 0001	q	123	0111 1011	{ Opening or left brace
114	0111 0010	r	124	0111 1100		Vertical line or pipe
115	0111 0011	s	125	0111 1101	} Closing or right brace
116	0111 0100	t	126	0111 1110	~ Tilde
117	0111 0101	u			

Table B-1   Decimal and binary values for common ASCII characters

The Hexadecimal System

The **hexadecimal numbering system** is a **base 16 system** because it uses 16 digits. As shown in Table B-2, the digits are 0 through 9 and A through F. Computer professionals often use the hexadecimal system to express addresses and instructions as they are stored in computer memory because hexadecimal provides convenient shorthand expressions for groups of binary values. In Table B-2, each hexadecimal value represents one of the 16 possible combinations of four-digit binary values. Therefore, instead of referencing memory contents as a 16-digit binary value, for example, programmers can use a 4-digit hexadecimal value.

Decimal value	Hexadecimal value	Binary value (shown using four digits)
0	0	0000
1	1	0001
2	2	0010
3	3	0011
4	4	0100
5	5	0101
6	6	0110
7	7	0111
8	8	1000
9	9	1001
10	A	1010
11	B	1011
12	C	1100
13	D	1101
14	E	1110
15	F	1111

Table B-2   Values in the decimal and hexadecimal systems

In the hexadecimal system, each column is 16 times the value of the column to its right. Therefore, column values from right to left are 1, 16, 256, 4096, and so on. Figure B-3 shows how 171 and 305 are expressed in hexadecimal.

Figure B-3   Representing decimal values 171 and 305 in the hexadecimal system

Measuring Storage

In computer systems, both internal memory and external storage are measured in bits and bytes. Eight bits make a byte, and a byte frequently holds a single character (in ASCII or EBCDIC) or half a character (in Unicode). Because a byte is such a small unit of storage, the size of memory and files is often expressed in thousands or millions of bytes. Table B-3 describes some commonly used terms for storage measurement.

Term	Abbreviation	Number of bytes using binary system	Number of bytes using decimal system	Example
Kilobyte	KB or kB	1024	one thousand	This appendix occupies about 85 kB on a hard disk.
Megabyte	MB	1,048,576 (1024 × 1024 kilobytes)	one million	One megabyte can hold an average book in text format. A 3½-inch diskette you might have used a few years ago held 1.44 megabytes.
Gigabyte	GB	1,073,741,824 (1,024 megabytes)	one billion	The hard drive on a fairly new laptop computer might be 160 gigabytes. An hour of HDTV video is about 4 gigabytes.
Terabyte	TB	1024 gigabytes	one trillion	The entire Library of Congress can be stored in 10 terabytes.

Table B-3   Commonly used terms for computer storage (*continues*)

(continued)

Term	Abbreviation	Number of bytes using binary system	Number of bytes using decimal system	Example
Petabyte	PB	1024 terabytes	one quadrillion	Popular Web sites such as YouTube and Google have 20 to 30 petabytes of activity per month.
Exabyte	EB	1024 petabytes	one quintillion	A popular expression claims that all words ever spoken by humans could be stored in text form in 5 exabytes.
Zettabyte	ZB	1024 exabytes	one sextillion	A popular expression claims that all words ever spoken by humans could be stored in audio form in 42 zettabytes.
Yottabyte	YB	1024 zettabytes	one septillion (a 1 followed by 24 zeros)	All data accessible on the Internet and in corporate networks is estimated to be 1 yottabyte.

Table B-3   Commonly used terms for computer storage

In the metric system, "kilo" means 1000. However, in Table B-3, notice that a kilobyte is 1024 bytes. The discrepancy occurs because everything stored in a computer is based on the binary system, so multiples of two are used in most measurements. If you multiply 2 by itself 10 times, the result is 1024, which is a little over 1000. Similarly, a gigabyte is 1,073,741,624 bytes, which is more than a billion.

Confusion arises because many hard-drive manufacturers use the decimal system instead of the binary system to describe storage. For example, if you buy a hard drive that holds 10 gigabytes, it actually holds exactly 10 billion bytes. However, in the binary system, 10 GB is 10,737,418,240 bytes, so when you check your hard drive's capacity, your computer will report that you don't quite have 10 GB, but only 9.31 GB.

Key Terms

The **decimal numbering system** is a numeric system that uses 10 digits, 0 through 9, arranged in columns to represent numbers.

The **binary numbering system** is a numbering system that uses two digits, 0 and 1, arranged in columns to represent numbers.

A **bit** is a binary digit.

The **American Standard Code for Information Interchange (ASCII)** is an eight-bit code that represents characters.

A **byte** is eight bits.

A **nibble** is four bits.

The **Extended Binary Coded Decimal Interchange Code (EBCDIC)** is an eight-bit code used in IBM mainframe computers.

Unicode is a 16-bit code used with languages such as C# and Java.

The **hexadecimal numbering system** is a number system that uses 16 digits, 0 through 9 and A through F, arranged in columns to represent numbers.

The **base 16 system** is the hexadecimal system.

Using The IDE Editor

The Visual C# Code Editor is like a word processor for writing source code. Just as a word-processing program provides support for spelling and grammar, the C# Code Editor helps ensure that your C# syntax is free of spelling and grammar errors. This support can be grouped into several categories that are described in this appendix.

IntelliSense

IntelliSense is Microsoft's name for the set of features designed to minimize the time you spend looking for help and to help you enter code more accurately and efficiently. The IntelliSense features provide basic information about C# language keywords, .NET Framework types, and method signatures as you type them in the editor. The information is displayed in ToolTips, list boxes, and Smart Tags. Features of IntelliSense include:

- Providing completion lists
- Providing quick information
- Providing parameter information
- Adding using statements

Providing Completion Lists

As you enter source code in the editor, IntelliSense displays a list box that contains all the C# keywords, .NET Framework classes, and names you have defined in your program that fit the current circumstances. This feature is called **completion mode**. For example, Figure C-1 shows a list box that makes suggestions based on what the programmer has typed in the Code Editor. If you find a match in the list box for the name you intend to type, you can select the item. Alternatively, you can press the Tab key to have IntelliSense finish entering the name or keyword for you.

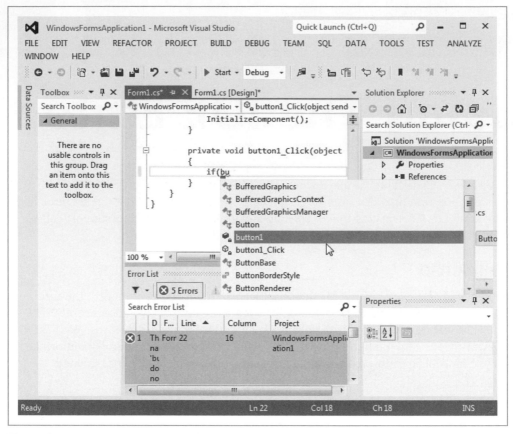

Figure C-1   A list displayed by IntelliSense

IntelliSense also supports a **suggestion mode**. In this mode, IntelliSense does not automatically complete identifiers, which makes it easier for you to type variable or method names without the completion list appearing. You can toggle between completion mode and suggestion mode by pressing Ctrl+Alt+Spacebar, or by pointing to IntelliSense on the Edit menu and clicking Toggle Completion Mode.

Similarly, when you enter a .NET Framework type or an identifier of a specific type into the Code Editor, and then type the dot operator (.), IntelliSense displays a list box that contains the members of that type. When you don't know what method or property you want for an object, typing its identifier and a dot can direct you to the appropriate choice. This technique sometimes teaches you about features you did not even realize were available.

Providing Quick Information

When you hover the cursor over a .NET Framework type, IntelliSense displays a Quick Info ToolTip that contains basic documentation about that type.

Providing Parameter Information

When you enter a method name in the Code Editor and then type an opening parenthesis, IntelliSense displays a Parameter Info ToolTip that shows the method's parameter list. If the method is overloaded, multiple method signatures are displayed, and you can scroll through them.

Adding `using` Statements

If you attempt to create an instance of a .NET Framework class without a sufficiently qualified name, IntelliSense displays a Smart Tag after the unresolved identifier. When you click the Smart Tag, IntelliSense displays a list of `using` statements to help you resolve the identifier. When you select a statement from the list, IntelliSense adds the `using` directive to the top of your source code file, and you can continue to write code at your current location.

Code Snippets

Code snippets are small units of commonly used C# source code that you can enter accurately and quickly with only a couple of keystrokes. To access the code snippet menu, right-click in the Code Editor, select Insert Snippet, and select Visual C#. Then, you can browse from the many available snippets, or you can create your own.

Wavy Underlines

Wavy underlines give you instant feedback about errors in your code as you type. A red wavy underline identifies a syntax error, such as a missing semicolon or mismatched braces. A green wavy underline identifies a potential compiler warning, and blue identifies an Edit and Continue issue. In Figure C-2, two wavy underlines appear (under `button1` and the closing curly brace that follows it) because the code in the last statement is not yet complete.

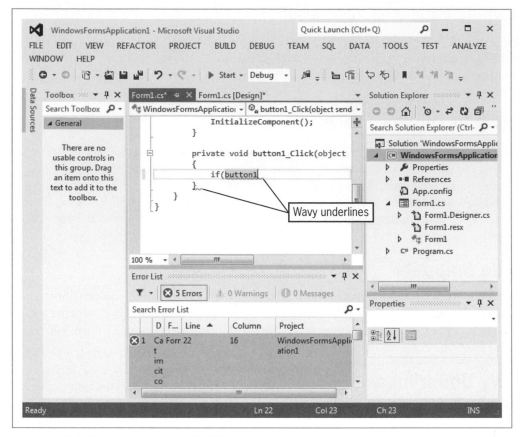

Figure C-2   Wavy underlines in Code Editor

Readability Aids

The editor assigns different colors to various categories of identifiers in a C# source code file to make the code easier to read. For example, C# keywords are bright blue, classes are blue-green, and comments are green.

Key Terms

IntelliSense is Microsoft's name for the set of features designed to minimize the time you spend looking for help and to help you enter code more accurately and efficiently.

Completion mode is an IDE editing mode in which suggestions are automatically provided for your code based on context.

Suggestion mode is an IDE editing mode in which completion mode is turned off.

Code snippets are small units of commonly used C# source code that you can enter accurately and quickly with only a couple of keystrokes.

Glossary

A

abstract class—a class from which concrete objects cannot be instantiated but can serve as a basis for inheritance. Contrast with *concrete*.

abstract method—a method that contains no statements and must be implemented by classes that derive from its class.

access specifier—a keyword that dictates which outside classes can use a method.

accessibility—describes limitations on how a method can be used.

accessors—methods in properties that specify how a class's fields are accessed. See *get accessors* and *set accessors*.

accumulated—describes totals that are added into a final sum by processing individual records one at a time in a loop.

actual parameters—arguments within a method call.

add and assign operator (+=)—an operator that adds the operand on the right to the operand on the left and assigns the results to the operand on the left in one step.

aggregate operators—in LINQ, operators that produce statistics for groups of data.

alias—an alternative name or pseudonym.

ambiguous—describes overloaded methods between which the compiler cannot distinguish.

American Standard Code for Information Interchange (ASCII)—an eight-bit code that represents characters.

ancestors—all the superclasses from which a subclass is derived.

Anchor property—an attribute that causes a Control to remain at a fixed distance from the side of a container when the user resizes it.

AND operator—an operator that determines whether two expressions are both true; it is written using two ampersands (&&). Also called the *conditional AND operator*. Contrast with *Boolean logical AND operator*.

anomaly—an irregularity in a database's design that causes problems and inconveniences.

applicable methods—the collection of potential methods that could be used by a method call.

application classes—classes that contain a Main() method and are executable programs.

application software—programs that allow users to complete tasks, in contrast with system software that the computer needs to complete tasks.

argument—the expression passed to a method.

array—a list of data items that all have the same data type and the same name, but are distinguished from each other by a subscript or index.

array element—one object in an array.

assembly—a group of code modules compiled together to create an executable program.

assignment—a statement that provides a variable with a value.

assignment operator—the equal sign (=); any value to the right of the assignment operator is assigned to, or taken on by, the variable to the left.

associativity—specifies the order in which a sequence of operations with the same precedence are evaluated.

at runtime—a phrase describing actions that occur during a program's execution.

attributes of an object—the characteristics of an object.

auto-implemented property—a property in which the code within the accessors is created automatically. The only action in the set accessor is to assign a value to the associated field, and the only action in the get accessor is to return the associated field value.

automatic properties—auto-implemented properties.

B

backing field—a field that has a property coded for it.

base—a keyword that refers to a class's immediate superclass.

base 2 numbers—binary system numbers.

base 10 numbers—decimal system numbers.

base 16 system—a mathematical system that uses 16 symbols to represent numbers; hexadecimal.

base class—a class that is used as a basis for inheritance.

behaviors of an object—the methods associated with an object.

betterness rules—the rules that determine the best overloaded method to execute based on the arguments in a method call.

binary files—files that can store any of the 256 combinations of bits in any byte instead of just those combinations that form readable text.

binary numbering system—a numbering system that uses two digits, 0 and 1, arranged in columns to represent numbers.

binary operators—operators that use two arguments: one value to the left of the operator and another value to the right of it.

binary search—an algorithm that attempts to find an item in a list by splitting the sorted list of objects in half repeatedly as the search gets closer to a match.

BinarySearch() method—a member of the System.Array class that finds a requested value in a sorted array.

BindingSource—an object that establishes a link from a database to a program.

bit—a binary digit.

bitwise operators—operators that are used to manipulate the individual bits of values.

black box—any device that can be used without knowing how it works internally.

block—a collection of one or more statements contained within a pair of curly braces.

block comments—comments that start with a forward slash and an asterisk (/*) and end with an asterisk and a forward slash (*/). Block comments can appear on a line by themselves, on a line before executable code, or after executable code. They can also extend across as many lines as needed. Compare with *line comments.*

bool—a data type that holds a Boolean value.

Boolean logical AND operator—an operator that determines whether two expressions are both true; it is written using a single ampersand (&). Unlike the conditional AND operator, it does not use short-circuit evaluation.

Boolean logical inclusive OR operator—an operator that determines whether at least one of two conditions is true; it is written using a single pipe (|). Unlike the conditional OR operator, it does not use short-circuit evaluation.

Boolean variable—a variable that can hold only one of two values: true or false.

break—a keyword that optionally terminates a switch structure at the end of each case.

byte—an integral data type that can hold an unsigned numeric value from 0 through 255.

C

C# programming language—a computer programming language developed as an object-oriented and component-oriented language. It exists as part of Visual Studio, a package used for developing applications for the Windows family of operating systems.

call—to invoke a method.

call stack—the memory location where the computer stores the list of locations to which the system must return after method calls.

called—describes a method that has been invoked.

called method—a method that has been invoked by another method.

calling method—a method that calls another method.

camel casing—a style of creating identifiers in which the first letter is not capitalized, but each new word is. Contrast with *Pascal casing.*

case—a keyword in a switch structure that is followed by one of the possible values that might equal the switch expression.

case label—identifies a course of action in a switch structure.

catch block—a block of code that can catch one type of Exception.

char—an integral data type that can store a character such as 'A', '4', or '$'.

character—any one of the letters, numbers, or other special symbols (such as punctuation marks) that comprise data.

character set—the group of all the characters used to represent data on a particular computer.

check digit—a digit calculated from a formula and appended to a number to help verify the accuracy of the other digits in the number.

CheckBox—a GUI widget that a user can click to select or deselect an option. When a Form contains multiple CheckBoxes, any number of them can be checked or unchecked at the same time.

CheckedListBox—a Control similar to a ListBox, with check boxes appearing to the left of each desired item.

child class—a derived class; a subclass; a class that has inherited from a base class.

class—a category of objects or a type of object.

class access specifier—describes access to a class.

class client—a program or class that instantiates objects of another prewritten class. Also called a *class user*.

class definition—the first class line that describes a class; it contains an optional access specifier, the keyword `class`, and any legal identifier for the name of the class.

class header—the first class line that describes a class; it contains an optional access specifier, the keyword `class`, and any legal identifier for the name of the class.

class user—a program or class that instantiates objects of another prewritten class. Also called a *class client*.

click event—an action fired when a user clicks a button in a GUI environment.

client—a method that uses another method.

closing a file—the process of making a file no longer available to an application.

code bloat—a term that describes unnecessarily long or repetitive program statements.

code refactoring—the process of changing a program's internal structure without changing the way the program works.

code snippets—small units of commonly used C# source code that are generated in the IDE using a few keystrokes.

collection—any data structure that holds objects of the same type.

Color—a class that contains a wide variety of predefined colors to use with `Controls`.

ComboBox—a `Control` similar to a `ListBox`, except that it displays an additional editing field that allows a user to select from the list or enter new text.

command line—the operating system's text interface.

command prompt—a request for input that appears at the beginning of the command line.

comment out—to turn a statement into a comment so that the compiler will not execute its command.

Compare() method—a method that compares two values. In the `String` class, it is a method that requires two `string` arguments.

CompareTo()—a method that compares objects; it is overridden in many classes, including `String`, and in the `IComparable` interface.

comparison operator—an operator that compares two values.

compiler—a computer program that translates high-level language statements into machine code.

completion mode—an IDE editing mode in which suggestions are automatically provided based on context.

Component—a class that provides containment and cleanup for other objects.

composed delegate—a delegate that calls the delegates from which it is built.

composite key—a unique record identifier constructed from multiple columns; a compound key.

composition—the technique of using an object within another object.

compound key—a unique record identifier constructed from multiple columns; a composite key.

computer file—a collection of information stored on a nonvolatile device in a computer system.

computer simulations—programs that attempt to mimic real-world activities to foster a better understanding of them.

concatenate—to join strings together in a chain.

concrete—nonabstract; describes classes from which objects can be instantiated.

conditional AND operator—an operator that determines whether two expressions are both true; it is written using two ampersands (&&). Also called the *AND operator*. Contrast with *Boolean logical AND operator*.

conditional operator—a ternary operator that is used as an abbreviated version of the `if-else` statement; it requires three expressions separated by a question mark and a colon.

conditional OR operator—an operator that determines whether at least one of two conditions is true; it is written using two pipes (||). Also called the *OR operator*. Contrast with *Boolean logical inclusive OR operator*.

Console.ReadLine()—a method that accepts user input from the keyboard.

constant—describes a data item when it cannot be changed after a program is compiled; in other words, when it cannot vary.

constructor—a method that instantiates (creates an instance of) an object.

constructor initializer—a clause that indicates another instance of a class constructor should be executed before any statements in the current constructor body.

contextual keywords—identifiers that act like keywords in specific circumstances.

Control class—a class that provides the definitions for GUI objects.

control statement—the part of a structure that determines whether the subsequent block of statements executes.

Controls—GUI components such as text fields, buttons, and check boxes that users can manipulate to interact with a program.

counted loop—a definite loop.

CSV file—a file that contains comma-separated values.

culture—a set of rules that determines how culturally dependent values such as money and dates are formatted.

D

data files—files that contain facts and figures; persistent collections of related records.

data hierarchy—the relationship of characters, fields, records, and files.

data redundancy—the unnecessary repetition of data.

data type—a description of the format and size of a data item as well as the operations that can be performed on it.

database—a collection of files that an organization needs to support its applications.

database management software—a set of programs that allows users to create table descriptions; identify keys; add, delete, and update records within a table; arrange records; write queries; create reports; and keep data secure.

dataset—a temporary set of data stored in a project.

DateTimePicker—a `Control` that retrieves date and time information.

dead code—statements that can never execute under any circumstances because the program logic "can't get there." Also see *unreachable*.

debugging—the process of removing all syntax and logical errors from a program.

decimal—a floating-point data type that has a greater precision and a smaller range than a `float` or `double`, which makes it suitable for financial and monetary calculations.

decimal numbering system—the system that uses 10 digits, 0 through 9, arranged in columns to represent numbers.

decision structure—a unit of program logic that involves choosing between alternative courses of action based on some value.

decrement operator (--)—an operator that reduces a variable's value by 1; there is a prefix and a postfix version.

decrementing—the act of decreasing the value of a variable, often by 1.

default—a keyword that optionally is used prior to any action that should occur if the test expression in a case structure does not match any case.

default constructor—a constructor that requires no parameters; it can be automatically supplied or written by a programmer.

default event—for a `Control`, the event or method generated when it is double-clicked in the IDE, as well as the event that users expect to generate when they encounter the `Control` in a working application.

default value of an object—the value initialized with a default constructor.

definite loop—a loop in which the number of iterations is predetermined. Also a *counted loop*. Contrast with *indefinite loop*.

delegate—an object that contains a reference to a method.

delimiter—a character used to specify the boundary between characters in text files.

derived class—a subclass; a class that has inherited from a base class.

deserialization—the process of converting streams of bytes back into objects.

design time—the period of time during which a programmer designs a program's interface and writes the code.

destructor—a method that contains the actions performed when an instance of a class is destroyed.

directories—structures used to organize files on a storage device; folders.

Directory class—a class that provides information about directories or folders.

do loop—a type of posttest loop; a loop that is tested at the bottom of the loop after one repetition has occurred.

Dock property—an attribute that attaches a `Control` to the side of a container so that the `Control` stretches when the container's size is adjusted.

do-nothing loop—a loop that performs no actions other than looping.

double—a data type that can hold a floating-point number with 15 or 16 significant digits of accuracy.

dual-alternative decisions—decisions that have two possible outcomes.

duck typing—the process of implicitly typing a variable. Also called *dynamic typing*.

dynamic typing—the process of implicitly typing a variable. Also called *duck typing*.

E

empty body—a block that has no statements in it.

encapsulation—the technique of packaging an object's attributes and methods into a cohesive unit that can be used as an undivided entity.

enhanced for loop—a version of the for loop that cycles through an array without specifying the starting and ending points for the loop control variable.

enumeration—a list of values in which names are substituted for numeric values.

Equals()—a method that determines equivalency. In the String class, it is the method that determines if two strings have the same value.

error list—a portion of the Visual Studio IDE that displays compiler errors.

escape sequence—a single character composed of two symbols beginning with a backslash that represents a nonprinting character such as a tab.

event—an object generated when a user interacts with a GUI object, causing the program to perform a task.

event-driven programs—programs that contain code that causes an event such as a button click to perform a task.

event handler—a method that performs a task in response to an event; an event receiver.

event receiver—a method that performs a task in response to an event; an event handler.

event sender—the control that generates an event.

event wiring—the act of connecting an event to its resulting actions.

EventArgs—a C# class designed for holding event information.

EventHandler—a class for events that do not use any information besides the source of the event and the EventArgs parameter.

exception—an error condition or unexpected behavior in an executing program.

exception handling—the set of object-oriented techniques used to manage unexpected errors.

explicit cast—purposefully assigns a value to a different data type; it involves placing the desired result type in parentheses followed by the variable or constant to be cast.

explicitly—purposefully. Contrast with *implicitly*.

exposes—associates a FileStream with a file.

Extended Binary Coded Decimal Interchange Code (EBCDIC)—an eight-bit code that is used in IBM mainframe computers.

extended class—a derived class; a child class; a subclass; a class that has inherited from a base class.

extension methods—static methods that act like instance methods.

F

fault-tolerant—describes applications that are designed so that they continue to operate, possibly at a reduced level, when some part of the system fails.

field—in a class, an instance variable. In a file or database, a character or group of characters that has some meaning.

File class—a class that contains methods that access information about files.

file position pointer—a variable that holds the byte number of the next byte to be read from a file.

finally block—a block of code that optionally follows a try block; the code within a finally block executes whether the preceding try block identifies any Exceptions or not.

fires an event—causes an event to occur. Also see *raises an event* and *triggers an event*.

fixed-pitch font—a font in which each character occupies the same width.

float—a data type that can hold a floating-point number with as many as seven significant digits of accuracy.

floating-point—describes a number that contains decimal positions.

flowchart—a tool that helps programmers plan a program's logic by writing program steps in diagram form, as a series of shapes connected by arrows.

focus—the state of a GUI component when the user's attention is drawn to it visually. When a component has focus, its action can be executed by pressing the Enter key.

folders—structures used to organize files on a storage device; directories.

Font—a class used to change the appearance of printed text on Forms.

for loop—a loop that contains the starting value for the loop control variable, the test condition that controls loop entry, and the expression that alters the loop control variable, all in one statement.

foreach statement or **foreach loop**—a statement used to cycle through every array element without using a subscript.

Form—a GUI interface for collecting, displaying, and delivering information.

Form Designer—a portion of the Visual Studio IDE in which applications are designed visually as opposed to using typed code.

formal parameter—a parameter within a method header that accepts a value.

format specifier—one of nine built-in format characters in a format string that defines the most commonly used numeric format types.

format string—a string of characters that contains one or more placeholders for variable values.

fragile—describes classes that depend on field names from parent classes because they are prone to errors; that is, they are easy to "break."

from—a LINQ keyword that indicates the collection or sequence from which data will be drawn.

fully qualified—describes a name that includes the class name as well as the identifier.

G

garbage—an unknown memory value.

get accessors—methods in properties that allow retrieval of a field value by using a property name.

getter—another term for a class property's get accessor.

gigabyte—approximately a billion bytes.

governing type—in a switch statement, the type that is established by the switch expression. The governing type can be sbyte, byte, short, ushort, int, uint, long, ulong, char, string, or enum.

graphical user interface (GUI)—an interface that employs graphical images representing controls the user manipulates.

group operator—in LINQ, the operator that groups data by specified criteria.

GroupBox—a Control that can be used to group other Controls on a Form; similar to a Panel but it has a Title property.

H

hardware—the physical devices associated with a computer.

has-a relationship—the relationship created using composition, so called because one class "has an" instance of another.

hash code—a number that should uniquely identify an object.

hexadecimal numbering system—a mathematical system that uses 16 symbols to represent numbers; base 16.

hide—to override a parent class member in a child class, making the parent class member invisible.

high-level programming language—a language that uses a vocabulary of reasonable terms such as "read," "write," or "add" instead of referencing the sequence of on/off switches that perform these tasks.

I

IComparable interface—an interface that contains the definition for the CompareTo() method.

identifier—the name of a program component such as a variable, class, or method.

if statement—a program statement used to make a single-alternative decision.

if-else statement—a statement that performs a dual-alternative decision.

immutable—unchangeable.

implementation hiding—the technique of keeping the details of a method's operations hidden.

implicit cast—the automatic transformation that occurs when a value is assigned to a type with higher precedence.

implicit conversion—the conversion that occurs when a type is automatically changed to another upon assignment.

implicit parameter—an undeclared parameter that gets its value automatically.

implicit reference conversion—the type of conversion that occurs when a derived class object is assigned to its ancestor's data type.

implicitly—automatically. Contrast with *explicitly*.

implicitly typed variable—a variable that has a data type that is inferred from the expression used to initialize the variable.

incrementing—the act of increasing the value of a variable, often by 1.

indefinite loop—a loop in which the number of iterations is not predetermined. Contrast with *definite loop*.

index—an integer contained within square brackets that indicates the position of one of an array's elements. Also see *subscript*.

infinite loop—a loop that (theoretically) never ends.

information hiding—a feature found in all object-oriented languages, in which a class's data is private and changed or manipulated only by its own methods.

inheritance—the ability to extend a class so as to create a more specific class that contains all the attributes and methods of a more general class; the extended class usually contains new attributes or methods as well.

initialization—an assignment made when a variable is declared.

initializer list—the list of values provided for an array.

inner loop—the loop in a pair of nested loops that is entirely contained within another loop.

instance methods—methods that are used with object instantiations.

instance of a class—an object; a tangible example of a class.

instance variables—data components of a class that exist separately for each instantiation. Also called *fields*.

809

instantiate—to create an object.

instantiation—a created object.

`int`—an integral data type that can hold a signed numeric value in four bytes.

integers—whole numbers.

integral data types—data types that store whole numbers; the nine integral types are `byte`, `sbyte`, `short`, `ushort`, `int`, `uint`, `long`, `ulong`, and `char`.

Integrated Development Environment (IDE)—a program development environment in which programmers select options from menus or by clicking buttons; an IDE provides helpful features such as color coding and automatic statement completion.

IntelliSense—Microsoft's name for the set of features designed to minimize program development time in the IDE.

interactive program—a program that allows user input.

interface—a collection of abstract methods (and perhaps other members) that can be used by any class as long as the class provides a definition to override the interface's abstract definitions. The interaction between a method and an object.

intermediate language (IL)—the language into which source code statements are compiled.

`internal`—a class access modifier that means access is limited to the assembly to which the class belongs.

`internal` **access**—a level of method accessibility that limits method access to the containing program.

intrinsic types—basic, built-in data types; C# provides 15 intrinsic types.

invoke—to call a method.

invoking object—the object referenced by `this` in an instance method.

invoking the event—calling an event method.

iteration—one execution of any loop.

iteration variable—a temporary variable that holds each array value in turn in a `foreach` statement.

J

jagged array—a one-dimensional array in which each element is another array.

just in time (JIT)—the C# compiler that translates intermediate code into executable code.

K

K & R style—a way of writing code so that the opening curly brace of a structure is on the same line as the control statement; it is named for Brian Kernighan and Dennis Ritchie, who wrote the first book on the C programming language.

key—a value that uniquely identifies a record.

key events—keyboard events that occur when a user presses and releases keyboard keys.

key field—the field used to uniquely identify records and to control the order of records in a sequential file.

keywords—predefined and reserved identifiers that have special meaning to the compiler.

kilobyte—approximately a thousand bytes.

L

`Label`—a `Control` object that typically provides descriptive text for another `Control` object or displays other text information on a `Form`.

left-associative—describes operators whose operations are performed from left to right.

length field—a field that contains the number of elements in an array.

Length property—a member of the `System.Array` class that holds an array's length. Also, a member of the `String` class that holds a string's length.

Leszynski naming convention (LNC)—a convention for naming database elements that is most popular with Microsoft Access users and Visual Basic programmers.

lexically—alphabetically.

line comments—comments that start with two forward slashes (//) and continue to the end of the current line. Line comments can appear on a line by themselves, or at the end of a line following executable code. Compare with *block comments*.

LinkLabel—a `Control` that is similar to a `Label`, but that provides the additional capability to link the user to other sources, such as Web pages or files.

LINQ (Language INtegrated Query)—a set of general-purpose standard query operators that allow queries to be constructed in C# using easy-to-understand syntax. LINQ is similar to SQL, and the compiler can check it for errors.

ListBox—a `Control` that displays a list of items the user can select by clicking.

literal constant—a value that is taken literally at each use.

literal string—a series of characters that is used exactly as entered.

local—describes a variable that is declared in the current method.

logic—the sequence of statements and methods that produce the desired results in a computer program.

logical AND operator—the ampersand (&).

logical OR operator—the pipe (|).

long—an integral data type that can hold a signed numeric value in eight bytes.

loop—a structure that allows repeated execution of a block of statements.

loop body—the block of statements executed in a loop.

loop control variable—a variable that determines whether loop execution will continue on each iteration.

loop fusion—the technique of combining two loops into one.

lower camel casing—a style of creating identifiers in which the first letter is not capitalized, but each new word is. Also called *camel casing*. Contrast with *Pascal casing*.

M

machine language—the most basic circuitry-level language.

magic number—a hard-coded number.

main menu—in the Visual Studio IDE, the list of choices that run horizontally across the top of the screen.

mandatory parameters—method parameters for which an argument is required in every method call.

matrix—a name frequently used by mathematicians when referring to an array. Also see *table*.

MaximumSize property—an attribute of a `Form` that has two values: `Width` and `Height`.

megabyte—approximately a million bytes.

menu strip—a horizontal list of general options that appears under the title bar of a `Form` or `Window`.

MenuStrip—a control that creates a menu strip.

method—an encapsulated series of statements that carry out a task.

method body—all the instructions contained within a pair of curly braces ({ }) following a method header.

method declaration—a method header or definition; it precedes a method and includes a return type, identifier, and an optional parameter list.

method definition—a method header or declaration; it precedes a method and includes a return type, identifier, and an optional parameter list.

method header—the first line of a method, which includes the method name and information about what will pass into and be returned from a method.

method node—in Visual Studio, a small box next to a code segment that developers click to expand or collapse the code.

method's type—a method's `return` type.

Microsoft Office Access—a relational database that is part of the Microsoft Office software suite.

MinimumSize property—an attribute of a `Form` that has two values: `Width` and `Height`.

mission critical—describes any process that is crucial to an organization.

modal window—a secondary window that takes control from a primary window. The user must deal with a modal window before proceeding.

MonthCalendar—a `Control` that retrieves date and time information.

multidimensional arrays—arrays that require multiple subscripts to access the array elements.

multifile assembly—a group of files containing methods that work together to create an application.

multiple inheritance—the ability to inherit from more than one class.

N

named constant—an identifier whose contents cannot change.

namespace—a scheme that provides a way to group similar classes.

nested `if`—a statement in which one decision structure is contained within another.

nested method calls—method calls placed inside other method calls.

new—a keyword used to create objects; also known as the `new` operator.

nibble—four bits; half a byte.

node—In the Visual Studio IDE, a box that appears on a vertical tree to the left of a list or a section of code and that can be expanded or condensed.

non-application classes—classes that do not contain a `Main()` method and therefore are not runnable programs; they provide support for other classes.

nonstatic—describes a method that requires an object reference.

nonvolatile—the type of computer storage that is permanent; it is not lost when a computer loses power.

normalization—the process of designing and creating a set of database tables that satisfies the users' needs and avoids many potential problems such as data redundancies and anomalies.

NOT operator (!)—an operator that negates the result of any Boolean expression.

O

object—a concrete entity that has attributes and behaviors; an object is an instance of a class.

object (or **Object**)—a class type in the System namespace that is the ultimate base class for all other types.

object initializer—a clause that assigns values to any accessible members or properties of a class at the time of instantiation without calling a constructor with parameters.

object-oriented approach—an approach to a problem that involves defining the objects needed to accomplish a task and developing classes that describe the objects so that each maintains its own data and carries out tasks when another object requests them.

object-oriented programming (OOP)—a programming technique that features objects, classes, encapsulation, interfaces, polymorphism, and inheritance.

one-dimensional array—an array whose elements are accessed using a single subscript. Also see *single-dimensional array*.

opening a file—the process of creating an object and associating a stream of bytes with it.

operands—the values that operators use in expressions.

operator precedence—rules that determine the order in which parts of a mathematical expression are evaluated. Also called *order of operation*.

optional parameter—a parameter to a method for which a default value is automatically supplied when no argument is supplied; a parameter is optional when it is given a value in the method declaration.

OR operator—an operator that determines whether at least one of two conditions is true; it is written using two pipes (||). Also called the *conditional OR operator*. Contrast with *Boolean logical inclusive OR operator*.

order of operation—rules that determine the order in which parts of a mathematical expression are evaluated. Also called *operator precedence*.

orderby operator—in LINQ, the operator that sorts a collection of data based on a field or fields.

orphaned method—a method that never executes in an application, and thus serves no purpose.

out of bounds—describes a subscript that is not within the allowed range for an array.

out of scope—describes a variable that is not usable because it has ceased to exist.

outer loop—the loop in a pair of nested loops that contains another loop.

output parameter—a parameter to a method that receives the argument's address; it is not required to have an initial value. Contrast with *value parameter* and *reference parameter*.

overload resolution—the process of determining which of multiple applicable methods is the best match for a method call.

overloading—using one term to indicate diverse meanings. In C#, methods are overloaded when there are multiple versions with the same name but different parameter lists.

override—a keyword used in method headers when a derived class inherits an abstract method from a parent.

overrides—the action that occurs when a method takes precedence over another method, hiding the original version.

P

Panel—a Control that can be used to group other Controls on a Form; similar to a GroupBox, but it does not have a Title property.

parallel array—an array that has the same number of elements as another array and holds corresponding data.

parameter array—a local array declared within a method header.

parameter list—the data types and parameter names that appear between parentheses in a method header.

parameter to a method—an object or reference that is declared in a method definition.

parameterless constructor—a constructor that takes no parameters; one that is called using no arguments.

parent class—a base class; a superclass; a class that is used as a basis for inheritance.

parse—to break an item into component parts.

Pascal casing—a style of creating identifiers in which the first letter of all new words in a variable name, even the first one, is capitalized. Contrast with *camel casing*.

passed by reference—describes how data is passed to a method when the method receives the memory address of the argument passed to it.

passed by value—describes how data is passed to a method when the method receives a copy of the argument passed to it.

path—the disk drive in which a file resides plus the complete hierarchy of directories.

permanent storage devices—hardware such as hard disks, USB drives, and compact discs that are used to store files.

persistent—describes storage that is nonvolatile.

PictureBox—a Control that displays graphics from a bitmap, icon, JPEG, GIF, or other image file type.

placeholder—in a format string, it consists of a pair of curly braces containing a number that indicates the desired variable's position in a list that follows the string.

polymorphism—the ability to create methods that act appropriately depending on the context.

populating an array—the act of providing values for all the elements in an array.

positional argument—an unnamed method argument that is assigned to a parameter list based on its position in the method call.

postfix increment operator—an operator that evaluates a variable and then adds 1 to it. This operator is represented by ++ after a variable.

posttest loop—a loop in which the loop control variable is tested after the loop body executes. Contrast with *pretest loop*.

precedence—a feature of operators that controls the order in which they are evaluated in an expression.

precision specifier—a specifier that controls the number of significant digits or zeros to the right of the decimal point in a format string.

prefix increment operator—an operator that increases the variable's value by 1 and then evaluates it. This operator is represented by ++ before a variable.

pretest loop—a loop in which the loop control variable is tested before the loop body executes. Contrast with *posttest loop*.

primary key—a value that uniquely identifies a record; the term is often used in databases.

private—an access specifier that indicates other classes may not use the method or variable that it modifies. When used as a class access specifier, it means access is limited to another class to which the class belongs.

private access—a level of method accessibility that limits method access to the containing class.

procedural program—a program created by writing a series of steps or operations to manipulate values.

program—a set of written computer instructions.

program comments—nonexecuting statements that document a program.

projection operator—in LINQ, an operator that projects, or sends off, specific data from a collection.

prompt—an instruction to the user to enter data.

propagating an exception—the act of transmitting an exception object unchanged through the call stack.

Properties window—a portion of the Visual Studio IDE in which properties and events are configured on controls.

property—a member of a class that provides access to a field of a class; properties define how fields will be set and retrieved. The value of an object.

proportional font—a font in which different characters have different pitches or widths.

protected—a keyword that provides an intermediate level of security between public and private access.

protected access—a level of method accessibility that limits method access to the containing class or types derived from the containing class.

pseudocode—a tool that helps programmers plan a program's logic by writing plain English statements.

public—an access specifier that indicates other classes may use the method or variable it modifies.

public access—a level of method accessibility that allows unlimited access to a method.

Q

query—a question that retrieves information from a database using syntax that the database software can understand.

query by example—the process of using database software to create a query by filling in blanks.

R

RadioButtons—GUI widgets, similar to CheckBoxes, except that when they are placed on a Form, only one RadioButton can be selected at a time; selecting any RadioButton automatically deselects the others.

raises an event—causes an event to occur. Also see *fires an event* and *triggers an event*.

random access file—a file from which records can be accessed in any order.

random access memory (RAM)—temporary storage in a computer.

range check—a series of statements that determine whether a value falls within a specified range.

range match—a process that determines whether a value falls between a pair of limiting values.

read from the file—to copy data from a file on a storage device into RAM.

read-only property—a property that has only a get accessor, and not a set accessor.

record—a collection of fields that contain data about an entity.

rectangular array—an array in which each row has the same number of columns.

recursive—describes a method that calls itself.

reference equality—the type of equality that occurs when two reference type objects refer to the same object.

reference parameter—a parameter to a method that receives the argument's address; it is required to have an initial value. Contrast with *value parameter* and *output parameter*.

reference type—a data type that holds a memory address. Contrast with *value types*.

relational database—a database that provides the capability to establish and maintain relationships between columns in the tables.

restriction operator—in LINQ, an operator that places a restriction on which data is added to a collection.

rethrow an Exception—to throw a caught Exception instead of handling it.

return statement—a method statement that causes a value to be sent back from a method to its calling method.

return type—the type of value a method will return to any other method that calls it.

Reverse() method—a member of the System.Array class that reverses the order of items in an array.

right-associative—describes operators whose operations are performed from right to left.

robustness—describes the degree to which a system is resilient to stress, maintaining correct functioning even in the presence of errors.

root class—the ultimate or first base class in a hierarchical ancestry tree.

root directory—the main directory of a storage device.

run time—the period of time during which a program executes.

runnable—describes files that are executable.

S

sbyte—an integral data type that can hold a signed numeric value from −128 through 127.

scientific notation—a numeric expression format that includes an *E* (for exponent) and that specifies a number of implied decimal places.

scope—the area where a variable or constant is known and can be used.

sealed class—a class that cannot be extended.

searching an array—the process of comparing a value to a list of values in an array, looking for a match.

select—a LINQ keyword that indicates what to select from a collection.

SELECT-FROM-WHERE—the basic form of the SQL command that retrieves selected records from a table.

self-documenting—describes a program element that is self-explanatory.

semantic errors—the type of logical errors that occur when a correct word is used in the wrong context.

sentinel value—a value that a user must supply to stop a loop.

sequence structure—a unit of program logic in which one step follows another unconditionally.

sequential access file—a data file in which each record is stored in order based on the value in some field.

sequential search—a search that is conducted by examining a list item-by-item in sequence.

serialization—the process of converting objects into streams of bytes.

set accessors—methods in properties that allow use of the assignment operator with a property name.

setter—another term for a class property's set accessor.

short—an integral data type that can hold a signed numeric value in two bytes.

short-circuit evaluation—the C# feature in which parts of an AND or OR expression are evaluated only as far as necessary to determine whether the entire expression is true or false.

side effect—an unintended consequence of an operation.

signature—a method's name and parameter list.

significant digits—specifies the mathematical accuracy of a value.

simple type—describes one of the following in C#: `byte`, `sbyte`, `short`, `ushort`, `int`, `uint`, `long`, `ulong`, `float`, `double`, `decimal`, `char`, and `bool`.

single-dimensional array—an array whose elements are accessed using a single subscript. Also see *one-dimensional array*.

snap lines—lines that appear in a design environment to help designers align new `Control`s with others that are already in place.

software—computer programs.

Solution Explorer—a portion of the Visual Studio IDE in which developers view and manage project files and settings.

`Sort()` method—a member of the `System.Array` class that arranges array items in ascending order.

source code—program statements.

standard numeric format strings—strings of characters expressed within double quotation marks that indicate a format for output.

`StartsWith()` method—a `string` method that returns `true` if its first `string` parameter starts with the characters contained in the second `string` parameter.

state of an object—the collective value of all an object's attributes at any point in time.

`static`—a keyword that indicates that a method will be executed through a class and not by an object.

step value—the amount by which a loop control variable is altered on each iteration, especially in a `for` loop.

stream—a pipeline or channel through which bytes are input from and output to a file.

`string`—a data type that can hold a series of characters.

strongly typed—describes a language in which severe restrictions are placed on what data types can be mixed.

Structured Query Language (SQL)—the most common language that database administrators use to access data in their tables.

subclass—a derived class; a child class; a class that has inherited from a base class.

subscript—an integer contained within square brackets that indicates the position of one of an array's elements. Also see *index*.

Substring() method—a method that can be used to extract a portion of a string from a starting point for a specific length.

suggestion mode—an IDE editing mode in which completion mode is turned off.

superclass—a base class; a parent class; a class that is the basis for inheritance.

switch—a keyword that starts a switch structure.

switch expression—a condition in a switch statement enclosed in parentheses.

switch structure—a structure that tests a single variable against a series of exact matches.

syntax—the set of grammar rules in a programming language.

syntax error—an error that occurs when a programming language is used incorrectly.

System namespace—a scheme built into the C# compiler that holds commonly used classes.

System.Array—a built-in class that defines fields and methods that belong to every array.

T

tab order—describes the sequence of controls selected when the user presses the Tab key in a program with a GUI interface.

table—a name frequently used by mathematicians when referring to an array. Also see *matrix*.

table adapter—a feature in C# programs that accesses a database that passes data back and forth between a dataset and the BindingSource.

tables—database files, so called because their contents are arranged in rows and columns.

ternary—describes an operator that requires three arguments.

TextBoxes—controls through which a user can enter input data in a GUI application.

text files—files that contain data that can be read in a text editor because the data has been encoded using a scheme such as ASCII or Unicode.

this reference—the reference to an object that is implicitly passed to an instance method of its class.

TLA—a three-letter abbreviation for *three-letter abbreviation*; it is the most popular type of abbreviation in technical terminology.

token—a block of text within a string that represents an entity or field.

Toolbox tab—a portion of the Visual Studio IDE that contains controls that can be dragged onto Forms.

transitive—inheriting all the members of one's ancestors.

triggers an event—causes an event to occur. Also see *fires an event* and *raises an event*.

truth tables—diagrams used in mathematics and logic to help describe the truth of an entire expression based on the truth of its parts.

try block—a block of code that might create exceptions that will be handled.

two-dimensional arrays—multidimensional arrays that have two or more columns of values for each row.

type inference—the process of implicitly typing a variable.

type precedence—a hierarchy of data types used to determine the unifying type in arithmetic expressions containing dissimilar data types.

U

uint—an integral data type that can hold an unsigned numeric value in four bytes.

ulong—an integral data type that can hold an unsigned numeric value in eight bytes.

unary operators—operators used with one operand.

Unicode—a 16-bit coding scheme for characters.

Unified Modeling Language (UML) diagrams—graphical tools that programmers and analysts use to describe systems.

unifying type—the type chosen for an arithmetic result when operands are of dissimilar types.

unreachable—describes program statements that can never execute under any circumstances because the program logic "can't get there." Also see *dead code*.

upper camel casing—a style of creating identifiers in which the first letter of all new words in a name is capitalized, even the first one; Pascal casing.

ushort—an integral data type that can hold an unsigned numeric value in two bytes.

using clause, or **using directive**—code that declares a `namespace`.

V

value parameter—a parameter to a method that receives a copy of the value passed to it. Contrast with *reference parameter* and *output parameter*.

value types—data types that hold a value; they are predefined types such as `int`, `double`, and `char`. Contrast with *reference type*.

var—a data type that creates an implicitly typed variable.

variable—a named location in computer memory that can hold different values at different points in time.

variable declaration—the statement that names a variable; it includes a data type, an identifier, an optional assignment operator and assigned value, and an ending semicolon.

verbatim identifier—an identifier with an @ prefix.

view—a particular way of looking at a database in database management systems.

virtual method—a method whose behavior is determined by the implementation in a child class.

visible—describes a class member that has not been hidden.

void—a keyword that indicates that a method does not return any value when called.

volatile—the type of computer storage that is lost when power is lost.

W

where—a LINQ keyword that indicates conditions for selecting records.

while loop—a structure that executes a body of statements continuously while some condition continues to be true; it uses the keyword `while`.

whitespace—any combination of spaces, tabs, and carriage returns (blank lines) in a program.

widgets—interactive controls such as labels, scroll bars, check boxes, and radio buttons.

wildcard—a symbol that means "any" or "all."

write to a file—to store data in a computer file on a permanent storage device.

Write() method—a method that displays a line of output on the screen, but the cursor does not advance to a new line; it remains on the same line as the output.

WriteLine() method—a method that displays a line of output on the screen, positions the cursor on the next line, and waits for additional output.

X

XML—an abbreviation of eXtensible Markup Language, which is a standard for exchanging data over the Internet.

XML-documentation format comments—comments that use a special set of tags within angle brackets to create documentation within a program.

Index

All bold page numbers indicate definitions